Peter Hess
Resisting Pluralization and Globalization in German Culture, 1490–1540

Peter Hess

Resisting Pluralization and Globalization in German Culture, 1490–1540

—

Visions of a Nation in Decline

DE GRUYTER

ISBN 978-3-11-135749-2
e-ISBN (PDF) 978-3-11-067492-7
e-ISBN (EPUB) 978-3-11-067500-9

Library of Congress Control Number: 2020946588

Bibliographic Information published by the Deutsche Nationalbibliothek
The Deutsche Nationalbibliothek lists this publication in the Deutsche Nationalbibliografie;
detailed bibliographic data are available on the Internet at http://dnb.dnb.de.

© 2022 Walter de Gruyter GmbH, Berlin/Boston
This volume is text- and page-identical with the hardback published in 2020.
Cover image: Anon. *Den rechten weg auß zu faren von Lißbona gen Kallakuth*. Nuremberg:
Wolfgang Huber, 1506. Title page. © Universitätsbibliothek Freiburg im Breisgau, Historische
Sammlungen (J 4672,m)
Typesetting: Integra Software Services Pvt. Ltd.
Printing and binding: CPI books GmbH, Leck

www.degruyter.com

Acknowledgments

This book has been in the making for over a decade and could not have been completed without the support of many colleagues and institutions, and I would like to express my gratitude to all of them. I would like to thank the Fritz-Thyssen-Stiftung for granting me a Herzog-Ernst-Stipendium that allowed me to do preliminary research at the Forschungsbibliothek Gotha for two months in the summer of 2007. The project came much more into focus during a six-month stay at the Herzog August Bibliothek Wolfenbüttel in 2014 when I wrote Part I of this book as well as outlines and some sections of Parts II and III. I would like to thank the College of Liberal Arts at the University of Texas at Austin, Dean Randy Diehl and Senior Associate Dean Richard Flores, for granting me release time in 2014 between my two terms as department chair, and again in 2018. The College of Liberal Arts also granted me a Humanities Research Award (2014–2017) that covered basic expenses during this stay as well as during shorter stays at the Herzog August Bibliothek Wolfenbüttel in the summers of 2015, 2016, and 2017 that were critical for completing the first draft of the book. Furthermore, I would like to thank the Herzog August Bibliothek Wolfenbüttel, Director Peter Burschel, and the Land Niedersachsen for providing me with a five-month research grant in summer and fall 2018. While the grant was for a different project, an English translation of Nikolaus Federmann's *Jndianische Historia* (1557) that I completed, my stay in 2018 also gave me the opportunity for additional research to revise my manuscript. The Herzog August Bibliothek Wolfenbüttel provides an ideal research environment that is actively supported by their professional staff of scholars and librarians and that allows scholars from around the world to engage with each other. It is hard to imagine that I could have written large chunks of my manuscript anywhere else. My own work has profited immeasurably from the input of many fellow researchers at the library. In particular, I would like to thank Jill Bepler, Volker Bauer, Elizabeth Harding, Gerlinde Strauß, and Uta Rohrig for working tirelessly to ensure productive stays for guest scholars like myself. Finally, I would like to thank the two anonymous peer reviewers for their constructive comments, as well as Elisabeth Kempf and Robert Forke, the two editors at De Gruyter, and my copy-editor Melanie Haupt for their work on my manuscript. While the book manuscript was concluded before the coronavirus pandemic, the professional staff at De Gruyter produced my book in the middle of it. To them go my special thanks.

Contents

Acknowledgments —— V

List of Figures —— XI

Introduction —— 1

Part I: **A World in Decline: Anxieties about Social and Political Order**

Chapter 1
Order and Discipline: Visions and Anxieties —— 15

Chapter 2
Gute Policey: Saving or Disrupting the Order? —— 28

Chapter 3
Defending Order and Discipline in *Dyl Ulenspiegel* —— 42

Chapter 4
A Dystopian Topsy-Turvy World —— 66

Chapter 5
Innovation and Progress as Agents of Decline —— 77

Chapter 6
History as Decline and Brant's Vision of the End of History —— 84

Chapter 7
The Communal Order and the Problem of Self-Interest —— 95

Chapter 8
The Decline of the Community: Common Good and Self-Interest as Literary Metaphors —— 107

Part II: Staying Home: Resistance to Expanding Spatial Horizons

Chapter 9
Spatial Expansion and Its Narratives —— 129

Chapter 10
From Chronicle to Cosmography (and Chorography):
The Rise of Synchronic Narratives of the World —— 136

Chapter 11
Ptolemy's Grid and the New Cosmography in Germany:
Waldseemüller and His Legacy —— 149

Chapter 12
Emancipation from Ancient Concepts of Space —— 172

Chapter 13
Spatial Discoveries: Anxieties and Rejection in Brant's Writings —— 181

Chapter 14
Spatial Anxieties in Literary Texts of the Early Sixteenth Century —— 201

Chapter 15
America and the Epistemological Crisis of Space: An Afterthought —— 213

Part III: Globalization and the Nationalistic Backlash in Germany

Chapter 16
Theory of Early Modern Globalization —— 233

Chapter 17
The Emerging Global Trade from a German Perspective —— 243

Chapter 18
The Backlash Against the New Economy —— 256

Chapter 19
Macro-Economic Critique of the Emerging Global Trade — 273

Chapter 20
Nationalistic and Xenophobic Responses to Foreign Influences — 289

Chapter 21
The Global Spice Trade: Breaching Traditional Values and Violating the Divine Order — 308

Chapter 22
The Backlash Against Globalization: The Rhetoric of Moral Decline and the Nostalgia Project — 328

Conclusion — 339

Bibliography — 359

Index — 385

List of Figures

Figure 1   Joseph Grünpeck. *Ein spiegel der naturlichen himlischen vnd prophetischen sehungen aller trübsalen/ angst/ vnd not.* Nuremberg: Georg Stuchs, 1508. Sig. a3r © Bayerische Staatsbibliothek München —— **68**

Figure 2   Sebastian Brant. *Daß Narren Schyff.* Basel: Johann Bergmann, 1494. Chapter 37, sig. F6v © Bayerische Staatsbibliothek München —— **73**

Figure 3   Hans Sachs. *Das schedlich Thier der Eygen nutz/ mit sein verderblichen zwölff Eygen schafften.* Nürnberg: Pankraz Kempf, c. 1535. Title page © Bayerische Staatsbibliothek München —— **109**

Figure 4   Martin Waldseemüller. *Der welt kugel. Beschrybung der welt vnd deß gantzen Ertreichs hie angezögt vnd vergleicht einer rotunden kuglen.* Strasbourg: Johann Grüninger, 1509. Title page and sig. B2r © Universitätsbibliothek Freiburg im Breisgau —— **151**

Figure 5   Anon. *Die reyse van Lissebone om te varenna dat eylandt Naguaria in groot Indien gheleghen.* Antwerp: Jan van Doesborch, 1508. Sig. C3r © John Carter Brown Library, Brown University, Providence, Rhode Island —— **160**

Figure 6   Sebastian Brant. *Daß Narren Schyff.* Basel: Johann Bergmann, 1494. Chapter 66, sig. L3v © Bayerische Staatsbibliothek München —— **188**

Figure 7   [Amerigo Vespucci]. *Das sind die new gefunden menschen oder volcker Jn form vnd gestalt Als sie hie stend durch den Cristenlichen Künig von Portugall/ gar wunnderbarlich erfunden.* Nuremberg: Georg Stuchs, 1505 © Herzog August Bibliothek Wolfenbüttel —— **218**

Figure 8   Anon. *Den rechten weg auß zu faren von Lißbona gen Kallakuth.* Nuremberg: Wolfgang Huber, 1506. Verso of title page © Herzog August Bibliothek Wolfenbüttel —— **245**

Figure 9   Martin Waldseemüller. *Carta marina.* Strasbourg [?]: s.n., 1516. Sheet four, detail © Library of Congress, Washington D.C. —— **253**

Figure 10 Daniel Hopfer. *Die Sprich Salomo das XI. Capitel.* [Broadsheet, Illustration to Proverbs 11:26.] Augsburg: s.n., 1534 © The Metropolitan Museum of Art, New York, N.Y. —— **263**

Figure 11 Hieronymus Brunschwig. *Apoteck für den gmeynen man. der die Ertzte zuersuchen. am gůt nicht vermügens/ oder sonst in der not allwege nicht erraychen kan.* Augsburg: Heinrich Steiner, 1529. Title page © Bayerische Staatsbibliothek München —— **314**

Introduction

Ambiguity, and in particular intolerance for ambiguity, are central categories in this book as the cultures of Humanism and of the Renaissance were ambiguous in nature.[1] Ambiguity is an umbrella term for phenomena of uncertainty of meaning, vagueness, or multiple possible meanings and interpretations.[2] Humanism explored multiple responses to moral, aesthetic, and political questions. Renaissance art created a space for individual expression and brought forth a broad range of forms, styles, and genres. Institutions were in flux, from urban governance to the imperial structure to the exuberant Papal Curia in Rome. Cultural norms were in flux as well, and so were trade practices, epistemological frameworks, and hermeneutic norms. The time around 1500 was marked by a loss of predictability and a loss of certainty about the known world.

This observation is relevant for our own historical moment as well, as we live in a period marked by a shrinking tolerance for ambiguity. The ambiguity that is now under pressure evolved in the years after the Second World War – which was triggered by the preceding intolerant age of ideologies and nationalisms. Since the collapse of the Soviet Union, tolerance for ambiguity has been receding and has been replaced by rigid thinking within stringent ideological frameworks. There are no questions or doubts in the worlds of Donald Trump, Viktor Orbán, Jair Bolsonaro, or Rodrigo Duterte, nor are there in the world of Brexit. They stand for a world that only knows right or wrong and that makes absolute and exclusive claims of owning the truth. No amount of scientific evidence will make climate change real to them. Their rise has to be seen as a backlash against the tolerance for immigration, refugee rights, gay and transgender rights, a diverse and multicultural society, and what is often dubbed "political correctness," that is the loss of perceived "authenticity" at the expense of civility and a cultured coexistence. The political discourses of the Trumpists in the United States or supporters of the AfD (Alternative for Germany) in Germany illustrate this trend. Their movements are carried by a yearning for purity and create a nostalgia for national origins where moral values were intact and unambiguous. This is the framework within which this study is so timely and relevant today.

Clearly, ambiguity and fluidity in the early sixteenth century were promoted and welcomed by many as they offered and created opportunities to reshape social and political structures, to expand spatial horizons, and to create

---

1 Bauer, *Die Vereindeutigung*, 25.
2 Bauer, *Die Vereindeutigung*, 13.

global trade networks of the kind the world had never seen before. This book is not about them, although their points of view will be considered in order to create a benchmark and to frame our discussion. This book is not about mapping the emerging diversity and multiple truths in the Renaissance world; rather, it is about the contravening responses to this ambiguity in Germany. This book is about those who rejected ambiguity and protested against it in a range of forms. Specifically, this book examines the politics of grievance; that is, the backlash against pressures on the political system, against spatial explorations both physical and intellectual, and against globalization in the rise of global trade networks in the early sixteenth century.

Globalization and spatial expansion around 1500 did not evolve in a cultural vacuum. In the early modern period, fundamental changes occurred in the way the world was imagined, which informed the quest for discoveries and the creation of global networks. This re-imagination of the world around 1500 was enhanced by the twin phenomena of pluralization and secularization, which opened up a space where ambiguity could be tolerated and that fueled the European Humanism of the fifteenth and early sixteenth centuries.

The term pluralization refers to the emergence of new or alternate knowledge and of competing realities that expressed themselves in an expansion of accepted and acceptable forms of representation and ultimately questioned the validity of established epistemological systems and their representations. Different or multiple responses to segments of reality in specific cultural and societal realms became conceivable and legitimate, which created significant ruptures in the early modern intellectual world.[3] A tolerance for ambiguity created some space for the acceptance of contradictions and of opposing premises and expectations. Demonstrating the multitude of ways to talk about the world with an ironic or skeptical distance became the native realm of much of Renaissance literature. Literature did not engage in a futile competition with philosophical or scientific imagination but rather created a sort of meta-discourse that refracted these fantasies.[4] This process of epistemological pluralization prepared the intellectual framework not only for the voyages of discovery, the Protestant Reformation, and the Scientific Revolution, but also for new patterns of social norms and human behavior. The emergence of new or alternate forms of knowledge was often explored in the form of the

---

3 Bleuler and Friedrich, "Pluralisierungen," 48.
4 Lobsien, "Die Pluralität der Welten," 143.

dialogue – a many-voiced and ambiguous genre that was reclaimed by European Humanism for that very reason.[5]

There was growing consensus that dissent was tolerable and indeed legitimate. We see that in models of confessional coexistence that were institutionalized in the Peace of Augsburg of 1555.[6] Accepted knowledge bases, such as Ptolemaic cosmography, now could be questioned, and new knowledge paradigms and methods for verifying truth claims could be conceived. Pluralization was one of the keystones of sixteenth-century thought:

> Writers from More to Leibniz make the collision between worlds – old and new, ancient and modern, imagined and real – central to their depiction of what has since been called the 'epistemological crisis' of the period, that increasing emphasis in the late sixteenth and seventeenth centuries on worldly plurality, contingency, and the limitations of human perception and knowledge.[7]

Pluralization rooted in probabilistic thinking was at the core of innovation from spatial explorations and the creation of global trade networks to technological and scientific innovation. To Steven Shapin, the Scientific Revolution was grounded in a "broadly probabilistic discourse institutionalized within early modern gentle society which permitted dissension without disaster."[8] A pluralistic worldview that was tolerant of ambiguity thus was a key catalyst for early modern culture.

Secularization refers to the loss of the centrality of religious institutions in the lives of human beings. In the late Middle Ages, the Church gradually lost control of imperial politics, of the emerging universities, but also of the private lives of individuals. The role of the Church and the balance between spiritual and worldly lives had to be renegotiated as laymen increasingly appropriated the realm of theology.[9] Sebastian Brant's *Narrenschiff* illustrates how a secular text could intrude into moral philosophy that the Church viewed as its own realm.[10] New technologies were critical as well: the moveable type allowed

---

5 Otterspeer, *In Praise of Ambiguity*, 60. Among the writers discussed in this study, Ulrich von Hutten was the most prolific author of dialogues. However, Hutten's dialogues, defying generic tradition, were not exploratory but rather dogmatic in character.
6 Bleuler and Friedrich, "Pluralisierungen," 49. Ironically, it is this formal recognition of two brands of Christianity that enabled the rise of a "confessionalist" culture that dwelled on confessional distinctions. For this aspect see Kemper, *Deutsche Lyrik*, vol. 2, 1–10.
7 Ramachandran, *The Worldmakers*, 6.
8 Shapin, *A Social History of Truth*, 66.
9 Funkenstein, *Theology*, 3–9.
10 The preacher Johann Geiler von Kaysersberg in turn used Brant's secular text as material for a series of sermons.

books to be printed for the market, which lay away from Church control, and new navigational tools allowed pioneering navigators like Columbus and Vasco da Gama to leave the relative safety of known shorelines. It is in this confluence of domestic factors informed by European Humanism with the rapid escalation of spatial explorations and corresponding commercial opportunities that we can locate the rise of a globalized culture around 1500, but also the backlash against it.

The Protestant Reform was only possible in a climate where alternate theologies were tolerable and where theologians like Martin Luther and others were given space to explore and redefine the basic tenets of Christianity, at least up to the point where the Church perceived a threat to its institutional primacy, as John Van Engen asserts: "The most striking feature of the fifteenth-century European Church was its forbearance with a complex variety of institutional and personal expressions that its sixteenth-century heirs would not allow."[11] Paradoxically, the Reformation represents a backlash against the tolerance of ambiguity displayed by the Church. Luther and his followers sought to close the ambiguous space with a more pure and literal biblical exegesis leading to a fundamentalist understanding of faith. The split of the Church ushered in a new period of a rigorous opposition to ambiguity as the new faith returned to a simple and unambiguous doctrine of salvation.[12] The tip of the iceberg was the "Tyranny of Virtue" in Geneva,[13] established by Guillaume Farel and Jean Calvin. Farel and Calvin installed a fundamentalist theocracy that was distinguished by a zero tolerance for ambiguity, which resembles the polities established by the Taliban or the Islamic State in our time.[14] While not all writers who rejected ambiguity also were adherents of the Reform, the Reformation nevertheless became an important tool to combat tolerance for ambiguity.

Ironically, the formal recognition of two brands of western Christianity in the 1555 Religious Peace of Augsburg, which in itself institutionalized religious tolerance, enabled the rise of a confessionalist culture that dwelled on confessional distinctions. The active early phase of the Reformation shaped a distinct anti-institutional and anti-clerical rhetoric in contemporaneous literary and political texts, but they did not fully internalize the institutionalized Reform program and therefore were not as clearly confessionally marked as texts written after 1555. Earlier texts often struggled with questions of faith and the search for the divine plan for salvation on a personal and individual level, which is

---

[11] Van Engen: "The Church in the Fifteenth Century," 309.
[12] Bauer, *Die Vereindeutigung*, 25.
[13] See Reinhardt, *Tyrannei der Tugend*, 129–179.
[14] Bauer, *Die Vereindeutigung*, 27.

why many texts discussed in this book carry an anti-clerical but not usually a confessional marker. Only the formalization of the two confessions in 1555 forced writers to align with one of the two camps and made confessional affiliation part of their identity, thus importing confessional issues into literary and political texts.[15] The Augsburg Peace therefore did not promote tolerance nor ambiguity and instead ushered in a new round of strife between the confessions.[16] A new tolerance for ambiguity only opened up again with the rise of the General Reform and Rosicrucian movements at the turn of the seventeenth century.[17]

This book seeks to examine the question how literary texts between 1490 and 1540 analyzed the perceived social and moral crisis, the dramatic expansion of spatial and epistemological horizons, and the growth of global trade networks. It asks why most texts discussed here reacted with derision and contempt to these transformations. It traces how poets clung to traditional models of world order "against the backdrop of the cataclysmic transformations" of the early modern period.[18] My aim is to read literary texts against the background of pluralization, secularization, disruptions in the political order, the instability of the spatial order, and the evolving globalized economic system. Reading literary texts in this context offers a new reading that is able to accommodate the apparent contradictions within the texts themselves and to address many misconceptions in literary scholarship. In that sense, the book is an investigation into the question how literature served as a response mechanism to address perceived disruptions of the established order, as a tool to manage crises and to repair perceived ruptures in the social fabric, and as a means to reestablish a stable order in the face of political and social upheaval and cultural decline.

The three thematic complexes in this study are all framed by these underlying issues. Each of its three parts looks at innovations and new developments informed by a growing tolerance for ambiguity but also analyzes the ambiguity-intolerant backlash against them. Part I deals with rising anxieties about disorder, the perceived loss of moral values, and the decay of social and political structures in an increasingly secular and pluralistic world. It traces political discourses on the divine order and its ramifications for the ideal organization of human society, but also on the legitimacy of urban governance, of the empire and on more general notions like *Policey* and the common good. Another issue under discussion is the rise of written law that often created insecurities at the local level. The backlash takes place in literary texts in the form of affirmation

---

15 Kemper, *Deutsche Lyrik*, vol. 1, 11.
16 Kemper, *Deutsche Lyrik*, vol. 2, 2–3.
17 Kemper, *Deutsche Lyrik*, vol. 1, 19.
18 Tang, *Imagining World Order*, 22.

of natural law, traditional values and morals, and the virtues of the common good, as well as in the form of heavy invectives targeting innovation and all forms of perceived transgressions against the traditional order.

The point of departure for Part II is the European exploration and spatial expansion around 1500. In what is sometimes referred to as early modern spatial turn, there was a rapidly rising interest in geographic and cosmographic knowledge, and spatiality became an important category of investigation. The recent interest in cultural studies in the spatial turn is a fortuitous coincidence. Fundamental changes occurred in the way the world was imagined in the Early Modern period, which informed the quest for discoveries and the creation of global trade networks. At the beginning of Part II, the representation of spatial expansion in narratives and cosmographies is discussed to establish the knowledge base and awareness in Germany. Among geographers and cosmographers, the insight grew that the knowledge of the ancients, particularly Ptolemy's *Geography*, no longer provided an adequate model to explain and map the world, as the story of Waldseemüller's two world maps illustrates. Spatial expansion therefore was tied to an emancipation from ancient concepts of knowledge. This is contrasted with hostile responses to travel, in particular to the voyages of discovery, and to the curiosity about remote corners of the world that dominated popular writing at the time. The focus will be on the many literary texts of the period that expressed resentments and opposition to spatial expansion. The last chapter looks at the question why America played little or no role in German imagination well into the sixteenth century.

Part III first establishes criteria to define Early Modern Globalization and looks at how this applies to Germany at the time. The bulk of the third part, however, is dedicated to the hostile German responses to all forms of global networking and to their cultural impact on Germany. Many writers expressed disdain for the merchant class because it engaged in usurious and predatory practices, such as generating unearned and excessive profits, taking interest, monopolizing and price gouging, hoarding, trading counterfeit merchandise, and selling below cost. All these issues were magnified by the long-distance trade with Arabia and Asia. The spice trade served as an illustration for the excesses of global trade that addicted Germans to luxurious imports while losing their traditional moral values. Asian imported spices were considered unhealthy for German consumers, caused Germans to disregard the healthy foods and spices grown on their own soil, disrupted the divine order, drained financial resources from Germany, weakened the moral fabric of the German nation, and provided long-distance merchants with unearned wealth. This caused German writers to see the German nation as morally weak and as losing its German identity. In response, they formulated a nationalist and xenophobic backlash against foreign influences that in their view made Germans weak, turned them into immoral and effeminate creatures, and stole their money. Many writers engaged in a nostalgia project that sought to reimagine and recreate a self-contained and strong German nation that was rooted in a pure and moral German past.

Strictly speaking, this is not a book about history. The focus is on textual representations, arguments, and discourses, not on historical events. Where historical events are discussed, they serve to establish the historical context and the proper intellectual environment and thus enhance the analysis of texts. Literary texts did not exist in a vacuum; rather, they responded to matters of concern in the society within which they were written. All arguments are supported by a close reading of texts. As textual evidence is central for close readings, this book contains a significant number of quotes from primary texts, some of them rather lengthy, in order to provide the proper context for the argumentation. Short quotes are often taken out of context and can be used to make misleading claims. Therefore, it is important to interpret text passages within their appropriate argumentative context and to use longer quotes to properly support the argumentative framework.

I quote from modern editions where available. In most cases, I consulted the original texts published in the early sixteenth century listed in the primary bibliography. A number of texts examined here were published in editions in the nineteenth century. I generally avoided their use as they generally are not very reliable and often normalized and simplified the Early New High German language used in the texts. There are some exceptions, such as the use of the edition of the works by Hans Sachs. All English translations are mine and are based on the original texts, except where noted otherwise. I translated German verse in prose to render meaning and context more precisely. The English translations are used in the body of the text for better readability, while the original German quotes are given in the notes.

This study is firmly anchored methodologically in literary studies, although it has an interdisciplinary outlook in a cultural studies mold. While literary analysis provides the tools for reading the texts examined here, not all of them could be characterized as literary, although many texts without literary ambitions also included poems. Brant's *Narrenschiff* shows that literature was largely understood to be part of ethics. Ethics in Humanism was primarily a pragmatic discipline whose objective was to teach a better life.[19] There was no clear theoretical

---

[19] Enrica Zanin, "Why is Boccaccio's *Decameron* in the Ethica Section?" Presentation at the annual meeting of the Renaissance Society of America, Toronto, 19 March 2019.

awareness of genres at the time, and hybrid and mixed forms were common. Genre boundaries were ill-defined, and there was no differentiation among fictional and non-fictional texts.[20] As ethical, political, and social discussions took place across a broad spectrum of genres, genres also play a subordinate role in this study.

The text genres discussed here vary greatly and run the entire spectrum of textual representations. They include prose narration, didactic poem, dialog, church hymn, proverb collection, broadsheet, but also less literary forms like political tract, legal treatise, decree, handbook on trade, herbal, medical text, chronicle, cosmography, map description, exploration report, travel account, pilgrimage account, book of sermons, almanac, news pamphlet, and so on. In spite of their superficial differences, they all share certain literary qualities, which allows us to discern how the literary imagination responded to, complemented, and most likely contested the emerging pluralization and globalization. While some texts under discussion are little known today, the inclusion of canonical texts serves to show that the developments traced in this book by no means represent marginal or fringe phenomena. Virtually all texts under discussion here, with the exception of travel accounts and of geographic or cosmographic texts, are part of the backlash described in this study. Targeted were real-world developments rather than other texts as such texts do not exist, the lone exception being Conrad Peutinger's writings in favor of globalization, monopolies, and self-interest.

Most of the texts examined here were written in the German vernacular. Vernacular texts served different audiences and pursued different purposes than texts written in Latin. Neo-Latin literary texts were mostly oriented on classical models, were highly rhetoricized artifacts, and served literate audiences that typically had a pan-European outlook.[21] The finely tuned rhetorical structure of Latin texts typically gave way to a broader, coarser, and more populist rhetoric, and authors writing in the vernacular did not have to follow the norms of learned discourse.[22] The Latin version of Geiler von Kaysersberg's sermons was more erudite, while the vernacular version was more polemical, direct, and hard-hitting.[23] Both literary and non-literary texts in the vernacular served localized audiences that often were only semi-literate, and their style and content therefore were more accessible. Vernacular texts had a much broader reach and therefore were more suitable to address a topic polemically or to have a specific political impact.

---

20 Kemper, *Deutsche Lyrik*, vol. 1, 37; Hess, "Poetry in Germany," 395–396.
21 Kühlmann, "Neo-Latin Literature," 282.
22 Müller, "Alte Wissensformen," 173.
23 Müller, "Erfarung," 317.

Many authors argued that vernacular texts guaranteed reaching not only a broader audience but also a more desirable audience. Sebastian Brant in 1502 published the first edition of Virgil's complete works and was known for his sophisticated Latin style. Yet, he frequently wrote in German. In his foreword to Ulrich Tengler's *Laÿen Spiegel* from 1509, he justified the use of the vernacular in this legal text with the lack of Latin skills among the intended audience.[24] Brant recognized that Latin texts had a very limited readership. In the case of legal texts, it could not be assumed that public officials in cities or administrators at princely courts could read Latin sufficiently to make use of the texts. Furthermore, the use of German in chanceries and at courts was pretty much established at the time. Similarly, the legal scholar Johannes Ferrarius explained that he wrote his legal text in German because this was the language of his urban and courtly audience of public servants, merchants, bailiffs, and others involved in governance and state administration.[25] German-language texts gave immediate access to a broad reading public, while Latin texts only reached a small elite audience. This is the key factor why the populist and polemical texts examined here were almost exclusively written in German.

The book deals with texts that were published roughly between 1490 and 1540. In the last decade of the fifteenth century, voyages of discovery increased in frequency and scope, and more importantly these voyages became known in a series of publications. Furthermore, the large southern German merchant-banking conglomerates rose to prominence in this decade and started to have an outsize influence both at the communal and imperial levels. In this decade, we also find a rapid increase in publications that took a critical attitude toward these changes and more generally toward the perceived demise of moral values, most notably Sebastian Brant's *Narrenschiff* from 1494. Anxieties about innovation and change and the polemics against the merchant-bankers peaked in the 1520s, the Imperial Diet seriously but ultimately unsuccessfully discussed measures against monopolies, and social conflict openly erupted in the Peasants' Revolt of 1524–1525. Not surprisingly, the anti-merchant and anti-globalist polemics also peaked in this decade.

However, this polemical and politicized literature rapidly subsided in the 1530s. The large merchant-bankers played a less prominent role in the public imagination, perhaps because their role and, along with it, the transformed urban economy had become normalized and accepted. Imported spices, long

---

24 Brant, "Doctor Sebastian Brannd vor reden," sig. ¢2r.
25 Ferrarius, *Von dem Gemeinen nutze*, sig. A4r-A4v.

the visible tip of globalized trade, had found entry into more urban middle-class households and thus no longer were the object of scorn. There were few texts discussing spatial discoveries past the mid–1520s, and their discussion, both supportive and dismissive, waned. Many early polemicists, like Sebastian Brant and Ulrich von Hutten, had died or were no longer active. There also seems to have been a growing acceptance, perhaps grudgingly, of the new status quo. Newer literary texts, notably those by Hans Sachs, were less political as moralizing invective was gradually displaced by more humorous but benign narratives. It is therefore appropriate to set the end point of this study approximately at 1540, even though there were some outliers in the 1540s. By then, political polemics appear to have waned, and a new generation of writers emphasized self-reflective, culturally aware, entertaining, panegyric, or didactic texts.

Part I: A World in Decline: Anxieties about Social and Political Order

> It ought to be remembered that there is nothing more difficult to take in hand, more perilous to conduct, or more uncertain in its success, than to take the lead in the introduction of a new order of things. Because the innovator has for enemies all those who have done well under the old conditions, and lukewarm defenders in those who may do well under the new.
> Niccolò Machiavelli, *The Prince* (1513)

Discourses about social order and its disruptions abounded in the late fifteenth and sixteenth centuries. They were fueled by the social, political, and economic transformations that accompanied the exponential growth of spatial knowledge and the establishment of global trade networks around 1500. Trade and commerce started to evolve rapidly, starting with the evolution of a proto-capitalist economy that began in Italy in the thirteenth century and took hold in Germany in the fifteenth century. Generally, economic development outpaced economic attitudes and moral norms relating to economic activity.[1] It is this tension between economic development and attitudes toward economic processes that led to concern about the stability of the social and political structures. Part I of this book traces responses to political transformations triggered by the rise of the long-distance merchant class and to corresponding shifts in the value system that governed political thinking. Literary texts covering all genres across the board, from church hymns to narrative prose, were dwelling heavily on this theme, which is an indication that writers were concerned about a threat to the order.

Historically, the conventional order was based on the organization of society into three classes or groups, namely those who pray (*oratores*), those who fight (*bellatores*) and those who produce (*laboratores*), as the monk Aelfric Grammaticus (955–1020) formulated it.[2] This was the foundation of the three basic estates in medieval society: clergy, nobility, and the third estate consisting of merchants, artisans and peasants. The estates were configured as "social corporations," each defined by its own set of privileges.[3] While this tripartite system remained operative in France until the French Revolution and was discussed by theoreticians of the Revolution, like Emmanuel Joseph Sieyès (1748–1836),[4] it did not find much attention in Germany past 1200.[5]

Many German cities liberated themselves from landed princes in the Middle Ages and were given vast privileges as free cities by the emperor. The self-confident citizens created their own urban social structures that were typically dominated by the patriciate. Other social categories were small merchants and shopkeepers, artisans and craftsmen, then disenfranchised groups like day laborers, servants, members of dishonest occupations, and Jews. In some cities, in particular in southern Germany and Switzerland, the guilds managed to amass considerable political power. Furthermore, noblemen and members of the clergy enjoyed special privileges in cities but were not involved in their

---

[1] McGovern, "The Rise," 224.
[2] Duby, *The Three Orders*, 102–106.
[3] Scott, *Society*, 27.
[4] For instance his influential pamphlet *Qu'est-ce que le Tiers État?* of January 1789.
[5] Kirschner, *Hermen Bote*, 77.

governance. Therefore, describing German society in terms of the three estates is not very useful. Rather, a differentiation in clergy, nobility, merchants, artisans and peasants was common, with the caveat that nobility and clergy formed their own hierarchy in urban contexts. Furthermore, variations allowed for further differentiation among urban citizens.

German cities in the fifteenth century enjoyed a system of self-governance that allowed many cities to operate like sovereign states. The economic recovery after the plague outbreaks of the fourteenth century led to economic opportunity for an expanding and ever more powerful class of merchants and artisans in German cities.[6] Local merchants typically formed the governing patriciate, but in many southern German cities the guild system was politically powerful as well. The growth of trading cooperatives and of large trading corporations in the fifteenth century gave rise to a class of wealthy long-distance merchants that threatened the existing power structure. Part I examines discourses that project visions of an ideal order as well as express anxieties about its demise.

---

[6] Scott, *Society*, 113–152.

Chapter 1
Order and Discipline: Visions and Anxieties

In the early sixteenth century, there was broad consensus that order was part of a divine plan and therefore represented an innate human need.[7] Christian Egenolff argued this in his *Chronic von an vnd abgang aller Welt wesenn* (*Chronicle of the Beginning and End of All Beings in the World*) from 1533: "And a divine order, as Paul teaches, is implanted into nature and reason, to protect the pious and to punish the evil."[8] The first threat to this natural order was the ejection from paradise. Yet, humans managed to live side by side in simple settlements following the norms of natural law for some time after that: "Thus they built houses, invented all kinds of arts, led a sweet sociable life and a civil and amicable coexistence, without any walls, defenses, armor, rule, authority, and war."[9] But soon some broke the peace and started to practice violence. Envy, disloyalty, theft, robbery, and murder became commonplace, and many left the path of virtue. Thus, the need arose to choose a leader who could protect people against evil deeds and keep the peace. Very soon, peoples chose their kings, built castles and walls around their villages, and armed themselves.[10] Conflicts and wars emerged and grew among these kingdoms, and the need arose to create a supreme monarchy, an imperial majesty, to control the other rulers.[11]

Egenolff made two important points here. First, he explained and justified the existence of the empire, which exercised control over other monarchies. Second, and more importantly, he argued that humans needed authoritarian rule in order to live together communally in peace. The pessimistic view was that humans ever since the fall from Paradise were not able to freely organize their affairs according to natural law. A functioning nobility and ruling monarchs were required to regulate coexistence among humans and to guarantee peace and prosperity. This is a key reason, according to Egenolff and others, that the natives of the West Indies had no kings nor any reliable system of governance and as such had to

---

[7] For instance, Bucer, *Das ym selbs niemant*, sig. c1r.
[8] Egenolff, *Chronic* (1533), fol. 86r: "vnnd ist ein götlich ordnung wie Paulus leret/ der natur vnd vernunfft eingepflantzt/ dem frommen zu schutz/ dem bösen zu straff."
[9] Egenolff, *Chronic* (1533), fol. 86r: "Derhalben bawten sie heuser/ erfanden allerley künst/ fürten ein süß gesellig leben/ vnd ein Burgerlich freuntlichs nachburlichs wesen bei einander/ on alle mawr/ wör/ harnasch/ herschafft/ oberkeyt vnd krieg."
[10] Egenolff, *Chronic* (1533), fol. 86v. Münster, *Cosmographia* (1544), sig. a3v-a4r, explained the rise of monarchic rule in a similar way.
[11] Egenolff, *Chronic* (1533), fol. 86v.

be classified as uncivilized.¹² Having a monarch or strong ruler who imposed order was an indispensable part of the divine order and thus represented the end stage of the development of human societies. As we will see in Chapter 6, the Holy Roman Empire of Maximilian I and Charles V therefore was seen as the ideal final stage of history.

Similarly, the historian and astrologer Johannes Carion (1499–1537), in his *Chronica* from 1532, viewed the divine imposition of order a historical necessity for the world to emerge from its original bleak and disordered condition. Based on Elijah's prophecy of the earth's six-thousand-year existence, the *Vaticinium Eliae*, Carion subdivided human history into three periods of two thousand years each:

> The world will last six thousand years, and then it will fracture. [...] That is for two thousand years the world shall stand desolate, that is without a government ordained by God's word. Then shall come the contraction and the law, and a government and service to God will be ordered anew through God's word, and this shall also last two thousand years. Then Christ shall come, and the period of the Gospel shall also last two thousand years.[13]

In its origins, the state of the world was thought to be desolate because it was without governance. Only in the second period God imposed his order, which allowed for the flourishing of the Assyrian, Persian, and Greek monarchies and later launched the Roman Empire that in its German reincarnation dominated the third and last period of the gospel. This allowed Carion to integrate the doctrine of the *translatio imperii* into the sequence of the four monarchies and simultaneously justify the Christian Occident's emerging leadership of the world.[14] Divinely inspired governance thus was not just important for human society to flourish, but it also was a prerequisite for the second coming of Christ and the subsequent end of history, culminating in the last judgment. To Carion, governance was the expression of divine will:

> I noted in the introduction that God conceived the world in four monarchies in order to sustain order, law, and punishment in the world. I reported this so that one can learn to

---

[12] Egenolff, *Chronica* (1535), fol. 107r.
[13] Carion, *Chronica*, sig. B1v: "Sechs tausent jar ist die welt/ vnd darnach wird sie zubrechen. [...] Das ist/ zwey tausent iar sol die welt stehen öd/ das ist one ein gefasset regiment durch Gottes wort/ Darnach sol die beschneidung vnd das gesetz komen/ vnd ein regiment vnd Gottes dienst/ durch Gottes wort von new geordnet werden/ das sol auch zwey tausent iar weren/ Darnach sol Christus kommen/ Vnd die zeit des Euangelij sol auch bey zwei tausent jaren haben." See also Green, "Translating Time," 163; Prietz, *Das Mittelalter*, 99–100.
[14] Carion, *Chronica*, fol. 56r. See also Münster, *Cosmographia* (1544), 27–28.

recognize and honor God's works in the authorities. This is why Scripture preaches to us so much about these monarchies.[15]

God's will and God's works were recognizable in the authorities he created. Thus, the value of the study of history, as Carion performed it in this *Chronicle*, was that it revealed God's hand behind it.[16] The characterization of God as the master of history, as envisioned in the Book of Daniel, thus rang true to Carion.[17] As its master, God also could ensure its end, which to Carion was very much the point of Daniel's vision.[18]

The radical reformer Sebastian Franck (1499–1542/43) was an unwavering advocate for the unlimited powers of the authorities. In his *Chronica, Zeytbuch vnd geschychtbibel von anbegyn biß inn diß gegenwertig MDXXXI. Jar* (*Chronicle, Annals and Bible of History from the Beginnings up to this Present Year 1531*), he argued that God had been using tyrannical governments as punishment for unruly societies since the Deluge. Worldly authorities were installed by God, and they could be good or tyrannical, depending on whether God intended it to be an instrument to maintain peace and welfare in the world or to punish the evil ones. This is why it was an act of heresy to resist worldly authorities, as the peasants had done in their revolt of 1524–1525:

> In sum, this is why the authorities are nothing other than a rod and servant of God to avenge the one who did evil, for the benefit of the good. This is why Paul […] recommends that the Christians should obey in all ways the godless heathen powers who were sovereigns over their territory, tyrannized it and led it violently. […] For there is no power, if it is not ordained by God, so that whoever opposes that power resists God's order.[19]

The Peasants' Revolt of 1524–1525 therefore held a real lesson for Franck. He described its horror and destruction with a purpose:

---

15 Carion, *Chronica*, sig. C3v: "Ich hab jnn der vorrede gemeldet/ das Got die welt jnn vier Monarchien gefast hab/ ordnung/ recht/ vnd straff jnn der Welt zu erhalten/ welche ich derhalben angezeigt habe/ das man lern Gottes werck/ jnn der Oberkeit erkennen vnd ehren/ Darümb auch die heilig schrifft vns viel von diesen monarchien prediget."
16 Prietz, *Das Mittelalter*, 104.
17 Prietz, *Das Mittelalter*, 100.
18 Carion, *Chronica*, sig. C3v.
19 Franck, *Chronica* (1531), fol. 240r: "Darumb ist in summa alle oberkeyt nichts anders dann ein růt vnd dienerin Gottes zur rach dem der übel handlet/ den gůten zů gůt. Darumb auch Paulus […] empfilcht […] das die Christen auch aller gottlosen heidnischen gwalt/ die zur selben zeit das regiment inn hielten/ tirannisierten/ vnd mit gwalt fůren/ […] solten gehorsam leisten in allen dingen/ […] dann es ist kein gewaldt/ dann von Gott verordnet/ also/ das wer sich der gwalt widersetzt/ Gottes ordnung widerstrebt."

> Enough said about all rebellion by way of example and deterrence, so that we should know that rebellion never was pleasing to God, and that the Gospel teaches us to suffer oppression and not to rise up.[20]

Like Luther, Franck held that the peasants were wrong to take matters into their own hands as it was up to God to punish the tyrants.[21] However, Franck remained an inconsequential outlier in the discussion of the nature of secular authority and political order as his spiritualist and mystical message was broadly and vigorously rejected in the Protestant world, including by Luther.

Urban self-rule, within the confines of the Holy Roman Empire, was commonly framed as a legitimate variant of monarchic rule within this system of order. Many political writers specifically addressed urban political structures within this larger context. Georg Lauterbeck (c. 1505–1578) in his *Regentenbuch Aus vielen trefflichen alten vnd newen Historien/ mit sonderm fleis zusammen gezogen* (*Regent Book, Drawn from Splendid Old and New Histories with Special Diligence*) from 1556, for instance, came up with a fairly differentiated urban structure that reflects the growing complexities of urban life and the nuances of urban governments. Lauterbeck stated that his text was modeled after Aristotle's *Politics*.[22] But it is not a mere translation as Lauterbeck specifically tailored it to the needs of cities and as he addressed specific sixteenth-century concerns.[23] Lauterbeck first mentioned the farmers, then "artisans, like bakers, shoemakers, tailors, carpenters, stonemasons, and the like."[24] The next groups were "merchants, shop keepers, and small sellers" as well as day laborers.[25] The fifth category were "those who engage in war"[26] with the clear limitation that only those were included who defended their city or fatherland, but not mercenaries who went to war for money. The last category included those who ruled the city:

---

20 Franck, *Chronica* (1531), fol. 237v: "Diß sey zum exempel vnd abschreckung von aller auffrůr genůg/ dz wir sollen wissen/ das Got kein auffrůr nie gefallen hat/ vnd dz Euangelium gewalt leiden vnd nit auffrůren leret."
21 Franck, *Chronica* (1531), fol. 238r.
22 Lauterbeck, *Regentenbuch*, fol. 137v.
23 Philipp (*Das ‚Regentenbuch'*, 110) calls the fourth chapter a mere translation.
24 Lauterbeck, *Regentenbuch*, fol. 137v: "Ackerleut," then "Handwergs leut/ [...] Als Becker/ Schuster/ Schneider/ Zimmerleut/ Steinmetzen/ vnnd dergleichen."
25 Lauterbeck, *Regentenbuch*, fol. 137v: "Kauffleut/ Kremer/ vnd Hocken" and "Taglöner."
26 Lauterbeck, *Regentenbuch*, fol. 137v: "die jenigen/ so sich Krieges gebrauchen."

And at last those who preside over the common good and the entire city, and who govern those and the common citizenry. Which is the most noble estate without which a city can in no way be and exist; which are judges, mayor, and council members.[27]

Beyond that, Lauterbeck listed the following groups not mentioned by Aristotle: "superintendents, school teachers, sextons, pastors and preachers," physicians, "legal scholars who are called jurists," and good builders and carpenters.[28] Lauterbeck saw all these social groups as necessary for a city to function properly, and it was also important that the groups worked together: "Wherever one wants to elevate one part or estate and suppress another, the government will not exist for long, because all these estates are needed to edify a city."[29] Lauterbeck concluded on a cautious, slightly ironic note: "Regardless, it often happens that one regards in highest esteem those estates which contribute the least to the city."[30] Lauterbeck, as well as other writers, was keenly aware of the gap between theoretical aspiration and practical governance.

While such lists could vary in the sixteenth century, Lauterbeck illustrated the degree of differentiation with which writers at the time saw their urban societies. Such classifications were commonly upheld by urban literary writers like Bote, Brant, Sachs, Fischart and many others. Beyond that point, the system remained static, and ideas of flexibility on a systemic level and social mobility on an individual level generally were not well-received, and the underlying concept of a rigid social order was not seriously questioned.

Descriptions of specific urban polities confirm this, like the *Tractatus de civitate Ulmensi* (*Treatise About the City of Ulm*), published in 1488 by the Dominican theologian Felix Fabri (1441–1502). In a detailed and differentiated fashion, Fabri described a stable and compartmentalized urban society that was based on inequality and lacked social mobility.[31] Long-distance merchants as a newer group were privileged but did not belong to the patriciate. As they

---

[27] Lauterbeck, *Regentenbuch*, fol. 137v: "Vnd zum letzten die jenigen/ so dem gemeinen nutz/ vnnd der gantzen Stad vorstehen/ dieselben vnd gemeine Bürgerschafft riegieren/ Welchs dann der fürnemlichste Stand ist/ daran ein Stad keins weges sein noch bestehen kan/ als da sein Richter/ Bürgermeister/ vnd Rethe/ etc."

[28] Lauterbeck, *Regentenbuch*, fol. 137v: "Superattendenten/ Schulen/ vnd Kirchendiener/ Pfarherrn vnd Predicanten;" "Ertzte;" "Rechts gelerte/ welche man Juristen nennet;" "gute Bawmeister vnd Zimmerleut."

[29] Lauterbeck, *Regentenbuch*, fol. 138r: "Wo man aber einen theil oder stand erheben/ vnnd den andern verdrucken wil/ da wirdt das Regiment nicht lang bestehen können/ denn es gehören diese Stende alle zu erbawung einer Stad."

[30] Lauterbeck, *Regentenbuch*, fol. 138r: "Aber vngeacht des/ treget sichs zum offtern mal zu/ das man die Stende am höchsten helt/ welche der Stad am wenigsten nützlich sein."

[31] Fabri, *Tractatus*, 101; Isenmann, *Die deutsche Stadt*, 699–708.

were the only class having relations with members of all the other classes, they were a socially more fluid class than the others.[32] Furthermore, the labor of merchants brought fame and wealth to the city of Ulm.[33] Fabri showed an unusual tolerance for the social and geographic mobility of long-distance merchants as a concession to his adopted hometown of Ulm, one of the most active merchant cities at the time.

A more allegorical example is *Van veleme rade byn ik eyn boek* (*Of Many Wheels Am I a Book*) by the Brunswick writer Hermann (or Hermen) Bote (c.1450–c.1520), commonly referred to as *Radbuch* (*Wheel Book*), which was published anonymously in Lübeck in 1492 or 1493.[34] Bote represented the political order of a free city that was an important member of the Hanseatic League. The son of a Brunswick master blacksmith, Bote served his native city as public official throughout his career. The title of the book plays on the homonymy of the words for "Rad" (wheel) and "Rat," which can mean both council and counsel.[35] In 1,392 Low German verses in paired rhymes, divided into eleven chapters, Bote developed the wheel as an allegory for the social structure of the time, which is represented as the foundation of human prosperity. The first chapter, the introduction, explains the allegory of the ten wheels discussed in the subsequent ten chapters: five wheels are useful and necessary for human life, while the five others are interlopers who try to disrupt the proper functioning and interplay of the five useful wheels.[36] Bote showed the world as a system of harmoniously interlocking wheels and used the wheel as a symbol for unity in diversity,[37] the five wheels jointly determining the course of the world, the "werlde loep," as Bote stated in the title of the book.[38] Bote stressed both the significance of each individual wheel as well as the importance of their collaboration for a higher purpose.[39] Yet, the wheel also could be the wheel of fortune shown in the ninth chapter, which symbolizes the changing fortunes that drive human life.

The ten chapters focusing on wheels are organized hierarchically from the most critically important and useful to the most harmful and detrimental. Each of the five useful wheels represents a social group that makes unique contributions to human society. The most central one is the millwheel in the second

---

32 Isenmann, *Die deutsche Stadt*, 706.
33 Fabri, *Tractatus*, 223–225.
34 Hayden-Roy, "The Masquerade," 6.
35 Blume, *Hermann Bote*, 29.
36 Bote, *Radbuch*, 73.
37 Wunderlich, "Nachwort," 149.
38 Baeumer, "Aufruhr," 139.
39 Wunderlich, "Nachwort," 149.

chapter that represents the dual authority of pope and emperor and is essential for the workings of the entire system. The third chapter features the cogwheel, which stands for the ruling princes who should practice good governance and implement imperial law. The capstan represents the nobility in general, who guarantee the safety and well-being of the producing classes. The wagon wheel in chapter five refers to the economic activity of merchants. It represents the noble free cities, above all the cities of the Hanseatic League of which Bote's native Brunswick was a prominent member. The wagon wheel is built out of five different types of wood of the highest quality and of four different metals,[40] representing the various social and occupational groups in the city who all have their distinct functions yet contribute their part for the good of the whole. The plow wheel, finally, stands for the peasantry. Peasants, like plows, should faithfully perform their duties on the land of the nobles and recognize existing law.[41] The chapter also includes a warning to the ignorant peasants to accept their subservient lives and to refrain from seeking social betterment. Bote reminds the members of all classes to consider their ranks and to act in accordance to that.[42] This is a clear reference to ongoing unrest in the peasant population, which eventually erupted in the Peasants' Revolt of 1524–1525.

The concluding five chapters parade the wheels that represent negative forces. Interestingly, women lead this group. Women are respresented as useful and charming, but also as mostly moody, untrustworthy, loquacious, and divisive.[43] The next three wheels stand for war, envy, hatred and discord, for evil supernatural forces, and for fools. The broken wheel, finally, is the source of all evil works and stands for all those who transgress against rules, norms, and laws, regardless of class, and thus constitute a threat to the established order. Bote included the wrongdoing by the authorities to the list of transgressions, which just like the misconduct of the subjects, could have a destabilizing effect.[44]

Bote's *Radbuch* perhaps was the first German literary text that in its entirety discussed the theoretical foundations of the social structure. The entire text served as an allegory that created the analogy between different types of wheels and different groups and classes within human society. The different importance and function of the five useful wheels served to justify the different estates and classes and their varying importance. Bote made it clear that this

---

[40] Bote, *Radbuch*, 93.
[41] Bote, *Radbuch*, 103.
[42] Bote, *Radbuch*, 105.
[43] Bote, *Radbuch*, 107–109.
[44] Blume (*Hermann Bote*, 29) reads the potential criticism of the authorities as the mark of a "modern" author.

order was ordained by God and that any infringements against it led to disorder, therefore representing a transgression against divine order.[45]

While later texts primarily focused on the breaks in the social order, Bote's text is balanced evenly between creating a vision for the proper functioning of the system of estates and showing the sources of the ruptures in the system, without resorting to a critique of specific vices practiced in Sebastian Brant's contemporaneous *Narrenschiff* (*Ship of Fools*). The five useless wheels did not contribute toward the common good and in many ways were disruptive to the workings of society and represented transgressions against the social order. The recognition of the existence of five useless wheels was important at the literal level as their wheel status recognized them as part of a system of wheels. On the allegorical level, the disruptive and transgressive element was an inherent part of human society and thus part of the divine plan. In that sense, Bote's text was still rather general and unsophisticated in terms of political thinking, while contemporaneous writers like Sebastian Brant developed their vision of the social order in more specific and differentiated ways.

Hermann Bote expressed similar views in his *Schicht boick* (*Chronicle of Uprisings*), a chronicle of political uprisings in Brunswick in the late Middle Ages. It was written between 1510 and 1514 and survived as an autograph but was not edited and published until 1880.[46] The text therefore had little impact beyond the small circle who had access to the illustrated manuscript. Instead of using wheels to define the role of each social group, he used the animal kingdom in the introduction to each of the six sections as an allegory to delineate his vision of a divinely ordained, hierarchical human order. In the *Schicht boick*, Bote chronicled six different political and social conflicts in his native Brunswick between 1292 and 1514 that erupted into open unrest and rebellion.[47]

His prologue is a plea to the citizens of Brunswick to pursue "the common good" that could not prevail if citizens pursued their own self-interest.[48] In his reading, uprisings such as the ones described here tended to be the fault of the ruling classes because there was disunion, envy, and even hidden hatred among the elites, as he explained in the prologue, or imprudent and arbitrary governance that did not serve the general public. The consequence of discord and disunion, said Bote, was that free cities fell under the control of landed princes: "But then it comes about that both parties lose life and goods, frequently at the

---

45 Blume, *Hermann Bote*, 29.
46 Blume, *Hermann Bote*, 53.
47 Hayden-Roy, "The Masquerade," 562.
48 Bote, *Das Schichtbuch*, 299: "dat ghemeyne ghut."

same time bringing the city under the control of the princes."[49] A second fault of the authorities was that they failed to control the common people and allowed them to act freely according to their own will: "And when a common burgher is not under control and under strict governance, that makes for disobedient burghers."[50]

Bote as a public official was well-informed about the history of his city, and his point of view must have been close to that of the city council. Members of the council presumably were his desired audience.[51] The last chapter, entitled "Uployp van twen schoten" (Uprising because of double taxation), refers to a crisis in Brunswick between 1512 and 1514. The uprising erupted while Bote wrote the text, and we have to assume that he added this chapter as a supplement because the main body of the text already had been completed.[52] Here, Bote was a participant and not just a chronicler. He narrated vividly how he was captured and abused by the rebels and very nearly executed.[53] Furthermore, Bote also had been temporarily relieved of his position in the customs office during the previous uprising of 1488.[54]

While Bote was a keen observer of the political life in Brunswick and recognized how lower classes were abused by the authorities, he was of the conviction that uprisings were illegitimate, counterproductive, and ultimately harmful to the common good.[55] His main focus was on the preservation of the corporate order, which was threatened by conflict among the patriciate and by imprudent currency and fiscal policies.[56] Strife and conflict thus were difficult to process for Bote as the desired state of concord was not compatible with upheaval and with the idea of historical change. The narration of the Brunswick conflicts thus had to end with Bote's claim that the old order was restored, "and they appointed a council as it had been before."[57] In spite of Bote's assertion, the conflict of 1374, the most violent of the six uprisings, brought profound and lasting change to the

---

49 Bote, *Das Schichtbuch*, 299: "unde kumpt denne ock vaken unde vele, dat eyn myt synem vyende vorlust liff unde ghud, unde bringet vaken de stede in de walt der fursten." Translation Hayden-Roy, "The Masquerade," 565.
50 Bote, *Das Schichtbuch*, 332: "unde wan de borger nicht in dwange sin unde in reygemente, dat maket ungehorsem borger."
51 Hayden-Roy, "The Masquerade," 562.
52 Blume, *Hermann Bote*, 89–90.
53 Bote, *Das Schichtbuch*, 456.
54 Blume, *Hermann Bote*, 87.
55 Baeumer, "Aufruhr," 465; Wailes: "The Childishness," 135.
56 Blume, *Hermann Bote*, 101.
57 Bote, *Das Schichtbuch*, 317, 22–23: "unde maketen dar eynen Rad wedder so tovoren was." See also Hayden-Roy, "The Masquerade," 567.

statutory make-up of the Brunswick council.[58] The historical record thus contradicts Bote's narrative of a continuous prevailing order.

While to Bote the biggest concerns were the stability of political order and social hierarchy as well as the threat emanating from unrest and upheaval, other writers expressed their anxieties about the failing order by focusing on the dangers emanating from individual transgressive behavior. It is in this context that the Basel lawyer and public official Sebastian Brant (1457–1521) published his highly didactic *Narrenschiff* (*Ship of Fools*) in 1494. In that sense, Brant rather than Bote set the paradigm. While the preoccupation with social order was pervasive in early modern literature, literary discussions mostly focused on individual transgressions against it. Brant did not question the divine origin of all order: "Therefore let God's foreknowledge and order based on foresight stand as it stands."[59] To Brant, the presence of an omniscient divine ordering hand was self-evident yet incomprehensible to humans. While Brant rarely reflected on the divine origin of creation and the worldly order in an overt manner, the entire *Narrenschiff* is spiked with biblical references, showing how deeply his work was infused by biblical thinking.

Brant's primary concern was the perceived gap between economic and social practices and the failure by the Church to provide proper guidance. He attempted to uphold late medieval economic attitudes that were largely informed by an economic system carried by the guild system and rejected the new economy that was dominated by merchant-bankers. He implicitly faulted the Church for not providing leadership in the face of this crisis. Furthermore, Brant took the liberty to elucidate human nature even though the explanation and interpretation of the human condition still was the prerogative of the Church.[60]

Brant's *Narrenschiff* was the most successful German-language book before Goethe's *Werther* (1774). There were seventeen German-language editions during Brant's lifetime[61] and a total of 77 editions, including translations into other languages, before 1600.[62] In 112 chapters, Brant described fools and their errant ways as a warning to the reader to refrain from foolish behavior described in the chapters. Brant's fools have sometimes been described as sinners, particularly in the older literature.[63] Many contemporaneous conceptions of fools

---

[58] Hayden-Roy, "The Masquerade," 567; Rüther, "Von der Macht," 127.
[59] Brant, *Narrenschiff*, ch. 57, v. 87–89: "Dar vmb loß gots fürwissenheyt | Vnd ordenung der fürsichtikeyt | Stan wie sie stat."
[60] Biehler, *Der Eigennutz*, 19.
[61] Rockenberger, *Produktion*, 97.
[62] Rockenberger, *Produktion*, 18.
[63] For instance Rosenfeld, "Brants Narrenschiff," 243; Bachorski, "Wie der Narr," 279.

included pranksters, jugglers, jokesters, and court jesters[64] or humans with intellectual or physical disabilities,[65] but all of these categories are absent from Brant's book. Brant defined fools more broadly as unwise, ignorant, immoral, and dull-minded individuals with flawed characters who threatened the moral fabric and social order in the process.[66]

Brant's notion of the fool was bound into a moral-theological context in that foolery was interpreted as an offense against God's will and works. For Brant, the fool embodied deviations from the norm that represented violations of the divine order.[67] This allowed for even minor deviations from the norm to be interpreted as foolery, that is vice. Literary representations of fools that operated on this principle were closely tied to the regulation of moral behavior.[68] In the introduction to the *Narrenschiff*, Brant revealed his bleak, apocalyptic vision: "The entire world lives in a dark night and is blindly frozen in sin. All streets and alleys are full of fools who do nothing else than engage in foolery."[69] Brant thus represented a negative anthropology in the Augustinian tradition. The fall from paradise caused humans to live out their days on earth as unreconstructed sinners.[70] Humans, in their reconfiguration as fools, thus by definition were corrupted and therefore threatened public morality and the stability of the social hierarchy, which is why Brant saw them in in need of moral guidance. Brant endeavored to address this perceived moral void and to repair these perceived ruptures in the social order by providing specific moral guidance that remarkably was mostly free of overt religious references and biblical teachings. Yet, foolishness also had an implied religious dimension in that the fool invariably was agnostic and distant from God: "He is a fool who does not want to believe Scripture regarding salvation, and who believes that he should live as if there was no God, nor hell, holding preaching and teaching in contempt as if he did not see nor hear."[71] Brant's text thus represents an extra-institutional religious response to a

---

64 Aurnhammer, "Sünder–Narr–Held," 276.
65 Bachorski, "Wie der Narr," 276.
66 Knape, "Der Medien-Narr," 253; Kuper, *Zur Semiotik der Inversion*, 59.
67 Neuber, "Verdeckte Theologie," 10.
68 Brüggemann, *Die Angst*, 41.
69 Brant, *Narrenschiff*, "vorred," v. 8–11: "Die gantz welt lebt in vinstrer nacht | Und dût in sünden blint verharren | All strassen/ gassen/ sindt voll narren | Die nüt dann mit der dorheit vmbgan."
70 Biehler, *Der Eigennutz*, 19–20.
71 Brant, *Narrenschiff*, ch. 11, v. 1–6: "Der ist ein narr der nit der geschrifft | Will glouben die das heil antrifft | Vnd meynet das er leben söll | Als ob kein got wer/ noch kein hell | Verachtend all predig vnd ler | Als ob er nit säh noch hör."

process of secularization that ran as a counter-movement to secularization in the early modern period.[72]

Brant's fools did not belong to a specific estate, social class, nor occupational category; to Brant, foolishness was ubiquitous. Fools ranged from beggars unwilling to work to princes endangering the cohesion of the empire with their selfish politics. It included every person in between, like unfaithful women, usurious merchants, or troubled clergy. Nobody was exempt from foolishness, and everybody was prone to committing one foolish act or another.[73] In his book, Brant sought to provide a consensus-based, comprehensive list of fools because only such a list could fully represent the range of transgressions that threatened the prevailing order. In Humanist rhetoric, a collection of *topoi*, often referred to as *loci communes*, did not just contain a large storehouse of thoughts and arguments. Rather, a correct and comprehensive collection of such *topoi* contained all of knowledge and thus had an epistemological function.[74] Sebastian Brant both in his prologue and his epilogue confirmed that he collected a comprehensive list of arguments to meet his didactic objectives.[75] The *Narrenschiff* intended to provide such a collection and thus a complete representation of reality.[76] Brant himself bragged about the comprehensiveness of his list of fools in his preface: "Here there is no shortage of fools. Each will find whatever he desires."[77]

Most other writers of the time diagnosed a general sense of malaise, depicted a web of disturbances of the established order, and expressed a great deal of anxiety about preserving order and repairing ruptures. A common theme in the literature of the late fifteenth and sixteenth centuries were transgressions against what was seen as the common good and perceived ruptures of the social order that was commonly framed as God-given, as the Catholic legal scholar Johannes Ferrarius confirmed: "All authorities and administrations are ordained by God. If someone rebels against them, he is rejecting God's order."[78] This theme was developed by followers of Luther as well. Luther himself forcefully condemned the

---

72 Lehmann, "Zur Erforschung," 10.
73 Brüggemann, *Die Angst,* 51.
74 Hess, "Zum Toposbegriff," 75–81.
75 Brant, *Narrenschiff*, "vorred" and "End des narrenschiffs." Brant used the word "gesamlet"(collected) in both instances. Wels (2010) demonstrates, using chapters 8 and 100 as examples, how Brant uses such collections of arguments to construe his chapters.
76 Müller, "Evidentia und Medialität," 70.
77 Brant, *Narrenschiff*, vorred, v. 47–48: "Hie ist an narren kein gebrust | Ein yeder findt das in gelust." Later (v. 87–88) he stated that compiling such a comprehensive list of fools caused a lot of work for him.
78 Ferrarius, *Von dem Gemeinen nutze*, fol. 8r: "Alle oberkeit vnd vorwaltunge sey von Gott verordnet/ da widder so sich iemant entpöre/ der widerstrebe Gottes ordenung."

uprising of the peasants in 1524–1525, which he saw as a godless rebellion against legitimate authorities. Otto Brunfels, who later became known for his herbals, reiterated this theme: "Rebellious is each who rises against his superiors whom he owes obedience, even if they rule in a tyrannical fashion. For all power is from God."[79]

---

[79] Brunfels, *Almanach ewig werend*, sig. C1r: "Vffrürisch ist ein yeder der sich vffbaumt wider seine oberen/ welchen er gehorsamen sol/ ob sye schon tyrannischer weiß herrschen. Wann yeder gwalt von Got."

Chapter 2
Gute Policey: Saving or Disrupting the Order?

It is not an accident that Bote wrote his *Radbuch* at a time when there was a growing concern about matters of state organization, both in the political literature and in everyday politics. One of the features was the strengthening of institutions of central administration from the communal level all the way to imperial administration.[1] A key tool was the *Gute Policey*, a term referring to laws, ordinances, and regulations issued by authorities to establish and enforce social norms, to achieve communal order, and to enhance the common good. The common good was a dominant theme in the political discourse of the sixteenth century.[2] *Gute Policey* was the expression of a growing insight into the need to give direction to communal life by way of legislation.[3] *Policey* was not interested in mediating individual differences of interests but rather in the order of the political system, of the polity as a whole.[4] Johannes Ferrarius stated as an objective the creation of written "permanent law"[5] that codified customary law, which had been passed down through generations: "This is why the written law is highly necessary, not just to govern by it, but also to give shape to customs as long as they promote the common good."[6]

The *Policey* stood for an acceleration of legislative activity on the level of the territorial state in the early modern period. Such efforts were rare in the late Middle Ages but had become exceedingly common by the eighteenth century.[7] Until the fifteenth century, landed rulers were mainly responsible for protection and high jurisdiction, while the political and social order was maintained by local political units or by the Church.[8] Thus, we see both a shift of legislation from the communal or urban level to the level of the territorial state and an increase in the number of laws. Thomas Simon identified three possible reasons why the early modern territorial state gradually took over the maintenance and

---

1 Hieber, "Policey," 1.
2 Blickle, "Beschwerden und Polizeien," 564.
3 Simon, *Gute Policey*, 168.
4 Simon, *Gute Policey*, 112. For a broader definition of the term *Gute Policey*, see Iseli, *Gute Policey*, 14–31.
5 Ferrarius, *Von dem Gemeinen nutze*, fol. 7v: "bestendig recht."
6 Ferrarius, *Von dem Gemeinen nutze*, fol. 7v: "Darumb das beschrieben recht hoch von nöten ist/ nit allein da durch zu regirn/ sonder auch den gewonheyten/ so fern die vor den gemeinen nutz sein mögen/ ein maß zu geben."
7 Simon, "Krise oder Wachstum," 1201.
8 Simon, "Krise oder Wachstum," 1203.

extension of the communal order in the late fifteenth and sixteenth centuries: (1) the declining capacity of local governments and of the Church to establish and maintain order, (2) a profound crisis of order that unsettled and destabilized society, and (3) and ongoing process of condensation, that is urbanization, more complicated webs of transaction, denser and geographically larger networks, and growing social interdependence.[9]

In Simon's reading, the third factor outweighed the other two. An increasingly complex society required a more intensive legislation at a higher political level, that of the territorial state.[10] However, a tighter web of social interdependences made the social system more susceptible to disruption.[11] The efforts to create more uniform legal codes was seen by many as a symptom for underlying uncertainty and instability, which explains why the popular literature responded anxiously and unfavorably. It was commonly believed that communal governments were best able to regulate communal affairs, which is why the intervention by princely governments was widely resented. Hermann Bote, for instance, anxiously rejected the new legal doctrine out of concern for the old corporative order that he saw threatened by it. The resistance to innovative, written territorial and imperial legal codes grew out of the perceived influx of foreign lawyers trained in Roman law and more generally of the intrusion of written Roman law into the German lands, as discussed in Chapter 20.

Martin Luther, for instance, considered a rigid legislative regime to be a sign of bad governance.[12] He stated this at the very beginning of his *Ein Sermon vom Neuen Testament* (*A Sermon About the New Testament*) from 1520:

> Firstly. Experience, all chronicles, and on top of that Holy Scripture teach us: the fewer laws, the better the justice, and the fewer commands, the more good deeds. And there never has been a community that was governed well for a long time that had a lot of laws.[13]

The idea that a community could not be primarily governed through legislation seems to have been commonplace at the time. *Policey* was not primarily

---

9 Simon, "Krise oder Wachstum," 1206–1207.
10 Simon, "Krise oder Wachstum," 1213.
11 Simon, "Krise oder Wachstum," 1211.
12 Simon, *Gute Policey*, 173–174. As Tacitus had famously stated, "The more corrupt the state, the more numerous the laws."
13 Luther, WA 6, 353, 5–9: "ZUm ersten. Das leret vns die erfarung, alle cronicken, dartzu die heyligen schrifft, das, yhe weniger gesetz, yhe besser recht, yhe weniger gepott, yhe mehr gutter werck, und ist noch nie keyn gemeyne odder yhe nit lang wol regirt, wo vil gsetz geweßen seyn." See also Luther, *Christian Nobility*, 451–452.

interested in expanding the legal corpus but rather in shoring up existing law with the goal of preserving or restoring the old order. *Policey* therefore was to be used with restraint.[14]

Legal scholar Sebastian Brant discussed the transition from natural law to an arbitrary and subjective legal code in his 1509 preface to the *Laÿen Spiegel* (*Layman's Mirror*) by Ulrich Tengler (1441–1511). As the title implies, the purpose of the text was to explain the legal code in the German vernacular to those without legal training, which included many officials in the service of cities or princes.[15] This was one of several legal texts Brant edited, in spite of the criticism of lawyers he had expressed in his *Narrenschiff*. God instilled natural law into humans as part of the act of creation. However, the natural law was crushed after the seduction by the snake in paradise, an act that created daily strife, envy, and disunity:

> Against that the faded natural law was no longer sufficient and compelling enough to teach and discipline humans with commands of statutes, out of divine providence, how they should live honorably, offend no one, and give to each his own. Such commands should be handled and administered by two swords conferred by the Almighty, one to the clerical and one to the secular estate.[16]

While the demise of natural law was regrettable, Brant did not hold it to be sufficient to deal with the complexities of contemporaneous life. Canon law and secular law, both also installed by divine authority, thus constituted a suitable alternative. In spite of a common theoretical aversion to change and innovation, to be discussed in Chapter 5, writers like Brant conceded that rapid changes in urban German society required appropriate adjustments in the legal structure.

For pragmatic reasons, therefore, it was necessary to consider new statutes as society was evolving at an ever more rapid pace, as Johannes Ferrarius noted:

> Because everyday something new transpires, and also because the circumstances of states and people and their affairs occur in such a way that they cannot be settled and governed through written or habitual law, therefore it is necessary to reflect on a new order or new statutes on occasion.[17]

---

14 Simon, *Gute Policey*, 174.
15 Knape, "Der humanistische Geleittext," 117–118.
16 Tengler, *Laÿen Spiegel*, sig. ¢1v: "Dargegen das verblichen natürlich gesatz/ nicht mer gnůg vnd not gewesen ist auß götlicher fürsichtigkait die menschen mit geboten des rechten zů vnderweisen vnd bezwingen/ wie sy ersamlich leben/ nyemands belaydigen/ vnd ainem yeden das sein geben solten. Solche gepot sollen durch zway swert/ der ains gaistlichen vnd das ander weltlichen stand von dem allmechtigen verlihen sein/ gehandthabt vnd verwalten."
17 Ferrarius, *Von dem Gemeinen nutze*, fol. 28v: "Dweil aber allen tag was news sich zutregt/ vnd auch gelegenheit der lande vnd leuthe/ vnd dero hendel/ ettwan der massen furfalln/ das

In spite of the aversion to legislation in principle, the perception of rapid change in society, which was stated and bemoaned almost universally by political and literary writers, prompted an increased consideration of *Gute Policey* in order to regulate these new developments and to outlaw new practices that were seen as detrimental to the common good. Change brought with it increased opportunity for transgressive behavior that, in Ferrarius's view, urgently needed to be curbed:

> This is why there has to be a law so that the rogue can be disciplined, the good one can be protected, and to each can be given what he deserves according to the law. For the law is a gift of God, a lesson from the wise, a punishment of transgressions, a link to the common good, according to which each deserves to live who is in the community.[18]

The law was not proactive and was not meant to design new visions of society, rather it was conservative and defensive of the status quo. The law also was not based on politics nor on the needs and desires of the sovereign but rather represented an attempt to preserve and restore order rooted in divine law and wisdom and was devoted to the punishment of transgressions and the promotion of the common good.

There was a pragmatic side to this discussion that considered both the need to maintain stability and to adjust the legislative body to new political, economic, and social environments. Georg Lauterbeck, for instance, tried to strike a balance between the two opposite poles in a chapter of his *Regentenbuch* (1556) with the programmatic title, "That one should not lightly make emendations to statutes, laws, and rules in a country or city."[19] Lauterbeck's focus clearly was on the preservation of the legal structure. In order to preserve stability, it was imperative "that a city stick with its order and firmly adhere to its statutes and laws which it once had implemented."[20] However, Lauterbeck's chapter title also hints at the

---

sie durch beschriebene Rechte/ odder herbrachte gewonheiten nit so statlich mögen entscheiden/ vnd regirt werden/ ist von nöten auff newe ordnung vnd statuten der gelegenheit nach zu dencken."

18 Ferrarius, *Von dem Gemeinen nutze*, fol. 3v: "Darumb müssen gesatz sein/ damit der schalck gezempt/ der gutte vor gewalt geschutzt/ vnd einem jeden was jme rechts halber gepurt/ mitgetheilt werde/ Dan das gesatz ist ein gab gottes/ ein lehr der weisen/ ein straff der vberfarung/ ein verbindung des gemeinen nutzes/ dar nach einen ieden zu leben gepurt/ der in der gemein ist."

19 Lauterbeck, *Regentenbuch*, fol. 111v-113r: "Das man leichtliche mit den Statuten/ Gesetzen vnd Ordnungen/ in einem Land/ oder bey einer Stad/ kein anderung machen sol."

20 Lauterbeck, *Regentenbuch*, fol. 112r: "das ein Stad bey jrer Ordnung bleib/ vnd vber jren Statuten vnd Gesetzen/ welche sie einmal bekrefftiget/ festigklich halte."

possibility of making changes. Changes were not entirely prohibited, but they should not be made lightly either. He sarcastically mentioned cities that changed their laws every four weeks with the result that none of them were observed and furthermore that all laws and ordinances in general were seen with contempt. Frequent changes to Lauterbeck were indicative of council members acting in their own interest and more generally of corruption. Stable laws therefore were essential for maintaining a stable order, and changes to laws had to be modest in scope and implemented thoughtfully. Yet, Lauterbeck was much more prepared to accept innovation as part of the political process than Ferrarius had been a generation earlier.

Early reformers attempted to link the notion of *Policey* to the divine order; see, for instance, Martin Bucer in his short tract *Das ym selbs niemant/ sonder anderen leben soll* (*That No One Should Live for Himself, but Rather for Others*) from 1523:

> Now we have to bear witness: as God immeasurably surpasses the wisdom and prudence of all humans, so also do the divine order and statute have to surpass the order and statute of humans to establish a just, honest, peaceful, and well-crafted policy [politzey] and to govern.[21]

In this text, Bucer represented a world where everything had a place in creation, as told in Genesis, and by analogy also had a place in the order of the world as it was created by God. For humans, there was an obligation to subject themselves to this divine order. The function of *Policey* was to create a worldly order that followed the precepts of the divine order.

While the notion of a divinely ordained order was not seriously challenged by other writers in the sixteenth century, most grounded the notion of *Policey* in a framework derived from a secularized moral philosophy and designed it as the primary tool to create a political structure that served the common good. Within that context, *Policey* dominated the political process from the late fifteenth century up to the beginning of the Thirty Years War. It included the entire system of authority-led public administration: it dealt with cultural, social, and religious issues and addressed the economic order, public safety, and infrastructure issues.[22] It embodied a more systematic, comprehensive, and proactive vision of the law and represented the beginning of the modern legislative

---

21 Bucer, *Das ym selbs niemant*, sig. c2r: "Nun müssen wir ye bekennen/ wie gott on masß übertrifft aller menschen weißheit vnd klůgheit/ also můsß auch göttlich ordnung vnd satztung/ aller menschen ordnung satzung/ ein rechte/ eerliche/ fridliche/ vnnd gantz wol angestelte politzey anzůrichten vnd regieren übertreffen."
22 Hieber, "Policey," 1.

process.²³ Even writers like Leonhard Fronsperger (1520–1575), one of the few writers in the sixteenth century who did not see the common good as the bedrock of an ideal society, strenuously argued in favor of *Gute Policey* as the foundation of state institutions. Fronsperger supported the universality of *Policey* in his tract *Von dem Lob deß Eigen Nutzen* (*Of the Praise of Self-Interest*) from 1564 that will be discussed more comprehensively in Chapter 8:

> The righteous, true, omnipotent and wise God and creator of all things created the world in such a way that all of it, as far as the circumference of it goes, is one single polity [*Policey*] and literally should be just like one state.²⁴

Fronsperger did not make a distinction between *Policey* and state – to him *Policey* was the very foundation of any state.

The political literature in the sixteenth century did not include fundamental innovations over earlier political literature. Many of the principles came out of the late medieval tradition of the *Fürstenspiegel*.²⁵ But the audience of such texts evolved over time: while they focused on advice for princes in late Middle Ages, they addressed everybody who was involved with governance, in particular urban administrators like members of city councils and public officials.²⁶ Furthermore, political advisers were held to the same standards as princes and thus also were addressees of these texts, as the Humanist writer Jakob Wimpfeling stated in his short tract *Agatharchia. Id est bonus Principatus* (*Agatharchia, that is, Good Government*; 1498):²⁷

> The councilors of the prince are just also. They are not indiscreet or tyrannical, rather just, prudent, sober, experienced, truthful; God-fearing, solid, steady; with impartial inquisitiveness and good judgment.²⁸

While political advice books still were addressed to rulers, their advisers were clearly included in the target audience.

---

23 Hieber, "Policey," 2–3.
24 Fronsperger, *Von dem Lob*, fol. 25v: "Es hat der recht war Allmechtig vnd weise Gott/ vnd schöpffer aller ding/ die Welt also erschaffen/ daß es alles so weit der vmbkreiß derselben ist/ ein eintzige Policey/ vnd gleichsam wie ein Statt seyn sol."
25 Simon, *Gute Policey*, 99. For an annotated list of *Fürstenspiegel* published between 1400 and 1600 see Singer, *Die Fürstenspiegel*, 49–144.
26 Simon, *Gute Policey*, 99.
27 For a comprehensive interpretation of Wimpfeling's *Agatharchia* see Singer, *Die Fürstenspiegel*, 173–249.
28 Wimpfeling, 1498: sig. a4v: "Iusti quoque Principis est: Consiliarios habere: non indiscretos aut thyrannos: sed iustos/ prudentes/ sobrios/ expertos/ veraces: Deum timentes: solidos etc. constantes: cum recto examine & bono deliberacionis."

As emerging territorial states increasingly relied on advisers and bureaucrats they too needed to be instructed in the art of ethical governance. Urban Rieger (Urbanus Rhegius, 1489–1541) in his influential *Enchiridion odder handtbüchlin eines Christlichen Fürstens/ darinnen leer und trost aller Oberkeit seer nützlich/ allein aus Gottes wort auffs kürtzest zusamen gezogen* (*Enchiridion or Small Handbook for a Christian Prince, in Which Teaching and Consolation for all Authorities Is Summarized in a Useful Way Solely Based on God's Word*) from 1535 stressed the importance of ethical advisers:

> Here we note that the advisers of a ruler should be pious, God-fearing, and wise people, not simply wise people in a physical, temporal way, but in a Christian way. Even though there are not so many of them, a single God-fearing man in a prince's council is a treasure nonetheless; he can avert so much evil and can be of critical use to an entire country.[29]

Wimpfeling and Rieger both recognized that political decisions were made by an increasingly broader group of people in need of instruction and moral support.

The legal scholar and politician Melchior von Osse (1506–1557) in his *Prudentia regnativa* (*Wisdom Ruling*), written in 1555 but only published posthumously in 1607, explicitly stated that advisers had to bring the identical list of virtues and qualifications to good governance as their sovereigns.[30] Officials who acted in a ruler's stead could not be devious and tyrannical, rather they had to be benign, fatherly figures.[31] In addition to these basic ethical requirements, which had to be met by both rulers and their advisers and officials, advisers also had a particular responsibility to be truthful to their masters:

> But the most deceitful vice [...] is the hypocrisy of the counsels, servants, and commanders when they tell their lords and report to them something else than what they fundamentally know to be true, and when they only make efforts to tell the lord what he likes to hear in order to receive his favor and to be in his graces. [...] This is against divine orders, against the law, and against good morals and the common good. In truth, these are the greatest enemies of a lord he may have on earth.[32]

---

29 Rieger, *Enchiridion*, sig. B3v-B4r: "Da mercken wir/ das eines Fürsten Rathmenner sollen frume/ Gottfürchtige vnd weise Leute sein/ Nicht allein weis nach dem fleisch/ auff das zeitlich [...] sondern Christliche weise leute. Wie wol solcher nicht alzu viel sind/ noch ists ein grosser thewerer schatz/ ein einiger Gottfürchtiger man jnn eines Fürsten Rat/ der kan viel vbels abwenden/ vnd trefflichen nutz bringen/ einem gantzen land."
30 Osse, *Prudentia regnativa*, 140.
31 Osse, *Prudentia regnativa*, 144–145.
32 Osse, *Prudentia regnativa*, 115–116: "Aber dz betrüglichste Laster/ [...] ist der Rähte/ Diener vnd Befehlhabere Heucheley/ wann sie jhrem Herren anders sagen vnd Bericht thun/ dann sie die Sache im Grund beschaffen wissen/ vnnd sich allein fleissigen dem Herren zu sagen was er gern höret/ darmit sie Gnad vnd Gunst erlangen/ oder erhalten/ [...] das wider Gottes

Osse took his argument a step further and showed how dependent rulers had become on their servants and advisers who had gained real influence and power and who had the opportunity to manipulate and even mislead their sovereigns. Osse's political advice books therefore had two audiences: in a traditional way, he sought to advise sovereigns how to be good rulers and to protect themselves against deceit. To that end, Osse dedicated an entire chapter to "How a sovereign should wisely appoint his court advisers"[33] and another one to how a sovereign could appoint rural officials who were able to execute his orders without abusing the rural populations.[34] Simultaneously, Osse taught advisers and counsels the same skills while reminding them of their ethical obligation to be truthful and loyal toward their sovereign and to keep his best interests in mind.

Political advice books in the sixteenth century increasingly addressed concerns about urban governance. The traditional focus of advice books was on the two core tasks of protecting the weak and of administering the law, as Johannes Ferrarius stated: "Thus we hold that the worldly authority has two chief offices, to protect and to administer the law."[35] Similarly, Michael von Osse asserted in his *Politisches Testament* (*Political Testament*) from 1555 that the ruler's divinely derived authority was particularly important in his paternal function as administrator of justice and protector of the weak.[36] Yet handbooks on governance also recognized that the tasks of urban governance were much broader and more specific. Ferrarius in recognition of this need added a large section to his handbook that expanded his focus on urban governance:

> In particular a city council on its honor and trust is obligated to undertake everything that may advance the well-being of the common city. Namely that the vices are punished, which are prostitution, public gambling, gorging, drinking, and many others as they are called, that disobedience is turned into obedience or is completely eradicated and cut off like a useless limb.[37]

Befehl/ wider Recht/ wider gute Sitten vnnd gemeinen Nutzen ist/ Dieses seynd in Warheit eines Herren gröseste Feinde/ die er auff Erden haben mag."
[33] Osse, *Prudentia regnativa*, 121–130: "Wie ein Regent seinen Hofraht weißlich bestellen solle."
[34] Osse, *Prudentia regnativa*, 130–140.
[35] Ferrarius, *Von dem Gemeinen nutze*, fol. 12r: "Also haben wir das die weltlich oberkeit zweyerley furnemliche ampt füret/ schutzen vnd rechtsprechen." Also fol. 44v.
[36] Osse, "Politisches Testament," 271. See also Simon, *Gute Policey*, 104–105. Similarly, Christian Egenolff in his *Chronic* (1533, fol. 86v) insisted that the authorities had the obligation to protect the poor against the power of the rich and prominent members of society.
[37] Ferrarius, *Von dem Gemeinen nutze*, fol. 44v: "Inn sonderheit gepurt einem Rath bei seinen ehrn vnd trawen/ alles das furzunemen/ das zu gedeyen gemeiner stat erschiessen mag/ das die laster/ als sein/ hurerey/ offentlich spihel/ fressen/ sauffen/ vnd andere alle sampt/ wie die

Ferrarius set no limits to the range of actions a city council might take, as long as these actions were motivated by the common interest. Not surprisingly, he first addressed the commonly mentioned issues of public morality. But the responsibility of the council far surpassed that:

> Further [the council] shall supervise all buying and selling in mills, bakeries, butcher shops, breweries, inns, annual and weekly markets, and in all other dealings that occur in cities. It also should sincerely address fraud in crafts each time, which should be handled in such a way that one can exist next to the other and can prevail in the community. [It also should make sure] that roads and paths will be improved, that new buildings will be erected for the community from which there will be no damage to neighbors nor public streets will be blocked nor sullied.[38]

In Ferrarius's account, the responsibilities of the city council had become very broad.[39] The council now had to supervise and monitor all economic activity in the city to prevent fraud and graft and to ensure honesty and integrity in all dealings. The council thus was not just responsible for maintaining social order but also economic stability. Beyond that, the city council also had to build, maintain, and clean streets and monitor construction projects to protect the public interest. From authors like Sebastian Brant, Hermann Bote, Hans Sachs, and others we know that there was a great concern with regulations in all these problematic areas. Ferrarius and other political writers were conceivably influenced by these debates. The political literature appears to have been largely reactive as it picked up issues particular to urban governance only after they had been exposed in other genres, particularly in literary texts. One major area of concern is missing from Ferrarius's text, however: the activities of merchants. Ferrarius only showed concern for the activities of small merchants who sold in markets at the retail level but did not consider the need for councils to address issues of large-scale trade and financial transactions in spite of the great anxieties expressed about them in the popular literature.

---

namen haben/ gestrafftt/ der vngehorsam zu gehorsam bracht/ ader aber gantz außgereutt/ vnd als ein vnnutz glidmas abgeschnittenn werde." See also Simon, *Gute Policey*, 105.

38 Ferrarius, *Von dem Gemeinen nutze*, fol. 44v: "Furters sal er ein auffsehens haben/ das es in Mölln/ Backheussern/ Fleischschirn/ Braw vnd Wirtzheussern/ Jar vnd wuchenmarckten/ Kauffen/ verkauffen/ vnd inn allen andern hantirungen/ so in Stetten gepraucht werden. Auch in handtwercken auffrichtig an betrug eines ieden zugehe/ vnd der massen gehalten werde/ das einer neben dem andern bleiben/ vnd sich in der gmein erhalten kunde/ Das wege vnd stege gebessert/ nawe bewe/ erstlich der gemein/ darnach keinem nachpaur zu schaden auffgericht/ noch die gemeine gassen versperr ader verunreint werden."

39 Simon, *Gute Policey*, 105–106.

In Ferrarius's view, a city could function properly only if it was "a school of discipline and example of all good public morals" supervised with integrity by council members.⁴⁰ Sebastian Brant devoted the second chapter of his *Narrenschiff*, entitled "von guten reten" (of good councils), to this topic. He bemoaned that too many sought office who did not have knowledge of justice nor of public affairs, nor were they interested in learning about them once in office. Like Brant, Ferrarius expressed anxiety about failures to achieve that high standard:

> Wherever this does not happen and the council forgets about its trusted leadership role, overlooks vices, and neglects the common good, this is where vices take over. Each only thinks of his own interests, defrauds his neighbor with usury, exploitation, and all kinds of fraud. God will withdraw his blessings, the community will be in decline, the council succumbs to sin and dishonor. It gets down to the saying: how the government is, so is the subject as well. For an evil, unfaithful mother seldom begets a pious daughter.⁴¹

For Ferrarius the city council took on the role of a sovereign who was responsible for legislation that enhanced public morality and the common good, and who also had the ethical duty to lead by example. Like literary texts at the time, he entered into a diagnostic mode, describing the social and political ills and then addressing the underlying issues having to do with poor and unethical governance, just like the literary texts by Sebastian Brant and Hans Sachs had done. Like Ferrarius, most writers suggested a range of specific areas where regulation was needed, but there were no common priorities across the board. Three areas emerged in the sixteenth century as favorite areas, however, where councils were prompted to take action: education, enforcement of public morality, and matters relating to religion and faith.⁴²

Urban governance played a central role in Georg Lauterbeck's *Regentenbuch* (1556). Lauterbeck dedicated the fourth out of five parts of his book specifically to the "Regiment der Stedte" (governance of cities). In twenty chapters, he outlined the function of city governments, which was overwhelmingly the preservation of the order. Councils had to protect the citizens and their assets, ensure the

---

40 Ferrarius, *Von dem Gemeinen nutze*, fol. 45r: "ein Zuchtschul vnd exempel aller guten Sitten."
41 Ferrarius, *Von dem Gemeinen nutze*, fol. 45r: "Wo aber das nit geschicht/ vnnd der Rath seine trawlich vorwesen in vergeß stellt/ vbersihet den lastern/ versewmet den gemeinen nutz/ da nemen die laster vberhandt/ ein ieder gedenckt seins besten/ bedreugt den nehisten/ mit wuchern/ verforteiln/ vnd allerhant betrug/ Gott entzeugt sein segen/ die gemeyn kompt in abfall/ der Rath fellt in sunde vnd schande/ vnd kompt auff den Spruch/ Wie die regierung/ so ist der vnterdan auch/ Dann ein bösse vntrewe mutter zeucht selten ein fromme dochter."
42 Simon, *Gute Policey*, 119–120.

proper education of the young, promote the common good, and create concord. The duties of citizens were to protect their city, to serve the government, and to refrain from any kind of rebellion against the authorities. The government's most important function by far was to curb social ills: idleness, excessive drinking and eating, a luxurious lifestyle, fashionable and inappropriate clothing, and of course the twin vices of greed and usury. There was no visionary program nor ambitious legislative agenda; a good council simply maintained peace and order in the community without implementing many changes.

The rapid broadening of the audience was the key reason why political texts in the sixteenth century for the most part were published in the vernacular as members of the targeted audience could no longer be trusted to be able to read Latin. Johannes Ferrarius used this as a justification for publishing his 1533 tract on governance in German:

> I very much considered publishing the text in the Latin language (as little as I know of it). But as I find that very few of those who are asked to govern know Latin or have experience with the Liberal Arts (as much as they should know about them), I wanted to compose it in the German language for the first time in order to serve every one.[43]

As Ferrarius was a well-educated university professor, writing the tract in Latin would not have been an obstacle for him; he was just being modest about his level of learning. This gives credence to his argument that writing the text in German made it accessible to a wider audience. But it also allowed citizens who were not involved with governance to inform themselves about the political process. Many texts were authored by public officials with experience in urban governance, such as the lawyer Johannes Oldendorp, who served as city syndic during part of his career.[44]

Urban Rieger, a follower of Luther's Reform, referred to another innovation for the genre in the extended title of his *Enchiridion odder handtbüchlin eines Christlichen Fürstens* (*Enchiridion or Small Handbook for a Christian Prince*) from 1535. Rieger used Augustine's title *Enchiridion*, which Martin Luther also had used as title for his *Small Catechism* from 1529. He claimed to have drawn his teachings "from God's word alone."[45] In the text, Rieger asserted that a prince

---

[43] Ferrarius, *Von dem Gemeinen nutze*, fol. A4r-A4v: "Jch were wol gesynt gewesen/ es inn Latinische sprache (wie wenig ich auch dero kan) zustellen/ aber dieweil ich befinde das die wenigsten so zu regirn auffgeworffen werden/ latinisch kunnen/ ader in den freyen kunsten erfarn sein (wie wol si dero wissen haben solten) hab ichs erstmals inn Deutsche sprach wollen fassen/ damit einem ieden zu dienen."

[44] Simon, *Gute Policey*, 99.

[45] Singer, *Die Fürstenspiegel*, 288–292.

needed to rule justly and wisely, but that this was impossible for the prince to achieve without faith and the grace of God:

> This is impossible for [the prince] to do without the specific grace of God, out of the natural powers of reasoning alone, because of the innate blindness that we have from the original sin, and because of the malice of the exasperating devil.[46]

The Christian ruler had the advantage over the ruler in classical antiquity as he was merely a tool of God who provided guidance to those who had faith in him, as opposed to the ancient ruler who had only his own reason to rely on.[47] Their reasoning powers were blinded by sin that was engineered by the devil; this blindness only could be overcome by divine grace. Classical rulers thus were prone to making mistakes:

> Among the heathens there were many wise and smart people. But with their reliance on reason, they committed many horrible mistakes in governance. For instance they could not govern a house in the right way, not to speak of an entire country.[48]

Rieger rejected the classical tradition as a source of wisdom in governance, and Aristotle in particular: heathens were too self-reliant on their own reasoning powers and did not recognize the importance of the guiding divine hand.[49] Rieger saw the rulers of classical antiquity as overly self-confident and even arrogant, but ignorant about the true workings of the world:

> Heathen princes rely on their own power and wisdom and do not know that all empires and governments do not hinge on human powers and providence but rather are in God's hand. He alone is the one who gives, places, holds, governs, protects, receives, and – if He wishes – takes it away. This is why [heathen princes] often fall hard and become targets of ridicule and shame.[50]

---

46 Rieger, *Enchiridion*, sig. B2v: "Das ist jme nu vnmüglich zuthun/ on sonderliche Gottes gnade/ allein aus krafft natürlichs verstands/ von wegen der angeborenen blindheit/ so wir von der sund haben/ vnd von wegen des leidigen Teufels arglistigkeit."
47 Rieger, *Enchiridion*, sig. A5v-A6r.
48 Rieger, *Enchiridion*, sig. B2v-B3r: "Vnter den Heiden sind viel weiser kluger leut gewesen/ Aber sie haben mit jrer vernunfft im Regiment manchen greulichen feelgriff gethan/ Vnd etwa ein haus nicht können mit jrer weisheit recht regieren/ wil geschweigen ein gantz land."
49 Simon, *Gute Policey*, 103.
50 Rieger, *Enchiridion*, sig. C8r: "Heidnische Fürsten verlassen sich auff jr eigene macht vnd weisheit/ vnd wissen nicht/ das alle Reich vnd Regiment/ nicht jnn menschlicher krafft vnd fürsichtigkeit stehen/ sondern jnn Gottes hand/ der ists allein der sie gibt/ setzt/ helt/ regiert/ schützt/ erhelt/ vnd auch wenn er wil weg nimpt/ Derhalben fallen sie auch offt schwerlich/ vnd werden zu spot vnd schanden."

By rejecting reason-based self-reliance as the basis for good and just governance, Rieger dismissed the classical tradition as well as the scholastic idea that reason could be a guiding principle in communal leadership. As human reasoning powers were afflicted by human sin, Rieger's overtly biblical approach to governance set serious limits to the value of human cognition.[51] Rieger's handbook represented a step toward the emancipation from classical notions of governance in Humanism and simultaneously maintained an interest in a faith-based approach to governance. When we turn to the texts of Sebastian Brant and Hans Sachs, we can see this faith-based approach as the implied model for good and just governance.

The emerging early modern territorial state not only relied on advisers and bureaucrats who were in need of proper guidance, but it also required stronger written public policy, commonly referred to as *Gute Policey*, that could be implemented more uniformly in the various territories of the state. *Policey* thus stood for a larger transformation of state: from *Herrschaft*, the rule of a sovereign who ruled a domain based on entitlements, to *Staat*, a state that covered a well-defined territory that was based on laws, and that was administered by bureaucrats. Many of the sixteenth-century texts paid more attention to issues arising in territorial states.[52] The trend toward written public policy manifested itself in legislation issued by the Imperial Diet, such as the *Reichsabschied* (recess) of 1512 and different versions of the *Reichspolizeiordnung* (imperial public policy ordinance) from 1530, 1548, and 1577.[53] Corresponding ordinances were issued by landed princes and by city councils as well. Handbooks were available for authorities who needed help, but of course these books also emboldened citizens to demand action from the authorities, particularly from city councils. A good example is the handbook by Johannes Oldendorp (1488–1567), which was first available in a Low German version in 1530 but reprinted in a High German version in 1597 under the title *Von Rathschlägen/ wie man gute Polizey vnd Ordnung in Stedten vnd Landen erhalten möge* (*Advice on How One Can Maintain Good Policy and Order in Cities and States*). Oldendorp made the modern distinction of two kinds of *Policey*: the first kind is the perennial kind that did not have to be changed or abolished, akin to a basic law or constitution. The second kind was temporal and intended to serve the needs of the time:

> Here you have to consider counsel that will advance, or not, the common good according to the needs of the time. And you must not forget to consider the advantage of the largest,

---

51 Simon, *Gute Policey*, 103.
52 Simon, *Gute Policey*, 99.
53 For a detailed discussion see Weber, *Die Reichspolizeiordnungen*.

not the smallest number of the subjects, otherwise vain injustice, unrest, and displeasure of all will result.[54]

In Oldendorp's pragmatic view, good governance was not an absolute; rather, it was the art of appeasing the citizenry. The implication is that there was a limited public sphere where opinions could be expressed. This offered intervention points for writers like Brant and Sachs to help formulate *Policey*.

The new focus on *Gute Policey* cannot be explained by a changing notion of statehood alone. Legislation tended to be reactive, as Oldendorp confirmed, and the perceived need for a significant expansion of legislation therefore points to deep-seated sense that society was in crisis – something that was expressed in a range of literary texts. Many of the issues that were subject to *Policey* were raised in literary texts as well, such as blasphemy, fashionable clothing, luxury, drinking and toasting, inflation, usury, hoarding, and other objectionable practices that were introduced and popularized by merchants. Based on the literary texts alone, it is difficult to assess whether they reacted primarily to concerns with *Policey* or to the underlying social, economic, and political issues. Most likely both patterns were at work. The catalogs of concerns raised by writers and covered by *Policey* had a significant overlap but were by no means identical. Furthermore, writers identified a much wider range of issues that were framed as potentially harmful to the social order.

---

54 Oldendorp, *Von Rathschlägen*, 35–36; "Hie kombt dir zu rathschlagen/ was dem gemeinen nutzen nach gelegenheit der zeit förderlichst sey oder nicht/ vnd diß vortheil mustu nicht vergessen auß der meisten vnd nicht der wenigsten zahl der vnterthanen zuermessen/ sonst würde eitel vnrecht/ auffruhr vnd aller vnlust darauß erfolgen."

Chapter 3
Defending Order and Discipline in *Dyl Ulenspiegel*

Sebastian Brant in his *Narrenschiff* (*Ship of Fools*) from 1494 developed a substantial catalogue of societal ills, and his preferred method to address them was general invective with the goal of prompting personal behavior modification. While Brant acknowledged the existence of laws as part of public order, he never directly promoted the idea of resolving issues that were important to him by way of legislation. Furthermore, he always used the word "gsatz" (laws, statutes), not the modern term *Policey*. Brant noted that laws frequently were absent or ineffective, as in his invective regarding the merchants' business practices: "And justice and law are silent about this."[1] Brant understood laws to be an important source of order but he did not turn to them to seek remedies for all the abuses he diagnosed in the *Ship of Fools*.

This is all the more surprising as Brant was a trained lawyer and a professor of law at the University of Basel when he wrote the *Ship of Fools*. From 1493 until his death, Brant was involved in the publication of a number of legal texts in the vernacular, most notably Ulrich Tengler's *Laÿen Spiegel* (*Layman's Mirror*) from 1509,[2] In the introduction to the *Clagspiegel* (*Lawsuit Mirror*) from 1516,[3] Brant expressed his expectation that citizens were familiar with ordinances and complied with them: "As one and every human has to be subject to the law, as it is written, [...] therefore everyone also is obliged to know the laws."[4]

Later literary writers, however, made specific references to *Policey*, most notably Hans Sachs. In his encomium *Ein lobspruch der Stadt Nürnberg* (*Encomium to the City of Nuremberg*) from 1530, he praised the city council for governing its citizens wisely and "with orderly government, good statutes and policies, charitably without any tyranny."[5] Sachs took a more critical stance in generic texts that did not specifically mention his native city of Nuremberg. In some poems he

---

[1] Brant, *Narrenschiff*, ch. 93, v. 28: "Vnd schwygt dar zů all reht/ vnd gsatz."
[2] Neuber, "Verdeckte Theologie," 17.
[3] According to Deutsch ("*Klagspiegel* und *Laienspiegel*," 90), the *Clagspiegel* was originally written by Conrad Heyden in 1436.
[4] Brant, *Der richterlich Clagspiegel*, sig. A2r: "NAch dem vnd ein yegklich mensch dem gesetz vnderthänig sein sol/ als geschriben steet [...] So ist auch ein yegklicher schuldig die gesetzd zů wissen."
[5] Sachs, KG 4, 195, v. 3–4: "Mit ordenlichem regiment, | Guter statut und policey, | Gütig on alle tyrannei."

mocked the futile attempts of *Policey* to promote the common good and to maintain the public order.⁶ In his didactic poem *Der eygen nutz, das greulich thir, mit sein zwölff eygenschafften* (*Self-Interest, that Awful Beast, with its Twelve Properties*) from 1527, he described self-interest as a monstrum, each of its body parts having a specific meaning: "Its boar's teeth mean that nobody can resist it, through laws, statutes, and policies."⁷ Even well-intended laws and policies were unable to curb the abuse of the common good by particular interests.

The rise of *Policey* increased the awareness of mostly urban middle-class writers, heightened their concern with political power, social order, and the common good, and, finally, increased awareness of the problems it tried to address. *Policey* also gave writers conceptual frameworks and the vocabulary to talk about social, economic, and religious issues. In this regard, the difference between Brant and Sachs is significant: while Brant and Sachs had a similar philosophical grounding, Brant sketched issues within a framework of individual morality and sought solutions in the realm of pragmatic moral philosophy. Sachs's writings often had a political angle. He understood the political nature of issues he was concerned with and suggested political action to address them. In the alternative, he chastised political leadership for their failure to provide appropriate legal frameworks.

German literary texts at the time rarely promoted political and social change. Writers around 1500 were typically burghers of free cities that rose in economic importance and political power in the fifteenth century. They were very much focused on preserving the political order that advanced the interests of their cities, which included the protective role of the emperor. Literary texts either promoted the current order or, more likely, bemoaned the fact that the order was threatened or was already crumbling. The world was seen by many as a *mundus perversus*, discussed in the next chapter, a topsy-turvy world rife with transgressive behavior that only could be met and rectified either with heavy invective or by satire. This is the framework within which many texts were written.

One of the most notable texts of this time period is the early prose narration *Ein kurtzweilig lesen von Dyl Vlenspiegel geboren vß dem land zů Brunßwick. Wie er sein leben volbracht hatt. xcvi. seiner geschichten* (*An Entertaining Reader About Dyl Ulenspiegel, Born in the Land of Brunswick. How He Passed His Life. 96 of His Stories*). While the text appeared anonymously, Hermann Bote was suggested as its author by Honegger in 1973. However, there is no evidence that

---

6 Sachs, KG 3, 589, v. 17–20; KG 22, 219, v. 32–35.
7 Sachs, KG 3, 495, v. 11–13: "So bedeuten sein eberzen, | das im kan nyemand widerstehn. | Durch gsetz, statut und policey."

Bote drafted a first Low German version in Brunswick around 1500, nor is there evidence that such a version ever existed,[8] perhaps with the exception of the fact that the titular protagonist was given the Low German name Ulenspiegel rather than the High German Eulenspiegel. The first known text is a small fragment of a High German version that was published in Strasbourg in 1510 or 1511.[9] The subsequent 1515 Strasbourg print is the oldest extant complete edition of the work.[10]

In 96 loosely connected stories, the book narrates the adventures of Dyl Ulenspiegel.[11] Yet, the book is not a biography as the episodes do not constitute a life story, with the exception of a few episodes at the beginning and at the end relating his upbringing and death. Ulenspiegel is a transient figure who is constantly on the move, which will be discussed in more detail in Chapter 14. He does not have geographic roots nor a secure social identity. At the center of each episode stands some trick or deceptive action, typically at the expense of another individual. Sometimes his actions lampoon the greed, pride, or narrow-mindedness of others, in particular members of the clergy. But in other instances, they target innocent people for no good reason, in particular craftsmen who just want to earn an honest living and have the misfortune of taking Ulenspiegel into their employ. His specialty is taking things literally, which invariably invites misunderstandings and confusion, but also leads to material damage and hurt feelings.

Ulenspiegel is routinely referred to as "schalck," which today has the connotation of a benign and merry prankster. The fact that the book became part of children's literature in Germany, most notably the narration by Erich Kästner (1938), has vastly enhanced Ulenspiegel's reputation as a funny and congenial prankster.[12] In the secondary literature, Ulenspiegel is generally seen as a sometimes subversive figure who unmasks society around him as egotistical

---

8 Schulz-Grobert, *Das Straßburger Eulenspiegelbuch*, 5–9.
9 A facsimile was reproduced as an unpaginated appendix of Honegger, *Ulenspiegel*.
10 I cite from the 1515 edition, printed by Johann Grüninger, except where noted otherwise. We do not know who authored the 1515 edition. Beise ("machen die docter," 34) claims that it was translated by the High German editor based on an alleged earlier Low German version. For a more complete publication history, see Honegger, *Ulenspiegel*, 11–82; Schulz-Grobert, *Das Straßburger Eulenspiegelbuch*, 1–127; Blume, *Hermann Bote*, 31–36; Beise, "machen die docter," 34–35.
11 Peter Honegger (*Ulenspiegel*, 101–116) proposed a different sequence of the stories and a different numbering system. As this is highly speculative, I follow the numbering of the 1515 edition and quote from it, unless stated otherwise.
12 Wunderlich, *Till Eulenspiegel*, 106–110. According to Ivanov-Dogaru (2014: 102), the Ulenspiegel figure appeared in more than 250 texts of children's and youth literature in the nineteenth century, typically as entertaining jokester.

and dysfunctional.¹³ However, this reading ignores the fact that the text used the term "schalck" consistently in the sense of rogue and villain.¹⁴ The victims in the narratives invariably see him as a wicked man, as does the narrator, who takes Ulenspiegel's evil nature as a given: "Ulenspiegel had become well-known in all lands because of his wickedness."¹⁵ The introduction of the 1515 Strasbourg print calls Ulenspiegel "a quick-witted, sly and cunning son of a peasant."¹⁶

In his *Schicht boick* (*Chronicle of Uprisings*), written between 1510 and 1514, Hermann Bote consistently used the term "schalck" to designate the rebels, like in the phrase "a venomous wicked man."¹⁷ Furthermore, he compared the vile rebels to a boy on horseback.¹⁸ It is not hard to recognize young Ulenspiegel from the second chapter of *Dyl Ulenspiegel* who performs his very first trick on horseback.¹⁹ This connection could indicate that Bote was the author or that the author was familiar with Bote's *Schicht boick*. Similarly, the frontispiece of the 1515 edition shows young Ulenspiegel on horseback.²⁰ Thus even in early childhood the author presents the protagonist as a villain who ridiculed the behavioral norms in his village in chapter two and inverted the communal solidarity into disunion in chapters four and eight.²¹ The author may have expressed a "general anxiety about the young, and the fear of the havoc they might do" that prevailed in the early sixteenth century.²² Yet, what we see here is the beginning of the protagonist's life-long career of questioning the familiar and of subverting established patterns of behavior and communal norms.²³ This is hardly the stuff his contemporaries were laughing about.²⁴

---

13 Bachorski, "Wie der Narr," 277; Classen, "Laughter," 485; Schwarz, "Leere statt Lehre," 102.
14 Wailes, "The Childishness," 127. The legal scholar Johannes Ferrarius (*Von dem Gemeinen nutze*, fol. 3v) used the term "schalck" in the same way. For Joseph Grünpeck (*Ein spiegel*, sig. aiv), "schalckheyt" is devastating the seeds and fruit of all the good deeds of Christians.
15 Anon., *Ein kurtzweilig lesen*, fol. 42v: "IN allen landen het sich Ulenspiegel mit seiner boßheit bekant gemacht."
16 Anon., *Ein kurtzweilig lesen*, fol. 2r: "ein behender listiger vnd durchtribener eins buren sun."
17 Bote, *Das Schichtbuch*, 466: "eyn vorgyftich schalck." For additional examples see Hayden-Roy, "The Masquerade," 566.
18 Bote, *Das Schichtbuch*, 451.
19 Wailes, "The Childishness," 135.
20 Apparently, this point was lost on the editors of the 1532 edition where Ulenspiegel still is shown on the frontispiece, but this time as an old, bearded man.
21 Röcke, *Die Freude am Bösen*, 220.
22 Strauss, *Luther's House of Learning*, 97.
23 Röcke, *Die Freude am Bösen*, 220.
24 Many scholars still discuss Dyl Ulenspiegel under the rubric of comical literature whose protagonist entertained and amused the masses, for example Melters, "*ein frölich gemüt*," 201–205.

From the beginning of the book, Ulenspiegel is represented as an individual who refuses to fit into any kind of social order. We never learn what social class he was born into. As discussed before, the introduction refers to him as the "son of a peasant," but the text itself does not bear this out. In two separate chapters Ulenspiegel rejects his mother's urging to enter an apprenticeship, despite the fact that his mother is impoverished and in need of support after his father's death: "Thus his mother became poor, and Ulenspiegel refused to learn a trade. He was sixteen years of age and romped about and learned many a mockery."[25] Ulenspiegel prefers hanging around engaging in mischief over working, and he also does not want to be tied down and locked into a position. Ulenspiegel declines to be defined socially and geographically and prefers to function in the margins of society.

By rejecting an apprenticeship, Ulenspiegel refuses to become a contributing member of society and thus to operate within the social order. As the author brought this up in two separate chapters, it is evident that he set up the repudiation of his own protagonist. Not surprisingly, Ulenspiegel's delinquent acts are mostly directed at the social class of craftsmen, the class he had been destined to join.[26] His disdain of craftsmen runs deep. He displays this attitude while introducing himself to one of the hostesses he meets during this itinerant life: "I am not a journeyman; rather, I am accustomed to tell the truth."[27] We can assume that this represents the world this urban author was most familiar with, and Ulenspiegel's wrongdoing could be best illustrated by exposing his attacks on the very occupational category that represented the backbone of the urban economy.

Ulenspiegel enters most adventures with an act of masquerade. He takes on roles as a doctor, apprentice, merchant, court fool, to mention just a few, and creates a fake identity by pretending to be somebody he is not.[28] Invariably, he changes clothes to facilitate his chosen role. In chapter 31, the narrator states that Ulenspiegel and his malice were so widely known that he could not return to a place where he had been "unless he was disguising himself so that one

---

[25] Anon., *Ein kurtzweilig lesen*, fol. 4v: "Also ward die müter arm vnd vlenspiegel wolt kei handtwerck lernen/ vnd was da bei sechzehen iar alt/ vnd dumelte sich/ vnd lernt mancherlei geuckerei." See also fol. 7r-7v.

[26] Blume, *Hermann Bote*, 36; Wunderlich, *Till Eulenspiegel*, 68.

[27] Anon., *Ein kurtzweilig lesen*, fol. 41r: "Ich bin nicht ein handtwerkßgesell/ sunder ich pfleg die warheit zu sagen."

[28] Hayden-Roy, "The Masquerade," 570.

would not recognize him."²⁹ In chapter 83, Ulenspiegel puts on different clothes to inflict further abuse on a female innkeeper whose dog he had killed in the previous chapter.

In addition to criminal energy, this also points to the unstable relationship between the protagonist's clothes and his body, which signals his unstable identity. Clothing at the time had a socially stabilizing function in that it helped others make correct assumptions about status and social identity of any individual. In encounters with strangers, clothing communicated class and status, which facilitated social, political, or economic transactions. By masquerading, Ulenspiegel consciously concealed his true identity and thus made it impossible for people in his environment to properly read his social status, which immediately gave Ulenspiegel an unfair advantage. These norms were codified by sumptuary laws whose purpose was to preserve the readability of clothes by maintaining the correlation between rank and wealth on one hand and clothing and general appearance on the other.

Sumptuary laws and related social commentaries responded to fears about a potential breakdown of the economic or moral order and thus served as a social control mechanism for the lower classes.³⁰ Ulenspiegel's deceptive use of clothing therefore was not just a tool to achieve his mischievous ends but also a serious violation of social norms and a transgressive act that exploited a core anxiety and thus was commented upon negatively by the narrator.³¹

The unstable relationship between his clothes and his body does not just express itself in the use of deceptive clothing but also extends to an insecure body image. Ulenspiegel leads a sexless life; while he recognizes sexuality in others, he never expresses a desire himself.³² The narrator relates to us that his landlady in Rome in chapter 34 perceives him as a beautiful man but does not develop the theme beyond this point. And in chapter 41, discussed in more detail below, both the wife of the blacksmith and her servant take an interest in Ulenspiegel, which he playfully rejects. Chapter 38 has to be read in the context of a protagonist who rejects all opportunities to be with women that arise. Here, Ulenspiegel claims in a confession that he had slept with the priest's maid. The enraged priest challenges and beats the maid, breaking the Seal of Confession in the process. Ulenspiegel uses that knowledge to blackmail the priest and forces him to surrender his horse. While the pastor misreads

---

29 Anon., *Ein kurtzweilig lesen*, fol. 42v: "es wer dan das er sich vercleidet dz man in nit kant."
30 Entwistle, *The Fashioned Body*, 90.
31 For a more comprehensive discussion of the transgressive use of clothing in early modern literature see Hess, "The Poetics of Masquerade."
32 Wailes, "The Childishness," 129.

Ulenspiegel as a sexual being, the reader understands that sexuality offers leverage exactly because it never is to be consumed by the protagonist.

This changes in one of the chapters added to the 1532 Erfurt edition. In chapter 97, Ulenspiegel has a woman whom he claims as his wife, who in turn cheats on him with the priest.[33] It appears that the editor of the 1532 edition had a different understanding of Ulenspiegel's personality and departed from the earlier concept of a sexless protagonist. He also misunderstood how important Ulenspiegel's sexlessness and secular celibacy is both as a narrative device and as yet another marker of his outcast existence.

There are a number of episodes where Ulenspiegel enters an inn to find the landlady at home alone, either because there is no husband or because he is away.[34] In some of these chapters, there are references that could be read as vaguely erotic, such as the encounter with a hostess in chapter 82 who keeps her furry dog on her lap at all times, until Ulenspiegel pulls off its fur. In a similar episode with erotic overtones in chapter 84, he places the bare rear end of a different hostess on hot embers as a form of punishment.[35] While there are no overt sexual references in these chapters, both women are home alone and thus not under male supervision. In both chapters, Ulenspiegel's punishment appears to be preemptive as it vaguely refers to the potentiality of sexually transgressive acts suggested by the women and is designed to dissuade them from seeing him as a sexual being. Ulenspiegel's immunity to potential erotic advances and his lack of a desire to have a wife further mark Ulenspiegel as an outcast who refuses to become domesticated and to subject himself to a marital order that was the very foundation of society.

In some chapters, Ulenspiegel targets the idea of communal solidarity – an idea upon which social cohesion in German cities around 1500 depended. In chapter 17, Ulenspiegel advises a hospital on how to heal patients and thus to relieve the hospital of overcrowding and the related excessive financial burdens. He tells patients that they all have to leave the hospital if they feel healthy. The last remaining patient, presumably the sickest one, would be burned and the ashes used as remedy to heal the others. As all the patients leave the hospital in a hurry, Ulenspiegel receives his reward and skips town

---

[33] Anon., *Von Vlenspiegel* (1532), sig. V3r-V3v.
[34] Anon., *Ein kurtzweilig lesen*, ch. 16, 30, 34, 82, and 84. See Wailes, "The Childishness," 130. In chapter 76, he encounters a peasant woman who is home alone.
[35] The word used to designate the rear end is "arß." The same word is used in chapter 91. The title of chapter 13 of Sebastian Brant's *Narrenschiff*, "Frow Venus mit dem ströwen ars" (Lady Venus with the ass of straw), illustrates the ambiguity of the reference.

quickly, before the patients return to the hospital one after the other. Ulenspiegel proceeds by talking to each patient individually:

> Thus Ulenspiegel went to the hospital and took along two servants. He asked each one of the patients where he ailed, and at the end when he walked away from a patient he implored him and said, what I am about to reveal you should keep with you as a secret and should not disclose to anyone. The patients agreed to that on their faith. Then he told each one of them separately, if I should help you sick ones to health und bring you back up on your feet, this is impossible for me to do unless I burn one of you to powder and give it to the others to drink, this I have to do.[36]

The key point is that Ulenspiegel makes an agreement with each patient individually and convinces them not to act as a member of the hospital community but rather to act individually by only looking out for themselves. Ulenspiegel in the pursuit of his own interests compels the patients to reject the idea of solidarity and to act against the interests of the community. This is a key point the text makes here: Ulenspiegel is an agent in the pursuit of individual interests at the expense of the common good and therefore is a threat to the social order.[37]

While Sebastian Brant frequently bemoaned the dire condition of the empire and its impact on the welfare of the cities, *Dyl Ulenspiegel* was almost exclusively focused on urban politics and individual transgressions. Chapter 63 is the exception in that it focuses on the political order within the empire. It is exceptional in a different regard as well: Ulenspiegel actually learns the craft of making eyeglasses in spite of the earlier assertion that he was not willing to learn a trade. While this is one of a number of inconsistencies in the narrative,[38] Ulenspiegel's unsteady lifestyle does not change as he is unable to find work, which is the point of the episode. His membership in a craft for the duration of a chapter is merely a narrative device in order to make the larger point.

---

36 Anon., *Ein kurtzweilig lesen*, fol. 22v-23r: "Also gieng vlenspiegel in spital vnd nam zwen knecht mit im/ vnd fragt die krancken/ ein ietlichen wz im gebrest/ vnd zů letsch wan er von eim krancken gieng so beschwur er in vnd sprach wz ich dir offenbaren wurt das soltu bei dir heimlich bleiben lassen von nieman offenbaren das sagten dan die siechen vlenspiegel bei grossem glouben zů daruff sagt er dan eim ietlichen bsunder/ sol ich nun vch krancken zů gesuntheit helffen vnd vff die füß bringen das ist mir vnmiglich ich verbren dan euwer einen zů pulver/ vnd gib dz den andern in den leib zetrincken/ dz můß ich thůn."
37 Kirschner, *Hermen Bote*, 94.
38 The Strasbourg editor of the 1515 print added several stories that were unlikely part of the Low German Brunswick original – if it ever existed. Furthermore, several stories were added from other sources, such as Stricker's *Pfaffe Amis* (c. 1240). For a discussion of this aspect see Tenberg, *Die deutsche Till-Eulenspiegel-Rezeption*, 59–65.

Chapter 63 opens with this statement by the narrator: "So angry and discordant were the prince-electors amongst each other that there was no Roman emperor or king."[39] Even though the historical reference vaguely points to the twelfth century, disunity among the prince-electors was a frequent theme in the literature around 1500. Conflicts among them were seen as a source of instability in the empire, which not only diminished the power of the emperor but also threatened the independence of cities like Strasbourg or Brunswick. While *Dyl Ulenspiegel* did not directly refer to contemporaneous politics, this can be read as a hidden critique of the disunity within the empire under Emperor Maximilian I.[40] As this reference does not factor into the plot of chapter 63, we have to read this as a gratuitous comment on an issue that was important to the author.

On his way to Frankfurt, Ulenspiegel encounters the archbishop and elector of Trier, who takes an interest in Ulenspiegel because of his odd clothing. Ulenspiegel identifies himself as a maker of eyeglasses from Brabant who is wandering around because he cannot find work. The bishop replies that there should be opportunity in this craft as people increasingly were afflicted by health issues and poor eyesight. Ulenspiegel replies that there is one problem with the theory, and with the permission from the archbishop to speak freely he engages in a monologue, the longest in the book:

> Gracious lord, this spoils the craft of the eyeglass makers, and there is reason to fear that it will die out entirely. For you and other great lords, popes, cardinals, bishops, emperors, kings, princes, councils, governors, judges in cities and states (God have mercy) now at this time turn a blind eye to what is right, which is motivated at times by gifts of money. However, one finds written of old times that the lords and princes, you being one of them, used to read and study the law so that no one would suffer injustice. And for that purpose they had many eyeglasses, and our craft was doing well. Also the clerics studied more at the time than they do now, and thus the eyeglasses sold well. Now they are getting so learned from the books they buy that they know by heart what they need to know, which is why they do not open more than one of their books in four weeks. This is why our craft is ruined, and I run from one state to the next and cannot find work anywhere. The decline has progressed so far that the peasants in the countryside practice this as well and turn a blind eye.[41]

---

39 Anon., *Ein kurtzweilig lesen*, fol. 87v: "ZOrnig vnnd zwitrechtig waren die Churfursten vnder einander also das kein romischer keiser/ oder künig wz."
40 For a more detailed discusstion of Sebastian Brant's veneration of Emperor Maximilian I see Chapter 6.
41 Anon., *Ein kurtzweilig lesen*, fol. 88r: "Gnediger her/ dz verderbt dz brillenmacher ha[n]twerck vnd ist zu besorge daz es noch abgang dan ir/ vnd a[n]dere groß herren/ babst/ cardinal/ bischoff/ keiser/ künig/ fürsten/ radt/ regierer/ richter der stat vnd land (got erbarmß) nun zur zeit durch die finger sehen wz recht ist/ dz zů zeite/ von gelt gaben sich vrsacht. Aber vor alten zeiten find ma[n] geschriben. Dz die herre vnd fürsten als vil ihr seint/ in rechte

First, he alleges that the ruling classes, from pope down to city council members, fail to provide good justice as they will turn a blind eye to the law through bribes. By contrast, rulers in the good old times read and studied the law books in order to administer equitable justice. In order to do so they needed eyeglasses. His craft now is in crisis because the rulers no longer read the law books and the clergy no longer read Scripture. While other chapters merely lampoon the weaknesses and shortcomings of individuals, here the ruling classes and the clergy are targeted more broadly. Like Bote in the *Radbuch* and the *Schicht boick*, the author of *Dyl Ulenspiegel* despised the unrest and disorder usually caused by the lack of good governance. Chapter 63 is different from the others as Ulenspiegel becomes a truth teller in the disguise of an honest craftsman looking for work. For a change, the transgressions in focus in this chapter are not his own.

Ulenspiegel's behavior is transgressive and destructive primarily in two ways: taking language literally and instrumentalizing fecal matter.[42] Ulenspiegel consistently exploits the space between literal and figurative meaning of words and idiomatic expressions; Ulenspiegel's abuse of language is his literalism.[43] Much has been written about Ulenspiegel's subversive use of language that runs through the entire book.[44] In a number of chapters, there is an implied metadiscourse on the nature of this language-based deception. My discussion here will be limited to some of those chapters.

From the beginning, there is evidence that Ulenspiegel consciously creates misunderstandings to gain his own advantage. In chapter 23, he visits the Danish court where he has this exchange with the king: "Ulenspiegel asked the king if he should believe his words. The king replied, yes, because he was acting

---

pflegte zů lesen vn[d] studieren/ vff dz niema[n]ß vnrecht beschehe vnd darzů hette sie vil brillen/ vnd da wz vnser hantwerck gut. Auch so studierten die pfaffen zů der zeit me [dan sie nun thůn] also giengen die brillen hinweg. So seint sie nun so gelert worden von den bücheren/ die sie koufen dz sie ihr zeit vßwendig kunnen darzů sie ir bůcher i[n]. iiii. wochen nit me dan eins vff thůn/ des halb ist vnser ha[n]twerck verdorben/ vnd ich louff vß einem land in dz ander vnd kan niergens arbeit über kumen/ der gebrest ist so weit kummen dz diß die buren vff dem land pflege [vnd durch die finger sehen]." As this passage contains several errors in the 1515 edition, I supplemented the parts in brackets from the 1519 edition that is almost identical (Anon., *Ein kurtzweilig lesen* (1519), fol. 88r).

42 Kirschner, *Hermen Bote*, 95.
43 Wailes, "The Childishness," 131.
44 Rusterholz, "Till Eulenspiegel;" Wunderlich, *Till Eulenspiegel*, 76. According to Beise ("machen die docter," 47–48), about half of all chapters are structured around the tension between the literal and figurative meaning of words.

according to his words."⁴⁵ Ulenspiegel finds out whether the king honors commitments, even if the literal interpretation of the commitment does not reflect its intent. The significance of this moment is that we see Ulenspiegel strategizing and knowingly plotting to exploit a misunderstanding. The test case is the king's promise of the best horseshoes for Ulenspiegel's horse. Ulenspiegel promptly has golden horseshoes put on his horse. When presented with the invoice, the king proves to be a man of his word. This is the only episode where Ulenspiegel backs down voluntarily. His attempt to ensnarl the king has failed, and he has the golden horseshoes removed from his horse again. This also is the only example where Ulenspiegel remains in the good graces of his master.

Chapter 15 explores a similar theme. Here, Ulenspiegel pretends to be a doctor who in this role tricks and humiliates a real doctor at a bishop's court in a rather public way: "Then the bishop and all courtiers began to laugh hard and spoke: it came to pass entirely according to your words."⁴⁶ Here, all bystanders comprehend Ulenspiegel's play with the meaning and interpretation of words and take his side. Like in chapter 23, the narrator wants us to know that Ulenspiegel's play with the meaning of words is conscious, calculating, and subversive and thus has to be interpreted as a transgressive act.

A number of chapters show how the damage Ulenspiegel inflicts on others is unjustified. Many of these chapters are directed against craftsmen whose sole interest is in making a living through honest work.⁴⁷ An example is chapter 43, in which Ulenspiegel works for a shoemaker. Because of misunderstandings, he cuts the leather to wrong sizes and ruins a total of three batches of leather. The master is unhappy about the financial loss but properly analyzes its root cause in this comment after the second batch is ruined: "Yes, my dear servant, this is how it is. My words were like this, but my intention was not like this."⁴⁸ While the shoemaker assumes some responsibility by recognizing his own role in misreading the discrepancy between the literal meaning of his words and the intended communication, he chases away Ulenspiegel after the third batch is ruined as he,

---

45 Anon., *Ein kurtzweilig lesen*, fol. 30v-31r: "Vlenspiegel fragt den künig ob er solt seinen worten glauben. Der künig sprach Ja dan er nach seinen worten thet."
46 Anon., *Ein kurtzweilig lesen*, fol. 20v: "Da ward der bischoff vnd alle hoflüt ser lachen vnd sprachen/ es ist gantz geschehen nach euwern worten."
47 In about 55 out of the 96 chapters, Ulenspiegel's adversaries are guild members, that is craftsmen.
48 Anon., *Ein kurtzweilig lesen*, fol. 61r: "ia mein lieber knecht/ das ist also/ mein wort waren also/ aber mein meinung wz nit also."

as well as the reader, now realizes that Ulenspiegel misunderstands things with malice and actively manipulates communication to create disorder.

Chapter 41, on the other hand, shows how even the truthful use of language can lead to deception, particularly if it plays on the expectation of Ulenspiegel's deceptive use of language. In Wismar, Ulenspiegel notices an attractive woman and her maid standing in front of a blacksmith's shop. He rips the shoes off his horse so he has a pretext to visit the shop the next morning. The blacksmith had heard of Ulenspiegel, is eager to talk to him and proposes a deal: "If [Ulenspiegel] could tell him an honest word that was truthful, he would give him a horseshoe for his horse for free."[49] Ulenspiegel responds that the blacksmith needs iron, coal, and wind in his bellows, and then he can perform his work. The statement is so obvious, commonsensical, and banal in its truth content that it implicitly ridicules the blacksmith. The blacksmith has to concede that this is a truthful statement and gives Ulenspiegel a horseshoe. The other three members of the household – journeyman, wife, and maid – also trade a true statement for a horseshoe, and so Ulenspiegel's horse has four shoes again. Everybody is happy, and Ulenspiegel rides away.

It can be argued that the reader is the victim of this chapter. The narrator's deception is to disappoint the reader's expectations and to deflate the anticipation of clever verbal savagery. Ulenspiegel fashions himself into a truthsayer, yet his statements are of utmost banality.[50] The reader expects a great revelation yet only hears statements whose truth content is self-evident. We expect an ironic tension between the different layers of meaning of the truth claim, but we get most trivial statements where no such ironic space exists. Ulenspiegel plays with the expectations both of the blacksmith and the reader. Here the trick consists of the absence of a trick, the deception in withholding the expected deception. In narrative terms, this is a very clever move: this pattern of intermittent reinforcement makes the reader eager to find out how Ulenspiegel's deceptive game plays out in future episodes.[51]

Yet, there is a subtle twist in his banal statements. Ulenspiegel, who had targeted this household because of the beauty of the two women, enjoys the veneration by the blacksmith and the adoration by the women in the story.

---

49 Anon., *Ein kurtzweilig lesen*, fol. 59v: "Wan er im auch künd ein war wort sagen dz warhafftig wer/ so wolt er seinem pferdt ein hůffysin geben."
50 Rusterholz, "Till Eulenspiegel," 19.
51 Similarly, Ulenspiegel in chapter 50 invites all taylors in Saxony to an assembly with the promise to reveal a secret that would benefit them and their children. His anticlimactic secret is that one should make a knot into the end of the thread after threading it through the eye of a needle.

Ulenspiegel's true statements for the two women have erotic overtones, and thus a second layer of meaning is revealed: he alleges that the wife of the blacksmith likes to look longingly at other men, and his statement to the maid contains this piece of advice: "Young maiden, when you eat, beware of beef so that you won't have to dig in your teeth, and so your belly won't be hurting."[52] This also could be read as advice to be sexually abstinent in order to avoid pregnancy. Her giddy response in the affirmative conveys that she understands all too well what Ulenspiegel is talking about. It appears that the two women understood the double meaning of these statements, but not the men. In this story, Ulenspiegel for a change is not the malicious interpreter and exploiter of semiotic ambiguity; rather, he is its source. Ulenspiegel not only understands that language has different levels of meaning, he also knows how to shape and manipulate such language to his advantage, even if it is just for a few fleeting flirtatious moments.

While in most chapters the meaning of words and of figures of speech is just the underlying mechanism of his mischief, they are at the center of the conflict in chapter 69, which focuses on Ulenspiegel's visit to a bathhouse in Hanover. The bath master wants his establishment to be referred to as "house of cleanliness" rather than as a bathhouse.[53] It is easy to relate to the re-branding effort, as bathhouses around 1500 had a questionable reputation and were increasingly regulated.[54] Ulenspiegel leaves a pile of smelly feces at its center with this explanation: "It is evident that this is a house of cleanliness because we enter it unclean and leave it clean."[55] He explains that he felt the need to cleanse his insides, so a house of cleanliness would be the perfect place to relieve himself. In his response, the bath master conveys that he understands the nature of the conflict: "Now I see very well that the words and the deeds are not all the same. Your words were pleasant to me, but your deeds are not appropriate, because your words were smooth but your works reek terribly."[56]

Ulenspiegel's deeds are based on a different interpretation of the neologism "house of cleanliness," and as usual he chooses the colloquially less obvious

---

[52] Anon., *Ein kurtzweilig lesen*, fol. 59v: "Megtelin wan du issest/ so hiet dich vor rindtfleisch/ so darffstu in den zenen nit grüblen/ vnd so thůt dir auch der buch nit wee."

[53] Anon., *Ein kurtzweilig lesen*, fol. 98r: "IN der badstuben zu honower vor dem leinthor wolt der bader nit das/ das es ein badstuben heißen solt/ sunder es hieß ein huß der reinikeit."

[54] Lindemann, *Medicine and Society*, 267.

[55] Anon., *Ein kurtzweilig lesen*, fol. 98v: "dz diß ein huß ist der reinikeit dz ist offenbar/ wan wir gon vnrein harin vnd rein wider harvß."

[56] Anon., *Ein kurtzweilig lesen*, fol. 98v: "nun sy ich wol das die wort vnd werck nit alle gleich seint/ dein wort waren mir angenem/ aber deine werck sein mir nit tau[g]lich wan dein wort waren sat/ aber deine werck stincken vbel."

Chapter 3 Defending Order and Discipline in *Dyl Ulenspiegel*

but more malicious interpretation. The bath master picks up on the alternate interpretations: "That cleanliness one practices in the latrine. This is a house of cleanliness from sweating, and you turn it into an outhouse."[57] In his clever comeback, he picks up on Ulenspiegel's dual meaning of the word cleanliness. Cleansing in Ulenspiegel's sense was taken care of in the "sprachhuß." The word around 1500 commonly referred to a latrine, but it could also designate a place of gathering, literally a place where words are exchanged.[58] Perhaps this is the bath master's ironic reference to Ulenspiegel soiling and debasing language with the result of turning the bathhouse into an outhouse.

Ulenspiegel is forced to back off, but he does not leave the premises before leaving a pile of excrement on the bath master's dining table. While this is a superficial victory for Ulenspiegel in the realm of fecal matter, he does not win the war of words. It is evident that the bath master in this episode wants to take linguistic control over his establishment by mandating how it should be referred to. As control of language is Ulenspiegel's domain, Ulenspiegel has to take up the challenge. This episode shows this key theme of the book more explicitly than most, namely the regulation of language and control of its meaning. The bath master uses language creatively to upgrade his business. Ulenspiegel's use of language, on the other hand, is rigid and is always used with the intention to offend, control, and inflict damage.

The same is true for his last encounter with his mother, who traveled to see him after hearing about his grave illness. This dialogue from chapter 90 shows that Ulenspiegel is sabotaging communication even in his last conversation with his mother while facing death:

> When she arrived where he stayed, she started to cry and spoke, my dear son, where are you sick?[59] Ulenspiegel said, dear mother, here between the trunk and the wall. Oh dear son, speak one more sweet word to me. Ulenspiegel said, dear mother, honey, that is a sweet herb.[60] The mother said, oh dear son, give me your sweet lesson I can remember you by. Ulenspiegel said, yes, dear mother, if you want to hear the sound of your business, turn your ass away from the wall so the stink will not go into your nose.[61]

---

57 Anon., *Ein kurtzweilig lesen*, fol. 98v: "die reinikeit pflegt man vff dem sprachhuß. Daz ist ein huß der reinikeit vom schwitzen/ vnd du machst darus ein scheißhuß."
58 Grimm, *Deutsches Wörterbuch*, vol. 16, 2759–2761.
59 The ambiguity in the first question, "wa bistu kranck," is difficult to translate. The mother's intent is to show surprise and confusion in the sense of "how could you be sick?" However, Ulenspiegel responds to the question of "wo," or where.
60 The second response is based on the similar sound of the words "wort" (word) and "krut" (herb) in Low German.
61 Anon., *Ein kurtzweilig lesen*, fol. 124v-125r: "Da sie nun zů im kam/ ward sie weinen vnd sprach. Mein lieber sun wa bistu kranck Vlenspiegel sprach liebe můter hie zwüschen der

By taking things literally, Ulenspiegel refuses to acknowledge what is intended to be said with words and reduces language to a tool of misunderstandings and into a means of talking past each other.[62] This dialogue makes clear that Ulenspiegel's intent is to disrupt and stunt communication, even in the moment when his mother visits him at his deathbed.

It has been claimed that Ulenspiegel breaks up rigid language and gives it new horizons of experience.[63] In fact, the opposite is the case: it is Ulenspiegel himself who deprives language of its dynamic range and interpretive openness by defining it through his rigid use of language. Taking things literally means reducing the meaning of words to their basic primary meanings and rejecting the use of words and expressions in figurative, metaphoric, and allegorical ways.[64] This is the underlying pattern of miscommunication in most episodes. By only accepting the narrowest and most advantageous interpretation of language, he manipulates communication and subverts all social transactions based on it. Communication, and by implication the underlying social order, only can function if all participants honor its conventions. Ulenspiegel subverts conventional norms of communication upon which the corporate social order depends, and he undermines societal interest in creating mutual understanding and consensus through verbal communication.[65] So the world is not topsy-turvy on its own; rather, for the most part it is a product of Ulenspiegel's dysfunctional communication.

Ulenspiegel's use of fecal matter is an extension of his inability to communicate. It is a mode of body language that functionally serves as a form of communication. Like Ulenspiegel's words, defecation only has a literal meaning: it has no pretense to mean something other than what defecation means in an immediate way – a sign of dislike, disrespect, and disapproval of another human being. In chapter 10, young Ulenspiegel in his first adventure away from home is instructed by the knight he serves to defecate on the "henep" (hemp) out of which the rope is made to hang thieves and robbers. Ulenspiegel thinks that he said "senep" (mustard) and acts accordingly. Ulenspiegel learns here that fecal matter has meaning and that it can be used as part of punishment for others. In chapter 12, he gets a pastor to defecate in his own church with a clever yet deceitful bet.

---

kisten vnd der wand. Ach lieber sun sprich mir noch zů ein sues wort. Vlenspiegel sprach liebe mŭter honig das ist ein süß krut. Die mŭter sprach ach lieber sun gib mir dein süß ler da ich dein bei gedencken mag. Vlenspiegel sagt ia liebe mŭter wan du wilt deins gemachs thön/ so ker den ars von dem wind so gat dir der gestanck nit in die naß."

62 Kirschner, *Hermen Bote*, 95.
63 Rusterholz, "Till Eulenspiegel," 20.
64 Kirschner, *Hermen Bote*, 95.
65 Kirschner, *Hermen Bote*, 96.

Fecal matter thus becomes the material he uses to trick people, to dish out punishment, or to exact revenge. Applications of fecal matter, as well as obscene acts, are forms of communication through body language that replace verbal communication and thus point to the dysfunction of social interactions. The text tells us that it is not the impurity of society that is unveiled through Ulenspiegel's acts of defecation, it is his own: they represent his transgressive energy to create social upheaval. Just like his use of language, his use of fecal matter is a subversive tool designed to dislodge the order of the world.

Dyl Ulenspiegel shows an imperfect world where greed, envy, and other shortcomings of a number of figures are highlighted in their interactions with the protagonist. In that sense, the name of the title figure has been taken literally as a wise owl that holds a mirror for his contemporaries, as the frontispiece of the 1515 edition implies.[66] But this is not really the main thrust of the book. At its center is a protagonist who operates in the margins of society, which enables him to commit his acts of transgression against the divinely ordained social order.[67]

Writers at the time, like Sebastian Brant, were extremely sensitive to conflict and unrest. Hermann Bote was extremely preoccupied with the political and social uprisings in his native city of Brunswick, and he was eager to show the temporality of these revolts by chronicling the return to the *status quo ante*. In his writings he expressed serious anxieties about the continued threat to the political order and strenuously argued in favor of its defense, both in his city and in the empire at large. This is the context within which we have to read *Dyl Ulenspiegel* as well. It articulates a warning against subversion and upheaval and a call to rein in the activities of mischievous and lawless figures in the margins who, like Ulenspiegel, threaten the established order.

Dyl Ulenspiegel had a significant impact on other literary texts in the sixteenth century, although subsequent texts referred to the titular protagonist as Eulenspiegel, the High German form of the name, rather than as Ulenspiegel.[68] There was concern at the time that the book would spoil the lower classes and particularly the German youth.[69] Georg Rollenhagen (1542–1609) in his *Froschmeuseler* from 1595, for instance, accused Eulenspiegel of corrupting the German youth. He assured his readers that his book would be more beneficial to the German youth: "It should be quite more useful than our world-famous

---

66 Wunderlich, *Till Eulenspiegel*, 55.
67 Blume, *Hermann Bote*, 25.
68 The discussion here makes use of both forms of the name, Ulenspiegel for the original and Eulenspiegel for versions by other writers.
69 Beise, "machen die docter," 33.

countryman Eulenspiegel, or than other shameful books as pfaff von kalenberg, kaziporus, rollwagen, etc."[70] Rollenhagen at the end of the century confirmed the outsized fame Ulenspiegel had acquired over time. But his facetious comments about *Dyl Ulenspiegel* and three other narrative texts, to which his own *Froschmeuseler* was very much indebted, also point to the questionable reputation these texts still enjoyed at the end of the sixteenth century.

Hans Sachs (1494–1576) was not only a prolific writer, but he also was the most productive adapter of episodes from *Dyl Ulenspiegel*. Sachs focused on Eulenspiegel in at least thirty-eight mastersongs. Of these, Sachs reworked seven as *Schwank* (short narrative) in verse or *Spruchgedicht* (spoken poem) with almost identical verses.[71] Furthermore, Eulenspiegel is the protagonist in four carnival plays written between 1553 and 1557. Sachs wrote all texts with Eulenspiegel references between 1533 and 1557.[72] Sachs owned the 1532 Erfurt edition of the book,[73] so it is not surprising that he started to write about Eulenspiegel in 1533. Among the episodes Sachs used were chapters 97 and 99 from the 1532 edition, both of which were not in the 1515 edition.

The very first Sachs text about Eulenspiegel from 1533 was simply entitled "Der Ewlenspiegel," which implies that Sachs at that time had no intention to dedicate additional poems to the Eulenspiegel figure. It is based on chapter 17, discussed above, where Eulenspiegel empties out a hospital full of sick people. The basic story is the same, although it now is set in Nuremberg. However, there are subtle but important differences in the conclusion. While the original text wraps up with a bitter complaint by the hospital administrator about the loss of funds and the deceit of patients, Sachs's version ends in benign laughter as the hospital chief learns how he has been tricked. Sachs ends with the administrator's conciliatory sentiment: "When he learned about the good farce, he had to laugh about the craftiness."[74] The term "schalckheit" thus loses the

---

[70] Rollenhagen, *Froschmeuseler*, 20, 22–25: "es solt etwas mer nutz schaffen/ denn vnser weltberümbter Landsman Eulenspiegel/ oder auch andere schandbücher/ der pfaff von kalenberg/ kaziporus/ rollwagen etc." The other narratives mentioned here are *Des Pfaffen Geschichte und Histori vom Kalenberg* (1473) by Philipp Frankfurter, *Katzipori* (1558) by Michael Lindener, and *Das Rollwagenbüchlin* (1555) by Jörg Wickram.
[71] I am indebted to the research project "De(kon)struktive Kommunikation im Eulenspiegelbuch" (2010–2014) at the Université de Lausanne, led by Alexander Schwarz, that listed most Sachs texts with an Eulenspiegel component. Unfortunately, this online resource no longer is available.
[72] Tenberg, *Die deutsche Till-Eulenspiegel-Rezeption*, 97.
[73] Sachs, KG 26, 179.
[74] Sachs, *Sämtliche Fabeln und Schwänke*, vol. 3, 110, v. 59–60: "Als er vernam den güeten schwanck, | Müest er der schalckheit lachen."

entirely negative connotation it had before; Sachs's use of the term is considerably more ambiguous.

Sachs did not return to Eulenspiegel for another five years. He wrote four mastersongs in 1538 and 1539 with an Eulenspiegel theme. The first mastersong in this group is *Des Ewlenspigels testament* (*Eulenspiegel's Testament*) from 1538[75] that is based on chapter 92. Here, a dying Eulenspiegel goads a greedy priest to reach into a purse into which he had defecated. While in the original version, the focus is on Ulenspiegel's legacy of mischief to which the priest had fallen victim, Sachs ends with a preachy reminder for all to respect the testaments of others and to allow things to take their predestined orderly course.

Chapter 97 from the 1532 edition, where the pastor has a fling with Ulenspiegel's woman, is worked into a 1539 mastersong entitled *Ewlenspigel mit dem prems* (*Eulenspiegel with the Muzzle*).[76] While the woman's status is ambiguous in the model, Sachs definitely makes her Eulenspiegel's wife. Eulenspiegel flees to Krems, leaving his wife and the pastor behind.[77] Sachs's ending gives the story a completely different spin:

> Modesty, discipline, and honor have become worthless. Nobody wants to take to heart the marital estate. Because of that, adultery is all too common; unfortunately, one finds it almost in all streets. As one is not punishing it harshly, it multiplies daily. Therefore, you pure and honest woman, safeguard your heart and body against adultery. Stick with your husband, then you will wear a crown of honor.[78]

Here, Eulenspiegel is not ridiculed, nor is the pastor scorned for his misdeeds. Instead, Sachs added a gloomy discourse on the decay of fidelity in marriage. Even though the pastor is the perpetrator in the story who seduced many women in his parish, Sachs's conclusion reminds wives to remain faithful to their husbands.

---

75 Sachs, *Sämtliche Fabeln und Schwänke*, vol. 3, 210–211.
76 "Prems" is the code word the priest utters when a woman passes by with whom he had relations. The word refers to the sting of the "Bremse," horsefly, and has sexual connotations. However, Sachs uses the word "brems" as a neuter noun, meaning muffle. In Sachs's usage, the word therefore loses its sexual connotation.
77 The text reads: "Vnd lies die půebin vnd den pueben siczen." Tenberg (*Die deutsche Till-Eulenspiegel-Rezeption*, 110) infers that Eulenspiegel leaves "Frau und Kinder." I would argue that the "půebin" refers to his adulterous wife and the "pueb" to the pastor.
78 Sachs, *Sämtliche Fabeln und Schwänke*, vol. 3, 220, v. 51–60: "Scham, zuecht vnd er ist worden klein, | Den estant wil nimant zw herczen fassen. | Des ist der epruch gar gemein, | Man fint in laider schir in allen gassen | Die weil man in nicht heftig straft, | Thůet er sich teglich meren. | Derhalb, dw raines pider weib, | Phůet hercz vnd leib | Vor epruch, halt dich an dein mann, | So tregst ein kron der eren."

Sachs did not return to the Eulenspiegel theme until 1546. Well over half the mastersongs about Eulenspiegel were written between 1546 and 1548. Sachs's mastersong "Der prillen macher" (The Maker of Eyeglasses), an adaptation of chapter 63 that was discussed earlier in this chapter, is indicative of how he repurposed the original *Dyl Ulenspiegel*. As discussed above, the original framed the chapter in the context of the discord among prince-electors threatening the well-being of the empire. Rulers didn't need eyeglasses because they were looking the other way when graft occurred. The charge was that prince-electors hurt the interests of the empire and by implication also of the cities, and that both ecclesiastical and worldly authorities covered up the corruption.

In Sachs's version, the idea of political authorities succumbing to corruption is toned down. Sachs instead blamed clergy for the decline of the craft of making eyeglasses: young monks running away and old monks knowing everything by heart, thus not needing to read.[79] However, this plot change did not lead up to anti-clerical or anti-Catholic polemics. In fact, Sachs's anticlerical polemic is quite restrained and less stinging than in the model, which is surprising given that Sachs was an unconditional follower of Luther's teachings. This is in sharp contrast to the mastersong *Die Wittenbergisch Nachtigall* (*The Nightingale from Wittenberg*) from 1523. Two years before the Reformation was officially introduced in his native Nuremberg, Sachs publicly expressed his support of Martin Luther and his demands while openly polemicizing against the pope and the Catholic Church. It appears that Sachs offered his views on large political issues only reluctantly after the Nuremberg city council reprimanded him in 1527 because of the perceived impropriety of his anti-papal polemics and temporarily prohibited the printing of his works.[80] Similarly, the mastersong *Ewlenspigel mit dem pabst* (*Eulenspiegel with the Pope*) from 1548, which is based on chapter 34, treats a visit with the pope in Rome as a surprisingly normal event without even a hint of criticism of the pope or his Church.

The poem about Eulenspiegel as the maker of eyeglasses illustrates how differently Sachs developed the didactic angle. Sachs added a moral lesson to his poems where the original added none. This is true for many of Sachs's mastersongs, particularly those that were based on chapters where Ulenspiegel in the earlier version acted maliciously. In *Dyl Ulenspiegel*, on the other hand, the

---

[79] Sachs, *Sämtliche Fabeln und Schwänke*, vol. 4, 63, v. 19–28: "Gaistlicher lewt sint vil gestorben | Die jungen münich laüffen raüs int welt, | Die alten küenens auswendig: | Darůmb lös wir kain gelt. | Der gleich künig vnd füersten, mag ich jehen | Pabst, pischoff vnd prelatten in der nehen | Nur durch die finger sehen. | Derhalb pedürffen der prillen gar nicht; | Derhalb mein hantwereck ellent ist, | Verstorben vnd entwicht."
[80] Hess, "German Poetry," 401–402; Bernstein, "Hans Sachs," 246.

protagonist himself was at issue because his mischief and unwillingness to integrate into society was the key destabilizing force. The critique of the protagonist and of the society in which he operated was driven by the dialogues and the plots. Just the rawness of his character, his malevolent disposition and his evil deeds were enough to get the point across. Plot and character drove the interpretation, and the reader could be trusted to arrive at the proper interpretation of both character and deeds.

Sachs returned to the plot of chapter 63 in a verse narration (*Versschwank*) in 1554, entitled *Ewlenspiegels disputation mit einem bischoff ob dem brillenmachen* (Eulenspiegel's disputation with a bishop about making eyeglasses). Eulenspiegel encounters a bishop who is en route to the diet in Worms, according to the narrative voice[81]: "There a diet was going to be held, and many princes stayed there. They should consider the common good, to aid and protect the Roman empire."[82] In contrast to the earlier mastersong, this version focuses on the discord within the empire and thus brings out the political dimension of the original *Ulenspiegel*.

In Sachs's text the bishop has the opportunity to respond: he blames wicked courtiers and shifty civil servants. Eulenspiegel counters that violent crime and infractions against the political and social order were common in Germany and mostly directed at the free cities and their citizens. He repeats his appeal to the princes:

> The princes should fend off such injustice and take care of it on their honor, and they should support the Roman Empire and not let it be ruined. Now the princes sit still quietly and look through their fingers [turn a blind eye]. That is why they do not require eyeglasses to maintain good eyesight.[83]

Crime and injustice thus happen when the empire is threatened by particular interests. However, the bishop laughs it off and invites Eulenspiegel to accompany him to the diet, just like in the model, but also concedes that the diet needs to act to restore justice to German lands.

---

81 In the 1515 text, the diet takes place in Frankfurt. At the time of Sachs's writing, the most recent diets took place in Worms (1535, 1544, 1545). The most recent Frankfurt diet took place in 1486. See Tenberg, *Die deutsche Till-Eulenspiegel-Rezeption*, 145, note 284.
82 Sachs, KG 9, 256, v. 12–14: "Alda solt werden ein reichßtag, | Und mancher fürste darzu lag. | Solten betrachten gmeinen nutz, | Römischem reych zu hülff und schutz."
83 Sachs, KG 9, 260, v. 5–12: "Solch unrecht soltn die fürsten wehrn | Und untersthen bey iren ehrn | Und dem römischen reych beystehn, | Es nit lassen zu drümmern gehn. | So sitzn die fürsten still mit rhu | Und sehen durch die finger zu. | Derhalb dürffens kein prillen nicht, | Zu behalten ein gut gesicht."

The ending of Sachs's didactic poem differs in significant ways. Sachs gives the bishop the last word. The bishop gets to adjudicate the conflict and formulate a final statement. Thus the authority of the sovereign is maintained, and Eulenspiegel ultimately has to subject himself to it. Furthermore, Sachs in his texts generally was interested in forging a compromise and building a consensus that castigated vices and transgressions but that was also committed to rebuilding the community and to pursuing the common good. The protagonist gets more leeway to castigate the authorities than in the earlier mastersong. Like in all the other Sachs texts, however, he still is not a free agent but rather has to subject himself to the compromise proposed by the bishop. Also in line with other Sachs texts, Eulenspiegel is not the unruly transgressor who embodies moral decay and social disruption through his personhood and his actions. Instead he becomes an agent of change by revealing transgressions committed by others and by generally diagnosing political and social disorder.

Sachs's four carnival plays based on the Eulenspiegel figure give us additional insight into how Sachs processed the plots from *Dyl Ulenspiegel* and reinterpreted both character and moral lesson. They are much longer than the original brief episodes and therefore offer opportunities to add new material. Furthermore, the dramatic form allows for a better development of the characters and requires the dialogues to be expanded in order to add plausibility, while it simultaneously reduces the role of the narrative voice.

In the play *Ewlenspiegel mit der pfaffen kellnerin und dem pfert* (Eulenspiegel with the priest's servant and the horse) from 1553, based on chapter 38 discussed briefly above, the Duke of Brunswick covets a pastor's horse, but the pastor is unwilling to give or sell it to the Duke. In both versions, the plot evolves along the same lines. Ulenspiegel promises to get the horse to the duke by subterfuge, and the Duke gives him a cash advance. Ulenspiegel goes to the pastor's house pretending to be indigent, and gets permission to stay at the house for a few days. He feigns mortal illness and requests a confession with the warning that he had sinned against the pastor. In the confession, Ulenspiegel tells the pastor that he had slept with the pastor's maid. The enraged pastor challenges and beats the maid, breaking the Seal of Confession in the process. Ulenspiegel threatens to report this to the bishop, unless the pastor gives him the horse. The pastor has no choice in the matter, and Ulenspiegel brings the horse to the duke and gets his reward.

There are subtle but significant differences between the two versions. Sachs's play opens with Eulenspiegel's monologue, in which he talks about his poverty and lack of shelter in the middle of a cold winter – a ploy we find in all four carnival plays and in a number of his other Eulenspiegel texts, which is designed to generate empathy for and a positive attitude toward the protagonist. The second difference is that the Duke in the play is essentially entitled to the horse, particularly as he is willing to pay. The original text on the other hand insists that the pastor is under no obligation to surrender the horse to the duke, a reference that was omitted by Sachs: "The pastor steadfastly denied that he wanted to leave the horse to him. And so the prince was not allowed to have the horse taken away, for the area was under the jurisdiction of the city of Brunswick."[84]

This sets up a different assessment of the story by the two authors. As the duke's wants are unjustified in the earlier text, Ulenspiegel's rogue actions to obtain the horse are unfair and even malevolent. The pastor is the innocent victim who is tricked into breaking confidentiality and loses both his horse and his maid due to Ulenspiegel's mischief. For Sachs, the pastor is the main culprit of the story in that he resists the legitimate wishes of his sovereign. He is presented negatively, like in the maid's unsubstantiated allegation that the pastor was a philanderer. The duke in his closing monologue asserts that the pastor deserved to lose his horse because he had refused to sell it. As Sachs signed off this final monologue with his own name, as he did in most texts, we must assume that this represents his point of view.

The role and perception of Eulenspiegel shifts accordingly. In *Dyl Ulenspiegel*, the protagonist is his own agent, an outcast, and a transgressive figure. The trick he plays on the pastor and the maid is vile and motiviated by his own greed. For Sachs, Eulenspiegel becomes a conscientious subject to the duke, who willingly fulfills the duke's wishes.[85] Upon delivering the pastor's horse, the duke offers him unlimited hospitality at court for which Eulenspiegel expresses his submissive gratitude: "Gracious Lord, I thank you for your clemency with which you think of me with grace."[86] Eulenspiegel in Sachs's play thus moves from an outcast to an insider, from a transgressor against the order to its supporter and enforcer of authority. The world still is in disarray and its social order under siege, but Eulenspiegel now has switched sides.

Even though Sachs's plotlines were almost identical to those found in *Ulenspiegel*, there are two key differences that offer a reinterpretation of the Eulenspiegel figure. First, Sachs handled the Eulenspiegel figure in a much more differentiated fashion. The original Ulenspiegel operated in the margins of society without occupation, social network, status, and moral standing. As an outsider who was unwilling to be a cogwheel in the system, he was not just

---

84 Anon., *Ein kurtzweilig lesen*, fol. 53v: "Der pfarer verneint allzeit dem fursten dz er dz pferd nit wolt verlassen/ so dorfft im der fürst auch dz pferd nit nemen lassen. Wan dz gericht wz vnder dem rad von Brunschwick."
85 Tenberg, *Die deutsche Till-Eulenspiegel-Rezeption*, 144.
86 Sachs, KG 17, 94–95: "Gnediger herr, ich danck ewr milt, das ir mein thut in gnad gedencken."

a transgressor through his actions but through his very being. Sachs's Eulenspiegel figure, by contrast, was marked as a member of society. In his song "Eulenspiegel mit der Kellnerin" (Eulenspiegel and the Waitress),[87] for instance, Eulenspiegel remains at the Wolfenbüttel court, performing his harmless tricks to everybody's amusement, but he remains an outcast in the original corresponding chapter 38. While often engaging in inappropriate acts, Sachs's Eulenspiegel is not mischievous by definition. Sachs often softens the reprehensible acts Ulenspiegel performs in *Dyl Ulenspiegel*. A good example is chapter 47, in which Ulenspiegel uses one of his somewhat belabored misunderstandings to boil his master's dog in the process of making beer in the town of Einbeck and is promptly chased out of town. In Sachs's version from 1551, entitled "Der hopff im bier" (Hops in the Beer),[88] the song ends with the remark that the Einbeck beer has tasted like boiled dog ever since. Sachs thus turned an evil deed into a harmless practical joke.

The second difference is that Sachs's versified episodes highlighted human foibles, vices, and sins.[89] The plots Sachs chose became the vehicle for his didactic and moralizing musings that often diverged substantially from the points established in the earlier template. In Sachs's writings we see the beginnings of a much more benign interpretation of Eulenspiegel as a benevolent and funny man who held a mirror to his contemporaries. While Sachs was concerned about the decay of the moral order as well, he used the stories to add his own invective with an emphasis on exposing individual behavior.

The larger context is that literary texts in the first quarter of the sixteenth century were heavily focused on large societal issues: globalization and pluralization, strife and disorder in the empire, economic pressures from large merchant bankers, and the perceived loss of the common good. In that context, the original Ulenspiegel posed a systemic threat. In Sachs's texts, on the other hand, Eulenspiegel became a depoliticized tool to demask immoral behavior that Sachs, unlike the earlier author, may have seen as reprehensible but not as a systemic threat. The transformation of the Ulenspiegel figure therefore should be seen within the larger cultural shift that took place around 1530, a shift away from the despair, grief and anger about the loss of the old political and social order toward an inward-looking program of individual moral improvement.

The concern about the social order conveyed in *Dyl Ulenspiegel* was misread by other contemporaries as well. Johannes Pauli (1455–1530) in his collection of

---

87 Sachs, *Sämtliche Fabeln und Schwänke*, vol. 4, 64–65.
88 Sachs, *Sämtliche Fabeln und Schwänke*, vol. 5, 153–165.
89 Tenberg, *Die deutsche Till-Eulenspiegel-Rezeption*, 124.

short stories from 1522, entitled *Von schimpff vnd ernst* (Mischief and Morality), used a couple of Eulenspiegel stories. In one of the stories, Eulenspiegel is simply referred to as "adventurer."[90] In another story, the narrator tells us about Xantus's servant who only cooks one lentil, as he is told literally, instead of lentil soup. The narrator reminds the readers: "One should complete a task according to the intention and will of the master. Such whimsical and strange stories you find in *Ulenspiegel*; he did exactly what he was told."[91] Here, the servant's transgression consisted of doing the opposite of what his master wanted him to do.[92]

Kaspar Scheidt's (1520–1565) *Grobianus/ von groben sitten/ und vnhöflichen geberden* (*Grobianus, of Coarse Manners and Impolite Gestures*)[93] from 1551 pointed to *Dyl Ulenspiegel* as a mirror so readers could recognize the inappropriateness of the public display of their bodily functions.[94] Grobianus, the titular conveyor of bad manners, recommends spraying one's own snot on a food platter with the result that everybody else will be too disgusted to eat the food. He then reveals the source of this trick: "That's written of Ulenspiegel: he did this little trick, too; everyone holds him high and worthy and they follow his book much more than all the lives of the philosophers. You too should follow this rule."[95]

The later writers, Sachs, Pauli, and Scheidt, framed Eulenspiegel as a relatively benign prankster, as opposed to his representation in *Dyl Ulenspiegel* as a rogue and villain. None of them picked up on the point that Eulenspiegel used language with the intention to offend, control, and inflict damage, and that his tricks were mean-spirited and malicious with the objective of hurting innocent artisans, servants, and shop-keepers. In the world of *Dyl Ulenspiegel*, the protagonist himself was at issue because his mischief and unwillingness to integrate into society was the key destabilizing force. Its author saw Ulenspiegel as a corrosive force posing a threat to the social fabric. The later writers no longer perceived Eulenspiegel as an existential threat, and they displayed a more relaxed attitude toward Eulenspiegel's transgressions. Instead, the misdeeds now were treated as individual shortcomings that needed to be exposed and modified.

---

[90] Pauli, *Schimpf und Ernst*, 558–559 (story 650).
[91] Pauli, *Schimpf und Ernst*, 336 (story 605): "Man sol ein ding thůn nach der meinung vnd dem willen des gebieters. Der verirten vnd seltzamen historien findestu in dem *Vlenspiegel*, der thet was man in hieß."
[92] Beise, "machen die docter," 47.
[93] The text is based on Friedrich Dedekind's *Grobianus. De morum simplicicate, libri duo.* Frankfurt: Eichorn, 1549.
[94] Wunderlich, *Till Eulenspiegel*, 55.
[95] Scheidt, *Grobianus*, sig. D2v. Translation Correll, *The End of Conduct*, 150.

Chapter 4
A Dystopian Topsy-Turvy World

According to Mikhail Bakhtin, carnival temporarily suspended hierarchical structures and "celebrated temporary liberation from the prevailing truth and from the established order."[1] The German carnival play of the fifteenth century grew out of this tradition. Yet, the gradual imposition of social discipline, described by Norbert Elias in *The Civilizing Process*, removed much of the space within which it was allowed to operate. The Reformation completed this process in areas that were under the control of Lutherans. The carnival plays by Hans Sachs were mostly written in a post-Reformation context and lost that tolerance for carnivalesque inversion. Rather, they functioned as short comedies that were conceived for a reading audience.

Handbooks on how to behave and how to control one's body mushroomed. Sebastian Brant contributed an early handbook on table manners in 1490, entitled *De moribus et facetijs mense. Thesmophagia* (*On Good Manners and Witty Conversation*), which was based on the *Phagifacetus*, a medieval handbook on table manners. Brant instructed an urban audience in proper conduct at table in a didactic text that alternates between Latin prose and German verse.[2] Of the many didactic texts designed to enforce civility and good behavior,[3] Kaspar Scheidt's (1520–1565) *Grobianus/ von groben sitten/ und vnhöflichen geberden* (*Grobianus, of course manners and impolite Gestures*) from 1551 sticks out.[4] The motto on the title page instructs the reader on how to read this book: "Read this booklet often and extensively. And always do the opposite."[5] By heaping praise on misbehavior, poor manners, and all kinds of social transgressions, the book created an inverted order that reflected a topsy-turvy world.

The carnivalesque became shorthand for a world that was out of kilter. No longer could temporary transgressions be seen as a release valve to relieve social pressures. Writers like Brant perceived the carnivalesque inversion as a transgressive threat to the established order.[6] Brant's reference that his *Narrenschiff*

---

[1] Bakhtin, *Rabelais and His World*, 10.
[2] Umbach, *Sebastian Brants Tischzucht*, 9.
[3] For instance Hans Sachs's didactic poem "Ein tisch-zucht" from 1534 (KG 4, 297–299).
[4] Scheidt's German text is based on an earlier Latin version by Friedrich Dedekind (1525–1598).
[5] Scheidt, *Grobianus*, title page: "Liß wol diß bůchlin offt vnd vil/ | Vnd thů allzeit das widerspil."
[6] The fact that Brant was carnival king in Basel in 1482 (Zeydel, *Sebastian Brant*, 65) appears to have done little to prevent a change in Brant's attitude.

was "printed in Basel during carnival, which one calls the consecration of the fools,"[7] is a clear indication that carnivalesque transgressions were not limited to the days leading up to Ash Wednesday, but rather that carnival now was happening every day of the year. Brant also added a chapter entitled, "Von fasnacht narren" (of carnival fools) to the second edition of his *Narrenschiff* (1495) to reinforce this point. The chapter ends with the dismayed realization that foolery is not limited to carnival season: fools remain fools during lent, that they make sure that they put on their caps during Easter week.[8] Brant inhabited an inverted world, one that was set up by the Antichrist against the divine order.[9]

Many moralistic and didactic texts reflected this grim vision of a world turned upside down. One example is the pamphlet *Ein spiegel der naturlichen himlischen vnd prophetischen sehungen aller trübsalen/ angst/ vnd not* (*A Mirror of the Natural, Celestial, and Prophetic Visions of All Afflictions, Fear, and Distress*) by the physician and astrologer Joseph Grünpeck (c. 1473–c. 1532). One of the woodcuts shows a church that stands upside down to signify the inversion that results from human sin (figure 1). A peasant occupies the priest's spot in the sanctuary, while the priest is plowing the field.[10] The image reinforces the thought that the Church and the social order are turned upside down. Another woodcut shows the sinking ship of the Church. It is reminiscent of an illustration to Brant's *Narrenschiff* and the text that alludes to the sinking of Saint Peter's ship.[11]

Other forms of inversion were common in the period as well. Perhaps the most interesting was the dystopia of the *Schlaraffenland* (Land of Cockaigne) that perhaps was most famously represented in the 1567 painting of the same name by Pieter Bruegel the Elder. The Land of Cockaigne was a ready-made place where all needs of humans were met without any labor and effort and therefore was associated with a number of sins, like gluttony, sloth, luxury, and lust.[12] While the vision of a world made out of ready-made food may appear appealing and even humorous, it described a dystopian place in the early modern imagination. Numerous writers used this motif and even devoted entire texts to it. Sebastian Brant dedicated chapter 108 to "Das schluraffen schiff."

---

[7] Brant, *Narrenschiff*, "End des narrenschiffs" [epilogue]: "Gedruckt zů Basel vff die Vasenaht/ die man der narren kirchwich nennet." Brant repeated the comparison of carnival to the consecration of the fool in the carnival chapter added in 1495 (ch. 110b, v. 31).
[8] Brant, *Narrenschiff*, ch. 110b, v. 112–115.
[9] Kuper, *Zur Semiotik der Inversion*, 60.
[10] Grünpeck, *Ein spiegel*, sig. A3r. See Kuper, *Zur Semiotik der Inversion*, 14.
[11] Grünpeck, *Ein spiegel*, sig. A5v. Brant, *Narrenschiff*, ch. 103, v. 62–63.
[12] Heinen, "Das Schlaraffenland," 241.

Figure 1: Joseph Grünpeck. *Ein spiegel der naturlichen himlischen vnd prophetischen sehungen aller trübsalen/ angst/ vnd not.* Nuremberg: Georg Stuchs, 1508. Sig. a3r. © Bayerische Staatsbibliothek München.

Hans Sachs discussed the theme in his didactic poem "Das Schlauraffen Landt" from 1530.[13]

The didactic poem "Der herzverkehrer" (The heart-inverter) by Hans Sachs from 1539 illustrates how allegories of inversion invoked anxieties about the social order. The full title of the poem indicates the program: "I am called the heart inverter, and I turned upside down the German land, as one can recognize in all estates."[14] The first-person narrator travels from Italy to Bern. On a

---

[13] Sachs, KG 5, 338–341.
[14] Sachs, KG 22, 217, v. 1–3: "Der herzverkehrer pin ich genant | Und hab verkert das tewsche land, | Wie man den spüert in allen standt."

mountainous trail, he encounters a tall and strong man who travels in the opposite direction. His appearance is bewildering as everything about him is topsy-turvy; he wears his pants on his arms, for instance. He claims that he wanted to do the same thing in Italy he had already achieved in Germany, namely turn everything upside down. What follows is a description in which the man lists all the things he had reversed in Germany, like turning bishops into worldly princes or subverting the justice system to make it unjust. He also interfered with the social order affecting cities: "I turned burghers into peasants. I brought many peasants within the city walls. I turned artisans into merchants and taught crafts to many burghers."[15] He blurred the boundaries between occupational categories and got many peasants to migrate into the city. By magnifying the inversion, Sachs gave voice to anxieties about the transformation of the city, particularly about the influx of rural migrants that caused great concerns among his contemporaries.[16]

The man's account of his activities reads like a catalogue of social ills of Sachs's time. The man closes with this summary that reads like a fool's tale in Brant's *Ship of Fools*:

> I made the common good small and self-interest big and common. I drove virtue away from Germany, yet vices remained in the city. So I turned everything upside down, and I forcefully nurtured the reverse. Through my cunning nobody wants to be what he really is and does not want to do what is up to him to carry out. Many things they like to do, but I get between target and bullet. This is, in sum, my business and labor, where I stand.[17]

The summary included a reference to self-interest, one of the main vices of his time, discussed in more detail in Chapter 7. Things having been better in the past is another important motif. Germany must have been a land of virtue in former times[18] as it has become a land of vices through inversion. Individuals

---

15 Sachs, KG 22, 218, v. 29–32: "Purger hab ich verkert in pawren, | Vil pawren pracht in die statmawren. | Hantwercker zw kauflewtn verkert | Vil purger habe ich hantwerck glert."
16 Nuremberg indeed was growing at the time. The growth in the city's economy created labor shortages which were largely met by in-migration. This increased urbanization, particularly in large cities like Nuremberg, was a northern and western European trend. See Hunt and Murray, *A History of Business*, 226–228.
17 Sachs, KG 22, 219, v. 10–20: "Gemainen nuetz den macht ich klain, | Den aignen nuetz gros und gemain; | Duegent hab ich aus Teutschland trieben, | Laster sint an der stat pelieben. | Also thet ich all ding verkeren, | Das widerspil gewaltig neren, | Das ein iglicher durch mein list | Gar nicht wil sein, was er doch ist, | Und nicht wil thun, was im zw-stet, | Und etlichs, das es geren det, | Ich zwischen zil und kugel kum. | Das ist in suma sumarum | Mein gescheft und arbeit, wo ich pin."
18 The nostalgia for an imaginary better past will be discussed in more detail in Chapter 20.

internalizing this inverted order, finally, aspired to belong to a different estate and class.

The ambition for social improvement filled early modern writers with anxiety as it represented a desire to challenge and reverse social order, which represented a transgression against both the existing order and the divine will that implemented it. To Brant, being discontent with one's own status was a basic form of foolishness. He frequently returned to this theme, targeting those fellow citizens who sought an inappropriate improvement in their lives. Chapter 29 has this epigrammatic pointed ending: "For each fool is flawed in that he does not want to be who he is."[19] Chapter 76 ends with a playful chiastic inversion of the end of chapter 29: "For each fool is flawed in that he wants to be who he is not."[20] Lack of self-knowledge and an improper desire to escape one's social status went hand in hand.

A good example is chapter 82, entitled "von burschem vffgang" (Of the rise of peasants), which is dedicated to the issue of social climbing in its entirety. At the beginning of the chapter, Brant engaged in the common topos of the good old times. He conjured up the image that peasants until quite recently led a simple and honest rural life in straw huts, until they started to drink wine and accrue a lot of debt. To Brant, fancy clothing was the most obvious marker of the peasants' desire for upward social movement:

> Linen does not appeal to them as before. The peasants do not want their short dresses anymore. It has to be clothing from Leyden and Mechelen, and entirely slashed and spread out, with all bright and shrill colors, and with the image of a fool on the sleeve.[21]

In six short lines, Brant summarized the key points commonly associated with the critique of fashion, ranging from the luxurious materials to the foreign origin of the cloth, the vivid colors, and the fashionable cut. Peasants were guilty of inappropriate desires, such as wanting the finest imported cloth from Leyden and Mechelen, considered to be of the highest quality at the time, indulging in inappropriate colors, and following the latest fashion trends like

---

19 Brant, *Narrenschiff*, ch. 29, v. 33–34: "Doch yedem narren das gebrist | Das er nit syn will/ das er ist."
20 Brant, *Narrenschiff*, ch. 76, v. 94–95; also ch. 76, v. 3: "Dann yedem narren das gebryst | Das er wil sin/ das er nit ist."
21 Brant, *Narrenschiff*, ch. 82, v. 13–18: "Jn schmeckt der zwilch nit wol/ als ee | Die buren went keyn gyppen me | Es můß sin lündisch/ vnd mechelsch kleit | Vnd gantz zerhacket/ vnd gespreit | Mit aller varb wild/ über wild | Vnd vff dem ermel eyn gouchs byld." A "gyppe" (or Gippe) is a short robe or jacket. "Gouch" literally means cuckoo, but also fool or rogue.

gashed garments.²² Since clothing served as a social marker, garments, colors and cuts all carried social meaning and were encoded in sumptuary laws.

The desire to willfully claim a higher social status than one was entitled to was almost invariably linked to the wearing of transgressive clothing, that is clothing which is more luxurious than the social status of its wearer might indicate. Clothing, and particularly its inappropriate use, therefore is a central motif in early modern texts that focus on socially transgressive behavior. A desire to wear the types of clothes that were reserved for higher social classes marked an inappropriate ambition to rise socially. Sumptuary laws were designed to preserve social distinctions in clothing and therefore to enforce social stability.²³ To Brant, therefore, the appropriation of elite clothing styles by peasants very much indicated a challenge of the social order and a prime transgression against it.²⁴ Brant also registered an implied critique of a rising urban consumer society in the fifteenth century, which increasingly created links between owning luxury goods, like fine garments or fashionable furniture, with social status and thus increased the fluidity in social structures.²⁵ As the ownership and the display of luxury goods in the course of the fifteenth century became less attached to social status and more dependent on the availability of economic resources to purchase them, the display or consumption of luxury goods easily could be seen as a tool to subvert the traditional social order. As we will see in Chapter 21, the consumption of exotic herbs and spices fell into this category as well, with similar consequences.

This transgressive energy that emanated from the peasants in Brant's argument permeated all of society. City dwellers acquired their vices from the peasants: "The city people now learn from the peasants how to increase evil. All cheating now comes from the peasants; every day they come up with a new way."²⁶ While the argument started out with the claim that the peasants were the teachers of evil, Brant transitioned to making peasants directly responsible for the economic ills of the city, such as hoarding commodities, manipulating

---

22 Breward, *The Culture of Fashion*, 42. For a comprehensive discussion of Renaissance fashion trends, see Mirabella, *Ornamentalism*, 2011.
23 Rosenthal: "Cultures of Clothing," 465.
24 Stallybrass and White, *The Politics*, 23. Typically, dressing up by the lower classes also was framed as a form of social deception. This element is missing here. For a more comprehensive discussion of clothing and identity, see Rublack, *Dressing Up*.
25 Pomeranz, *The Great Divergence*, 114.
26 Brant, *Narrenschiff*, ch. 82, v. 19–22: "Das statt volck yetz von buren lert | Wie es jnn boßheit werd gemert | All bschysß yetz von den buren kunt | All tag hant sie eyn nuwen funt."

prices, and gouging inflation that impoverished many – all allegations commonly leveled at merchants at the time.

The second half of chapter 82 opens up to generalizations. Brant gives us a scornful account of people of all social ranks who are in the process of climbing the social ladder. This list also includes women desiring material goods they cannot afford, which makes their husbands poor. The chapter concludes with this condemnation: "In all lands there is disgrace as no one is satisfied with his estate. No one considers who their ancestors were. Thus the world is full of fools."[27] The conclusion reminds the reader that ancestors are not honored anymore, thus renewing the reference to the better past. To Brant, not only were the traditional values and honest simple lives of the ancestors in play, but also the idea of cultural continuity. The desire for social improvement threatened the connection with the past and therefore with the traditional national character. At stake was not just the stability of the social order but also the viability of traditional German values.

The beginning of chapter 37 exposes the transgressive nature of social climbing by explaining its consequences: "He is a fool who climbs up high so that one sees his shame and disgrace. He always seeks a higher rank, yet does not regard the wheel of fortune."[28] Brant created the analogy between a fool's desire for social rise and an upward ride on the wheel of fortune. The woodcut to the chapter makes this link even more evident than the text: it shows a ship's wheel that is turned by a crank whose extension reaches to a divine hand in the top left corner of the image (figure 2). Three figures hang onto the wheel: a human figure with a donkey's head on the rise, a donkey on top, and a human figure with fool's cap with the lower body of donkey on the downside. The message of both text and image was that social rise was illusionary and temporary as the wheel of fortune did not allow anyone riding it to remain on top. The phrase "schand vnd schmoch" in the second line indicates an interesting ambiguity. Ordinarily we would translate this as "shame and disgrace." Yet, we are told that this is something we can see with our own eyes as the fool is climbing up. The word "schand" therefore also refers to the fool's private parts that are exposed in the act of climbing. The social climber is exposing himself both literally and allegorically as a social climber who commits a shameful act, namely seeking a higher status in a licentious and unscrupulous way. But the social climber is not just exposed as transgressor of societal norms. The reference to the wheel, and

---

[27] Brant, *Narrenschiff*, ch. 82, v. 60–63: "Inn allen landen ist groß schand | Keynen benügt me/ mit sym stand | Nyemans denckt wer syn vorderen woren | Des ist die welt yetz gantz voll doren."
[28] Brant, *Narrenschiff*, ch. 37, v. 1–4: "Der ist eyn narr der stiget hoch | Do mitt man säch syn schand vnd schmoch | Vnd sůchet stäts eyn höhern grad | Vnd gdencket nit an glückes rad."

Figure 2: Sebastian Brant. *Daß Narren Schyff*. Basel: Johann Bergmann, 1494. Chapter 37, sig. F6v. © Bayerische Staatsbibliothek München.

ever more so to the divine hand in the woodcut, makes it clear that he also is in violation of divine norms, of the order ordained by God.

Chapter 56, entitled "von end des gewalttes" (Of the end of violence), uses the identical woodcut showing the wheel of fortune. The chapter presents a critical examination of the use of gratuitous force and violence by powerful leaders in world history. Why Brant, or the printer, chose to recycle the woodcut is unclear as it does little to enhance the core message of the chapter, although it could have been intended to show the cyclical nature of empires. In the text, there is only one brief reference to the wheel of fortune: "That is why you powerful ones should be reminded that you are in the grace of fortune. But be wise and think of your end so that God will not turn the wheel on you."[29] What this reading of the wheel of fortune has in common with the idea presented in chapter 37 is that, metaphorically speaking, a wise person will not engage with the wheel of fortune as the fall is an inevitable part of the cycle. In chapter 56, princes and other authorities can avoid the fall by the judicious use of force in the performance of governance functions. While this passage corresponds to the point made in the woodcut, the use of the wheel metaphor seems forced in the context of the chapter.

Brant's use of the wheel of fortune deviated greatly from the cyclical vision of history common in classical antiquity, which lived on in Neo-Stoic philosophy in the early modern period.[30] Here, it is not the fateful cycle of history that elevates humans in order to make them tumble at their peak, nor is it a Neo-Stoic vision of the renunciation of worldly life in order to escape the vagaries of fate. The wheel is a metaphor representing inappropriate rise: those tempted by the wheel can hang on to it to advance in society. But there is no way to hang on to the advancement and to stay on top because God keeps turning the wheel. Yet, this is not a Stoic vision: God may be turning the wheel, but humans are under no obligation to get on it. In fact, this is inadvisable as God will undo any gains made on the wheel. So, in Brant's reading, only fools actually will get on it with the misguided hope to get to the top: the rise is always temporary, and the rewards are elusive. The ideal human therefore will refrain from engaging with the wheel and instead will stay put and seek stability and constancy in everything he does.

Urban Rieger later expressed a similar view in his *Enchiridion* (1535), discussed above. As only non-believing and heathen rulers were exposed to the hard fall, Christian faith protected against the vagaries of fate and promoted

---

[29] Brant, *Narrenschiff*, ch. 56, v. 39–42: "Har by mercken jr gwaltigen all | Ir sitzen zwor jn glückes fall | Sindt witzig/ vnd trachtend das end | Das gott das radt/ üch nit vmb wend."
[30] Pietsch, "Grundstrukturen historischer Abläufe," 20–21.

wise and stable governance.³¹ The ideal then was not to seek change, both in personal and in communal life, but to statically trust in God's providence. As Brant explained in the following chapter 57, entitled "Furwissenheyt gottes" (God's providence), God's will and judgment were concealed and his reasons unknowable. As the order God imposed on the world could not be understood, it could not possibly be challenged: "For that reason, let God's omniscience and the order of providence stand as it stands. Do right and well. God is merciful and full of grace."³² God's providence was omniscient but unintelligible. Everything was uncertain, except God's grace and mercy for those who accepted his order. Attempts to question or challenge the divine order were akin to a transgressive reversal of order. The woodcut for the chapter shows this graphically: a fool sits on top of a crab that is walking backwards. The backwards walk of the crab allegorically stands for the reversal of the order.³³ The fool who challenges the order, therefore, is decidedly moving in the wrong direction.

Similarly, Sebastian Münster in the dedication to his *Cosmographia* (1544) rejected the role of *fortuna* and argued that God was firmly in charge of the rise and decline of empires. To Münster, it was futile to explain the rise and fall of empires with categories like fate or reason. He reminded King Gustav I Vasa, to whom he dedicated the text, that God was the true master over the world and its order:

> It comes from the hand of God who gives and takes according to His own predilection and who shows with His deeds that He is the lord, not in heaven alone but also on earth and on the wide oceans. All things are negotiated through Him, and nothing happens out of luck or chance, that is out of fortune or misfortune, as humans would have it; rather everything happens out of divine knowledge and order.³⁴

God steered history according to his own plan, and humans could do little more than setting up governance in compliance with the ordained divine order. To Münster, it is the purpose of the *Cosmographia* to show these unstable patterns of the past to drive home the point that there is permanence only in the

---

31 Rieger, *Enchiridion*, sig. C8r.
32 Brant, *Narrenschiff*, ch. 57, v. 87–90: "Dar vmb loß gots fürwissenheyt | Vnd ordenung der fürsichtikeyt | Stan wie sie stat/ thů recht vnd wol | Gott ist barmhertzig/ gnaden vol."
33 Henkel and Schöne, *Emblemata*, 727. The modern German expression "Krebsgang" conveys the same idea.
34 Münster, *Cosmographia* (1544), sig. a2v: "Es kompt von der hand Gottes/ der gibt vnd nimpt nach seinem gefallen/ vnd erzeigt mit seinen thaten/ dz er der herr ist/ nit allein im himmel/ sunder auch auff der erden/ vnd in dem weyten möre/ vnd alle ding durch jn verhandlet werden vnd nichts ex fortuna vel casu/ dz ist von glück oder onglück/ die die menschen daruon reden/ sunder alles auß dem wissen/ ja ordnungen Gottes geschicht."

system of order imposed by God, albeit with the reminder that true stability could only ever be found in eternal life.

In the light of a topsy-turvy world, what emerged was a yearning for a static and permanent vision of history where the social order ideally remained stable and where change usually had negative connotations. Any kind of change or innovation had to be rejected because of its destabilizing and transgressive potential. A historical model based on stability invariably interpreted innovation as a disturbance. The discrepancy between this theoretical claim on one hand and the rapid social and economic evolution of the urban society in the sixteenth century on the other could not be starker and explains the heavy-handed invectives many contemporaneous writers leveled at the society they lived in.

The fact that the economic reality evolved at a much more rapid pace than social and moral norms created great potential for conflict and was one of the root causes for a backlash against innovation generally and economic progress specifically. Sebastian Brant saw the rapidly changing world around him with a great deal of anxiety because he read innovation as a sign of decline that followed a period of constancy and strength. The chasm between the likes of the merchant Jakob Fugger the Rich (1459–1525), the wealthiest man of his time and standard-bearer of the new economic system, and the intellectual Sebastian Brant (1457–1521) was unbridgeable. In his diagnosis, the order and stability his German forefathers had fought for and achieved was under attack, which he perceived to be the fundamental crisis of his time. The metaphor of "geschwinde Zeiten," which was a common shorthand in early modern writings to designate a crisis, emphasizes the element of change in the diagnosis of crisis.[35] And it is this crisis, more than any other, that Brant sought to address in his *Narrenschiff*.

---

35 For example Ferrarius, *Von dem Gemeinen nutze*, sig. A4r: "the common people in these troubled times, many of them having fallen away [from God]" ("die gemeynen inn diesen geschwinden zeiten/ bey etlichen inn abfall geraten"). See also Postel, "Geschwinde Zeiten."

Chapter 5
Innovation and Progress as Agents of Decline

Ulrich von Hutten (1488–1523), in his guaiacum tract from 1519, reported a conversation with a doctor whom he had asked about the efficacy of guaiacum to treat syphilis. The doctor responded that he did not know as Aristotle did not mention it and he had not seen it, guaiacum being a recent import from Hispaniola. Hutten's reply, that "a new disease requires a new medicine that is still completely unknown to us,"[1] is remarkable given the hostile attitude toward innovation and foreign influences he otherwise displayed in his guaiacum tract as well as in other texts.[2] Therefore, the fact that a new disease could appear in Europe during his lifetime, apparently out of nowhere, must have been unsettling, aside from the fact that Hutten himself suffered and eventually died from it. This quote also is a good example for how evolving pragmatic circumstances could challenge his staunch opposition to change, innovation, and progress.

The rejection of innovation and progress was a commonplace in German literature of the fifteenth and sixteenth centuries, well beyond the temporal scope of this study. Johann Fischart (1546–1590) stated in 1577 in an exemplary fashion what his contemporaries held to be true: "For the cities flourish here when virtue remains in old bloom. But where one acts out of character and provokes new customs every day, there innovation settles in, which hardly ever led to success in any country."[3] Change and innovation were not compatible with maintaining a wholesome, moral lifestyle and upholding traditional values. Progress and novelty were intractably linked with social and moral decline.

While Fischart summarized the sixteenth-century attitude, Sebastian Brant set its tone. His desire to maintain social and political stability was reflected in most literary and political texts of the late fifteenth and sixteenth centuries. The political ideal was to achieve the *tranquillitas ordinis* (tranquility of order) as Augustine had defined it in Book 19 of the *City of God* as "well-ordered concord."[4] Once this status had been achieved, improvement was impossible to

---

[1] Hutten, *Von der wunderbarlichen artzney*, sig. E4r: "dz ein newer brest ein neuwe artzney erfordert/ vnd vnß dz noch gar vnbekant wer."
[2] Discussed in more detail in Chapter 20.
[3] Fischart, *Das Glückhafft Schiff*, sig. A3r: "Dann also grünen die Stätt hie | Wann tugend bleibt bey alter plüh/ | Aber wo auß der art man schlegt/ | Vnd täglich newe bräuch erregt/ | Da kumpt gewiß ein Newerung | Die selten eim Land wol gelung."
[4] Augustine, *The City of God*, 690–691: "Peace between man and God is the well-ordered obedience of faith to eternal law. Peace between man and man is well-ordered concord. Civil

bring about. This explains why Brant and other writers were so insistent on maintaining order, as we have seen in the previous chapters. For the same reason, these same writers also had an extreme aversion to change and innovation. For instance, Brant was critical of the new urban economy (chapter 48) and of the belief that it offered access to easy prosperity without the corresponding hard work (chapter 57). In Brant's static model of history, which will be discussed in more detail in Chapter 6, there was little room for innovation as he did not see it as being compatible with a stable order.

Brant's disdain for innovation had a biblical component. Chapter 11, entitled "verachtung der gschrift" (contempt of Scripture), juxtaposes the truth of Scripture with the new stories presented by heretics and other tempters. The double meaning of "gschrift" is instrumental here; as the title of the chapter indicates, Scripture now is held in contempt, replaced by fanciful writings:

> If someone came, resurrected from the dead, one would run there one hundred miles in order to hear the new tales from him, about what was the essence of hell, if many people were sent there, if one is pouring new wine there, and other monkey business like that. Now we have so many written texts.[5]

People were beguiled by new and sensational stories, like a resurrected man telling fables about hell. The sarcastic question whether new wine was poured in hell no doubt is a reference to Acts 2:13, in which the image of men full of new wine serves as a scornful metaphor for those who lack wisdom and insight. So, newness becomes shorthand for being misinformed and misdirected, for not being in the possession of the real truth whose only source is biblical Scripture. The "affen spil," literally monkey game, reinforces the idea as the monkey commonly was associated with the devil. Brant's message is that all the new stories are the devil's work. He weaves in a critique of the onslaught of new information, presumably enabled by the printing press, which makes it difficult for humans to distinguish between deceitful new information and old biblical truth. The woodcut reinforces this idea: we see a man wrapped in linen and sitting on his open casket. A fool is standing next

---

peace is a similar concord among the citizens. The peace of the celestial city is the perfectly ordered and harmonious enjoyment of God, and of one another in God. The peace of all things is the tranquillity of order. Order is the distribution which allots things equal and unequal, each to its own place."

5 Brant, *Narrenschiff*, ch. 11, v. 7–14: "Kem einer von den dotten har | So lieff man hundert mylen dar | Das man von jm hort nuwe mer | Was wesens jn der hellen wer | Vnd ob vil lut fůrend dar jn | Ob man ouch schanckt do nuwen win | Vnd des glich ander affen spil | Nůn hat man doch der gschrifft so vil."

to him and obviously talking to him. The fool is standing on two books, each foot on one book, as if the books were the soles of his shoes. The artist makes it look like books, and the deceitful knowledge drawn from them, carried the fool to this spot.

Brant added the historical example of Hans Böhm (or Behem, 1450–1476), often referred to as the Drummer of Niklashausen an der Tauber. In 1476, Böhm claimed to have had a vision of the Virgin Mary. Based on that vision, Böhm preached social transformation and pushed for a revolt against the authorities. This quickly led to unrest in the Tauber valley, which was one of the first peasant revolts. Böhm was apprehended by soldiers of the bishop of Würzburg, tried for heresy, and executed.[6] Brant tells us that many still were in search of the "chapel and hermitage of the bagpiper of Niklashausen."[7] The focus of Brant's account was not so much on Böhm's treason and heresy, but rather on the town of Niklashausen having become a place of pilgrimage for ordinary people still spellbound by this tale. The seductive power of Böhm's deception and heresy was that people liked to hear "new stories and legends"[8] but were not interested in divine wisdom and faith. It is this fateful attraction humans had toward everything that was new and sensational that was so detrimental to the community and to faith.

Brant's chapter four, entitled "Von nuwen funden" (of innovations), addressed the issue of innovation more comprehensively. Here, Brant assailed any kind of innovation in society, as the motto verses to the chapter stress: "Whoever makes new finds throughout the land will cause much irritation and shame and will hold the fool by his hand."[9] While title and motto verses targeted change in general, the body of the chapter more narrowly focused on innovations that relate to the human body. The title itself implies that as "Von nuwen funden" refers to new finds, to innovations, but also can be read more narrowly to refer to new fashions. The first few lines mark the transition to the focus on the body: "What used to be a shameful thing one now regards simply and lightly. It used to be an honor to wear a beard. Now the womanish men

---

[6] For a full account, see Wunderli, *Peasant Fires*. Hartmann Schedel tells us the story in his *Nuremberg Chronicle* from 1493 (fol. 255r). In chapter 54 of his *Narrenschiff*, Brant defines the bagpipe as the coarse instrument of the fool ("Eyn sackpfiff ist des narren spil," ch. 54, v. 7) who loathes the harp, the instrument of wisdom, and the lute, the instrument of poetry, both instruments played by educated, sophisticated people.
[7] Brant, *Narrenschiff*, ch. 11, v. 17–18: "kappel vnd klusen | Des sackpfiffers von Nickelshusen."
[8] Brant, *Narrenschiff*, ch. 11, v. 27: "nuw mär vnd sag."
[9] Brant, *Narrenschiff*, ch. 4, v. a–c: "Wer vil nüw fünd macht durch die land | Der gibt vil ärgernyß vnd schand | Vnd halt den narren by der hand."

have learned and grease themselves with monkey grease."[10] The chapter presents a catalog of transgressions against ways to dress and present one's body beyond shaving one's beard: wearing fashionable dress and luxurious jewelry, chasing ever-changing fashion trends, greasing one's hair or bleaching it in the sun, and showing too much skin by wearing revealing clothing – all of which Brant viewed as violating old German customs and as being shameful to the German nation.

In his conclusion, Brant chastised both those committing these transgressions and those neglecting to censor them. However, for Brant wearing fashionable clothes and displaying novel body techniques also were metaphors for innovation and change in general, which threatened social stability at its core. Brant's chapter expressed his anxiety about both: "For one innovation quickly yields to another. This shows that our mind is feeble and unsettled all the way to being shameful. Much innovation is in the entire land."[11] Mixed in with his opposition to innovation was his despair about the fickle human mind that made humans susceptible to the temptations of change. His stance here was typical for the entire *Narrenschiff*: Brant developed no vision for the present other than fending off innovations that he viewed as threats to the established order. His orientation was backwards in that he cherished an idealized past that now appeared lost, and his focus was entirely on critiquing a present that had abandoned the pristine past.

The desire for a stable political and social order and the aversion against innovation generally were critical elements in the political writings of the time. Again, the seminal text *Von dem Gemeinen nutze* (1533) by Johannes Ferrarius serves to illustrate the connection. His third chapter is entitled "That the worldly authorities have been ordained by God and appointed to lead the community by necessity."[12] In a key passage that refers to Paul the Apostle, Ferrarius asserted that worldly authorities were ordained by God and endowed with divine authority:

> All authorities and administrations are ordained by God. If someone rebels against it, he is rejecting God's order. They do not carry the sword vainly but rather as servants of God in order to punish the evil ones.[13]

---

10 Brant, *Narrenschiff*, ch. 4, v. 1–5: "Das ettwan was eyn schantlich dyng | Das wygt man yetz schlecht vnd gering | Eyn ere was ettwan tragen bert | Jetzt hand die wibschen mann gelert | Vnd schmyeren sich mit affen schmaltz."
11 Brant, *Narrenschiff*, ch. 4, v. 21–24: "Dann ein fundt kum dem andern wicht | Das zeygt/ das vnser gmüt ist licht | Vnd wanckelbar in alle schand | Vil nüwrung ist jn allem land."
12 Ferrarius, *Von dem Gemeinen nutze*, fol. 8r: "Das die weltliche Oberkeit von Gott verordnet/ vnd der gemeine als notwendig vorgesatzt sei."
13 Ferrarius, *Von dem Gemeinen nutze*, fol. 8r: "Alle oberkeit vnd vorwaltunge sey von Gott verordnet/ da widder so sich iemant entpöre/ der widerstrebe Gottes ordenung/ dieweil sie das schwert tregt nit vergeblich/ sonder als Gottes dienerin/ zur straff der bösen."

The sovereigns and his administrators bore the sword as an extension of divine justice. The rulers and their governments were good in principle as they derived their authority and power from God.

However, the divine origin of the power and authority of rulers wasn't just anchored in Scripture but also was evident from the order of nature:

> And if we wanted to remain silent about Scripture, or to set it back, it still would become evident from nature and be proven adequately that the worldly authority is from God and very necessary. For whoever views the perimeter of the world will find nothing other than God's work, created and shaped very delicately and orderly, in such a way that each part enters as component of His order, completes His works, and does not obstruct the other in its domain. Thus the sun is assigned to the day and the moon and stars to the night. And so each piece of creation is put ahead of its own effect and is guided to see the other.[14]

Scripture is not required to understand the divine origin of the world as nature itself tells us the story of an ornate and orderly creation willed by God. Each part of creation has its own, specific purpose in the divine plan, but also combines efforts with others in the interest of the whole.[15]

In analogy to the components of the universe, the parts of the human body work together as well. Each body part has its own function yet simultanously serves the other parts and the body as a whole as well: "Throughout the entire body there not a single part that in its normal workings doesn't look out for the others."[16] In Ferrarius's representation, the body becomes an elaborate metaphor for the workings of the community, which is governed by the head and served by various parts of the body in various capacities:

> And when we look at the whole human, as he is composed out of body and soul, we find that the philosophers not without reason call him microcosm, that is the small world. For the world was created orderly and ornately and put in motion, and it was created for us

---

14 Ferrarius, *Von dem Gemeinen nutze*, fol. 9v: "Vnd ob wir der schrifft alhie wolten geschweigen/ oder die hindan setzen/ so wurde sichs doch auß der natur ereugen/ vnd gnugsam beweisen/ das die weltlich oberkeit von Gott/ vnd sehr nöttig ist/ Dan wer in den vmbkreyß der welt schawet/ der findet nit anders dan Gottes werck gantz zierlich vnd ordentlich geschaffen vnd gestalt/ dermassen das ein iedes stuck in seiner ordenung hereintritt/ sein werck volnbrengt/ vnd keines dem andern in den beuelch greifft. Also ist die Sonn dem tag/ der Mon vnd stern der nacht zugeordenet/ vnd sunst ein jedes gescheft seinem eigen werck vorgesetzet/ vnd auff das andere zu sehen gericht."
15 Simon, *Gute Policey*, 128.
16 Ferrarius, *Von dem Gemeinen nutze*, fol. 9v–10r: "Vnd also fur vnd fur ist kein glidmas am gantzen leib/ das inn seinem ordentlichen werck nicht stehe/ vnd auff das andere sehe."

by the Almighty in His image as a wondrous thing so that we can honor and praise Him in it. Therefore we find nothing in the human being that is not perfect.[17]

Just as a head is required for the body parts to function and collaborate, a king is required to coordinate the estates and to main a communal order. The terminology promotes this analogy as the "haupt" is both the head of the body and the head of state. Comparing the workings of the human body with the workings of the state was a commonplace of political literature in the early modern period.

Ferrarius's analogy between divine creation, the human body, and the body politic implied that both the human body as the microcosm of creation and the analogous political order had to be perfect because they were God-given. Just like the human body, the political body could not have been created by humans but rather was ordained by a larger force.[18] As part of divine creation, the political order was not negotiable for Ferrarius: "Therefore we conclude that the worldly authority is from God."[19] Ferrarius conceded that non-believers were capable of organizing good governments as well. But if they were not designed to serve the honor of God they were destined to disintegrate and fall, as the examples of Athens and Rome proved.[20]

As the basic political structure was given by God, it could not really be improved upon as it already had been optimized, by design, functionality, and inner harmony. In fact, the very concept of change was alien to the nature of the political order.[21] Rulers and city councils could stray from the God-given path, but such behavior invariably had to be seen as transgressive and even sinful – which empowered urban writers to criticize the behavior of their rulers and masters. Ferrarius reminded city councils that the community would sink into disorder and vice if they did not maintain good government practices, and that the council itself would fall into sin and dishonor.[22] Attempts to change

---

[17] Ferrarius, *Von dem Gemeinen nutze*, fol. 10r: "Vnd wan wir also den gantzen menschen/ als er mit leib vnd sehel zusamen bracht ist/ anschawen: so befinden wir/ das er nit vnbedacht von den Philosophis Microcosmos/ das ist/ die kleine welt genant wirdt. Dan wie die welt ordenlich vnd gezirlich geschaffen/ bewegt wirdt/ vnd als ein wunderbarlich ding von dem almechtigen/ jn darin zu ehren vnd preissen/ vns furgebildt ist/ Also befinden wir auch nichts an dem menschen das nit volkommen sei."
[18] Simon, *Gute Policey*, 128.
[19] Ferrarius, *Von dem Gemeinen nutze*, fol. 11r: "Also haben wir das die weltlich oberkeit von Gott ist."
[20] Ferrarius, *Von dem Gemeinen nutze*, fol. 10r–10v.
[21] Simon, *Gute Policey*, 128.
[22] Ferrarius, *Von dem Gemeinen nutze*, fol. 45r.

and improve the system therefore were seen with great suspicion, both by political writers and by the culture at large, as a large number of literary texts indicate. Changes to the system were invariably seen as leading to the deterioration of the prevailing order. Where order and stability had been achieved, any kind of innovation was detrimental to their maintenance.[23]

Both political and literary writers therefore shied away from proposing changes to the existing system as changes were associated with the loss of order. Rather, they were focused on the past, on how to preserve the traditional order and how to restore it once it had been disrupted and lost. For this reason, literary texts of this time never developed a vision for a better social organization. Instead, writers like Brant, Hutten, or Sachs focused on lacking morals, adverse events, and disruptions of the order. Their texts indulged in a nostalgia for a better past rather than developing a vision for a better future. Attempts at reform at any level therefore were couched in terms of restoring earlier, better organized, and more just conditions.[24] Martin Luther's reforms found so much support precisely because they were widely understood as efforts to bring the Church back to its pristine origins in early Christianity.

---

[23] Simon, *Gute Policey*, 129.
[24] Simon, *Gute Policey*, 129.

Chapter 6
History as Decline and Brant's Vision of the End of History

Many in the early sixteenth century believed that a final political and social organization had been achieved, at least theoretically. The focus of political and literary texts therefore was to maintain the order, fight transgressions against it, and attempt to restore it where it had failed. As argued in the previous chapter, political, economic, and social innovation was regarded with a great deal of distrust, and the pragmatic and utilitarian innovation that surged in contemporaneous society engendered a great deal of anxiety. The prevailing political models described here did not offer a fitting category for innovation, which therefore could not be integrated into political thinking even though pragmatically it was omnipresent in sixteenth-century urban life.

Attempts to integrate change and innovation into political thinking did not occur until the middle of the century. Georg Lauterbeck, in his *Regentenbuch* (1556), conceded that laws could be adjusted cautiously, "depending on opportunity of time and course of events" and if there was a good reason to do so, "except for what God himself and nature changed."[1] Lauterbeck signaled a subtle shift toward a new understanding of history, however without acknowledging that this eventually would undermine the established order rooted in the notion of unchanging stability. In a subtle way, Lauterbeck moved away from the strict notion that the human order had already achieved its optimal order. While he accepted the notion of change as being part of nature, he did not integrate the idea of an evolving human history in his text and his theory.

In the period under examination, the empire was commonly seen as the guardian of stability and the defender of the German place in history. Most German writers of the sixteenth century therefore sang high praises of empire and emperor, but also openly called on emperors to do more to ensure peace and stability and to secure a stable place in history for the empire. It was very common for writers like Sebastian Brant to call on emperors to be more vigilant about the Turkish threat,[2] for instance, and the pamphlet literature on this issue is quite voluminous.

---

[1] Lauterbeck, *Regentenbuch*, fol. 112v: "nach gelegenheit der zeit vnd leuffte;" "ausgeschlossen was Gott selbs vnd die natur verandert haben."
[2] Brant, *Narrenschiff*, ch. 99, v. 129–130.

Chapter 6 History as Decline and Brant's Vision of the End of History — 85

The core idea that defined the place of the empire in history was the *translatio imperii ad Germanos*. It described history as a linear succession of dominant empires where power was transferred from one to the next. It was derived from the theory of the four empires formulated in the Book of Daniel (Daniel 2:21), which prophesied that the apocalypse would set in at the end of the fourth empire. Church father Jerome (347–420), in his commentary on the Book of Daniel, defined the four empires as Babylon, Persia, Greece, and Rome. Jerome's commentary was influential for the Christian doctrine of the succession of empires.[3] Johannes Carion, in his *Chronica* (1532), referred to this sequence of empires in his justification of German primacy in the Holy Roman Empire:

> There were four monarchies in succession. First the Assyrians ruled, then the Persians, then the Greeks, then the Romans. And God chose the Germans ahead of other nations for this honor and authority over the world to its end.[4]

Carion referenced the Book of Daniel as the source of the theory of the four empires,[5] which established the historical pattern in which power and supremacy migrated from Asia to Europe, from the Orient to the Occident:[6]

> Thus the sovereignty over the world migrated from the Orient to the Occident, and from Asia to Europe. Then Asia subsequently declined little by little, not only in power, but also in discipline, virtue, governance, and all kinds of goods, until the time of the Romans. Then the Barbarians invaded and completely destroyed it, which had been the most beautiful part of the world where the highest wisdom, holiness, and power had resided and now became a den of thieves. Thus the high gifts from God now are in the Occident as the world nears its end.[7]

---

3 Hirschi, "Konzepte von Fortschritt," 38. Hirschi (*The Origins of Nationalism*, 41) points out that the westward movement of empires implied in the Book of Daniel can be traced in the imperialist thinking in early modern France, Britain, and later even the United States.
4 Carion, *Chronica*, sig. B2r: "vnd sind nach einander vier Monarchien gewesen. Erstlich haben regiert die Assyrier/ darnach die Persen/ darnach die Greken/ darach die Römer/ Vnd hat Gott die Deudschen für andere Nation/ zu dieser ehre vnd hoheyt der welt/ auffs letzt gezogen." Carion referenced Daniel as the source of the theory of the four empires (sig. C4r and fol. 170r). The identical passage can also be found in Johannes Egenolff, *Chronic* (1533), fol. 1v. Köbel (*Glaubliche Offenbarung*, sig. A4v) identified the Babylonian, Carthagian, Macedonian and Roman empires as the four leading empires.
5 Carion, *Chronica*, sig. C4r and fol. 170r.
6 Prietz, *Das Mittelalter*, 103–106.
7 Carion, *Chronica*, fol. 56r: "Vnd ist nu die hoheit der Welt von Orient/ jnn Occident/ vnd aus Asia jnn Europa gewandelt/ vnd hat Asia hernach fur vnd fur abgenomen/ nicht allein an macht/ sondern auch an zucht/ tugent/ regimenten/ vnd allerley gütern/ bis zur Römer zeit/ da die Barbari darein gefallen/ vnd habens gantz verwüstet/ das der schönest teil auff erden/ da

The Christian Occident not only assumed political leadership but also began to lead the world in morality, virtue, and good governance. The word "Occident" in European history referred to the western half of the Roman Empire after its division of 395. After the demise of Rome, the divine gifts were transferred to the "Occidentalisches Reich" (Occidental Empire) that since Charlemagne had been ruled by Germans.[8] The common view was that the Franconian Empire under Charlemagne became the seamless continuation of the Roman Empire in the ninth century. Sebastian Münster serves as a good example for how the argument in support of this claim unfolded. In his *Cosmographia* (1544), Münster dedicated an entire chapter to the question "When and how the empire came to the Germans."[9] He repeated the standard theory that the empire in its final incarnation originated with the Romans but was transferred to the Greeks, that is the Byzantine Empire, after the fall of Rome. As the Byzantine rulers showed little interest in Italy and neglected to support the papacy in Rome, western leaders took action:

> This is why the rulers in Italy, including the pope, made common cause and made Charles, the king of the Franks, emperor over Italy, France, and all other countries who were located toward the sunset. They also parted ways with the emperor in Constantinople in the year 801 after Christ's birth.[10]

Christian Egenolff in his *Chronic* (1533) similarly argued that the Greeks in Constantinople were negligent in their governance obligations to Rome, which is why the Romans turned to Charlemagne as emperor over the Occident.[11] Egenolff thus closed the continuity gap at both ends. First, he sustained the fiction that the Byzantine emperors maintained imperial control in the West until 800 so the Byzantines legitimately could pass on the imperial crown. Second, Egenolff, like Münster, represented Charlemagne's elevation as a choice by the Romans rather than a takeover by the Franconian kingdom. In this narrative, there was neither a temporal gap nor a lapse in legitimacy.

---

die höhist weisheit/ heiligkeit/ vnd macht gewesen ist/ itzund schier gantz ein morder gruben ist. Also sind nu die hohen Gottes gaben jnn Occident nach dem die welt zum ende nahet."
[8] Zedler, *Universal-Lexicon*, 25, 321. See also the article "Occidentalisches Reich" in Ersch-Gruber, *Allgemeine Encyclopädie*, 3, 1, 243–260.
[9] Münster, *Cosmographia* (1544), 163–164: "Wann vnd wie das keyserthům an die Teütschen kommen ist."
[10] Münster, *Cosmographia* (1544), 163: "[...] darumb wurden die öbersten in Jtalia mit samt dem Bapst der sachen eins/ vnd machten Carolum den künig von Franckrich keyser über Jtaliam/ über Franckrich vnnd alle andere länder/ die gegen der sonnen vndergang gelegen waren/ vnnd wichen ab von dem Constantinopolitanischen keyser/ anno nach Christi geburt 801."
[11] Egenolff, *Chronic* (1533), fol. 87r. Also Köbel, *Glaubliche Offenbarung*, sig. A5r.

In the next step, Sebastian Münster argued that the imperial crown was transferred to Germany, not France, primarily based on the fact that Charlemagne the emperor was German and not French, as the French and Italians claimed. Charles, in Münster's argumentation, was born in Germany, spoke German, lived in Germany, converted much of Germany to Christianity, and held imperial diets in German cities like Regensburg, Worms, and Aachen. In sixteenth-century Germany, this was the canonical view of how Germany came to be the leader of the Christian Occident.[12]

The coronation of King Otto I as Roman emperor by Pope John XII in Rome in the year 962 marked the recognition of the East Franconian Empire as the successor of the Franconian Empire. This act later was construed as evidence that the Roman imperial crown legitimately had been transferred into German hands.[13] Münster made that connection in his historical narrative as well:

> He [Otto I] received the imperial crown in Rome in the year of the lord 937. Rudolf, king in Burgundy and in Arles, subjugated himself to him and promised allegiance to the German Roman Empire, and thereafter his son Conrad.[14]

The fact that Münster got the year wrong – Otto I became German king in 936 – is not significant compared to the key argument that the pope himself recognized the legitimacy of the German claim, followed by the King of Burgundy.

The German Empire continued to be seen as the legitimate successor of the Roman Empire, which was indicated by its designation first as Roman Empire, then as Holy Roman Empire (*Sacrum Imperium Romanum*) starting in the thirteenth century, and finally as Holy Roman Empire of the German Nation (*Heiliges Römisches Reich Deutscher Nation*) starting in the fifteenth century. This evolution of the nomenclature, first to refer to the Christian character of the empire and then to its German leadership, indicates how carefully the idea of continuity of empire was construed and emended over time. Furthermore, the fact that the emperor was elected by the seven most prominent princes of the empire not only added legitimacy but also, in the words of Christian Egenolff, ensured that the empire would never descend into tyrannical rule.[15] The *translatio imperii* therefore represented a long tradition of stability and

---

12 Similar argument in Köbel, *Glaubliche Offenbarung*, sig. A5r.
13 Hirschi, "Konzepte von Fortschritt," 39.
14 Münster, *Cosmographia* (1544), 167: "Er hat die keyserlich kron zů Rom emfangen anno domini 937. Vnder disem hat Růdolphus künig in Burgund vnd zů Arelat [Arles] sich gethon vnd verpflicht zů dem Teütschen Römischen reich/ vnd nachmals sein sun Conradus."
15 Egenolff, *Chronic* (1533), fol. 86r.

continuity. It also guaranteed the preservation in perpetuity of the imperial idea under German and Christian leadership.

Writers around 1500 generally held the empire in high esteem. In part, this was due to the fact that the emperor guaranteed the independence of free imperial cities and insulated them against territorial claims by surrounding princes. A good example is Sebastian Brant's lifelong veneration of Emperor Maximilian I (1459–1519) in a number of poetic works.[16] A long panegyrical section dedicated to Maximilian I is embedded in chapter 99, entitled "von abgang des glouben" (of the loss of faith).[17] The chapter starts out with the observation that faith had been diminished by an army of heretics, primarily the Turks. Brant relates in some detail how the Turks had vanquished Christian empires and diminished Christianity. The second half of chapter 99 is a brief history of the empire, starting out with the early Roman Empire:

> O Rome, you had kings at first. You were indentured to them for many years. But then you were led into freedom when you were governed by a communal council. But then one pursued pride and wealth and great power, and citizens fought other citizens. No one paid attention to the common good. So the power mostly dissipated, and at last you became subject of an emperor.[18]

Brant linked disunity with political deterioration. More importantly, in this context he showed the cyclical nature of history in classical antiquity.[19] The initial royal government was removed by an elected communal government, the senate. However, the rise of disunity and the pursuit of self-interest caused the Republic to falter, until an emperor seized power and abolished the liberties the Romans had enjoyed. From here on, the empire went through a history of decline, which according to Brant lasted 1,500 years. Therefore, the beloved Emperor Maximilian I, according to the theory of the *translatio imperii*, was a latter-day successor to this first Roman emperor. The delicate issue for Brant

---

[16] For Brant's role as Maximilian's panegyrist see Harrison, "Virgil, Sebastian Brant, and Maximilian I;" Mertens, "Sebastian Brant, Kaiser Maximilian."
[17] Brant, *Narrenschiff*, ch. 99, v. 155–165. Maximilian I was much admired by the writers and artists of German Humanism.
[18] Brant, *Narrenschiff*, ch. 99, v. 95–104: "O Rom/ do du hatst künig vor | Do waßt du eygen/ lange jor/ | Dar noch jnn fryheit wardst gefürt | Als dich eyn gmeyner rott regiertt | Aber do man noch hochfart staltt | Noch richtům/ vnd noch grossem gwalt | Vnd burger wider burger vacht | Des gmeynen nutzes nyeman acht | Do wart der gwalt zům teil zergon | Zů letzst/ eym keyser vnderthon."
[19] Polybios designed a system that cycled between monarchic, democratic, and oligarchic governance, all three existing in benign and malignant variants. See Pietsch, "Grundstrukturen historischer Abläufe," 16.

was that the empire at the time, according to Brant himself, had hit rock bottom, with some assistance by the Turks.

The German predominance over the empire was also threatened by the French king, who saw himself as the legitimate heir of Charlemagne's Franconian empire. This is the foundation for a second *translatio* theory, the *translatio studii*. It held that the French assumed the lead in the cultural realm directly from the Byzantine empire. The French Crown developed a project in the thirteenth century to make Paris the capital of Christian universal learning with the University of Paris at its center, which was claimed to have been founded by Charlemagne.[20] While German intellectuals around 1500 conceded cultural deficits,[21] like Conrad Celtis (1459–1508) in his poem "Ode ad Apollinem" (1486), they also demanded the advancement of a German vernacular culture to close this gap and to fend off competing French claims to lead the empire.

In response to these concerns that Germany might lose control over the empire, Brant likened the decline of power to the waning of the moon. Implied in this analogy is the idea of a cycle: just as the moon starts waxing after the new moon, the historical cycle starts to reverse itself as well. To Brant, the empire had hit a low point in power and cohesion, and Maximilian was valiantly attempting to reverse the decline. Brant blamed the estates for thwarting Maximilian's efforts to restore the empire to its former greatness, as he explained in this lengthy analysis:

> Many cities have brought themselves under their own control and do not respect emperors anymore. Each ruling prince breaks off a part of the goose so that he will have a feather from it. That is why it is no great surprise that the empire is naked and bare. Each [new emperor] is required not to demand what is rightfully his; instead everyone is allowed to maintain the status he had enjoyed before. You princes look through God what harm will arise from this. If the empire were to fall you would not prevail forever either.[22]

In their selfishness, the princes were plucking the goose, the imperial eagle, denuding it entirely. A particular problem for Brant was the practice of the *capitulatio caesarea* which provides that newly elected emperors had to confirm old

---

20 Hirschi, "Konzepte von Fortschritt," 39.
21 Hirschi, "Konzepte von Fortschritt," 47.
22 Brant, *Narrenschiff*, ch. 99, v. 119–132: "Vil stett sich brocht hant jnn gewer | Vnd achten yetz keyns keysers mer/ | Eyn yeder fürst/ der ganß bricht ab | Das er dar von eyn fäder hab/ | Dar vmb ist es nit wunder groß | Ob joch das rich sy blutt/ vnd bloß | Man byndt eym yeden vor das jn | Das er nit vordern soll das syn/ | Vnd lossen yeden jn sym stadt/ | Wie ers biß har gebruchet hadt | Durch gott/ jr fürsten sehen an | Was schad/ zů letst dar vß werd gan/ | Wann joch hyn vnder kem das rich | Ir blyben ouch nit ewigklich/."

privileges of the estates and also make new concessions, thus gradually eroding imperial powers over time to the detriment of the empire. While in the previous section Brant had blamed the Turks for harming the influence of the empire, the underlying reason for the decline of the empire in this passage was the lack of support from cities that cherished their political independence and from landed princes who prioritized their own dynastic interests.

This self-inflicted weakness caused by crumbling internal cohesion opened the door for the Turks to further weaken the empire. Humanists like Brant sought to use the Turkish threat as an instrument to promote nation building, but they were disappointed to see that princes prioritized the territorial squabbles over forming a united front against the Turks.[23] Humanists like Bebel, Wimpfeling, Celtis, Brant, and others called for a halt to all strife between German estates to support the common good an in particular to preserve the national honor.[24]

Brant's text presented the pursuit of unity and of the common good as solutions: only if there was cohesion and collaboration among the estates of the empire could the empire flourish; in their absence, discord would destroy this great empire. At this point, it becomes evident that Brant subtly switched the historical model from a cyclical historical narrative to a stability discourse focused on the present with Maximilian at its core. While the cyclical model could explain classical history, Brant envisioned a stable empire under German command that had the aspiration and potential to provide permanent leadership in the Christian Occident. To Brant, Maximilian represented the stability that could transcend the cyclical vagaries of history – if only unruly cities and princes did not hinder his work. Brant referred to this moment when the Germans were entrusted with the leadership in the empire as the moment of the paradigm shift: "The reputation of the Germans was much praised. They had achieved such fame that they were entrusted with the empire. But the Germans became diligent at destroying their empire themselves."[25]

The empire now had achieved its final state as Germans had been entrusted with its leadership and as the *translatio imperii* had been fulfilled. From here on out, the focus had to be on safeguarding the empire and protecting the German claim to its leadership. Classical history thus had little to tell to Germans as the

---

[23] Hirschi, *Wettkampf der Nationen*, 301.
[24] Hirschi, *The Origins of Nationalism*, 103. This was a common theme among German men of letters, all the way to *Letzte Posaun Uber Deutschlandt* (1663) by Johann Amos Comenius.
[25] Brant, *Narrenschiff*, ch. 99, v. 140–144: "Der tütschen lob was hochgeert | Vnd hatt erworben durch solch rům | Das man jnn gab das keyserthům/ | Aber die tütschen flissen sich | Wie sie vernychten selbst jr rich."

focus now was on the preservation in perpetuity of what Germans had achieved as leaders of the empire. This is why Brant never developed a political vision beyond securing the supremacy of the empire. To Brant, progress therefore was detrimental as the historical developments, at least ideally, had reached their terminal state.[26] Brant engaged in a perennial balancing act between a vision of an empire that fulfilled the divine design for a terminal world order, leading up to the end of time, and a desperate struggle against forces that endangered the implementation of this vision.

To Brant, there was only one historical truth, that of the succession of the four empires culminating in German hegemony. Since this was the only truth, it had to be valid over time, thus rejecting a notion of history as an open-ended and ambiguous process. Brant saw the events of his time with so much trepidation because they invariably detracted from Maximilian's ideal last empire that was so close yet so elusive. The heavy invective of his *Narrenschiff* was designed to re-establish a status quo ante, a moral and cultural purity of the Germans as they allegedly existed at the inception of the German Empire. A return to the simple, pure and unadulterated origins of the German nation therefore was paramount for the completion of Germany's historical destiny.

Chapter 56, entitled "von end des gewalttes" (the end of power), had set up the historical pattern of the temporality of a succession of empires which had enabled Germany to assume a preeminent role in the Christian Occident. It argued that all power was temporal and that all empires ultimately met their demise. The motto overtly references this pattern: "Never was power on earth so great that it did not take an end with time when it had run its course and its hour had arrived."[27] Empires in Brant's view were not exempt from the temporality of worldly things. The cyclical idea of the historical process is enhanced by the woodcut (which is identical to the one used in chapter 37): it shows a wheel of fortune in support of the idea of the temporality of empires.

In the text of the chapter, Brant reviewed a number of empires that had risen and fallen over time, mostly because of poor governance and gratuitous use of force. While the current German empire was not explicitly exempt from this pattern, the chapter closes with an expression of hope that it may be lasting and extend its rule over the entire globe: "The Roman Empire [of the German Nation] will remain as long as God wills it. God set its time and scope.

---

26 Kuper (*Zur Semiotik der Inversion*, 61) maintains that Brant bemoaned the absence of progress in the midst of chaos and destruction. But there isn't any evidence that progress was a meaningful category in Brant's thinking.
27 Brant, *Narrenschiff*, ch. 56, v. a-c: "So groß gewalt vff erd nye kam | Der nitt zů zytten/ end ouch nam | Wann jm syn zyl/ vnd stündlin kam."

May he ordain that it will become so large that the entire earth will be subject to it, as it should be by law and statutes."[28] The question of whether the German Empire will find an end or not is left open, but it could be ever-lasting if that was God's will, that is ever-lasting up to the eschaton. Brant expressed the hope that it would grow so powerful that its reach would span the globe and the confidence that this indeed was the intended divine design.

In chapter 99, Brant similarly expressed the confidence that Emperor Maximilian I one day would exert control over the Holy Land[29] and reiterated the idea that the pious king could bring the world under his leadership if the imperial estates were to collaborate in harmony.[30] At the same time, Brant conceded that Germany was at great risk of losing its predominance in Europe as well as its internal stability, and for that reason the thrust of Brant's efforts was entirely on the preservation and restoration of its former greatness. He called on the princes to do their part in the preservation of the empire: "But you lords, kings, states, you should not tolerate such a disgrace. You should stand by the empire, so the ship will continue to sail upright."[31] This appeal to the princes capped Brant's restoration agenda. The ship here stood for the empire: it had nowhere to go – the goal was to maintain it in its upright position and to keep it sailing.

Brant was such a fervent supporter of the imperial idea and specifically of Maximilian I that he moved away from Basel back to his native Strasbourg in protest in 1501, after Basel had joined the Swiss Confederation.[32] The Swiss, in turn, had defeated Maximilian in the Swabian War of 1499 and subsequently gained defacto independence from the empire, thus delivering a serious setback to Brant's vision of restoring the unity of empire and bringing about the end of history through Maximilian I. The Swiss Confederation was not perceived as a separate nation by contemporaries like Brant but rather as a renegade part of the empire

---

28 Brant, *Narrenschiff*, ch. 56, v. 90–94: "Das römsch rich blibt so lang got will/ | Got hat jm gsetzt syn zytt/ vnd moß | Der geb/ das es noch werd so groß | Das jm all erd sy vnderthon | Als es von recht/ vnd gsatz solt han."
29 Brant, *Narrenschiff*, ch. 99, v. 159–162.
30 Brant, *Narrenschiff*, ch. 99, v. 169–172.
31 Brant, *Narrenschiff*, ch. 99, v. 151–154: "Aber jr herren/ künig/ land/ | Nit wellen gstatten solch schand | Wellent dem Römschen rich zů stan | So mag das schiff noch vff recht gan."
32 Brant referenced his anti-Swiss stance in a 1512 didactic poem entitled "Sebastianus Brand in Helvetios" that is partly in Latin and partly in German (Brant, *Kleine Texte*, vol. 1.2, 574). For Brant's views on the Swiss Confederation see Hirschi, "Eine Kommunikationssituation zum Schweigen."

that collaborated with Germany's enemies in a treasonous fashion.[33] Brant was not alone in his anti-Swiss attitude: many southern German intellectuals shared this view. The Strasbourg writer Jakob Wimpfeling, for instance, published a polemical pamphlet entitled *Soliloquium pro pace Christianorum et pro Helvetiis ut resipiscant* (*A Soliloquy for the Peace of Christians and for the Swiss so that They May Come to Their Senses*) in 1505. The subtitle of the text, "In honor of the king of the Romans and of the princes,"[34] indicates that Wimpfeling, like Brant, strongly supported the imperial cause.

Brant was not the only author who projected their nationalistic hopes onto the figure of Maximilian I.[35] Maximilian's death in 1519 changed the dynamic as an international field of candidates was vying for the succession, and the loss of German control of the empire suddenly became a real possibility.[36] The election of King Charles I of Spain was the least problematic outcome as he at least was a Habsburg, even though his personal and political life was clearly centered in Spain. Nevertheless, a number of Germans had high hopes in the early years of Charles's reign, namely that he would wrest Germany from papal control and stop France's expansionist designs. Martin Luther had initially hoped that the new German emperor would spearhead his Church reform, and like Brant he supported a strong imperial hand: "Therefore let the German emperor be the rightful and free emperor, and not suppress his power nor his sword through such blind actions of Papist hypocrites, as if they should govern independently over the sword in all matters."[37]

Ulrich von Hutten asked his contemporaries to welcome the new emperor "as a restorer of German liberties."[38] But elsewhere, Hutten expressed the cautious hope that Charles had enough Germanness in him to assert German interests against the pope: "So I hope that King Charles will be courageous, that there is German blood in him, and that he will with honor perform his duties to resist the pope forcefully."[39]

---

33 Hirschi, *Wettkampf der Nationen*, 299.
34 Wimpfeling, *Soliloquium*, title page: "Ad honorem Regis Romanorum et principum"
35 Hirschi, "Konzepte von Fortschritt," 51.
36 Hirschi, "Konzepte von Fortschritt," 51.
37 Luther, *An den christlichen Adel deutscher Nation*; WA 6, 465,18–21: "Darumb last den deutschenn keyszer recht unnd frey keyszer seinn, vnnd seine gewalt noch schwerdt nit nyderdrucken durch solch blind furgebenn Bepstlicher heuchler, als solten sie auszgetzogenn ubir das schwerdt regieren in allen dingenn."
38 Hutten, *Gespräch büchlin*, sig. k4v: "Ja vnd das jn yederman grüsse einen widerbringer der teütschen freyheit."
39 Hutten, *Clag vnd vormanung*, sig. c4r: "So hoff ich künig Carles müt/ | das sey in jm ein Teütsches blůt/ | vnd werd mit eeren üben sich | dem Bapst entgegen gwaltiglich."

Yet, Charles chose to make Spain the center of his life, both personally and politically. The restoration of the German polity remained an elusive objective. The empire as central institution and as focal point for the nationalistic identification of so many writers around 1500 continued to weaken due to many factors, such as loss of control over Italian domains, continuous conflict between emperor and princes, the military successes of the Turks, the inability to control an increasingly monopolistic economy, and the divisions created by the Reformation. Jacob Köbel's reminder to the prince-electors in 1532, thirteen years into Charles's reign, that they should mentor and advise the young Spanish king on the Roman throne indicates doubt that Charles would be able or willing to restore the empire to its former glory.[40]

The idea of a general political and moral decline was closely correlated with the notion that there had been better times in the past that needed to be restored. There was a common nostalgic belief that in former times the old Germans were pure, brave, modest, and simple, an idea that will be discussed in more detail in Chapter 22. Many writers idealized this old German culture that had been displaced by the decline of cultural and moral values, and as a result the topos of the moral old Germans leading an honest and simple life was quite common. The organizational plan for a Christian society did not rely on creating something new; rather, it drew its ideals from the oldest and purest models. In a worldview that did not assign an important role to history, the beginnings of religious and political communities offered guidance because they revealed the pure and unadulterated divine will present at their inception.[41] These old and pure Germans had been entrusted with the empire after all, and therefore the restoration of their morality, values, and cultural norms was important for the preservation of the empire. Many writers also bemoaned a loss of connectedness and of civic cohesiveness. They diagnosed a rise of the pursuit of self-interest, and in particular of predatory commercial practices like hoarding (*fürkauf*), at the expense of the common good. The final two chapters of Part I will examine this more closely.

---

40 Köbel, *Glaubliche Offenbarung*, sig. A5v.
41 Bauer, *Die Vereindeutigung*, 28.

Chapter 7
The Communal Order and the Problem of Self-Interest

One of the great themes of the moral literature of the late medieval and early modern periods was the *Gemeinnutz* or *Gemeinsinn*, the common good. The focus on the common good, the *bonum commune*, in political theory has its roots in classical antiquity and was mediated by Thomas Aquinas into Neo-Aristotelian political ethics in the Middle Ages[1] where the term served to legitimize princely rule. In Humanism, the idea of the common good was increasingly seen as the key principle around which to organize the communal political structure.

The common good formed a shared ideological foundation for conduct books in the late 15th and 16th centuries. The pursuit of the common good, both at the individual and communal levels, was seen as a guiding principle of political theory in the late medieval and early modern periods,[2] and it remained a dominant theme through the tool of *Policey* in the political literature of the sixteenth century.[3] Communal values were seen as the antidote to avarice and the pursuit of personal gain, which were almost universally condemned. The common good also was a key term in the political rhetoric in the early modern period, and it was commonly associated with *gute policey*.[4] It was instrumentalized for different political purposes, and its importance was close to that of divine law.[5] Opposing sides in the same conflict often fought over the legitimacy of its use for their purposes: revolting peasants verus their masters, citizens versus city councils, and reformers versus members of the Catholic Church.[6] Reformers justified their notion of Christian renewal by claiming a common interest while framing the Roman Church as an institution in pursuit of its own self-interest.[7]

Ulrich von Hutten was perhaps the most combative polemicist against the Roman Church. His anti-clerical rhetoric was expressed in many texts, like his *Clag vnd vormanung gegen dem übermässigen vnchristlichen gewalt des Bapsts zů Rom* (Lament and Warning Against the Excessive, Un-Christian Power of the

---

1 Droege, *Gemeinnützigkeit*, 16.
2 Schulze, "Vom Gemeinnutz," 597.
3 Blickle, "Beschwerden und Polizeien," 564.
4 Blickle, "Beschwerden und Polizeien," 549.
5 Blickle, "Beschwerden und Polizeien," 564.
6 Blickle, "Beschwerden und Polizeien," 564.
7 Blickle, *Die Reformation im Reich*, 66–68.

Pope in Rome) from 1520. Here, Hutten lamented the predatory behavior of the Roman Church, which sought to amass worldly power and wealth at the expense of the empire and of ordinary Germans, and therefore posed a singular threat to the Christian order and to the common good. In a nationalist reference to the common good in the subtitle of the tract, he dedicated the pamphlet "to the use and benefit of the German fatherland of the German nation."[8]

Birgit Biehler compellingly argues how notions of common good and of self-interest, its antithesis, were central to Luther's teaching.[9] However, we should resist the temptation to see the doctrine of the common good as exclusive part of Lutheran dogma and as anchored in Reformation theology.[10] Rather, the issue was part of a larger secularization discourse that pre-dated the Reformation and that evolved separate from the Reformation. The Reformation made use of the existing debate surrounding self-interest, for its own moral philosophy promoting the common good, as well as in its anti-papal rhetoric.

Fighting self-interest, which was rooted theologically in the deadly sin of avarice, was an important theme in pre-Reformation texts as well, as this passage from chapter 10 of Brant's *Narrenschiff* on the topic of true friendship illustrates: "Self interest displaces all law, all friendship, love, kinship, family. One finds nobody like Moses today who loves others as he loves himself."[11] While Brant's focus was on the social and political implications, self-interest is characterized as a sinful category in opposition to the Christian precepts of charity and brotherly love.

Hans Sachs's short play *Comedia: Die ungeleichen kinder Eve, wie sie Gott, der Herr, anredt* (*Comedy: The Unequal Children of Eve, How God, the Lord, Speaks to Them*; 1553)[12] illuminates the theological foundations of the support of communal values without engaging in confessional rhetoric. The play is set at the house of Adam and Eve who, after their eviction from Paradise, have a family with twelve sons. One day, God decides to visit them to see how they are raising their sons and to test their catechetical knowledge. God's questioning on matters of faith soon makes it evident that the sons fall into two groups: six good

---

8 Hutten, *Clag vnd vormanung*, title page: "dem vatterland Teütscher Nation zů nutz vnd gůt". For a more comprehensive discussion of Hutten's nationalism and anti-Roman polemics, see Chapter 20.
9 Biehler, *Der Eigennutz*, 28–64.
10 Biehler, *Der Eigennutz*, 156. Biehler in her otherwise fine monograph fails to embed "Eigennutz" into a larger, pre-Reformation discourse.
11 Brant, *Narrenschiff*, ch. 10, v. 19–22: "Der eigen nutz vertribt all recht | All frintschafft lieb sipschafft/ geschlecht | Kein fyndt man Moysi jetz gelich | der andre lieb hab/ als selbst sich."
12 Sachs, KG 1, 53–87.

sons, led by Abel, and six evil ones, led by Cain and supported by the devil. God is not pleased to see so much godlessness and tells Abel to instruct his evil brothers. Cain is irate about this plan and kills his brother Abel.

Throughout the play, Abel is compliant with rules, obedient to his parents, and eager to perform labor that benefits the entire family. While the other five good sons do not develop distinct personae in the play, all six wicked ones do. Cain is impulsive and aggressive and filled with pride, envy, and anger. The other five have qualifiers attached to their names in Sachs's instructions that are indicative of their chief characteristics: Dathan the rabble-rouser (who also likes to gamble), Achan the thief, Nabal the glutton, Esaw the lecher, and Nemrot the tyrant. In a vague reference to the seven deadly sins, Cain and his evil brothers glorify eating, drinking, stealing, cheating, fornicating, and fighting. Sixteenth-century notions of masculinity and male honor included exactly these sins and transgressions of young urban males.[13] For citizens like Sachs, they created a great deal of anxiety in cities like Nuremberg. As the six rotten and wicked sons prepare for their meeting with God, each gives a pep talk to his brothers. Nemrot describes his desires in this way: "You brothers, I also have a tradition: I would much prefer to be violent, to rule over the common world, over the rich and the poor, and to lead into war, rather than to have mercy."[14] The inclusion of tyranny among the vices appears to be Sachs's innovation, which allowed him to denounce the abuse of power through oppression and injustice and thus to implicitly chide the anti-communal behavior and practices of princes.[15] To Sachs, both the use of violence and the abuse of power were infractions against the community, and this is what Nemrot's sins had in common with his brothers' sins.

In Sachs's play, vices were used to critique individualistic and antisocial behavior and to legitimate social hierarchy.[16] In a literal sense, the overlap between the sins of the six sons and the seven deadly sins was only partial, but both represented infractions against the community. By bringing these social infractions into the form of sins, Sachs's opposition to Humanist individualism and pluralization took on a theological dimension. His reliance on the seven deadly sins, rather than on the Decalogue with its more individualistic catalogue of sins, further reinforced the anti-communal character of sin. In a larger context, it was indicative of the late medieval and early modern obsession with

---

13 Crowther, "Raising Cain," 317.
14 Sachs, KG 1, 77, v. 29–33: "Ir brüder, ich habe auch den sitt: | Ich wolt vil lieber gwaltig sein | Und herrschen in der welt gemein | Uber die reichen und die armen | Und krieg füren an als erbarmen."
15 Crowther, "Raising Cain," 317.
16 Crowther, "Raising Cain," 304.

maintaining order and of anxieties about its collapse. Maintaining social order required an unconditional fight against the deadly sins, and Sachs's play made the claim that this link between socially disruptive and self-centered behavior and sin went all the way back to Adam and Eve.

The play also contains a clear message about social hierarchy that can be traced back to the Fall from Paradise. By giving Abel powers over Cain, God shows that he is not concerned with equality. God's hierarchy was not accepted by the six wicked sons as indicated by their sinful acts. It is their rebellion against social hierarchy ordained by God that motivates the fratricide. The gender hierarchy has its roots in the original sin as well: Sachs has Eve accept sole responsibility for having eaten the forbidden fruit, and she concedes that she had to accept a subservient role to Adam as a result of her sin. The result is a hierarchical and unequal world. Even the title of the play states that Eve's children are unequal, which Eve accepts as part of divine punishment. God himself addresses Eve's six wicked children in disgust:

> Oh what a faithless pack that thinks nothing at all of God, neither of faith nor prayer! You only pursue the earthly delights, that which feels good to flesh and blood and which Satan suggests. That is why you will have to become grim and wretched people on earth.[17]

What all their sins have in common is that they serve earthly self-interest at the expense of the common good. God goes on to enumerate the base occupational and social categories they will have to fill in perpetuity, such as farmers, wood choppers, day laborers, mercenaries – and shoe makers. The mentioning of shoe makers is a cheeky, self-ironic quip referring to his own occupational category rather than a doubtful comment on the divine origin of the social order that arises from the Fall from Paradise. Even though Sachs's account of the origins of social hierarchies has biblical roots and is an expression of his faith, his play does not dwell on confessional rhetoric.

Sachs in his discussion of self-interest did not depart in significant ways from Sebastian Brant, whose *Narrenschiff* (1494) predated the Reformation. Brant's thinking about communalism was rooted in the guild system that held solidarity and communal life in high regard. Late medieval guilds regulated trade and crafts in a way that gave all its members an opportunity to make a living. Their cartel-like organization determined production methods, defined

---

[17] Sachs, KG 1, 80, v. 24–31: "O wie ein gar glaublose rott, | Die ganz und gar nichts helt von Gott, | Weder vom glauben noch gebet! | Hängt nur an dem irdischen stet | Was wol thut ihrem fleisch und blut | Und der Sathan ein blasen thut! | Derhalben so müst ir auff erden | Hart und armutselig leut werden."

quality standards, and generally prevented competition, which put the guilds in opposition to the emerging proto-capitalist system that was carried by merchants, and in particular by the huge trading conglomerates like the Fugger and Welser corporations of Augsburg. The guilds also had para-military obligations, and their social and economic support of members experiencing hardship indicated that guilds were interested in community-building beyond shared economic interests. Johannes Ferrarius in his political tract of 1533 represented the guilds as the core of the community:

> For this reason we should not view guilds as just serving the guilds themselves and their members but also the community, considering that they are also limbs [members] of the community. For as we look at guilds by themselves, each one of them in its craft and trade is a community of its own.[18]

Guilds thus were seen as the backbone of the urban communal structure, supported even by intellectuals and public officials like Brant and Ferrarius, who were not part of the guild system themselves.

To be sure, Brant also commented critically on guild members, craftsmen, and artisans. He dedicated his entire chapter 48 to this group. The chapter is unusual as it is one of only two chapters without a motto and without a title.[19] Brant used a full-page illustration showing four ships, all filled with members of various guilds who are carrying the tools of their trade. One of the ships displays the main heraldic element in Basel's coat of arms: the bishop's crozier. This is the most overt reference to the city Brant called home at the time of writing the *Narrenschiff*. This may have been a jab at the pro-Swiss policies of Basel that he opposed, or more likely at the disproportionate political power the guilds had in Basel at the time. With great disdain, Brant described disunity among guild members, their pursuit of self-interest, as well as their greed, laziness, and unethical business practices. Brant also scorned the desire of journeymen for upward mobility: "each journeyman wants to become a master."[20]

---

18 Ferrarius, *Von dem Gemeinen nutze*, fol 53v: "Sollen dero wegen die zunfft nit alleyn auff jrer zunfft vnd zunfftgnossen frommen sehen/ sonder auch der gemein/ nach dem sie auch glidmasse der gemeyn sein/ dann so wir die zünffte fur sich selbst ansehen/ ist ein jede inn jrem handwerck vnd gewerbe ein eigen Commun."
19 The other chapter without title and motto is the weighty chapter 103 that is commonly given the title "Vom endkrist" (The End Christ).
20 Brant, *Narrenschiff*, ch. 48, v. 7: "Jeder knecht/ meyster werden will." On the inappropriate desire to rise socially, see also *Narrenschiff*, ch. 29, v. 33–34; ch. 37, v. 1–4; ch. 76, v. 3; ch. 76, v. 95; ch. 82, v. 30–51.

The thought of a social group not performing their God-given task was intolerable to Brant. In his view, leaving one's traditional social class and occupational category was not an option.[21] Brant vigorously defended the traditional social order that was based on firmly assigned estates and condemned the ambition of the lower classes. Perhaps his censure of craftsmen was so harsh because Brant as a more highly ranked and academically trained public official and legal scholar feared the competition for himself and his peers. Nevertheless, Brant's critique also focused on the perceived loss of what had made the guilds strong: their communal values and their contributions to the welfare of the city.

Public-mindedness, *Gemeinsinn*, and the pursuit of the common good were virtues and ethical norms that Brant promoted throughout his writings. In his preface to the pamphlet *In Laudem Traiani Caesaris* (*In Praise of Emperor Trajan*) from 1520, which he dedicated to the newly elected Emperor Charles V, he praised Trajan for promoting "the common benefit to the Holy Roman Empire."[22] This thinly veiled reminder on how to govern properly was really addressed to Charles V. As Maximilian I had been a champion of free cities, his death in 1519 distressed urban leaders like Brant. The concern was that Charles, whose life focus had already shifted to Spain, would not be nearly as perceptive to the needs of free cities like his native Strasbourg. This pamphlet was bound together with a similar one praising Emperor Titus; both appeared under the title *An den allerdurchleüchtigsten Großmechtigsten Fürsten und Herren/ Herrn Carolum den fünfften Römischen Keiser vnnd Hyspanischen [König]* (*To the Most Serene Omnipotent Prince and Lord, Lord Charles the Fifth, Roman Emperor and Hispanic [King]*). The two pamphlets were not historical in character; rather, they have to be read in the generic context of the Renaissance education of a Christian prince. It is remarkable, then, that Brant tried to instill the same communal values in the young emperor as he did in guild members. As we have seen before, Brant's message was traditional, but his medium contemporary.

Redefining the role of the individual in a collectivist society was one of the great themes of Humanist thought. While Brant conceded free space for the individual to make decisions for himself in matters of faith, there was little room for individualism in the tightly woven social fabric of the city, as Brant defined it. Not surprisingly, *Gemeinsinn* and *Gemeinnutz* were social values central to Brant's *Narrenschiff* as well. Being community-minded was a key quality of a wise man,

---

21 Rosenfeld, "Brants Narrenschiff," 241.
22 Brant, *An den allerdurchleüchtigsten*, sig. C7v: "den gemeinen nutz des heiligen Römischen Reichs."

while a fool, by contrast, did things by and for himself: "A wise man is useful to his community; a fool carries his club alone."[23] The pursuit of self-interest ran counter to the collective interests of the urban community: "Whoever does not value the common good as much as self-interest that he desires, him I hold to be a foolish dunce. What is common also belongs to each."[24] Each individual was not just a contributor to but also a stakeholder in the common good. Brant even saw the pursuit of self-interest as running counter to legal principles: "self-serving interest displaces all law."[25]

In chapter 99, entitled "von abgang des glouben" (the loss of faith), the theme of community is central. The three-verse motto establishes the connection: "I ask you, lords big and small, to consider the use for the community. Leave the fool's cap to me alone."[26] Brant reminded the princes that communal thinking was central for a community of faith and that it was up to the lords to enforce it, lest they be stuck with the fool's cap themselves. Again, maintaining a community-based society is not mainly up to the individual. Rather, it falls to the authorities to mandate and enforce it.

But the motto did not explain the theme of the chapter – the loss of faith, for which Brant blamed the princes in the first few verses of the chapter. Brant then explained the loss of faith with the advancement of the Turks on the Balkans who displaced Christians and the Christian faith. It was the disunity among the princes that, according to Brant, prevented the Christian leaders from intervening and that allowed the Turks to expand the Ottoman Empire well onto European soil.

In a delicate argument he praised the Republican Senate in ancient Rome as the positive, community-minded counter-example.[27] The Romans had lived in serfdom and oppression, but unity and collaboration in the Senate led to freedom and prosperity. But soon, greed, a desire for power and wealth, and infighting among citizens imperiled this achievement. Brant reduced the problem to this one statement: "Nobody paid attention to the common good."[28] The consequences, in Brant's

---

23 Brant, *Narrenschiff*, ch. 42, v. 7–8: "Eyn wyser ist nütz der gemeyn | Eyn narr syn kolben dreitt alleyn." A "Kolben" is club-like weapon. But in the context of fools, it becomes the fool's weapon, that is one of the attributes of the fool, like the fool's cap.
24 Brant, *Narrenschiff*, ch. 10, v. 25–28: "Wem nit der gmein nütz jst als werd | Als eigen nutz des er begert | Den halt jch für ein närschen gouch | Was gmeyn ist/ das ist eigen ouch."
25 Brant, *Narrenschiff*, ch. 10, v. 19: "Der eigen nutz vertribt all recht."
26 Brant, *Narrenschiff*, ch. 9, v. a-c: "Jch bitt üch herren groß/ vnd kleyn | Bedencken den nutz der gemeyn | Lont mir myn narrenkapp alleyn."
27 Brant, *Narrenschiff*, ch. 99, v. 95–110.
28 Brant, *Narrenschiff*, ch. 99, v. 102: "Des gmeynen nutzes nyeman acht."

mind, were the loss of freedom, the end of the republic, and the subsequent decline of empire. Brant summed up the point: strength came through unity while division brought decline.[29] Every member of society bore responsibility for unity: "Pious kings, princes, nobles, common people, may they soon win and force around the entire world, if only all stick together."[30]

In Brant's view, members of all social classes were required to assume responsibility for the common good, each according to his own status. As Hermann Bote had explained in his *Radbuch* from 1492/93, the world was a system of interlocking wheels of which each had to play a distinct role. Each had a vital part to pay, and each was required for the whole to function. While Brant did not use this metaphor, it is well-suited to explain his worldview. Like Brant, Bote recognized hatred, envy, and pride as the primary distractions as they led to discord that in turn disrupted the functioning of the system of wheels. Like Brant, Bote also stood for an unconditional preservation of the traditional social and political order. In their view, a hierarchical system was a prerequisite for social peace.

Communalist thinking in Brant's *Narrenschiff* can be read as an implied rejection of individualism that was emerging in Humanist thought. While Brant recognized a role for individual thinking, individual decisions were subservient to communal considerations. Therefore, it is not without irony that Brant developed a strong individualistic authorial voice in his book. While Brant preached communal values, he did so in a highly individual and personal voice and in a medium that opened the door for individual expression. The book as a medium was the most powerful tool of pluralization, yet Brant used the book to oppose individualism and pluralization. While the book seemed an appropriate venue for Brant to discuss his ideas, he also promoted a new medium that could not be controlled and that was capable of accommodating and disseminating dissenting viewpoints. This basic dilemma informed Brant's conflicted and even paradoxical view on books.

One of the pioneering theoretical treatises promoting communal organization based on the *bonum commune* was *Von dem Gemeinen nutze/ in massen sich ein ieder/ er sey Regent/ ader vnterdan/ darin schicken sol/ den eygen nutz hindan setzen/ vnd der Gemeyn wolfart suchen* (*Of the Common Good, Whereby Everyone, Be He a Regent or a Subject, Should Commit to Suppress Self-Interest and Seek the Welfare of the Community*), published in 1533 by the Marburg professor Johannes

---

29 Brant, *Narrenschiff*, ch. 99, v. 133–136.
30 Brant, *Narrenschiff*, ch. 99, v. 169–172: "Frům künig/ fürsten/ adel/ gmeyn | Das sie die gantze weltt alleyn/ | Gewynnen/ vnd vmbbringen baldt | Wann man alleyn sich zamen haldt."

Ferrarius, or Eisermann. It is worth considering Ferrarius in this context as he theorized and systematized the ideas Sebastian Brant and Hermann Bote promoted in their literary writings forty years earlier.

In his preface, Ferrarius deplored the fact that the Golden Rule, formerly the foundation of simple, harmonious communal life, no longer had any validity as people only pursued their self-interest at the expense of others:

> For human innocence lapsed into evil, obedience plummeted, and civic beliefs, with all virtues, decayed noticeably. Nobody wants to do for the other anymore what he would like to be done for himself. Each one is trying to figure out how he can take advantage of the other. Things literally got down to the phrase that one man is the other's wolf.[31]

Paraphrasing Plautus, he described human predatory behavior in a simile that Thomas Hobbes later made famous with the succinct formulation "homo homini lupus."[32] According to Ferrarius, this led to the lamentable current state where communal life was dominated by vices that were willfully committed by community members. The ideal was a community where good order created harmony, which he likened to the metaphor of the harp common in medieval political literature,[33] which, while having different strings, emitted harmonious sounds and thus stood for good order in the city:

> For many voices of a stringed instrument played together create a harmony and a separate, consonant note that is lovely. Likewise, in a city or community all pieces have to sound together, must be coordinated, and none can take over another's duties. Out of this grows a harmony and lovely tone, which we call the common good.[34]

Like in Bote's *Radbuch*, separate but equally important parts – wheels for Bote and strings for Ferrarius – allegorically represented different segments of human society who all had to cooperate harmonically to create a peaceful, congruous, and prosperous community.

---

31 Ferrarius, *Von dem Gemeinen nutze*, Vorrede, sig. A2r: "Dann der menschlich einfalt ist zur bößheit geratten/ der gehorsam gefallen/ vnd der burgerlich glaub/ sampt allen tugenden/ in mircklichen abfall komen/ Es wil keiner mehr dem andern thun was er gern wölt/ man jme thete/ vnd tracht ein jeder wie er den andern möcht vber das sehel werffen/ Jst damit beynaw auff das wort komen/ das ein mensch des andern wolff sey."
32 Thomas Hobbes drew upon this proverb in the dedication his *De Cive* (1642).
33 Simon, *Gute Policey*, 127.
34 Ferrarius, *Von dem Gemeinen nutze*, fol. 21r: "Dann viel stymmen eins seyten spiels mit einander vergliechen machen harmoniam/ vnd ein zurtheilten gleichlautenden thon/ der lieplich ist. Also in einer statt ader Commun müssen alle stucke zusammen stymmen/ sich vergleichen/ vnd keins dem andern in sein ampt fallen/ Daraus kompt ein harmonia vnnd schoner lieplicher thon/ das wir nennen ein gemeinen nutz." Similar argumentation also on fol. 49r.

Yet, this harmony was elusive, as was the good order it was supposed to evoke. A lack of proper discipline and education for Ferrarius was at the core of the problem. A gross and willful neglect of parental duties allowed the rise of a young generation that no longer could function as full members of society: "Finally, as they are supposed to become adults and be of use to the community, they can do no more than gamble, drink, swear, curse, and in sum go idle."[35] Ferrarius's definition of "gemein nutz," common good, very much followed what Brant had in mind for his own community of fools:

> It is important to know that *res publica*, or the common good, is nothing other than a good common order in a city or in another community. Its sole pursuit is that one can exist next to the other and thus can keep peace more appropriately with genuine, honorable conduct. And it is called common good, because here no one shall consider his own interests alone, but rather will assist others so that his neighbor not only will not be hindered but also will be supported (where the need arises). This is why I called it a civil society.[36]

Like Brant, Ferrarius made the connection between communal thinking and public order – in fact, the term *res publica* in his view is synonymous with *gemein nutz*, the common good, whose purpose is to create conditions where citizens do not put their self-interest ahead of the interests of the community. It is remarkable that he called his ideal community a "burgerliche geselschafft" – a term he claims to have coined. This is a term we commonly associate with the rise of a civil society that is by definition not linked to the authorities and that allows civic communities to thrive in a privately organized realm. Terminologically, this may be an allusion to Cicero's *societas civilis*.

To be sure, Ferrarius did not envision a society in which the urban middle classes were emancipated from the authorities and led self-empowered lives. In his view, the city council in an urban context very much acted as an authority that had the task of maintaining the common good: "Furthermore, a city council should have an eye exclusively on the common good, because it also is a member

---

[35] Ferrarius, *Von dem Gemeinen nutze*, sig. A2v: "zu luzt wann sie angehende leuthe werden/ solten der gemein etwas nutz sein/ so kunn sie nit mehr dan spilen/ sauffen/ schweren/ fluchen/ vnd in summa/ mussiggehen."
[36] Ferrarius, *Von dem Gemeinen nutze*, fol. 19r-19v: "[...] ist zu wissen/ das Respublica/ oder gemein nutz nit anders ist/ dan ein gemein gutte ordenung einer statt/ oder einer andern commun/ darinn allein gesucht wurd/ das einer neben dem andern bleiben kunde/ vnd sich desto statlicher mit vffrichtigem vnuerweißlichem wandel im friden erhalten. Vnd wird darumb der gemein nutz genant/ das inn dem fall keiner auff sein eigen sache allein sehen sall/ sonder denen also furstehen/ das sein nachpaur dadurch nit allein nit gehindert/ sondern auch (wo es die noth ergreifft) gefurdert werde. Darumb hab ichs auch ein burgerliche geselschafft gnant."

of the ruling elite and head, whose authority is directed toward [the common good]."[37] The term "burgerlich" indicated his focus on an urban middle-class world and its *cives*, citizens, or burghers. In that sense, a "burgerliche geselschafft" designated a society in which each member knew what his civic duties were and performed them according to class and estate under the tutelage of the city council. This was Sebastian Brant's vision in his literary texts as well.

Ferrarius's ideal citizen very much owed obedience to the authorities. While the authorities had to impose order and enforce the law assertively, their actions, too, could not be self-serving and had to focus on the common good:

> Firstly, each authority shall ensure that their policies are directed toward the common good and neglect their own particular interests. For such is the principle and core of a government devised this way that it seeks the protection of the subjects and not of the rulers. Otherwise, it would not be called government but rather a selfishness.[38]

While citizens were required to be obedient, the authority of the rulers was not without limits. Rulers were bound by the same ethical rules in that they worked for the common good and could not pursue their particular self-interests.

Just like Bote and others before, Ferrarius used the body as a metaphor for the hierarchical structure of the state throughout his book.[39] Ferrarius explained the analogy between body and state at great length:

> There is no part throughout the entire body that in its proper functioning is not looking out for the others. So that the body parts do not go astray, each remains within its orders, and each performs its duties to address the needs of the body. The head is placed above all other body parts so that each of them does not stray, stays within its mandate, and performs its duties to sustain the body. In the head reason governs no differently than a king does in his palace. This is how it came that each government or authority was called a head.[40]

---

37 Ferrarius, *Von dem Gemeinen nutze*, fol. 43r: "Es sal auch ein Rath allein den gemeinen nutz vor augen haben/ Dann er ist auch ein glidmaß der Herrschafft/ vnd haupts/ welchs ampt sich allein dahin richtet."
38 Ferrarius, *Von dem Gemeinen nutze*, fol. 23r: "Zum ersten sal ein iede Oberkeit darauff sehen/ das jre furhaben auff den gemeinen nutz gericht sey/ vnd jres eigen nutzs vergeß/ dann solchs ist das principal vnd hauptstuck einer vorgenomen regirung/ das der vnterdanen/ vnd nit der regenten nutz gesucht/ sunst were es kein regiment/ sonder ein eygennutzickeit gnant."
39 The absolutist theory of state, most notably in Thomas Hobbes's *Leviathan or the Matter, Forme and Power of a Commonwealth Ecclesiastical and Civil* (1651) used the body as a metaphor for the organization of state as well.
40 Ferrarius, *Von dem Gemeinen nutze*, fol. 9v-10r: "Vnd also fur vnd fur ist kein glidmas am gantzen leib/ das inn seinem ordentlichen werck nicht stehe/ vnd auff das andere sehe. Damit aber die glidmas nit irren/ ein iedes inn seinem beuelch bleibe/ vnd zu notturft des leibs sein

The analogy between body and community makes six distinct points. Firstly, it explains how a human society and the human body were analogous because the individual parts in both occupied different ranks in the hierarchy and performed different tasks. Secondly, it states why a coordinator or ruler was needed. As the head governed and controlled the body, its parts, and its functions, the ruler as head of government ruled his subjects. It is noteworthy that Ferrarius pointed out that the word *Haupt* (head) could designate both the central, governing parts of the human body and of a social organization. Thirdly, as the body with its distinct parts was part of divine creation, therefore the same could be said by way of analogy for the organization of state. A fourth point is that the body parts worked together harmoniously and without conflict, as did the wheels in Bote's *Radbuch*. Hierarchy in these systems remained unquestioned and indeed unquestionable, and by way of analogy the same was true for human society as well. This is a key reason for the disdain so many authors expressed for social upheaval and challenges to political rule.

Later in the text, Ferrarius added a fifth dimension of the analogy: just as body parts could not exist on their own and in isolation, the members of the human society could not live alone. As they needed each other to survive, it was in their self-interest to work together. Working for the common good in human society therefore was not just a reasonable and ethical thing to do, it was part of the divine plan and essential for the survival of the human community.[41] The sixth point of analogy was that both the human head and the king as head of state were ruled by reason. It is this concept of reason that was anchored in morality, which is yet another point of connection with Sebastian Brant.

It bears repeating here that the pursuit of the common good as a basic objective of the state was so heavily promoted by religious and political thinkers and literary writers in the sixteenth century exactly because its relevance and validity were increasingly in doubt. The desperate call to consider the common good was quite anachronistic as it did not correspond to the economic reality of urban merchants and artisans discussed in Part III. Moral philosophy and ethical norms were out of step with the new patterns of economic behavior and were largely unable to provide guidance. Sebastian Brant and many other literary figures of the time, like Hans Sachs, Hermann Bote, the author of *Dyl Ulenspiegel*, Ulrich von Hutten, and Johann Fischart, were among those who strongly reacted to the perceived loss of moral and ethical standards and general sense of crisis in their urban environments.

---

werck volbringe/ ist das haupt vber sie aller gesetzt/ darinn die vernunfft nit anders dan ein könig in seinem schloß regirt. Daher es kummen/ das ein jede regirung oder oberkeit ein haupt genent wurde."
41 Ferrarius, *Von dem Gemeinen nutze*, fol. 21v-22r.

Chapter 8
The Decline of the Community: Common Good and Self-Interest as Literary Metaphors

Hans Sachs represented a world similar to that of Sebastian Brant in a number of ways. Both Brant and Sachs were citizens of important merchant cities in southern Germany – Brant in Basel and Strasbourg and Sachs in Nuremberg – and represented the type of self-confident burgher of a free city. In their thinking, both were rooted in the guild system; Sachs as master shoemaker was even a guild member. Both viewed the emperor as a guarantor of the independence of their cities and thus generally represented empire and emperor in positive terms.[1] There are notable differences as well: while Brant was a university-trained lawyer who read and wrote Latin with ease, Sachs had no university training, although he claimed to have learned Latin during his school years in his autobiographical poem *Summa aller meiner Gedichte vom 1514. Jahr an bis ins 1567. Jahr* (*Sum of All My Poems from the Year 1514 Until the Year 1567*) from 1567. While Brant wrote a wide range of texts for equally varied audiences, Sachs wrote exclusively in German for an urban middle-class audience – the same audience Sebastian Brant targeted with his *Narrenschiff*. While Brant wrote in a pre-Reformation context, Sachs publicly swore allegiance to the Lutheran cause in 1523.[2] Nevertheless, Sachs's views on *Eigennutz* seemed to have differed little from those of Brant.

Eigennutz, self-interest, was the theme of Hans Sachs's didactic poem *Der eygen nutz, das greulich thir, mit sein zwölff eygenschafften* (*Self-Interest, that Awful Beast, with its Twelve Properties*; 1527). In the space of 388 rhymed doggerel verses, the first-person narrative tells the story of a nightly dream, framed by sequences of falling asleep and waking up. The narrator is restless because of worries about economic conditions:

> One night I lay in bed sleeplessly. I was consumed by heavy thoughts, why all trades on earth now have become scarce, tight, and meager, as well as food and drink and all merchandise. Whatever God makes grow all year long rises up to the highest [price]. No

---

1 Brant's support of the emperor was discussed above. Sachs wrote a number of poems reflecting upon that, such as "Kayserlicher mayestat Caroli der V einreyten zu Nürnberg in des heyligen reichs stat, den xvi tag Februarii deß 1541 jars," (Sachs, KG 2, 381–394) which describes the emperor's visit to Nuremberg in 1541.
2 Hess, "German Poetry," 401–402.

merchandise is sold the way it used to be. This is why the poor common man can barely afford his food.³

The poem starts out with a diagnosis of crisis. The marketplace does not work anymore, food is scarce and expensive, and poor people are suffering. The narrator tries to find a reason for this and falls asleep over this question.

In the following dream sequence, which is the core of the text, an old man with wings appears and takes him up high so they can get a better look at the world. He identifies himself as Menippus from Lucianus's satires. What they see is people taking advantage of each other and crawling like ants in an utterly disorderly and even chaotic world where villages are burning and humans are screaming in despair. The passage creates vivid imagery that graphically illustrates Sachs's own anxieties about the perceived crisis of his time. A horrible animal enters that had caused the utmost destruction on the world below (figure 3). The narrator demands to know more about this monstrum that features body parts from different animals.⁴ Menippus responds: "Indeed it is nothing good. It is called and is self-interest."⁵ The twelve body parts allegorically stand for different aspects of self-interest. Using a monstrum to represent self-interest allegorically was a novel idea as there was no standard allegorical figure.⁶

The "löwen-haupt" (lion's head) represents the authorities who abuse their subjects with undue financial demands and thus are at the core of the problem of self-interest:

> Firstly, the lion's head signifies that self-interest numbs the authorities and that they oppress their subjects. Self-interest sucks dry the people with heavy taxes, interest, and drudgery, with tithes, fiefs, and hunts, with harsh treatment and punishment, with indulgences, ban and pallium, annuities, confession, sacrifice, shrine, dispensations, and similar money-strings of many kind.⁷

---

3 Sachs, KG 3, 491, v. 3–12: "Eins nachts ich ungeschlaffen lag. | Viel schwer gedancken ich auß wag. | Warumb all hendel yetz auff erden | So klemb, spitzig und zucker werden, | Auch speiß und tranck, auch alle wahr. | Das Gott lest wachsen uber jar, | Stayget als auf das höhest auff. | Kein wahr steht mehr im alten kauff. | Derhalb der arm gemeine man | Sein narung hart erschwingen kan."

4 Sachs published an almost identical version of the poem around 1535 with the title *Das schedlich Thier der Eygen nutz/ mit sein verderblichen zwölff Eygen schafften*. This version has a title illustration showing the monstrum that is reproduced here.

5 Sachs, KG 3, 494, v. 19–20: "Es ist fürwar nichts guts. | Es haist und ist der aygen nutz."

6 Biehler, *Der Eigennutz*, 153.

7 Sachs, KG 3, 494, v. 24–34: "Erstlich bedeut das löwen-haubt, | Das aygner nutz die herrschafft taubt.| Das sie trucken ir unterthan | Mit schwerer stewer, zinst und fron, | Mit zehent, lehen und gewildt, | Mit straff und wandel gar unmildt, | Mit ablaß, bann und pallium, | Anaten, beicht, opffer, heylthumb, | Dispensieren und simoney | Und dergleich gelt-strick

Figure 3: Hans Sachs. *Das schedlich Thier der Eygen nutz/ mit sein verderblichen zwölff Eygen schafften*. Nürnberg: Pankraz Kempf, c. 1535. Title page. © Bayerische Staatsbibliothek München.

---

mancherley | Thut eygner nutz die lewt auß saugen." "Simoney," literally the sin of Simon, refers to corruption.

Sachs paints a bleak picture of the authorities of his time, both worldly rulers and the princes of the Church, who treated their subjects in an unjust way. They also created a web of financial schemes and of corruption to maintain power and to support their luxurious lives.

It is worth mentioning that Sachs arrived at a different assessment of the government of his native city of Nuremberg in his poem *Ein lobspruch der Stadt Nürnberg* (*Encomium to the City of Nuremberg*, 1530). Here, he idealized his own city, its citizens, and its wise government.[8] He praised his fellow citizens in glowing terms as "an industrious people, rich and very powerful, smart, skillful, forward-looking."[9] Sachs expressed his unqualified support for the type of polity Nuremberg represented, namely the free imperial city with its independence from landed princes. His idealization of the city is based on an analogy between the architectural order in the layout of his city to its social order, which guarantees wise governance: "I viewed all things close and far; adornment and grace of our common city, harmony in the community and the council, order among the ranks of the citizens, a wise and careful government."[10] Wise, benevolent governance and harmonious civic order are rooted in the idea of the common good: "Also the council and the community are in agreement and of one mind, and they protect each other. From that grows the common good, which gives the city permanence."[11]

The upbeat assessment of the political structure in his own city has to be contrasted with his general cultural pessimism expressed in other texts. In the generic context of the encomium, a positive assessment was expected, and Sachs therefore was willing to overlook the serious political difficulties in Nuremberg at the time. Furthermore, harsh critique directed at specific individuals or identifiable groups was frowned upon in the early modern period. It must have seemed opportune for Sachs as a well-known member of the community to please the political leadership and his fellow citizens. Sachs had a vested interest in the continued representation of the guild system in city governance as it guaranteed his own privileges. Therefore, he had no incentive to anger the city elders.

---

8 Hess, "German Poetry," 410.
9 Sachs, KG 4, 193, v. 18–19: "Ein embsig volck, reich und ser mechtig, | Gescheyd, geschicket und fürtrechtig."
10 Sachs, KG 4, 198, v. 28–32: "All ding besichtigt nahe unnd weyt,| Geschmück und zier gemeiner stat, | Eynigkeit der gemein und rat, | Ordnung der burgerlichen stend, | Ein weiß, fürsichtig regiment."
11 Sachs, KG 4, 195, v. 12–16: "Also ein rat und die gemein | Einhellig und einmütig sein | Und halten da einander schutz. | Darauß erwechst gemeiner nutz. | Auß dem so hat die stat bestant."

Hans Sachs returned to the theme of good governance and public morality a number of times. One of the most curious such efforts is the didactic poem *Von dem teuffel, dem die hell will zu eng werden* (*Of the Devil for Whom Hell Became too Crowded*) from 1540, which appears to have a Nuremberg connection as well. A first-person narrator wanders through the forest on a Saturday night on a business-related journey to Neustadt an der Aisch, which is located about forty kilometers northwest of Nuremberg. Saturday night, Saturn's day, often was seen as the night when evil spirits were encountered and therefore was seen as the devil's day.[12] Not surprisingly, he encounters the devil who himself is traveling on business. The devil is looking for good stone masons and carpenters who can help him build a larger hell as it is populated beyond capacity.

The narrator tries to talk the devil out of his project to build a larger hell with his claim that the number of sinners has decreased: "I took heart and said: So look! During Ulysses's time, hell was as big as an entire country. But now few heathen souls are in it. How could hell be bursting if now almost all of us are Christians? Even fewer of us [Christians] are entering it."[13] Sachs implied that the recent Reformation was the reason why fewer were finding their way to hell. Now that real Christianity had arrived, so the argument, enlarging hell no longer would be required. The devil responds that Christians, both of a secular or clerical estate, did not uphold the principles of their faith and that all Christian lands were drenched in sin. The devil asks for a more thorough explanation, to which the narrator responds: "Yes, I said, you do injustice to us because now the entire humankind has converted back to God, as this is preached and taught now and people are admonished to do penance."[14] Here Sachs's claim that the Reformation has brought people back to God becomes evident.

The narrator now engages in a lengthy monologue that forms the core of the text. He spares no details to praise the virtues of the new Christian society. He discusses humans and their virtues group by group: clergy, worldly authorities, merchants, artisans, and peasants. All the vices that were commonly associated with particular groups now have given way to their opposite virtues. The

---

12 Bächtold-Stäubli, *Handwörterbuch*, vol. 7, 918–936.
13 Sachs, KG 3, 587, v. 10–16: "Ich fieng ein hertz und sprach: So schaw! | Die hell ward zu Ulissis zeyt | Gleich eynem gantzen lande weit, | Doch wenig haidnischer seel darinnen: | Wie möcht di hell dir yetz zerrinnen, | So wir schier alle Christen seyn? | Unser faren noch wenger dreyn."
14 Sachs, KG 3, 587, v. 23–27: "Ja, sprach ich, du thust uns unrecht, | Weil ietz das gantz christlich geschlecht | Ist widerumb zu Gott bekert, | Weyl man also predigt und lert | Und das volck zu der buß vermant."

pope, the cardinals and the bishops have become humble, practice a simple life in modesty and abstinence, and fight heresy with Scripture. The ironic nature of this list becomes apparent at the onset, as the idea of Lutheran teachings being adapted by the pope and the other princes of the Church is illusionary. This sets the tone for the other claims: the rulers are peace-loving and not one bit tyrannical. The merchants are no longer pursuing their own self-interest and have abandoned their much-maligned business practices, like hoarding (*fürkauff*), usury, and fraudulent financial transactions. Artisans now deliver quality work and no longer engage in unfair competition. And the peasants pay their taxes and rents and are obedient. Social life has become orderly as well: there is no marital strife, wives are acquiescent, children well-raised, and people do not commit sins like adultery, fornication, gluttony, drinking, sorcery, theft, and fraud. The narrator ends his monologue with the plea to the devil not to go through with his hell expansion plans. The devil responds angrily: "You mendacious man. You said not a single true word."[15] The narrator promises evidence, and the devil agrees to a pact: the narrator has until the following Thursday to find ten pious witnesses who will confirm his account. If so, he will go free, and the devil will stop his construction project. At this point, the devil disappears.

The narrator now goes out to look for the ten pious men who meet the criteria. He looks for ten years but does not find a single one. Everybody he talks to about this calls him a liar, and it now becomes evident to the reader that the world of virtue the narrator represented in his rosy description does not exist, and the irony of his representation of the world becomes evident. Maria Müller sees this text as a response to the encomium to Nuremberg that Sachs had written ten years and one day earlier. In her reading, the citizens of Nuremberg, still virtuous at the time of the encomium, were now rotten through and through.[16] But the ten-year span between the two poems likely is accidental; Sachs easily could have matched the dates rather than setting them one day apart. While the reference to Nuremberg is very specific in the encomium, it is circumstantial in the story about the devil. The praise in the encomium is directed at Nuremberg and its citizens exclusively, within the generic parameters discussed above. The facetious praise in the 1540 text explicitly includes all of Christianity and is by no means understood as a reference to Nuremberg specifically – with the exception of the fact that the devil wants Nuremberg stone masons and carpenters because of their reputation for quality work.

---

15 Sachs, KB 3, 591, v. 32–33: "Du verlogner man, | Du hast kein wares wort geredt."
16 Müller, *Der Poet der Moralität*, 152. *Ein lobspruch der Stadt Nürnberg* is dated 20 February 1530 and *Von dem teuffel, dem die hell will zu eng werden* is dated 21 February 1540.

As the narrator is not able to deliver on his promise within five days, and not even within ten years, the devil wins the bet. Yet, he is unable to claim his prize because the narrator, unlike the protagonist of the later *Faustbuch*, has not committed a sin in the process. Rather, salvation comes through the grace of God, and the narrator expresses confidence that Christians will be cleansed of their sins because God through baptism extends the salvation that was promised through Christ's death. The devil could be captured and bound so he could not do harm to the narrator, and sin and hell could be overcome. The text closes with the Lutheran expression of faith: "Whoever believes will be blessed, says Hans Sachs."[17]

But why would Hans Sachs have his naive and ignorant narrator give an idealized account of the world that so obviously was inaccurate? Why would he create this image of a utopian world that was quickly unmasked and discredited because he saw the real world as a dystopia? The narrator contextualized the newly found moral life within a Reformation context. He maintained the illusionary and fictitious claim that the Reformation had turned humans into moral beings who lived in an idealized community where self-interest was absent. In 1523, Martin Bucer had expressed the hope that the religious renewal would restore the order by abating sin that was so instrumental in the decay of the public order.[18] Almost two decades after Sachs had publicly embraced Luther's teachings in the same year, he must have arrived at the conclusion that the Reformation failed to combat perceived evil in society and to have a positive impact on public morality. The ironic play in the text with the newly found moral life may well represent the expectation he himself once had and now understood to be unrealistic and elusive.

The text represents a distressing recognition of the fact that the Reformation had not changed sinful daily life, as transgressions were as rampant as they had been before. But the conclusion hints at an element of hope in the theological realm: the centrality of faith and of forgiveness through divine grace in Lutheran doctrine creates the confidence that the devil can be overcome and sins can be forgiven. Sachs's point that little had changed in the post-Reformation urban environment and that humans still were sinners as before, as he witnessed it in Nuremberg, puts his own ardent and enthusiastic endorsement of the Lutheran cause in *Die wittembergisch nachtigal* (*The Wittenberg Nightingale*) from 1523 in perspective. It represents an implicit admission that confessional differences did not greatly impact public morality and mattered little in the way his fellow

---

17 Sachs, KG 3, 592, v. 37: "Wer glaubt, wirdt selig, spricht Hans Sachs."
18 Bucer, *Das ym selbs niemant*, sig. b1v.

citizens conducted their lives. More broadly put, public morality did not have a distinct confessional dimension, and confessional issues did not significantly drive moral philosophy.

In that sense, the Nuremberg encomium was a bit of an outlier as it was very specifically embedded in the Nuremberg context. It can be read as an illustration of Sachs's range as a writer, but its message cannot be seen as reflective of Sachs's view on politics and the human condition in the abstract. For that, we have to return to the 1527 poem *Der eygen nutz, das greulich thir, mit sein zwölff eygenschafften*. As mentioned above, the lion's head represents fledgling governance. The other body parts are associated with a range of unsavory aspects of the monstrum called self-interest, such as general inflation caused by the eyes of the basilisk, verbal injury and deception by the tongue of the viper, the insatiable nature of self-interest by the heart of a toad, and its pervasiveness across all social classes and estates by the wings of the dragon. The boar's teeth indicate that self-interest cannot be legislated and regulated "by laws, statutes, and policies"[19] because it is so invasive that it takes on a dynamic of its own that also affects the authorities, as we have seen above. Self-interest is framed as the source of all evil and is seen as bringing misery and starvation to the masses.

Four body parts are reserved for four different economic groups – they represent the four middle sections among the twelve body parts. The throat of the crocodile is an allegory for the insatiable greed for money displayed by the bankers and money lenders:

> Further, the throat of the crocodile signifies that self-interest can satisfy no one with hoarding, usury, and financing, with luxury and graft, liens on meadows, fields and barns, and with inflation on wine, grains, and houses. With cash it pursues many transactions. With deferred securities, everything is left to it. With malice it is selling short many, until they are forced from house and farm. Thus self-interest amasses lots of money. This burdens the whole world.[20]

Sachs described abusive and ruinous financial transactions and trading practices in some detail, such as the much-maligned practice of hoarding goods to

---

[19] Sachs, KG 3, 495, v. 13: "durch gsetz, statut und policey."
[20] Sachs, KG 3, 495, v. 35–496, v. 11: "Auch deut der schlund des cocodrillen, | Das aygner nutz kan nyemand stillen | Mit fürkauff, wucher und finantzen, | Mit popitzen und alifantzen | Leyhen auff wiesen, äcker, schewrren, | Wein, koren unnd hewser vertewren. | Mit müntz er auch vile wechsel treybt. | Verstandtne pfand, im alles bleibt. | Mit griffen gschwind manchen verkürtzt, | Biß er von hauß und hof in stürtzt. | Des samlet aygner nutz groß geldt. | Des ist beschwert die gantze welt."

artificially limit their supply.²¹ We have to assume that as a master shoemaker and shop owner he had a certain understanding of the business practices and good reason to criticize them.

Not surprisingly, merchants, and in particular large, well-networked trading companies fare no better in Sachs's text. Sachs thinly disguised them as stomach of the wolf. They make their money with trading, buying cheaply, creating monopolies, selling expensively, bribing, cheating by using false measurements and fraudulent invoicing, and making illegitimate profits by selling on credit. These practices in Sachs's analysis were responsible for massive inflation, which was generally viewed as a key factor for poverty and hunger at the time. Sachs added one more sentence that appears out of context here: "Labor does not mean much to [the monstrum]."²² From the perspective of a guild member who worked with his hands to produce a useful material object, such speculative financial transactions indeed did not look like honorable labor. As a consequence, Sachs did not consider earnings from these activities to be legitimate. This is in line with how other literary texts represented labor in the sixteenth century, and the motif of a merchant's unearned and thus illegitimate income through financial manipulations was common in the literature of the sixteenth century.²³ Interestingly, this view was not entirely shared by Martin Luther, who considered the earnings of merchants legitimate as long they complied with his teaching on just price.²⁴

The section on the claws of a gryphon is devoted to artisans, the social group Sachs belonged to. At thirty-two verses, it is the longest of the sections dedicated to the twelve body parts. The first seven verses describe how artisans act in self-interest through competitive behavior and thus "break their order and statutes."²⁵ The claws have to be read as a threat to the guild system that comes in the form of innovation as well as competitive thinking and behavior among artisans, which all were considered disruptive for the system.²⁶ To Sachs, guilds formed the backbone of the economic, social and political order in the city, so the subversion of the guild system by the competitive behavior by some of its members constituted a real threat to the social order in the city.

---

21 This will be discussed in more detail in Chapter 18.
22 Sachs, KG 3, 496, v. 26: "Die arbeyt gilt ihm kaum so viel."
23 An example is chapter 93 in Brant's *Ship of Fools*. The idea of unearned income often is associated with usury, as discussed in Chapter 18.
24 Luther, *Von Kauffshandlung*, sig. A4r.
25 Sachs, KG 3, 497, v. 1: "brechen ir ordnung und gesetz."
26 Biehler, *Der Eigennutz*, 154.

The artisans are the only group who are also framed as victims of the changing economy, particularly poor artisans who run a small shop: "On the other hand, the rich is subcontracting the poor. And he wants to have the labor for a bargain price and wants to cook a soup from it too."[27] Sachs referred to changes in the urban economy where small artisans increasingly became subcontractors in a growing workshop or putting-out system.[28] Merchants, particularly large trading conglomerates like the Fuggers, Welsers, and others, pursued vertical integration schemes in which artisans, like shoe makers, became de-facto contract workers.[29] This system became common in artisanal work with textiles, metal, wood, and leather. Merchants provided workers with raw materials, purchased back the finished products with a slim margin for the workers, and pocketed significant profits when reselling them wholesale or retail.[30] This practice in part was designed to circumvent guild rules, and it definitely contributed to downward pressures in wages and outright poverty among some artisans.[31]

Even peasants, represented here as the feet of a buffalo, are seen critically. Sachs shows peasants engaged in deceptive behavior, like moving property markers, watering down milk, cutting wood to a shorter length, and selling rotten eggs. Most notably, they are not willing to fulfill the duties of their estate: "They are unruly in many ways and disobedient toward their masters; they even want to avoid paying their interest."[32] In line with the norms of the time, Sachs did not view the peasants, the poorest and least privileged group at the time, as victims of a changing economy. Peasants were a constituency without advocacy and representation.

The last body part is the tail of the scorpion, which rhetorically serves to summarize all evils brought forth by self-interest. With stark language and frequent use of asyndeton, Sachs describes how self-interest brings discord, conflict, war, destruction, and hunger. What is more, it disrupts human interactions and destroys morality and social fabric:

---

[27] Sachs, KG 3, 497, v. 7–10: "[...] Dargegen | Der reich den armen thut verlegen | Und will die arbeyt wolfeyl hon, | Ein suppen sieden auch darvon."
[28] For an overview of the Verlagswesen see Isenmann, *Die deutsche Stadt*, 876–881; for contemporary criticism see Kießling, "Problematik."
[29] Hunt and Murray, *A History of Business*, 178.
[30] Scott, *Society*, 252–254.
[31] Scott, *Society*, 97–98.
[32] Sachs: KG 3, 498, v. 3–5: "Sind widerspenstig manigfalt | Sind seer unghorsam ihren herren, | Wolten sein gar unzinßbar geren."

> At all times self-interest tears apart, spoils, misleads, feasts on, and flushes away everything just like a downpour, namely all good manners, discipline, and virtue. It spoils the old and the young, both in the upper and lower classes. That is why you should not be surprised that everything came to a head in all lands and principalities.[33]

Sachs's narration ends here and returns to the narrative frame: the monster tries to seize the narrator, who then wakes up from his dream.

Sachs portrayed self-interest as this corrosive, pervasive force that affected all parts of society. Worse than the material effect causing poverty and hunger was the spiritual one, as it led to a decline of virtue and public morality. The text thus serves as an illustration for how Sachs saw moral and economic issues not as distinct but rather as intertwined and inseparable. The critique of self-interest followed moral and even religious mandates, but it also targeted the new proto-capitalist economy as the main culprit for moral decline. Sachs thus projected a unified world view in which theological, economic, social, and political concerns did not inform separate realms[34] but rather became part of the same literary discourse.

The final section, entitled "Beschluß" (conclusion), takes on the form of a prayer. Sachs, who identifies himself as speaker in the last line, asks God for his help and protection. This caps his negative anthropology, which resembles Brant's: humans are shown to be depraved and incapable of helping themselves. The authorities are seen as part of the problem as well, as they are greedy themselves and take advantage of their subjects instead of protecting them against all the excesses and abuses. By not issuing new ordinances to combat the impact of self-interest nor enforcing existing ones, the authorities abdicate their role as just rulers and God's representatives on earth who administer the divine order. By calling on God to resolve a matter that could be settled by drafting and enforcing prudent public policy, Sachs expresses a lack of confidence in their integrity and leadership skills. But the prayer also serves as a rhetorical device to communicate the urgency of the issue. Sachs aims to shame individuals into abandoning the pursuit of self-interest and pressure authorities into issuing new ordinances and regulations that promote the common good.

Eight years later, Sachs wrote another didactic poem on the topic of self-interest, entitled *Klag der brüderlichen lieb uber den aygen nutz* (*Lament of Brotherly Love About Self-Interest*, 1535), which is considerably shorter with its

---

33 Sachs, KG 3, 500, v. 16–24: "Wann aygner nutz zu aller zeyt | Zerreist, verderbt, hinfürt, verschlembt, | Recht wie ein güß all ding verschwembt | All gute sitten, zucht und tugend, | Verderbt das alter und die jugendt | Durch-auß bey obern und bey undern. | Darumb darffst du dich nit verwundern, | Das alle ding auffs höchst ist kummen | In allen landen, fürstenthummen."
34 Biehler, *Der Eigennutz*, 159.

144 doggerel verses. The two texts share important elements, most notably a narrative frame that introduces the theme. The economic analysis is analogous: self-interest promotes deceit, usury, hoarding, and crafty financial schemes, and it causes inflation, poverty, and hunger. The titles of both texts reference "eygen nutz" (self-interest), and their introductions describe the problem of inflation as point of departure. In other words, both texts start out stating an economic problem and its ramifications for humans.

The protagonist, this time wandering during the daytime, meets Caritas, who serves as the main allegorical figure in this text and is represented as a care-giving woman nursing two children.[35] Caritas is not defined as love of God but rather as the brotherly love alluded to in the title. In contrast to the monstrum of the 1527 poem, Caritas is a positive figure who has a voice in the story rather than one who is the object of the narrator's commentary. Caritas narrates the trauma of her victimization by another allegorical figure, self-interest. In an odd twist, self-interest has bitten off Caritas's feet.[36] The disfigured Caritas is forced to remain in hiding in the forest and therefore is no longer able to play a role in society. What is more, she has accepted defeat and now awaits the last judgment, which according to her assertions is near.

The wanderer, still shaken by Caritas's grievous injury, takes leave and offers this final reflection:

> The human is so very rotten due to self-love, which is passed down to us. Thus I and me, to me and mine govern alone on the entire earth. That in the words of the Christ the Lord the last judgment is very near, because love is so ice cold and self-interest governs with force, the deluge of all misery. May God turn it to the best! wishes Hans Sachs.[37]

The conclusion of the poem, presumably in Hans Sachs's own voice, is taking on a theological interpretation by linking self-love with the original sin, making self-interest man's inescapable destiny. The demise of brotherly love and the undisputed rule by self-interest will trigger the last judgment. This linkage of the dominance of self-interest with the last judgment is a reference to Luther's

---

[35] On the image of the nursing Caritas, see Freyhan, "The Evolution," 83–85.
[36] Caritas sometimes is shown as standing in bags of gold and money. Perhaps the idea is that self-interest in its greed did not just gobble up the wealth but also the legs of Caritas.
[37] Sachs, KG 3, 305, v. 29–38: "Das der mensch ist so gar verderbet | Durch eygne lieb, die auff uns erbet. | Das ich und mich, mir und das mein | Regiert auff gantzer erd allein, | Das nach des Herren Christi sag | Bald künfftig ist der jüngste tag, | Weil die lieb ist so gar erkalt | Unnd eygen nutz regiert mit gwalt | Die sündfluß alles ungemachs. | Gott wends zum besten! wünscht Hans Sachs."

theology: Luther read the spread of self-interest as a sign for the impending end of the world.[38]

The two poems end in a remarkably different fashion. While the 1527 text expands on the worldly effect of self-interest with economic and social consequences and ends in a prayer directed to God, the later text takes on a theological argumentation, but ends in an assessment of the divine implications, rather than in a direct plea to God.[39] Sachs presents the victory of self-interest and the impending last judgment as theological certainty; there is no plea to God to interfere, just a generic wish that God may turn everything around. By accepting the truth of human sinfulness, both texts are based on negative anthropology by showing a bleak world irreversibly corrupted by self-interest. The dichotomy between self-interest and common good, which was the foundation of the texts we have considered so far, is transformed into a dichotomy between self-interest and brotherly love.

In its theological reading, Sachs's poem *Klag der brüderlichen lieb uber den aygen nutz* certainly represents a low point in the literature about the common good. In terms of social and political analysis, it is an expression of deep anxieties about the evolving proto-capitalist economy that put increasing pressures on the guild system and its members and that threatened to disrupt the traditional social and political order in the city. Sachs's two poems discussed here, and in particular the later one from 1535, are good examples for the paradoxes of pluralization. Sachs took advantage of the emancipatory push of the Reformation – particularly in the Lutheran doctrine of universal priesthood – as it gave him the latitude to infuse his economic and social analysis with his own exegetic ramblings, which would have been impossible in a much more dogmatically controlled Catholic environment. In Sachs, we see the paradoxical case of a writer who enjoyed the benefits of pluralization by engaging in theological arguments as a lay person, while utterly condemning the economic and social ramifications of pluralization and upholding an inflexible, traditional moral code that does not allow space for alternate views and that no longer corresponds with the new social realities.

The views about the nature and indeed the primacy of the common good expressed by writers like Sebastian Brant, Ulrich von Hutten, Martin Bucer, Johannes Ferrarius, Hans Sachs, and many others are representative for literary discourses as well as for economic ethics of the late fifteenth and sixteenth centuries. Yet, their vehement pleas in support of the common good

---

38 Biehler, *Der Eigennutz*, 158.
39 Biehler (*Der Eigennutz*, 158) claims that "Sachs [beendet] das Gedicht konsequenterweise mit einer Anrufung Gottes, der allein die Herrschaft des Eigennutzes brechen könne."

appear like a last-gasp effort to salvage a vanishing value system and therefore are a strong indication of shifting attitudes. The concept of self-interest gained significant pragmatic acceptance in economic and political circles in the sixteenth century.[40] The texts discussed in Chapters 7 and 8 therefore can be read as a backlash against this shift in values. Moreover, the anxieties about the loss of traditional order and values that are the focus of Part I of this book pivoted in this vigorous justification of the common good, which served as a last line of defense.

Conrad Peutinger (1465–1547) served as the first intellectual apologist for the pursuit of self-interest in Germany. He vigorously opposed planned measures to curtail monopolies in the first three decades of the sixteenth century.[41] Peutinger argued that there was no law nor moral imperative to restrict the pursuit of one's own interests, to make profits, and even to accumulate wealth.[42] Peutinger's position was picked up on a theoretical, systematic level only in the second half of the sixteenth century, first in the tract *Von dem Lob deß Eigen Nutzen* (*The Praise of Self-Interest*; 1564) by the German soldier and military writer Leonhard Fronsperger (1520–1575). Fronsperger was a Lutheran from Ulm but spent his career serving in the imperial army. As such, he became one of the most prominent military writers of the sixteenth century.[43] Just like Brant and Sachs, Fronsperger saw his time as a period of crisis that posed a threat to the social order. In his view, both clergy and nobility were not performing their duties in support of their societies, which left the peasants with too much responsibility. The result was "disorder and divisiveness"[44] that would have been even worse "if I, self-interest, would not have come to aid in many ways."[45] Self-interest, which speaks in the first person in this text, describes itself as the savior of society and the deterrent for crisis.

This text has been read as a complete reversal in attitudes about self-interest, anticipating Bernard Mandeville's *The Fable of The Bees* (1705) and Adam Smith's *The Wealth of Nations* (1776),[46] who defined self-interest as the primary factor for the growth in the national economy.[47] However, it has been

---

[40] Schulze, "Vom Gemeinnutz," 602–604.
[41] This is discussed in more detail in Chapter 19.
[42] Schulze, "Das Wagnis," 275–276.
[43] Biehler, *Der Eigennutz*, 178–182.
[44] Fronsperger, *Von dem Lob*, fol. 17r: "vnordnung vnd zertrennung."
[45] Fronsperger, *Von dem Lob*, fol. 17v: "wo ich Eigner Nutzen sachen nicht etlicher massen zu hilff komme."
[46] Schulze, "Vom Gemeinnutz," 604–608.
[47] Fiori, "Individual and Self-Interest."

argued that Smith's notion of self-interest was not identical to selfishness or greed. Rather, self-interest was regulated by a need for mutual cooperation and a desire for approval.[48] Birgit Biehler's careful analysis similarly shows a more differentiated picture regarding Fronsperger,[49] and a close reading of his text bears this out.

The first-person narrator, the impersonator of self-interest, started out by admitting that self-interest was not well-received at the time. Then he compared self-interest to wine that could be healthy and delightful but harmful if abused[50] and to flattery, which he presented as morally objectionable, but which at the same time could prevent conflict and facilitate social relations.[51] He went on to claim that many realms of life were unthinkable without self-interest playing a pivotal role. Nobody was getting married out of concern for the common good, for instance, but rather was motivated by "naturally self-serving affect or naturally implanted desire."[52] His comment in the margins summed up the point: "In matrimony each is seeking his own interest."[53] Remarkably, matrimony was not just rooted in Scripture but also in common sense: "One has to recognize that marriage is the singular sustainer and extender of the human genus, not just out of a requirement by Holy Scripture but also out of human reason."[54] Fronsperger recognized human reason as a source of authority equal to the authority of the Bible. By challenging commonly accepted basic cultural notions, such as the primacy of the common good, he pushed an unconventional and pluralizing rhetoric.

In the following chapters, Fronsperger showed how central self-interest was for providing people with food and clothing. Farmers or artisans did not produce out of the desire to feed and clothe others; rather, they were motivated by their desire to provide for themselves and their own families. Merchants were entirely motivated by self-interest:

> For which merchant ever traveled across the oceans and risked his life and livelihood in order to bring spices and other merchandise from India, which serve humans not just for

---

48 Werhane, "The Role of Self-Interest," 670.
49 Biehler, *Der Eigennutz*, 177–206.
50 Fronsperger, *Von dem Lob*, fol. 4r.
51 Fronsperger, *Von dem Lob*, fol. 5v–6r.
52 Fronsperger, *Von dem Lob*, fol. 13r: "natürlich eigennützig affect/ oder natürlich eingepflantzte begirlichkeit."
53 Fronsperger, *Von dem Lob*, fol. 13r: "Jm Ehestand suchet jeder sein eigen nutzen."
54 Fronsperger, *Von dem Lob*, fol. 12r: "Also/ daß man bekennen müsse/ nicht allein auß zwang der heyligen Schrifft/ sonder auch auß menschlicher vernunfft/ daß der Ehestand sey ein einziger erhalter vnd erweiter deß menschlichen Geschlechts."

sustenance but also for the maintenance of health, just for the common good, if he was not motivated by self-interest and avarice?[55]

As economic activity was motivated by the desire for personal gain, so was secular and religious governance. Government, in Fronsperger's argument, did not happen because of the princes' desire to serve the common good, but because of their desire to be in charge. This could be a mixed blessing, as Fronsperger conceded, as the pursuit of self-interest also contained the potential for conflict and war.

Fronsperger was not an unconditional apologist for self-interest. Rather, he was an undogmatic pragmatist who did not take a great interest in intricate philosophical or theological points. To him, the common good was a theoretical construct that did not correspond to a reality he experienced as military leader and publicist: "One talks about the common good, but nobody knows it, nobody has seen or recognized it. Yet, everybody scolds me because of it."[56] Fronsperger did not oppose the notion of the common interest. Rather, as a theoretical artifice without practical value it was not a useful category for his pragmatic discourse. Self-interest, on the other hand, was a tangible, pragmatic category that warranted an emotionally detached examination.

Nevertheless, Fronsperger showed a great interest in embedding his observations in Scripture. In chapter sixteen, he based his discussion on Matthew 19: 17–24 where a Christian asks Jesus what he has to do to be saved. While in Matthew, Jesus lists most of the Ten Commandments, according to Fronsperger the response is reduced to this: "He should love God and his neighbor as himself."[57] Fronsperger's marginal notes sum this up: "The common good is that one help the other."[58] Fronsperger rejected the standard interpretation of Jesus's concluding metaphor, namely that it was easier for a camel to go through the eye of a needle than for a rich man to enter into the kingdom of God (Matthew 19:24). There was no need for the rich man to give away his wealth charitably for the sake of his salvation as Jesus's teachings were intended to be spiritual in nature:

---

55 Fronsperger, *Von dem Lob*, fol. 18v: "Denn welcher Kauffmann ist je vber Meer gefahren/ hat sein Leib vnd Leben gewagt/ daß er Specerey oder andere Kauffmannschafft so den Menschen nicht allein zu der Speiß/ sonder auch zur gesundheit höchlich dienet/ auß Jndia herüber brechte/ gemeinem nutz zu gut/ wenn jn nicht Eigner nutz oder geitz darzu reitzte."
56 Fronsperger, *Von dem Lob*, fol. 37v: "Man redt von gemeinem Nutz/ vnnd kennet jhn doch niemand/ hat jhn auch niemand gesehen/ oder erkennt/ Aber dennoch schilt mich jedermann dargegen."
57 Fronsperger, *Von dem Lob*, fol. 31r: "Er solt Gott lieben vnd den Nechsten als sich selbs."
58 Fronsperger, *Von dem Lob*, fol. 31r: "Gemeiner Nutz ist/ dz einer dem anderen zu hilff komme."

"In my opinion, the meaning is generally more spiritual than physical, meaning that one should love God and one's neighbor spiritually."[59] According to Fronsperger, wealth did not have to be given away in a physical form. If that was the case, wealth would simply be transferred to others who had not produced it. The metaphor of the camel and the eye of the needle therefore took on a different meaning:

> That he should be prepared to serve his neighbor with all that God has bestowed upon him, be it in terms of body, reason, art, honor, or possessions, and to help maintain the before-mentioned great rules in praise and honor of God.[60]

Honoring God was best accomplished through brotherly love, which became the guiding ethical principle throughout Fronsperger's text.

Fronsperger recognized an obvious chasm between the ethical literature on the common good and what he observed as real human behavior and its consequences.[61] His perspective was informed by economic processes he observed empirically, not by abstract ethical norms. This "new respect and even justification for private gain" has been referred to as "economic humanism," a term John F. McGovern defined as "an appreciation of the economic activity of individuals."[62] Fronsperger was a rare voice defending the economic status quo in spite of the broad critique in the literature. Yet Fronsperger did not reject the common good as an ideal. While he dismissed it as an end in itself as it was promoted by most books and pamphlets of the time, his rootedness in the notion of neighborly love reframed rather than refuted the idea of communal interest and grounded it more firmly in religious thinking. At the same time, Fronsperger's text offered more discretionary, individualistic space to translate religious principles into ethical action and thus became an important voice for pluralization.

Yet, Fronsperger's views were not broadly received at the time. Only by the beginning of the seventeenth century was the notion of self-interest normalized as a legitimate category of reason of state in the writings of Hugo Grotius (1583–1645), the theoretician of international law.[63] More conventional views on

---

59 Fronsperger, *Von dem Lob*, fol. 32r: "So ist doch meins erachtens der verstand inn gemein mehr Geistlich denn Leiblich/ Also daß Geistlich Gott vnd deinen Nechsten lieb haben."
60 Fronsperger, *Von dem Lob*, fol. 33v: "Also daß er bereit ist mit allem dem/ das jm Gott verliehen hat/ es sey an Leib/ Vernunfft/ Kunst/ Ehr oder Gut/ seinem nechtsten zu dienen/ vnd obgemelte grosse Policey Gott zu Lob vnd Ehr/ helfen zu erhalten."
61 Biehler, *Der Eigennutz*, 187.
62 McGovern, "The Rise," 225.
63 Tang, *Imagining World Order*, 61.

the primacy of the common good prevailed up to that point, both in literary and ethical texts. A good example is Paul Negelein's (1562–1627) *Vom Burgerlichen Standt* (*On the Bourgeois Estate*), a handbook for the urban middle classes published in 1600. He presented a conventional viewpoint: "Whatever concerns an entire community should be privileged over the singular interest."[64] He drew a well-established analogy between the human and political bodies that Johannes Ferrarius in his *Von dem Gemeinen nutze* (1533) had used.[65] Just like each part of the body had its own, separate function, so did each member of society – an analogy that also justified the hierarchical structure of the social order. The structure of the community followed the same pattern: "Likewise, the beautiful, gorgeous edifice of the common good will topple by necessity wherever self-interest has taken over and each only takes an interest in his own penny."[66]

Negelein's tract also had Neo-Stoic elements that were lacking in earlier treatises. He dispassionately appealed to individuals to use self-knowledge and general conflict avoidance to maintain the communal order. The most important element was self-control with the demand "that no one should desire too much for himself, but rather should be content with the little that he has."[67] The polemic against self-interest thus added a different, a-political dimension in the seventeenth century: the Neo-Stoic renunciation of material luxuries in the pursuit of individual contentment and happiness.

---

[64] Negelein, *Vom Burgerlichen Standt*, 323: "Was ein gantze Gemein betrifft/ sol dem eigenen vorgezogen werden."
[65] Ferrarius, *Von dem Gemeinen nutze*, fol. 9r–10r.
[66] Negelein, *Vom Burgerlichen Standt*, 323: "Eben also auch der schöne herrliche Baw deß gemeinen Nutzes/ wo der eigen Nutz vberhand genommen hat/ vnd ein jeder nur auff seinen Rap gedenckt/ über ein hauffen fallen muß."
[67] Negelein, *Vom Burgerlichen Standt*, 328: "daß ihme keiner zu viel begern/ sondern mit dem wenigen so er hat/ sich begnügen lassen soll."

Part II: **Staying Home: Resistance to Expanding Spatial Horizons**

> There is talk of a new astrologer who wants to prove that the earth moves and goes around instead of the sky, the sun, the moon, just as if somebody were moving in a carriage or ship might hold that he was sitting still and at rest while the earth and the trees walked and moved. But that is how things are nowadays: when a man wishes to be clever he must [...] invent something special.
>
> – Martin Luther, Table Talk No. 4638 (1539)

It is a commonplace that the period around 1500 was marked by European exploration and expansion. We also witness an "unprecedented explosion in mobility, in regard to both increased range and frequency of travel."[1] The Portuguese explored the coast of West Africa throughout the fifteenth century,[2] culminating in the first voyage around Africa by Vasco da Gama in 1497–1499 to connect with the spice markets in India. Likewise, the Spaniards sought to reach East Asian markets in a westerly direction, beginning with Columbus's first journey of 1492–1493. While the Spaniards only made a permanent connection with Asia with the founding of the port of Manila in 1571, they managed to build up a vast colonial empire in the Americas in the interim.

In the Early Modern period, fundamental changes occurred in the way the world was imagined, which informed the quest for discoveries and the creation of global trade networks. In a feedback loop, discoveries and networks in turn affected how the world was imagined. Perhaps the most important innovation in Early Modern Europe was a fundamental change of intellectual conceptions of space and of the human relationship to it. The link between knowledge and space was famously established by Petrarch when he climbed Mont Ventoux in 1336 just to gain a different perspective on spatial relations. At the tail end of Humanism, Francis Bacon in the famous frontispiece to his *Novum Organum* (1620) showed ships sailing into the open space past the Pillars of Hercules at the Strait of Gibraltar that had marked the end of the known world since antiquity. The newly discovered endlessness of geographic space thus became a metaphor for limitless human knowledge.

A central and radical innovation in the imagination of space was the development of linear perspective, which, in the words of Robert T. Tally, "not only enabled more 'accurate' pictorial representations in the visual arts but also occasioned a wholesale re-imagining of space and of human spatial relations."[3] Linear perspective allowed for a more accurate pictorial representation of three-dimensional space, allowed for a precise capture of human spatial relations, and thus altered the human experience of space and place.[4] Linear perspective thus allowed for a different interpretation of the world.[5] The medieval view of space that was based on the Aristotelian view of spaces as finite and discontinuous was no longer tenable as a mathematically ordered, infinite, homogeneous, and

---

1 Harris, "Long-Distance Corporations," 275.
2 For the interaction between the Portuguese and African polities in the fifteenth century see Bennett, *African Kings and Black Slaves*.
3 Tally, *Spatiality*, 17.
4 Tally, *Spatiality*, 17–18.
5 Goldstein, *The Social and Cultural Roots*, 151.

isotropic notion of space emerged.⁶ Medieval Europeans saw their place in the world in relation to the Holy Land, represented by the centrality of Jerusalem in the medieval *mappamundi* that was as much dedicated to biblical instruction and the representation of the divine plan as to geographical information. T-O maps had an easterly orientation, placing Asia on top.⁷

The emerging heliocentric worldview und the understanding of the earth as an endless sphere were indebted to geometry, mathematical calculation, empirical observation, and pragmatic experience. They were also amplified by instruments like the sextant, the compass, and, later, the telescope. This changed the focus of map making: the representation of the transcendental, theological meaning was displaced by the pragmatic need to give an accurate rendition of physical space that could be used for commerce and navigation.⁸ The two large-scale world maps produced by Martin Waldseemüller in 1507 and 1516 captured this transformation in spatial thinking and representation in an exemplary fashion.⁹ The production of the first surviving globe by Martin Behaim in 1492, the famous *Erdapfel* (earth-apple),¹⁰ and the subsequent creations by the globe maker Johannes Schöner coincided with the desire to see the world as a three-dimensional space that had lost its sense of a privileged directional orientation.

Given the magnitude of this transformation, it is not surprising that socially constructed space and spatial relations became central features in texts across the generic spectrum, a circumstance that has been described as a spatial turn.¹¹ Part II of this book investigates the textual evidence for a spatial turn but also traces a growing resistance against it, particularly in popular literature. The resistance took on multiple forms, such as negative representations of travel and indeed of any kind of mobility, and rejection of new discoveries and critical treatments of their epistemological consequences. Part III will examine how these changed notions of space affected economic processes and their perception.

---

6 Tally, *Spatiality*, 19.
7 Tally (*Spatiality*, 20) points out that the term "orientation" itself means "facing east."
8 Tally, *Spatiality*, 20–21.
9 Hessler and Van Duzer, *Seeing the World Anew*.
10 Leitch, *Mapping Ethnography*, 21.
11 Tally uses this term as a heading in *Spatiality*, 11–43.

Chapter 9
Spatial Expansion and Its Narratives

The spatial expansion around 1500 was accompanied by a rising number of narratives that focused on it. Travel and explorations thus increasingly became an integral part of a public discourse that did not elude even those who had no travel experience.[12] The range of these narratives is vast. The late medieval pilgrim reports to the Holy Land in many ways served as a blueprint for the new reports.[13] Bernhard von Breydenbach in his *Peregrinatio in terram sanctam* (*Pilgrimage to the Holy Land*, 1486), for instance, described modes of travel, cities and other landmarks found along the way, and encounters with locals, particularly non-Christian populations.[14] At the same time, these pilgrim reports insisted that travel took place exclusively in the pursuit of spiritual cleansing and salvation and not out of curiosity and worldly gratification. This justification was important as the false and nefarious pilgrim had become a literary commonplace in the late Middle Ages.[15] The Nuremberg patrician Hans Tucher the Elder (1428–1491), for instance, insisted that he traveled to the Holy Land in 1479–1480 "with the intent and idea to pursue God's honor and the salvation of my soul, but not for the sake of fame, curiosity, nor some other frivolity."[16] Tucher was well aware of the contemporaneous anxieties that surrounded travel.

Reports relating to the establishment of Portuguese trade ventures played an important role in expanding knowledge of hitherto unknown areas of Africa and Asia and in creating the awareness of rapidly expanding trade networks in Germany. The first such report in Germany was the anonymous *Den rechten weg auß zu faren von Lißbona gen Kallakuth* (*To Travel on the Right Path from Lisbon to Calicut*) from 1506 that chronicled Vasco da Gama's pioneering voyage around Africa. Balthasar Springer's (d. 1509) *Die Merfart vnd erfarung nüwer Schiffung vnd Wege zů viln onerkanten Inseln und Künigreichen* (*The Ocean Voyage and Discovery of New Navigation Routes and Paths to Many Unknown*

---

12 Treue, *Abenteuer und Anerkennung*, 15.
13 Legassie (*The Medieval Invention of Travel*, viii) views late medieval pilgrimage reports as a form of "literate labor" that engaged in "a prolonged cultural debate about the individual and collective benefits of voyages to various parts of the world."
14 Mozer, "Vorwort," XXI–XXIV.
15 Legassie, *The Medieval Invention of Travel*, 5–6.
16 Tucher, *Nach Cristi*, title page: "jn willen vnnd maÿnung allein vmb gotes ere vnd meiner sel seligkeit vnd keines růmes/ firbitzes/ noch anndere leichtfertigkeit willen."

Islands and Kingdoms) from 1509 is a first-hand account by a Welser factor who had traveled to India in 1505–1506; it is richly illustrated with woodcuts by Hans Burgkmair.

Subsequent travel reports from Spanish encounters in the Americas had the added function of official accounts to justify actions performed in the West Indies in the name of the Spanish Crown, known as *probanza de mérito*. Publications of such narratives also sought to relate the wonders of lands far away and relied on their entertainment value, particularly in parts of Europe without direct involvement with the colonial project, like Germany. These narratives have in common a relatively unproblematic relationship with non-European spaces, which were mostly framed in terms of their novelty, although accounts of encounters with non-Christians represented challenges, both in terms of actual events and their textual representations. The only German-language text of this kind was Nikolaus Federmann's *Jndianische Historia* (*Indian History*), which was written around 1532 but only published in 1557. It chronicled his time as military leader in Venezuela in 1530–1531.

A number of these narratives entered Germany early on. Initially, German translations of the famous Columbus letter and of the even more influential accounts by Amerigo Vespucci were printed in Germany. German printers also were responsible for publishing some of the earliest illustrations of the Americas that were most commonly inspired by Vespucci's *Mundus Novus*. This includes the famous engraving printed in Augsburg by Johann Froschauer around 1503 that is believed to be the first visual representation of New World anthropophagy.[17] Until 1550, more texts relating to the Americas were published in Germany than in any other area of Europe,[18] which is primarily due to the preeminence of German printers in cities like Basel, Strasbourg, Augsburg, and Nuremberg and to the prominent role of the Frankfurt book fair, which remained the unchallenged center of the European book trade in the early modern period.[19] While there is surprisingly little evidence for a strong reception of these texts in Germany, they nevertheless made knowledge about spatial discoveries available to a wide range of German readers.

Compilations of texts relating to European discoveries became common already in the first decade of the sixteenth century, and they played an important role in the popularization of the knowledge about the newly discovered lands. Early such compilations contain texts of different provenance and covering

---

[17] Leitch, *Mapping Ethnography*, 137.
[18] Sixel, "Die deutsche Vorstellung," 46–47.
[19] Pettegree, *The Book in the Renaissance*, 79.

different genres, and they also do not distinguish between discoveries in Asia and in the Americas as America was seen as an island archipelago belonging to Asia well into the sixteenth century. One of the earliest compilations is Jobst Ruchamer's *Newe vnbekanthe landte Und ein newe weldte in kurtz verganger zeythe erfunden* (*New Unknown Lands and a New World Found in the Recent Past*) from 1508. It is a translation of a compilation published in Italian in 1507 by Fracanzano da Montalboddo under the title *Paesi Novamente retrovati*.[20]

In the introduction to the German edition of the anthology, which was not part of Montalboddo's text, Ruchamer asserted his desire to acquaint German readers with "such wondrous and hitherto unheard-of things which in many places contradict the writings of the old masters of nature and erudite scholars."[21] Ruchamer expressed awe and wonderment "that the Christians undertook such distant, dangerous, unknown, and marvelous travels or journeys by ship."[22] He made it clear that this was new knowledge the Ancients knew nothing about. To Ruchamer, the travel that led to these discoveries was entirely legitimate, particularly as it had been ordered by the kings of Portugal and Spain. Furthermore, the findings were so spectacular and interesting that they easily justified the journey of exploration:

> For they found in these places wondrous, beautiful, and entertaining islands with naked, black people with strange and unheard-of customs and manners, also strange and wondrous animals, birds, prized trees, spices, many kinds of precious stones, pearls, and gold, which are held in high esteem by us but considered common there.[23]

Ruchamer conveyed admiration for the strange foreign lands described here and for the explorers who generated the knowledge represented in his compilation. Even the wildness and nakedness of native populations were not grounds for negative comments, and his attitude toward the discoveries was generally marked by curiosity and wonderment.

---

20 Ankenbauer, *Paesi novamente retrovati*. For the reception of Montalboddo's compilation in Germany see Pieper, *Die Vermittlung*, 137–140.
21 Ruchamer, *Newe vnbekanthe landte*, "vorrede," sig. A1v: "so wunderbarliche vnd byßhere vnerhörte dinge/ welche auch an etlichen orten den geschrifften der alten Natürlichen Mayster vnd hochgelerten wyderwertig sein."
22 Ruchamer, *Newe vnbekanthe landte*, "vorrede," sig. A1v: "das die Christen sulche weythe/ verliche/ vnbekanthe vnd wunderbarliche rayße ader schieffarthe gethan haben."
23 Ruchamer, *Newe vnbekanthe landte*, "vorrede," sig. A1v: "Dann sie an den selbigen orthen gefunden haben/ wunderbarliche schöne vnd lustige jnseln/ mit nackenden schwartzen lewten seltzamer vnd vnerhörten sitten vnd weyse/ auch seltzamen vnd wunderlichen thyeren/ geflügeln köstlichen bawmen/ spetzereyen/ mancherley edeln gestayne/ berlen vnd golde/ welche bey vns hoch geacht/ vnd daselbste bey jnen gemayn sein."

The positive attitude toward the discoveries in part was due to the higher purpose they served, as Ruchamer noted in the conclusion of his introduction:

> May many recognize and investigate the great miraculous wonders of God the Almighty who created and adorned the world with many kinds of humans, lands, islands, and strange creatures (as indicated above), which all before this time had been unknown in Christendom and in our nation. And what is almost miraculous is that the Christians undertook such distant, dangerous, unknown, and wondrous travels or journeys by boat.[24]

In Ruchamer's argument, even the recently discovered parts of the world were part of God's creation, as was the diversity among humans, other creatures, and landscapes; diversity was innate in God's design of the world and thus was worthy of being explored and becoming subject of his creation narrative. The implication is that even those humans who had lived completely outside of the known Christian realm were worthy as God's children. What is more, Ruchamer admired the curiosity of the travelers and framed the courage to face the dangers of travel to the unknown parts of the world as miraculous.

Paratexts to travel narratives, both compilations and editions of single texts, generally conveyed a positive attitude toward travel and discoveries. On the title page of his *Merfart* from 1509, Balthasar Springer (d. 1509) asserted that he had "gesehen vnd erfaren" (seen and experienced) everything he was writing about.[25] In the first paragraph of the text, Springer repeated that he had personally witnessed everything he described, and specifically "the wondrous newly found lands, kingdoms, islands, and regions."[26] The sense of wonderment was common in these narratives as it implied a sense of admiration for God's creation, which then legitimately could be experienced by travelers without running afoul of edicts against curiosity.

The 1507 German edition of John Mandeville's travels made the reference to "erfarung," the experience made during travel, in the title of the book: *Von. der. erfarüng. des. strengen. Ritters johannes. von. Montauille.* (*Of the Experience*

---

[24] Ruchamer, *Newe vnbekanthe landte*, "vorrede," sig. A1v: "Auff das meniglich erkennen vnd erkündigen mochte/ die großen wunderbarlichen wunder gottes des almechtigen/ der die welte mit so mancherley geschlechten der menschen/ landen/ jnseln vnd seltzamen creaturen (wie oben angezaygt ist) erschaffen und gezyerthe hat/ welches alles vor dyser zeite/ bey der Christenhayte vnd vnser natione ist vnbekante gewesen. Vnd auch welches vast wunderbarlich ist/ das die Christen sulche weythe/ verliche/ vnbekanthe vnd wunderbarliche rayße ader schieffarthe gethan haben."

[25] Borowka-Clausberg (*Balthasar Sprenger*, 83–84) supports this claim of a factual and realistic representation.

[26] Springer, *Merfart*, sig. A2r: "die wunderbarlichen new erfunden lande/ kunigreich Jnseln vnd gegene." Springer sometimes is referred to as Sprenger.

of the Brave Knight John of Mandeville). The introductory paragraph justified the purpose of this German translation:

> So that the Germans also may read in it of many wondrous things that are described here, of foreign lands and strange animals, of foreign people and of their faith, of their nature, of their clothes, and of many other miracles.[27]

The editor stressed the virtues of getting to know wondrous things, foreign countries and their people, and generally framed the encounter with the non-European other in positive terms. The experience of the world was praised without apparent limitations to human curiosity. The post-script, perhaps the work of the Strasbourg printer Johannes Knobloch, again praised many forms of travel because it increased knowledge and insight into important matters and urged readers to seek out the unknown:[28]

> One reason why one travels through many countries is to achieve knighthood, the other because of worship, the third because of commerce, the fourth in order to experience marvels, and the fifth because of devotion and love.[29]

In the eyes of this editor, there were no limitations for travel as all forms were legitimate, even travel motivated by curiosity and by a desire to experience the marvels of the world. As the entire universe was God's creation, the desire to explore it was endorsed by the editor: "I want to reveal the itineraries and countries to all those who want to experience the lands, and also to those who want to recognize God through his miraculous works."[30] Like Ruchamer's introduction, the paratexts from the 1507 German Mandeville edition mentioned the two most common justifications for travel that emerged in the late Middle Ages: "to recognize God through His miraculous works" and the genuine interest in foreign lands and people.[31]

---

27 Mandeville, *Von der erfarüng*, sig. A1v: "Vff das die teütschen auch mügen darinne lesen. von mannigen wunderbaren sachen die dar in geschriben stönd/ von fremden landen und seltzamen thieren/ von fremden leuten vnd von iren glauben. von irem wesen. vnd von iren cleidern vnd von vil andern wundern."
28 Müller, "*Erfarung*," 312.
29 Mandeville, *Von der erfarüng*, sig. M6r: "Darumb durch fert einer vil landes durch ritterschaft der ander durch andacht/ der trit durch kauffmanschatz/ der vierde wunder zů erfarenn/ der funfft vmb mynn vnd lieb."
30 Mandeville, *Von der erfarüng*, sig. M6r: "wil ich denen die dy land erfaren/ auch denen die got durch syn wunderwerck erkennen wöllen die weg vnd land [...] allent halben verkünden."
31 Müller, "*Erfarung*," 312.

This tolerance and even admiration of strange people in foreign lands goes back to Augustine's *City of God* (XVI, 8), in which Augustine argued that alien people and monstruous races, as Pliny had described them in his *Natural History* (VII, 2, 15–16), very much were part of God's creation and had to be accepted as such. Based on Augustine, a number of German commentators took the trouble to explain how these stories of strange and alien people in fact aided Christian contemplation and thus further integrated the newly discovered lands and peoples into a unified vision of God's creation.[32] Hartmann Schedel must have remembered these lines from Augustine when he argued in his *Nuremberg Chronicle* (1493) that the monstrous races described by Pliny very much were part of God's design of the world and thus a natural part of this world: "For as the the almighty God knew in what likeness and diversity he created the beauty of the world, he also wanted to introduce monstrous humans into the world."[33] Schedel's argument is particularly significant because Schedel did not seek to legitimize a travel narrative but rather presented this argument in a chronicle. But as we will see in the discussion of Sebastian Brant's *Narrenschiff*, which was published almost simultaneously, this viewpoint was not shared universally at the time.

While there were a number of German-language travel texts published shortly after 1500, their number decreased in the second decade of the sixteenth century as interest in the discoveries generally appears to have waned. Pieper notes that new discoveries after 1503, such as the discovery of the Isthmus of Panama and of the Pacific Ocean in 1513, were barely noted outside of the Iberian Peninsula.[34] Germans traveling to foreign lands played a subordinate role in the narratives of the first half of the sixteenth century. This changed only with first-person accounts of their New World adventures by Nikolaus Federmann (1557), Hans Staden (1557), and Ulrich Schmidel (1567). What the three texts have in common is that their stories were clearly anchored in a sense of place and space.

Later sixteenth-century German travel narratives focusing on the adventures of one single explorer or adventurer followed the emerging pattern of Spanish accounts of the New World that were mostly framed as a *probanza de mérito*, that is reports to the Spanish Crown on conquest activities and on individual merits of the reporting conquistador. While the humanity of the indigenous peoples was a given, their descriptions focused on the resources they

---

[32] Johnson, *The German Discovery*, 38–40.
[33] Schedel, *Nuremberg Chronicle*, fol. 11v: "dann als der almechtig got wißet mit was gleichnus vnd manigformigkait er die schön der werlt beschuff do wolt er auch wundergestalte menschen in die werlt einfüren."
[34] Pieper, *Die Vermittlung*, 26.

had to offer to European invaders and on the adversarial relationships with them. The narratives typically began with the protagonists departing from their European base and concluded with the journey back home, the main focus of the narrative being on the locus of exploration. These texts, too, framed travel as a positive experience, and the foreign spaces were represented in a way that instilled curiosity in the reader. A good German-language example is Hans Staden's *Warhaftige Historia vnd beschreibung eyner Landtschafft der Wilden/ Nacketen/ Grimmigen Menschenfresser Leuthen/ in der Newenwelt America gelegen* (*The True History and Description of a Country Populated by a Wild, Naked, and Savage Man-Eating People, Located in the New World, America*), published in 1557. The focus of Johann Dryander's dedication of the text was not a justification of travel and exploration; rather it served to affirm the truthfulness of Staden's narrative in the context of his outlandish allegations of cannibalism by the Tupinambá in Brazil. The legitimacy of Staden's adventure seems self-evident as it was not even flagged as a potential issue.

All these travel narratives are not the focus of Part II as they generally were concerned with travel and spatial expansion and uncritically framed them in a positive light as generic norms required. Dedications and introductions to these texts generally had the task to justify and legitimate travel and adventure; their function was not a critical examination of travel and spatial exploration. From a rhetorical viewpoint, the justification of the exploration narratives in paratexts is self-evident, like in Ruchamer's introduction. Furthermore, the narratives themselves served to validate journeys to countries and territories far away and to justify the actions of Europeans in these lands. These texts were briefly discussed here to illustrate that there were widely divergent discourses on this topic between the late fifteenth and the middle of the sixteenth century. This chapter also served to establish a knowledge base for the period and a benchmark for later discussion of the rejection of this literature and the spatial concepts represented here.

The key questions for the remaining chapters of Part II are these: how was the impact of the European spatial expansion felt and represented in German culture in the first half of the sixteenth century? How was the knowledge of the spatial expansion integrated, framed, and related in general texts that did not describe travel and had no explicit spatial agenda? What were the cultural responses to the expansion of spatial horizons and to the notion of travel for the sake of discovery? And, more generally, what were the responses to growing insight that the classical world view, which was based on the existence of three continents grouped around the Mediterranean, was no longer tenable? The key argument of the subsequent chapters is that in popular literary texts a powerful counternarrative developed, one that rejected the discoveries and the narratives associated with them.

Chapter 10
From Chronicle to Cosmography (and Chorography): The Rise of Synchronic Narratives of the World

Chronicles have a long history going back to Antiquity, peaking in the late Roman period.[1] Chronicles are prose texts that give an overview of historical events in chronological order, typically beginning with biblical history and leading up to the present. With the growing interest in human history in the late Middle Ages, chronicles rose to new prominence.[2] At the same time, chroniclers started to add information about cities, territories, and empires. The premise of this chapter is that chronicles increasingly included some geographic and even cultural information. This chapter therefore will trace the gradual transformation of chronicles, the formation of hybrid genres, and the rise of cosmographical and chorographical texts that privilege spatial, cultural, and anthropological over chronological information.

In the late Middle Ages, chronicles became important vehicles to lay claim to territories or to prove the legitimacy and heroic history of ruling dynasties. Chronicles of princely houses legitimized their dynastic claims, and regional chronicles served to assert the autonomy of territories and to form regional identities. Examples of the former are the Bavarian chronicles by Ulrich Fuetrer (c.1430–1496) and by Johannes Aventinus (born Johann Georg Turmair, 1477–1534). A number of Swiss chronicles attempted to achieve the latter: they sought to legitimize the freedom and sovereignty of the Swiss Confederation within the confines of the empire and recounted its political and military rise. Prominent examples are the *Weisses Buch von Sarnen* (*White Book of Sarnen*, 1470–1472) by Hans Schriber, the chronicles by Diebold Schilling father and son, and the later chronicles by the Humanist Aegidius Tschudi.[3]

The best-known and most important general chronicle of the late fifteenth century is the *Nuremberg Chronicle* by Hartmann Schedel (1440–1514), also known as *Liber Chronicarum*,[4] which was published in a Latin and then German

---

1 Leitch, *Mapping Ethnography*, 19.
2 For an overview of medieval chronicles in the vernacular, see Gärtner, "Die Tradition," 57–71.
3 Johannes Carion in his *Chronica* (fol. 156r) noted the existence of a number of Swiss chronicles.
4 In line with traditional manuscript practice, the *Chronicle* does not have a proper title page. Its first page is the title page of the index, which identifies the text as s chronicle. (Füssel,

edition, both in 1493.[5] This was perhaps the most important incunable printed in Germany other than the Gutenberg Bible, and it certainly was the most complex printing project before 1500.[6] It has to be regarded as the prototype for the vast cosmographic literature in the sixteenth century. It is lavishly illustrated with 1,804 woodcuts printed from 652 different wood blocks and thus was technologically advanced and even experimental; it is the most heavily illustrated book of the fifteenth century.[7]

The printer Anton Koberger published a separate broadsheet advertisement in which he applauded the singularity of the project and its centrality for the self-representation of the city of Nuremberg: "Nothing like this has hitherto appeared to increase the delight of men of learning and of everyone who has any education at all: the new book of chronicles with its pictures of famous men and cities which has just been printed at the expense of rich citizens of Nuremberg."[8] At the same time, Schedel's book was intellectually cautious and adverse to innovation in the knowledge it represented. Rather it was a compilation of existing knowledge based on recent authorities.[9] We have to assume that Schedel was primarily a compiler, using a number of sources in manuscript and printed form.[10] The novelty was in the aspiration to include all of world knowledge in a vast and ambitious project that plainly entertained the "ambition to place Nuremberg at the centre of an encyclopedic rendering of world history."[11]

The *Nuremberg Chronicle* gives an overview of the Seven Ages of the World, a medieval tradition of structuring human history from Creation to the Last Judgement that was still used in some chronicles around 1500. The book is subdivided into the Seven Ages, each corresponding to a distinct phase of biblical history, in analogy to the seven days of creation. The first five Ages tell the biblical and classical histories until the birth of Christ. The Sixth Age ranges from the birth of Christ to the days of Schedel. It takes up more than half of the *Nuremberg*

Hartmann Schedel, 634.) This is the reason why different titles are used to refer to the book, such as *Schedelsche Weltchronik* in German.

5 The Latin text was drafted by Schedel himself, while the Nuremberg city official Georg Alt provoded the German translation. For the process of translation, see Green, "Text, Culture," 114–132, and Green, "Translating Time," 162–177.
6 Ashcroft, "Black Arts," 6.
7 McLean, *The 'Cosmographia' of Sebastian Münster*, 116.
8 Quoted in Pettegree, *The Book in the Renaissance*, 41.
9 Ashcroft, "Black Arts," 6; Leitch, *Mapping Ethnography*, 19.
10 Vogel, "Schedel als Kompilator," 73–97. For a thorough discussion of the sources and the production of the book see the monograph by Reske, *Die Produktion*.
11 Pettegree, *The Book in the Renaissance*, 41.

Chronicle and includes the vast majority of the famous city woodcuts.[12] From the beginning of the book, Schedel sought to tell the parallel biblical and classical histories; he even called Plato the Moses from Attica.[13] Schedel unsuccessfully attempted to reconcile a medieval Christian teleology with the Humanist vision of classical revival and the dawn of a new era.[14]

Yet, the biblical and classical strands of history remain strangely juxtaposed and are not integrated into a unified vision. Schedel failed to fuse biblical and secular history into a singular narrative, as McLean states.[15] Moses, the "divine prophet and chronicler,"[16] for instance, predated the Trojan War by some years and thus was put in a common chronological order yet stood in no relation to Greek history. When the two narratives were in competition, he privileged the biblical narrative: "But in the way Moses talks about how God created the world, he refutes three errors by Plato, Aristotle, and Epicurus."[17] The Platonic theory of matter and form did not apply because God created the world out of nothing, without pre-existing and prepared matter.[18] The six days of creation were related to the twelve celestial spheres, the illustrations showing an increasing number of spheres being created stage by stage.[19] The woodcut illustrating the finished creation on the seventh day shows the Ptolemaic spheres with the earth consisting of four elements at its center.[20]

In his account of the five Ages from creation to the birth of Christ, the biblical narrative was interrupted by the history of ancient cultures with the goal to achieve an integrated chronology. But early on, the narrative was interjected by descriptive and explanatory sections. Schedel took the description of Paradise, with the four rivers emanating from a spring within Paradise, as an opportunity for a geographic or cosmographic digression that not only named the four rivers – Ganges, Nile, Tigris, and Euphrates – but also described their geographies and provided other noteworthy information.[21] The segment on Noah's Ark was

---

[12] Schedel used 90 folios to cover the first five ages but 163 to cover the sixth (Gärtner, "Die Tradition," 59).
[13] Schedel, *Nuremberg Chronicle*, fol. 1r.
[14] Ashcroft, "Black Arts," 9.
[15] McLean, *The 'Cosmographia' of Sebastian Münster*, 115.
[16] Schedel, *Nuremberg Chronicle*, fol. 2r: "gottlich prophet vnd geschicht beschreiber."
[17] Schedel, *Nuremberg Chronicle*, fol. 2r: "Aber in dem das Moyses spricht das got beschaffen hab so stelt er damit ab drey irrung Platonis Aristotilis vnd Epicuri."
[18] Schedel, *Nuremberg Chronicle*, fol. 2r.
[19] Schedel, *Nuremberg Chronicle*, fol. 2v–5r.
[20] Schedel, *Nuremberg Chronicle*, fol. 5v. For a discussion of the cosmological dimension see Rowan, "Chronicle as Cosmos."
[21] Schedel, *Nuremberg Chronicle*, fol.7v–8v.

supplemented by an extensive description of misshapen and malformed human beings, complete with twenty-one small illustrations derived from Pliny's catalogue of monstrous races.[22] His later narration of the post-Noah genealogy was interrupted by a two-page world map largely in a Ptolemaic tradition that shows the three continents with subsequent descriptions. Aside from some islands off West Africa, the map does not feature any discoveries made in the fifteenth century.[23] Nevertheless, at the end of the book Schedel described the Portuguese discovery of a number of islands off the African coast exceeding the representation on the map.[24]

Schedel's *Nuremberg Chronicle* is famous for the many woodcuts showing important European cities. Thirty-two of the *Chronicle*'s city views were pioneering visual representations of the locations they represented.[25] They are inserted at that point in the historical narrative where the city in question first appears in the narrative. Not surprisingly, the city of Jerusalem is shown as the first city woodcut.[26] Like all the other city woodcuts, it is accompanied by a brief history and description of the city. Subsequent city woodcuts represent Ninive, Cairo, Trier, Damascus, Babylon, Rhodos, and Corinth. Trier made the list of the oldest cities because Schedel believed that it was founded by Assyrians who had to flee their homeland,[27] and "this is the place where this legend fits in according to a synchronous view of time."[28] Surprisingly, he counted cities like Paris, Mainz, and Venice among the oldest as well because he believed them to have been founded by Trojans displaced by the Trojan War. The city views thus were a reflection of the Humanists' growing preoccupation with geography.[29]

Schedel included other descriptive sections, such as a section that defined islands and described some sample islands, or a segment on the land of the Amazons.[30] Schedel believed that the nobility as a ruling class had its origins in the post-Babel period. Therefore, he delivered a justification of the existence of the nobility and of the hierarchical structure of society.[31] In the post-Babel

---

22 Grafton, *New Worlds*, 58; Leitch, *Mapping Ethnography*, 26–30.
23 Leitch, *Mapping Ethnography*, 17.
24 Schedel, *Nuremberg Chronicle*, fol. 285r–285v.
25 Leitch, *Mapping Ethnography*, 31.
26 Schedel, *Nuremberg Chronicle*, fol. 17r.
27 Schedel, *Nuremberg Chronicle*, fol. 23r. Likewise, Anon., *Der Oberrheinische Revolutionär*, held the king of Trier to be the original German monarch who ruled over the ancient world (145–148).
28 Füssel, *Hartmann Schedel*, 7.
29 Leitch, *Mapping Ethnography*, 30.
30 Schedel, *Nuremberg Chronicle*, fol. 19r–19v.
31 Schedel, *Nuremberg Chronicle*, fol. 20r.

world, so Schedel, the population grew rapidly, and with it the need to protect the general population against people who had evil intentions. Furthermore, elite rulers were needed because most could not handle governance. In addition, a noble status could be a reward for bravery or in recognition of wealth used to feed the poor and needy. So Schedel's narrative was infused with social and political theory and commentary.

His description of the Sixth Age begins with the story of Christ that is embedded in the history of Roman rule. The history from the birth of Christ to the present is told as a parallel story of "the Christian empire and the highest papal bishopric."[32] The end of the Sixth Age is marked by enmity between the Christian occident, led by Maximilian I, the King of the Romans, and the Ottomans who at the time of writing controlled a vast portion of the formerly Christian Balkans. Like Sebastian Brant and other German Humanists, Schedel engaged in panegyrics of Maximilian, who in Schedel's interpretation represented the last hope to unite Christianity in order to turn back the invasion of the Turks and to protect Hungary and Germany against their advances. Suddenly, the narrative switches to an apotheosis of Maximilian, who rides triumphantly into Rome on a chariot and ushers in a new age. Conrad Celtis, the poet laureate, would celebrate the events in immortal songs, and the historian Antonius Sabellicus would ensure his afterlife in the history books.[33] The description of the Sixth Age ends with Schedel's acknowledgment that history was incomplete and its end yet to be written: "For the description of more stories or future events the following few sheets were left blank."[34] Schedel thus confirmed that the historical narrative was privileged in his book in spite of the many descriptive insertions.

The brief Seventh Age focuses on the coming of the Antichrist, the end of the world, and the Last Judgement.[35] In the final paragraph, he called his work "the book of the stories of the ages of the world and of the descriptions of the most famous and notable cities."[36] Here, he elevated the descriptions of the cities to a level equal to that of the historical narrative, thus contradicting what he had said just a few pages before. But the book does not end here. Schedel added a substantial but unsystematic appendix, largely drawn from

---

32 Schedel, *Nuremberg Chronicle*, fol. 95r: "das cristenlich keyserthumb vnd dz höhst babstlich bistumb."
33 Ashcroft, "Black Arts," 8; Schedel, *Nuremberg Chronicle*, fol. 258r–258v.
34 Schedel, *Nuremberg Chronicle*, fol. 258v: "Zu beschreibung mer gschihten oder künftiger ding sinn hernach ettliche pletter lere gelassen."
35 Schedel, *Nuremberg Chronicle*, fol. 259r–262v.
36 Schedel, *Nuremberg Chronicle*, fol. 262v: "das bůch von den geschihten der alter der werlt vnd von beschreibung der berümbtisten vnd namhaftigisten stett."

Enea Piccolomini,[37] in which a number of regions and states are described with the excuse that these descriptions had reached him only after he had completed the book. These are mostly territories and states that were not covered in the historical account, such as territories within Germany, states in Eastern Europe, and contemporaneous nation states, such as Spain, Portugal, France, and England. No longer is there an attempt to create a historical narrative around them. The book ends with a two-page map of Germany by Hieronymus Münzer, the first map of Germany ever printed in a book.[38]

As the title page of the index of the *Nuremberg Chronicle* indicates, the book sees itself as part of the chronicle tradition. Its basic inner structure is entirely chronological and stands in the traditional view of the Seven Ages. The Seventh Age marks the end point of history, not unlike the end stage of history Sebastian Brant envisioned, as discussed in Chapter 6. Schedel made allusions to the beginning of a new age associated with Maximilian's rule, like in the vision of Maximilian's triumphal entry into Rome, which was simultaneously an apotheosis of Maximilian and evoked images of the Last Judgement – which in Schedel's view undoubtedly was the telos of human history. But Schedel's hints at a new age also made a nod to emerging Humanism, such as his panegyrics of the printing press that enabled the knowledge of the Ancients to be disseminated[39] and the commendation of early German Humanist thinkers, such as Johannes Regiomontanus[40] and Conrad Celtis.[41]

In spite of all the cultural and geographic references, these elements remain subordinate to the chronological principle. It would therefore be an overstatement to call the *Nuremberg Chronicle* "the largest printed atlas of its time."[42] First, the book only contains two maps: the world map close to the beginning of the work and the map of Germany at the very end. Second, the geographical information remains subsidiary throughout the *Chronicle*. At the same time, it is evident that Schedel attempted to break out of the chronicle format in favor of a more cosmographic frame of the world by infusing the chronology with spatial narratives. Furthermore, the woodcuts that illustrate the creation story in the first few pages of the book can be read as an attempt to map the story of creation. While history and chronology were still central to Schedel's project, his cosmographic interest is evident, and with it the trend to integrate elements of spatial

---

37 McLean, *The 'Cosmographia' of Sebastian Münster*, 117.
38 Füssel, *Hartmann Schedel*, 666.
39 Schedel, *Nuremberg Chronicle*, fol. 252v.
40 Schedel, *Nuremberg Chronicle*, fol. 255r.
41 Schedel, *Nuremberg Chronicle*, fol. 258v.
42 Leitch, *Mapping Ethnography*, 19.

genres into chronicles. However, the different epistemologies made it impossible for Schedel to fuse chronology and cosmography into a single text in a compelling fashion.

The chronicle tradition lived on in texts like the highly successful and influential *Chronica* by the Brandenburg court astrologer and historian Johannes Carion (1499–1537),[43] first published in 1532 and reprinted numerous times.[44] The Wittenberg reformer Philipp Melanchthon influenced the text and heavily edited later editions.[45] Yet, the relatively slim 1532 edition avoided confessionally marked references, presumably to make it marketable to Catholic audiences as well.[46] Carion subdivided human history into three periods of 2,000 years each, adapting the framework of the earth's 6,000-year existence from the prophecy of Elias (or Elijah), the so-called *Vaticinium Eliae*.[47] The first period reached from Adam to Abraham, and the second from Abraham to the birth of Christ. The third period lasted into the present and was not complete yet, but Carion's millenarian vision reminded the reader that, based on Elias, the completion of the last set of 2,000 years was fast approaching: "Now in this year 1532 after the birth of Christ approximately 5,474 years have passed since the beginning of the world. Therefore, it is hoped that we are not far from the end."[48] While Schedel's eschatological vision was attached to the person of Emperor Maximilian I and celebrated the apotheosis of Maximilian as the conqueror of the infidels and as the unifier of the Christian occident, Carion was firmly anchored in Lutheran millennialism.

The secondary organizational principle of Carion's chronicle was the vision of the four empires based on Daniel, as discussed in Chapter 6. The first three empires – the Assyrian, Persian, and Greek monarchies – were all located in the second period between Abraham and the birth of Christ. The fourth empire, however, had its roots in Ancient Rome in the second period, but thanks to the

---

43 Carion was a German astrologer, also known also for historical writings. He served as court astrologer to Elector Joachim I Nestor of Brandenburg. Carion's *Chronica* became an important work in Protestant millenarian thought.

44 In 1532 alone, at least three editions were published in Wittenberg and one each in Augsburg and Marburg. The text was reprinted multiple times until 1624. While the 1532 edition was mostly Carion's work, later editions were heavily edited by Melanchthon and others. For a list of editions of Carion's *Chronica* see Prietz, *Das Mittelalter*, XVII–XXVIII.

45 Prietz, *Das Mittelalter*, 31–38.

46 Prietz, *Das Mittelalter*, 11. Nevertheless, Prietz (*Das Mittelalter*, 661) refers to Carion's book as "erstes protestantisches Geschichtswerk" (first Protestant work of historiography).

47 Green, "Translating Time," 163; Prietz, *Das Mittelalter*, 99–100.

48 Carion, *Chronica*, fol. 169r: "Nu sind jnn disem jar nach der geburt Christi 1532 ongeferlich 5474 jar nach anfang der welt/ Derohalben zu hoffen/ wir sind nu nicht fern vom Ende."

Chapter 10 From Chronicle to Cosmography (and Chorography) — 143

transfer of power to the Germans at the time of Charlemagne, commonly referred to as *translatio imperii*, it lasted into the present and indeed would be the final empire, as envisioned by Brant also, completing the millennial vision. In spite of the millennial speculation and occasional forays into prognostication, Carion's narrative remained dedicated to chronology throughout which, in the case of the fourth empire, was based on the chronology of emperors. While Carion, like Schedel, pursued a vision of the end of time, he was not interested in importing cosmographic knowledge into his chronicle, nor was he adapting the commonly used scheme of the Seven Ages (*aetates*) employed by Schedel.

Schedel's struggle with adapting a chronicle to a cosmographical format reverberates in the *Chronica* by the Frankfurt printer Christian Egenolff (1502–1555).[49] Egenolff's text was mostly a derivative compilation, and its reception and impact were limited. But Egenolff published three different editions in the years 1533, 1534, and 1535, which document both the progression in his thinking and the resulting conceptual changes. It becomes evident that Egenolff struggled both with the integration of new cosmographic knowledge into his chronicle and with the emerging genre of the cosmography itself.

The first chapter of the main body of the first edition from 1533 is entitled "Instructions on How Chronicles Have to Be Understood and Read in an Orderly Fashion. By Johannes Carion."[50] As Carion had done before him, Egenolff promoted the periodization into three segments of 2,000 years, based on the prophecy of Elias, and subdivided the history of human civilization into four distinct monarchies. Yet, Egenolff also brought in the analogy between the seven days of creation and the seven *aetates* of humanity, which had been the organizing principle of Schedel's *Nuremberg Chronicle*. Like Schedel, Egenolff was weaving cosmographic information into a chronological narrative, at least early in his text:[51] he included segments on misshapen human beings representing monstrous races,[52] on the origin of the nobility,[53] and on the Amazons,[54] just like Schedel had done. Egenolff also inserted segments on the cities of Trier, Rhodos, Troy, Paris, and Mainz, which Schedel had discussed in the same order early in his

---

[49] Egenolff learned the trade of bookprinting in Strasbourg but moved to Frankfurt in 1530 to set up his own shop. He printed about 400 books by many influential authors, some illustrated by Hans Sebald Beham and Virgil Solis. He became the first important printer and publisher in Frankfurt. He also issued compilations, most notably his *Chronica*.
[50] Egenolff, *Chronic* (1533), fol. 1r: "Anleytung/ wie Historien ordentlich zu fassen vnd zu lesen seindt. Joannis Carionis."
[51] Egenolff up to fol. 16r closely followed Schedel's model.
[52] Egenolff, *Chronic* (1533), fol. 4v.
[53] Egenolff, *Chronic* (1533), fol. 6v.
[54] Egenolff, *Chronic* (1533), fol. 9r.

text. Both the level of specificity and the placement of these digressions within the text show how closely Schedel served as a model.

But at this point, Egenolff's text takes a different turn by inserting the history of the Israelites, which was taken verbatim from Kaspar Turnauer's *Von dem Jüdischen vnnd Jsraelischen volck vnnd jren vorgeern* (*Of the Jewish and the Israelite People and Its Predecessors*), published in 1528.[55] Egenolff then returned to the narration of the four empires, dropping the concept of the seven ages and instead orienting himself on the model of the four monarchies used by Carion. The survey of the Persian Empire is followed by the most substantive part of the book, comprising well over half of it: the history of the Roman Empire, illustrated with medallion portraits of all the emperors,[56] with a heavy focus on the empire since Charlemagne. While these latter parts of the book were more closely oriented on Carion, the book ends with a detailed discussion of contemporaneous events, such as the wars against the Turks and the Peasants' Revolt, which Carion only touched on lightly. While the chorographic impulse was evident on the first pages of Egenolff's *Chronic*, it ended entirely in a chronicle mode.

The second edition of Egenolff's *Chronica*, published in 1534, is structurally similar to the first edition. While he added new materials, they are most evident toward the end of the book. For instance, he added a section on German castles and the dynasties that occupied them. Most remarkable is a five-page section entitled "The great inflation at the time of Charles V," which is a five-page millennialist invective of the practices of usury and hoarding, leading to inflation, hunger, and misery.[57] Egenolff added two appendices, both taken from *Chronica, Zeÿtbůch und geschÿcht bibel von anbegyn biß inn diß gegenwertig M.D.XXXI. jar* (*Chronicle, Annals and Bible of History from the Beginnings up to this Present Year 1531*), published by Sebastian Franck (1499–1542/43) in 1531. They are "Chronicle and short treatise of the name of heretics and related teachings" and "Twenty confessions or sects of the single Christian faith."[58] The latter offers brief descriptions of Christian religious practices in different parts of the world.

In the second edition, Egenolff was consciously adding information that went beyond historical narratives without changing the basic structure of the

---

55 Egenolff, *Chronic* (1533), fol. 16r–34r.
56 Egenolff, *Chronic* (1533), fol. 52v–129v.
57 Egenolff, *Chronica* (1534), fol. 161v–164r: "Die groß Thewrung zur zeit Caroli. v." For more on this topic see Chapter 18.
58 "Chronic/ vnd kurtzer begriff der Ketzer namen vnnd fürnemige leren" and "Zweintzig Glauben/ oder Secten/ alleyn des eynigen Christen glaubens."

Chapter 10 From Chronicle to Cosmography (and Chorography) — 145

book. In the third edition, published in 1535, the changes are much more pronounced. It was greatly influenced by Sebastian Franck's *Weltbůch: spiegel vnd bildtniß des gantzen erdbodens von Sebastiano Franco Wördensi in vier bůcher/ nemlich in Asiam/ Aphricam/ Europam/ vnd Americam/ gestelt vnd abteilt* (*World Book: Mirror and Image of the Entire Earth, by Sebastian Frank from Donauwörth, Namely Represented and Subdivided in Asia, Africa, Europe, and America*). Egenolff's third edition begins with an extensive cosmographic description of the world based largely on Franck and copies from the *Weltbůch* extensively.[59] However, this initial section only covered the three traditional continents that formed the Ptolemaic world. Some material from earlier editions was integrated, such as the segment on misshapen monstrous races that in this edition became part of the description of Africa.[60]

Next follows the actual chronicle portion of the book, which is largely based on the two earlier editions and still includes the text segments from Johannes Carion's *Chronica* (1532).[61] It ends with the election of Maximilian I as Roman King in 1486 and the alliance of the city of Basel with the Swiss Confederation in 1494. At this place in history, Egenolff inserted his description of America with the title "Of America, the fourth part of the world, found in the year 1497."[62] America thus was not part of the synchronic description of the world but rather of the diachronic historical part. In a sense, America, and with it other newly discovered lands in Africa and Asia, were still part of a historical narrative and thus history in the making, rather than fully integrated into a synchronic account of a contemporaneous world. The section begins with the alleged discovery of America by Amerigo Vespucci in 1497 and fits neatly into the chronological narrative. The text segments were all copied from Franck's *Weltbůch*.

Egenolff's text then returns to Europe and gives an account of contemporaneous imperial history, from the battles with the Ottoman Turks to the Peasants' Revolt and the Münster Rebellion of 1535. The text also includes the account of recent inflation and Carion's chronicle of heretics, which were already part of the second edition. Egenolff's text thus represents a hybrid form. While the 1533 and 1534 editions were clearly structured as chronicles whose narratives were mostly oriented on the chronology of events, the 1535 edition made a more serious attempt at turning the book into a cosmography, taking Franck's *Weltbůch*

---

[59] Egenolff, *Chronica* (1535), fol. 1r–31v.
[60] Egenolff, *Chronica* (1535), fol. 3r–3v. Martin Waldseemüller in his *Carta marina* from 1516 on sheet four places the monstrous races in India.
[61] Egenolff, *Chronica* (1535), fol. 32r–103v.
[62] Egenolff, *Chronica* (1535), 103v–108v: "Von America dem vierdten theyl der Welt/ Anno M. cccc.xcvij. erfunden."

as a model. But in contrast to Franck, Egenolff still treated the New World as part of contemporaneous history rather than as part of an emerging new world view. Egenolff clearly recognized that the world around him was expanding at a rapid pace, but information about the fringes of the world was still difficult to obtain and equally difficult to integrate into existing genres and knowledge systems. The three editions of his *Chronica* illustrate his attempts to move away from a Creation-based narrative without having found a form that could adequately represent the changing contours of his world.

It is Sebastian Franck's *Weltbůch* from 1534 that made a huge step toward fully establishing the new cosmographic paradigm. Throughout the sixteenth century, new cosmographies appeared that chronicled the advancements in knowledge about space and summarized the current state of geographical knowledge. Cosmography as the "representation of the *imago mundi*" had its own medieval tradition, deriving its knowledge from heterogeneous sources, including Christian cosmology, classical writers, and travel accounts.[63] However, the older cosmographic tradition was quite eclectic and unsystematic and lacked the generic focus it developed in Humanism. Furthermore, cartography, one of the core functions of cosmography, before the Early Modern period was largely based on theoretical speculation rather than empirical observation.[64]

Cosmography in the sixteenth century was a "mathematically based system for measuring the earth."[65] Franck in his *Weltbůch* (1534) offered this definition:

> Cosmography is a complete, full, actual description of the world, and what is understood to be the universe, such as the four elements, stars, sun, moon, planets, and circle out of which the upper celestial sphere is made. It offers the opportunity to measure each place and the latitude of the pole through symmetry. It indicates cause and differences of all climates, day and night, the four directions of the world, the movement of rise and fall of the fixed and moving stars, and whatever belongs to the course of the heavens, such as the latitude of the poles and of the parallels of the equatorial zone, circles, climate zones, etc. through the mathematical arts.[66]

---

63 Cattaneo, "European Medieval," 36–38.
64 Cattaneo, "European Medieval," 41.
65 Johnson, *The German Discovery*, 219, note 2; McLean, *The 'Cosmographia' of Sebastian Münster*, 47; Cormack, "Good Fences," 644–650.
66 Franck, *Weltbůch*, fol. 2v: "Cosmographia sey [...] ein gantze folle eygentliche beschreibung der welt/ vnd was mit des himmels vmbschweyff/ begriffen wirt/ als der vier element/ stern/ Sunn/ Mon/ der Planeten vnd circkel darauß die über himlisch Spher wirt gemacht/ der auch die gelegenheit eins yeden ort/ vnd die höhe des Poli durch Simetriam abmißt/ vrsach vnd vnderscheyd anzeygt aller climat/ tag vnd nachts/ der vier angel der welt die bewegung auffgang vnnd nidergang der gehefften vnd irrenden stern/ vnnd was zů des himmels lauf

Cosmography used astronomical principles to measure the world mathematically in order to establish a geometric grid, a coordinate plane of latitude and longitude. Cosmography was considered part of astronomy and thus of the *quadrivium* and differed from geography because it divided the land through the circles of the sky, not through topographical features on the surface of the earth, such as mountains and rivers.[67] Cosmography was a "theater of the world [...] that connects the elemental earth to the order and movement of heavens within a single, ordered, and harmonious creation: a cosmos or world machine."[68] Cosmographers mapped out the space where human events could unfold and therefore represented an attempt to explain the world spatially rather than historically.[69]

Geography, by contrast, "is a description of the world as it is experienced and recognized in its attributes and is like a depiction of the most noble places, mountains, forests and rivers."[70] Franck drew a sharp contrast between the two disciplines:

> Geography is distinguished from Cosmography in that it measures the earth and makes distinctions with mountains, rivers, and oceans; cosmography on the other hand through the compass of the skies.[71]

Through concentrating on the predictable skies rather than on the malleable surface of the earth, Renaissance cosmographers imparted a system of order and harmony of the world that was rooted in mathematics and geometry.[72]

Geography thus was a more localized extension of the representation of the world as a geometric plane of coordinates established by cosmography: it measured and represented topographic features, such as mountains, rivers, and human settlements, on a local scale and set them into a spatial relation with each other. Cosmography and geography thus prepared the ground for a much broader description of locations that included anthropological and cultural information. This less mathematically precise, more qualitative mode of description led to chorography, which allowed for the inclusion of both geographic

---

gehört/ als die höhe des Poli/ der Paralel zonis mittagischen/ circkel/ Climata. etc durch Mathematische kunst anzeygen/ [...]."
67 Johnson, *The German Discovery*, 52.
68 Cosgrove, "Globalism and Tolerance," 856.
69 Cosgrove, "Globalism and Tolerance," 856.
70 Franck, *Weltbůch*, fol. 3r: "ist ein Beschreibung der welt/ wie sy erfaren/ gesehen/ vnd yr gelegenheit erkent wird/ vnd gleich ein abmalung der fürnempsten ort/ berg wäld/ flüß."
71 Franck, *Weltbůch*, fol. 3r: "Geographia [...] wirt von Cosmographia vnderscheyden/ das sy das erdtrich mißt/ vnd vnderscheydet mit bergen/ flüssen/ vnd mör/ Cosmographia aber durch die circkel des himmels."
72 Johnson, *The German Discovery*, 52.

and non-geographic information. The anonymous *Canon oder außlegung diser gegenwertigen Mappen* (*Canon or Interpretation of the Present Maps*) from 1533 defines chorography as the "description of cities and countries."[73] The city representations in Schedel's *Nuremberg Chronicle* thus have a chorographic dimension in that they represented localized specifics supporting qualitative descriptions that incorporated non-geographic features into the narrative. As spatial relations became increasingly important in the culture of the sixteenth century, chorography became an important tool in a range of genres, including literary representations, like in Johann Fischart's *Das Glückhafft Schiff von Zürich* (*The Lucky Boat of Zurich*) from 1577.[74]

Sebastian Franck was not just theoretically versed but also carefully observed the difference between chronicles and forms of cosmographic writings in his own books.[75] He authored three major texts on this spectrum, and he wrote all of them in the German vernacular in order to reach both the educated elites and a semi-literate general population.[76] In 1531, he published his *Chronica*, a general chronicle, followed in 1534 by the *Weltbůch*, a cosmography examining contemporaneous issues. Both of these works had a comprehensive, global agenda. His *Germaniae Chronicon* from 1538, by contrast, focused on the history of Germany from Noah to Emperor Charles V.

---

73 Anon., *Canon oder außlegung*, sig. A3r: "Chorographia/ das ist Stet vnd Länder beschreibung."
74 Hess, "Travel as Projection of Civic Virtue."
75 Müller, "Alte Wissensformen," 173.
76 Franck, *Chronica* (1531), sig. a2r.

Chapter 11
Ptolemy's Grid and the New Cosmography in Germany: Waldseemüller and His Legacy

Martin Waldseemüller (1472/75–1520) and Lorenz Fries (1489–1531) were among the early propagators of cosmographical theory in Germany.[1] Cosmographies were influential as they enhanced geographical knowledge and affected the thinking about space in sixteenth-century culture, as explicitly stated by Waldseemüller and Fries. Most importantly, Humanist cosmography sought to transform and eventually replace the Ptolemaic model that was no longer able to support the rapid pragmatic expansion of spatial knowledge. At the same time, there was a palpable tension between the new projections of space in cosmographies and the representation of space in literary texts and other forms of cultural expression, as we shall see in Chapters 13 and 14. This tension was due in part because the cosmographic model was rooted in empiricism and thus disregarded biblical accounts of creation, and in part because it operated with the presumption that spatial exploration was not just legitimate but also beneficial.

The Humanist scholar and map maker Martin Waldseemüller, who was part of a small Humanist scholarly community in the provincial town of Saint Dié in Lorraine,[2] published a text entitled *Der welt kugel. Beschrybung der Welt vnd deß gantzen Ertreichs* (*The Sphere of the World. Description of the World and of the Entire Earthly Realm*) in the aftermath of the publication of his huge world map of 1507.[3] Here, Waldseemüller provided a largely Ptolemaic view of the world. His cosmos followed the conventional Ptolemaic model: the universe was a system with the four elements at the center, the sublunar world, encircled by concentric

---
[1] Johnson, *The German Discovery*, 49.
[2] Little is known about Waldseemüller. After studies in Freiburg, where he met his collaborator Matthias Ringmann, both Waldseemüller and Ringmann moved to Saint Dié around 1505. Both remained there for the remainder of their lives; Ringmann died in 1511 and Waldseemüller in 1520. We know little about their sources of information and about their networks outside of Saint Dié.
[3] For more on the Waldseemüller map, see Hessler (*The Naming of America*) and Lester (*The Fourth Part*). The lone surviving copy of the 1507 map, as well of the 1516 *Carta marina*, was owned by the globe maker Johannes Schöner who had them bound together in what is known as the *Schöner Sammelband*, now at the Library of Congress. After Schöner's death in 1547, his entire library was purchased by Georg Fugger. The Fuggers owned it until 1656. (Hessler and Van Duzer, *Seeing the World Anew*, 3.) This is a good example for how large corporations kept their geographic knowledge up to date.

rings representing the planets and the celestial world. In Ringmann's and Waldseemüller's cosmography, the earth was a sphere at its center, not just a circle[4]: "All of the earth is compared to a sphere or an apple, as you can see here."[5] The reference is to an illustration where the globe is covered by a grid consisting of longitudinal and tropical lines, which he carefully described in his text (figure 4). The purpose of the detailed description is that the reader could understand and experience the structure of the world for himself:

> If you desire to recognize said things, and much more, put the sphere in front of you and look for the rings or circles with their names, as described before. Like this you will find everything by yourself without instructions, if only you can read.[6]

Once the reader learned how to read the grid, he could also use it to find specific places on earth that were defined by their specific coordinates on the grid, like the three continents, but also more narrowly defined spaces. Waldseemüller showed how the Ptolemaic model was at once expandable in theory but factually obsolete when he discussed the discovery of America:

> Now we have found a new island or world, a fourth part of the earth, much larger than Europe but not as well developed, etc. And one should call it America because of its discoverer, and it is located on the sphere next to Europe and Africa, further out toward the occident.[7]

Waldseemüller defined America as its own, fourth continent, which in his assessment was much larger than Europe.

Waldseemüller was famously the first person to label the new continent "America," both on his 1507 world map and on his accompanying globe gores, and de facto gave the continent its name.[8] Waldseemüller's famous 1507 world

---

4 Lehmann, *Die Cosmographiae Introductio*, 61.
5 Waldseemüller, *Der welt kugel*, sig. B2v: "Das gantz ertrich würt vergleicht einer kuglenn oder apffel/ als du hie sichst."
6 Waldseemüller, *Der welt kugel*, sig. C2v: "Ob du nun begerest diese gesagten ding alle zů erkennen vnd noch vil mer So setz die kugell für dich vnnd sych die Ring oder zyrckel mit iren namen wie vorstat. So findestu das alles von dir selb augensichtlich on vnderweisung/ so du allein lesen kannst."
7 Waldseemüller, *Der welt kugel*, sig. C3v: "Noch so hat man ietz erfunden ein nüwe insel oder welt ein fierd theil des ertreichs/ vil grösser dan Europa ist aber nitt so wol erpuwen etc. vnd die mag man von irem erfinder America heissen vnd ligt an der kugel neben Europa vnd africa vssen gegen nidergang zerechnen."
8 On Waldseemüller's role in the naming of the new continent, see Fernández-Armesto, *Amerigo*, 183–192; Johnson, "Renaissance German Cosmographers;" Obhof, "Der Erdglobus;" Pietschmann, "Bemerkungen." McGuirk, however, claims that the land mass commonly seen

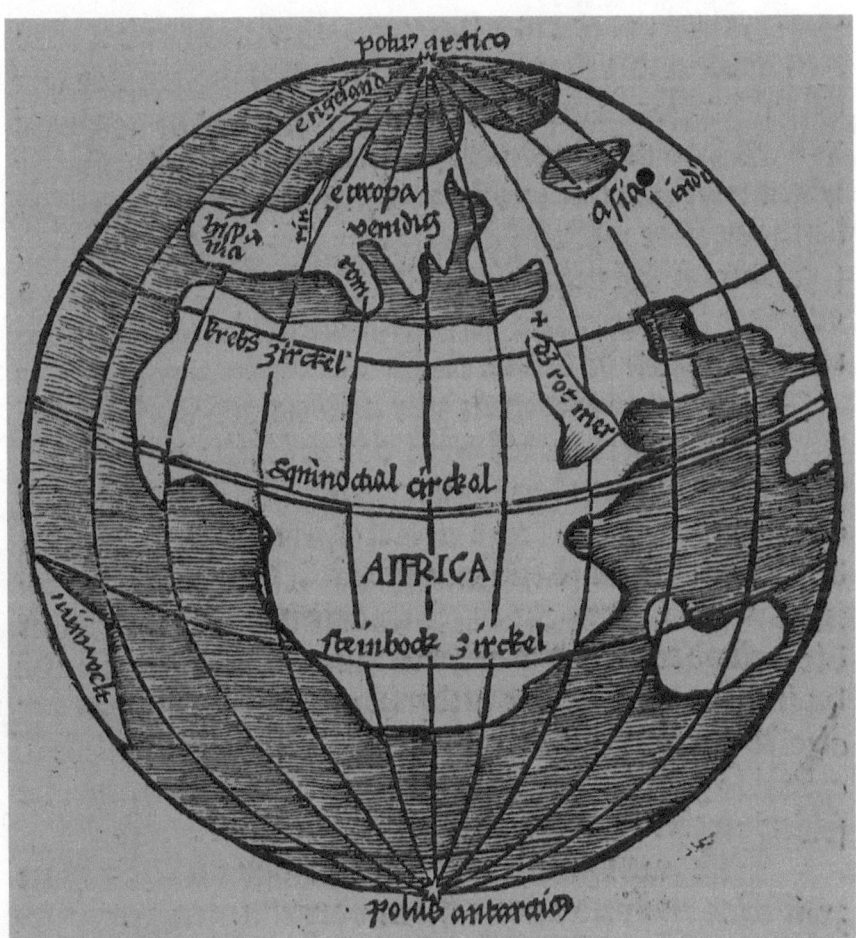

Figure 4: Martin Waldseemüller. *Der welt kugel. Beschrybung der welt vnd deß gantzen Ertreichs hie angezögt vnd vergleicht einer rotunden kuglen*. Strasbourg: Johann Grüninger, 1509. Title page and sig. B2r. © Universitätsbibliothek Freiburg im Breisgau.

---

as North America actually is "Asia, Cuba and a fabrication, all in one" ("The Presumed North America," 88). Furthermore, Lehmann ("The Depiction of America," 11–13) argues that the claim of the existence of a new continent on Waldseemüller's map was based on political rather than geographic considerations.

map, entitled *Universal Cosmography according to the Tradition of Ptolemy and the Discoveries of Amerigo Vespucci and Others*,[9] was the first map to show open water between America and East Asia years before the commonly acknowledged first discovery of the Pacific Ocean by Vasco Núñez de Balboa in 1513.[10] Waldseemüller showed the portraits of both Ptolemy and Vespucci on top of his map, and he made the erroneous claim that Amerigo Vespucci had found this new continent in 1497.[11]

Matthias Ringmann (1482–1511), Waldseemüller's collaborator in Saint Dié, published a Latin edition of Vespucci's *Mundus Novus* in Strasbourg under the title *De ora antarctica per regem Portugallie pridem inventa* (*Recently Discovered by the King of Portugal at the Edge of Antarctica*) in 1505. The *Cosmographiae introductio* (*Introduction to Cosmography*), published by Waldseemüller and Ringmann in Saint Dié in 1507, also included a reprint of Vespucci's *Quatuor Navigationes* (*Four Voyages*). The book was intended to accompany Waldseemüller's world map and globe gores and provided the commentary to the map: "The earth is now known to be divided into four parts. The first three of these are connected and are continents, but the fourth part is an island because it has been found to be surrounded on all sides by sea."[12] Waldseemüller placed a text box on sheet twelve of the 1507 map, where he further expanded on the concept of his map:

> Even though most of the Ancients were interested in marking out the extent of the world, many things remained unknown to them; for instance, in the west, America, named after its discoverer and that is now known to be a fourth part of the world. Another, to the south, a large part of Africa, which begins about seven degrees this side of Capricorn and extends in a great expanse southward, well past the torrid zone and the Tropic of Capricorn. A third example, found in the east, is the land of Cathay and all of southern India, past one hundred and eighty degrees of longitude. All of these places we have added to the ones that were known before, so that those who are interested and love knowledge of this kind may see all that is known to men in the present day, and that they may approve of our work. This one request we have to make, that those who may not be acquainted with geography shall not condemn all that they see before them until they

---

9 Cattaneo, "European Medieval," 54. The original Latin title is *Universalis cosmographia secundum Ptholomaei traditionem et Americi Vespucii aliorumque lustrationes*. See also Van Duzer, "Waldseemüller's World Maps," 14.
10 This discrepancy has given rise to the speculation that there may have been an earlier expedition to the Pacific of which Waldseemüller had knowledge. (Lester, *The Fourth Part*, 9.)
11 Fernández-Armesto, *Amerigo*, 188. In the cartouche on sheet nine of his 1507 world map, Waldseemüller reported that Vespucci discovered these territories and islands during four journeys between 1497 and 1504.
12 Hessler, *The Naming of America*, 101.

have learned what will surely be apparent to them later on, when they have come to understand what they see.[13]

This statement contains two radical innovations that represented a departure from Ptolemaic thinking. First, Waldseemüller now talked about four parts of the world, giving America the status of its own continent. Second, this new continent was an island, completely surrounded by water and oceans. As mentioned above, this implied the existence of a body of water between America and Asia. It also deviated from Ptolemy as this new part of the world was not connected to any of the others. In Ptolemy's view, the three continents were connected and ultimately represented one single land mass, surrounded by a larger ocean that had different names but represented a single body of water. While it appears to have been Waldseemüller's intention to designate America as the fourth continent, and the representation of America on his 1507 map supports that claim, the portrayal of America as an island befuddled later writers exactly because it did not fit the Ptolemaic definition of a continent, because the size of this island was unknown, and because it could be argued that these newly found islands were consistent with the islands Ptolemy had located in East Asia, at the very edge of the world.[14]

It is remarkable that Columbus's accomplishments did not register with Waldseemüller nor with Ringmann. Renate Pieper, in her detailed analysis of the role of information networks for the dissemination of knowledge about America in the empire, points to lacking ties between Germany and Spain as a reason why there was little information on the voyages of Columbus and other Spanish activities in the New World.[15] The interest in Columbus in Germany had generally decreased and his prestige had waned after 1497[16] as did the interest in the discoveries in the Atlantic in general,[17] particularly after the Portuguese started to travel to India along the African coast.[18] Pieper arrives at the conclusion that the quality of information about America available in Germany was poor, in spite of a large number of printed references to America. Pieper argues that new and accurate information was primarily disseminated in

---

13 Translation Hessler and Van Duzer, *Seeing the World Anew*, 46. The ninth chapter of Ringmann's accompanying commentary (Waldseemüller and Ringmann, *Cosmographiae introductio*, sig. C3v) makes the same point. See also Lehmann, *Die Cosmographiae Introductio*, 163–170.
14 These islands were represented on the Martellus world map of c. 1491 as well as on the 1507 Waldseemüller world map, but not on his 1516 *Carta marina*.
15 Pieper, *Die Vermittlung*, 85–86.
16 Pieper, *Die Vermittlung*, 97–99.
17 Pieper, *Die Vermittlung*, 101.
18 Pieper, *Die Vermittlung*, 118.

manuscript form. There was ample manuscript traffic from Spain to Italy but not to Germany, which means that Germany was largely cut off from new information out of Spain until at least 1515,[19] and perhaps longer. The use of modern means of communication and dissemination of information in the form of the printing press in Germany ironically led to a loss of accuracy and speed of the information flow.[20]

The texts attributed to Amerigo Vespucci (*Mundus Novus, Quatuor Navigationes*), on the other hand, which described Vespucci's participation in Portuguese expeditions, were highly successful in Germany. Generally, information from Portugal, through Italian intermediaries, was more readily available in Germany.[21] Furthermore, the Moravian printer Valentim Fernandes, who lived in Lisbon from 1495 until his death in 1518 or 1519, supplied southern German merchants and intellectuals with reliable information about Portuguese activities. Vespucci's *Mundus Novus*, first published in Paris in 1503, was printed a total of nineteen times in the empire north of the Alps between 1504 and 1506, including an edition by Matthias Ringmann in Strasbourg in 1505.[22] While Vespucci's tales were largely fictitious, they made the sensational claim that a new continent separate from East Asia had been found – the source of Waldseemüller's claim – and also offered titillating tales of anthropophagy.[23] The preference for the printed word and lacking access to information from Spain caused the Saint Dié circle to incorrectly assess the roles Spain and Portugal played in the discoveries, and it led to their fateful determination that Vespucci was the true discoverer of America in their 1507 publication project.[24] Ironically, the consequential naming of this new continent in this small provincial town was the result of lacking or faulty information and of insufficient communication networks.[25]

Waldseemüller must have recognized his error as he dropped the name in later publications. In his 1516 *Carta marina*,[26] Vespucci played a lesser role. Instead, the text in the cartouche on sheet ten credited Columbus with the discovery of the New World, specifically mentioning his voyage of 1492, while

---

[19] Pieper, *Die Vermittlung*, 119.
[20] Pieper, *Die Vermittlung*, 161.
[21] Pieper, *Die Vermittlung*, 141.
[22] Pieper, *Die Vermittlung*, 134–135.
[23] Pieper, *Die Vermittlung*, 134.
[24] Pieper, *Die Vermittlung*, 141.
[25] Pieper, *Die Vermittlung*, 161; Davies, *Renaissance Ethnography*, 50.
[26] According to the Library of Congress, the 1516 *Carta marina* was printed on twelve sheets, has a total size of 128 x 233 cm, the same as his 1507 world map. Van Duzer's recent *Martin Waldseemüller's 'Carta marina' of 1516* could not be considered for this study.

Pedro Álvares Cabral and Vespucci were given secondary and tertiary credit. America lost its status as continent, and the word "America" disappeared entirely: North America was labeled "Terra de Cuba, Asie partis" (land of Cuba, part of Asia) and South America now was called "Terra nova" at its Caribbean coast and "Brasilia sive terra papagalli" (Brazil or land of the parrot) further south. The large text box with Waldseemüller's address to the reader and the blank cartouches on sheet nine take up all the space where South America and particularly its Pacific coast would be located, and the map does not show an ocean west of America. The visual ambiguity built into the 1516 map left it open whether America indeed was a new continent or a group of islands off East Asia. While the 1507 map was influenced by Vespucci's view of this new continent, Waldseemüller's 1516 *Carta marina* reflected Columbus's view of the newly discovered lands.

Even though the 1516 map lacks the striking boldness of the 1507 map, it reflects the state of knowledge much more accurately. The rehabilitation of Columbus and the refusal to show the as of yet unknown Pacific coasts of North and South America are indications for that. Most importantly, all remnants of the Ptolemaic concepts were removed. The critical examination of Ptolemy had already influenced the 1507 map as Waldseemüller confirmed in his *Cosmographiae introductio* from 1507:

> All that we have said here in our Introduction to Cosmography will provide sufficient understanding only if we tell you that in designing the layout of our world map we have not been faithful to Ptolemy in every respect, particularly in the layout of the new lands, where on the nautical charts we find that the equator has been placed differently than Ptolemy represented it. Therefore, when you see this do not think it is our mistake, for we have represented it this way purposely, because at times we have followed Ptolemy and at other times the nautical charts.[27]

The analysis of the 1507 map shows that the representation of the world known to Ptolemy, and in particular the Mediterranean and the Middle East, very much was indebted to the Ptolemaic tradition.[28] An example is the "horn" of Africa shown across from Gibraltar, which has the appearance of earlier Ptolemaic maps but is no longer present on the 1516 map.[29] The 1507 map also shows Ptolemy's erroneous assumption that the equator was crossing West Africa rather than the Gulf of Guinea, as correctly shown on the 1516 map, and it places a large number of islands south of Japan.

---

27 Translation Hessler, *The Naming of America*, 106.
28 Hessler and Van Duzer, *Seeing the World Anew*, 50.
29 Hessler and Van Duzer, *Seeing the World Anew*, 34.

The 1516 *Carta marina* radically eliminated all knowledge that was attributed to ancient philosophy and geography and instead relied on contemporaneous sources, such as marine charts and travel reports. Waldseemüller explained his principles in a cartouche on sheet nine of the map:

> Moved by these considerations, and in the interest of the common utility of scholars, I have added this second image of the world to my first, so that while in the first one there is an image of the whole world, land and sea, according to ancient authors, in this one would shine forth not just the new and present face of the world, but together with the things added in the intervening times, the usual matters of the mortal world, and natural change should be clear, so that you have (if I may say so) in one view what things are transitory and how, what they were like in ancient times, and how they certainly will be in the future. Therefore, in accordance with modern custom, it seemed good to call this image and description of the whole world a Carta marina, in which, as far as the depiction of the oceans, I have followed the common and tried-and-true indications of nautical charts, while in the depiction of the Mediterranean, Asia, and Africa I have made ample use of recent authors' travel narratives, regional maps, descriptions of countries, and the accounts of some recent explorers.[30]

This text is a powerful testament to the rapid evolution of Waldseemüller's cartographic thought, to his resolve to depart from Ptolemy's geographic thinking, and to his uncompromising willingness to correct his own mistakes, including the retraction of the word and the concept of America, and to revamp his entire map.

Yet, Lorenz Fries still used the term "America" in the small world map which he added to his 1522 edition of Ptolemy's *Geography*, published by Johann Grüninger in Strasbourg. Fries published his own *Carta Marina Navigatoria* in 1525, again printed by Grüninger, which was a three-quarter-sized, less sophisticated version of Waldseemüller's 1516 *Carta marina* with captions in the vernacular, but also printed on twelve sheets.[31] Here, Fries used the term "the newly found land" and its Latin equivalent "Terra nova."[32] However, in his commentary on the map, entitled *Uslegung der mercarten oder Cartha Marina* (*Interpretation of Ocean Maps or Nautical Chart*, 1527), Fries still used the name "America" and referred to it as the fourth continent[33] even though he had listed the three continents Europe, Africa, and Asia just a few pages before.[34]

---

30 Translation Hessler and Van Duzer, *Seeing the World Anew*, 50.
31 No copies of the 1525 edition remain, but there is one copy each of the 1530 and 1531 editions; my comments are based on the 1530 edition located at the Bayerische Staatsbibliothek in Munich. See Hessler and Van Duzer, *Seeing the World Anew*, 66–68.
32 Fries, *Carta Marina Navigatoria* (1530), "Dz nüv erfunden land."
33 Fries, *Uslegung der mercarten*, sig. A6v.
34 Fries, *Uslegung der mercarten*, sig. A3v.

The ambiguity of America's status as a continent lingered well into the second half of the sixteenth century. Heinrich Bünting's *Itinerarivm Sacrae Scriptvrae* (*Travel book through Holy Scripture*) from 1581 contains a map where the three traditional continents are represented as clover leaves, with Jerusalem as the stem at the center that holds them together in the manner of traditional T-O maps. In the bottom right corner, Bünting showed part of a land mass called "America the New World."[35] The next map, an actual representation of the world, also showed America in the bottom left corner. In the accompanying text, he explained that he was not discussing America here because it was not part of Scripture.[36] While Bünting acknowledged the existence of America as a "fourth part of the world," he did not accord it full status as a continent because it lacked biblical status.

While Waldseemüller recognized his own error, the term "America" continued to be used in Germany to designate the newly found lands to the west, although not consistently.[37] German sources credited Vespucci with the discovery of America well into the 1530s, and 1497 was the commonly assumed date of discovery.[38] Even Nicolaus Copernicus in his groundbreaking *De Revolutionibus* (1543) reiterated the cosmography presented in Waldseemüller's and Ringmann's *Cosmographiae introductio*:

> Beyond that meridian, where [Ptolemy] left unknown land, the moderns have added Cathay and territory as vast as sixty degrees of longitude, so that now the earth is inhabited over a greater stretch of longitude than is left for the ocean. To these regions, moreover, should be added the islands discovered in our time under the rulers of Spain and Portugal, and especially America, named after the ship's captain who found it. On account of its still undisclosed size it is thought to be a second group of inhabited countries. There are also many other islands, heretofore unknown.[39]

Copernicus still ascribed the discovery of America to Vespucci, paraphrasing Waldseemüller's description of America in the *Cosmographiae introductio*, thus showing Waldseemüller's lasting influence on sixteenth-century cosmography.[40]

In spite of this grave and consequential error, Waldseemüller's work is important because of the compelling implications of his grid: the world had become a known place, at least theoretically. His readers understood that: the mathematician, globe maker, and astronomer Johann Schöner (1477–1547) owned both

---

35 Bünting, *Itinerarivm Sacrae Scriptvrae*, vol. 1, 4–5: "AMERICA Die Newe Welt."
36 Bünting, *Itinerarivm Sacrae Scriptvrae*, vol. 1, 7.
37 A good example is Johann Schöner's *Opusculum geographicum* from 1533, sig. C4r.
38 For example Sebastian Franck's *Weltbůch* (1534) and the third edition of Christian Egenolff's *Chronica* (1535) discussed later.
39 Copernicus, *On the Revolutions*, 10.
40 Hessler and Van Duzer, *Seeing the World Anew*, 19.

maps and drew a series of red grid lines over the entire 1516 map and over portions of the 1507 map in order to transfer the coordinates of various places to his globes.[41] While there still were many blank spots on the map, the grid allowed for newly discovered lands to be placed on the correct spot on the map immediately, as the example of America exemplified. Maps could be improved by adding newly found territories or by adding more detailed information, but they did not have to be reconceptualized and redesigned. The grid helped to create a unified world view out of the disparate pieces contributed by different navigators and merchants, and in turn also facilitated future voyages that would add to the geographic knowledge base.

It is important to remember that Ptolemy had originally developed a grid that made any spot on the world definable by mathematically calculated coordinates indicating the longitude and the latitude of any spot of the known world.[42] Portuguese navigators as well as Columbus and Vespucci relied on Ptolemy's *Geography* and its maps during their voyages.[43]

Methodologically, Humanists still could learn from Ptolemy: "Ptolemy's *Geographia* explains the methods of obtaining data about the world, and of using this data to construct representations of the earth."[44] Humanist cosmography and cartography thus were very much indebted to Ptolemy[45] as he lent the legitimacy of ancient authority to Humanist mapmakers.[46]

An example is the anonymous pamphlet entitled *Den rechten weg auß zu faren von Lißbona gen Kallakuth* (*To Travel on the Right Path from Lisbon to Calicut*), published in Nuremberg in 1506. The text gives a brief account of the Portuguese explorations in Asia, in particular the voyage of Vasco da Gama, and highlights the spices, medicines, precious stones, and animals sent from India to Lisbon. (Refer to the illustration on the cover of this book.) The frontispiece of the text shows a Portuguese and Indian standing at opposite edges of the same landmass. The Indian, along with the tree next to him, stands at a right angle to the Portuguese, thus indicating a different position on the globe. A triangle at the center of the image reinforces the idea that the two men stand at a right angle to each other yet share a space that can be defined geometrically, representing the

---

[41] The two maps, bound together and known as *Schöner Sammelband*, are located in the Library of Congress [G1015 .S43 1517]. The Schöner copy is the lone surviving copy for both maps. For more on Schöner's globe making, see Van Duzer, *Johann Schöner's Globe*.
[42] Geus, "Ptolemaios," 49.
[43] Gautier Dalché, "The Reception," 327–333.
[44] McLean, *The 'Cosmographia' of Sebastian Münster*, 49.
[45] Olwig, *Landscape*, 32.
[46] Johnson, *The German Discovery*, 54.

90 degrees of longitude between Lisbon and Calicut.⁴⁷ Similarly, the anonymous *Die reyse van Lissebone* (*The Journey from Lisbon*) from 1508 shows a woodcut with two separate images standing at a ninety-degree angle to each other (figure 5). The first shows three Europeans, the figure on the left perhaps being Vespucci, while the image standing on its side shows two inhabitants of America. The two images are joined by a triangle. Both illustrations thus attempted to represent the shape of the world as a sphere.⁴⁸

The 1506 text is preceded by another woodcut showing a crude map of the Old World represented as a globe-like sphere on which the Ptolemaic grid is superimposed. The anonymous author added a descriptive comment about the map:

> This sphere of the earth according to Ptolemy's description will teach and instruct you of the location of the lands according to line and degree. Also, the figure below contains all the following descriptions of new islands and lands, which were found recently but which had been unknown to the philosophers for a long time. In this figure, one can also find Nuremberg, Lisbon, and Calicut marked with dots and single letters.⁴⁹

Ptolemy is both confirmed and dismissed in the same paragraph: on one hand, credit is given to Ptolemy for the method by which the map is constructed. On the other hand, the text proudly declares that the map shows parts of the world that were unknown to the Ancients, like Ptolemy. Furthermore, the map only marks three cities, none of them of significance in the classical world, but all of them hubs of the contemporaneous global trade system.⁵⁰ The introduction to the map makes a vague reference to America, but neither does the map itself nor the main body of the text. However, the map shows the entire continent of Africa, not just the northern half. This text shows the ambivalence toward Ptolemy: Ptolemy still was accepted as an authority, and his *Geographia* remained a popular book in the sixteenth century, while at the same time his knowledge base was seen as limited and dated.⁵¹ Ironically, this ambivalence is

---

47 Borowka-Clausberg, *Balthasar Sprenger*, 4.
48 Borowka-Clausberg, *Balthasar Sprenger*, 7–9.
49 Anon., *Den rechten Weg*, [2]: "Dise spere nach Ptholomeus beschreybung des erdreychs wirdt euch lernen vnd vnderweysen die gelegenhait der landen bey welcher linien vnd gradus Auch ist die nach gesetzt figur/ in jr halten alle nach geschribne ding von newen Jnseln vnd landen die man yetz in kurtz gefunden hat/ das dan den Philosophi lange zeyt verporgen ist gewesen. Man findt auch darin verzeichnet Nurnberg/ Lißbona vnd kallakuth mit punckten vnd einzalig buchstaben in der figur."
50 On the map, Nuremberg and Calicut are marked with small circles and initial letters N and K while Lisbon is only marked by a small circle.
51 Ramachandran, *The Worldmakers*, 5.

Figure 5: Anon. *Die reyse van Lissebone om te varenna dat eylandt Naguaria in groot Indien gheleghen*. Antwerp: Jan van Doesborch, 1508. Sig. C3r. © John Carter Brown Library, Brown University, Providence, Rhode Island.

highlighted by a typographical error in the map as well.[52] The bottom of the map indicates south, as was the new norm in cartography. The top of the map, however, is labeled east, a relic of old T-O maps that had an east-west orientation.

The competing claims by Portugal and Spain to the Moluccan spice islands illustrate how maps using a Ptolemaic grid could be used to gain territorial advantage. The conflict erupted after the Spanish Magellan expedition had reached the area in 1521, an area already claimed by Portugal. In 1529,

---

52 Borowka-Clausberg, *Balthasar Sprenger*, 3.

the Treaty of Saragossa settled the issue in Portugal's favor; however, the Spanish Crown received the handsome compensation of 350,000 ducats in return. Two mapmakers in the services of the Spanish Crown, Diogo Ribeiro[53] and Giovanni Vespucci,[54] produced maps in the years before 1529 that moved the Moluccas further east, presumably to support the Spanish claim. The Vespucci map used a polar perspective to demonstrate that the Moluccas were located to the east of the extended line established in the Atlantic by the Treaty of Tordesillas in 1494. The fact that both Ribeiro and Vespucci participated in the negotiations on the Spanish side shows that their geographic expertise and their ability to manipulate the grid was valued.[55] In the aftermath, the Welser Company hired Ribeiro as their own map maker and to produce the large Welser world map in 1530.[56]

The Augsburg Humanist Conrad Peutinger offers a further instructive example for the ambivalence toward Ptolemy. When Anton Welser, his father-in-law, Ambrosius Höchstetter, and Conrad Vöhlin brought natives of India to Augsburg, Peutinger noted their arrival in his personal copy of Ptolemy's *Cosmographia*, as if he intended to amend Ptolemy's description of the world.[57]

In spite of his critique of Ptolemy, Waldseemüller himself participated in modern editions of Ptolemy's works and contributed maps for them. While Ptolemy was still an accepted authority, Humanists were eager to point out flaws in his work. Chief among them was the fact that his longitudinal data contained significant errors and thus was highly unreliable.[58] Ptolemy also overestimated the east-west dimension of the known world considerably, and Ptolemaic maps were thought only to show 180 degrees of the world, not the full 360 degrees. As a result, explorers like Columbus vastly underestimated the distance to East Asia.[59] Map makers created the illusion of relative proximity between Europe and

---

53 Häberlein, *Aufbruch*, 164–165.
54 Heitzmann ("Wem gehören die Molukken?") describes a Spanish map by Giovanni Vespucci from 1523 or 1524 that was recently discovered in the holdings of the Herzog August Bibliothek Wolfenbüttel, as well as a similar 1524 map by Vespucci at Harvard University, both using a polar perspective.
55 Brotton (*A History*, 201) claims that the Portuguese had three map makers in their delegation and the Spanish five, including Alonso de Chaves and Nuño García in addition to Ribeiro and Vespucci.
56 Häberlein, *Aufbruch*, 164–65. Only two segments of the map are still extant.
57 Leitch, *Mapping Ethnography*, 73; also 214, n. 46.
58 The problem to accurately assess longitude persisted throughout the Early Modern period and was only resolved by John Harrison (1693–1776). See Sobel, *The True Story*.
59 Geus, "Ptolemaios," 43–45.

East Asia, like the world map by Henricus Martellus (Heinrich Hammer) created around 1491 with which Columbus likely was familiar.[60] Martellus positioned Japan far off the coast of Asia at the edge of the map, thus implying relative proximity to Europe on the other side of the map, and placed a number of small islands that were mentioned by Ptolemy to its south.[61] Columbus thus had every reason to believe that he had arrived in the East Indies. It is this misconception that may have prevented Columbus from claiming to have discovered a new continent, which in turn made his accounts less alluring. Only the accounts of his third voyage of 1498–1500 implied that mainland had been found.[62]

In his introduction to the text, Waldseemüller explained the basic idea behind the grid concept he developed and employed here:

> I put together the following outline and interpretation, which is common to the entire world. For this is useful and good for all humans, as will be made clear later. So that everyone, be he learned or uneducated, can assess and understand what is presented to him daily, in sermons and otherwise, of many lands in which God and His Saints performed miracles and revealed the genuine Christian truth to the entire world, from which no one shall back off.[63]

His intention was to create a visual representation of a spatial model that granted the opportunity to develop an understanding of the structure of the world even to uneducated people so that they could understand geographic references used by preachers.

In a poem that concludes his introduction, Waldseemüller emphatically asserted that the New World was included in his description of the world as it was part of God's miraculous creation:

---

[60] Hessler and Van Duzer, *Seeing the World Anew*, 19.
[61] The fact that Japan was an island was known from Marco Polo's account. Waldseemüller in his 1507 world map represented this part of the world virtually identically to the Martellus map, with the addition of America that now separates Europe and Asia. According to Van Duzer, Martellus was an important source for Waldseemüller's 1507 map. (Van Duzer, "Waldseemüller's World Maps," 8.) Waldseemüller completely re-designed the representation of Asia in his 1516 map.
[62] Pieper, *Die Vermittlung*, 100.
[63] Waldseemüller, *Der welt kugel*, sig. A2r: "hab zůsamen bracht diß nachgonde exposition vnnd vßlegung/ in einer gemeyn der gantzen welt/ Dan sollichs nützlich vnd gůt ist allen menschen/ als dan hernach/ klarlich vermerckt wirdt/ vff das ein yeder/ er sey gelert oder vngelert/ ermessen vnnd verston möge/ Was im teglich an predigen vnnd sunst vorgesagt wirt von mangerley land darinn got vnd seine heiligen allenthalben wunderzeüchen gethon/ vnd die rechte cristenliche warheit geoffenbaret aller welt/ deren sich nieman entschuldigen mag."

The heaven and the entire earth are described here without peril, and in addition the New World is included here as well. Whatever miraculous works God created, this booklet will talk about it.[64]

The accompanying woodcut shows the creation of Eve – a clear reference that cosmography had its origin in the creation of the world and that it had to be viewed as part of the creation narrative.[65] In the woodcut, Eve is emanating from Adam's side with the newly created animals watching, while Adam is sleeping on the ground. Eve, her feet still stuck in Adam's side, is turning to God, and her finger is almost touching God's finger. What is remarkable is that God's finger is seeking out Eve's finger and not Adam's, as is the case in Michelangelo's iconic fresco in the Sistine Chapel, referred to as the *Creation of Adam*, created a couple of years later.[66] Michelangelo's version of creation sees Adam as the crowning achievement, and the near-touch of the fingers is interpreted to allude to the fact that the human was created in God's image. But in Genesis 2:21–23, the creation really only is complete with the creation of Eve. In the same way, America is simultaneously an afterthought and symbol that creation is not complete without it. Just as creation was only complete once Eve had been created, the creation narrative of the earth only was complete once it included America.

Waldseemüller was working toward an unexcited and factual method of talking about space, which he saw as one of the reference points in the cultural framework of the time. He helped integrate spatial knowledge into cultural discourses and thus gave the rhetoric of discoveries an aura of normalcy. In a text box on sheet twelve of his 1507 world map, Waldseemüller urged his readers to be patient and to try to learn about contemporaneous cosmography before condemning it: "This one request we have to make, that those who may not be acquainted with geography shall not condemn all that they see before them until they have learned what will surely be apparent to them later on, when they

---

64 Waldseemüller, *Der welt kugel*, sig. A2v: "Der hymel vnd die gantze erde | Wirt hie beschriben on geferde | Vnd dartzů die neüwe welt | Wirt auch hie bey getzelt | Was wunderwerck got hat geschaffen | Diß büchlin hat on vber klaffen."
65 Sebastian Münster's *Cosmographia* (1544) contains a similar representation of the creation of Eve as well. The page bears the title "Beschöpffung der welt ein anfang aller historien/ vnd vrsprung der gantzen Cosmographei" (Creation of the world, a beginning of all histories and origin of the entire cosmography). To Münster, cosmography had its origin in the creation of the world.
66 Hartmut Schedel's *Nuremberg Chronicle* contains a similar woodcut (fol. 6v). But there are significant differences: in Schedel's version, God is holding Eve's arm with one hand while raising his other in a gesture of blessing. Also, no animals are present.

have come to understand what they see."[67] The implication was that traditional systems of order were insufficient as long as they did not include current geographic knowledge. This was not acceptable to those who rejected the rhetoric of discoveries. The resulting tension is at the core of the backlash against spatial knowledge and globalizing trends in the culture of the early sixteenth century that will be discussed in Chapters 13 and 14.

Subsequent cosmographic writings continued to explore this tension. An important text that established the cosmographic tradition in Germany was *Cosmographia liber* (Book of Cosmography), a relatively slim but richly illustrated and influential book published in 1524 by the mathematician and astronomer Peter Apian (Petrus Apianus, 1495–1552). The book has two main parts: the first discussing the principles of cosmography, which to Apian was defined by its mathematical approach, and the second providing cosmographical data.[68] In a textbook fashion, Apian systematically developed a methodology on how the world could be measured and understood using mathematical and geometric principles, giving data points on the structure of the spheres, the division of the heavens, the geography of the earth, its parallels and meridians, climate zones, winds, and islands and peninsulas. He instructed readers on how to build and use instruments of measurement and how to use them for map making. He taught learned students the methods for calculating the latitude and longitude of a place and the trigonometry necessary for calculating distances.[69] In that sense, Apian's text was an introduction to a world in which maps and globes representing an increasingly complex world held a certain fascination but also became an essential tool for success in sixteenth-century society.[70]

Apian's Dutch colleague Gemma Frisius (born Jemme Reinerszoon; 1508–1555), the annotator of the 1529 edition of Apian's *Cosmographia liber*, expressed this novelty and joyful wonderment in the preface of his own *De principiis astronomiae et cosmographiae* (*Of the Principles of Astronomy and Cosmography*, 1530). There, Frisius stated that he wrote the book

> because new parts of the earth are surveyed by the day now, [parts] which these [ancient] authors did not mention, a fact for which they should not be blamed. Also, because new names of regions spring up continuously, spreading considerable confusion among students. Last of all, because we recently brought out a globe, designed with

---

67 Translation Hessler and Van Duzer, *Seeing the World Anew*, 46.
68 Broecke, "The Use of Visual Media," 132.
69 McLean, *The 'Cosmographia' of Sebastian Münster*, 124.
70 Broecke, "The Use of Visual Media," 133.

great effort from the descriptions of ancient authors and the navigations of the Spanish and Portuguese, but encountered many who ignored its splendid and joyous use.[71]

Frisius took great delight that knowledge of the world was growing at a breathtaking speed, beyond what the Ancients ever could have known.

The second part of Apian's book offers a brief survey of the four continents, America being on equal footing with the other three continents. The illustration of a globe early in the book shows "America" as a separate continent.[72] Like Waldseemüller and other German sources before him, he claimed that America, also referred to as "Novus Mundus," was discovered by Vespucci in 1497, and he repeated other standard topoi, such as the natives going naked and practicing anthropophagy.[73] The last third of the book lists places on all four continents and gives longitudes and latitudes for all of them.[74] Each place on earth thus is describable by its coordinates on the world grid. Apian listed a total of 1,417 places, all with longitudes and latitudes. The book thus turns into a work of reference, providing data so that other practitioners of cosmography did not have to make the complicated calculations themselves.[75]

But Apian was not interested in providing detailed geographical or anthropological information about various parts of the world; rather he wanted to teach the methods that would allow readers to see the world as a grid to which they could attach information they had generated themselves. Steven Vanden Broecke argues that the cosmographic work by Apian and Frisius probably has to be seen as "didactic tool for use in a non-institutionalized context."[76] While his work was rooted in academic astronomy, he also relied on artisanal cartography and on scientific and navigational instruments. Displaying images of maps, globes, and instruments therefore served to legitimize cosmography and helped prepare the way for later cosmographic and chorographic works.

Mapping projects after Waldseemüller proceeded in a very similar fashion. Lorenz Fries picked up Waldseemüller's and Apian's theoretical and methodological frame and referenced it in the title of his 1527 book, *Uslegung der mercarten oder Cartha Marina Darin man sehen mag/ wo einer in der wellt sey/ vnd wo ein ytlich Landt/ Wasser vnd Stadt gelegen ist (Interpretation of Ocean Maps or Nautical Charts, in Which One Can See Where One Is in the World, and Where*

---

71 Frisius, *De principiis astronomiae*, sig. A1v.; translation Broecke, "The Use of Visual Media," 133.
72 Apian, *Cosmographicus Liber*, 2.
73 Apian, *Cosmographicus Liber*, 69.
74 Apian, *Cosmographicus Liber*, 70–104.
75 McLean, *The 'Cosmographia' of Sebastian Münster*, 124.
76 Broecke, "The Use of Visual Media," 143.

Every Land, Body of Water, and City Is Located). In his book, Fries offered an interpretation of Waldseemüller's magnificent second world map, the *Carta marina* from 1516 and of his own *Carta Marina Navigatoria* from 1525 that was inspired by Waldseemüller's chart, yet lacked its sophistication and detailed representation.[77] We have to assume that Fries had access to some notes from Waldseemüller, who had died in 1520.[78] Just like Waldseemüller, Fries asserted the indebtedness of his approach to Ptolemy while simultaneously dismissing Ptolemy's insights as impractical. The point of Fries's ocean map was to create a framework of orientation for the mariner:

> Everywhere on this map markings or lines were drawn across the ocean that intersect repeatedly, which may seem quite strange to many. To explain briefly, you should know that these markings mean nothing other than the needles according to which mariners orient their voyages from one port to the other where they plan to travel, and also according to which they know to turn into or from the wind.[79]

Invoking Waldseemüller as his model, Fries asserted that the maps were drawn "in appropriate size, using the best skills, and following exact geometric measurements."[80] The maps helped the user easily find the three continents, but also the "seven climates as they were applied by the Ancients."[81] In Fries's model the climate zones served as latitudinal zones that helped fine-tune his geographic grid system. Fries added an index that included numeric coordinates with the intent to help readers find the desired locations, like countries, cities, and islands on the maps.[82]

As indices were a new feature of the printed book in the early sixteenth century,[83] Fries felt compelled to add detailed information on this novel concept and on how to use it. By doing so, he incidentally also explained how his geographic mapping system worked:

---

[77] No copies of the original 1525 map are extant, only one copy each of the 1530 and 1531 editions. See Hessler and Van Duzer, *Seeing the World Anew*, 66–68.
[78] Johnson, *Carta marina*, 96.
[79] Fries, *Uslegung der mercarten*, sig. A3r: "ES sind allenthalben in diser karten riß oder linien gezogen durch dz mer welche zum dickrenmal krütz weis vbereinander gond/ das da manchen gar seltzam bedunckt. Kürtzliche diß zůerkleren/ sol tu wissen dz dise riß nit anders bedüten dan die nadlen/ nach welchen die Marinalen ire schiffert richten von einem port zů dem andern/ dahin se dan faren wöllen/ auch nach welchen sie wißen den winden zů vnd von zůgeben."
[80] Fries, *Uslegung der mercarten*, sig. A1v: "in zimlicher grösse/ nach rechter kunst vnd gewisser messung der Geometry."
[81] Fries, *Uslegung der mercarten*, sig. A4r: "siben climat/ wie sie von den alten gebrauchet worden."
[82] Fries, *Uslegung der mercarten*, sig. A4v.
[83] Pettegree, *The Book in the Renaissance*, 294–295.

If you want to know in which climate zone a country, island, or region is located, find in the register where this city or island is mentioned. Note the first number you find next to it and search for it on the map. On the left-hand side you see the climate zone in which this city, island, or region is located. Take this as an example. A foreign merchant travels from Alexandria to Frankfurt am Main to visit the trade fair and wants to know in which climate zone Frankfurt is located. So he goes to the letter F in the index, finds Frankfurt, and then sees the number 47. He looks for this number next to the border on the left-hand side and sees noted the seventh climate zone. This indicates to him that Frankfurt is located in the seventh climate zone.[84]

The example is as instructive as it is remarkable: apparently, a merchant traveling from Alexandria to Frankfurt on business was realistic enough to serve as a credible hypothetical example. The example shows how broad Fries' own mental map was and how he tried to promote a new spatial thinking that had a global frame of reference. It is this expanded global outlook that more conservative intellectuals at the time found very difficult to accept, as Chapters 13 and 14 will argue.

While Fries did not promote geographic innovations as thoroughly as Waldseemüller, he included an eighth climate zone in the north as these arctic territories had not been known and described by the Ancients.[85] He also included a section on the New World in his text: "The new land described here is, called America, is approximately as big as a fourth part of the entire world."[86] While he did not explicitly call America a fourth continent, the claim that it was as large as a fourth of the world de facto gave it a continental status. He repeated Waldseemüller's claim that America was discovered by Amerigo Vespucci in 1497 and therefore bore his name.

The included sample map shows southern Portugal, the West African coast, and the islands of Madeira and Porto Santo.[87] A line is drawn from Portugal to

---

84 Fries, *Uslegung der mercarten*, sig. A4r: "So du nun wissen wilt/ in welchem climat ein land/ insul/ stat oder gegne gelegen sei/ so nim in dem register war/ wo die selbe stat oder insul ston/ vnd die ersten zal so du daneben findest/ die sůhe in der carten/ gegen der lincken hand am ort vnd zůhand sichstu dabei dz climat dar in die selbig stat/ insul oder gegne gelegen ist. Deß nim dir ein sölich exempel/ Es kumpt ein frembder kauffman von Alexandria gen franckfurt an mein in die meß/ vnd wil wissen in welchem climat frankfurt lig/ so get er hienach in dz register im bůchstaben. F. findet franckfurt/ vnd daby zů dem ersten. 47. Dise zal sucht er neben der leisten gegen der lincken hand/ vnd sicht dabei verzeichnet die. 7. climat dz gibt im anzeigung dz frankfurt im sibenden climat gelegen ist."
85 Fries, *Uslegung der mercarten*, sig. A4r.
86 Fries, *Uslegung der mercarten*, sig. A6v: "Das new lant hie beschriben/ America genant/ ist gar nahent als gros als ein vierdes teil der gantzen welt."
87 In the copy at the Herzog August Bibliothek Wolfenbüttel [A: 10.3 Geogr. 2°] the hand-colored sample map is glued in between folio XIII and XIV.

these islands, and a ship is traveling along this line. Latitudes are marked numerically in both lateral borders. Climate zones are marked as well: the fourth zone is between the 35th and the 30th parallel, the third zone below that. Furthermore, a scale indicates distances; the implication is that the map was drawn to scale.

Waldseemüller's erroneous claim that Vespucci had discovered America in 1497 was repeated by Christian Egenolff in the third edition of his *Chronica*, published in 1535. Egenolff added a section "Of America, the fourth part of the world, found in the year 1497,"[88] which was not included in the earlier editions from 1533 and 1534. Egenolff identified the West Indies as new islands with the status of a continent that was discovered by Vespucci: "America the New World, or called the fourth part of the world, has its name from its discoverer Amerigo Vespucci."[89] Waldseemüller and Ringmann also were the source for the claim that America was completely surrounded by water, rather than Vespucci. While it has been long known that Vespucci is an unreliable source, Waldseemüller and Ringmann also misrepresented Vespucci.[90]

Egenolff, like most other contemporaneous writers, stressed that this large new continent was not known to Ptolemy nor to the other Ancients. But his text shows that the New World was still a hazy concept, at least in Germany, in that all lands not known to the Ancients are referred to as New World, including recently discovered parts of Africa. The next sub-heading in the America section is entitled "New World that was found in the year 1455 below Portugal"[91] and reports the explorations of the West African coast by the Venetian Alvise Cadamosto on behalf of the Portuguese Crown. This is followed by an account of a Portuguese expedition to India in 1500, led by Pedro Álvares Cabral; Egenolff did not mention the pioneering journey to India by Vasco da Gama in 1497–1499.

The next section discusses the "voyage of the King of Castile by Christopher Columbus."[92]

It focuses on the discovery of the islands of Hispaniola and Cuba in 1492. If Egenolff knew about Columbus's 1492 journey, why did he credit Vespucci's 1497 journey as the moment when America was discovered? It is possible that

---

[88] Egenolff, *Chronica* (1535), fol. 103v: "Von America dem vierdten theyl der Welt/ Anno M. cccc.xcvij. erfunden."
[89] Egenolff, *Chronica* (1535), fol. 103v: "America die new Welt/ oder der vierdtheyl der Welt genant hat von jrem erfinder Amerigo Vespucio den namen."
[90] Lehmann, "Amerigo Vespucci," 20–21.
[91] Egenolff, *Chronica* (1535), fol. 104r: "Newe Welt so mann gefunden hat/ Anno etc. M.cccc. lv. vnderhalb Portugal."
[92] Egenolff, *Chronica* (1535), fol. 105r: "schiffart des königs von Castilia durch Christophorum Columbum."

Egenolff did not associate Hispaniola and Cuba with the New World, just as Columbus was not aware of having discovered a new continent? It is also possible that he uncritically accepted Waldseemüller's narrative and for some reason failed to see the larger picture. But even more puzzling is the subsequent section on the "boat voyage by Albericus Vespucci,"[93] just a few pages after the section about Amerigo Vespucci mentioned above. Did Egenolff not recognize that Albericus and Amerigo were one and the same person? Albericus was a common Latinization of Amerigo, and as a result both Alberico and Alberigo were used as Vespucci's first name.[94]

The last two sections of the chapter on America focused on the narratives by Hernán Cortés and by Johann Boemus whose *Omnium gentium mores, leges et ritus* (1520) was influential throughout the sixteenth century.[95] It is evident in all the text segments on discoveries that Egenolff uncritically anthologized text segments by different writers, but selected and copied from a single source: Sebastian Franck's *Weltbůch*, published in 1534.[96] Several of these segments are first-person narratives, told in the voice of the original author. Egenolff made no attempt to properly integrate these segments in his own third-person narrative to enhance its cohesion. It looks like Egenolff put this chapter together at the last minute and in haste, and it is evident that his knowledge of the subject matter was minimal.

The fact that not even a major publisher based in Frankfurt could make sense of these narratives is evidence that knowledge about Spanish and Portuguese explorations was still sketchy and tentative in Germany in the 1530s and that the scope of the colonial expansion that was well under way at that time was poorly understood, in spite of the rapidly growing interest in cosmography. Only toward the middle of the sixteenth century did the majority of cosmographers and mapmakers consider America a continent, even though the evidence still was inconclusive.[97] We also have to remember that Egenolff's text grew out of the chronicle tradition, as mentioned before, and that the inclusion of synchronous geographic information led to a messy

---

[93] Egenolff, *Chronica* (1535), 107r: "schiffart Alberici Vesputii."
[94] There is a line of scholarship making the claim that Alberico was Vespucci's birth name, last made by Forbes, "The Use," 53.
[95] Johnson (*Cultural Hierarchy*, 30) calls the book "arguably the most widely cited and reprinted cosmography of its day."
[96] Egenolff's section on the New World (*Chronica* (1535), fol. 103v–108v) is lifted almost verbatim, but selectively from the corresponding but much more comprehensive section of Sebastian Franck's *Weltbůch* (Franck, *Weltbůch*, fol. 210v–239r).
[97] Davies, "America and Amerindians," 351.

transitional text drawing from different generic traditions. But at the same time, the temptation offered by Franck's text to start to fill geographic information in the blank spots on the (imaginary) emerging cosmographic globe may have been too great for Egenolff to pass up.

Waldseemüller, Fries, and Egenolff's third edition[98] made the point that the earth as a sphere could be calculated and known mathematically – even though geographic knowledge of the non-European world still was scant. A geometric grid had been imposed on it that made it possible to describe the world accurately and to "know" those parts of the world that had not been explored yet. Geographic knowledge now had a location on a mathematically calculable grid. No longer were there unknown parts of the world as each spot on Earth had coordinates and therfore its place on the grid, and as such was at least theoretically known.

The invention of the globe in the late fifteenth century has to be seen in connection with the rise of cosmography: the globe depicts "the shape of the earth" and thus "emphasizes the mobility of the geometric center."[99] The geometric projections that form the basis of both cosmography and the three-dimensional representation of the world on a globe make it possible to distinguish between a culturally and ethnically determined center of the world and a geometrically determined center that was movable and adjustable.[100] This enabled Father Mateo Ricci to produce a world map in China in 1584 where the Pacific, and with it China, held the central position while Europe was placed at the periphery.[101] While cosmography and the globe enabled the distinction between cartographic and cultural centrality, the texts examined in the next section will show that this notion was very much contested and that the potential loss of geographic centrality was rejected, particularly in popular culture.

The movability of the center and the mathematical-geometric method of describing space made it possible to gradually develop geographic knowledge, and new discoveries thus no longer fundamentally reshaped the way Humanists thought about the world; rather, discoveries simply helped fill in the blank spots on the map. For this reason, later discoveries did not have an impact comparable to those around 1500 as they no longer had the capacity to challenge the basic concepts of spatial organization.

This is not to say that cosmographers had an unequivocally positive attitude toward the idea of spatial expansion. Sebastian Franck, for instance, in

---

98 Egenolff, *Chronica* (1535), fol. 1v.
99 Mignolo, *The Darker Side*, 370, note 8.
100 Mignolo, *The Darker Side*, 222.
101 Mignolo, *The Darker Side*, 219–223.

his *Weltbůch* (*World Book*) from 1534 very much doubted the noble intentions behind the quest for the discovery and appropriation of the entire world:

> A large part of [the world's] location, size, and expanse would be unknown now if the use of force by the great Alexander and by the Romans had not unlocked the world. And most recently in the past hundred years, in particular, the rule of the Venetians, the curiosity and gold hunger of the merchants, and the ocean voyages by the kings of Portugal and Spain have discovered many territories and peoples, yes even a new world, which were unknown to us before.[102]

Franck believed that the conquests by Alexander the Great and by the Romans in the classical period were critical for the expansion of the known geographic world. The word "gwalt" describes the use of force, in the sense of *potestas*, in order to achieve control. Franck viewed the discoveries and conquests of more recent times in the context of the expansion of trade, promoted by foreign powers like Venice, Portugal, and Spain, and of the lustful accumulation of riches. The words "fürwitz" and "goldthunger," both attributes of merchants, were connotated negatively: "Fürwitz," curiosity, was commonly associated with the deadly sin of *curiositas*, while "goldthunger," literally hunger for gold, tied into the topos of unearned and undeserved wealth – that was part of usury discourses – and into the deadly sin of greed and avarice. These are some of the key topoi we will encounter in the literature hostile to the spatial expansion.

---

[102] Franck, *Weltbůch*, Vorred, fol. 1r: "Nun von der gelegenheyt grösse vnd weitte der selben wer auch ein grosser teyl vnbekant/ wa nit des grossen Alexanders vnd der Römer gwalt die welt hetten auffgeschlossen/ vnd sunderlich zůletzt yetz in hundert jaren der Venediger herrschafft/ der Kaufleüt fürwitz vnd goldthunger/ vnd des Künigs von Portugals vnd Hispanien mörfart/ vil land vnd leüt/ ja gleich neüwe welt/ vns vormals vnbekannt/ hetten gefunden."

Chapter 12
Emancipation from Ancient Concepts of Space

In the early sixteenth century, the rising trade hubs like Lisbon and Antwerp became new melting pots where people and ideas from all over the world came together. In 1503, the imperial secretary and Humanist Johannes Collaurius (d. 1508/9) excitedly wrote to Conrad Celtis from Antwerp:

> We have arrived in this land [Antwerp] where no day passes on which I would not call you a thousand times. You would here see, among many other noteworthy things, Portuguese sailors who relate astounding tales. You would wonder at the absurd statements of all the ancient writers who have asserted that things are not to be found in human nature, unless they themselves had discovered and seen them. You would see here another kind of map for navigating to the Antarctic pole and men who would relate to you marvelous and unheard things. [...] I am unable to write about all that we have seen and heard. Another world has been found unknown to the Ancients![1]

Collaurius picked up on the tension that existed between the classical world view, as represented by Ptolemy, and the pragmatic knowledge generated by mariners and merchants that gradually eroded the influence of Ptolemy's *Geography*. Collaurius's statement makes clear that Ptolemy offered no "intellectual niche" to integrate new geographic information obtained by empirical observation.[2]

Narratives containing geographic descriptions invariably entered a complex and potentially conflictual relationship with the classical tradition, and many writers of the early sixteenth century pointed out with pride that contemporary geographic knowledge by far surpassed that of the Ancients. Around 1500, Italian chronicles and cosmographies started to make the claim that the newly found territories were extraordinary and had not been described by classical authorities.[3] German sources followed this argumentation quickly, first in subtle ways, but soon much more overtly.

Gregor Reisch inserted a large fold-out world map in his *Margerita philosophica*, published in Freiburg in 1503. Following Ptolemy, a land mass encloses the Indian Ocean on the map. On the portion of the landmass that connects to southern Africa in an easterly direction, Reisch added this caption: "Here is not land, but ocean. In it there are islands of extraordinary size unknown to

---

1 Translation Spitz, *Conrad Celtis*, 103–104.
2 Phillips, "The Outer World," 31.
3 Pieper, *Die Vermittlung*, 110.

Ptolemy."[4] While the visual representation in the map still was indebted to Ptolemy, the inscribed text was not. Thus the tension played out in a single map. A similar example is Martin Waldseemüller's map of southern Africa in the 1513 Strasbourg edition of Ptolemy's *Geographia*, entitled "modern map of the second part of Africa."[5] At its center, it bears the inscription: "This part of Africa remained unknown to the Ancients."[6]

As mentioned above, Jobst Ruchamer in the foreword to his 1508 German edition of Fracanzano da Montalboddo's influential compilation of discovery texts, the *Paesi Novamente retrovati* (1507), argued that the Ancients had known nothing about the wondrous lands his book was about to describe.[7] Similarly, Michael Herr's compilation of New World discovery texts, based on a Latin compilation by Simon Grynaeus and published in 1534, turned the ignorance of the Ancients into a programmatic point that is communicated in the very title of the book: *Die new welt, der landschaften vnnd Insulen, so bis hie her allen Altweltbeschrybern unbekant/ Jungst aber von den Portugalesern vnnd Hispaniern jm Nidergenglichen Meer herfunden* (*The New World of Landscapes and Islands, Which Were Not Known to the Famous Ancient Cosmographers and Describers of the World, but Which Were Found Recently by the Portuguese and Spaniards in the Occidental Ocean*). The heading of the first chapter of the main body of the text repeats the first half of the title and then asserts that these newly discovered parts had been unknown to classical authorities like Ptolemy, Strabo, Pomponius Mela, Dionysos, and others.[8]

Likewise, areas in northern Europe were alleged to have been unknown to the Ancients. Johannes Eck makes this point in the introduction to his 1518 German translation of the *Tractatus de duabus Sarmatiis, Asiana et Europiana* (*Treatise on the Two Sarmatias, Asian and European*) by Maciej Miechowita. Eck praised the validity of this text "considering that said doctor Maciej Miechowita is at home in Poland and that his description is more credible than that of other Latin or Greek writers who had never seen these lands."[9] Eck dedicated his

---

4 Translation Grafton, *New Worlds*, 57.
5 Ptolemy, *Claudii Ptolemei*, [263]: "Tabula Moderna Secunde Porcionis Aphrice."
6 "Hec pars Aphrice antiquioribus mansit incognita." Translation Johnson, *The German Discovery*, 74.
7 Ruchamer, *Newe vnbekanthe landte*, "vorrede," sig. A1v.
8 Herr, *Die new welt*, fol. 1r.
9 Eck, *Tractat*, sig. A1v: "in ansehung/ das bemelter doctor Mathis von Miechaw in poln anhaym/ vnd seiner beschreybung mer weder andern lateinischen oder kriechischen schreybern/ die solche lanndt nye gesehen/ [...] zů gelauben ist."

translation to Jakob Fugger, no doubt fully aware of the Fuggers's thirst for novel geographical information. Similarly, the Swedish Catholic theologian Olaus Magnus (1490–1557) claimed in the pamphlet that accompanied his famous 1539 *Carta Marina* that the Scandinavian kingdoms shown on the map "were unknown to all Greek and Latin historians to date."[10]

While most cosmographers used an incrementalist approach to differentiate their knowledge base from that of the Ancients, Sebastian Franck in his *Weltbůch* (1534) painted a stark contrast between the modern view of the world as a sphere and Ptolemy's antiquated world view whose descriptions were barely recognizable to Franck:

> There is a great difference between the ancient and the modern scribes of the world and travelers on the topic of the location, form, and names of the round, spherical, perfect world and its peoples and provinces. For Ptolemy calls nearly all things differently than our contemporary merchants, mariners, and cosmographers. [...] I consider this not a small reason for the many turnovers of governments, as happened also in Germany.[11]

Ptolemy not only named things differently, he also conceptualized them differently. After calling the earth a round, spherical, perfect world, Franck focused on the discontinuities of cosmography, in particular on the discrepancies between ancient and modern cosmographers. In the book title Franck signaled that he relied on "credible, experienced world writers" rather than on classical authorities.[12] While the ancient cosmographers like Ptolemy were philosophers, the modern geographical authorities were merchants, mariners, and cosmographers who took a pragmatic, commercially motivated or political interest and based their insights on empirical observation and experience, not on speculation and theoretical reasoning. To Franck, the practical, pragmatic knowledge of modern merchants, travelers, and cosmographers eclipsed the merely theoretical construct presented by Ptolemy, which was why the likes of Ptolemy, Strabo, or Pliny could no longer be accepted as authorities. Franck asserted

---

10 Magnus, *Ain kvrze Avslegvng*, sig. A1v: "alle Kriechischen und Lateinischen gschichtschreibern bisher unbekant."

11 Franck, *Weltbůch*, Vorred, fol. 2v: "Nun ad propositum von der gelegenheyt form vnd nammen der runden kugelten vollkummenen welt/ vnnd yhrer völcker vnnd prouintzen ist ein grosser span vnder den alten vnd neüwen weltschreibern vnd landtfarern/ dann Ptolomeus schier all ding anders nennt/ dann vnsere yetzigen kaufleüt/ mörherren/ vnd Cosmographi/ [...]. Dises acht ich auch nitt ein kleine vrsach sein die vilfeltig verkörung der Regiment/ wie auch in Germania geschehen."

12 Müller, "Alte Wissensformen," 177.

that Ptolemy made up a lot of geographic references and names and even pondered whether Ptolemy was a liar or merely ignorant.[13]

But to Franck the free-thinking mystic and spiritualist, truth also was a matter of faith: truth was buried deep in the world and ultimately only could be accessed through God.[14] This is why he dedicated his text "dem Gottseligen leser" (to the Godly reader) so that he may recognize God's works in his heart.[15] To Franck, it was a matter of faith why the books of the Ancients could not be trusted:

> For in this new divine school of rebirth belongs nothing other than a new, divine, born-again human, so that in God's school are nothing but God's children. [...] Why then would it be a surprise that all books written by humans are full of lies? What can be said about something untruthful that is true, about something impure that is pure? [...] All this I say so that we do not draw on books so much for the consolation and confidence in our lives, nor hold them to be God, nor ever put them into our heart next to God and his omnipotent living word.[16]

In contrast to the Ancients, modern men were reborn in Christ and therefore did not need to rely on the deceitful books of the Ancients. It is the experience of divine creation that gives humans an understanding of the outwardly, physical world.

Franck already indicated his program in the title of his 1534 cosmography, *Weltbůch: spiegel vnd bildtniß des gantzen erdbodens von Sebastiano Franco Wördensi in vier bůcher/ nemlich in Asiam/ Aphricam/ Europam/ vnd Americam/ gestelt vnd abteilt* (*World Book: Mirror and Image of the Entire Face of the Earth by Sebastian Franck of Donauwörth, Presented and Subdivided in Four books, namely in Asia, Africa, Europe, and America*). While the title page gives America the unequivocal status as an equal continent, the heading at the beginning of the main body of the text is more ambiguous: "Geography, mirror and image of Asia, Europe, and Africa, also of the newly found world."[17] This indicates that

---

13 Franck, *Weltbůch*, Vorred, fol. 2v. On the argument that Ptolemy may have been a liar or plagiarist see Geus, "Ptolemaios."
14 Franck, *Weltbůch*, Vorred, fol. 4r.
15 Franck, *Weltbůch*, Vorred: fol. 1r.
16 Franck, *Weltbůch*, Vorred, fol. 5r: "dann in dise neüwe götliche schůl der widergeburt gehört nicht dann ein neüwer götlicher widergeborner mensch/ das in Gottes schůl nicht dann Gottes kinder seyen. [...] Was ists dann wunder das aller menschen bůcher voll lugen seind? Was kan von einem lugenhafftigen waars gesagt werden/ von eim vnreynen reyns? [...] Diß alles sag ich darumb/ dz wir vnser leben trost vnnd datum nit so gar auff bůcher setzen/ noch für Gott halten/ oder ye neben Gott vnd sein allmechtigs lebendigs wort in vnser hertz setzen."
17 Franck, *Weltbůch*, fol. 2r: "Geographia spiegel vnd bildtniß Asie/ Europe/ vnnd Aphrice/ auch der neüw gefundenen welt."

even Franck was unsure what this New World was and how to integrate it into the existing geographical framework.

The fourth chapter, entitled "America, the fourth book of this Geography, of new, unknown worlds, islands, and landmasses that were found recently,"[18] carries on this ambiguity. Franck again stressed that the Ancients, Ptolemy in particular, knew nothing about this new part of the world. While the fourth part begins with the mythical discovery of America by Vespucci in 1497, it soon shifts to the Portuguese explorations along the coast of Africa and to the description of the kingdoms at the tip of West Africa and of some location in the Indian Ocean. The part of Africa that was known to the Ancients, including Ethiopia, Egypt, the Mediterranean coast, and West Africa to Mauretania, had been covered in the first part about the continent of Africa.[19] The narration then returns to the canonical narratives: the chapter is essentially a summary of various narratives by discoverers. But only half of the chapter focuses on America,[20] while the other half deals with voyages to different parts of the world, including relatively detailed descriptions of sub-Saharan Africa. The fourth chapter thus is not strictly about America, but more broadly about the "newly found world."

While Sebastian Franck delivered a sharp rhetorical break with the Ptolemaic tradition, Ptolemy still provided the structure of his *Weltbůch*: the first three parts deal with the world as it was known to the Ancients. The fourth part deals with the New World in the broadest sense, namely the world new to Ptolemy, whether it was located in America, Africa, or Asia. While Franck on the surface recognized America as the fourth continent, he could not escape Ptolemaic categories of thinking about the world and thus struggled to make a compelling case for America as the fourth continent. The quality of information available to Franck and his contemporaries differed greatly: while Franck could draw on a long descriptive canon covering the Ptolemaic world for the first three sections of the book, there was little illustrative material on the post-Ptolemaic "new world" available to him. As a result, the bulk of the text covering these newly discovered parts of the world consists of excerpted travel and conquest narratives penned by explorers and compilers. These text segments generally failed to render a sense of place, which was a key objective of the evolving cosmographic and chorographic project.

---

18 Franck, *Weltbůch*, fol. 210v: "America das vierdt Bůch diser Geographey von neüwen vnbekanten welten/ Jnseln/ vnd erdtriche/ so neüwlich erfunden worden seind."
19 Franck, *Weltbůch*, fol. 5v–21v.
20 Franck, *Weltbůch*, fol. 220r–234v.

In his *Cosmographia* (1544), Franck's fellow cosmographer Sebastian Münster (1488–1552) took a different, incrementalist approach that recognized Ptolemy's role as a pioneer of cosmography. Münster maintained the traditional division into three continents.[21] This was not unusual as the American discoveries to sixteenth-century scholars were not qualitatively different from the new accounts of Africa and Asia, as was the case with Franck as well. For Münster, this "new world" included most of Asia as much as it did America.[22] Of the six chapters, one is theoretical, three deal with different parts of Europe, and the remaining two deal with Asia and Africa. The small section on the New World is attached to the chapter on Asia.[23] It is interesting to note that only the 1628 edition of Münster's *Cosmographia* recognized America as a full-blown continent and dedicated an entire book to it.[24] Münster took a much more conciliatory approach toward Ptolemy and discussed the more limited knowledge of the Ancients in a moderate, almost apologetic tone:

> Ptolemy was a widely experienced man, and he described a large part of the world. Yet much remained concealed to him that was only discovered over the past thirty or forty years. The tip that you see in the general map of Africa reaching over the winter circle only was found and became known in our time. [...] Likewise, the great islands of America, Paria, Cuba, Hispaniola, Ziprangri, Francisca, and many more were unknown to the Ancients before our times, as was the far-flung part of the country of India. Also, in our times the country of Calicut became the subject of great fuss, but it has been a well-known country for a long time, particularly among the neighboring states, because it is located between Arabia and the island of Taprobane [Sri Lanka]. [...] But the new and unprecedented navigation made it known to us, which is why inexperienced people hold it to be a new island.[25]

Münster saw Ptolemy as a man of experience and integrity who was hindered by the limited knowledge of the time. He added that until forty years prior,

---

21 Davies, "America and Amerindians."
22 Rubiés, "Travel Writing," 137.
23 Münster, *Cosmographia* (1544), 636–642.
24 Lopes, "Außerordentliche und kuriose Denkwürdigkeit," 82.
25 Münster, *Cosmographia* (1544), 22: "Es ist Ptolemeus ein wyt erfarner mann gewesen/ wie er auch ein groß theyl der weldt beschriben hat/ aber es ist jm vil verborgen gewesen/ das erst in dryssig oder viertzig jaren ist erfunden. Die spitz so du in der general tafel in Africa sihst über den winter circkel ghan/ ist erst zů vnsern zyten erfunden vnd bekant worden/ [...]. Deß glichen die grosen inseln America/ Parias/ Cuba/ Hispaniola/ Zipangri/ Francisca/ vnd andere vil mer sind vor vnsern zyten den alten vnbekant gewesen/ wie dann auch das vßer theyl des lands Jndien. Es ist auch by vnsern zyten das land Callikut in ein groß geschrey kommen/ dz doch ein alt bekant land ist gewesen/ nemlich den vmbseßern/ dann es zwüschen Arabiam vnd der inseln Taprobanam gelegen ist/ [...] aber die nüw vnd fürhin onerhört schiffung hat es vns bekant gemacht/ dz doch die onerfarnen menschen für ein neüw insel halten."

most navigation took place in the Mediterranean.[26] He downplayed the significance of the discoveries: they were merely an expansion of the known world. According to Münster, discoveries southward in Africa to the Cape region, the discovery of new islands in Asia, that is the New World, and the discovery of Calicut and its region were unduly sensationalized as India had been known all along. Furthermore, in Europe more territory was discovered "toward the midnight [arctic] pole."[27]

The tension between the text and the maps, however, is palpable. While the text promotes an incremental increase in knowledge, the maps demonstrate how the conceptualization of the world had shifted fundamentally. The double-page world map that follows the introduction carries the title "Ptolomaisch general tafel" (Ptolemaic general map), but it shows "AMERICA seu insula Brasilii" (America or the island of Brazil) as a full-blown continent.[28] It is followed by the "Ptolomaisch ander general tafel" (second Ptolemaic general map) that shows the extent of Ptolemy's universe. Just the comparison of the two maps shows that the difference is not incremental. Rather, it becomes obvious that Humanist cosmography had rendered Ptolemy obsolete, in spite of Münster's lip service. Furthermore, Münster added a map of the *Novus Orbis* (New World) to his edition of Ptolemy's *Geographia universalis*, which first appeared in 1540.[29] The map shows both North and South America, and it also was the first map to use the name "Mare pacificum" for the Pacific Ocean.[30] Münster added this map, as well as others, to later editions of the *Cosmographia* as well,[31] further accentuating the tension between the restrained text and the open representation of America in his map material.

In discussing the new discoveries, the relationship of Renaissance culture with Antiquity initially framed the discussion. Humanists referred to the traditional metaphor of the dwarf standing on the shoulders of a giant, indicating that modern writers were perhaps less significant overall but that their comulative

---

26 Münster, *Cosmographia* (1544), 22.
27 Münster, *Cosmographia* (1544), 23: "gegen dem mittnächtigen polus."
28 Davies ("America and Amerindians," 356–357) arrives at a different conclusion: she claims that the maps "sustain the tripartite worldview."
29 McLean, *The 'Cosmographia' of Sebastian Münster*, 168.
30 Reprinted in Johnson, *The German Discovery*, 76. The image is also available here: https://library.princeton.edu/visual_materials/maps/websites/pacific/pacific-ocean/pacific-ocean-maps.html (last accessed on 11 May 2020).
31 Münster, *Cosmographia* (1548), map 28. The caption reads: "Die newe weldt der grossen vnnd vilen Jnslen von den Spaniern gefunden."

knowledge was greater than that of the Ancients.[32] This argument was a harbinger for the ideological quarrel of Ancients and Moderns that would emerge later in the sixteenth century and carried over into a number of other areas. Germans often expressed pride in their invention of the printing press, which allowed Germans to disseminate information more rapidly and reliably than the Ancients ever could. Humanists generally noted that the Ancients knew nothing about the territories discovered more recently and increasingly insisted that the Humanists' level of knowledge had now surpassed that of the Ancients, often with a reference to Virgil, who had forecast that there was unknown land beyond the Pillars of Hercules.[33]

It is this pragmatic knowledge based on exploration that enabled the Spanish conquest and other colonial pursuits, unencumbered by the antiquated word view of the Ancients. These colonial projects in turn enlarged the pragmatic knowledge base. The European exploration of America required a pragmatic approach that replaced the bookish nature of classical notions of nature and experience. The Spaniards institutionalized the gathering of all empirical evidence and generally of all useful practical information about the New World in the *Casa de la Contratación* and thus implicitly dismissed classical authorities as sources of important information: "Experience gained in explorations and in contact with other cultures increasingly displaced classical sources in the authority for knowledge. The natural products of the New World lacked referents in the classical sources."[34] Adapting European agricultural products and practices to a colonial context required practical knowledge that only could be gained by experimentation, not by relying on classical sources:[35] "The disparities between classical knowledge and the New World experience forced a slow reorganization of existing epistemological models."[36] The empirical practices promoted by the colonial institutions at the service of the state allowed Spain to control and commodify the natural resources that were the very foundations of colonial rule. Thus, the discovery of America affected the role of classical knowledge in two ways: first, the discovery of America forced Europeans to rethink the Ptolemaic conception of the world. And second, the need for pragmatic

---

[32] Strosetzki, "Die Idee von Fortschritt," 4; Stock, "Antiqui and Moderni," 370–374. A number of Humanists noted when writing about newly discovered lands, that this was "extra Ptolomaeum," not in Ptolemy. (Wuttke, "Humanismus," 533–535.)
[33] Wuttke, "Humanismus," 496. However, there also were some Humanists who claimed that the ancients already had made some of these discoveries. (Wuttke, "Humanismus," 519.)
[34] Barrera, "Local Herbs, Global Medicines," 164.
[35] Barrera-Osorio, *Experiencing Nature*, 23–24.
[36] Barrera-Osorio, *Experiencing Nature*, 103.

solutions in a challenging colonial environment forced the colonists to debunk the theoretical and speculative natural philosophy propagated by the Ancients. As this process was carried by Spanish institutions of state, its impact reached well beyond the borders of the Spanish empire.

This is the kind of historical progress to which Sebastian Franck had alluded: spatial expansion was ultimately linked to the process of history: "Even today, new lands, islands and people are found daily, so that the opinion that there are uncountable worlds and that the world is without end likely has to be seen as true."[37] To Franck, history was dynamic, living, and changeable:

> As history not without reason is called a master of life by the Ancients, which lives and puts living examples in front of our eyes, so that all books of law altogether teach only with empty letters and are relevant to dead people, therefore we took this labor upon ourselves not unwillingly.[38]

Here too, Franck's pragmatism is evident: it is living history that overtakes the dead letters of books. But in contrast to the model of the Ancients, Franck's concept of history also included a dynamic concept of space whose central metaphor was the world as a round, perfect, infinite spherical space. As mentioned before, Franck alleged that Ptolemy had given different names to places than modern merchants, mariners, and cosmographers had.[39] But this works both ways: the moderns in fact renamed places Ptolemy had known, and they gave names to places Ptolemy had not known. By naming and re-naming, the moderns were taking away power from the Ancients, and they asserted the primacy of their conception of space that was emancipated from ancient geography.

Franck's dynamic notion of history differed substantially from Sebastian Brant's view of a historic trajectory that had found its terminal state in the German Empire and had thus ceased to be dynamic, as discussed in Chapter 6. As the next chapter will show, Brant and others also rejected the dynamic notion of space propagated in Franck's *Weltbůch* and, more importantly, as promoted and implemented pragmatically by merchants, explorers, mariners, and colonizers.

---

37 Franck, *Weltbůch*, fol. 3v: "auch teglich noch heüt neüw land Insel vnd leüt gfunden werden/ das schier die meynung für war möcht angsehen werden/ es seind vil vnzalbar welt vnd das die welt on end sey."
38 Franck, *Weltbůch*, Vorred, fol. 2r: "Demnach weil die historia ein meysterin des lebens nitt vnbillich von den alten wird genent/ die da lebt/ vnd lebendige exempel für die augen stelt/ das alle gsatzbücher auff einen hauffen nur mit todten bůchstaben leeren vnd dem gestorben menschen fürhalten/ [...] haben wir vns nit vngern zů diser arbeyt gegürtt."
39 Franck, *Weltbůch*, Vorred, fol. 2v.

Chapter 13
Spatial Discoveries: Anxieties and Rejection in Brant's Writings

As discussed in the previous chapter, cosmography and chorography reflected the most advanced thinking about space in the early sixteenth century, in part because they were no longer entirely beholden to the classical tradition and managed to detach themselves from classical precepts, and in part because they continually integrated empirical information into their knowledge base that rapidly became available at the time, mostly informed by the latest discoveries by the Portuguese and the Spaniards. Cosmography and chorography operated outside of the established, conservative academic world and thus were not indebted to academic orthodoxy; instead they were informed by a new understanding of the world as a global commercial space.

Resistance to travel had its roots in medieval concerns about the maintenance of social order.[1] As travel writers and cosmographers were gradually working new geographic information into their texts, they encountered considerable resistance and even hostility in the popular culture against travel, but also against the exploration of space and more broadly against this new geography. In particular, German writers contested the movability of the geographic center and by implication of the cultural center introduced by cosmography. Using Sebastian Brant as an example, I will argue that there was a backlash in popular culture against the conception of space as it was developed by travel literature, cosmography, and related genres. While popular travel texts did not participate in this polemic as they generally put a positive spin on the travels reported there, texts that did not focus on the expansion of space tended to take a much more negative attitude against spatial discoveries, narratives relating them, and texts that propagated this new Humanist spatial thinking. This reveals a line of conflict within Humanism, which by no means was a uniform movement. On one hand, a pragmatic strand of Humanism evolved that was eager to integrate empirical knowledge into their writings, even if that meant disowning classical writers, as discussed in the previous chapter. On the other hand, urban intellectuals drafted popular texts that were very much focused on the preservation of the political, social, and economic order, as we have seen in Part I. These writers were also resisting the integration of new geographic information into their knowledge base. The following section will focus on these writers and their argumentation.

---

[1] Legassie, *The Medieval Invention of Travel*, 4.

Sebastian Brant's *Narrenschiff* from 1494 set the stage for the negative reception of spatial knowledge in sixteenth-century Germany. Brant discussed this topic most extensively in chapter 66, entitled "von erfarung aller land" (Exploration of all lands). With 154 verses, it was by far the longest chapter up to this point, which marks its importance; all previous chapters had a length of either 34 or 94 verses. Here, Brant uttered these well-known lines: "Furthermore, they since found everywhere in Portugal and Spain gold islands and naked people, about whom one could not say anything before."[2]

There is ample evidence that Sebastian Brant knew the *Columbus Letter* (1493), as two Latin editions of the *Letter* were published in Basel in 1494. The second Basel edition also included Carlo Verardi's *In laudem Serenissimi Ferdinandi Hispaniarum Regis* (*In Praise of the Most Serene Ferdinand, King of Spain*). It was published by Johann Bergmann von Olpe, who also published Brant's *Narrenschiff* later in the same year. Sebastian Brant even contributed a dedicatory poem to King Ferdinand entitled "In Baethicum triumphum congratulatio S. Brant" (Congratulations on the victory in the Baetic Cordillera from S. Brant).

Brant's text is a panegyrical poem of twenty-eight verses in praise of the Spanish *reconquista* of 1492, the reclaiming of control over Granada from the Arabs.[3] The poem also contains a vague reference to the journey of Columbus and the resulting control of some remote islands by the Spanish Crown:

> Already you have under your rule a territory that extends from the Pyrenees to the great Iberian fields. A territory that reaches from the Ocean to Cádiz, and that also includes the kingdoms found in the sea.[4]

The fact that Brant was aware of Columbus's journey does not mean that he understood the importance of this discovery. In other words, Brant knew the *Columbus Letter* and knew of Columbus's explorations on behalf of King Ferdinand, but he did not know "America," that is the true significance of Columbus's discovery, as will be discussed in more detail in Chapter 15.

This panegyrical poem stands in contrast to his position in the *Narrenschiff*, in which Brant framed spatial expansion in very negative terms. While Brant appears to endorse and even praise Ferdinand's efforts at spatial exploration, we

---

[2] Brant, *Narrenschiff*, ch. 66, v. 53–56: "Ouch hatt man sydt jnn Portigal | Vnd jnn hispanyen vberall | Golt/ jnslen funden/ vnd nacket lüt | Von den man vor wust sagen nüt."
[3] Pieper, *Die Vermittlung*, 111. [Verardi], *In laudem Serenissimi*, fol. aa1v.
[4] Brant, *Kleine Texte*, vol. 1.1., 136–137, v. 15–18: "Iamque tenes quicquid pyrenaeo clauditur arco, | Abluit et si quos magnos Iberus argos. | Quicquid ab extremis disterminat oceanus vel | Gadibus, addo etiam regna reperta mari."

have to keep in mind that this poem belongs to a specific generic tradition whose norms it follows. The point of a panegyrical poem is to praise the person addressed in it, particularly if it is a royal figure. This includes a positive assessment of the person's attributes and accomplishments regardless of the author's own views. To censor Ferdinand for the explorations he sponsored thus would have been inappropriate in this context even if we assume that Brant opposed explorations in principle. For this reason, it also is not appropriate to use this poem to construe the argument that Brant supported spatial explorations.[5]

This brings us back to the question of how Brant's reference to gold and naked people, two key descriptors so common in New World discourses, is contextualized in chapter 66 of the *Narrenschiff* and what the chapter tells us about Brant's notion of space and his attitude toward travel. From the very first moment of discovery, gold served as a seductive lure for European explorers of the New World with the promise of easy access to wealth. As quoted before, Sebastian Franck saw "the merchants' curiosity and hunger for gold" as the primary motivation for the explorations.[6] Gold therefore was shorthand for the seductive, negative role of wealth and the immoral luxurious life promised by the explorations.[7] It tied into suspicions of unearned wealth and into reservations regarding excessive luxury.

However, the gold that was found during voyages of exploration was not condemned universally. As discussed above, Jobst Ruchamer in the introduction of his anthology of exploration texts from 1508 admired the explorers for finding "many kinds of precious stones, pearls, and gold, which are held in high esteem by us."[8] While Ruchamer did not associate negative connotations with nakedness and gold, we have to keep in mind that Ruchamer in his introduction was eager to promote his anthology. Genre matters, and as in other contexts, we cannot automatically generalize remarks made in the front matter of a book.

The nakedness of the islanders has been compared to the nakedness of Adam and Eve in paradise where nakedness stood for the purity of the soul.[9] There are examples for a positive reception of nakedness in Renaissance culture, but only in contexts where moral purity is undisputed, such as in Alciato's emblem 196

---

[5] Wuttke ("Humanismus," 496–497) takes this poem as evidence for Brant's support of explorations.
[6] Franck, *Weltbůch*, Vorred, fol. 1r: "der Kaufleüt fürwitz vnd goldthunger."
[7] Nikolaus Federmann, for instance, by his own account was singularly motivated to enter the interior of Venezuela in his entrada of 1530–1531 by the hope to find gold.
[8] Ruchamer, *Newe vnbekanthe landte*, "vorrede," sig. A1v: "mancherley edeln gestayne/ berlen vnd golde/ welche bey vns hoch geacht." See the discussion of this quote in Chapter 9.
[9] Klaffke, "*Es sey die alte Welt*," 36.

that shows a naked, domesticated Venus.[10] In other texts about the New World, as well as in accompanying visual representations, nudity is typically connected to other moral deficiencies, like anthropophagy and promiscuity, and more generally to the savage nature of the natives. Brant also condemned showing off too much skin in his own text. In the preface of the *Narrenschiff*, he made plain that women were among the fools as well. Their biggest vice was that they craved current fashions that called for wearing pointed shoes and openly cut dresses that revealed their breasts.[11] Brant disapproved of women who dressed according to the latest fashion, stating, "They go around like wild animals."[12] Women thus reverted to a wild animalistic state, more commonly associated with the indigenous naked people who inhabited the newly found islands. Brant projected an image of an animalistic, sinful, and lapsed nature,[13] a nature that had lost its innocence with the original sin.

In chapter 4, Brant chastised German women for showing too much neck and cleavage[14] and concluded: "Yuck, shame on the German nation where one bares and lets see what nature wants to be covered."[15] Nudity for humans was against the natural order. Nature wanted humans to dress and cover their nakedness. Therefore, nakedness to Brant was shameful and immoral. If the natives of the islands all went naked, they were clearly outside of the realm of divine order, and their existence was far from paradisiacal. Their nakedness served as an indicator for the moral depravity of its inhabitants. Nakedness was not a marker for moral purity but rather for moral perils.

As we will see, Brant's reference to gold islands and naked people was part of a longer diatribe against the investigation of the world. Gold and nudity were shorthand for a futile quest for knowledge fueled by curiosity. Those who sought out, in person or in their writings, the marvels at the edges of the earth could easily lose their way amid sensual delights and transient pleasures that brought the soul no closer to God.[16]

---

10 Alciato, *Emblematum libellus*, 222–223. In the 1542 Paris edition used here, Venus is naked in an enclosed domestic space, representing domestic virtue. (In the original 1531 Augsburg edition, the naked Venus stands outdoors.) The inscriptio reads, "A woman's reputation, not her beauty, should be known to the world."
11 Brant, *Narrenschiff*, "vorred," 117–118. Neuber, "Verdeckte Theologie," 10–11.
12 Brant, *Narrenschiff*, "vorred," 122: "Sie gänd har wie die wilden their."
13 Neuber, "Verdeckte Theologie," 11.
14 Brant, *Narrenschiff*, ch. 4, v. 6.
15 Brant, *Narrenschiff*, ch. 4, v. 27–29: "Phuch schand der tütschen nacion | Das die natur verdeckt wil han | Das man das blöst/ vnd sehen lat."
16 Johnson, *The German Discovery*, 38.

A central yet unexpected rhetorical strategy Brant used against spatial exploration was confronting the voyages of central figures in classical antiquity about their travel habits. Over 32 verses of chapter 108, he presented the Odyssey, a protoype of ancient voyages, as a two-part allegory.[17] In the first half, Brant indirectly praised Odysseus as a wise man whose exceptional wisdom kept him alive during his adventurous journey: "Homer thought of all of this so that one may pay attention to wisdom."[18] The pursuit of wisdom was the point of Homer's story, yet Brant did not endorse Odysseus's wisdom. The second half relates the story of Odysseus's return home to Ithaca where he was killed as an imposter because nobody recognized him, other than the dogs. He was clubbed to death by his son Telegonus from his relationship with Circe. Brant thus fused the conciliatory Homeric ending with that of the Telegony.[19]

Brant insisted that Odysseus managed to survive on his journey through trickery and deceit, and his journey was further put into question by his inability to return home safely. Brant concluded that Odysseus would have lived and been a wiser man had he stayed home and tended to his own business. The basic flaw of his endeavor, namely the very fact that he engaged in a journey, caught up with him when he was killed unglamorously upon his return by the offspring that resulted from his trickster life. His journey thus was a transgression against the domestic order he left behind with the consequence that reentering his tranquil domestic space was impossible. Brant modified this canonical Homeric myth in order to point to the foolishness of travel and concluded the story with this moralizing statement: "A wise man keeps himself at home."[20] In Brant's reading, Odysseus became a charter passenger of the Ship of Fools.

In chapter 66, Brant retold the story of Hercules.[21] Hercules set two pillars, one in Africa and one in Europe, to mark the edges of the known world. His interest was in the open space beyond that, and his goal was to find the end of the world. But he showed disdain for all wondrous works ("wunderwerck") and was killed through the ruse of a woman. While Brant did not establish a direct causality, it was the same carelessness and arrogance that caused him to disregard God's wonders. He desired to see the end of the world and did not anticipate suffering the most shameful death at the hands of a woman.

---

17 Brant, *Narrenschiff*, ch. 108, v. 69–101; Aurnhammer, "Sünder–Narr–Held," 139–140.
18 Brant, *Narrenschiff*, ch. 108, v. 69–70: "Homerus hatt diß als erdacht | Do mit man hett vff wißheyt acht."
19 Aurnhammer, "Sünder–Narr–Held," 141.
20 Brant, *Narrenschiff*, ch. 108, v. 129: "Eyn wis man/ sich do heym behalt." In Dante's *Inferno* (Canto 26), Odysseus's wanderlust also gets a negative reading, but here it is based on his ruses.
21 Brant, *Narrenschiff*, ch. 66, v. 69–76.

Hercules appeared in different contexts in Brant's *Narrenschiff*, most notably in the retelling of the Choice of Hercules in chapter 107.[22] On the surface, Hercules made the right choice by choosing the nondescript and unerotic but industrious and virtuous woman over the beautiful, voluptuous and pleasure-seeking woman. However, in Brant's reading there was only the appearance of a free choice. For a Christian, there was only one right choice that led to a virtuous and God-pleasing life. The other choice led to the transgressive and sinful life of a fool.

The Hercules story in chapter 107 is not linked to Hercules in chapter 66. Brant was not interested in relating Hercules, or other classical figures, as a consistent character throughout the text. Rather, Brant used mythological fragments, often in a reframed version, for his own didactic purposes. In Brant's *Narrenschiff*, classical knowledge served as a storehouse of topoi rather than a source of true wisdom. This is not to say that Brant did not take classical texts seriously: Brant the learned Latinist was a serious connoisseur of classical literature, as his magisterial 1502 edition of Virgil's complete works, the first ever to appear in print, shows.

Bacchus is another classical figure whose travel Brant censored. Bacchus traveled in order to teach people how to drink wine and to make beer.[23] Furthermore, his teacher Silenus delighted in an easy life of entertaining women while being drunk.[24] To add insult to injury, the Ancients created a holiday to celebrate the legacy of the god Bacchus long after his death, even though his life of drunkenness had found a lonely and sorrowful end.[25] The fact that Brant dedicated 32 verses connecting travel with inebriation indicates just how central the theme was for Brant,[26] a theme for which he does not appear to have had literary models.[27]

We can gain a further clue when we examine how Brant framed chapter 66. It was entitled "von erfarung aller land" (Exploration of all lands), but the motto of the text makes it clear that his focus was much broader: "Whoever measures sky, earth, and ocean and thereby seeks lust, joy, and erudition, he should seek to fend off the fool."[28] The motto warns of the perils of measuring

---

[22] Brant, *Narrenschiff*, ch. 107, 17–36. See Hartweg, "Sebastian Brants Anlehnung;" Stieglecker, *Die Renaissance eines Heiligen*, 411–416.
[23] Brant, *Narrenschiff*, ch. 66, v. 77–82.
[24] Brant, *Narrenschiff*, ch. 66, v. 83–94.
[25] Brant, *Narrenschiff*, ch. 66, v. 95–103.
[26] Brant, *Narrenschiff*, ch. 66, v. 77–108.
[27] Rupp, *Narrenschiff*, 197–198.
[28] Brant, *Narrenschiff*, ch. 66, v. a–c: "Wer vß mißt hymel/ erd/ vnd mer | Vnd dar jnn sůcht lust/ freüd/ vnd ler | Der lůg/ das er dem narren wer."

the earth, that is the theoretical discipline of cosmography, to gain lust, joy, or doctrine, that is knowlege whose generation is not governed by strict theological criteria. Only things that were revealed by God could be experienced and investigated by humans.[29] To Brant, those who sought knowledge for its own sake were fools, and he reiterated this theme throughout the chapter.

The woodcut illustration for chapter 66 shows a cosmographer in a fool's costume measuring the world with a compass (figure 6). The world is shown as a disk with four concentric rings representing the sublunar world with its four elements: earth, water, air and fire.[30] One end of the compass is firmly placed at the center of the earth. However, the earth, in a departure from standard representations, is not at the center of the three other rings, indicating that measuring the earth will be inherently faulty and even impossible to achieve. Furthermore, a cosmographer in a fool's dress is distracted by another fool sitting on his back. Motto and pictura of the chapter thus signal that measuring the world, as cosmographers did, was a futile and foolish undertaking.

The first section of the text, consisting of 18 verses, endorses this view and reads like a wholesale condemnation of cosmography:

> I do not hold to be wise at all the one who uses all his sense and industriousness to explore all cities and lands. He takes the compass into his hand, so that it will tell him how wide, how broad, how long, how wide the earth is, how deep and far the ocean extends, and what is contained in the outermost sphere. And how the ocean holds up at the end of the world so that it does not fall off into the depths. Whether one traveled around the entire world. What people live below each line [degree of latitude]. Whether there are people beneath our feet, or whether there is nothing, and how they keep upright without falling into the air. How one calculates with a rod so that one sees the entire world with its help.[31]

This is an indictment of the work of the cosmographer whose curiosity made him ask questions that reveal his excessive and vain curiosity. At the same time, Brant showed a remarkable familiarity with the cosmographic questions of his time. Brant raised some urgent questions, such as what was the nature of

---

29 Rupp, *Narrenschiff*, 188.
30 I do not agree with Rupp's assertion (*Narrenschiff*, 191) that the woodcut shows a sphere rather than a disk.
31 Brant, *Narrenschiff*, ch. 66, v. 1–18: "Ich halt den ouch nit jtel wiß | Der all syn synn leidt/ vnd syn fliß | Wie er erkund all stett/ vnd landt | Vnd nymbt den zyrckel jn die hant | Das er dar durch berichtet werd | Wie breit/ wie lang/ wie witt die erd | Wie dieff/ vnd verr sich zieh das mer | Vnd was enthalt den letsten spör/ | Wie sich das mer zů end der welt | Haltt/ das es nit zů tal ab felt | Ob man hab vmb die gantz welt fůr | Was volcks wone vnder yeder schnůr/ | Ob vnder vnsern füssen lüt | Ouch sygen/ oder do sy nüt | Vnd wie sie sich enthaltten vff | Das sie nit fallen jnn den lufft/ | Wie man vß mit eym stäcklin räch | Das man die gantze welt durch säch."

Figure 6: Sebastian Brant. *Daß Narren Schyff*. Basel: Johann Bergmann, 1494. Chapter 66, sig. L3v. © Bayerische Staatsbibliothek München.

Chapter 13 Spatial Discoveries: Anxieties and Rejection in Brant's Writings — **189**

the outer edges of the universe or whether the ocean really dropped off into a precipice at the edge of the world. However, these were rhetorical questions as Brant's own sources held the earth to be a sphere rather than a disk.[32]

The subsequent rhetorical questions appear to accept the spheric shape of the world as they focus on whether humans lived on the opposite side of the earth and how they stayed on the ground rather than falling into space. The distrust of cosmography becomes evident in the flippant and sarcastic closing remark that calculations done with a simple calculating tool could help one see and understand the world.

The second section of the text deals with classical precursors of modern cosmographers, like Archimedes, Dikaiarchos, Ptolemy, Pliny, and Strabo, and their futile efforts to calculate the world.[33] To Brant, the fate of Archimedes was exemplary as he knew how to calculate circles, yet his lack of common sense caused him to be killed by soldiers who had disrupted his circles. Most notably, Ptolemy had subdivided the world into 180 degrees, but Ptolemy had to concede that only 25 degrees were known and explored land. To Brant, it was vain to calculate the world in theory while otherwise having no knowledge of it.[34] Brant summed up the absurdity of measuring everything with the derisive closing remarks of this section: "Pliny calculates it in feet, while Strabo makes miles out of it."[35]

The subsequent section lists the recent discoveries made by Portugal and Spain discussed above. Brant then used Pliny to chastise the vain desire to calculate the world in his own time:

> Pliny the master says that it is absurd to want to understand the size of the world, to even go beyond that, and to calculate everything beyond the ocean. In this regard, human reason is very much in error in that it tries to reckon these things all the time yet cannot reckon itself.[36]

Using Pliny, Brant argued that it was foolish to try to calculate the world as Ptolemy had done and as contemporaneous cosmographers were doing. This

---

[32] Rupp, *Narrenschiff*, 191.
[33] Brant, *Narrenschiff*, ch. 66, v. 19–48.
[34] Brant, *Narrenschiff*, ch. 66, v. 37–48. Rupp, *Narrenschiff*, 197.
[35] Brant, *Narrenschiff*, ch. 66, v. 47–48: "Plynius rächt das mit schritten vß | So machet Strabo mylen druß."
[36] Brant, *Narrenschiff*, ch. 66, v. 59–66: "Plinius der meyster seitt | Das es sy eyn vnsynnikeit | Wellen die größ der welt verston | Vnd vsser der/ by wilen gon | Vnd rächnen biß hynder das mer | Dar jnn menschlich vernunfft jrrt ser | Das sy solchem noch rächen allzyt | Vnd kan sich selb vß rächen nitt."

also is a first reference to the conclusion of the chapter, namely that the efforts of cosmographers to calculate and understand the world stood in the way of a true self-knowledge as a Christian.[37]

This is followed by the sections where he censored the travels of Hercules, Bacchus, and Silenus mentioned above. He then returned to his theme, as he stated himself, and offered this preliminary conclusion:

> Even though this art [cosmography] is valid and true, he nevertheless is a great fool who in his mind considers so little that he wants to know alien things and understand them in their essence, yet cannot recognize himself. [...] Many have explored distant and foreign lands, yet none of them ever knew themselves.[38]

This is the core theme that weaves through this chapter like a red thread: exploration to Brant was a narcissistic endeavour beset by the deadly sin of curiosity, which stood in the way of true self-knowledge and thus of a pious, god-pleasing life.

Once again Brant returned to the false praise of the Ancients. In the following section, he recognized how Odysseus, Pythagoras, Plato, and Apollonius had gained worldly knowledge through their explorations in what appears to be a conciliatory move. He attested that Odysseus continually "improved himself with good instruction,"[39] yet we know that Brant disapproved of Odysseus's travel elsewhere in the *Narrenschiff*. And in his conclusion to chapter 66, Brant made it plain that this worldly wisdom is futile in the face of divine judgment: "Whoever now undertakes such journeys by ship and on land in order to generate wisdom, he would better reject that, although that would not be enough. For the person whose mind is set to wander will not serve God at all."[40] Exploring foreign lands therefore was not a legitimate pursuit; rather, it was a misguided and foolish adventure that did not generate real insight and that created distance from God.[41] Travel and exploration were ungodly activities, as much as the quest for knowledge may

---

[37] Rupp, *Narrenschiff*, 196.
[38] Brant, *Narrenschiff*, ch. 66, v. 117–122 and v. 131–132: "Ob schon dis kunst ist gwyß vnd wor | So ist doch das eyn grosser tor | Der jn sym synn wygt so gering | Das er well wissen frömde ding | Vnd die erkennen eygentlich | Vnd kan doch nit erkennen sich [...] Vil handt erkundt/ verr/ frömbde lant | Do keyner nye sich selbs erkant."
[39] Brant, *Narrenschiff*, ch. 66, v. 136: "mert sich stät jn gůtter ler." Müller, "*Erfarung*," 313, reads this line as Brant's approval of Odysseus's travels.
[40] Brant, *Narrenschiff*, ch. 66, v. 149–154: "Wer yetz solch reyß vnd lantfar dät | Das er zů nem jnn wißheit stät | Dem wer zů vber sehen baß | Wie wol doch nit genůg wer das/ | Dann wem syn synn zů wandeln stot | Der mag nit gentzlich dienen got."
[41] Heimann, "Curiositas und experientia," 265.

have been tempting to Brant's Humanist sensibilities. In his conclusion, Brant left no doubt that travel and exploration stood in contradiction to Christian self-knowledge that served divine insight rather than empirical worldly competence. To Brant, travel and service to God stood in profound and fundamental opposition. The lack of Christian self-knowledge was a central motif in Brant's *Narrenschiff*, and this gave him the opportunity to censor a number of classical authorities whose spatial explorations were proof to Brant that they lacked Christian morals and self-understanding.

Brant's underlying point is clear: travel, discovery, and generally the expansion of the spatial realm represented a destabilization and disruption of the social, political, and moral order. The central metaphor of the book, all fools being passengers of a ship that travels without purpose and aim, reinforces this idea. Brant thus set the stage for the negative reception of spatial knowledge in sixteenth-century Germany. While his text rejected the discoveries, the rising number of empirical descriptions of far-away places at the time created an epistemological anxiety and antagonism that permeates Brant's text. Brant's brand of Humanism, which was rooted in academic learning, very much put a premium on topical knowledge that was anchored in imported book knowledge and hermeneutic traditions and that was required by Humanist rhetoric.[42] The topical knowledge about geography, as promoted by Brant, was tied into a theologically determined cosmology. It was therefore conceptually impossible to find new land; one could only recover what the ancient authorites had already described.[43]

Brant's world view was still informed primarily by biblical and classical texts, while merchants, cosmographers, and mapmakers promoted a pragmatic and adaptable worldview based on empirical observation that quickly incorporated new accounts of distant lands. Brant's topical knowledge thus stood in sharp contrast with new forms of generation of knowledge promoted by texts describing travel and exploration, which were based on first-hand experience and empirical observation. New frames of reference evolved, which were rejected in a roundabout way by Brant as well as by others. This was not just a question of genre and communicative context but also of method. Brant broadly rejected new forms of pragmatic knowledge generation because they were not compatible with his brand of traditional Humanist learning. Questions of cultural contact and of alterity were

---

42 Hess, "Zum Toposbegriff."
43 Hassauer, "Volkssprachliche Reiseliteratur," 269–270.

not a matter of interest nor concern to Brant as his intellectual framework was shaped by deductive reasoning firmly anchored in biblical and classical narratives.

In his sermons on Brant's *Narrenschiff*, given in Strasbourg in 1498 and 1499, the preacher Johann Geiler von Kaysersberg (1445–1510)[44] picked up on the travel theme as well. In sermon 33, he censored those who wanted to see the world: "The seventh bell is for those who want to see the world. They are travelers who roam about and want to see other countries for the sake of worldly honor."[45] He particularly scolded students who took up their studies in far-away places like Paris, Bologna, or Krakow. His sermon 65, entitled "Von landfarer narren" (Traveling fools), in the printed version from 1520 used the same woodcut that illustrated Brant's chapter 66 discussed above. In seven sections, he explicitly mirrored Brant's hostile attitude toward travel, each of them alluding to one of the deadly sins. The biggest folly was to travel "solely for the sake of knowledge."[46] Travel was also dishonoroable if motivated by envy of others, by a desire to brag about the places one has seen, by slothful lethargy, by the pursuit of love interests, or by an unsettled and disquiet mind. He held long-distance merchants who traveled as far as India for their merchandise in particular contempt.[47]

Sebastian Brant condemned other forms of travel as well. In chapter 92, which focused on arrogance and pride, Brant targeted those who pursued a university eduction in Romance countries, particularly Italy and France: "Many a fool holds himself in such high regard because he returned from Romance lands, where he had become wise in the schools: in Bologna, Pavia, and Paris, in sapience at the high school in Siena, and also at the school in Orléans."[48] Brant conceded that learning was first at home in Athens and then got transferred to Italy, and by extension to France. Reminiscent of the logic of the *translatio studii*, the cultural companion to the *translatio imperii*, Brant argued that higher learning had definitely arrived in Germany, so travel to a foreign university was a futile and foolish act.[49] Generally, a person was a fool who traveled through many lands and to places of learning like Rome, Jerusalem, or Pavia,

---

44 According to Israel ("Sebastian Brant," 49), Brant and Geiler met at Basel University in 1475. Israel discusses their long friendship.
45 Geiler, *Des hochwirdigen doctor*, fol. 81r: "DJe sibent schel ist die welt wöllen sehen. Es seint landfarer/ die daraffter vagieren die land besehen vmb weltlicher eer willen."
46 Geiler, *Des hochwirdigen doctor*, fol. 183v: "allain vmb des wüssen willen."
47 This aspect will be discussed in more detail in Chapters 18 and 19.
48 Brant, *Narrenschiff*, ch. 92, v. 11–16: "Manch narr halt sich gar hoch dar vmb | Das er vß welschen landen kum | Vnd sy zů schůlen worden wiß | Zů Bonony/ zů Pauy/ Pariß | Zůr hohen Syen jnn der Sapientz | Ouch jnn der schůl zů Orlyens."
49 Brant, *Narrenschiff*, ch. 92, v. 11–30.

yet did not learn about arts nor virtue, as he argued in chapter 34.[50] Brant concluded that travel alone was not honorable, unless something unique could be learned from it.[51]

A central part of Brant's thinking was that modern exploration and travel did not serve self-knowledge. However, Brant seemed open to the pilgrimage, in which contemplation and prayer were interwoven with the travel experience and where the end point of travel was a place of contemplation, devotion, and religious renewal. Brant did not openly promote the pilgrimage, but pilgrims were always carefully exempt from the fools who traveled. The illustration to chapter 17, entitled "Von vnnutzem richtum" (Useless wealth), shows a wealthy man in his house in front of a large box with coins. Outside sits a poor man whose sore feet are licked by two dogs, referencing the biblical story of the rich man and Lazarus (Luke 16:19–31).[52] The poor man carries a pilgrim's staff, and his hat is adorned with the shell of Saint James (*Jakobsmuschel*), attributes marking him as a pilgrim. While Brant felt no compassion toward beggars and generally slothful poor people,[53] this figure marked both as Lazarus and as a pilgrim was clearly exempt from the author's scorn.[54] Brant treated beggars more harshly: to him, they were lazy and deceptive people who often were criminals and amassed significant assets. One of the beggar's worst tricks was that he acted "as if he wanted to travel to Santiago [de Compostela]."[55] In other words, the duplicitous beggar lived well by pretending to be a pilgrim.

In Brant's view, it was acceptable to be a pilgrim. He only targeted false pilgrims – those who received alms intended for true pilgrims and thus enriched themselves. It is not within the logic of the *Narrenschiff* to praise contemporaries and their lifestyles. Their absence from the ship was Brant's mark of approval. Pilgrimages had a long tradition in Germany and were seen as legitimate in the late Middle Ages as they were not motivated by curiosity and a desire for discovery. However, the fact that Brant did not exclude all forms of travel as illegitimate does not alter our findings presented here.

Brant returned to the topic of discoveries in his introduction to Ulrich Tengler's (1447–1511) *Laÿen Spiegel von rechtmässigen ordnungen in Burgerlichen vnd peinlichen regimenten* (*Layman's Mirror of Lawful Ordinances of Civil and*

---

50 Brant, *Narrenschiff*, ch. 34, v. 11–18.
51 Brant, *Narrenschiff*, ch. 34, v. 25–26.
52 Lorentzen, *Johannes Bugenhagen*, 99–100.
53 See chapter 63, entitled "Von bettleren" (of beggars).
54 In chapter 83, "von verachtung armut" (of contempt of povery), Brant praised a Christian charitable life in poverty as just and virtuous.
55 Brant, *Narrenschiff*, ch. 63, v. 72: "Als wolt er zů sant Jacob faren."

Penal Governance), first published in 1509.⁵⁶ The *Laÿen Spiegel* was a handbook covering the legal foundations of sociey, written in German for an urban lay readership, as Brant claimed in his introduction.⁵⁷ This may have been an exaggeration as such popular legal texts in the vernacular often served public officials who played an active role in the legal system,⁵⁸ as Brant himself conceded later in his introduction.⁵⁹ One of Tengler's objectives was to popularize Roman law with a German-speaking audience. But the text also sought to explain the law in the vernacular in order to invoke a code of conduct,⁶⁰ just as Brant had done in a different generic context in his *Narrenschiff*. With a total of fourteen editions, the book remained influential in Germany throughout the sixteenth century. Brant's introduction highlighted Tengler's erudition and praised his text because it served the common good.

Brant praised scholars who put their wisdom on paper and made it available in print to benefit all nations. He then compared these learned people with discoverers:

> All the while there are a number of others who, after traveling with Spanish fleets between the Pillars of Hercules, circumnavigated the entire land of Africa and sailed through the Arabian, Persian, and Indian oceans, and also found new islands and territories. They hold that their effort, labor and work was hard and well worthy of a reward, great fame, and high honors.⁶¹

Just like in chapter 66 of the *Narrenschiff*, the main focus is on the Portuguese discoveries in Africa and Asia. While there is a vague reference to newly found islands and territories, there still is no mention of America nor a recognition that a fundamentally different part of the world had been discovered. The function of this passage within the framework of Tengler's text is unclear, beyond

---

56 Ulrich Tengler's family belonged to the lower nobility. Little is known about his education; it is unlikely that he had extensive university training in law. Rather, Tengler was a practitioner who had a distinguished career as public official in several southern German jurisdictions. This is the perspective he introduced into his *Laÿen Spiegel*, his only known publication. It remained influential throughout the sixteenth century. It is unclear what connection Tengler had with Sebastian Brant.
57 For a detailed discussion of Brant's introduction see Knape, "Der humanistische Geleittext."
58 Schumann, "Beiträge studierter Juristen," 451.
59 Tengler, *Laÿen Spiegel*, fol. 2v.
60 Neuber, "Verdeckte Theologie," 17.
61 Tengler, *Laÿen Spiegel*, fol. 2r: "Wiewol auch daneben ettlich annder/ nach dem sy durch die Hyspanischen Schiffungen/ von den Heraculischen sewlen/ mit vmbfarn des gantzen lands Affrica/ das Arabisch/ Persisch/ vnd Jndisch möre vnd Golffen durchswayffende/ auch erfindung neüwer Jnsulen und land. Sich bedüncken lassen jr müe/ arbait vnd werck schwär/ vnd ainer belonung/ hohes berůmbs vnd Eeren wol wirdig zu sein."

the panegyrical statement that Tengler's accomplishments surpassed those of the book-writing scholars and of the explorers in distant lands.

In the research literature, this passage is generally seen as endorsing the discoveries and as praising those who gained experience through travel.[62] Yet, a closer examination of the passage does not support this conclusion. This remark about discoveries is entirely devoid of context as discoveries do not play a role in Tengler's text. The only context is the panegyrical topos of outdoing,[63] which implies that Tengler's book was more significant than all the discoveries made over the past century. Furthermore, Brant's language creates a distance to the discoveries: Brant's phrase "sich beduncken lassen" implies that the author did not share the discoverers' own view that their deeds were indeed worthy of praise and fame.[64] Within this panegyrical framework, Brant tells us that the discoverers were important only in their self-assessment while Tengler's learning and accomplishments were universally lauded. Thus the discoverers were not at the core this argument, and at the same time, there was only the appearance of praise for them. Brant's point was that the accomplishments of a man whose book contributed to the maintenance of public order were much more significant than those of travelers and discoverers who did not contribute toward the common good.

Later in the introduction, Brant returned to the issue of discovery, this time comparing Tengler to Hercules:

> Therefore our Tengler has to be compared with Hercules's thirst quite favorably and justly, because he is not linked with the description of one single poem, nor with the discovery of unique islands, territories, gulfs, or oceans. Rather, as the laudable Emperor Justinian says, he is the right one who dared, through the middle of a deep and bottomless ocean, to take on an unspeakable labor about a great and high thing, both in body and spirit.[65]

---

62 Heimann, "Curiositas und experientia," 275; Wuttke, "Humanismus," 508–509; Klaffke, "Es sey die alte Welt," 33.
63 Curtius, *European Literature*, 162–165. The original German edition was published in 1948.
64 "Sich beduncken lassen" or "sich bedünken lassen" was a common phrase around 1500 without stated subject, meaning "they believe" or "they make the claim." See Grimm, *Deutsches Wörterbuch*, vol. 1, 1238.
65 Tengler, *Laÿen Spiegel*, fol. 2r–2v: "Deßhalben diser vnnser Tenngler der gedürstigkait Herculis gar wol vnd billich zůvergleichen ist/ in dem das nit mit beschreybunng ains aintzigen gedichts/ noch mitt erfarunng aintziger Jnsulen/ lande/ Golffen oder möres/ Sonnder als der loblich Kayser Justinianus spricht. Durch mitel des tieffen vnd grundlosen möres/ der rechte sich gewaget Vnd ainer nitt wol säglichen arbait vnderwunnden ains grossen vnd hohen dings/ leibs vnd gemüts vnnderstanden."

Hercules here is associated with his thirst. Presumably, this is a reference to Propertius's Elegy IV.9, where Hercules forcibly entered a sacred grove, which was open only to women, in order to quench his thirst in the creek. Presumably this is the poem Brant referred to.[66] Like in the *Narrenschiff*, Hercules is represented as a transgressor who lacks discipline and self-knowledge.[67] Hercules's desire to discover the world by sailing beyond the pillars is only alluded to here, a connection Brant had made explicit in the *Narrenschiff*.[68]

By contrast, Tengler went through great efforts to get to the bottom of his chosen topic, metaphorically speaking, by completing his laudable summary of extant law. This is the significance of the reference to Emperor Justinian, whose *Institutiones*, the sixth-century codification of Roman law, served as the model for Tengler.[69] Brant made a reference to Justinian's introduction that described the nature of the work of compiling the vast volumes of ancient law: "And sailing as it were across the mid-ocean, [we] have now completed, through the favor of heaven, a work that once seemed beyond hope."[70] To Brant, the model for Tengler therefore was the civic-minded Justinian, not the transgressor Hercules. By comparing Tengler to Justinian, Brant credited Tengler with publishing the first summary of German law. Tengler again was shown to be a tireless servant of the truth and a faithful supporter of the divine order. And Brant confirmed his distrust of travel and discovery.

A final work by Sebastian Brant on this theme was "Eyn Chronick über Teutsch land/ zuuor des landes Elsas/ vnd der loblichen statt Straßburg/ durch Sebastian Brant versamlet" (A chronicle about Germany and especially of the land of Alsace and the laudable city of Strasbourg, collected by Sebastian Brant). It was published in 1539 by Caspar Hedio (Kaspar Heid; 1494–1552) as an appendix to his *Ein außerlesne chronick von anfang der Welt* (*Select Chronicle from the Beginnings of the World*). While Hedio's text indeed is a chronicle, the

---

66 Fischart in chapter 3 of his *Geschichtsklitterung* (56) made a reference to the thirst of Hercules as well.
67 Neuber ("Verdeckte Theologie," 21) arrives at the opposite conclusion, namely that the accomplishments of Hercules could not be surpassed, not even by Tengler. This is implausible as it contradicts the logic of panegyrics.
68 Brant, *Narrenschiff*, ch. 66, v. 69–76.
69 Knape, "Der humanistische Geleittext," 123–124. Knape does not discuss the references to the discoveries of unknown lands.
70 The complete second paragraph of the Proœmium reads as follows: "2. When we had arranged and brought into perfect harmony the hitherto confused mass of imperial constitutions, we then extended our care to the vast volumes of ancient law; and sailing as it were across the mid-ocean, have now completed, through the favor of heaven, a work that once seemed beyond hope." (Iustinianus, *The Institutes of Justinian*, 1–2.)

use of the word for Brant's appendix is a misnomer. Rather than a chronicle, it is a description of Brant's native upper Rhine valley and a collection of itineraries covering Alsace, southern Germany, and the Swiss Confederation.[71] As such, it also covers the extent of Brant's own travel experience. Little is known about the origins of this fragmentary text; we have to assume that Brant worked on it between 1513 and his death in 1521.[72]

In his introduction, Brant stressed the fact that Germany was a much larger and more developed state than what Pliny, Strabo, and Ptolemy had described. Brant's Germany extended from the Swiss Alps to the shores of the North Sea and included the Rhineland, which the Romans had seen as their own.[73] In his descriptions, Brant drew on contemporaneous rather than classical sources, such as Schedel's *Nuremberg Chronicle*, maps, travelogues, and in particular on pilgrimage itineraries and reports.[74] Brant listed bridges across the Rhine as well as tolls and ferries and gave expert advice on horses and on transporting merchandise. He also gave hints about shortcuts, the comfort level of certain roads, road conditions during different seasons, and places to spend the night. Much of Brant's text must have been based on personal experience as there are no earlier published sources for this information.[75]

This pragmatic turn perhaps had to do with his own life experience. A native of Strasbourg, Brant had lived in Basel for a quarter century before returning to Strasbourg in 1501. From 1502 until his death, Brant was the chief of the city administration of Strasbourg. Thus the text only covers the world known to him through his own personal travel experiences. We therefore have to assume that Brant considered regional travel within one's own geographic horizon not just acceptable but legitimate and normal. In this context, we can appreciate that Brant did not reject all forms of travel outright. Brant embraced pilgrimages as well as regional forms of travel to conduct government and private business. These forms of travel had already been acceptable in the late Middle Ages because they served a legitimate purpose yet were not motivated by curiosity, that is by a desire for discovery and for expanding spatial horizons. Yet, it is important to remember that Brant was not receptive to most other forms of travel, and in particular to those devoted to the discovery of new lands. While there were other voices that expressed wonderment at the new discoveries and

---

71 For a general introduction to itineraries, see Denecke "Strassen, Reiserouten," 1992.
72 Heimann, "Curiositas und experientia," 267.
73 Brant, "Eyn Chronick," 732.
74 Heimann, "Curiositas und experientia," 272.
75 Heimann, "Curiositas und experientia," 271–272.

that accepted these new worlds as part of divine creation, Brant created a powerful counternarrative that remained influential in the first half of the sixteenth century.

Sebastian Franck picked up Brant's theme of Germans knowing foreign countries but not themselves in the introduction of his *Germaniae Chronicon* from 1538:

> Whoever observes the Germans will find this curiosity, deficiency, and apish manner about them. They pay attention to, seek, examine, marvel about, etc. everything except for their own affairs. Thus, they travel and wander through all lands up to the outermost islands in the New World. They espy with curiosity all things, yet do not know themselves. And they are not even lacking a club, as it is the manner of fools. They would much sooner marvel about, know, curiously imitate, and investigate everything before they even knew who they were themselves.[76]

It is important to note that Franck made this statement in a German chronicle. In the generic context of his cosmographical writings it would have been inappropriate and indeed counterproductive. In this passage, Franck clearly referenced chapter 66 of Brant's *Narrenschiff*. Like Brant, Franck associated travel and exploration with sinful curiosity and linked the lustful quest for knowledge and discovery of foreign lands with an absence of self-knowledge. Franck used Brant's motif of the fool, and he identified the club (*Kolben*) as one of the insignia of the fool, as Brant had established it in the introduction to the *Narrenschiff*.[77] When Germans wandered to the most remote islands in the New World, they did not do it physically. Rather, it was an act of apish imitation in that they metaphorically wandered along a trail of curiosity with their minds, soaking up written accounts of voyages of discovery while neglecting the Christian path to self-knowledge.

Yet Franck's world view was much more inclusive. The fact that Germans demonstrated excessive curiosity could not negate that real human beings lived on these remote islands. While Brant sought to dehumanize them by stressing their nakedness, Franck took a more generous and inclusive view. The question whether the inhabitants of the New World were indeed human was an important one in the colonial debates of the early sixteenth century and was only

---

[76] Franck, *Germaniae Chronicon*, sig. bb2r: "Demnach wer der Teutschen acht hat/ der findt dissen fürwitz/ mangel/ äffische art an jn/ das sie aller ding ehe acht haben/ sůchen/ nachfragen/ verwundern/ etc. dann jres eygnen dings/ da faren vnnd durchwanderenn sie alle land/ biß zů den eussersten Jnseln/ inn new welt/ erspeen/ fürwitzig all ding vnd sich selbs wissen sie nit/ vnd gefelt jn so gar jr kolb nit/ wie doch der narren art/ das sie all ding ehe verwundern/ wissen/ fürwitzig nachthon vnd erfragen/ dann das sie wisten wer sie selbs weren."

[77] Brant, *Narrenschiff*, vorred, v. 132; also ch. 42, v. 8. The club is shown in the woodcut illustrating chapter 111.

settled by Pope Paul III in his bull *Sublimis Deus* of 2 June 1537.[78] As the natives of the New World were humans, according to the bull, they also could not be enslaved. There had been a scholarly discussion on this question up to this point, and Sebastian Franck was perhaps the only German participating in it. In his *Weltbůch* from 1534, he stressed that he was intent on describing all parts of the world without prejudice:

> For the marvelous customs and thousand papacies described herein will give you much understanding and take you far, because you must acknowledge that these strange people, laws, and jurisdictions are still human and must be accepted as humans and not held to be geese. Also remember that the world is wide and almost unending and filled with the very works of God that he cannot hate, and that a Turk, heathen, etc. was equally created in the image of God and is a creation of God as is a German.[79]

Franck humanized the non-European others because they were part of divine creation as well. As they too were created in the image of God and equally loved by him, it is imperative for Christians to do the same, "because God is also the God of the heathens."[80]

The contrast between the two Franck quotes is remarkable and only can be resolved if we read both in their respective generic contexts. The second quote, while earlier, comes from Franck's world book, his cosmography. Its generic tradition required an empirically based description of the world, including the "marvelous customs" and "thousand papacies," that is the multitude of religions. The first quote is from his German chronicle, which by definition was a Germanocentric text telling the history of the Christian empire that was rooted in Biblical narratives. In this generic context, seeking knowledge about the new edges of the world seems irrelevant and indeed inappropriate.

Second, the two quotes cover different argumentative contexts. The latter quote from the *Weltbůch* addressed divine creation as a whole and argued that in a strictly theological argument no part of the world was privileged over others and thus equally loved by God. But a mere description of the indigenous

---

[78] Neuber, "The Red Indian's Body," 93; Davies, *Renaissance Ethnography*, 220. The bull sometimes is referred to as *Veritas ipsa*.
[79] Franck, *Weltbůch*, fol 3r: "Nun die wunderbarliche sitten vnd tausent bapstumb hierinn beschriben werden dir vil verstand geben vnd weit bringen/ weil du dise seltzeme leüt/ gsatz/ vnd ordinacion auch menschen vnd menschlich můßt lassen bleiben/ vnd nit für genß achten/ auch gedencke das die welt weit vnd schier vnendtlich ist/ mit eitel Gottes wercke/ die er nit hassen kan/ besetzt/ vnd das ein Türck/ Heyd. etc. eben so wol zů der bildtniß Gots erschaffen/ vnnd ein werck Gottes ist/ als ein Teütscher." Translation partially based on Johnson, *The German Discovery*, 39.
[80] Franck, *Weltbůch*, fol 3r: "weil Gott auch der Heyden gott."

people of these remote islands was not an endorsement of their religions, cultures, values, and lifestyles. The first quote focused on what constituted a virtuous Christian life as Germans should live it. In this context, the traditional prejudice against curiosity prohibited the exploration of the world out of inquisitiveness. The mere existence of a different world that existed on the fringes did not justify its exploration. Here Franck accepted Brant's point that undue curiosity detracted from self-discovery and thus needed to be curbed.

Franck made this argument in his *Weltbůch* as well, as discussed above. Modern discoveries were primarily motivated by "the curiosity and gold hunger of the merchants."[81] But most importantly, the mystery of divine creation could not possibly be experienced by reason and empirical observation alone: "For the world, God's work and creation, albeit finite, is deeper, more perfect and more occult than a quill could reach or a tongue could pronounce."[82] Franck showed the limitations of cosmography: only the surface of divine creation was visible to humans and thus describable, while its allegorical, tropological, and anagogical levels of meaning were so unspeakable, mysterious and concealed that they were beyond human cognition. This delineated the boundaries of curiosity that even applied to the genre of cosmography.

---

81 Franck, *Weltbůch*, Vorred, fol. 1r: "der Kaufleüt fürwitz vnd goldthunger."
82 Franck, *Weltbůch*, Vorred, fol. 1r: "Dann die Welt/ Gottes werck vnd geschöpff/ wiewol endtlich yedoch tieffer vollkummner vnnd verborgner/ dann eynich feder erreychen oder ein zung außsprechen mag."

Chapter 14
Spatial Anxieties in Literary Texts of the Early Sixteenth Century

German popular literature in the early sixteenth century seldom addressed spatial discoveries and the transgressive desire to travel directly. Perhaps the first German literary text in which the spatial turn was normalized in a similar way is Jörg Wickram's novel *Von Gůten vnd Bösen Nachbaurn* (*Of Good and Evil Neighbors*), published in 1556, which traces the adventures of a merchant from Brabant in Lisbon and represents long-distance trading as an honorable occupation. Curiosity for unknown places was portrayed positively as in this justification for making a detour on the way home to Lisbon: "Yet curiosity tickled him as he wanted to see Venice and their manner."[1] As this chapter will show, literary texts before 1550 either ignored the spatial turn or commented on it negatively by associating it with the creation of new opportunities for transgressive behavior.

A literary text that has often been compared to Wickram's novels is the anonymous *Fortunatus*, a highly popular and successful prose narration. It was first printed in Augsburg in 1509 and published and translated many times after that.[2] Its author is unknown, and the text must have been written shortly after 1482, as it appropriated an itinerary from the travelogue describing the journey to the Holy Land by Hans Tucher the Elder, which was published in Augsburg that year.[3] The social identity of Fortunatus and his family fluctuates greatly, and the narrator's description as "a noble burgher" reflects this ambiguity.[4] The origins of the family are in the urban patriciate but the titular hero prefers to move in courtly circles and participate in knightly tournaments with costly horses, even if he has to abandon his family to do so.[5] His life's story has aspects of a fairy tale due to the magical elements he controls, a magic purse that gives him cash in local currency whenever he opens it, and a magic hat that allows him to travel wherever he wishes. In spite of the magical and supernatural elements, the story is narrated in a sober and factual narrative style.

---

[1] Wickram, *Von Gůten vnd Bösen Nachbaurn*, 166: "wiewol er fast gern haim in Portugal gefaren wer/ noch kitzlet in der fürwitz/ das er Venedig und ir monier gern gesehen."
[2] Steinmetz ("Welterfahrung," 210) points out that the novel still occupied third place at the Frankfurt book fair in 1569.
[3] Speth, *Dimensionen*, 9; Herz, *Studien*, 28.
[4] Anon., *Fortunatus*, 5: "ain edler burger".
[5] Anon., *Fortunatus*, 6.

Fortunatus travels the world between Alexandria and London in his guise as a merchant. While he performs trade activities, he operates outside of a competitive market system as his magic purse gives him limitless funds. His travels cover the known world from his base in Cyprus – a clear indication that *Fortunatus* was firmly anchored in the late medieval Venetian Mediterranean system rather than in the emerging Portuguese Atlantic system. During a visit to Alexandria, where he is acquiring pepper through lavish gifts to the sultan, he decides to travel to the land where the pepper is grown.[6] His journey to Persia and India is not arduous, thanks to the magic hat. There is only a reference in passing that travel to Persia on horseback follows the classic overland route. In other words, Fortunatus is not sailing around Africa, a route that was known in Germany at the time of publication. There is no description of these alien lands at all with the cheeky remark that a separate big book would have to be written and that a curious reader should read John Mandeville's book.[7]

Unlike the later texts discussed in this chapter, *Fortunatus* did not treat discoveries, travel and long-distance trade as problematic categories. Fortunatus's activities as a merchant cannot be taken seriously because of his magical supply of endless money. The travel horizon was that of late medieval pilgrimage reports, such as that by Hans Tucher, including Fortunatus's obligatory visits to sites in the Holy Land. Furthermore, his journey to Asia is entirely in the realm of fantasy. The narrator does not raise concerns with any of the travels in the novel. The text still operated in the mold of late medieval adventure tales whose protagonists had courtly aspirations and therefore were able to travel within the confines of their estate.

At no point in the novel is the narrator critical of Fortunatus and his two sons, in spite of significant moral failings. We have to assume that the author was more interested in an adventure tale than in a morality tale, and perhaps he also was more focused on the development of the individual's subjectivity in the novel.[8] The only critical remarks can be found in the paratexts written at the time of publication and unlikely to have been penned by the author.[9] The epilogue features a serious critique of Fortunatus, who had chosen wealth over wisdom because of his impudent and misguided nature. Therefore, he was responsible for bad luck and

---

[6] Anon., *Fortunatus*, 107–108.
[7] Anon., *Fortunatus*, 107.
[8] Prager, *Orienting the Self*, 123–160.
[9] Steinmetz ("Welterfahrung," 212) notes that the brief afterword only appeared in the 1509 edition, but not in the later prints.

for his demise and that of his sons.[10] It is this moralizing editorial that clumsily attempted to bring the text in line with the concerns expressed by most literary texts around 1510.

At that time, space was primarily experienced as the anxiety-inducing intrusion of the foreign into Germany,[11] most notably the threat of a Turkish invasion that captured the literary imagination throughout our period. The other major theme was the rapid rise of imported goods after the Portuguese opened the sea route around the Cape of Good Hope and thus dramatically increased access to Asian markets. The rising global trade and its perceived impact on Germany will be discussed in Part III. In that context, it was not foreign travel itself but rather the subsequent intrusion of foreign goods and their economic, political, and cultural effect from a localized German perspective were the focus of discussion.

Literary texts in the period under discussion were contextualized in local cultures that seldom looked beyond the known world, *Fortunatus* being the rare exception. A good example is Hans Sachs, whose prolific writings were all set in his native Nuremberg and surroundings. As a shoemaker, he had no need to travel, and his travel experience was limited to a five-year period as a journeyman. After that, he never left Nuremberg again. In his own autobiographical poem *Summa all meiner gedicht* (*Sum of All My Poems*) from 1567, he mentioned a number of cities he visited as journeyman, ranging from Passau and Salzburg to the southeast of Nuremberg and Cologne and Aachen to the northwest. He does not appear to have engaged in foreign travel. His own biography thus followed the expected norm: travel was only justifiable if it served a socially accepted purpose, such as commerce or improvement of skills. As Sachs joined the Lutheran reform movement as early as 1523, a pilgrimage, the other form of legitimate travel, was out of the question for Sachs.

Not surprisingly, the road in Sachs's writings was often portrayed as a space at the margins of civic order. It was a location away from secure urban spaces where suspect characters operated and where the established social order could fray or break down. A good example is his verse narration entitled *Von dem teuffel, dem die hell will zu eng werden* (*The Devil to Whom Hell Became too Tight*) from 1540, which is discussed in Chapter 8. In the frame narration, the first-person narrator walks through the forest from Nuremberg to nearby Neustadt an der Aisch on a Saturday night. To his horror, he encounters the devil in the forest in the middle of the night. However, the devil merely is interested in finding out why so many souls had been coming to hell, causing a shortage of space. The devil challenges

---

10 Anon., *Fortunatus*, 194–195.
11 For a definition of German and Germany see Chapter 17.

the protagonist, who had doubts about the devil's tale, to find him ten pious men. After wandering around for ten years, the protagonist still had not met the challenge. But there is a happy end after all: by becoming a pious man himself, he is able to overcome hell and Satan with God's help.

Der farendt Schuler im Paradeiß (*The Traveling Student in Paradise*) from 1550 is a simple carnival play whose protagonists are a traveling student, a peasant woman and her second husband. As he introduces himself, the student brags about his travel experience: "Know that I am a traveling student and that I am traveling all over back and forth. I just came from Paris about three days ago."[12] The plot hinges on a simple misunderstanding. The peasant woman understands "paradise" instead of "Paris" and asks the student whether he had seen her late first husband there. The tricky student quickly seizes the opportunity and responds in the affirmative, offering to take presents to him. The peasant woman is delighted, and the student quickly goes on his way. Upon hearing the story, the second husband gets angry with his dumb wife and rides after the student, who promptly swindles the peasant out of his horse. He tells his wife that he gave the horse to the student so he would get to paradise faster. At the end, marital bliss is restored: the second husband has to realize that he is not any smarter than his wife, and the wife is happy about the unexpected generosity of her second husband.

In both stories, the road is a treacherous space where the social order cannot be guaranteed and where legal norms are tenuous. The traveling student is marked as untrustworthy just by virtue of the fact that he is a transient and thus has the opportunity to escape unrecognized and without consequences whenever the need arises. The urban audience of the play must have recognized immediately that the peasant woman made a mistake by trusting him. Sachs made it evident why travelers were not to be trusted: they stood outside the local social order and the tools of social discipline and even law enforcement did not apply here. In his writings, Sachs projected the idealized image of a tightly knit, mobility-averse community where outsiders commonly occupied marginal spaces and became the transgressors and thus the disruptors of the social order.

In the poems, stories, and plays by Hans Sachs, the road is generally the space where one meets unsavory characters who clearly operate outside of the social order or who even want to upend it. The latter is the case in the didactic poem *Der herzverkerer* (*The heart-turner*) from 1539. The narrator meets a strange man in the Alps, on the road from Rome to Bern, who wears all his clothes in the

---

[12] Sachs, KG 14, 73, v. 8–11: "Wiß, ich bin ein farender schuler | Vnd fahr im lande her vnd hin. | Von Pariß ich erst kummen bin | Itzundt etwa vor dreien tagen."

wrong places. He confesses that he is the person who debases everything and who has created the *mundus perversus*. The narrator asks him what he turned upside down in Germany. The man offers a long list of all the social upheavals he created and offers this summary: "I made the common good very small and the self-interest big and common. I drove virtue out of Germany, but vices remained in the city. So I perverted everything."[13] At the end the narrator begs God to show the path to salvation: "Thus we will be converted to follow you on your road according to your word, each of us away from our own evil road and from our twisted path and trail."[14] The road metaphor is central here as Sachs used no fewer than four synonyms in this passage. Sachs not only asked God for a safe path to him but also to make all roads safe by removing evil and vice from them.

The prose novel *Dyl Ulenspiegel*, published in Strasbourg in 1515, focused on a transient figure as the protagonist and displayed an unusual awareness of the narrative function of space.[15] The text consists of 96 loosely connected episodes, or chapters, that do not tell a real biography, with the exception of the chapters narrating his youth and his death.[16] The first nine episodes tell us the story of Ulenspiegel's childhood and youth. We never learn his father's occupation, and the household therefore is never described as a specific space defined by the work performed therein, nor as a space indicating social class and status in the community.[17] Soon, the family moves to a different town, and his father dies when Ulenspiegel is still very young. Ulenspiegel grows up without roots in the community, and space never becomes a source of identity during Ulenspiegel's upbringing.

His first trick, showing his bare rear end while riding a horse with his father, happens while moving in space. The river as transitional space plays a central role in the early episodes. On the way home after the baptismal festivities, Ulenspiegel is dropped into a creek by his inebriated godfather and nearly drowns. The river as a transitional space is thus marked as a danger zone.[18] As a result, Ulenspiegel is baptized three times in three different spaces, as the narrator cheekily states at the end of the first chapter: the proper baptism in the Ampleben castle chapel, nearly

---

13 Sachs, KG 22, 219, v. 10–14: "Gemainen nuetz den macht ich klain, | Den aignen nuetz gros und gemain; | Duegent hab ich aus Teutschland trieben, | Laster sint an der stat pelieben. | Also thet ich all ding verkeren."
14 Sachs, KG 22, 220, v. 12–15: "So werden wir zw dir pekert | Ider von seinem poesen weg, | Von seim verkerten steig und steg | Auf dein strassen nach deinem wort."
15 For the discussion of other aspects of the text, including Hermann Bote's possible authorship, see Chapter 3.
16 Blume, *Hermann Bote*, 31.
17 Jahn, "Raum für Schwänke," 67–70.
18 Jahn, "Raum für Schwänke," 70.

drowning in the muddy creek, and being washed off in a bucket at home in nearby Kneitlingen. By virtue of his strange baptism, he defied social categorization at birth, which gave him license to operate in different social realms throughout the narrative.[19]

In chapter 3, he tightens a rope across the river, walks across it, falls victim to a trick and plunges into the river, reinforcing the idea of the river as a problematic space. Back on the tightrope in chapter 4, he uses the same space to take revenge. He tricks his onlookers into taking off their left shoes with the pretense that he needed them to perform a trick on the tightrope. Ulenspiegel drops all the shoes in a single pile and watches their owners scramble as they attempt to recover their matching shoe from the big pile.

His unsteady, adventurous, nomadic, and socially unmarked life begins in chapter nine when he is hiding in a basket containing an empty beehive in order to catch thieves who had stolen other beehives.[20] He falls asleep and is carried away by two thieves. When he wakes up in the morning, he finds himself in a strange and unknown place: "Then he crawled out of the beehive and did not know where he was. So he went on his way."[21] In a sense, he was abducted and released in a new, alien environment. Leaving is not a deliberate choice nor a constructive act; rather, the result of an apparently random abduction. This episode signals the end of his youth and firmly establishes the pattern of Ulenspiegel's unsteady itinerant life marked by repeated changes of location.

The literature at the time made it clear that the life of a wanderer and vagrant was not socially respectable. Chapter 63 of Sebastian Brant's *Ship of Fools* is one massive rant against wandering beggars who enriched themselves with their deceptive and predatory behavior, by faking poverty, ailments, and piety and by peddling images of saints and fake relics. Similarly, Thomas Murner's *Narren bschwerung* (*Exorcism of Fools*) from 1512 berated mendicants who moved around the country with fake relics.[22] The anonymous *Liber vagatorum der betler orden* (*Book of Wanderers, the Order of Beggars*) from 1510 associated wandering with an unsteady life of a beggar, swindler, fake pilgrim, and even master of the occult arts. The pamphlet introduced readers to 28 different types of drifters and beggars and gave specific reasons why one should not give anything to them. Their mobility and corresponding lack of social integration made these people outcasts who were not to be trusted. Ulenspiegel in the various

---

19 Kirschner, *Hermen Bote*, 92.
20 Kirschner, *Hermen Bote*, 92.
21 Anon., *Ein kurtzweilig lesen*, fol. 11v: "da kroch er vß dem yemenstock/ vnd weßt nit wa er was/ also gieng er einen weg vß."
22 Murner, *Narrenbeschwörung*, 181, ch. 16, v. 77–78.

episodes resembles a great many of the types of vagrants represented in the *Liber vagatorum*. The reader of *Dyl Ulenspiegel* no doubt understood that much of Ulenspiegel's trickery was attributed to vagrants, beggars, tricksters, and hucksters of religious images and relics.[23] Without a doubt, neither the author nor his readers understood Ulenspiegel to be the benign jokester as commonly assumed today.

Like the first nine chapters, the last seven chapters of *Dyl Ulenspiegel* form a unit as well, telling the story of the protagonist's illness and death. The remaining chapters, the bulk of the book, are loosely structured episodes telling Ulenspiegel's many adventures. He stays in each town for one or two episodes, just long enough to unfold his mischief, and he is typically forced to flee by locals victimized by his tricks. Thus, he loses the last remnants of his social markers, those associated with his life with his mother. As Ulenspiegel steadfastly refuses to learn a trade in his youth,[24] he is not marked in terms of occupational category and social identity. And in chapter nine, he loses the marker associated with place – place of origin and a permanent place of residence.

Wandering through German lands, apparently without any particular plan or purpose, is the narrative staple of this book, as the narrator confirms repeatedly. In in chapter 27, Ulenspiegel moves on to the state of Hessen "because he had wandered throughout the state of Saxony and was known very well."[25] The same motif appears a few chapters later: "Ulenspiegel had become well-known in all lands because of his wickedness. And where he had been once before he was not welcome, unless he wore deceptive clothing so that one could not recognize him."[26] He dresses up in a religious robe so that people cannot identify him and instead hold him to be a priest, and he also travels with a peddler of relics, another social misfit.[27] Ulenspiegel thus spreads his web of infringements all over Germany, and he runs out of places to go as the story progresses. In a sense, his death is the logical consequence of him running out of safe spaces where he can perform his mischief without already being known and seen with mistrust. The text thus develops a topography of rejection: the narrator lets us know that things happen in specific places for a specific reason and

---

23 Röcke, *Die Freude am Bösen*, 227.
24 This is mentioned twice in Anon., *Ein kurtzweilig lesen*, fol. 4v and fol. 7r–7v.
25 Anon., *Ein kurtzweilig lesen*, fol. 35r: "da er dz land zů Sachsen fast vmb vnd vmb gwandert hat/ vnd fast wol bekant wz."
26 Anon., *Ein kurtzweilig lesen*, fol. 42v: "IN allen landen het sich Ulenspiegel mit seiner boßheit bekant gemacht/ vnd wa er vor ein mal gewesen waz da wz er nit wilkum es wer dan das er sich vercleidet dz man in nit kant."
27 Anon., *Ein kurtzweilig lesen*, fol. 43r.

projects an imaginary map of where Ulenspiegel has been and where he is no longer welcome.

Chapter 25 offers a good example. We learn that Ulenspiegel is forbidden to ever enter the duchy of Lüneburg again under penalty of death because of earlier mischief he had performed there. True to form, Ulenspiegel disregards this order and promptly encounters the Duke of Lüneburg in a forest. Ulenspiegel kills and guts his horse and stands in the horse's hollow corpse as the duke approaches and demands an explanation. Ulenspiegel responds: "Merciful and high-born prince. I am worried about being in your disfavor, and I am very much in fear. So I have heard all my life that everyone should have his peace within his four posts."[28] The duke understands the legal reference and lets him go. The horse's four legs that surround him literally mark the four corners of his personal domain and idiomatically invoke the doctrine in German law that the four posts, either the four corners of the house or the four fence posts, demarcated the domestic sphere where a German could live in peace.[29] The irony of course is that he performs a literal meaning of the law in order to subvert it.

The narrator meticulously enumerates the locations of Ulenspiegel's misdeeds, and the specific geographic names introduced by the narrator serve to authenticate the narrative and represent his effort to impose a geographic order onto the narrative.[30] While the narrative is informed by the spatial turn of the early sixteenth century, the geographic order is ritually disrupted by the titular protagonist. His constant geographic movement is designed to disturb and subvert this order and to create a map of deception. The disruption of the geographic order is thus closely linked to Ulenspiegel's disruption of the social order discussed in Chapter 3.

Ulenspiegel's three trips outside Germany appear to disrupt this pattern. Both visits to the courts of Denmark and Poland are successful in that his trickery does not challenge the authority of the ruler. In chapter 23, he reverses the financial damage to the king of Denmark, and in chapter 24, his trickery is directed against another jester at the Polish court. Rather than chasing him out of the country, both kings maintain warm relations with Ulenspiegel and invite him to stay. The end of chapter 23 indicates that Ulenpiegel remains at the Danish court until the king's death, although there is no clue as to the duration

---

28 Anon., *Ein kurtzweilig lesen*, fol. 33v: "Gnediger vnd hochgeborner fürst/ ich besorg mich euwer vngnad/ vnd förcht mich gantz vbel/ so hon ich all mein lebtag gehört/ das ein ietlicher sol frid haben in seinen vier pfelen."
29 This is commonly referred to as *Hausfrieden*. Osenbrüggen, *Der Hausfrieden*, 11. Also Grimm, *Deutsches Wörterbuch*, vol. 13, 1597.
30 Jahn, "Raum für Schwänke," 77–78; Wunderlich, *Till Eulenspiegel*, 33.

of this stay. At the Polish court, Ulenspiegel wins the competition against the local court jester to the king's amusement, gets his reward, and rides away in good standing. These two episodes at foreign courts show that Ulenspiegel can play nice if it was important to him, but also that the criticism implied in his mischief is directed at his fellow Germans.

The third foreign trip leads him to Rome in what appears to be the mockery of a pilgrimage. Chapter 34 begins with the reminder of Ulenspiegel's mischief: "Ulenspiegel was hallowed with cunning mischief. When he had tried all shenanigans he remembered the old proverb: Go to Rome as a pious man, come back as a good-for-nothing."[31] The sarcastic use of the religious term "geweiht," consecrated or hallowed, for his proclivity for mischief signals the narrator's disapproval of both the pilgrimage in specific and Ulenspiegel's moral make-up in general. Only once he has gone through all possible forms of mischief does he remember his lapsed commitment to faith. The critical proverb, however, is used ironically here as Ulenspiegel is not traveling to Rome as a pious man, nor does he return as a better person, as the narrator confirms at the end of the chapter.[32]

In Rome, he bets with his landlady that he would be able set up a meeting with the pope for her in exchange for a handsome sum of money. The trick he uses to achieve this goal does not victimize anyone in spite of its deceptive intent: everybody is happy at the end, and he receives the promised monetary reward and leaves town. While he frequently lampoons members of the clergy in other chapters for their pettiness and greed, the papal court is not targeted in any way. It becomes apparent that the author did not intend to criticize the Church as an institution, only its flawed members in Germany. As in the other two foreign adventures, he is not chased out of town, nor does he cheat or abuse anyone. The author presents an inverted geographic order: while he unleashes his abusive behavior and sharp invective on the members of his own national community to the point that he leaves behind a web of places where he is no longer welcome, he does not victimize his competitors in foreign locations, very much the opposite of what we would expect in the cultural context of the early sixteenth century.

---

31 Anon., *Ein kurtzweilig lesen*, fol. 47r: "MJt durchtribner schalckheit was Vlenspiegel geweihet. Als er dan alle schalckeit versûcht het/ da gedacht er an das alt sprichwort. Gang gen Rom frummer man/ kum herwider nequam."

32 Chaper 84 describes the adventure after his return from Rome. Here, Ulenspiegel engages in the same pattern of abuse as before; the journey to Rome appears to have left no impact, as the end of the chapter indicates (Anon., *Ein kurtzweilig lesen*, fol. 118r): "And Ulenspiegel left the house and laughed and said: this is how one should carry out the journey to Rome." ("vnd vlenspiegel get vß dem huß vnd lacht vnd sprach also sol man die rom fart volbringen.")

When Ulenspiegel falls ill and senses his impending death in chapter 89, he seeks shelter in a monastery. The chapter begins with this statement:

> When the time came when Ulenspiegel had passed through all countries and he had become old and grumpy, a remorseful quiet came over him, and he resolved that he wanted to enter a monastery, given his poverty, in order to conclude his life well and to serve God for the rest of his life so that he would not be lost when God was passing judgment over him.[33]

This move is not without irony as monastic life promises a stable and sedentary existence without geographic mobility – which is the exact opposite of how he had conducted his life to date. The ironic distance with which the narrator relates this turn of Ulenspiegel's life allows doubts as to Ulenspiegel's motivation. The abbot mercifully welcomes Ulenspiegel and assigns him the easy job of gatekeeper. This assignment is not without irony. While Ulenspiegel never accepted and respected physical borders and personal boundaries in his entire life, he now is put in charge of guarding and regulating the boundary separating the monastery from the outside world and of controlling the movement of others. The abbot instructs him to allow entry to only every third or fourth beggar to make sure that beggars do not use up the monastery's food supplies. Ulenspiegel extends that restriction to everybody who wants to enter, thus creating a great deal of upheaval. Ulenspiegel is relieved from his position and is eventually forced to leave the monastery after playing another trick.

It becomes clear that Ulenspiegel is not able to maintain a sedentary life even though this would have been in his interest, given his poor health. After a couple of more adventures, Ulenspiegel dies, and even his funeral is marked by transgressive spatial elements. During the memorial, a group of pigs knocks over his casket (chapter 94), and during the burial one of the ropes breaks so he ends up being buried standing upright in his grave (chapter 95).

While the protagonist Ulenspiegel serves as a mirror to censure the immorality and the pettiness of his contemporaries, he himself is an imperfect being and a transgressor who violates scores of social norms. It is his mobility that makes him so effective as a tool of satire and invective and so vulnerable as an object of scorn. His itinerant life is the key factor that turns him into a social misfit. It reflects his unwillingness to become a contributing member of society and his inability to become socially viable by entering an occupational category. His mobility allows him

---

[33] Anon., *Ein kurtzweilig lesen*, fol. 123r–123v: "NUn bei der zeit als Ulenspiegel alle Land vmb louffen het/ vnd was alt und verdrossen worden da kam in ein galgen ruw an/ und gedacht wie er sich wolt in ein closter ergeben/ mit seiner armůt/ vnd sein zeit vol schleißen/ vnd got dienen sein leben lang/ für sein sünd wan got vber in gedůt/ dz er nit verloron würd."

to avoid social classification and stands metaphorically for his unstable identity and lacking morality. Just as for Brant, unchecked mobility represented uncontrolled and uncontrollable agency that was deeply suspect to the author of *Dyl Ulenspiegel*. The presentation of the protagonist as a vagabond and buffoon allows for a projection of diffuse fears of change through unchecked mobility, change that threatened social norms and civic order.[34]

Dyl Ulenspiegel showed a keen awareness of geographic spaces and thus was one of the first literary texts reflecting a rising interest in space and geography, providing evidence for the impact of the spatial turn on popular culture. However, this new spatiality was projected with suspicion as it made it more difficult to exercise social control and moral discipline. The author viewed spatial mobility as a vehicle of transgression that enabled a life in the margins outside of social control mechanisms. The text's geographic order was inverted in that the mental map of Germany was gradually filled with places where Ulenspiegel no longer could go, thus developing a negative cosmography where locations were removed from the map rather than added. By showing how the new spatial dimension created the opportunity for the protagonist's transgressive behavior in the narrative, he implicitly provided a critique of the spatial turn.

This intellectual world of social projection in literary texts stood in stark contrast to the practices of travel, spatial discovery, long-distance trade, and the connection of regional networks that had become the norm for the new elites, that is merchants, bankers, mariners, cosmographers, chroniclers and others who drove the spatial expansion with commercial ambition and strategic intent and who chronicled these exploits. Late medieval culture had rejected travel, other than pilgrimage and the pursuit of regional trade, but this was rarely a contentious issue in society and literature as there was broad consensus on this point. The rapid uptick in travel activity around 1500, both in terms of frequency and distance of travel, disrupted this consensus. This provoked a backlash among literary writers who were firmly anchored in a stable and static urban society hostile to all forms of innovation: vernacular culture was vastly opposed to the practices of travel and exploration.

Reports of new discoveries did not have a significant effect in Germany,[35] with the exception of a brief interest in the sensational and mostly fake accounts by Vespucci, and the public discourse in the vernacular was largely dominated by the

---

34 Röcke, *Die Freude am Bösen*, 221.
35 Pieper, *Die Vermittlung*, 112–113.

voices critical to travel and discoveries.[36] Perhaps the most profound response came from Sebastian Brant, who condemned the explorations by the Portuguese and the Spaniards as a form of godless curiosity. Literary writers frequently addressed geographic mobility and invariably associated it with social outcasts who operated in the margins of society and used their mobility for their transgressive acts. Discovery and mobility were thus seen as sources of destabilization of the social cohesion and political order by German popular culture between 1490 and 1540.

---

[36] The textual evidence presented here clearly contradicts Treue (*Abenteuer und Anerkennung*, 36) who claims that sceptics like Sebastian Brant or Kaspar Stiblin in his *Commentariolus de Eudaemonensium Republica* (1555) were drowned out by the general enthusiasm for foreign countries and exotic cultures.

Chapter 15
America and the Epistemological Crisis of Space: An Afterthought

These four verses from Sebastian Brant's *Narrenschiff* from 1494 have generally been read as the first mentioning of America in a German literary text:[1] "Furthermore, they since found everywhere in Portugal and Spain gold islands and naked people, about whom one could not say anything before."[2] For three reasons, this claim does not withstand closer examination. Firstly, Brant mentioned Portugal before Spain, as the Portuguese discoveries were much more sustained and significant at the time, looking back on almost a century of African exploration and colonization. Brant must have viewed the discoveries made by Columbus as merely part of a larger pattern rather than as a singularly important event.

Secondly, America was not a known concept in 1494. At the time, Columbus had only completed one journey. There was only one text bearing witness, the famous *Columbus Letter* that was presumably written by Columbus on 15 February 1493 on his journey back to Europe. His letter makes it very clear that he assumed that he had landed on some Asian islands. The momentous nature of his discovery was entirely obscure at the time and certainly not apparent to Columbus himself, nor to the readers of his letter. It has been argued that Brant's descriptor "jnn hispanyen" as the place where gold was found refers to the island of Hispaniola rather than Spain.[3] But the locator phrase read as a whole, "jnn Portigal vnd jnn hispanyen," makes it clear that Brant talked about both Portugal and Spain as the nations that had made the discoveries in unknown parts of the world.

Two editions of the *Columbus Letter* were published in Basel in 1494.[4] Brant knew at least the second Basel edition that was published by Brant's own publisher Bergmann von Olpe in 1494. The *Letter* was issued together with Carlo Verardi's *In laudem Serenissimi Ferdinandi Hispaniarum Regis*,[5] to which Brant

---

1 Jantz, "Amerika," 311; also Neuber, "Verdeckte Theologie," 15; Sievernich, "Entdeckung und Verdeckung," 47; Klaffke, *"Es sey die alte Welt,"* 32.
2 Brant, *Narrenschiff*, ch. 66, v. 53–56: "Ouch hatt man sydt jnn Portigal | Vnd jnn hispanyen vberall | Golt/ jnslen funden/ vnd nacket lüt | Von den man vor wust sagen nüt."
3 Neuber, "Verdeckte Theologie," 12. This argument is important for Neuber as he seeks to make the point that Brant was aware of the singularity of Columbus' discovery – which is implausible as Columbus himself was not clear about the significance of his discovery.
4 Pieper (*Die Vermittlung*, 111) argues that the first Basel edition was published in 1493.
5 [Verardi], *In laudem Serenissimi*, fol. dd5v–ee6v.

contributed a panegyric poem. The title page to the second part of the book containing the *Columbus Letter* reads *De Jnsulis nuper in mari Jndico repertis* (*The Islands Recently Discovered in the Indian Ocean*).⁶ In other words, Bergmann the printer and Brant as collaborator and perhaps editor located the islands Columbus had discovered in the Indian Ocean as part of Asia. Brant thus had no knowledge of a continent that is known as America today. Similarly, the Brant disciple Johann Geiler von Kaysersberg in his sermons on the *Narrenschiff* from 1498–1499 firmly located the new islands found by King Ferdinand in Asia.⁷ The existence of a new continent located between Europe and Asia was only fully accepted in Germany in the 1530s. Furthermore, German sources into the 1530s defined Vespucci's 1497 journey as the moment of discovery. As discussed in Chapter 11, the concept of the "New World" typically included all newly discovered lands, and even cosmographers in the first half of the sixteenth century struggled with the question of whether America should be designated as a proper fourth continent.⁸

Thirdly, Brant also mentioned the discoveries of new lands near the Arctic circle in the previous four verses: "Yet, since then [the time of Pliny and Strabo] many new lands were found behind Norway and Thule, like Iceland and Lapland, which all before were not known."⁹ These were newly discovered lands as well. Like other writers, Brant did not differentiate between discoveries in different parts of the world. In line with the thinking of the time, the new discoveries were merely extensions at the fringes of the known world:¹⁰ The Arctic territories in the north of Europe, sub-Saharan territories in Africa discovered by the Portuguese, and now these islands found by Columbus that were presumably located somewhere in Asia. Neither Brant's text nor the historical context would indicate that Columbus's discovery was different or even privileged in any way. Brant merely wanted to establish the fact that modern Europeans were expanding spatial horizons in every direction.¹¹ In Germany, it

---

6 [Verardi], *In laudem Serenissimi*, fol. dd5v.
7 Geiler, *Des hochwirdigen doctor*, fol. 134r.
8 Pieper (*Die Vermittlung*, 112) claims that two thirds of the Americana published north of the Alps by 1503 referred to these four verses from Brant's *Narrenschiff*. Yet, America was not a known concept at that time so this is a questionable frame of reference.
9 Brant, *Narrenschiff*, ch. 66, v. 49–52: "Noch hat man sythar funden vile | Landt/ hynder Norwegen vnd Thyle/ | Als jßlant vnd pylappenlandt | Das vorhyn alls nit was erkandt."
10 Johnson, *The German Discovery*, 61.
11 Wuttke ("Humanismus," 496) claims that German Humanists between 1493 and 1534 often praised the discovery of America as a unique major accomplishment. While it is true that many Humanists stressed that their knowledge of the world surpassed that of the ancients, the discovery of America never was privileged or singled out as the major factor. Furthermore, the

became clear only well after 1500 that these newly found islands in the Atlantic Ocean were distinct from the East Indies.[12]

Brant's verses were inspired by Columbus, who claimed that most rivers in Hispaniola contained gold and that all the people he had encountered "go naked, as their mothers bore them, men and women alike."[13] The Columbus letter was published in twenty-two editions in Europe between 1493 and 1496 and thus was widely known.[14] The only other source referring to "America" is Hieronymus Münzer's travel report about his journey to France, Spain, and Portugal in 1494–1495 that contains a passage congratulating King Ferdinand and Queen Isabel on the discovery of the new Indian islands.[15] Pieper claims that two thirds of all "Americana" that were published north of the Alps referred to these four lines by Sebastian Brant, and much of the rest were editions of the Columbus letter. Yet, Brant had no concept of a new continent discovered by Columbus nor a reason to believe that the discovery of Hispaniola by Columbus was different in any way than the ongoing discoveries of new islands off the coast of Africa by Portugal. Other than this being the first major Spanish expedition since the conquest of the Canary Islands in the early fifteenth century, there is little that seemed exceptional about Columbus's voyage. It is therefore inappropriate to subsume these verses under the rubric of "Americana." It has been noted that Columbus's journey found virtually no resonance in Germany,[16] and the failure to understand its true significance was likely the reason for it.

The reports authored by Amerigo Vespucci changed the reception of the New World in Germany, even though much of his reporting was false. His first letter was published in Paris in 1503 with the title *Mundus Novus* and describes his participation in a Portuguese expedition to the coast of Brazil in 1501–1502. There was a total of twenty-eight editions of the letter in Europe between 1504 and 1506, nineteen of them in the empire north of the Alps.[17] Vespucci stated in his introduction that there was a new inhabited continent south of the equator. Vespucci represented the view of the Portuguese in whose service he had

---

magnitude of Columbus's discovery was not recognized until well after 1500, as I argue here. See also Ehrlicher, "Die ‚Neue Welt'," 358.

12 Pieper, *Die Vermittlung*, 111. Wuttke ("Humanismus," 500–503) lists a number of responses to America by German writers, all after 1500.
13 Columbus, *The Four Voyages*, 117.
14 Pieper, "Between India and the Indies," [5].
15 Vogel, "Amerigo Vespucci," 55.
16 Vogel, "Amerigo Vespucci," 55–56.
17 Pieper, "Between India and the Indies," [5]; Pieper, *Die Vermittlung*, 103–104, 134–135. According to Davies (*Renaissance Ethnography*, 79), there were 22 Columbus editions and 60 Vespucci editions in Europe by 1530.

traveled that these newly discovered lands differed from Asia, its cultures, and its treasures. He contradicted the Spanish belief that these were hitherto unknown regions of Asia.[18] The Augsburg *Mundus Novus* reprint from 1504 for the first time disseminated information about a possible new continent. It is this line of thinking that inspired Waldseemüller and Ringmann to publish their map and supporting texts in 1507 that recognized these lands as a continent and called it America.[19]

Vespucci's *Four Voyages* was first published in Italian in Florence in 1504 or 1505. As discussed above, Matthias Ringmann and Martin Waldseemüller included a Latin translation as *Quattuor Americi Vespucij Nauigationes* (*Four Voyages of Amerigo Vespucci*) to their *Cosmographiae Introductio* (1507), their introduction to cosmography and geography, which was published in Saint Dié in 1507. The book was republished by Johannes Grüninger in Strasbourg in 1509, again containing both parts. In the same year, Grüninger published a German translation of the *Quatuor Navigationes* with the title *Diß büchlin saget wie die zwen durchlüchtigsten herren her Fernandus. K. zů Castilien vnd herr Emanuel. K. zů Portugal haben das weyte mör ersůchet vnnd funden vil Insulen/ vnnd ein Nüwe welt von wilden nackenden Leüten/ vormals unbekant* (*This Booklet Says How the Two Most Serene Lords, Lord Ferdinand King of Castile and Lord Emanuel King of Portugal, Searched the Wide Ocean and Found Islands and a New World of Wild, Naked People that Were Formerly Unknown*). The colophon at the end of the book contains this concluding remark, which was not present in the Latin original: "How you should understand the sphere and the description of the entire world you will find and read about afterwards."[20] It stands to reason that the reference is to Martin Waldseemüller's *Der welt kugel* (*The Sphere of the World*), which was also published by Johannes Grüninger in Strasbourg in 1509, and which was discussed in Chapter 11. While the text has some similarities with the *Cosmographiae Introductio*, it is not a translation. Thus, Waldseemüller wrote his cosmography in the vernacular not just as a commentary for his world map of 1507 but also to accompany the German translation of Vespucci's *Quatuor Navigationes*.[21] This is further evidence that Waldseemüller regarded the Vespucci text as vital evidence for his cosmography.

Many of these early German prints were illustrated, more so than their non-German counterparts. The 1494 Basel edition of the Columbus letter, for instance,

---

[18] Pieper, *Die Vermittlung*, 104.
[19] See the detailed argumentation in Chapter 11.
[20] [Vespucci], *Diß büchlin saget*, sig. F6r: "Wie du aber dye kugel vnd beschreibung der gantzen welt verston soltt/ würst du hernach finden vnnd lesen."
[21] *Der welt kugel* and *Diß büchlin saget* are bound together in the copies at Freiburg University Library, the Württembergische Landesbibliothek Stuttgart, and the Huntington Library.

with which Sebastian Brant likely collaborated, has five woodcuts showing ships, landscapes, and even an urban scene on Hispaniola. Two woodcuts show caravels of the kind the Spaniards used at the time. One woodcut shows a galley, however, which certainly was not used for a transatlantic passage.

Vespucci's *Mundus Novus* inspired German printmakers even more. Several German *Mundus Novus* editions featured woodcuts, showing the Portuguese king, Amerindians, or Portuguese ships. But they were very basic woodcuts that did not convey anthropological information, other than the nakedness of the natives. There is no concept of the violent first contact; in fact, neither violence nor anthropophagy were even implied in the images. Also, there were no landscapes, human settlements, and only very rudimentary ships. But at the same time, two broadsheets were produced that were clearly inspired by Vespucci's *Mundus Novus*. They featured the most sophisticated and differentiated representations of the New World to date.

The very first illustration representing anthropophagy in the New World was a woodcut on a single-page broadsheet produced by Johann Froschauer in Augsburg, perhaps as early as 1503.[22] The first sentence of the caption has a title function: "This image shows us the people and the island that were found by the Christian King of Portugal or by his subjects."[23] While we know today that Vespucci's third voyage of 1501–1502, described in *Mundus Novus*, led to the eastern coast of Brazil, the caption shows no awareness of place. The location is generically described as an island, just like the locations visited by Columbus were described as islands as well.

The short description of the scene is unexcited; the anthropophagy is almost incidental in the final part of the caption: "They also eat each other, even those who were slain, and hang their meat into the smoke. They live to 150. And they have no government."[24] The woodcut shows a peaceful group of natives dressed only in feather skirts. In the center is a mother taking care of her three children. But there is also part of a human body hanging over the fire, and one of the natives is gnawing on a human arm. On the horizon, we see two Portuguese caravels approaching over the open waters, presumably ready to invade, to impose Christian order, and to install a government which they do not have.

---

22 Grafton (*New Worlds*, 76) dates it to 1505.
23 [Vespucci], *Dise figur anzaigt*: "Dise figur anzaigt vns das volck vnd insel die gefunden ist durch den cristenlichen künig zů Portugal oder von seinen vnderthonen." The full text is reproduced and translated in Davies, *Renaissance Ethnography*, 79–81.
24 [Vespucci], *Dise figur anzaigt*: "Sy essen auch ainander selbs die erschlagen werden vnd hencken das selbig fleisch in den rauch. Sy werden alt hundert vnd fünffzig iar. Vnd haben kain regiment."

The other broadsheet was published by Georg Stuchs in Nuremberg in 1505 (figure 7). Its title is very similar to that of the Augsburg print: "These are the newly found humans or people in form and figure, as they stand here, found quite marvelously by the Christian King of Portugal."[25] The one-page text makes it clear that it is drawn from Amerigo Vespucci's *Mundus Novus*. But the broadsheet text does not tell the story of Vespucci's voyage and instead only focuses on the description of the Amerindians, which is given in an abbreviated form. The description is condensed to the essential information, such as the warm tropical climate, the nakedness of the natives, their lack of governance and of private property, their sexual permissiveness, and their anthropophagy.

Figure 7: [Amerigo Vespucci]. *Das sind die new gefunden menschen oder volcker Jn form vnd gestalt Als sie hie stend durch den Cristenlichen Künig von Portugall/ gar wunnderbarlich erfunden.* Nuremberg: Georg Stuchs, 1505. © Herzog August Bibliothek Wolfenbüttel.

The brief description concludes with this statement: "And without a doubt I believe that the worldly paradise on earth is not far from this landscape. So it is manifest

---

25 [Vespucci], *Das sind die new gefunden menschen*: "Das sind die new gefunden menschen oder volcker Jn form vnd gestalt Als sie hie stend durch den Cristenlichen Künig von Portugall/ gar wunnderbarlich erfunden."

and evident that we sailed through the fourth part of the world."[26] It is evident that the editor of this text was interested in working out the tensions in Vespucci's text. On one hand, natives led lives that were transgressive in many respects, and on the other, the scene was set in an idyllic landscape that resembled paradise and was described as a fourth part of the world distinct from the three known continents.

The woodcut shows a rugged shoreline landscape, but it also picks up on that tension. We see a narrow gap in the ocean that is lined by steep cliffs on both sides and that opens up into a bay. Three Portuguese caravels are sailing through the gap, awaited by two groups of native warriors who are hiding on either side of the gap; they are armed with bows, arrows, and clubs but are wearing only girdles of feathers. Interestingly, the men in the illustrations are bearded, in contrast to most texts describing Amerindians that asserted that they were unable to grow beards. Just as in the Froschauer woodcut, the Portuguese are about to take possession of the land, and the violent first contact appears imminent. The image itself shows neither moral depravity nor anthropophagy of the natives; yet their representation in the text makes it abundantly clear that the Portuguese intervention is more than justified.

The German reception of Vespucci's *Four Voyages*, which was first published in Italian in 1504 or 1505, was not as intense as that of his earlier text. As discussed above, the Humanist circle around Waldseemüller and Ringmann published a Latin version in 1507 in Saint Dié and again in Strasbourg in 1509, and also a German translation in Strasbourg in 1509. The German translation features five woodcuts, including the frontispiece. Two of the five woodcuts show anthropophagy. The first illustration within the text shows naked Amerindians chopping up human arms and legs, presumably in preparation for a feast.[27] The third text illustration shows a Portuguese mariner being seduced by three naked native women, while a fourth kills him from behind using a human bone as a club.[28] In spite of the rather alluring and explicit illustrations of the German Vespucci prints, and particularly those published in the German vernacular, the Vespucci reception waned rather rapidly after 1509, as the Columbus reception had done before.

The first German-language anthology containing travel and discovery reports was Jobst Ruchamer's *Newe vnbekanthe landte* (*New Unknown Lands*, 1508), a translation of Fracanzano da Montalboddo's Italian compilation *Paesi Novamente retrovati* (1507). Much of the book is dedicated to the Portuguese voyages to Africa

---

26 [Vespucci], D*as sind die new gefunden menschen*: "vnd on zweyffel halt ich ob das irdisch paradeis auff erdtrich das dz nit verr von diser lantschafft sey. So ist küntlich vnd offenbar dz wir den vierden theyl der welt durch schyfft haben."
27 [Vespucci], *Diß büchlin saget*, sig. B1v.
28 [Vespucci], *Diß büchlin saget*, sig. E4v.

and Asia; only a small part renders texts relating to the Spanish conquests, chiefly reports of Columbus's first three voyages and Vespucci's *Mundus Novus*. Just like Waldseemüller, Ruchamer appears to have had no knowledge of Columbus's fourth journey to the New World.[29] Ruchamer's text had a limited impact; only the compilation by Michael Herr in 1534 picked up some of Ruchamer's texts.[30]

Ruchamer's anthology and the 1509 Vespucci translation by the Waldseemüller circle represented a temporary end point in the German reception of texts relating to Spanish explorations and conquests in the New World. Waldseemüller soon must have recognized that he vastly overestimated Vespucci's role in the discovery of the New World. With that, Waldseemüller's claim to a fourth continent disappeared, as is evident in his 1516 *Carta marina* discussed in Chapter 11.

While a significant number of German prints before 1510 contained information about America, they all went back to just two sources: Columbus and Vespucci. There was no awareness that Columbus and Vespucci talked about the same region of the world, nor that this region would eventually be recognized as its own new continent. Thomas Murner's description of newly discovered territories in his *Narren bschwerung* (*Exorcism of Fools*) from 1512 illustrates this point: "One says about King Ferdinand, how he found many new islands near the land of Calicut. Many spices were found there, and silver and gold were found there as well."[31] Murner was conflating two narrative strands, the Columbus Letter portraying the Spanish King Ferdinand as the sponsor and the discovery of gold and silver and the Portuguese narratives describing the location of these new islands near Calicut and the spices found there. More importantly, Murner located all new discoveries in Asia and showed no awareness of a new continent. This text passage makes evident that the quality of information available to Murner and other writers was low as Germany had little access to Iberian communication networks that could have expanded the knowledge base.[32] Once the novelty of the Columbus and Vespucci accounts had worn off, the interest in the New World discoveries in Germany dropped as well.

Some of the privileged information made it into print in the form of printed general-interest information pamphlets, commonly referred to as "Newe zeittung." A small number of these reports appeared in the years after the fascination with Vespucci had ended. They described and named the geography of the New World

---

29 Pieper, *Die Vermittlung*, 143.
30 Pieper, *Die Vermittlung*, 137–140.
31 Murner, *Narrenbeschwörung*, 208, ch. 24, v. 12–16: "Man seit von künig ferinandt, | Wie er vil nüwer inselen fand | By dem calecutter land, | Darinn man fand vil spetzery, | Silber, goldt was ouch da by."
32 Pieper, *Die Vermittlung*, 135.

with more specificity. The first was *Copia der Newen Zeytung auß Presillg Landt* (*Copy of the New Newspaper from the Brazilian Land*) that describes the 1511–1512 Portuguese expedition organized by Christopham de Haro and Dom Nuno Manuel. The report had been sent to the Fuggers in manuscript form by their factor in Lisbon and was printed in three editions in Augsburg and Nuremberg in 1514.[33] In makes clear that trade was the motivation for this Portuguese voyage: the ship returned to Lisbon with foodstuffs (*victualia*), spices (*specerey*), and Brazilwood (*Presil holtz*), but the report also mentions the "purchased young boys and girls,"[34] that is young slaves, on the ship. This is generally seen as the first report about Brazil in Germany. The text reports the pilot's claim that Malacca could be reached on this route and thus tentatively locates Brazil in Asia to the west of Europe, yet it does not make the connection with Spanish discoveries in the same region nor with notions of a new continent.

There appears to have been more geographic clarity by the end of the decade. Ulrich von Hutten in his syphilis tract from 1519, entitled *Von der wunderbarlichen artzney des holtz Guaiacum genant* (*On the Miraculous Medicine Called Guaiacum Wood*), mentioned the origin of the guaiacum wood, one of the remedies promoted at the time to treat syphilis: "Its use came to us from the island called Hispaniola, located toward the sunset near America, the land that extends toward midnight in its length."[35] Hutten located Hispaniola to the west near America. He implied that America extended considerably to the north. While there is no clear indication how Hutten understood the status of America, he assumed that it was a landmass more significant than Hispaniola itself. Hutten's assertion that the inhabitants of Hispaniola successfully used the guaiacum wood to treat syphilis gives the impression that the disease was indigenous to the island. Adding to the geographic confusion is Hutten's claim earlier in the book that syphilis first had appeared in Naples in 1493,[36] the same year Columbus had returned from his first journey. However, the belief in Germany at the time was that America was discovered by Vespucci only in 1497. Furthermore, Naples was not one of the ports that was in contact with the colonies in America. Hutten thus presents two incompatible stories of the origin of the disease, which only can be explained by Hutten's lack of

---

33 Pieper, *Die Vermittlung*, 134; Aymoré, *Die Jesuiten*, 121.
34 Anon., *Copia der Newen Zeytung*, sig. A3v: "voller erkauffter Jungen knaben vnnd maydlen."
35 Hutten, *von der wunderbarlichen artzney*, sig. C1r: "Sein bruch ist zů vns kumen vß der Jnselen Spangnola genant/ die ligt zů dem nidergang der sonnen/ bey America dem landt da es sich zů Mitternacht hin erstrecket nach seiner lenge."
36 Hutten, *von der wunderbarlichen artzney*, sig. B2r.

geographic knowledge. In other words, it appears that Hutten did not understand the true significance, size, and location of America.

The conquest of the Aztec Empire by Hernán Cortés resulted in a different quality of reporting in Germany. Contrasting with Vespucci's accounts of savage and overly sexualized Amerindians, Cortés projected an image of a civilized and orderly Aztec culture. The most important German text reporting on Cortés is *Newe zeittung. Von dem lande. Das die Sponier funden haben ym 1521. iare genant Jucatan*. (*New Pamphlet of the Land that the Spaniards Found in 1521, Called Yucatán*), published in Erfurt in 1522. Its focus is the conquest of Mexico by Cortés, here referred to as Yucatán, which is told over the first eight pages of the pamphlet. It was based on the 1522 edition of *De orbe novo* by Peter Martyr d'Anghiera, a compilation that included the first three volumes of his *Decades*, and Cortés's letters to Charles V.[37] The last three pages of the *Newe zeittung* included bulletins covering other newsworthy items: events at the imperial court in Brussels and the Turkish occupation of Budapest.

Much of the text describes the Aztec city of Tenochtitlán, now Mexico City. Tenochtitlán is portrayed as a large and sophisticated city in a European mold:

> In the middle of that lake lies a large city of 70,000 people. The Christians call this city Great Venice, and three other cities lie in the middle of the same lake. Great Venice has five gates, and each gate has a bridge leading to the firm land. And on these five bridges they have many drawbridges with their towers, which is why the city cannot be conquered. [...] The city called Great Venice is extraordinarily rich in gold and in merchandise made out of cotton and honey. It holds a market every day, and daily 40,000 to 50,000 come to the market. They use copper coins, and they have weights and measurements.[38]

The author calls Tenochtitlán "Great Venice" and thus sets up this large and powerful European merchant city as point of comparison. The city is heavily fortified like a European city, reachable only on heavily fortified bridges. They have a very active cash-based market economy. This is a far cry from the other New World communities described in earlier texts that did not know personal property and thus were not market-based. One of the two woodcuts shows

---

37 Johnson, *Cultural Hierarchy*, 34–39.
38 Anon., *Newe zeittung*, sig. A3r-A3v.: "mitten ym dem selben Sehe leyt eyn grosse Stadt/ von lxx Tausent vetzeres/ welche stat die Christen nennen gross Venedig/ liegen sonst noch drey Stete/ yn dem selben Sehe/ vnnd das groß Venedig hat funff pfortten/ vnd ein ytliche pfordt hat ein Brucke/ biß auffs lande/ vnd auff den selbigen funff brucken/ haben sie vil schlege brucken mit yren thürmen/ darumb die stat nicht zugewynen ist/ [...]. Die stat groß Venedig gnant Jst auß der massen reich an golde/ vnd baumwollen war vnd honig/ hat alle tage margkt do/ kummen teglich xl. biß in funfftzig tausent mhan zum margt prauchen kupferm müntze/ haben gewicht vnd moß vnder yne."

Tenochtitlán as a European city with its bridges and fortifications. The inhabitants of Tenochtitlán were fully dressed and wore European clothes. Both the text and this woodcut "made the representational leap into a world somewhat familiar to the reader."[39] So the great news was that a mercantile and well-organized city had been found in the New World. Interestingly, the story ended with a peaceful arrangement between the Aztecs and the Spaniards; the subsequent violent submission of Tenochtitlán was not known to the author of this text.

The second letter by Hernán Cortés to Emperor Charles V was published in Nuremberg in 1524 as *Praeclara Ferdinandi Cortesii*. The interrelationship between political order, high civilization, and architecture was expressed in the stunning and well-known map of Tenochtitlán, which was added to the book.[40] The map shows the location of the city in the middle of the lake as well as the bridges that led to the city. The center of Tenochtitlán is laid out as a square. Three years later, Albrecht Dürer published *Etliche vnderricht zu befestigung der Stett/ Schloß vnd Flecken* (*Comprehensive Instruction on the Fortification of Cities, Castles, and Villages*) in 1527, which was the first architectural treatise in a modern European language and which brought the new Humanist discipline of urban planning to Germany.[41] Dürer's book contains the map of a carefully planned ideal city with a large, square central plaza and a road system that was laid out as concentric squares around this plaza, which resembles the map of Tenochtitlán to a remarkable degree.[42]

Laying out cities in a grid or checkerboard design was first practiced by the Spaniards in the areas of southern Spain that were reclaimed from the Muslims.[43] Santo Domingo, the first Spanish city in the New World, was built on a grid, designed by the governor Nicolás de Ovando in 1502. The grid became the norm for newly founded Spanish cities, and Charles V in his settlement ordinances of 1526 mandated that new settlements "shall be divided into squares, streets, and lots in ordered, straight lines commencing from the central square, from which shall issue the streets leading to the main roads and gates."[44] The 1524 Nuremberg map of Tenochtitlán is by far the most detailed representation we have of this fabled Aztec city. It is therefore difficult to assess to what extent it accurately rendered the layout of the city or whether it was influenced by the ideal of urban design in

---

39 Johnson, *Cultural Hierarchy*, 39.
40 Johnson, *Cultural Hierarchy*, 39.
41 The pioneering treatise on architecture, promoting principles of city planning, was *De re aedificatoria* by Leon Battista Alberti, written around 1450 and printed in 1485.
42 Johnson, *Cultural Hierarchy*, 39–41.
43 Ortiz Crespo, "The Spanish American Colonial City." 23.
44 Ortiz Crespo, "The Spanish American Colonial City." 24.

the early sixteenth century, which was already actively practiced by the Spaniards in the region.[45]

This was not Dürer's first encounter with Aztec culture. During a visit to Brussels in August 1520, Dürer viewed the famous Aztec treasures that had been given to the conquistador Hernán Cortés by the Aztec ruler Moctezuma and that were exhibited there.[46] Dürer described the gold artifacts and textiles enthusiastically in his diary.[47] However, Dürer lacked the iconographic frame of reference to view these extraordinary pieces of art, and there is little evidence that the experience had an effect on his own work.[48] Yet, when the map of Tenochtitlán was published in his home town four years later, he already had an awareness of the cultural significance of the city.

To return to the *Newe zeittung* from 1522, the pamphlet did not just praise the civilizatory achievements of the Aztecs, but it also associated the non-European other with the devil. The first of the two woodcuts shows life in Tenochtitlán in five panels. The center right panel shows the arrival of the Spaniards by boat. The top left shows Tenochtitlán as a European city. But the top center panel shows the ritual killing of babies whose bodies are thrown down the stairs in the bottom panel. The top right shows the association of the European-looking burghers of Tenochtitlán with the devil. The text explains in some detail how Aztec kings staged a ritual before they went to war during which twelve to eighteen children were sacrificed to ensure the support of the devilish idol in battle. While the inhabitants of Tenochtitlán may have reached a high level of commerce, civilization, and governance, Aztec religious practices were increasingly perceived as idolatrous and troubling exactly because the newly encountered Aztecs could not be perceived as simple primitives. It is also conceivable that the text was influenced by the polemics against idolatry by the radical reformer Andreas Karlstadt the same year.[49]

It is not surprising that the "trope of America as a false paradise ruled by demons"[50] appeared exactly at the moment when Europeans first discovered an advanced civilization in Mexico. Descriptions of civilization, good governance,

---

45 Ortiz Crespo, "The Spanish American Colonial City." 23–24.
46 Smith, "Albrecht Dürer as Collector," 24–25.
47 Sahm, *Dürers kleinere Texte*, 133.
48 Hess, "Marvelous Encounters." We know from Dürer's famous "Rhinocervs" woodcut from 1515 that he was curious about the newly discovered world. His description of the rhinoceros states that it was "brought to Lisbon to the omnipotent King of Portugal, Emanuel, from India" ("Hat man dem großmechtigen Kunig von Portugall Emanuell gen Lysabon pracht auß Jndia").
49 Johnson, *Cultural Hierarchy*, 54.
50 Cañizares-Esguerra, *Puritan Conquistadors*, 167.

Chapter 15 America and the Epistemological Crisis of Space: An Afterthought — 225

and idyllic landscapes had to be countered by invoking the trope of an "emasculating false paradise" ruled by demons.[51] The distrust of discovering new parts of the world displayed by Sebastian Brant and others was taken to a higher level here. Anxieties of space opened up by the discovery of the New World culminated in the association of these spaces with devil worship.

The dedication letter by Michael Herr for his compilation *Die New welt, der landschaften vnnd Insulen* (*The New World of Landscapes and Islands*) from 1534 picked up this theme. Herr framed it more broadly by talking about foreign peoples in general:

> Those who recognize the same God as the creator of all things were for the most part seduced by the shameful Muhammad and by the priests who followed him. But those who serve the devil directly, like the ones from Calicut, they could not give any other reason for their deeds, like those from Hispaniola and Cuba. For what their priests teach them, this is how the devil rewards his apostles after they have done their work.[52]

The Lutheran Michael Herr promoted the image of indigenous priests serving as the devil's apostles and blamed them for the devil worship by both the people of the West Indies and of Calicut.[53] Herr represented a growing trend to associate the non-European other with the devil, be it in the Orient or in the New World.[54] Part of this trend was the theme of associating New World gold with devil worship. The German conquistador Nikolaus Federmann noted how gold ornaments given to him by indigenous nations in Venezuela in 1530–1531 were associated with devil worship. Federmann described how a cacique (native leader) sent a woman to him with a present: "The Indio woman returned and brought me a golden gem, which was a satanic effigy, of the kind they wear on their chest as ornaments."[55]

---

51 Cañizares-Esguerra, *Puritan Conquistadors*, 167.
52 Herr, *Die new welt*, sig. *3v: "Welche under den selben Gott/ den schöpfer aller ding herkennen/ die seind das gröst theil von dem schantlichen Machumet verfürt worden/ und von seinen nachkomenden der Pfaffen. Welche aber stracks dem Teufel dienen/ als die von Calechut/ die künden auch kein andere ursach jres thûns geben/ gleich als die aus Hispaniola oder Cuba/ dann das sie jre Pfaffen also leren/ doch so lont der Teufel seinen Aposteln auch nach jrer arbeit."
53 Johnson, *The German Discovery*, 41.
54 Cañizares-Esguerra (*Puritan Conquistadors*, 163–169) traces this trend in the second half of the sixteenth century. Particularly the anthologies published by Theodore de Bry (1528–1598) and Levinus Hulsius (1546–1606) focused on devil worship in the New World.
55 Federmann, *Jndianische Historia*, sig. N2r: "Nu aber die India khame wider/ bracht mir ein güldene kleinoth/ das was ein teüflische bildtnus/ so sie zů jrer zier an der brust tragen." The *Jndianische Historia* was probably written in the 1532 or 1533 but published only in 1557.

In sum, a limited number of German texts dealt with the New World before a wave of cosmographic texts attempted to integrate it into their overall structure of the globe in the 1530s. Their take on America did not reflect the importance of these discoveries and was quite limited in scope as the influx of new knowledge beyond the Vespucci texts was modest. In German writings, the territories of the New World were generally seen as islands without a firm location on the world map. There was no awareness that they formed a separate continent distinct from the lands discovered by the Portuguese in Africa and Asia, and there was no imagination and language to discuss these discoveries and to assess their significance.

Germans also were poorly informed about both the activities and the thinking in the Iberian world in regard to this new continent, with the notable exception of the merchant-banker elites in Augsburg and Nuremberg who had access to their own private information networks.[56] To be sure, Columbus himself did not develop a full understanding of where he had been and what he had discovered, but the Spaniards nevertheless acted very swiftly on these discoveries. By 1500, the Spaniards were constructing stone houses in Santo Domingo on the island of Hispaniola, and in 1502 they paved the Calle de las Damas. Just one decade after the arrival of Columbus, the Spaniards were erecting a permanent and fortified city with the clear intent to set up durable settlements and to subjugate and colonize the region. There was little general awareness in Germany of these Spanish activities. In the first quarter of the sixteenth century, only the large merchant houses had access to this information through their own networks, and they responded by expanding their presence in Portugal and Spain. The fact that the Welser merchant house opened a trading post in Santo Domingo in 1526[57] remained largely unnoticed in Germany. Furthermore, no princely houses in Germany showed an interest in participating in the colonial conquest, perhaps because they were more focused on tensions within the empire.[58]

None of these German texts noted that both the Portuguese and the Spaniards were in the process of building global empires supported by fortified outposts in

---

[56] Johnson, *Cultural Hierarchy*, 2. See also Keller and Molino, *Die Fuggerzeitungen*. Benedikt Reiff in his 1861 edition of Lucas Rem's diaries added an appendix (111–172) containing previously unpublished reports and letters received by the Welser Company of Augsburg. Rem was employed by the Welsers at the time.

[57] Häberlein, *The Fuggers of Augsburg*, 80.

[58] Similarly, the French Crown showed no interest in colonial ventures in the sixteenth century, as Schwitter ("Das Desinteresse am Neuen," 68) argues. However, some trade with the New World, particulalry to Portuguese possessions, were organized by merchant cities in northern France.

order to engage in global trade, although the Portuguese commercial activities were discussed in Germany, which will be examined in Chapter 17. The strategic intent is evident in the Treaty of Tordesillas of 1494, in which Pope Alexander VI divided up the newly discovered and the yet to be discovered parts of the world into Spanish and Portuguese spheres of influence and conquest.[59] The treaty, supplemented by the Treaty of Saragossa in 1529 to create a line of demarcation in Asia, represented an early attempt at creating a world order, with the Catholic Church in the cental role of arbiter. Yet, all these attempts to order the globe went unnoticed in Germany.

Many important discussions took place in the Catholic Iberian world in which Germans did not participate, such as whether Amerindians were human and could thus be converted, a question that was settled affirmatively by the bull *Sublimis Deus* by Pope Paul III in 1537.[60] The lone German exception was Sebastian Franck who in his *Weltbůch* from 1534 vigorously argued that the natives of all newly found territories were children of God and therefore human.[61] Other issues, like how to set up contact and communication with the non-European other, whether Amerindians could be enslaved and how to set up a colonial administration, mattered in Spanish discourses, but none of this trickled down into the German conversation in the first half of the sixteenth century.

A continuous narrative about the New World gradually emerged in the cosmographic literature of the 1530s and 1540s as the question of America as a continent was revisited, but there were few traces in the contemporaneous popular literature. A better understanding of America as a distinct space only emerged after 1550 with the publication of first-person accounts by Nikolaus Federmann, Hans Staden, and Ulrich Schmidel. All three had spent a significant amount of time in South America as mercenaries in the service of the Spaniards or Portuguese and as participants in the Iberian conquest and colonization of Latin America. All three narratives developed a distinct sense of place, had an acute awareness of geography, and above all created a sense of German participation and agency in the colonial theater.

Ulrich Schmidel served as mercenary in the Pedro de Mendoza expedition to the Río de la Plata (La Plata River) starting in 1534 and lived in the region, mostly in Asunción, until his return to Germany in 1554. His narrative, *Neuwe*

---

[59] Alexander VI in a couple of bulls from 1493 already had drawn a vertical line through the Atlantic, dividing Portuguese and Spanish spheres of influence. Furthermore, a number of bulls throughout the fifteenth century recognized Portuguese conquests off the coast of Africa, as Vogel ("'America,'" 11) argues.
[60] Davies, *Renaissance Ethnography*, 220.
[61] Franck, *Weltbůch*, fol 3r. See the discussion in Chapter 11.

Welt: Das ist/ Wahrhafftige Beschreibunge aller schönen Historien von erfindung viler vnbekanten Landschafften/ Jnsulen vnnd Stedten, (*New World, that is Truthful Descriptions of all Beautiful Narrations About the Discovery of Many Unknown Landscapes, Islands, and Cities*), was published in 1567. Hans Staden traveled to Brazil twice as part of Portuguese missions between 1547 and 1554. His account, *Warhaftige Historia vnd beschreibung eyner Landtschafft der Wilden/ Nacketen/ Grimmigen Menschenfresser Leuthen/ in der Newenwelt America gelegen* (*The True History and Description of a Country Populated by a Wild, Naked, and Savage Man-Eating People, Located in the New World, America*), published in 1557, was quite sensational because Staden claimed to have been a captive of the Tupi people, who intended to cannibalize him. Both Schmidel's and Staden's texts were illustrated with remarkable woodcuts, were reprinted and anthologized, and thus left an imprint on the German imagination in the second half of the sixteenth century.

The testimonial by Nikolaus Federmann (1506–1542) is the most relevant in this context. Federmann described his journey to the north coast of South America in 1529–1531, where he participated as a military leader in the attempted colonization of modern-day Venezuela by the Welser merchant house of Augsburg. He described his adventures in his *Jndianische Historia: Ein schöne kurtzweilige Historia Niclaus Federmanns des Jüngern von Ulm erster raise* (*Indian Chronicle: A Beautiful and Entertaining Story of the First Journey by Nicholas Federmann the Younger of Ulm*). The text, while written in the early 1530s, was published posthumously only in 1557 and was never reprinted nor anthologized. We must assume that its impact in Germany was minimal. Federmann was keenly aware that he operated in a space the Spaniards called *Las Indias* or *Indias Occidentales*. He developed a clear sense of orientation and direction and displayed a remarkable awareness of space, which was common for conquistadors operating in the Spanish realm.

While Federmann described the conquest and the violent first contact in detail, he also highlighted the participation of the Welser Company of Augsburg in the Spanish colonial project. The Welsers had secured the rights to colonize and exploit these territories in a contract with the Spanish Crown in 1528.[62] The Fuggers also participated in trade deals in the New World around 1530.[63] However, these commercial activities by the two Augsburg companies in the New World went largely unnoticed in Germany, perhaps because none of these ventures were commercially successful. They will be discussed in more detail in Chapter 17.

---

62 Simmer, *Gold und Sklaven*, 757–770.
63 Häberlein, *The Fuggers of Augsburg*, 80–82.

Chapter 15 America and the Epistemological Crisis of Space: An Afterthought

This demonstrates that the Fugger and Welser corporations, as well as other merchant bankers in Augsburg and Nuremberg, had access to privileged information or operated their own information networks, which allowed them to make decisions about investment and trade opportunities. Ironically, much of that information was disseminated in hand-written letters. Through their trade and communication networks, the Fuggers and Welsers had access to privileged information that was not intended for public consumption and therefore was never printed.[64] The result was an information imbalance: the merchant-banker elites had access to geographic knowledge which remained concealed to most Humanists and certainly to popular culture. The Fuggers, Welsers, and other corporate leaders therefore developed a global outlook that allowed them to act as global players who were able to use their knowledge to amass unimaginable wealth, particularly through their participation in the Portuguese trade network that included most of Asia. The uninformed masses and even the old urban elites had no access to this privileged information, yet warily witnessed the rapidly growing wealth and political power of the merchant-banker elites. The conflict erupting along this line of cleavage is the topic discussed in Part III.

---

64 Lach, *Asia in the Making of Europe*, vol. 1, book 1, 91–92.

Part III: **Globalization and the Nationalistic Backlash in Germany**

Navigare necesse est
Im Anfang war das Gewürz

Stefan Zweig, *Magellan*

Chapter 16
Theory of Early Modern Globalization

Current discussions frame globalization primarily in terms of the internet technology that evolved from the microelectronics revolution of the 1970s and that has created new global information grids that allow humans to communicate and network at astounding speeds. Manuel Castells, one of the earliest theorists of a technology-driven notion of globalization, in his trilogy *The Information Age: Economy, Society and Culture* (1996–1998) defined the internet as a central institution of contemporary globalization. The end of the Cold War, marking the victory of market economies over socialist models, was seen equally as a catalyst for globalization and a force that gave rise to an economy-based definition of globalization that was heavily reliant on global institutions like the World Trade Organization, the International Monetary Fund, and the World Bank.[1] The term globalization itself became fashionable in the early 1990s to coincide both with the end of a bipolar world order and the rapid rise of the internet.[2]

However, Castells in a 2006 essay conceded that globalization can be observed throughout history in different forms: "the conflictive interaction between global networks and communal identities is not a specific feature of the Information Age but a critical social dynamic in all forms of human organization throughout history."[3] Recent definitions of globalization have become more expansive and allow for the inclusion of earlier periods of history as phases of globalization. Jürgen Osterhammel and Niels Petersson see three basic traits of globalization that easily can be applied to the early sixteenth century.[4] First, globalization diminished the significance of the state and shifted the power away from the state toward markets and large, transnational corporations. An example is the outsize power of the Fugger Company[5] and its ability to thwart regulatory attempts by the Imperial Diet, the deliberative and legislative body of the Holy Roman Empire, to curb its predatory practices. Second, globalization affected

---

[1] Economic historians tend to use data sets to assess and define early modern globalization. Zwart (*Globalization*, 31–77) gives a survey of quantitative definitions of globalization.
[2] Osterhammel and Petersson, *Geschichte der Globalisierung*, 7.
[3] Castells, "Nothing New," 158.
[4] Osterhammel and Petersson, *Geschichte der Globalisierung*, 11–12.
[5] Wüst ("Das Bild der Fugger") documents the outsized reputation of the Fugger Company in the sixteenth century.

Note: Parts of this chapter were previously published in a different and abbreviated form in Hess, "Protest From the Margins."

cultural processes, driven by innovations in communication technology, such as the internet today or the printing press around 1500. This could lead to cultural homogenization, but paradoxically could also promote heterogenization by provoking a backlash in defense of local particularities and practices. We could read the rise of German nationalism at the time as such a backlash. And third, categories of space and time were profoundly altered and compressed. This is evident in the rise of cosmographic writings in the early sixteenth century, discussed in Chapter 10, that sought to displace the primacy of chronological and biblical narratives in favor of spatial representations, and in the representation of the world as a navigable grid that is the foundation for the creation of global networks.[6]

Ever since Immanuel Wallerstein's seminal 1974 book, there has been a growing consensus that the term globalization does not exclusively apply to the contemporary world and that the term can be applied to earlier phases in history. In *The Modern World-System*, Wallerstein launched an ongoing debate about whether the age of European expansion around 1500 can be characterized as a phase of globalization. He developed the concept of the "Modern World-System" whose origins he located in the rise of the "European World-Economy" around 1500.[7] Wallerstein recognized that both the explorations and a new capitalist society were prerequisites for such a "world-economy." However, the success of global trade around 1500 was largely due to the absence of a dominant single state. This enabled merchants to operate in a transnational space that could not be controlled by any state actor alone.[8]

Later critics, like Kenneth Pomeranz, assert that Wallerstein's argumentation was too Europe-centered and that it neglected the existence of equally wealthy trading nations along the Indian Ocean basin.[9] Pomeranz points out that there was comparable wealth in Europe and Asia around 1500. His key question is when and why European economic development pulled ahead of that of Asia in a process Pomeranz describes as *The Great Divergence* (2000). Pomeranz argues that this divergence began later than previously assumed and developed only between 1750 and 1850. Prasannan Parthasarathi presents a similar argument in *Why Europe Grew Rich and Asia Did Not: Global Economic Divergence, 1600–1850* (2011). Others, like Broadberry and Bishnupriya, paint a more differentiated picture by claiming, "by the eighteenth century the more economically advanced parts of Asia should be seen on the same level as the more peripheral, rather than the most developed,

---

6 Osterhammel and Petersson, *Geschichte der Globalisierung*, 11–12.
7 Wallerstein, *The Modern World-System I*, 67.
8 Wallerstein, *The Modern World-System I*, 127.
9 Pomeranz, *The Great Divergence*, 8; also Parthasarathi, *Why Europe Grew Rich*, 4, and Subrahmanyam, "Introduction," 16.

parts of Europe."[10] While this debate has little impact on the argument presented here, it confirms how critical the examination of early modern global connections has become in current scholarship. However, the key feature of early modern globalization, the linkage of the Indian Ocean trade system with the Atlantic world, is not under dispute. The result was that separate regional networks now became connected and that global patterns of interaction were restructured.[11]

Recent historiography has confirmed globalization as a key feature of the early modern period. Ronald E. Seavoy's study *Origins and Growth of the Global Economy* (2003) locates the beginnings of the global economic expansion in the fifteenth century, however without justifying the claim. The recently completed *Cambridge World History* further illustrates this point. Volume six, published in 2015, carries the title *The Construction of a Global World, 1400–1800 CE*. In his introduction, Sanjay Subrahmanyam identifies connectivity as one of the key themes of the volume and as one of the drivers of early modern history: "This is a period characterized by an intensification of long-distance contacts."[12]

A 2002 article by O'Rourke and Williamson reinvigorated the question when globalization began. The authors ridiculed "the 1490s big bang theory" because of the largely qualitative nature of the argumentation.[13] Instead, they argue that "the only irrefutable evidence that globalisation is taking place is a decline in the international dispersion of commodity prices or what might be called commodity price convergence."[14] This purely quantitative metric led the authors to the hypothesis that globalization did not set in until the Industrial Revolution, and specifically until the 1820s. In response, other economic historians more generally presuppose a continuous exchange of products and "sustained interactions" among the world's major regions "on a scale that generated deep and lasting impacts on all trading partners."[15]

While many economic historians investigate global trade networks and specific data points like price convergence and market integration, cultural historians focus on cultural influences and world systems. As a result, many alternate points of view have been formulated as to when globalization began. One such world-system was the Medieval Islamic sphere of cultural influence that extended from the

---

10 Broadberry and Bishnupriya, "The Early Modern Great Divergence," 3.
11 Fäßler, *Globalisierung*, 60–61.
12 Subrahmanyam, "Introduction," 7.
13 O'Rourke and Williamson, "When Did Globalisation Begin," 24.
14 O'Rourke and Williamson, "When Did Globalisation Begin," 24.
15 Flynn and Giráldez, "Path Dependence," 83. De Vries ("The Limits of Globalization," 713–714) refers to the two definitions as "hard globalization" and "soft globalization."

Mediterranean into East Africa and Southeast Asia.[16] Others argue that globalization began with the unification of the Eurasian landmass by the Mongol conquests in the thirteenth century[17] or with the subsequent age of Chinese overseas exploration during the early Ming Dynasty (1405–1433).[18]

A commonly postulated starting point of globalization is the conquest of the Americas, thus locating the start of globalization at the beginning of the sixteenth century. However, 1492 is not a useful date to mark the beginning of globalization. First, there was no awareness of a new continent until well into the sixteenth century, as argued in Chapter 15. Second, the economic significance of this discovery was not felt in Europe until after 1540. The impact of Vasco da Gama's journey to India around Africa in 1497–1499 was felt much more immediately. The most common view, favored here, is that significant global connections began around 1500 with the voyages of Vasco da Gama, Christopher Columbus, and their followers.[19] In other words, "The year 1500 marks an important turning point in world history [...]. The European discoveries made the oceans of the earth into highways for their commerce and conquest."[20] A variant of this view holds that globalization began in 1571 with the establishment of the port of Manila by the Spaniards, effectively creating a permanent link between Spanish America and the Pacific and Indian Ocean trade systems.[21]

Justin Jennings in his *Globalizations and the Ancient World* (2011) offers a useful methodological model for discussing globalization in a pre-modern context. To Jennings, an earlier era of globalization era has to show both evidence for "a significant leap in interregional interaction" as well as for corresponding "social changes that are associated with the creation of a global culture."[22] His definition of pre-modern globalization makes the important point that globalization cannot be defined on the basis of empirical, quantitative evidence alone but rather must include qualitative cultural factors. Jennings provides the foundation for the discussion of globalization in this chapter: "All globalizations should (a) be triggered by a surge in long-distance connections that (b) caused the specific array of cultural changes associated with the creation of a global culture."[23] Both Castells and Jennings see long-distance connections and global networks as prerequisites for globalization.

---

16 Abu-Lughod, *Before European Hegemony*, 8 and 286.
17 Findlay and O'Rourke, *Power and Plenty*, 108.
18 McCants, "Exotic Goods," 437.
19 McCants, "Exotic Goods," 436.
20 McNeill. *A World History*, 295.
21 Flynn and Giráldez, "Path Dependence," 82 and 99.
22 Jennings, *Globalizations*, 13.
23 Jennings, *Globalizations*, 21.

The expansion of European networks, ushered in by the voyages of Columbus, Vasco da Gama and others, certainly constituted such a globalization moment, particularly as these voyages led to the Spanish colonization of the New World, to the establishment of permanent and fortified Portuguese outposts along the coasts of Africa, India, and China, and to the substantial restructuring of global trade networks in the sixteenth century.[24] Obviously, there were older civilizations whose network included all of the world known at that time, as Jennings argues, but never before had the globe been seen as a sphere that could become a spatial plane on which humans could move at will and develop colonial and commercial nexuses literally anywhere on the planet. The Spaniards and the Portuguese around 1500 built truly global networks, to be followed by the British and Dutch later in the sixteenth century. The effect of the arising global trade networks was felt all over Europe, even in countries like Germany, which were only marginally involved in intercontinental trade.

Cosmographers like Christian Egenolff increasingly described an interconnected world promoted by discoverers and merchant-bankers and defined the world as an endless sphere: "It is a unanimously decided and certain matter for all geographers and cosmographers that the form and center of the universe is round; the same they also suppose for the earth as for the heavens."[25] As new lands, islands, and people were found on a regular basis, Egenolff claimed that "the world has innumerable parts, but they make up one world that does not have an end, for something new can be found daily in the works of our wondrous God who never can be fully understood."[26] While God still was the creator of this endless world, the creation narrative no longer framed the discussion. Rather, the world had become a modular sphere on which new discoveries could be located. While these discoveries were new to humans, they all had their God-given space on this endless, spherical globe.

The Portuguese spice trade, which was of great importance to German merchant houses, symbolically stood for sixteenth-century globalization: "the spice trade is an early manifestation of global scope and global intent coming together."[27] It is in the form of the spice trade that Germany first was confronted

---

[24] O'Rourke and Williamson, "Did Vasco da Gama Matter," 677–680.
[25] Egenolff, *Chronica* (1535), fol. 1v: "BEy allen Geographis vnnd Cosmographis/ ist diß einhellig beschlossen vnd gewiß/ das der welt form vnd centrum rundt ist/ eben dasselbig halten sie auch von der erden wie vom himmel."
[26] Egenolff, *Chronica* (1535), fol. 2v: "es seind vil vnzalbar welt/ vnd das die welt on end sey/ dann täglich findt sich etwas newes/ in den wercken des wunderbarlichen Gottes/ der nit auß zulernen ist." Egenolff copied this passage from Franck, *Weltbůch*, fol. 3v.
[27] MacGillivray, *A Brief History*, 8.

with these new global trade networks. While trade with Asia has older origins, the Italian trading system arising in the thirteenth century did not extend beyond the Mediterranean and was merely an appendage of the Asian trading system.[28] Steiner points out that these networks were built mostly by non-state actors at a time when the classic attributes of modernity, like state administration, a capitalist economic system, and a scientific knowledge culture were not fully developed yet.[29] Dozens of southern German companies in Augsburg, Nuremberg, and several secondary centers of trade were active participants in these long-distance networks,[30] as Chapter 17 will discuss in more detail.

The Fugger and Welser companies of Augsburg, as well as other southern German companies, had European networks of factors and developed a strong presence at the ports where the new trade routes entered Europe. The Fuggers maintained an extensive pan-European information and intelligence network,[31] while the Welsers had a number of travel accounts translated to keep their key agents informed.[32] The Moravian printer Valentim Fernandes, who lived in Lisbon from 1495 until his death in 1518 or 1519, was an important source of geographic, political, military, and economic information for southern German merchants and intellectuals. He corresponded with Conrad Peutinger in Augsburg, among others, who collected the letters from Fernandes and made them available in manuscript form to the Welser merchant house.[33] Peutinger even printed some of these reports in his collection *Sermones conuiuales* from 1506 that "demonstrate the very early proprietary interest the Augsburgers had in India."[34] Later, Peutinger also acquired some of Fernandes's papers.[35]

The voyages around 1500, unlike previous voyages, induced a European expansion and served as a catalyst for a process of transformation that created

---

28 Reinhard, *A Short History of Colonialism*, 20.
29 Steiner, *Colberts Afrika*, 21.
30 Häberlein, *The Fuggers of Augsburg*, 97.
31 Johnson, *Cultural Hierarchy*, 2. Pieper, *Die Vermittlung*, 222–226. An odd and curious broadsheet from 1531, *Wunderbarliche geschicht anzeygung*, shows just how important these news networks were for the flow of trivial news as well. It claims that "the Fugger gentlemen and other gentlemen here in Augsburg received information from Portugal that a large whale was sighted on January 18."
32 Johnson, *The German Discovery*, 218, note 122.
33 According to Leitch (*Mapping Ethnography*, 214, n. 48), this collection still exists in the Bavarian State Library Munich under the heading "De insulis et peregrinationibus Lusitanorum." Wintroub (*The Voyage of Thought*, 20) erroneously claims that this collection was printed in 1506.
34 Leitch, *Mapping Ethnography*, 74.
35 Häberlein, *Aufbruch*, 184–186; Wintroub, *The Voyage of Thought*, 19–20.

new global networks and ended the isolation of many nations and compelled them to relate to one another.[36] This expansion led to an "unprecedented explosion in mobility, in regard to both increased range and frequency of travel."[37] Most of this travel was not private but rather corporate in nature; that is, travel served the activities of corporate entities that stood in contractual relationships with state actors or at least were authorized by them.[38] These journeys prove that in the last decade of the fifteenth century, for the first time in history, the globe in its entirety had become knowable and indeed at least theoretically known, "thanks to technical innovation, commercial ambition and strategic intent."[39]

This made it possible to explore all parts of the world and to fill in the blank spots on the world map. Up to the end of the fifteenth century, frontiers were not just constructed to delineate spatial arrangements but they also demarcated boundaries of humanity.[40] What happened around 1500 is the systematic penetration of the world and of these boundaries, which resulted in the linkage of spaces and networks of interaction that had been hitherto unconnected. According to Paula Findlen, "tentative encounters in the era of Columbus gave way to new connections with far more transformative consequences."[41] These are evident in the establishment of a permanent Portuguese trade system and in the rapid and systematic colonization of Latin America by the Spaniards.

These rapidly growing trade networks and colonial possessions required a mechanism to regulate the expansion, in which the Catholic Church played an important role. The assumption was that God held authority over the entire earth, including parts hitherto unknown, and that it therefore fell to the Church to supervise their proper division and administration. The papal bull *Inter Caetera* of 1493 conferred title over territories to the west of existing Portuguese possessions to the Spanish Crown. In the more precise Treaty of Tordesillas (1494), Pope Alexander VI divided up the newly discovered and yet to be discovered parts of the world into a Spanish and a Portuguese sphere of influence. The Treaty of Saragossa (1529) defined a comparable line of demarcation in East Asia.[42] The two treaties indicate that the signatory parties had a global outlook and attempted to create a new, globalized

---

36 Steiner, *Colberts Afrika*, 21.
37 Harris, "Long-Distance Corporations," 275.
38 Harris, "Long-Distance Corporations," 276–277.
39 MacGillivray, *A Brief History*, 19.
40 Mignolo, *The Darker Side*, xi.
41 Findlen, "Early Modern Things," 5.
42 Fäßler, *Globalisierung*, 60.

world order, with the Catholic Church at its center in the role of arbiter. This also is evident in the bull *Sublimis Deus*, issued by Pope Paul III in 1537, which declared that Indians were true human beings who had specific rights, were capable of receiving the Christian faith and therefore were capable of becoming European.[43]

Castells and Jennings also see cultural responses to global networks, including the reassertion of communal identities and other forms of backlash, as a mandatory part of the globalization dynamic. The primary cultural change effected by globalization was a gradually emerging holistic vision of the world fueled by a "relentless intellectual and cultural drive to uncover a comprehensive vision of the whole."[44] This is based on a reconceptualization and compression of the categories of time and space, a precondition for the creation of global networks.[45] In the large European trade centers like Antwerp, Lisbon, and Venice, but also Nuremberg and Augsburg, a global awareness arose that included knowledge about Asia and eventually also America.[46] In the late fifteenth century, new elites of wealthy merchant bankers, like Jakob Fugger "the Rich" (1459–1525), emerged who maintained vast, secretive trade webs and who understood the world in its interconnectedness and acted as global players.

Globalizations throughout history invariably affected local communities. Cultural changes triggered by these global networks, the second factor identified by Castells and Jennings, thus unleashed a considerable conflict potential by challenging the conventional static concept of a world based on biblical creation and hostile to any change and innovation. Opposite from the globalists stood Humanist and civic leaders and scholars, like Sebastian Brant and Ulrich von Hutten, who viewed the rapidly growing global networks as a threat to the political, social, and moral order. Few understood the global networks within which the Fuggers and others performed their trade activities. Yet global activities always had a local impact that was keenly felt. The so-called silver crisis in Germany was caused by the heavy outflow of silver and copper to Antwerp and Lisbon, to be shipped to Asia to buy spices. Silver coins were minted with a low silver content, which depressed their value and hurt poor people in particular.[47] Spice imports, in addition to financial claims made by papal emissaries, drained Germany of financial resources, and foreign influences were seen as diminishing the viability of a

---

[43] McGrane, *Beyond Anthropology*, 14.
[44] Ramachandran, *The Worldmakers*, 6.
[45] Osterhammel and Petersson, *Geschichte der Globalisierung*, 12.
[46] Häberlein, *Aufbruch*, 20.
[47] For a comprehensive discussion see Rössner, *Deflation*, 485–664.

strong, virtuous German culture. Then as now, the privileged downplayed the consequences of their schemes and practiced "sanctioned ignorance"; that is, they developed blind spots that allowed them to ignore the domestic social cost of their globalizing agenda.[48]

Obviously, globalization around 1500 did not evolve in a cultural vacuum. Rather, fundamental changes occurred in how the world was imagined, which informed the quest for discoveries and the creation of global networks. This reimagination of the world around 1500, discussed in Part II, was enhanced by the twin phenomena of pluralization and secularization, discussed in more detail in the Introduction, that fueled the European Humanism of the fifteenth and early sixteenth centuries. The period around 1500 in Germany constituted a moment of dislocation between a secularized, globalized elite culture driven by explorers, mariners, and merchants and an inherently inward-looking static local culture that resisted the erosion of traditional cultural values, which was blamed on globalizing processes. The objective of Part III is to demonstrate how such a globalization conflict played out in Germany in the early sixteenth century, and the subsequent chapters will trace different aspects of the backlash against the felt effect of globalization. The next chapter will explore the extent of German involvement in global activities and the knowledge about globalization that was available in Germany. Subsequent chapters will analyze a range of texts that stood in opposition to globalization in the early sixteenth century. To many German intellectuals, explorations and the rising global trade system posed a threat to the stability of the economic and political system and more generally to the social and moral order. For this reason, the new global networks were almost universally rejected.

The polemical responses are traced here in distinct thematic groups: changing economic practices in Germany, the rising global trade networks, nationalistic and xenophobic polemics in Germany, global trade as violation of the divine order, and globalization as the root of moral decline. In contrast to the travel narratives, the texts discussed here explored the globalization context much more critically and commented on the perceived expansion of spatial knowledge with a great deal of apprehension. Texts in the vernacular in particular took on a populist tone, responded negatively to the expansion of space and to its consequences, and helped propagate resentment against global networks. The term "populist" may appear anachronistic in this context in that a public sphere and a civil society in the modern sense did not exist. However, the term is legitimate as

---

[48] The term "sanctioned ignorance" was first used by Spivak, *A Critique of Postcolonial Reason*, 2.

many texts at the time used an emotion-laden rhetoric to frame politics as a battle between virtuous, ordinary people and a nefarious, corrupt elite that worked against the interests of the common people. We can pinpoint a veritable backlash against globalization and against groups and individuals who promoted it and who were seen as profiting from it.

Chapter 17
The Emerging Global Trade from a German Perspective

German merchant houses had a long-standing involvement with international trade. The Fugger Company, based in Augsburg, was already trading in Venice in the 1470s and owned a permanent chamber in the *Fondaco dei Tedeschi* in Venice starting in 1489.[1] From there, the Fuggers and other companies imported goods into Germany, generally in return for metals and metal products. Imported goods were commonly referred to as *specery* or *specerey*, which included fine and exotic spices for culinary purposes as well as herbs and other substances for medicinal use, but also fragrances.[2] The term also could include other foodstuffs, like sugar, textile dyes, and alum for metal processing.[3] Scholastics distinguished between goods that were necessary to sustain life, goods that allowed for a life commensurate with an individual's rank and estate, and goods that were excessive and superfluous.[4] *Specerey* referred to luxury items belonging to the last category. These goods did not address daily needs but rather belonged to the morally suspect category of conspicuous consumption.

The commercial activities of the late fifteenth century were inscribed in the globe produced by Martin Behaim (1459–1507) in Nuremberg in 1492. Behaim, a German cosmographer and explorer, is known to have worked in the Antwerp branch of the Hirschvogel Company of Nuremberg as early as 1478. He traveled to Lisbon for the first time around 1480 and became the Lisbon agent for the Hirschvogels no later than 1484. His task was to provide the company with economic information about the West African markets recently discovered by the Portuguese.[5] Behaim participated in Portuguese expeditions to the Azores and along the West African coast, perhaps as far south as Namibia.[6] Behaim lived in Lisbon until his death in 1507, with the exception of the period between 1490 and 1493 when he resided in his native Nuremberg. During this period, Behaim created his famous globe, which is the oldest surviving terrestrial globe, commonly referred to as *Erdapfel* (earth apple).[7] Behaim's globe includes text cartouches that

---

1 Häberlein, *The Fuggers of Augsburg*, 49–50.
2 Zedler, *Grosses vollständiges Universal-Lexicon*, vol. 38, 1215.
3 Schmitt, "Atlantische Epansion," 130.
4 Isenmann, *Die deutsche Stadt im Mittelalter*, 585.
5 Knabe and Noli, *Die versunkenen Schätze*, 81.
6 Lach, *Asia in the Making of Europe*, vol. 2, book 2, 327–328.
7 Pietschmann, "Bemerkungen," 369.

describe natural products and their places of origin, including spices from West Africa and Asia. Furthermore, Behaim described the stations of the Venetian spice trade using the land route, with the caveat that the Venetians did not travel further than the eastern Mediterranean.[8] While the Portuguese discovery of the sea route to Asia a few years later gave Europeans access to Asia and increased the volume and importance of the Asian trade substantially, Behaim's globe provides evidence that cosmographers were aware of global commercial networks long before the big discoveries by Vasco da Gama and Columbus became known.

The successful opening of a sea route to India around Africa by Vasco da Gama in 1497–1499 ushered in a profound and rapid transformation in the global trade system.[9] It led to the ascent of Lisbon as new hub of the global trade in spices and fine garments. In 1501 the Portuguese set up the *Casa da Índia* to promote exploration of and trade with the Orient. Antwerp assumed the role as the major port of entry into northern Europe for Asian goods imported by the Portuguese and their clients. The first shipment of pepper via the Cape route arrived in Antwerp in 1501,[10] and Vasco da Gama's economically successful second journey in 1503, which resulted in a huge shipment of spices, permanently altered the structure of the spice trade.[11]

In Germany, there was an appreciable awareness of Asia and travel to Asia in the first half of the sixteenth century because imported goods were readily available and because there were several first-hand German accounts describing it. German involvement in the Portuguese spice trade became known in Germany through travel narratives. The fact that the European expansion around 1500 was driven by commercial interests was not lost on German contemporaries. The early texts describing voyages to India elaborated on their economic motivation. The anonymous pamphlet entitled *Den rechten weg auß zu faren von Lißbona gen Kallakuth* (*To Travel on the Right Path from Lisbon to Calicut*), published in Nuremberg in 1506, was likely written by a participant in Vasco da Gama's second voyage to India in 1502–1503. The map at the beginning of the text shows only three cities, all major commercial centers: the port cities of Calicut and Lisbon as well as Nuremberg, a major center of the metalworking industry (figure 8).[12]

---

[8] Eser, "Gewürze auf dem Behaim-Globus," 143.
[9] O'Rourke and Williamson, "Did Vasco da Gama Matter," 674. The Cape itself already had been reached by Bartolomeu Dias (c. 1450–1500) in 1488.
[10] Findlay and O'Rourke, *Power and Plenty*, 206; O'Rourke and Williamson, "Did Vasco da Gama Matter," 677; Häberlein, *The Fuggers of Augsburg*, 53.
[11] O'Rourke and Williamson, "Did Vasco da Gama Matter," 657.
[12] Borowka-Clausberg, *Balthasar Sprenger*, 2–3.

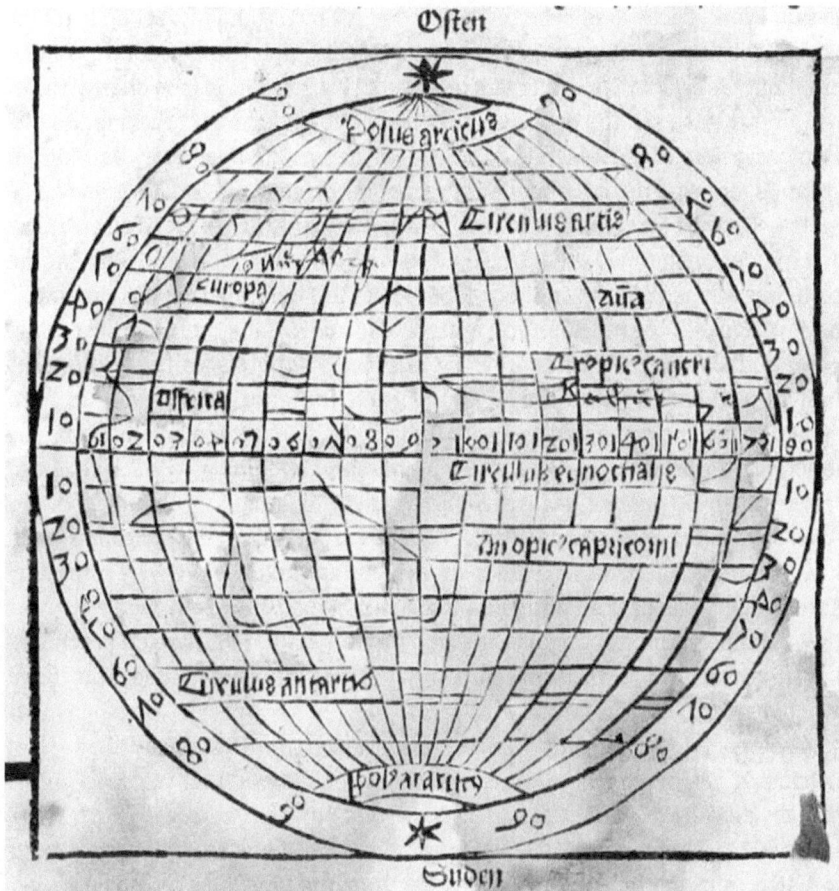

Figure 8: Anon. *Den rechten weg auß zu faren von Lißbona gen Kallakuth.* Nuremberg: Wolfgang Huber, 1506. Verso of title page. © Herzog August Bibliothek Wolfenbüttel.

Southern German merchant companies set up shop in Lisbon to take advantage of this new trading opportunity very quickly.[13] The first southern German firm to establish direct relations with Portugal was the company Anton Welser, Conrad Vöhlin, and Associates of Augsburg in the fall of 1502; it managed to conclude a commercial contract with King Manuel I of Portugal in February 1503. In

---

13 For a comprehensive discussion of the German involvement in the Portuguese overseas trade in the early sixteenth century see Pohle, *Deutschland und die überseeische Expansion Portugals*, 97–254.

the same year, Lucas Rem, who in 1518 started his own company, set up an office for the Welser Company in Lisbon and represented their interests in the trade with India until 1508.[14] The Fuggers of Augsburg arrived in Lisbon shortly thereafter, and they seized the opportunity to negotiate preferential access to the distribution system of the emerging Portuguese pepper trade as early as 1504, in exchange for deliveries of copper to be carried as cargo to the Indian Ocean.[15]

The German merchant companies, led by the Fuggers, Welsers, and Hirschvogels, financed and outfitted three vessels that were part of the Portuguese expedition to India of 1505–1506, led by Francisco de Almeida.[16] The Portuguese needed foreign capital to support the expensive East India fleets, and the German companies were able to supply significant amounts of silver and copper from the Alps and from Hungary, which were in high demand in commercial exchanges with India.[17] The journey was chronicled by the Welser agent Balthasar Springer in *Die Merfart vnd erfarung nüwer Schiffung vnd Wege zů viln onerkanten Inseln und Künigreichen* (*The Ocean Voyage and Discovery of New Navigation Routes and Paths to Many Unknown Islands and Kingdoms*) from 1509.[18] Both Springer and the earlier anonymous author therefore were intimately knowledgeable about the Portuguese trade with Asia.[19] However, the Portuguese Crown claimed a monopoly over the trade with Asia in 1506, which precluded further participation of German companies in trade missions to Asia. The crown monopoly ended only in 1570.[20]

Another important early source of information in Germany was Jobst Ruchamer's *Newe vnbekanthe landte Und ein newe weldte in kurtz verganger zeythe erfunden* (*New Unknown Lands and a New World Found at a Recently Past Time*), published in Nuremberg in 1508. It was a compilation of a number of travel reports translated from the Italian, including several reports describing Portuguese journeys to India. The report of Vasco da Gama's three-month sojourn in Calicut in summer 1498 described the busy port and trading post of Calicut: "During this time, they saw an infinite number of ships. They estimated their number to be

---

14 Häberlein, *The Fuggers of Augsburg*, 51; Dauser and Ferber, *Die Fugger und Welser*, 41–42.
15 Jardine, *Worldly Goods*, 290.
16 Häberlein, *The Fuggers of Augsburg*, 51–52.
17 Häberlein, *The Fuggers of Augsburg*, 51–52.
18 Springer, *Merfart*, sig. A2r. For a summary of the 1505–1506 journey, see Imhoff, "Nürnbergs Indienpioniere," and Borowka-Clausberg, *Balthasar Sprenger*, 14–56.
19 For a more detailed discussion of European publications on journeys to Asia see Lach, *Asia in the Making of Europe*, vol. 1, book 1, 154–171.
20 Häberlein, *Aufbruch*, 87–88.

1,500, which came here in order to do trade in spices."[21] German readers were made to understand that Calicut was a large and well-stocked market that offered almost endless trading opportunities for European merchants.

Texts like these completely changed what Germans knew about Asia and the ways they learned about it. Before Vasco da Gama, Eurasian trade mostly used land routes, typically along the old Silk Road, and it was extremely rare for a single person to travel the entire length of the Eurasian trade routes.[22] The Venetians, for instance, did not travel to the Asian markets directly; rather they bought spices and silk at the markets in Alexandria, Aleppo, and other cities in the Levant where the goods were sold by Arabic or Ottoman merchants. As a result, Europeans had no first-hand information about Asia. Furthermore, reports like the one by John Mandeville turned out to be fiction.[23] The voyages from Lisbon directly to Asia, commanded by Vasco da Gama, Francisco de Almeida, and others, therefore didn't just open up a new trade route. They also provided new and much more reliable sources of information about Asian markets, cultures, systems of governance, religions, and geography.

The impact of the Portuguese involvement in the Asian trade was swift as spice prices fell and the Venetian monopoly in the spice trade vanished quickly.[24] In contrast to other scholars, Subrahmanyam argues that the Venetian spice trade never collapsed, resulting in a duopoly,[25] while the European consumption of pepper increased.[26] Subrahmanyam concedes that the Venetians had some supply problems in the first decade of the sixteenth century because of political unrest in the Mamluk regime.

The trade of the Fugger Company was focused on Antwerp, where they opened an office in 1493, rather than on Lisbon. Antwerp's significance as a port rose when the Portuguese decided to bring pepper to the European markets via Antwerp. The first shipment of Portuguese pepper arrived in 1501, and the Portuguese opened the royal Portuguese trading post, the *Feitoria de Flandres*, in 1508. Because the Portuguese needed mostly copper and silver for their trade with Asia and Africa, southern German merchants, who largely

---

21 Ruchamer, *Newe vnbekanthe landte*, sig. e1r: "in welcher zeyte sie sahen/ ein vnentliche zalle der schyffe/ schatzten sie wol auff tausent vnd funffhundert/ so sie hine komen vmb der kauffmanschafft willen der spetzery [...]."
22 Pomeranz and Topik, *The World That Trade Created*, 41. The inscriptions on Martin Behaim's globe of 1492 discussed at the beginning of this chapter confirm this.
23 Pomeranz and Topik, *The World That Trade Created*, 41–42.
24 Jardine, *Worldly Goods*, 289–290; O'Rourke and Williamson, "Did Vasco da Gama Matter," 674–677.
25 Subrahmanyam, "The Birth-Pangs," 270–274.
26 Wright, "The Medieval Spice Trade," 37.

controlled the trade in these commodities, became their most important commercial partners, with Antwerp as the main hub of these trade activities.[27] The direct trade between southern German merchants, in particular the Fuggers who controlled the lion's share of the trade in mining products, and the Portuguese Crown made spices more accessible in Germany,[28] but their visible engagement in global trade also added to the anti-merchant rhetoric of the time.

The strategic cooperation between agents of the Portuguese Crown and representatives of the Augsburg merchant houses in Lisbon and Antwerp played a central role in procuring metals for the Portuguese Asian trade between 1500 and about 1540.[29] Two astounding archaeological finds of 2008 confirm this. The merchant ship *Bom Jesus*, which was owned by King João III, shipwrecked off the coast of Oranjemund, Namibia, in 1533. It was en route from Lisbon to India and carried 1,845 copper ingots, weighing a total of 16–17 metric tons, which were mostly marked with the Fugger trident seal.[30] The second merchant ship sank near the town of Ngomeni, Kenya, in the early sixteenth century. It contained about 20 tons of copper ingots, also marked with the Fugger trident seal, in addition to some mercury and other merchandise.[31]

In spite of the rapid growth of the Portuguese spice trade, the economic significance of imported spices was modest as compared to the production that was supplied and consumed locally and regionally.[32] Even in major trading nations, only about two percent of the gross domestic product was generated by long-distance trade in the sixteenth century.[33] While exotic spices were assailed in many written testimonials of the time, their comparative economic and culinary significance was modest. Adam Lonitzer in his *Kreuterbuch* (*Herb Book*) from 1564, for instance, discussed individual herbs and spices over 418 pages,

---

27 Häberlein, *The Fuggers of Augsburg*, 53.
28 As Smith ("Profits Sprout," 391–392) points out, the Portuguese neither controlled the production of the spices in Asia nor their distribution in Europe. Rather, the Portuguese Crown sold the bulk of spice supplies in private contracts to consortia of merchant capitalists throughout Europe, like the Fuggers and Welsers.
29 Häberlein, *Aufbruch*, 14; Rössner, *Deflation*, 108.
30 Werz, "Saved from the Sea," 91; Hauptmann, Schneider, and Bartels, "The Shipwreck of Bom Jesus," 189; Knabe and Noli, *Die versunkenen Schätze*, 161–166. Knape and Noli (129–160) give an extensive description of the Bom Jesus and its equipment.
31 The find was only made public in 2015: https://archaeologynewsnetwork.blogspot.com/2015/07/500-year-old-portuguese-shipwreck-found.html#7JpAZ5wHog7Z7pdT.97 (last accessed on 11 May 2020).
32 Osterhammel and Petersson, *Geschichte der Globalisierung*, 42.
33 Parker, *Global Interactions*, 69.

of which only a small section of seventeen pages at the end was dedicated to imported varieties.[34] Furthermore, not all spice books participated in this polemic against imported spices. Balthasar Beck in his *Herbarius* from 1527 regularly pointed to the foreign origin of spices but never took issue with the fact that spices might be from India or Arabia.[35] Likewise, Leonhart Fuchs (1501–1566) in his *New Kreüterbůch* (*New Herb Book*, 1543), as well as Lonitzer, simply stated the provenance of non-native spices.[36] The discrepancy between the actual size of global trade and the outsized discourses opposing it illustrates to what extent this had become a symbolic issue representing much larger cultural controversies. This is not a phenomenon that can be explained with quantitative, empirical data alone.

The fact that only a handful of spices, which could all be transported easily, like pepper, ginger, nutmeg, cloves, cinnamon, and saffron, were actually imported in the early sixteenth century raises the possibility that these discourses on this limited issue served to support a more general xenophobic, anti-merchant, and anti-luxury polemic. The consumption of imported spices in the early sixteenth century was still largely an elite phenomenon and was a symbol of wealth and status for the upper class, but increasingly also for the middle class.[37] Due to the growth of luxury consumption among the very wealthy in the sixteenth century, many goods considered luxuries in the late Middle Ages gradually became everyday goods for the middle class.[38] Their trade, while limited in volume, could be highly profitable; Lisa Jardine refers to pepper as "the merchants' 'black gold'."[39] Thus the discourses were not just about merchants engaging in long-distance trade and about imported spices; rather they functioned as part of an anti-globalization rhetoric. Contemporaries understood Germany to be affected by and indeed part of the emerging global system and, more importantly, also diagnosed and rejected an array of cultural changes prompted by it. Thus, the evidence presented here substantiates the claim that the early sixteenth century met the definition of globalization as proposed by Jennings and Castells.

German merchants also made several attempts to participate in colonial projects in the New World. The Welser Company started to engage in the Spanish

---

34 Lonitzer, *Kreuterbuch*, fol. 336r–343r.
35 In contrast to Fuchs and Lonitzer, Beck did not create a separate section where he discussed imported spices.
36 Fuchs, *New Kreüterbůch*, sig. Mm3v-Mm5v; Lonitzer, *Kreuterbuch*, fol. 336r–343r.
37 Albala, *Eating Right*, 210. Flynn and Giráldez ("Path Dependence," 91) argue that not all imports from Asia should be considered luxury items.
38 Pomeranz, *The Great Divergence*, 114.
39 Jardine, *Worldly Goods*, 53.

trade shortly after 1500. By 1510, the Welsers had branch offices in Saragossa and Valencia, and in 1525 they opened an office in Seville, the Spanish port that handled all commerce with the West Indies. In 1526, the Welsers established an office in Santo Domingo on the island of Hispaniola,[40] then the commercial and political hub of the emerging Spanish colonial empire, and started to operate plantations on Hispaniola.[41]

The most ambitious commercial as well as colonial project by a German merchant-banker was the *asiento* (contract) of 1528, in which the Spanish Crown ceded to the Welser Company of Augsburg the right to colonize and exploit the territory of what is Venezuela today.[42] The Welsers were required to bring 300 well-armed soldiers from Europe, to found at least two villages within two years, populated by 300 settlers each, to build three forts, and to bring in 50 German-born miners.[43] The venture never turned a profit, in part because the Welser operatives were more interested in short-term gain, like looting gold, than in building cities and setting up mines. The Welsers ended their Venezuela operations in 1546 after the murders of Bartholomäus VI Welser and Philipp von Hutten in Venezuela and also withdrew from Santo Domingo. The contract was formally terminated in 1556.[44] Nikolaus Federmann, a military commander for the Welser Company, wrote a first-person account on the early phases of this project. Its impact was minimal because it was only published in 1557.

In 1530, the Fugger agent Veit Hörl negotiated a contract with the Spanish Council of the Indies regarding the rights to a huge conquest zone on the Pacific coast from Chinca, Peru, near present-day Pisco, south to the Strait of Magellan, including all of present-day Chile. Hörl signed the contract in June 1531, but Charles V did not ratify it for unknown reasons even though he had earlier signaled approval.[45] A Fugger fleet failed to reach the area via the Strait of Magellan in 1532–1533, and the Fuggers abandoned the project in 1534. The huge distance to Chile and the extreme difficulty of traveling there, as well as waning Spanish support, perhaps motivated by the successful colonization of Peru by Francisco Pizarro starting in 1532, were likely the main factors for this decision.[46]

---

40 Häberlein, *The Fuggers of Augsburg*, 80.
41 Denzer, *Die Konquista*, 50.
42 Großhaupt, "Der Venezuela-Vertrag," 3. Denzer, *Die Konquista*, 52–54.
43 Simmer, *Gold und Sklaven*, 758.
44 Denzer, *Die Konquista*, 21.
45 Häberlein, *The Fuggers of Augsburg*, 80.
46 Denzer, *Die Konquista*, 55–57. For a detailed discussion of the Fugger involvement in the New World see Kellenbenz, *Die Fugger*, vol. 1, 149–164.

Furthermore, both the Fugger and Welser companies participated in the expedition to the Río de la Plata (La Plata River), commanded by Pedro de Mendoza, in 1534–1537.[47] The Fuggers and the Welsers each contributed a ship, fully outfitted and manned by Germans. Ulrich Schmidel, who later wrote about this expedition, was one of the mercenaries on the Fugger ship.[48] However, the German investments did not pay off as no sustainable trade opportunities arose from this expedition. The Spaniards were focused on colonizing the interior of the continent and set up their main base in Asunción, the current capital of Paraguay. The Spaniards were forced to abandon the coastal settlement in what is now Buenos Aires, thus depriving them of the only viable port.[49]

Both the Fugger and Welser companies declined opportunities to get involved more directly in the colonial project.[50] All these activities were little-known in Germany and did not become part of a larger discourse. Accounts that told these stories of German involvement in Venezuela and the La Plata region, written by Nikolaus Federmann and Ulrich Schmidel, were not published until 1557 and 1567, respectively, and had limited reception in Germany.

There was no lasting impact of the German New World adventures in the first half of the sixteenth century. The participation of the Welser and Fugger companies in the conquest did not lead to permanent German colonies nor to significant and sustained trade relations. After the end of the Welser engagement in Venezuela in 1546, no other German entities were seriously involved in colonial projects until German unification in 1871. The lone exception was the failed Brandenburg colonial project in West Africa in the late seventeenth century.[51]

While the Welsers maintained economic interests in Hispaniola until 1547, their share of the emerging transatlantic trade was small. While the Portuguese were able to tap into an extant, vibrant trade system in the Indian Ocean basin and thus were able to bring significant amounts of imported goods from Asia to the European markets without delay, economic resources in the New World, such as mining operations and plantation agriculture, had to be built up gradually with the investment of a significant amount of capital. As a result, the transatlantic trade only started to pick up in the second half of the sixteenth century, a time when German trading corporations were no longer active in the

---

47 Asúa and French, *A New World of Animals*, 29.
48 Morison, *The European Discovery*, 564; Asúa and French, *A New World of Animals*, 29.
49 The Spaniards maintained a small settlement 1536–1541. Buenos Aires was founded a second time only in 1580.
50 Smith, "beschreibung eyner Landtschafft," 2; Denzer, *Die Konquista*, 55.
51 German interests, sponsored by the Electorate of Brandenburg, founded Groß Friedrichsburg, now Pokesu, at the Gold Coast of Ghana in 1682 and operated it until 1717.

New World. Furthermore, the flow of information about the New World slowed considerably after the hype surrounding Columbus and Vespucci had died down. While Germans had ready access to information about Asia and Asian trade, information about the New World was scarce until the middle of the sixteenth century.

The Portuguese trade network left its imprint on German maps and in cosmographies as well. This is evident in the differences between Martin Waldseemüller's two oversized world maps discussed in Chapter 11, the world map from 1507 and the *Carta marina* from 1516. The 1507 map was still Ptolemaic at its core, albeit with the sensationalistic addition of the American continent. The *Carta marina*, on the other hand, was based on recent navigational charts and travel accounts. It sought to eradicate the influence of ancient philosophers like Ptolemy, but also curtailed the speculative representation of America. It strongly emphasized the pepper trade in its representation of Asia. Its title, *Carta marina navigatoria Portvgallen navigationes*, indicates that the map was a nautical chart greatly informed by the voyages and discoveries of the Portuguese, although the continuation of the title indicates that the map represents all of the known world, land and oceans.[52] Perhaps influenced by the rapidly growing trade relations, the focus of the map is on the Lusitanian world, while the representation of America is less pronounced than in the 1507 map and the Pacific Ocean is missing altogether.

A text box on sheet twelve in the bottom right corner of the *Carta marina* lists where all the spices and other goods came from that were traded in Calicut, now Kozhikode, and shipped to Europe from there. The map itself shows seven small men on sheet four, some of them working with plants (figure 9).[53] The accompanying text identifies them as pygmies and explains that they are harvesting pepper: "In these mountains pepper grows in great abundance, planted by the pygmies, who are in continual battle against cranes."[54] It is remarkable that Waldseemüller incorporated global commerce into his map, and it is evident

---

[52] The full title is *Carta marina navigatoria portvgallen[siorum] navigationes atque tocius cogniti orbis terre marisque formam naturamque situs et terminos nostri[s] temporibus recognitos et ab antiquorum traditione differentes eciam quorum vetusti non meminerunt autores, hec generaliter indicat.* (A Nautical Chart that Comprehensively Shows the Portuguese Voyages and the Shape of the Whole Known World, Both Land and Sea, and its Nature, its Regions, and its Limits as They Have Been Determined in Our Times, and How They Differ from the Tradition of the Ancients, and also Areas Not Mentioned by the Ancients.) Translation Hessler and Van Duzer, *Seeing the World Anew*, 49.
[53] Van Duzer, "A Northern Refuge," 226.
[54] Translation Van Duzer, "A Northern Refuge," 228.

that he was not only interested in but also knowledgeable about the Asian spice trade. The cartouche on sheet seven describes Calicut as the major commercial port in the Indian Ocean basin, and the cartouche on sheet twelve – the largest text box on the entire map with the exception of Waldseemüller's address to the reader on sheet nine – lists all the spices traded in Calicut, complete with price information. Furthermore, the long text box on sheet seven describes Calicut, its governance and local customs as well as the luxury goods available at its markets, such as spices.

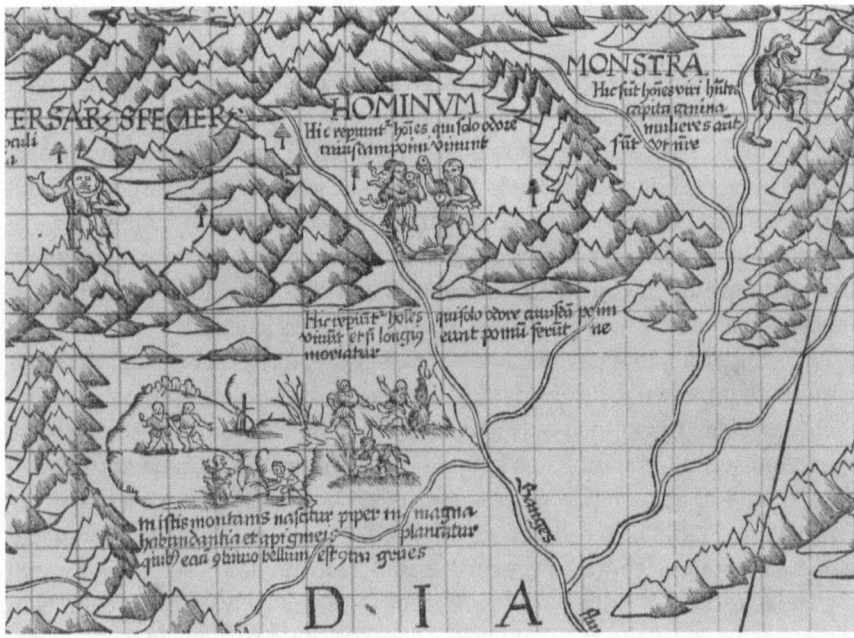

Figure 9: Martin Waldseemüller. *Carta marina*. Strasbourg [?]: s.n., 1516. Sheet four, detail. © Library of Congress, Washington D.C.

The *Carta marina* reflects a profound rethinking and reconceptualization of the world. The 1507 world map by and large was indebted to Ptolemy's view of the world, with the exception of the daring representation of America, and sought to complement Ptolemy as much as to refute him. His 1516 map, on the other hand, was designed as a nautical map – although with extensive information on the interior of the continents – and relied on medieval and contemporaneous accounts even in areas where there were ample sources in the Ptolemaic tradition, such as the Mediterranean and the Middle East. These modern sources were travel accounts, ranging from Marco Polo to Ludovico di Varthema, and nautical charts that rapidly gained in accuracy, such as the chart by Nicolo de Caverio, dated between 1503 and 1505. As contemporaneous navigation was fueled by commercial interests, particularly easier access to Asian markets, commercial interests also informed many parts of the map, and in particular the text inserts describing commercial activities in Calicut, Ceylon (Sri Lanka), Pegu (Bago, Myanmar), and a number of islands in Southeast Asia.

Like Waldseemüller in his 1516 map, Lorenz Fries in his *Uslegung der mercarten oder Cartha Marina* (*Interpretation of Ocean Maps or Nautical Charts*, 1527) and in his accompanying world map, the *Carta Marina Navigatoria* (1525), focused on the representation of ocean navigation and trade relations. He only described three German cities in the text. All of them, Antwerp, Strasbourg, and Augsburg, were major commercial centers. He singled out Antwerp as "the most noble merchant city in German lands"[55] and described it as a hub for global commerce: "Many large ships come here, loaded with silk, cloth, gold, spices, Brazilwood, strange animals, birds, many kinds of fish, and all kinds of people from Portugal, Castile, England, Venice, Barbaria, and from all kinds of places."[56] Antwerp is described in terms of its significance for global commerce, and the people who could be found there mostly originated in countries and cities with a leading role in the international trade system at the time, Portugal first and foremost.

It is important to remember two key facts. First, the texts investigated so far indicate that there was a considerable awareness of the trade with Asia, even if the Asian trade constituted only a small fraction of all economic activity at the time. And second, America was still not on the horizon as a trade partner and as a source of imported goods as late as 1527. The difference was that the Portuguese, and later the Dutch and the British, gained access to a large and well-functioning Asian trade network as well as to Moluccan spice islands and the Malabar coast of India.[57] The Europeans were relatively marginal players in the Asian markets, and the Portuguese therefore could participate immediately without disrupting them.[58] While Vasco da Gama in 1499 claimed the entire Indian Ocean for the king of Portugal, as there was no recognized European jurisdiction,[59] the Portuguese in reality only managed to gain control over a few

---

[55] Fries, *Uslegung der mercarten*, sig. B1r: "die fürnemste kaufmans stat in tütschem landt."
[56] Fries, *Uslegung der mercarten*, sig. B1r: "Es komen dahin uil groser schif geladen mit seiden/ tůch/ gold/ specerey/ presilien holtz/ seltzamer thierer/ Vögeln mancherley fischen/ mancherlei volck/ von Portugal/ Castilia/ Engelland/ Venedig/ Barbaria vnd allenthalben her."
[57] MacGillivray, *A Brief History*, 8.
[58] Fäßler, *Globalisierung*, 61.
[59] Parker, *Global Interactions*, 21.

outposts like Goa, Malacca, and Macau. Europeans during the first centuries of contact were unable to project power in Asia and therefore had to trade according to local rules.[60]

The Spaniards, on the other hand, had to build from scratch a colonial administration and an export-oriented economy in the Americas, including plantation agriculture and mining operations, in order to gradually build a transatlantic trade system. This gave the Spaniards extensive control over their American colonies, but the effect of the transatlantic trade on the global economy grew only gradually and not until after 1540. Therefore, the discovery of America did not have economic consequences for Germany until much later in the sixteenth century, and there was little public awareness in Germany of how the colonization of the Americas progressed. When we turn to negative responses to the new global trade arising in the early sixteenth century in Germany, we have to keep in mind that the target of criticism invariably was the Portuguese trade with India and beyond, as well as the German participation in it.

---

60 Pomeranz and Topik, *The World That Trade Created*, 5–6.

Chapter 18
The Backlash Against the New Economy

In the absence of an economic theory at the time, we have to reconstruct economic thought from a number of statements in various texts. While micro-economic comments on specific economic practices were common, macro-economic arguments were infrequent and never had the entire national economy in view. Merchants as those members of the economy who did not directly participate in the production of foodstuffs or manufactured goods traditionally stood at the center of critical examination.

The critique of merchants has roots in medieval ethics, which viewed excessive profits and unearned income as immoral and unbecoming of a Christian, based on Matthew 19:24. Merchants in the late Middle Ages were increasingly seen as representatives of a new urban culture that was susceptible to the deadly sins of *superbia* (pride), *avaritia* (avarice), and *invidia* (envy).[1] The Franciscan Berthold of Regensburg (d. 1272) was a relentless critic of merchants, accusing them of usury, hoarding, giving credit, pawning, fraud, and theft.[2] The *Reformatio Sigismundi*, which originated around 1439 in the context of the Council of Basel,[3] discussed the classical socio-economic themes, like the profits of merchants, monopolies, fraud, indulgences, usury, hoarding, bad measurements, and bad coins,[4] but in a radical turn also demanded the breakup of the large trading companies.[5] Usury (*usuria*) in a narrow sense was defined as demanding and taking interest payments for a loan. More broadly, usury also could include excessive prices beyond what was considered a just price (*iustum pretium*), price inflation due to speculative intermediate trade or purchase on credit, or gains through monopolies.[6] The critique of merchants thus had a long history. Yet, it resurfaced with new vigor in the early sixteenth century and specifically took on the large merchant-banking corporations and their business practices in the context of the new global trade networks.

---

1 Voltmer, "Krämer, Kaufleute, Kartelle," 405.
2 Voltmer, "Krämer, Kaufleute, Kartelle," 406–407. Voltmer discusses a range of late medieval authors.
3 The text went through eight printed editions between 1476 and 1522 (Scott, *Society and Economy*, 200).
4 Rössner, *Deflation*, 525–526; Isenmann, *Die deutsche Stadt im Mittelalter*, 970; Voltmer, "Krämer, Kaufleute, Kartelle," 437–438.
5 Isenmann, *Die deutsche Stadt im Mittelalter*, 972.
6 Isenmann, *Die deutsche Stadt im Mittelalter*, 960; Gilomen, "Christlicher Glaube," 121–125.

Needless to say, taking interest and profiting from financial transactions were commonplace in the international business world in the early sixteenth century. Writers who represented the interests of merchants and bankers, like Conrad Peutinger, vigorously defended these practices. Another example is Matthäus Schwarz (1497–c.1574) who started to work for Jakob Fugger in 1516 and served the Fugger Company as chief accountant throughout his career. In his manuscript of 1518, commonly referred to as *Dreierlay Buchhaltung* (*Three-Fold Bookkeeping*),[7] Schwarz represented the business world in positive terms. His only point of criticism focused on an irresponsible merchant who overburdened himself with debt due to real estate purchases or a luxurious lifestyle: "After that, one goes bankrupt, settles with the creditors, gives them barely one third. The rest he stole from them."[8] Schwarz did not belabor the point with a moralizing commentary as the irresponsible merchant simply harmed his creditors without affecting the common good.

On the other hand, a number of texts with a religious orientation criticized usury and other commercial practices that led to massive unearned wealth well into the sixteenth century. Martin Luther was suspect of wealth "not from tilling the soil or raising cattle" and saw the Fuggers of Augsburg as paragons of excessive wealth accumulation: "In this connection, we must put a bit in the mouth of the Fuggers and similar companies. How is it possible in the lifetime of one person to accumulate such great possessions, worthy of a king, legally and according to God's will?"[9] A later example is Georg Witzel's *Wider den Vnchristlichen Wucher/ vnd grosse Schinderey dieser itzigen bösen zeit* (*Against the Unchristian Usury and Great Drudgery of These Evil Times*) from 1539. Witzel represented avarice as the root cause of usury, hoarding, and other forms of self-interest. Witzel's text, like most others of this kind, viewed it as immoral and un-Christian to amass wealth and to live in luxury, while their neighbors lacked clothing and were starving.[10] The appeal, however, was for charity rather than for changes in the economic and legal system.

In texts with an economic or political orientation, the legitimacy of interest payments always stood in the foreground. By the early sixteenth century, a consensus

---

[7] Schwarz revised the text in another manuscript version in 1550. The Elbing manuscript of the text was first published in print by Alfred Weitnauer (*Venezianischer Handel*) in 1931. A different manuscript (CVP 10720 at the Austrian National Library) was published in a critical edition in Westermann and Denzel, *Das Kaufmannsnotizbuch*, 257–496.
[8] Schwarz, "Dreierlay Buchhaltung," 270: "Alßdann macht man banca rotta, vergleicht sich mit seinen creditori, gibt inen etwan kaum ⅓. Das ubrig hat er in gestolen."
[9] Luther, *To the Christian Nobility*, 462. Similarly also 406.
[10] Witzel, *Wider den Vnchristlichen Wucher*, sig. A8r–B2r.

had emerged that an interest rate of five percent was legitimate. Ever since the Council of Constance of 1414–1418 had recognized limited interest as a necessity, writers were attempting to create a separation between interest and usury.[11] Even Martin Luther conceded that four, five, and even six percent interest was legitimate on some loans as long as the deal was not motivated by avarice and greed.[12] The Catholic legal scholar Johannes Ferrarius agreed that the taking of modest interest could be legitimate as long as a deal benefited all parties.[13] As usury still was considered a violation of biblical precepts, it was up to state authorities to define the circumstances under which the taking of interest was tolerable.[14] Even as late as 1556, the matter was far from settled, as Georg Lauterbeck's *Regentenbuch* indicates: "There are many and various opinions about usury, both with theologians and jurists; the same with merchants, nobles, great lords, and other worldly persons."[15]

Yet, most popular texts continued to reject the taking of interest outright. The Strasbourg preacher Johann Geiler von Kaysersberg acknowledged that the theological and ethical norms regarding certain business practices were in flux and that some contemporaneous theologians and jurists justified the practice of taking interest. In his *Christenlich bilgerschafft zům ewigen vatterland* (*Christian Pilgrimage to the Eternal Fatherland*) from 1512, Geiler discussed the pilgrim's "shoes of virtue" as an elaborate allegory against innovative thought.[16] As new shoes were uncomfortable, caused blisters, and hindered the journey, the pilgrim needed to rely on old, well-worn shoes. In analogy to that, a Christian going through life needed to rely on traditional theological and moral precepts and reject "unreasonable advice and judgment of the theologians and also of the jurists who are soulless."[17] The prime example Geiler used was the widely practiced taking of interest. Based on the new morals, a merchant could feel justified to take interest and acquire other illegitimate wealth: "From one hundred gulden that I loaned I always take five. I have this and that illegitimate asset, but I can trade it with God's consent."[18] Geiler thus staunchly

---

11 Rössner, *Deflation*, 211.
12 Luther, *On Commerce and Usury*, 206.
13 Ferrarius, *Von dem Gemeinen nutze*, fol. 52r–52v.
14 Simon, *Gute Policey*, 156.
15 Lauterbeck, *Regentenbuch*, fol. 132v: "ES seind viel vnnd mancherley Opiniones vom Wucher/ beide bey den theologen vnd Juristen/ desgleichen bey den kauffleuten/ denen vom Adel/ grossen Herrn/ vnnd andern Weltlichen Personen."
16 Geiler, *Christenlich bilgerschafft*, fol. 90r–101v.
17 Geiler, *Christenlich bilgerschafft*, fol. 93v: "vnuernunfftige ret vnd vrteil der theologen/ vnd ouch der iuristen/ die do selloß sint."
18 Geiler, *Christenlich bilgerschafft*, fol. 94r: "Jch nym von hundert gulden die ich gelihen hab allwegen fünff. Jch hab das vnd das vnrechtfertig gůt/ mag ich also thůn mit gott." Geiler also rejected usury in *Doctor keiserszbergs Postill*, part II, fol. 17r.

opposed the taking of interest and rejected new ethical norms that took a softer stance.

Many Reformation-era Lutheran texts continued to reject all forms of interest. The anonymous broadsheet entitled *Hie kompt ein Beüerlein zu einem reychen Burger* (*Here Comes a Peasant to a Rich Burgher*) from 1522 presents a conversation between a peasant and a merchant about the question whether a mortgage payment should be considered usurious. The peasant, who represents the narrator's viewpoint, argues that annual mortgage or rent payments for a loan on a piece of property are usury by another name and accuses the merchant of making his money off the backs of poor people.[19] A pastor and a monk join the conversation, both taking the merchant's side. The pastor concedes that the Church generates income the same way. The peasant humbles the three with his moral conviction and theological insight: "I hear indeed that you have a different God than we poor people. We have our lord Jesus Christ, and he forbade such lending money for profit."[20]

Similarly, the Basel reformer Jakob Strauß (1480–1533) viewed all forms of interest as "un-Christian tyrannical usury."[21] He saw interest as a violation of the precept of brotherly love and chastised the decision by the Council of Constance to allow it: "Interest that was, as one says, eased to five gulden per hundred at the Council of Constance is deliberately usurious interest."[22] Finally, the anonymous Lutheran author of the dialogue *Der Wůcherer Meßkram oder Jarmarkt* (*The Usurers' Kermis or Annual Fair*), published in 1544, condemned usury because many practiced it under the pretense of Christian love.

Of concern was not just the taking of interest for loans but also concealed forms of interest and profit taking.[23] The trial against the Basel merchant Ulrich Meltinger and his conviction for financial irregularities in 1494 left behind a unique set of documents that give us insight into how merchants could circumvent usury laws. Meltinger could conceal interest or profits in the conversion of coins into guilders when credits were paid back,[24] and he also was accused of keeping interest

---

[19] The term used here is "guldt" or "güldt," sometimes referred to as "gülte" or "gilte." On the use of the term in medieval texts see Peters, "zins und gülte," 2017.
[20] Anon., *Hie kompt ein Beüerlein*, fol. 3r: "ich hör wull ir hapt ein andern gott dan wir armen/ wir haben vnsern hern Jhesum Christum/ der hatt solichs gelt leyhen verbotten vmb genuß."
[21] Strauß, *Das wucher zu nemen vnd geben*, sig. A2v: "vnchristlichen Tyrannischen wucher."
[22] Strauß, *Haubtstuck*, fol. 2r (Thesis 8): "Die zinß im Concilio zů Costnitz/ wie man sagt/ nachgelassen/ auff hundert fünff gulden/ seinnd wissenlich wůcherzinß."
[23] Isenmann, *Die deutsche Stadt im Mittelalter*, 963–966.
[24] Steinbrink, *Ulrich Meltinger*, 66.

payments off the books.²⁵ Peasants who owed him interest paid interest in wine,²⁶ while others paid interest in the form of deliveries of freshwater fish during lent.²⁷

Similarly, Sebastian Brant in his *Narrenschiff* from 1494 exposed the trick of lenders who recorded a larger amount than the amount that was actually loaned: "Instead of ten one records eleven in the ledger."²⁸ Brant also was one of the writers who extensively represented issues in the domestic economy as having a direct impact on the general population, such as *Wucher* (usury) and *Fürkauf*. *Fürkauf* in broad terms designated the highly profitable intermediary trade in food and other commodities, and more specifically the hoarding and monopolizing of basic commodities with the intent of driving up prices.²⁹ Sebastian Brant targeted these practices in his *Narrenschiff*:

> Who buys up and stores in his house all the wine and grains in the entire land just to store it, yet fears neither sin nor shame? So that a poor man will find nothing and will die of hunger with wife and child? For this reason there is much inflation now, and it is worse this year than last. For wine was barely worth ten pounds. In one month it came to pass that it now is valued at thirty. This also happens with wheat, rye, and grains.³⁰

Brant recognized how poverty and starvation were connected to hoarding and the resulting sharp rise in the price of basic foods, like grains and wine. He gave us the moving, archetypal example of a man who perished with wife and child because of the greed of the merchants. Brant hit a raw nerve, and this view dominated in the first half of the sixteenth century. For instance, the broadsheet *Vom wucher. Furkauff vnd Tryegerey* (*Of Usury, Hoarding and Graft*), published in Augsburg around 1535, included not just this quote but the entire chapter 34 from Brant's *Narrenschiff* with only minor changes.³¹

---

25 Steinbrink, *Ulrich Meltinger*, 201.
26 Steinbrink, *Ulrich Meltinger*, 153.
27 Steinbrink, *Ulrich Meltinger*, 163.
28 Brant, *Narrenschiff*, ch. 93, v. 21: "Für zehen schribt man eylff jnns bůch."
29 Kießling, "Problematik und zeitgenössische Kritik," 178.
30 Brant, *Narrenschiff*, ch. 93, v. 4–14: "Der hynder sich koufft jnn syn huß | Alls wyn/ vnd korn jm gantzen land | Vnd vörchtet weder sünd noch schand | Do mit eyn arm man nützet fynd | Vnd hungers sterb mit wib/ vnd kynd | Do durch so hat man yetz vil dür | Vnd ist/ dann värnyg/ böser hür | Nůn galt der wyn kum zehen pfundt | neym monat es dar zů kundt | Das er yetz gyltet dryssig gern/ | Alls gschicht/ mit weyssen/ rocken/ kern." Also Geiler, *Des hochwirdigen doctor Keiserspergs narenschiff*, fol. 184r. The pagination is disorganized and faulty. I am following the handwritten corrections in the digitized copy in the ONB.
31 The broadsheet also included most of Brant's chapter 102. See Jäger, "Texte aus Sebastian Brants Narrenschiff." Voltmer ("Krämer, Kaufleute, Kartelle," 413) claims that the broadsheed was published in 1515.

Efforts to curb various forms of interest payments took on a new sense of urgency as the activities of the big German merchant-banking companies, like the Fuggers and Höchstetters of Augsburg, gradually became more widely known in the early sixteenth century and unleashed a public outcry around 1520.[32] This debate coincided with the rapid rise in global trade with exotic foods and spices, which created even more opportunity for such market manipulations, fraudulent trade practices, and the illegitimate accumulation of wealth. There was a growing perception in the early sixteenth century that these practices had escalated to a much higher level or that they represented a new problem altogether.

The legal scholar Christoph Cuppener (1466–1511) in 1508 published one of the first German tracts disapproving of these new deceptive commercial practices,[33] entitled *Ein schons buchlein czu deutsch. doraus ein itzlicher mensche. was standes er sey. lernen mag. was wucher und wucherische hendel sein* (*A Beautiful Booklet in German, from Which Contemporary Humans, Regardless of Estate, May Learn what Is Usury and Usurious Trade*). Cuppener claimed that usury and the usurious hoarding of foodstuffs were new practices not known in German lands up to that point.[34] Cuppener also targeted the practice of *fürkauf*, which he viewed as a particularly egregious usurious practice: "Furthermore, those merchants are true usurers who buy up grains or other merchandise that they do not need in the hope that inflation will occur and with the intention to make a large profit from it."[35] In Cuppener's view, hoarding led to inflated prices and excessive profit margins.[36]

The practice appears to have been so widespread that Martin Luther made it a central point in his tract *Von Kauffshandlung vnd wucher* (*On Commerce and Usury*) from 1524. To Luther, hoarders were "manifest thieves, robbers and usurers," as their practices were selfish and predatory, as Luther defined it:

> Again, there are some who buy up the entire supply of certain goods or wares in a country or a city, so that they may have those goods solely in their own power and can then fix and raise the price and sell them as dear as they like or can. Now I have said above that the rule that a man may sell his goods as dear as he will or can is false and unchristian. It is far more abominable that one should buy up the whole supply of a particular good for that purpose.[37]

---

32 Jardine, *Worldly Goods*, 343.
33 Johnson, *The German Discovery*, 131.
34 Cuppener, *Ein schons Buchlein*, title page and sig. F5v.
35 Cuppener, *Ein schons Buchlein*, sig. F5v: "Also sein wiederumb die kaufleute warhaftige wucherer. dy do getreit einkaufen. ader ander war vberflussig in der entlichen hoffnung. das teurunge werden sal. vnd gedencken grossen gewin doraus czu haben."
36 A similar argument also in Bock, *Teütsche Speißkammer*, fol. 118v; Franck, *Von dem grewlichen laster*, sig. C2v.
37 Luther, *On Commerce and Usury*, 182.

Luther called on princes and cities to provide a reserve supply of food staples to insulate the poor people from the effects of hoarding in the name of "a right and good Christian providence for the community and for the good of others."[38]

Numerous broadsheets, pamphlets, and texts of different kinds were published in the first half of the sixteenth century covering the issue of buying up and hoarding goods. Otto Brunfels in his *Almanach ewig werend* (*Eternal Almanach*) from 1526, for instance, quoted Proverbs 11: "Whoever is holding back grains, the people will curse. But blessings will come over the one who is selling them."[39] The artist Daniel Hopfer (1471–1536) used the same verse as a motto for an etching published in Augsburg in 1534 (figure 10). Hopfer shows the merchant hoarding food on the left side as a large, gluttonous man who sits on a pile of bags filled with grains while anxiously protecting the bags with his hands. Empty-handed people in vain try to get him to sell his merchandise. The merchant on the right, by contrast, is opening his bags and is freely selling his grains to grateful customers. The religious overtones are evident in the illustration as well: while the hoarder is surrounded by devilish figures, the honest merchant is blessed by the dove above him, representing the Holy Spirit, and by the divine hand.

The practice of hoarding was criticized in many literary texts as well, for instance in the writings by the Nuremberg writer Hans Sachs. His so-called *Romanus-Dialogue*[40] from 1524 attempted to give the theme of greed and hoarding a decidedly Lutheran spin. The two debaters have programmatic names: Romanus represents the Catholic clergy, while Reichenburger is a wealthy burgher: "The content is an argument, which our Romanists cry out from the pulpit, and wherever they have space, with a high-pitched voice in order to blaspheme the evangelical teachings, in particular with the cursed greed."[41] Both use a number of biblical quotes to support their argumentation. Reichenburger recounts the standard Lutheran critique, like indulgences, oblations, the doctrine of good deeds and the sacraments that are for sale.

---

38 Luther, *On Commerce and Usury*, 183. Similarly Hans Sachs in *Von dem teuffel, dem die hell will zu eng werden* from 1540: "Kein fürkauff ist mehr in der stat. Allein der gmayn zu eym vorrat." (Sachs, KG 3, 589).
39 Brunfels, *Almanach*, sig. B3v: "Prouerb. xi. Wer korn ynnhelt/ dem flůchen die leüt. Aber der segen kumpt über den so ers verkaufft."
40 Published in Nuremberg in 1524 as *Ein Dialogus/ des inhalt/ ein argument der Römischen/ wider das christlich heüflein/ den Geytz/ auch ander offenlich Laster etc. betreffend* (*A Dialogue on the Argument of the Romanists Against the Christian Community Regarding Greed and Other Public Vices*). The text also is in KG 22, 51–68.
41 Sachs, *Ein Dialogus*, sig. A1v: "des inhalt ist ein Argument/ so vnnsere Römische/ mit hoher Stimm außschreyen auf der Cantzel vnd wo sie raum haben/ die Ewangelischen leer zulestern/ fürnemlich mit dem verfluchten geytz."

Figure 10: Daniel Hopfer. *Die Sprich Salomo das XI. Capitel*. [Broadsheet, Illustration to Proverbs 11:26.] Augsburg: s.n., 1534. © The Metropolitan Museum of Art, New York, N.Y.

Ironically, it is the priest Romanus who demonstrates how greed leads to a bad state of economic affairs. He relentlessly targets abuses like usury, dishonest deals, fraudulent numbers and measurements of weights and lengths, dishonest invoices, coercive practices, trade with inferior or spoiled merchandise, hoarding, and other economic practices that served to optimize profits. Reichenburger, as wealthy merchant, is unable to mount a credible defense as Romanus specifically takes on the monopolies of large corporations:

> Greed also governs corporate shareholders, such that they buy up merchandise in large quantities, out of the hands of others, and grab it for themselves, such as spices and whatever is their trade and business, add a surcharge on it as they please, and thus burden country and people. Is this good evangelical practice?[42]

---

[42] Sachs, *Ein Dialogus*, sig. A3r–A3v: "Auch regiert der geyz in geselschafftern/ also/ das sie etlich war zů hauff auff kauffen/ andern auß den henden/ vnd dann zů sich bringen/ als spetzerey/ vnd was dann jr handel vnd gewerb ist/ machen damit ein auffschlag wenn sie wöllen/ beschweren also landt vnd leüt/ ist das gůt Ewangelisch."

Romanus also very effectively targets the putting-out system and merchants who squeezed every penny out of workers in their employ on a piece-work basis:

> Furthermore, greed governs mightily among the merchants and merchant-employers who pressure their laborers and piece-workers when they bring to them their work and trifles or carry them home. The employers criticize their work sharply. Then the poor worker stands by the door trembling, with wringing hands, but silently, so that he would not lose the grace of the merchant because he had borrowed money on his labor already. Then the merchant reckons with him as he pleases. If the poor man forfeits his own money in addition to his labor the rich man rejoices because of his good bargain, and he believes that he did right by him.[43]

Sachs allowing the Catholic priest to levy these charges unchallenged in the first half of the dialogue, as well as him positioning a rich merchant as Protestant spokesperson, is surprising and indicates that Sachs did not think through the confessional configuration of this dialogue,[44] perhaps because the confessional configuration in his native Nuremberg was quite fluid at the time. His didactic poem entitled "Mercurius, ein got der kaufleut" (Mercury, a God of the Merchants) from 1526, brings some of the same charges against merchants while leaving out confessional rhetoric.[45]

Yet, in the second half of the dialogue, Reichenburger develops the theme that a Christian has no obligation toward lazy, deceitful, and immoral people who abuse the Christian charity Romanus is promoting. It is legitimate, for instance, to collect a debt from a drunk, a gambler, a philanderer, or a grifter.[46] He insists that many beggars are just lazy, and giving money to them makes them become dependent on charity:

> If one were to give everybody what they demanded, many of them would depend on that and would pursue only beggary and would not work. Not all of those who beg are needy.

---

43 Sachs, *Ein Dialogus*, sig. A3v–A4r: "Weyter regirt der geytz gewaltigklich vnter den kauff herren vnd verlegern/ die da drucken jre arbeiter vnd stückwercker/ wenn sie jnen jr arbeyt vnd pfennwerdt bringen oder haim tragen/ da thadeln sie jn jr arbeyt/ auffs hinderst/ dann steet der arm arbeyter zitrent bey der thür/ mit geschoßnen henden/ stilschweygent/ auff das er des kauff herren huld nit verlier/ hat etwan vor gelt auff die arbeyt entlehent/ alßdann rechent der kauff herr mit jm wie er wil/ büst der arm sein aygen gelt ein/ zů seiner arbeyt/ dann frewt sich der reich/ des gůten wolflen kauffs/ maynt er hab ihm recht gethan."
44 Ozment (*The Age of Reform*, 267) sees Sachs's unusually positive view of wealth "as an idication of the Reformation's accommodation to established power and surrender of its original high social ideals in the mid-1520s."
45 Sachs, KG 3, 512–516.
46 Sachs, *Ein Dialogus*, sig. B2v.

That is why one has no obligation to give to all of them, for whoever is not working should not be eating.[47]

While Romanus insists that these unworthy people should be dealt with by the legal system, to Reichenburger a wealthy Christian has to make the moral determination whether a poor person is worthy of charity and welfare, and the burden of proof now rests with the person requesting it. The view presented here is that protecting one's own resources against the undeserving other serves the common good.[48]

To Reichenburger, being rich is not morally suspect per se. Only those who fall victim to the moral pitfalls of wealth will not enter God's kingdom. He cites many biblical examples:

> Thus Abraham, Isaac, Jacob, David, Job, and many Church fathers were wealthy, but did not put their hopes in their wealth. So, it is possible that one is wealthy yet does not put one's heart into the wealth, as Paul teaches.[49]

The accumulation of wealth, and more broadly the pursuit of self-interest, therefore is compatible with being a Christian. In this dialogue, Sachs took on the distinctly Lutheran view that the Christian was the "steward over temporal goods."[50] However, later writings did not repeat this rather controversial Lutheran viewpoint. The *Romanus-Dialogue* was one of four Reformation dialogues Sachs wrote in 1524, a year before his native Nuremberg joined the Lutheran movement, and we have to assume that Sachs wrote these dialogues in this historical moment to generate support for the Reform movement. In later writings, he returned to a more conventional critique of merchants and of the pursuit of self-interest.

This is evident in Sachs's didactic poem *Der eygen nutz, das greulich thir, mit sein zwölff eygenschafften* (*Self-Interest, this Gruesome Animal, with Its Twelve Properties*) from 1527. Here, Sachs described self-interest as a *monstrum*, a gruesome animal with twelve body parts from different species, each representing a different aspect of self-interest. The "cocodrillen-schlund," the maw of a crocodile, serves as an allegory for insatiable greed: "The maw of the

---

47 Sachs, *Ein Dialogus*, sig. C1r: "Sölt man yedem geben nach seinem beger/ verließ sich mancher darauff/ vnd lege auff der betlerey/ vnd arbeytet nit/ sie seind nit all noturfftig die betlen/ darumb ist man jn nit allen schuldig zů geben/ wann wer nit arbeyt/ der sol nit essen."
48 Mellor and Shilling, *Re-forming the Body*, 118.
49 Sachs, *Ein Dialogus*, sig. B4r: "Also waren Abraham/ Isaac/ Jacob/ Dauid/ Job/ vnd vil väter/ reich/ setzten aber kain hoffnung darein/ ists nit noch möglich daß man reich sey vnd doch das hertz nit auf die reichtumb setz/ wie Paulus lert."
50 Sachs, *Ein Dialogus*, sig. B3v: "schaffner [...] vber das zeytlich gůt." See also Dutschke, "Bauernkrieg und bürgerliche Opposition," 69.

crocodile signifies that self-interest cannot satisfy anybody with hoarding, usury, and financial scams, with splurging and swindling, lending on meadows, fields and barns, inflating prices on wine, grains and houses."[51] Sachs listed a number of ways that merchants and bankers could manipulate financial arrangements at the expense of common people. Sachs concluded, "This burdens the entire world."[52]

A number of texts made the connection between merchants who manipulated markets and common people who suffered hunger and death as a result, particularly after Martin Luther condemned the practice in his tract *Von Kauffshandlung vnd wucher* (*On Commerce and Usury*) from 1524, whose second part was based on *Ain Sermon von dem wucher* (*A Sermon on Usury*) from 1520.[53] One of the more remarkable and interesting examples among the many testimonies is a secular song by Teus Bronner (dates unknown), entitled *Ein new lied/ von dem fürkauff/ vnd vnbillichem wucher der gesellschafften vnd kaufflewten* (*A New Song About Hoarding and Illegal Usury by Corporations and Merchants*). It contains 21 stanzas with 13 verses each and was published in Nuremberg in 1542.

Bronner described in great detail how merchants took advantage of artisans and peasants, pushing them deeper into poverty. The eighth stanza describes the basic pattern of the abuse:

> Indeed, all grains that will grow henceforth are sold for several years out, and the poor community is suffering. They come with an enormous grievance. The grains are not passed out, I say, but rather locked up in storage. So food is getting ever more expensive. This is caused by the massive hoarding. Enough of all goods grew last year as this year. If only this usury could be punished.[54]

Bronner outlined a strategy we would describe as hedging today. Harvest yields were sold years ahead of time and food supplies locked away in order to reduce the merchants' exposure to risk and to maximize their profits. According to Bronner, this happened at the expense of poor people who suffered because of

---

51 Sachs, KG 3, 495–496: "Auch deut der schlund des cocodrillen, | Das aygner nutz kan nyemand stillen | Mit fürkauff, wucher und finantzen, | Mit popitzen und alifantzen | Leyhen auff wiesen, äcker, schewrren, | Wein, koren unnd hewser vertewren." For a more comprehensive discussion of this poem, see Chapter 8.
52 Sachs, KG 3, 496: "Des ist beschwert die gantze welt."
53 Skrine, "Images of the Merchant," 189.
54 Bronner, *Ein new lied*, sig. A3v: "All Frücht so künfftig wechst fürwar/ | die sind verkaufft auf etlich jar/ | verderbt die arm gemeyne. | So kummen sie mit grosser klag/ | die Frücht geben nicht wol ich sag/ | schliessends in kasten eine. | So wirdt die narung wider theür/ | macht ja das groß fürkauffen/ | All ding wechst gnug gleych fert als heür | thet man den wucher straffen."

rising prices and starvation. Wealthy, usurious merchants had nothing to fear as their misdeeds went unpunished: "The usurers are not punished now. This one notices in this world, as everybody is pursuing dishonest deals."[55] In spite of recognizing the injustice, he advised the poor and disadvantaged in the last two stanzas to endure their plight and trust in God, while abstaining from rebellion. The most remarkable aspect of this text is that this is a song in the didactic and political popular song (*Sangspruch*) tradition, to be performed publicly. The choice of genre indicates that this was an issue of great concern that reverberated in the popular culture of the time.

Hoarding was not just a German problem, and some writers observed that the emerging global trade offered new opportunities to manipulate markets. The cosmographer Sebastian Münster in the 1556 edition of his *Cosmographia* described hoarding as a phenomenon that afflicted the newly globalized economic system:

> But Damianus [de Goes], a Portuguese, [...] accuses the hoarders who buy up all the spices and pressure all the middlemen so that the common people throughout Europe have to make up for it. These harmful hoarders one should drive out of the country and not tolerate in all of Europe.[56]

This statement referring to Damião de Góis (1502–1574), an important Portuguese Humanist philosopher and chronicler, was not included in earlier editions of the *Cosmographia*.[57] Münster targeted powerful trade conglomerates that clearly manipulated the nascent global trade system. He recognized this as a pan-European problem and demanded a pan-European strategy to fight the practice. Münster, like the other sources discussed here, appeared helpless in the face of massive market distortions imposed by trading corporations and long-distance merchants. The consensus was that food was a commodity and public resource. It

---

55 Bronner, *Ein new lied*, sig. A5v: "Die wucherer strafft man yetzt nicht/ | das spürt man wol in diser welt/ | yeder sich nach finantzen richt."
56 Münster, *Cosmographei* (1556), 88: "Aber Damianus ein Portugalleser [...] beschuldiget die fürkäuffer die alle gewürtz an sich kauffen vnd andere vnderkäuffer dermassen strecken/ das sie der gemein man durch das gantz Europa müß entgelten. Dise schedliche fürkäuffer solt man zum land herauß treiben vnd im gantzen Europa nit tolen." Damião de Góis, latinized Damianus de Goes, was a friend of Erasmus and well-connected in European Humanist circles. Münster had met Góis during his visit of Basel in 1533. (Lach, *Asia in the Making of Europe*, vol. 2, book 2, 19.) It is important to point out that Góis justified the exclusive policy of the Portuguese and, like Conrad Peutinger, defended the practices of the large merchant houses. (Lach, *Asia in the Making of Europe*, vol. 2, book 2, 22–23.) On the disputes between Münster and de Góis see McLean, *The 'Cosmographia' of Sebastian Münster*, 178–180.
57 Johnson, *The German Discovery*, 164. It is unclear why this conciliatory remark towards de Góis was included in this posthumous edition of the *Cosmographia*.

needed to be managed more efficiently to serve the common good in the face of threats presented by the rapidly rising global trade.

In addition to market manipulations, merchants were frequently accused of fraudulent practices, such as manipulating quality or quantity of the merchandise they were trading. Johannes Ferrarius considered "fraudulent merchandise, false weights, incorrect scales, inflated prices, surcharges"[58] to be antisocial and godless acts. Such practices were not just harmful in economic terms, but they also violated the public trust and harmed the common good:

> This is not traded honestly, rather outside of faith, which is a foundation of civil society. For when things evolve to the point where one cannot have trust or faith in the other, and where one does no longer appear to be trustworthy to the other, this is where the common good has already collapsed.[59]

Trust was an important common good that served as a foundation for the moral and social order.[60] A number of texts pointed to the obligation of princes and city councils to ensure that weight and size of the merchandise sold in their jurisdictions conformed with the established norms.[61]

The control of quality standards was an equally vexing problem. Ferrarius bemoaned the practice of selling goods of inferior quality for the full price.[62] Merchants also stood accused of altering the merchandise they were selling, in particular of adding other, less costly substances to the merchandise in order to maximize profits. Sebastian Brant referred to this practice in his *Narrenschiff* (1494): "Instead of gold one now adds copper. Mouse dung one mixes in with pepper."[63]

Similarly, Christoph Cuppener in his 1508 tract on usurious commerce discussed extensively how dishonest merchants mixed cheap metals like lead with gold or silver or diluted expensive food items like wine, but in particular spices like pepper, saffron, and ginger.[64] The spices he mentioned were all imported, suggesting that the risk of being defrauded was considered much higher with

---

[58] Ferrarius, *Von dem Gemeinen nutze*, fol. 51v: "betrug der war/ falsch gewicht/ falsche wage/ verthewrung/ auffsatz." Similarly Sachs, *eygen nutz*, KG 3, 496.
[59] Ferrarius, *Von dem Gemeinen nutze*, fol. 51v: "das ist nit vffrichtig gehandelt/ sonder vsserhalb dem glauben/ der ein fundament der burgerlichen geselschaft ist/ dan wo die sachen da hin gespielt werden/ das einer dem andern nit mehr darff vertrawen ader glauben/ vnd auch einer dem andern kein Glauben mehr beweist/ da ist der gemeyn nutz algeretz gefallen."
[60] On the connection between trust and the social order, see Shapin, *A Social History of Truth*, 3–16.
[61] Ferrarius, *Von dem Gemeinen nutze*, fol. 44v and 50v; Lauterbeck, *Regentenbuch*, fol. 136v.
[62] Ferrarius, *Von dem Gemeinen nutze*, fol. 51v.
[63] Brant, *Narrenschiff*, ch. 102, v. 67–68: "Für golt man kupfer yetz zů rüst | Müsdreck man vnder pfeffer myst."
[64] Cuppener, *Ein schons Buchlein*, sig. F3v–F4r.

imported goods, in part because these spices tended to be expensive, and in part because foreign traders could be trusted even less than their German counterparts. Hieronymus Bock (1498–1554) complained that many merchants sold ground ginger that included dried bread and that other spices contained substances like oak bark, sawdust, and fine earthen materials in order to maximize profits.[65] And Otto Brunfels (1488–1534) warned of composite spices and medicines, which opened the door to all kinds of fraud.[66]

Imported spices were regarded as particularly susceptible to fraudulent foreign substances because they were profitable and because their foreign origin made it virtually impossible to ascertain their quality and purity. Not surprisingly, many sources addressed the issue of corrupted or spoiled herbs and spices. A good example is Bock, who dedicated an entire chapter of his *Teütsche Speißkammer* (*German Pantry*) to the "Warning of counterfeit spices from numerous peddlers."[67] Here, Bock described a number of fraudulent practices of diluting spices and contended that foreign, imported merchandise was particularly susceptible. In Bock's analysis, the fraud was systemic and victimized common people first and foremost:

> Everything happens on the back of the poor man who shall and must remain poor and overburdened. The office holders who have jurisdiction in these things do not take this seriously, look through their fingers, let it sneak by, claiming that this is not their job. Furthermore, one often finds rulers who are secretly in bed [with the perpetrators]. They would be sorry if the fraud and the secret practices came to light.[68]

Bock described an environment of collusion where government officials supported the fraudulent trade practices of the merchants or at least looked the other way.

Paracelsus, born Philippus Aureolus Theophrastus Bombastus von Hohenheim (1493–1541), objected to the practice of importing medicines from overseas in his tract *Beschreibung etlicher kreüter/ auß dem Herbario Theophrasti Paracelsi* (*Description of Numerous Herbs from the Herbarium of*

---

65 Bock, *Teütsche Speißkammer*, fol. 107r.
66 Brunfels, *Contrafayt Kreüterbůch*, sig. b1v.
67 Bock, *Teütsche Speißkammer*, fol. 107r–108r: "Warnung vor falscher specerei etlicher Landtstreicher."
68 Bock, *Teütsche Speißkammer*, fol. 107r: "Es gehet aber alles vber den armen man/ der sol vnnd můß allzeit arm vnnd vberladen sein/ die amptuerweser/ so vber dise ding gesetzt/ achtens nit hoch/ sehen durch die finger/ lassens hin schleichen/ vermeinen es gehe sie nichts an/ zůdem findt man etwan befelch haber/ die heimlich vnder der deck ligen/ denen leidt were/ das der betrug vnd heimliche pracktic ans liecht kommen solten."

Theophrastus Paracelsus), written around 1525–1526.[69] To Paracelsus, importing herbs was too laborious and too costly, particularly since the German soil provided an abundance of herbs suitable to cure any imaginable illness.[70] In his view, the added prestige of imported goods prompted Germans to pay more for them, which gave merchants good profit margins, while accepting diminished health benefits. He alleged that doctors knew about this deceptive scheme, "namely the fraud by merchants, storekeepers, sellers, etc., that they bring the merchandise across the oceans, nothing without being counterfeited. The same is true also for those who store and re-sell it."[71] Paracelsus believed that the whole chain of trade was corrupted, but he singled out the merchant class that imported the spoiled goods into Germany as the main profiteer of this fraudulent scheme. The victim was the patient who, fearing death, did not have a choice other than consuming the counterfeit medicines in the hope of getting well again.[72]

Sebastian Münster in the 1556 edition of his *Cosmographia* focused on the larger context. He asserted that the Portuguese had established a trade monopoly by controlling the trade route to India around Africa, which did damage not just to the German economy, but also to the economies of France, England, and Denmark:

> Accordingly, Paulus Jovius, a learned man in Italy, writes that the navigation by the Portuguese not only makes the road to India much more difficult for other countries but that it also ensures that the spices come to us with a large profit for the Portuguese but with a noticeable damage to us. For what is of a good quality they keep and what is worth nothing they sell to us at the highest price.[73]

---

[69] The tract was first published in 1570 as part of *Ettliche Tractatus Des Hocherfarnen vnnd berümbtesten Philippi Theophrasti Paracelsi*. Sudhoff in his 1930 edition (*Theophrast von Hohenheim*, III) claims that the text was written around 1525–1526. See also Heinrichs, *Plague, Print, and the Reformation*, 57.

[70] Paracelsus, "Beschreibung Etlicher kreüter," 286. Moran ("The Herbarius," 104) provides a rather free translation.

[71] Paracelsus, "Beschreibung Etlicher kreüter," 289: "nemlich den betrug der kauffleuten/ kremern/ verkeuffern/ etc. das sie die ding vber Meer bringen/ nichts ohn gefelscht/ dergleichen auch von denen/ die es behalten/ vnd widerverkauffen." See also Moran, "The Herbarius," 105.

[72] Paracelsus, "Beschreibung Etlicher kreüter," 289–290; Moran, "The Herbarius," 105.

[73] Münster, *Cosmographei* (1556), 88: "Demnach schreibt Paulus Jouius ein gelertmann/ in Jtalia/ das der Portugalleser Schiffung nit allein andern landschafften verschlecht die straß in Jndiam/ sunder sie macht auch daß das gewürtz zů vnß kompt mit einem grossen gewin der Portugalleser vnnd vnsern mercklichen schaden. Dann was gůt ist behalten sie/ vnd das nichts sol verkauffen sie vns auff dz teüwrest." This statement was not included in earlier editions of the *Cosmographia*. The reference probably is to Paolo Giovio (1483–1552), an Italian physician, historian, biographer, and prelate.

Münster recognized that other routes to India, notably the Venetian land route through the Levant, could not compete against the Portuguese sea route around Africa and that the Portuguese used their primacy in Asian navigation to control the spice trade. He also alleged that they abused their dominant market position by selling spices of inferior quality to Germany at premium prices. Münster's argument was not simply nationalistic; rather, his critique targeted the system of trade. He identified the Portuguese as manipulators of the new global system of trade, with Germany, France, England, and Denmark at its victims.

In the face of so much fraud and market manipulation, authors of spice books like Otto Brunfels and Hieronymus Bock urged Germans to reject imported spices entirely. Germany offered a large number of healthy spices that were comparable to those that were imported from Asia. Given the availability of viable domestic alternatives, the use of expensive imported spices represented unnecessary, wasteful spending that only enriched wealthy foreign merchants.[74] Hieronymus Bock in the foreword to the second edition of his *Kreüter Bůch* (*Herb Book*) from 1546 opposed composite spices because the quality, authenticity, and possible foreign origin could not be verified.[75]

A few texts focused on merchants as potential victims in foreign locations and offered advice on how to reduce the risk of being defrauded in foreign trading posts. Michael Herr suggested that the anthology of discovery and travel texts that he edited and translated into German could help merchants understand global trade. In his introduction to *Die new welt, der landschaften vnnd Insulen, so bis hie her allen Altweltbeschrybern unbekant* (*The New World of Landscapes and Islands Which Were Not Known to the Famous Ancient Cosmographers*), published in 1534, Herr praised the usefulness of his book to merchants, among others:

> It may be of use to merchants and to those who do business in other countries. To them, it may be highly beneficial. Firstly, because they learn here where each merchandise comes from and how it is transported from one place to another. Also how a merchandise is traded against another. Also how one recognizes the good [merchandise] against the spoiled and forged [merchandise].[76]

---

74 Brunfels, *Contrafayt Kreüterbůch*, 291; Bock, *Kreüter Bůch*, 1546, sig. a4v; Bock, *Teütsche Speißkammer*, fol. 92v.
75 Bock, *Kreüter Bůch*, 1546, sig. a4r-a4r. The 1539 first edition of the Herb Book touches on the topic but does not develop it to the same extent.
76 Herr, *Die new welt*, sig. *4v: "kaufflleut vnd die so gewerb in andern landen treiben/ den mag es zuuor hochdienstlich sein. Zum ersten/ wann sie hie leren wo her ein yede war kum/ vnd auch wie sy von einem orth zů dem andern bracht werd. Do bey wie ein war gegen der andern verstochen wird. Auch wo bey man die gůten erkennen mag vor den verlegnen vnd gefälschten."

While the anthology contains little useful pragmatic information for merchants, Herr using this argument to promote his book is an indication that this was a significant issue.

Lorenz Meder's (d. 1561) *Handel-Buch* (*Trading Book*) from 1558, a handbook for merchants, cautioned that merchants who bought spices in Lisbon from the King of Portugal did so at their own risk. Meder offered an implicit critique of what has been dubbed "sixteenth-century southern European crown capitalism."[77] Meder warned in particular of ground spices in Lisbon, such as pepper, ginger, cloves, cinnamon, nutmeg, and mace, because those were commonly mixed with dust, straw, stones, and earth.[78]

Meder pointed to an increased risk of doing business in foreign locations because merchants had to deal with unfamiliar local trade practices and with different legal standards. As foreign merchants, they had little cultural currency and legal standing in cities like Lisbon. One possible solution was organizing trade in the diaspora. Merchants with the same nationality created communities of trust in many important commercial hubs. Within these national houses, fraud was less common, and support was available in dealing with local merchants or authorities.[79] This also helps us understand that the thrust of this argument was not meant to evoke sympathies for merchants but rather serves as evidence for deeply held xenophobic beliefs. As foreigners could not be trusted, particularly in foreign locations, German merchants abroad required assistance, no matter how reprehensible their actions might otherwise be.

---

[77] Kocka, *Capitalism*, 55; also Reinhard, *A Short History of Colonialism*, 21–29.
[78] Meder, *Handel-Buch*. fol. 26r.
[79] Pomeranz and Topik, *The World That Trade Created*, 7.

Chapter 19
Macro-Economic Critique of the Emerging Global Trade

A detailed critique of merchants at the micro-economic level led to a more comprehensive and systemic macro-economic critique of the emerging global trade. Points of discussion were the massive market manipulations, the monopolies, the outlandish profits made in international trade, the sheer size of some of the corporations, and the fact that the expanded international trade was depriving Germany of significant financial resources and generally hurt the German economy. Ulrich von Hutten even argued that cities and merchants were unknown to the old Germans and that the urban merchant culture was inherently un-German and therefore constituted a harmful foreign innovation.[1] The moralizing undertone common in anti-merchant polemics connected to the luxury debate or to the misgivings about excessive travel. Given the modest economic significance of border-crossing long-distance trade at the time, as compared to local and regional production and consumption,[2] the strong publicist response against the large merchant-banking companies and their global trade activities is quite surprising.

The political backlash against these large economic conglomerates and their business practices started in the last decade of the fifteenth century. The merchant-bankers were first discussed at the Imperial Diet of Worms in 1495,[3] and the monopoly discussion started around 1500, reaching its peak between 1521 and 1530.[4] Monopolies (*monopolia*), which were typically synonymous with the large merchant companies, were first tackled at the Imperial Diet of Cologne and Trier of 1512.[5] The discussion of monopolies at various diets primarily focused on the spice trade and on mined commodities,[6] that is exactly on the two sectors of the economy that were most affected by the Portuguese trade with Asia. The Diet acknowledged in a decree of 16 August 1512 that "many large corporations of merchants arose in the empire in recent years" and moved to restrict the

---

[1] Hutten, "Die Anschawenden," sig. x2v.
[2] Osterhammel and Petersson, *Geschichte der Globalisierung*, 42.
[3] Bauer, "Conrad Peutingers Gutachten," 145.
[4] Johnson, *The German Discovery*, 133; Bauer, "Conrad Peutingers Gutachten," 1. For a summary of the *Monopolstreit* see Johnson, *The German Discovery*, 133–140; Isenmann, *Die deutsche Stadt im Mittelalter*, 972–977. For a more comprehensive discussion see Mertens, *Im Kampf gegen die Monopole*.
[5] Isenmann, *Die deutsche Stadt im Mittelalter*, 973.
[6] Isenmann, *Die deutsche Stadt im Mittelalter*, 974.

hoarding and monopolizing of commodities, like spices (*specerey*), metals, and some textiles.[7]

The newly elected Emperor Charles V, in his electoral capitulation (*capitulatio caesarea*) of 3 July 1519, had to commit to reining in "the large merchant companies, which so far have governed with their money, acted without restraint, and through price gouging brought much disruption to the empire, on whose inhabitants and subjects they inflicted significant harm, disadvantage and hardship."[8] Sensing an anti-merchant mood, the electors forced the emperor to accept some rather harsh anti-merchant rhetoric. The *Polizeiordnung* (police ordinance),[9] passed at the Diet of Worms on 17 April 1521, picked up much of the language of the 1512 ordinance. Its title, "Of inappropriate hoarding, also the prohibition of monopolies for members of corporations and other individual persons," was programmatic, and its objective was to thwart the attempts by the large merchant corporations to create new monopolies and to inflate the prices of their merchandise in inappropriate ways.[10] It is noteworthy that the recently developed trade in imported spices played a prominent role in the deliberations and decrees of the diet as both were subjected to monopolistic control exerted by the King of Portugal and the secondary monopoly of the merchant companies that controlled the distribution in the empire.

The merchant cities of Augsburg and Nuremberg responded to this threat to their business model. Conrad Peutinger, the Augsburg city manager (*Stadtschreiber*), represented the Augsburg merchant-bankers as their counsel and lobbyist. Peutinger also had familial ties to Augsburg financial interests as he was married to Margarete Welser (1481–1552), the daughter of Anton Welser the Elder (1451–1518) and the sister of Bartholomäus V Welser (1484–1561).[11] Peutinger had a substantial collection of travel reports focusing on Asia and

---

[7] Senckenberg, *Zweyter Theil derer Reichs-Abschiede*, 144: "viel grosse Gesellschafft in Kauffmannschafften in kurtzen Jahren im Reich aufgestanden." See also Mertens, *Im Kampf gegen die Monopole*, 16–17; Rössner, *Deflation*, 215.

[8] *Deutsche Reichstagsakten, Jüngere Reihe*, vol. 1, 872, §19: "die grossen geselschaften der kaufgewerbsleut, so bisher mit irem gelt regirt, irs willens gehandelt und mit teurung vil vngeschicklichkeit dem reich, des inwonern und underthan merklich schaden, nachteil und beswerung zugefugt."

[9] Police ordinance is a literal translation. The term *Polizei* (or *Policey*) refers to policy as well as the attempt to create a system of law and order through ordinances.

[10] *Deutsche Reichstagsakten, Jüngere Reihe*, vol. 2, 351: "Von unzimblichen furkaufen, auch den gesellschaftern und ander sonder person verbotten monopolien."

[11] Zäh, "Konrad Peutinger," 449–451.

America, both printed and in manuscript form,[12] and he was an important intellectual trailblazer of globalization in Germany. Between 1522 and 1530, Peutinger wrote a total of six legal opinions on behalf of the large merchant-bankers against monopoly legislation considered by the Imperial Diet.[13] Peutinger turned to Johannes Eck for a theological argument to legitimize the global flow of capital, interest of five percent, and monopolies in the commodities trade.[14] Peutinger presented both legal and economic arguments in support of the merchants: "Peutinger mentioned the interdependency of economic processes, creating a picture of economic dynamics that were essentially the consequence of institutions securing private property rights and individual entrepreneurship striving for profit."[15] If indeed there were manipulations in the pepper trade, the trade policies of the king of Portugal were at fault and not the activities of the German merchants.[16]

In a departure from traditional thinking, his argumentation reconceptualized the notion of the common good: "He said that the richer the merchants, the more they are in number, the larger will be their business volume and turnover and accordingly the benefit of the common good."[17] Peutinger presented his theory that the common good was enhanced by economic activity that was entirely motivated by self-interest and contradicted centuries of scholastic thinking by doing so.[18] Furthermore, he argued that the growth of the national economy as well as the economic well-being of the poor depended on the entrepreneurial spirit and prosperity of the elites and thus promoted a version of trickle-down economics – which has defined the Republican economic platform since Ronald Reagan. We have to remember that Peutinger wrote as a lobbyist on behalf of larger commercial interests, his Humanist learning notwithstanding. Self-interest serving the common good was a novel concept that did not gain more acceptance until Leonhard Fronsperger expressed similar ideas in his *Von dem Lob deß Eigen Nutzen* (*Of the Praise of Self-Interest*) from 1564.[19]

The outflow of financial resources that resulted from the German involvement in the new global trade became a concern in political circles early on.

---

12 Häberlein, *Aufbruch*, 174–176. Some reports and correspondence by Peutinger were reprinted in Greiff, *Tagebuch des Lucas Rem*, 111–172.
13 Reprinted in Bauer, "Conrad Peutingers Gutachten." For a discussion see Mertens, *Im Kampf gegen die Monopole*, 60–63; 103–106; 158–160.
14 Roper, *Martin Luther*, 117.
15 Rössner, "Introduction," 144.
16 Isenmann, *Die deutsche Stadt im Mittelalter*, 976.
17 Rössner, "Introduction," 145. See also Bauer, "Conrad Peutingers Gutachten," 193.
18 Isenmann, *Die deutsche Stadt im Mittelalter*, 976.
19 See the discussion of this text in Chapter 8.

As early as 1507, Emperor Maximilian I addressed the financial drain in his instructions to the imperial estates at the Diet of Constance. Maximilian demanded steps against the import of silken clothes and gold jewelry from Italy because of the resulting drain of financial resources and impoverishment of the general population.[20] A prohibition of the importation of foreign luxury goods was never considered, in spite of the contentious debate. However, there were many regulatory measures to ban hoarding and other trade practices that were deemed harmful, first at the Diet of Worms in 1521.[21] Yet, whatever the Diet discussed and resolved had a limited impact. In an emerging global market system, imperial laws were often ignored, difficult to enforce, and deemed insufficient to curb economic manipulations, as the significant amount of literature on this topic indicates.

The extensive discussion of the global trade at the Diet of Nuremberg in 1522–1523 is a case in point.[22] A committee report described how merchants quickly became exceedingly wealthy because of the Portuguese spice trade in spite of heavy losses at sea.[23] The Diet subsequently tried to limit the capital stock of any one merchant company to 50,000 florins and to three branch offices,[24] at a time when the Fugger firm held assets worth millions of florins and when their Antwerp branch alone held 100,000 florins' worth of copper reserves.[25] This illustrates how poorly even the members of the Diet understood the size and reach of the commercial conglomerates they were attempting to regulate. Conrad Peutinger argued that they served a larger common good and that limiting the size of German corporations would benefit foreign competitors.[26]

The Diet also attempted to establish limits by levying taxes on foreign specialty goods like spices, gold, silver, silk cloth, brocade, other foreign cloth, sugar, and other kinds of seasonings.[27] The Diet ultimately settled on an import duty of four percent.[28] Jakob Fugger objected in a letter to Charles V in 1523, in which he reminded the emperor of his level of indebtedness to the Fuggers.[29] A delegation was sent to the emperor in Spain that compelled him to repeal the

---

20 Janssen, *Frankfurts Reichscorrespondenz*, 737.
21 Mertens (*Im Kampf gegen die Monopole*) discusses economic legislation at imperial diets in the sixteenth century extensively. See also Johnson, *The German Discovery*, 141.
22 Mertens, *Im Kampf gegen die Monopole*, 39–60.
23 *Deutsche Reichstagsakten, Jüngere Reihe*, vol. 3, 587–588.
24 Isenmann, *Die deutsche Stadt im Mittelalter*, 975.
25 Jardine, *Worldly Goods*, 346.
26 Häberlein, *The Fuggers of Augsburg*, 66.
27 Johnson, *The German Discovery*, 142.
28 Häberlein, *The Fuggers of Augsburg*, 66.
29 Jardine, *Worldly Goods*, 346.

import duty as well as to end pending suits against several Augsburg firms alleging that they had violated monopoly laws. In the edicts of Madrid and Toledo from 1525, Charles V decided the monopoly issue in favor of the merchant companies, thus ending the efforts of the Diet, representing the imperial estates, to rein in the economic influence and political power of the large merchant companies.[30] Charles V now officially supported the globalizing agenda of the large southern German merchant companies. The diets of 1526, 1529, 1530, and 1532 further debated the monopoly issue but without tangible results.[31]

The publicist backlash against the globalized trade system began in the 1490s as well. The Strasbourg preacher Johann Geiler von Kaysersberg in his sermons on Brant's *Narrenschiff*, given in Strasbourg in 1498 and 1499, merged Brant's points into a more coherent critique of long-distance merchants:

> The sixth bell is to travel far away out of avarice. Everybody knows with what kind of care and labor merchants travel far away. They flee poverty through water and over land all the way to India. So many strange customs, such wild clothes and strange sins come to our lands, which are brought here from foreign lands by avaricious merchants and by travelers. They leave as fools and come back as much bigger fools in their strange and foolish clothes, and many fools followed them. King Ferdinand found many islands in the upper sea, or in the high sea.[32]

This is one of the very first sources to assess the activities of long-distance merchants in a critical manner. Geiler's list of complaints against merchants was long: their travel was motivated by greed and avarice, they traveled as far as India, they brought back alien customs, new sinful behavior, and outlandish clothes, and they came back as much bigger fools. Geiler, like Brant before him, held the expansion of the spatial system to be disruptive of the spatial order that he believed to be divine in origin. Geiler also mentioned the discoveries made on

---

30 Häberlein, *The Fuggers of Augsburg*, 67; Mertens, *Im Kampf gegen die Monopole*, 73–85.
31 Isenmann, *Die deutsche Stadt im Mittelalter*, 977.
32 Geiler, *Des hochwirdigen doctor Keiserspergs narenschiff*, fol. 134r: "Die sechßt schel ist daraffter faren vß geitigkeit/ iederman weiß mit was sorg vnd arbeit die kaufleut daraffter faren/ biß gon india sie fliehen armůt durch wasser vnd erdterich/ es kummen souil seltzammer sitten/ so wilde cleider vnd seltzame sünd yn vnsere land/ die von den geitigen kaufleuten/ vnd den landfarer herkummen/ die sie vß frembden landen herbringen. Sie faren narren hinweg vnd kummen noch vil grösser Narren herwider yn iren seltzamen/ vnnd nerrischen cleidern/ vnd haben vil narren nachfolget. Der künig ferdinandus hat vil insulen gefunden in dem oberen mör/ oder im hochen mör." Geiler referred to the subheadings in his sermons as "schel" (bell), alluding to the bells that adorned the dress of fools in Brant's text. It is unclear what Geiler meant with "oberes mör" (upper sea). Historically, this referred to a mythical ocean in the north of Assyria. As Geiler refers to the islands of King Ferdinand, we have to assume that the reference is to the Atlantic Ocean, although this was probably not clear to Geiler.

behalf of King Ferdinand "in dem oberen mör" (in the upper sea). The upper sea may be a reference to a body of water suspected in Asia north of the Persian Gulf. Geiler must have assumed that the mariners who traveled on behalf of Ferdinand ended up somewhere in Asia. Geiler at the time of writing most likely was not aware of America as the fourth continent, which explains his focus on India as the locus of discovery.[33] Assuming that this text was drafted by Geiler in 1498 or 1499, before Vasco da Gama had returned to Lisbon from his first circumnavigation of Africa, Ferdinand's discoveries described by Columbus and Vespucci indeed represented the most recent discoveries.

Ulrich von Hutten's polemical critique of the consumption of luxury goods imported from foreign lands makes a similar point, although his argumentation was more detailed and his perspective was much more focused:

> No spice one turns down, nor any delicacy. It does not hurt if it is expensive. Or if it is brought back from India, grown in Arabia, or comes from the new island. Serve it up, the Fuggers will bring more of it.[34]

In Hutten's view, the Fuggers preyed on the moral weakness of Germans in order to generate excessive wealth:

> Our forefathers lived very modestly. However, our foods are not tasty to us anymore. We sell ours so that we can buy others for it, those that were brought over the ocean by the Fuggers. They became rich because of our cravings and built themselves such beautiful houses. These very servants of our lust have amassed such wealth that they surpass every ruling prince.[35]

For Hutten, the Fuggers stood for all large merchant companies. They took advantage of the moral shortcomings of the Germans. They were also responsible for the fact that Germans no longer had a taste and desire for their own, locally grown food and instead lusted for the finer imported varieties. The larger argument, however, was that the Fuggers became immensely wealthy in the process. Hutten thus expanded the anti-Fugger polemic of the time,[36] whose thrust

---

[33] For a discussion of German awareness of the discovery of America see Chapter 15.
[34] Hutten, "Feber das Erst," sig. b4v: "Kein wurtz man spart/ noch spetzerey. | Schadt nit/ ob das schon tewer sey. | Obs sey geholt auß Jndia/ | Gewachsen in Arabia. | Kumm auß der newen Jnsel her. | Tragt auff/ die fucker bringens mer."
[35] Hutten, *von der wunderbarlichen artzney*, sig. H3r: "vnsere vorfarn hondt gar messigklich gelebt/ aber vns schmacken vnsere früchten nit/ wir verkauffen die vnseren das wir andere darumb kouffen/ die/ die Fucker vber mör hat bringen/ darůb sie vnser schelligkeit reich seint worden/ vnd gar schöne hüser gebuwen hondt/ die selben vnsers wollusts diener haben in reichtum so hoch zů genumen/ daz sie ein yedn fürsten vbertreffen."
[36] Rössner, *Deflation*, 214.

was directed against their financial practices, their quest for monopolies, and their outsize influence in imperial politics. With Hutten, the Fuggers also became the focal point of the new scourge of importing foreign goods, and particularly of foreign food and spices.

Hutten understood the increased opportunities for market manipulation offered by the emerging global trade. The same is true for Martin Luther, who opposed long-distance trade for this very reason. Luther also brought the anti-luxury topos into his argument:

> But those foreign trades, which bring from Calicut, India, and other such places, wares such as costly silks, gold-work, and spices, which minister only to luxury and serve no useful purpose, draining away the wealth of land and people – these trades ought not be permitted, if we had government and princes.[37]

Luther alluded to the inherent problem for princely and urban governments to regulate and control these global trade networks. Even worse, princely governments did not even attempt to do so and thus were derelict in performing their duties.

Issues like hoarding, usury, and generally the market dominance of the large merchant-banking conglomerates led to a discussion of monopolies. In a series of sermons given in Strasbourg in the summer of 1509, Johann Geiler von Kaysersberg detailed the merchants' sinful business practices.[38] One of the sermons, held on 25 July 1509,[39] targeted monopolies:

> Firstly, I say that said monopolies and cartels are against reasonable natural law. Note how in a human body one member serves the entire body. My eye sees my feet, the feet go and carry the entire body, my mouth eats for the stomach, the stomach accepts the food and distributes it to the entire body and to all members. And if you had a block standing on your shoulder that was harmful for the entire body and that was pulling away resources, of which other members needed to live, then you would cut it away and would ask what it was doing here. Therefore, I say that we here in Strasbourg are all one body, and we are its members. If there now is a member, a merchant who is a monopolist, he is harmful to the other members.[40]

---

37 Luther, *On Commerce and Usury*, 173–174.
38 The sermons under the heading "Von dem Wannenkremer vnd der kaufleut hantierung" (On the Business of Hawkers and Merchants) were recorded by the Franciscan Johannes Pauli and published in 1517 as part of a larger collection of sermons entitled *Die brösamlin doct. Keiserspergs* (*The Bread Crumbs by Doctor Kaysersperg*). See Voltmer, "Krämer, Kaufleute, Kartelle," 419.
39 Voltmer, "Krämer, Kaufleute, Kartelle," 439.
40 Geiler, *Die brösamlin*, fol. 94v–95r: "Zu dem ersten sprich ich. Das semlich Monopolii vnd stupferei ist wider das vernünfftig natürlich gesatz wann du sihest in eim leib des menschen dz ein glid dem gantzen leib dienet/ mein aug das sicht den füssen/ die füß gond vnd tragen den gantzen leib/ der mund isset dem magen/ der mag nimpt die speiß vnd teilt es dem

Geiler tied his argument into common visions of a natural order, in which individuals organically played a discrete role as part of a larger whole.[41] Those pursuing monopolies and cartels violated divine law and thus committed a deadly sin,[42] but they also disrupted the social order and harmed the common good. By enriching themselves at the expense of others, monopolists moved outside of the natural body of the society and needed to be extracted from it.

Hans Sachs described the mechanism of hoarding and monopolizing at the height of the discussion in his didactic poem *Der eygen nutz* (*Self-Interest*) from 1527. Sachs allegorized self-interest as a monstrum whose body parts by definition belonged to different animals and pursued their own interests and thus represented the antithesis of an organically grown natural order. These disparate interests represented by the monstrum were devastating the economic and social system:

> Furthermore, the wolf's stomach signifies that self-interest sends down its throat all metals, wax, and imported delicacies through corporations and trading posts, by dealing, bidding, and selling, by bundling and selling merchandise, and by assessing a surcharge on all merchandise that is much more expensive on credit than it is in cash.[43]

Sachs alleged that merchant-bankers and their branch offices were buying up and hoarding all kinds of commodities, thus cornering and monopolizing the market and ensuring excessive profits.

The Fugger Company of Augsburg was frequently singled out as an example of a corrupt and abusive merchant-banking company. A key factor in the polemics against the Fuggers was their sheer size, their disproportionate political influence and their corrupt practices. Johannes Agricola (1494–1566) described the exclusive and corrupt trade arrangements between the Fuggers and the King of Portugal in his *Drey hundert Gemeyner Sprichworter/ der wir Deutschen vns gebrauchen* (*Three Hundred Common Proverbs that We Germans Use*) from 1529:

---

gantzen leib auß vnd allen glidern vnnd hettest du ein klotzen vff der achßlen ston/ der dem gantzen leib schedlich wer/ vnnd züg ansich/ dauon andere glider leben/ solten/ du schnittest in hinweg vnnd sprechest was sol er da züston. Also sag ich/ wir hie zü Straßburg seind alle ein leib/ vnnd wir seint glider. Jst nun ein glid/ ein kauffman ein stüpfer/ der den andern glideren schedlich ist."

41 For a comprehensive discussion of this issue, including the use of the human body as allegory for political organization, see Chapter 1.
42 Geiler, *Die brösamlin*, fol. 94v.
43 Sachs, KG 3, 496: "Weyter bedeudt des wolffes magen | Das aygner nutz schlickt in sein kragen | All metall, wachs und spezerey | Durch gsellschafft und durch factorey, | Mit tauschen, stechen und verkauffen, | All wahr zusam kuplen und verkauffen, | Und auffschlag machen in all wahr, |Auff porg viel thewrer, wann umb par."

> In the German lands we now have a merchant, Jakob Fugger, who pushed trade so hard like nobody can remember so that there has not been anyone like him since the beginning of the world. Germans have quite some reputation in the world because of him. The gracious and honorable Hans von Dolzsch, the chief administrator of the wise Duke Frederick, Elector of Saxony, says that said Fugger, when he concluded the deal with the King of Portugal in order to establish a monopoly over the spice trade, gave the King a present of such magnificence that it would have been appropriate, if not excessive, if one emperor had given it to another. Before that agreement, all spices were priced moderately. But afterwards, they raised the prices of the spices as they pleased.[44]

Agricola was well aware of the unique economic importance of the Fuggers, of their efforts to establish monopolies in all branches of the economy, and of the nature of the arrangement the Fuggers closed with the Portuguese Crown, including a massive bribe, to secure their monopoly over the spice trade.

Furthermore, Agricola bemoaned the fact that ruling princes did not enforce existing laws and that the large merchant-bankers could establish their monopolies unhindered:

> Imperial law forbids monopolies and the hoarding of goods, but nobody now is treated better than said corporations and monopolizers. They say that there is no ruling prince in Germany who is not in debt to Fugger, which is why they do not enforce imperial laws and let everyone do as they please.[45]

Agricola didn't just condemn the Fuggers but also the inability of the political system to curb their power and to protect the population because so many princes were personally indebted to the Fuggers.

---

44 Agricola, *Drey hundert Gemeyner Sprichworter*, fol. 132r–132v: "Wir haben ytzt in Deutschen landen einen kauffman/ welcher bey mannes gedencken den handel so hoch getriben hat/ daß sein gleichen von anbegyn der welt nie gewesen ist/ den Jacob Fucker/ des die Deutschen vor der welt einen grossen rhum haben. Der gestrenge vnd ehrenfest Hanß von Doltzsch/ des weisen Hertzogen Fridrichs Churfursten zu Sachsen Marschalck sagt/ daß der Fucker/ do er den kauff gemachet hat mit dem Konig von Portugalien/ also daß sie den wurtzkauff allein haben sollen/ dem Konig ein solch geschenck geben hab/ daß es auch gnug were/ wo nicht zuuil/ wenn es ein Keyser dem andern schenckte/ Vnd vor der vnterhandlung waren alle wurtze bessers kaufs/ hernach aber haben sie die selbigen gesteygert nach yhrem wolgefallen."
45 Agricola, *Drey hundert Gemeyner Sprichworter*, fol. 132v: "Die Kayserlichen Rechte verpieten Monopolia/ die furkeuffe/ aber ytzt ist niemand besser noch baß gehalten/ denn die selbigen gesellschaffter vnd furkeuffer/ Man sagt/ es sey schier kein furst Deutsches landes/ der sey dem Fucker schuldig/ darum halten sie auch vber den Keyserlichen Rechten nicht/ vnd lassen einen yglichen thun was er nur wil." This was a common complaint. Geiler von Kaysersperg stated this in a sermon in 1509 (Geiler, *Die brösamlin*, fol. 95r).

What is more, the new global trade system developed such a cultural pull that young men were urged to join merchant-banking corporations at a young age before completing their education:

> The most noble cities in the German lands don't allow anyone to learn the liberal arts and languages anymore. Rather, as soon as a boy knows how to read and write in German he has to go to Frankfurt, Antwerp, and Nuremberg and has to learn arithmetic and business affairs."[46]

Agricola lamented the fact that young boys were asked to fully immerse into the world of business before acquiring a comprehensive education.

A further point of critique was the significant outflow of financial resources triggered by the global system of trade that was thought to be harmful to the German economy. Martin Luther demanded in *To the Christian Nobility of the German Nation* from 1520 that the worldly authorities should "restrict the traffic in spices, which is another of the great ships in which money is carried out of the German lands."[47] Luther also turned against "boundlessly excessive and costly dress," which led to impoverishment. In his view, God provided for everything humans needed:

> God has certainly given us, as he has to other countries, enough wool, flax, linen, and everything else necessary for the seemly and honorable dress of every class. We do not need to waste fantastic sums for silk, velvet, golden ornaments, and foreign wares.[40]

Here, too, it was the imported goods that inflicted the most serious economic damage on Germany.

Ulrich von Hutten polemicized against this aspect of the global trade as well. In his dialogue *Praedones* (*The Robbers*, 1521), he admonished the merchant class because they robbed Germany of immense sums of money every year by "importing large quantities of the most frivolous products into this country and sending ever larger amounts of money to foreign countries."[49] The city of Frankfurt was identified as the hub of the gold trade where merchants from all countries came to buy and sell and where the Fuggers dominated trade with their vast reserves in gold: "Merchants from all lands come here who buy and sell. Here, the merchants pile up their money, and here the Fuggers have whole mountains of gold

---

46 Agricola, *Drey hundert Gemeyner Sprichworter*, fol. 133r: "Die furnemsten stedte Deutsches landes lassen ytzt niemand mehr kunste vnd sprachen lernen/ sondern so bald ein knab Deutsch schreiben vnd lesen kan/ so muß er gen Franckfordt/ Antwerp vnd Nurmberg/ vnd muß rechen lernen/ vnd des handels gelegenheyt."
47 Luther, *To the Christian Nobility*, 461.
48 Luther, *To the Christian Nobility*, 460.
49 Hutten, *Praedones*, fol. 22v.

lying around."⁵⁰ Martin Luther addressed the economic impact of the outflow of silver and gold as well, again through the city of Frankfurt, and made it part of his polemic against global trade:

> God has cast us Germans off. We have to throw our gold and silver into foreign lands and make the whole world rich while we ourselves remain beggars. England would have less gold if Germany let it keep its cloth; and the king of Portugal, too, would have less if we let him keep his spices. You calculate yourself how much gold is taken out of Germany, without need or reason; from a single Frankfurt fair, and you will wonder how it happens that there is a single *heller* left in German lands. Frankfurt is the gold and silver sink, through which everything that springs and grows, is minted or coined here, flows out of the German lands.⁵¹

Luther specifically mentioned English cloth and Asian spices traded by the king of Portugal as culprits for the economic drain. Just like Lorenz Meder after him, Luther identified the king of Portugal as the person profiting most from the German spice trade. The Portuguese Crown indeed operated the pepper market as a royal monopoly until 1570.⁵² In Luther's analysis, this outflow of German silver led to the indebtedness of German states and cities. As he asserted in the passage quoted earlier, global trade also hurt individuals and led to widespread poverty because luxury goods imported from India, such as precious silk, golden artifacts, and spices, deprived common people of the financial resources to cover their basic needs.⁵³

It has been argued that these luxury imports from India and China were paid with silver and gold from the New World mines in Mexico and Peru.⁵⁴ But significant quantities of New World silver only started to arrive in Europe around 1540.⁵⁵ The silver from the Americas started to displace the German silver in the trade with Asia in the 1540s and remained the dominant commodity traded with Asia until the 1640s.⁵⁶ Before that, the Asian trade was paid mostly with German

---

50 Hutten, "Vadiscum," sig. g2r: "Hye her kummen auß allen landen/ die do kauffen vnd verkauffen. hie bringen die kauffleüt ir gelt zů samen hie haben die fucker gantze berg von golt ligen."
51 Luther, *On Commerce and Usury*, 174.
52 Findlay and O'Rourke, *Power and Plenty*, 206; Smith, "Profits Sprout," 392; Jardine, *Worldly Goods*, 345. For more on the Portuguese crown capitalism, see Reinhard, *A Short History of Colonialism*, 21–29.
53 Luther, *On Commerce and Usury*, 173–174.
54 Jennings, *Globalizations*, 24.
55 Rössner, *Deflation*, 108; Schmitt, "Atlantische Epansion," 134–136.
56 Flynn and Giráldez, "Path Dependence," 84.

silver as the empire produced about 80 percent of the world's silver around 1500.[57] Until 1498, only modest amounts of German silver were exported to Portugal. The export volume rose exponentially after the Portuguese discovered the Cape route to Asia.[58] In the first three decades of the sixteenth century, a large amount of silver was exported from Germany to places like Milan, Antwerp, and Lisbon, much of it to pay for the trade in Asian spices and silk. In the same time frame, the Welser Company regularly delivered large amounts of silver from Germany to the *Casa da Moeda* in Lisbon.[59] In return, southern German merchants were directly participating in the Portuguese spice trade through Lisbon and later through Antwerp.[60]

Bad coins became a significant and heavily publicized economic and political issue after 1450.[61] Minting coins with a lesser metal content was advantageous to the authorities due to the lower cost, but consumers, and in particular poor peasants, in their transactions were frequently able to claim only part of the imprinted value of the coin. Sebastian Brant took up the issue in his *Narrenschiff*: "The old coins are all worn down and could not exist any longer if one had not mixed in an additive. Coins weakened more than a little; bad money has become common now."[62] Brant described a crisis of coins that only could be addressed by adding other materials to them, presumably adding cheaper metals like copper to silver coins. This led to a devaluation of coins, that is bad coins that could not hold their original imprinted value.

Poor people who were dependent on lower-denomination silver coins disproportionately suffered the consequences. Johannes Agricola described the abusive mechanism:

> There is such fraud regarding coins that a poor man has to give up on much food and pay a premium if he wants to have good coins. That is why really bad coins are commonly circulating, but the good coins remain stashed away and are not released except for with usury.[63]

---

57 Rössner, *Deflation*, 108. According to Rössner (*Deflation*, 251), virtually the entire production from the Schwaz and Mansfeld silver mines around 1500 was exported, als well as over one quarter of the Saxon production.
58 Rössner, *Deflation*, 304.
59 Rössner, *Deflation*, 104.
60 Rössner, *Deflation*, 274.
61 Rössner, *Deflation*, 485–488.
62 Brant, *Narrenschiff*, ch. 102, v. 41–45: "Die alte müntz ist gantz hardurh | Vnd möcht nit lenger zyt beston | Hett man jr nit eyn zůsatz gethon | Die müntz die schwächert sich nit kleyn | Falsch geltt/ ist worden yetz gemeyn."
63 Agricola, *Drey hundert Gemeyner Sprichworter*, fol. 132v: "Es ist ytzt der muntz halben solcher betrug/ daß ein armer man/ wo er wil gute muntze haben/ etwas vil an seiner narung

Ownership of good coins, especially those minted out of gold, required significant financial resources, while poor people had no access to good coins and thus suffered the economic consequences of bad currency in the form of poverty and hunger.

The practice was commonly seen as fraudulent, as Agricola's commentary illustrates, but it did not violate any legal norms. As silver coins became the standard in most German territories in the late fifteenth century,[64] the substantial export of German silver to Portugal in the early sixteenth century led to a silver shortage in Germany. The silver content of coins, and in particular of small coins, was lowered frequently, which depressed their value. The Diet of Worms recognized the connection between the monopolies of large merchant houses and the outflow of silver and gold out of Germany: "Specifically, many gold and silver coins were taken out of the empire into foreign lands through [monopolies], and in return they imported merchandise that is more harmful than useful to the German lands."[65] The resulting economic problems were so significant, particularly for the poor, that the Diet of Nuremberg in 1522–1523 discussed the issue again.[66] The self-interested monstrum in Hans Sachs's didactic poem *Der eygen nutz, das greulich thir, mit sein zwölff eygenschafften* (1527) speculated in coins as well: "With coins he pursues many exchanges."[67] Hans Sachs recognized the speculative opportunities offered by the uncertain valuation of coins at the expense of the poor.

In the Peasants' Revolt of 1524–1525, the silver shortage became an important issue.[68] The Joachimsthal mining ordinance of 1518 promised payments to the miners exclusively in locally minted silver coins. However, a 1521 poem asserted that the mine operators did not comply with this agreement and paid the miners with bad coins.[69] The dissatisfied miners participated in the Peasants' Revolt and expressed their demands in their Joachimsthal articles of 20–23 May 1525.

---

verlieren muß/ vnd auffgeldt geben/ Daher es kompt daß eyttel bose muntze geng vnd gebe ist/ aber die gute muntze bleibt da dynden/ vnd kompt nicht herfur/ denn allein mit wucher."
64 Rössner, *Deflation*, 85.
65 *Deutsche Reichstagsakten, Jüngere Reihe*, vol. 2, 353: "Namblich so wurdet dardurch vil golds und silbermunz aus dem raich in frembde land bracht, und bringen dagegen vil war, die Teutschen landen mer schaden weder nutzen."
66 Rössner, *Deflation*, 104–105.
67 Sachs, KG 3, 496: "Mit müntz er auch vile wechsel treybt."
68 Der *Oberrheinische Revolutionär* (*Upper-Rhenish Revolutionary*) stressed the importance of good coins for the economic well-being of the masses alreay in 1509–1510 (Anon., *Der Oberrheinische Revolutionär*, 383).
69 Mittenzwei, *Der Joachimsthaler Aufstand*, 68.

In the third article, the miners lamented "that in spite of many pledges silver is transported away from this laudable mine and not minted here."[70] The miners thus had to endure inferior pay while the silver from their mine was exported to satisfy the trading needs of the large merchant companies.

Many arguments against long-distance trade and its domestic impact were based on traditional anti-merchant topoi, although specific points typically referred to newly arising issues. To be sure, the new economy had its own vocal supporters who were generally associated with the Augsburg and Nuremberg trade networks, most prominently Conrad Peutinger, Willibald Pirckheimer, and travel writers like Balthasar Springer. Opposition to the new trade came from many writers in the upper Rhine area between Strasbourg and the Swiss Confederation, such as Sebastian Brant, Johannes Geiler von Kaysersberg, and Ulrich von Hutten. The many merchant cities in this region lost their significance with the re-orientation of the European trade system. An interesting addition to this group was the Nuremberg writer Hans Sachs, who opposed merchants based on his own social identity as shoemaker and guild member – a social group that became increasingly dependent on merchants in the early sixteenth century.

A key factor in their opposition was a static view of the economy and more generally of the political system. Chapter 6 outlined a static view of history promoted by German intellectuals around 1500, in which the empire under Maximilian I had completed the vision outlined in the Book of Daniel (Dan. 2:21) and thus had brought world history close to its predestined end point. Political changes and innovations induced a great deal of anxiety as each one of them harbored the potential to move society away from the final destination of history that had seemed so near. Similarly, economic evolution and growth were anathema to these conservative writers. Their political tracts thus focused on a stable, inflexible order in the sixteenth century that provided a stable and constant level of economic resources for its members instead of growing the economy and promoting increasing prosperity.[71] The guild system embodied this view: it sought to maintain a stable number of participants in any branch of the economy and fixed the conditions under which they could perform their labor, from restricting the materials and tools used in the shops to controlling quality and fixing prices. Their objective was not to grow businesses and the entire economy, rather it was to guarantee a stable and predictable income to its

---

[70] Kobuch and Müller, *Der Deutsche Bauernkrieg*, 120: "das uber vielfeltige zusage die sylber von diesem loblichen bergwerg gefurt werden und nit hie vermuntzt." See also Sieber, "Der Joachimsthaler Aufstand," 49.
[71] Simon, *Gute Policey*, 159.

membership. The guild system thus exemplified the static view of the economy and is a primary reason why urban intellectuals responded so negatively to the rapid economic transformation triggered by long-distance trade, in particular the new global economic networks.

The efforts by authorities thus were limited to maintaining and restoring the traditional economic order, while explorations and the expansions of space, as well as the subsequent growth of the global trade and of the financial sector, were rejected because of their disruptive and transgressive potential. Princely states before the period of mercantilism were not equipped to pursue an active economic policy and certainly did not encourage economic innovation. Rather, the role of the economic policy was limited to managing damaging disruptions. The focus was on fighting perceived abuses, as illustrated by the attempts by the Imperial Diet to curb monopolies, but authorities were unable to regulate the rapidly expanding financial system and to contain operators of predatory global networks like Jakob Fugger.

This inability by the authorities to respond to perceived economic excesses sharpened the populist polemics against the new globalized economy.[72] The Reformation theologian and pamphleteer Johann Eberlin von Günzburg (1465–1533) illustrates how radical the backlash against the new economic order could be. In 1521, Eberlin published a series of fifteen pamphlets, commonly referred to as the *Fünfzehn Bundesgenossen (Fifteen Confederates)*,[73] which were influential in southern Germany.[74] The series projected a new utopian society based on Lutheran principles. In two of the pamphlets, he designed the utopian community of Wolfaria. The tenth pamphlet focused on the religious and moral order of Wolfaria and designed a communal order where innovation had no place, while the eleventh established its worldly organization, including restrictive rules for the merchant class:

> All Fuggery should be abolished. There shall be no more than three partners in a company. No wine should be offered here that does not grow in our country. No cloth should

---

[72] The term "populist" may be a bit anachronistic in this context in that a public sphere and a civil society in the modern sense did not exist. However, the term is legitimate in this context as politics indeed were framed as a battle between virtuous, ordinary people and a nefarious, corrupt elite that worked against the interestest of the common people.

[73] The *Fifteen Confederates* were published as separate pamphlets in the Basel edition used here. The text exists in other editions as well, such as the combined Augsburg edition, also of 1521, with the title *Ain klegliche klag an den Christlichen Römischen kaiser Karolum wegen Doctor Luthers vnd Ulrich von Hutten (A Lamentable Lament to the Christian Roman Emperor Charles on Behalf of Doctor Luther and Ulrich von Hutten)*.

[74] Kießling, "Problematik und zeitgenössische Kritik." 175.

be offered here that was not produced in our country. No crops should be offered in our country that were not grown here, except if needed to alleviate great bodily distress.[75]

The first concern was the banishment of large merchant corporations, like the Fugger Company, from this utopian space, using the term "fuckery" (Fuggery) as generic term. In general, companies were to be kept small. Of equal importance was that foodstuffs and of other merchandise could not be imported. Only cloth made in Wolfaria and only wine and foodstuffs grown in Wolfaria could be sold there. Eberlin thus opposed exactly those parts of the economic system that advanced the goals of globalization. The subsequent chapters will examine these points more closely.

---

[75] Eberlin von Günzburg, *Ein newe ordnung*, fol. 2v: "Alle fuckery soll ab gethon werden. Jn keiner geschellschafft söllen meer dann dry sein. Kein wein der in vnserem land nit wechßt/ soll härin gefürt werden. Kain tůch das in vnserem land nit gemacht wirt soll härin gefürt werden. Kain frucht die in vnserem land nit wechßt/ soll härin gefürt werden/ man müß es dann zů grosser lybs not haben." The term "fuckery" (Fuggery) refers to the Fugger merchant house in Augsburg.

Chapter 20
Nationalistic and Xenophobic Responses to Foreign Influences

The animus against foreign merchandise has to be seen in the context of general nationalist and xenophobic impulses of the time. The fifteenth century was not just a period of growing global connections but also a period of rising nationalism, often referred to as Humanist nationalism. It was structured differently from modern nationalism, the roots of which are commonly seen in the nineteenth century. The concept of Humanist nationalism was developed in scholarly literature in the fifteenth century, grouped around the ideas of national languages, national stereotypes, and civic patriotism.[1] It also could contain a xenophobic element, namely, the rejection by educated elites of foreign influences, in particular foreign goods like fashionable garments and fine foods, Roman law, and the Italianized papacy that was seen as draining German financial resources. This phenomenon, in contrast to modern nationalism, was not a mass movement and had little effect on governance, which remained largely determined by non-nationalist political, dynastic, and religious institutions and structures until the French Revolution.[2]

The term Germany refers to the scholarly concept of a German nation, which arose in the fifteenth century to designate a community that shared the same language and culture. The term *natio Germanica* originally came out of the Council of Constance (1414–1418), in which participants were subdivided into five *nationes* (*Gallicana*, *Italica*, *Anglicana*, *Germanica*, and *Hispanica*), each representing a voting bloc.[3] The *natio Germanica* therefore designated one of the five nations in the Christian occident.[4] These *nationes* played a central role in the formation of national identities in the scholarly community.[5] It led to an occasionally fierce and moralizing competition among Humanists representing different

---

[1] Hirschi, *The Origins of Nationalism*, 10–13.
[2] Hirschi, *The Origins of Nationalism*, 3. For a comprehensive discussion of Humanist nationalism see Hirschi, *The Origins of Nationalism*, 119–179.
[3] Initially, there were only four nations. The Iberian representatives arrived in Constance two years late. They demanded the formation of a fifth *natio*, the *natio Hispanica*, which was approved (Hirschi, *The Origins of Nationalism*, 83). Ulrich Richental (*Das Konzil zu Konstanz*, 2,181) confirmed in c. 1430 that the Spaniards were late, but in his account their absence gave the English the opportunity do demand their own status as a nation.
[4] Hirschi, *The Origins of Nationalism*, 81–85; Knape, "Humanismus, Reformation," 113.
[5] Hirschi, *The Origins of Nationalism*, 82–88.

national and progressively vernacular traditions, which will be discussed in Chapter 20. The *natio* quickly became a politicized and contested concept as there were more aspirants to the status of *natio* than the five recognized ones. A further distinction was made between the *nationes principales*, referring to the official voting bodies, and *nationes particulares* that were defined by common ancestry, territory, or language. The number of *nationes particulares* varied; there may have been as many as thirty-six.[6]

Ulrich von Richental, the author of the *Chronicle of the Council of Constance* (c. 1430), defined Germany as the lands where German was spoken:

> Germany, these are German lands where German is spoken. The Holy Roman Empire, the Kingdom of Bohemia, the Kingdom of Hungary, the Kingdom of Poland, the Duchy of Lithuania in Russia [. . .]. Whatever Christians live there, they belong to the German nation.[7]

Richental included many areas where Slavic languages or Hungarian were spoken, which shows how aspirational the concept of nations developed at Constance really was, but also how the distinction between the two concepts of *nationes principales* and *nationes particulares* was not always maintained.

This notion of a German nation was supported by the simultaneous ascent of the German vernacular as a cultural and political language.[8] Ulrich von Hutten addressed his anti-papal tract of 1520 to the "fatherland of the German nation," which he defined through its common German language.[9] The terms Germany and German nation in the understanding of the time referred to a community where German was commonly spoken, and this is how these terms are used in this chapter.

In the second half of the fifteenth century, Tacitus, whose *De Germania* had been discovered in 1455, became a source of topoi that could be used to talk about the ancient Germans and in many ways anchored the anti-Romance rhetoric of many German Humanists.[10] A nationalistic misinterpretation of Tacitus served to create the generally accepted myth of the old

---

6 Hirschi, *The Origins of Nationalism*, 85.
7 Richental, *Das Konzil zu Konstanz*, 2,182: "Germani, das sind tütschi land und die da tütsch sprechend; das hailig Römsch Rich, das küngrich zu Beham, das küngrich von Ungern, das küngrich von Polan, die hertzogthům ze Littow in Russenlanden [. . .]. was darin cristen lüt sind, die gehorend zů der nacion Germanica."
8 Knape, "Humanismus, Reformation," 113–116.
9 Hutten, *Clag und vormanung*, title page: "dem vatterland Teütscher Nation zů nutz vnd gůt;" also sig. b2r: "Now I shout at the fatherland of the German nation in its own language." ("Yetzt schrey ich an das vatterland Teütsch nation in irer sprach.")
10 Hirschi, *Wettkampf der Nationen*, 326.

Germans leading a simple and virtuous life and promoted a cult of pure originality, territorial, ethnic, and moral.[11] In this view, their bravery and virtue earned them freedom and independence and prompted the transfer of the imperial crown to Germany under Charlemagne.

The German nation was vaguely associated with the empire and more frequently with the person of the emperor, but it did not correlate with established political practice nor align with imperialist, dynastic, and religious principles.[12] The term empire, by contrast, referred to the polity that was governed by the emperor and the Imperial Diet and was commonly referred to as Holy Roman Empire. Initially, the empire was not the focal point of patriotism as the terms *patria* and *imperium* were barely linked; rather, terms like *patria Germania* or *teutsch vatterland* were associated with the German nation.[13] The distinction between the empire and the German nation was increasingly blurred by the idea that the empire was German in character, leading to the official designation *Heiliges Römisches Reich Deutscher Nation* (Holy Roman Empire of the German Nation) at the Diet of Cologne in 1512.[14] This is evident in Ulrich von Hutten's definition of the Imperial Diet: "It is an assembly of the council of princes, and of the common German nation."[15] There are numerous examples of this terminological blending in the first half of the sixteenth century. Martin Schrot (d. 1576), for instance, used the terms "Deütschland," "Deütsch Nation," "heyligs Römisch Reich," and "Vatterland" interchangeably in his song about the "Present Unrest of the German Nation" published in 1546.[16]

Conrad Celtis was one of the most important disseminators of German nationalistic ideas. While Celtis wrote exclusively in Latin and always valued the learning of the ancient Greeks and Romans, he urged Germans to assert themselves against hegemonial aspirations of the contemporaneous Italian and French cultures. In his inaugural lecture at Ingolstadt University in 1492, known as "Oratio in Gymnasio in Ingelstadio Publiae Recitata" (Public Oration Delivered in the University of Ingolstadt), Celtis reminded Germans that they were the custodians of the Roman Empire and therefore should strive to live up to cultural norms worthy of that status:

---

[11] Hirschi, *The Origins of Nationalism*, 168–170; Hirschi, *Wettkampf der Nationen*, 320.
[12] Hirschi, *The Origins of Nationalism*, 3.
[13] Hirschi, *Wettkampf der Nationen*, 43.
[14] Knape, "Humanismus, Reformation," 116.
[15] Hutten, "Die Anschawenden," sig. t4r: "Es ist ein versamlung zům rat der Fürsten/ vnd gemeyner Teütschen nation."
[16] Schrot, *Vrsprung vnd vrsach*.

> Do away with that old disrepute of the Germans in Greek, Latin, and Hebrew writers, who ascribe to us drunkenness, cruelty, savagery, and every other vice bordering on bestiality and excess. Consider it a great disgrace to be ignorant of the histories of the Greeks and Latins, and the height of shame to know nothing about the topography, the climate, the rivers, the mountains, the antiquities, and the peoples of our region and our own country, in short all those facts which foreigners have so cleverly collected concerning us.[17]

Celtis internalized the Italian viewpoint that Germans were culturally inferior barbarians who were unable to build a civilized society.[18] In his view, Germans had to learn their own history and prioritize the study of their own nation. Celtis also used this self-deprecating argument as a tool to promote a German elite culture.[19]

At the same time Celtis called on Germans to return to the moral purity of the ancient Germans and to resist the temptation of corrupt foreign cultures:

> To such an extent are we corrupted by Italian sensuality and by fierce cruelty in exacting filthy lucre, that it would have been far more holy and reverend for us to practice that rude and rustic life of old, living within the bounds of self-control, than to have imported the paraphernalia of sensuality and greed which are never sated, and to have adopted foreign customs.[20]

Celtis thus set the tone for the next generation of German writers who were less subtle in their nationalistic messaging, and he signaled that national stereotyping was a two-way street. Celtis and his followers engaged in an increasingly fierce competition with other Humanists representing different national and increasingly vernacular traditions. Many expressed an awareness of a cultural deficit, yet expressed confidence that Germans were catching up with other nations and in some ways surpassed them.

The growing consensus in Germany at the time was that the more cultured neighbors to the west and to the south had gotten soft and degenerate. Hutten himself developed this argument in his dialogue *Die Anschawenden* (*The Observers*) from 1521. The conversation on the topic begins with the observation that the Italians considered not just the Germans to be barbarians, but also other Europeans, including the French.[21] Hutten then turned the argument around by claiming that it really was the Italians who were afflicted by barbarism:

---

17 Celtis, "Oratio in Gymnasio," 43. For a modern German edition see Müller, *Die 'Germania generalis.'*
18 Hirschi, *Wettkampf der Nationen*, 302–303.
19 Hirschi, *Wettkampf der Nationen*, 305.
20 Celtis, "Oratio in Gymnasio," 53.
21 Italian Humanists, with few exceptions, indeed painted non-Italians as barbarians. See Hirschi, *The Origins of Nationalism*, 152.

[Phaeton] The Germans thus are considered to be barbarians. [Sol] As Rome judges, no less than the French as well, and all other peoples outside of Italy. However, if one wants to see good morals and a respect for friendly association, also aspiration for virtue, consistency of disposition, and honesty, then this is a well-civilized nation; the Romans on the other hand are afflicted by utmost barbarism. For firstly, they are a people spoiled by softness and an effeminate life. Secondly, they are afflicted by a great fickleness and more than womanish inconstancy, little faith, fraud, and malice, with which they surpass all.[22]

While for the Italians, the Germans were unfit for civilization, Hutten turned the argument into a moralistic rejection of their effeminate and immoral life, excessive luxury, and lack of faith.[23] Then he compared German vices with those of the Italians:

Since ancient times, Germans have been drunkards and prone to gluttony. Furthermore, it has never been a disgrace with them to be drunk. [. . .] This affliction is inbred to them, as fraud is to Italians, thievery to Spaniards, pride and over-confidence to the French, and other deficits to others.[24]

Johannes Aventinus in his *Bayerische Chronik* (*Bavarian Chronicle*) told the wild story of German conquests in the ancient world. When the Goths, Bavarians, and other Germans conquered Athens, the Germans put the books of the Greeks on a pile with the intent of burning them. A German soldier advised against it with a curious explanation:

Leave the books to the fools, the Greeks. As they deal with them, they become nothing but women who are too inept for war and who are not allowed to defend themselves. It is better and to our advantage if they deal with books and quills than with armor and weapons.[25]

---

22 Hutten, "Die Anschawenden," sig. u2v: "[Phaeton] Seind dann Teütschen nach für barbarisch geacht. [Sol] Als Rom vrteylet/ nit weniger dann auch Frantzosen/ vnd allen ander völcker außwendig Jtalien. Wil man aber gůte sitten/ vnd achtung freüntlicher beywonung/ auch fleyß der tugent/ beständigkeit der gemüt vnd redlicheit ansehen/ so ist dises ein wol gesitte nation/ vnd dargegen die Römer mit der aller ausserlichsten barbarey verstallt. Dan erstlich seind sye von weychmütigkeit/ vnd weybischem leben verdorben leüt. Darnoch ist bey jnen grosse wanckelmütigkeit/ vnd mer dann weybische vnbeständigkeit/ wenig glaubens/ betrug/ vnd boßheit/ damit sye allen fürtreffen."
23 Hirschi, *The Origins of Nationalism*, 314–315.
24 Hutten, "Die Anschawenden," sig. y1v–y2r: "Es seind aber Teütschen von alter her trüncker/ vnd der fullery geflyssen. Jst auch bey jnn nye schand gewesen/ truncken sein. [. . .] Dißer gebrechen ist jnn angeboren/ als dem Jtalianer betrug/ Hispaniern dieberey/ Frantzosen stoltz vnd übermůt/ anderen andere mängel."
25 Aventinus, *Bayerische Chronik*, 2,239: "last den narren, den Kriechen, die püecher; weil sie damit umbgen, werden si lauter ungeschickt zu kriegen weiber daraus, die sich nit weren dörfen; ist besser und uns wägerer, si gen mit der schrift und feder dan mit dem harnisch und

In Aventinus's reading, books and erudition are enemies of a virile masculinity as displayed by the old Germans. In his twisted argument, the Germans allowed the Athenians to keep their books so they would not become hardened fighters like the Germans and instead would sink into effeminate decadence. His nationalistic rhetoric thus had a distinct anti-intellectual flavor, which served to turn German shortcomings in this realm into a strength.

Italians were commonly associated with the merchant culture that was increasingly gaining traction in Germany. The character of Italians therefore was associated with the attributes of greedy merchants, as Hutten spelled it out:

> At all times one sees the Italians as nasty, stingy, and greedy. They demand much, always seek profits, cheat, break promises, and practice craftiness. They conceal hatred and envy amongst each other, murder secretly, deliver poison, always think of fraud, and always surround themselves with unfaithfulness. None of them believes the other. They do nothing publicly or sincerely, and I believe that they have a pale complexion because of this.[26]

The dysfunction and dishonesty of the Italians is not just a moral question; rather it has a physiological dimension as well.

The anonymous author of the allegorical poem *Die welsch gattung* (*The Italian Kind*), which was published in Strasbourg in 1513, was one of the most polemical anti-Italian writers. The text identified the Italian wars as the greatest source of instability that also threatened the empire. Furthermore, he viewed Italy as the source for greed, usury, self-interest, and general moral decay. He repeatedly warned of the harmful Italian cultural influence, but also of commercial goods from Italy: "That is why, Germany, beware: do not get attached to the Italian goods."[27]

In general, the vices of the Germans appeared more benign than those of members of other nations. At the very least, Germans no longer had to be ashamed when compared with other nations. Many authors engaged in a comparable cultural critique and nationalistic competition. Aventinus, for instance,

---

wer umb." His *Bayerische Chronik*, while written c. 1526–1533, was first published in 1556. See Hirschi, *The Origins of Nationalism*, 173. Hirschi, *Wettkampf der Nationen*, 335.

26 Hutten, "Die Anschawenden," sig. u4v: "Dann die Jtalianer sycht man zů allen zeiten hässig/ karg vnd geytzig sein/ vil begeren/ nach gewinn stellen/ betryegen/ glauben brechen/ vnd hinderlist üben/ sich in haß vnd missgunst vntereinander selbs verdecken/ heymlich mörden/ gifft geben/ allweg nach betrug dencken/ vnd mit vntrew vmbgehen/ jrer keiner dem anderen glauben/ nichts öffentlich oder auffrichtlichen thůn/ vnd glaub dz sye darumb bleych von farben seint." Similarly also Murner, *Narrenbeschwörung*, 372, ch. 73, v. 55.

27 Anon., *Die Welsch-Gattung*, 179, v. 334–335: "Darumb, Teütschland, hab dich jn hůt, | Hab nit zů lieb yetz das welsch gůt."

berated the French in a similar way, contrasting the effeminate French courtly civilization with the manly German warrior culture.[28]

Ulrich von Hutten was perhaps the most intemperate nationalistic German writer of the period. He developed his nationalistic ideas in many of his texts, most prominently in his dialogue *Praedones* (*The Robbers*) from 1521, where his xenophobic tendencies became evident. Here, Hutten identified four types of robbers: street robbers, long-distance merchants, legal scholars, and members of the Catholic clergy. Ordinary street robbers did the least harm because they were aware of their transgressions and because the damage they inflicted merely was of a material nature.[29] The other three types of robbers, on the other hand, acted with a sense of entitlement and damaged the common good.[30] The merchants were depriving Germans of their virtue as well as financial resources by importing useless spices from abroad, as discussed in the following chapter. The legal scholars were seen as recent foreign arrivals who sought to disseminate the principles of Roman law in a country that had not known a written legal tradition.[31] The members of the clergy, finally, ensured the influence of the pope and sucked financial resources out of Germany to support the Roman Curia.[32]

Hutten's xenophobia in *Praedones* went beyond lashing out at foreign customs being copied and foreign imports being esteemed by Germans. Foreign influences were at the core of the moral decline Hutten saw in contemporaneous Germany. The old Germans did not know lies, dissimulation, infidelity, usury, deceit. Their virtues were sullied by foreigners who introduced vices into the German culture. "O alienage" (O peregrinatem), Hutten exclaimed wistfully in his *Praedones*.[33] His xenophobic argument was that the triad of merchants, lawyers, and clergy were contaminating his countrymen with undue foreign influences and hence were disrupting the German social and moral order. Members of these three groups were among the most mobile and well-educated segments of society, had occupations that transcended national boundaries, and had most in common with Renaissance Humanists.[34] Merchants and jurists were members of a new elite that threatened the traditional social order by establishing foreign practices in Germany. The clergy, under the influence of the Curia,

---

28 Aventinus, *Bayerische Chronik*, 1,118.
29 Hutten, *Praedones*, fol. 21v.
30 Hutten, *Praedones*, fol. 21v.
31 Simon (*Gute Policey*, 173–174) documents the resistance to the rise of written law in the early sixteenth century, often referred to as *Gute Policey*.
32 Hirschi, *The Origins of Nationalism*, 168.
33 Hutten, *Praedones*, fol. 23r.
34 Hirschi, *The Origins of Nationalism*, 178.

redoubled its efforts to drain Germany of crucial financial resources. Hostility to these groups thus formed the core of a nationalist program that prominently featured the opposition to the importation of foreign goods, particularly herbs and spices.

It was assumed in the early sixteenth century that Germans had lived according to natural law throughout their history and that it provided the foundation for the justice system before the late fifteenth century. Natural law was thought to be close to divine law; Martin Luther saw them as identical. In his view, natural law was instilled by God in all humans, enabling them to make a distinction between right and wrong.[35] The rise of the written Roman law thus gave rise to a range of issues for the administration of justice: "uniform law versus diversity of customs, central versus distributed power, authority versus freedoms."[36] Any kind of new positive law meant a curtailment of local practices and therefore was met with reservation and even hostility. Literary texts from that time are full of anti-lawyer polemics.

One of the most prominent critics of the rise of positive law was Sebastian Brant, who ironically was a lawyer himself.[37] In chapter 71, entitled "Zancken vnd zu gericht gon" (Quarrelling and Going to Court), Brant described a legal system where legal maneuvers delayed and obscured justice to the point where the fees for foreign lawyers exceeded the value of the matter at hand and deceived the judges with their hollow talk: "One has to hire expensive jurists and bring them here from countries far away, so that they can whitewash the issues and deceive the judges with their babble."[38] Under natural law, common sense prevailed, while the new system of written law required the assistance of a lawyer in order to entangle the judge in a web of verbal deception. While legal disputes could formerly be resolved locally, learned foreign lawyers who were skilled at understanding and manipulating the new legal standards were now required. In chapter 79, Brant similarly reinforced the idea that lawyers were only motivated by their own gain while justice was not served and the legal system as a whole suffered. We have to keep in mind that the thrust in his *Narrenschiff* was a general critique of

---

35 Strauss, *Law, Resistance and the State*, 211.
36 Strauss, *Law, Resistance and the State*, 240.
37 As discussed in Chapter 2, Brant edited a number of legal texts. There, he conceded pragmatically that canon law and secular law were necessary to regulate an increasingly complex society. The *Narrenschiff*, by contrast, was a vessel that allowed Brant to send a more populist message and to apply a more fundamental critique of a world gone awry.
38 Brant, *Narrenschiff*, ch. 71, v. 21–24: "Man mŭß yetz köstlich redner dyngen | Vnd sie von verren landen bringen | Das sie die sachen wol verklügen | Vnd mit geschwätz/ eyn richter betrügen." Geiler von Kaysersberg argues in a similar way in his sermons on Brants *Narrenschiff* (*Des hochwirdigen doctor Keiserspergs narenschiff*, fol. 141v).

culture and society and of all its stakeholders and participants. This did not preclude a more pragmatic approach to the function of written law in his legal writings, as discussed in Chapter 2.

Martin Luther believed in settling legal disputes according to local customs and held a rigid legislative regime to be a sign of bad governance.[39] This informed his antipathy against Roman law and more generally against lawyers:

> Secular law – God help us – has become a wilderness. [. . .] It seems just to me that territorial laws and customs should take precedence over general imperial laws, and that the imperial laws be used only in case of necessity. Would God that every land were ruled by its own brief laws suitable to its gifts and peculiar character. This is how these lands were ruled before these imperial laws were designed, and as many lands are still ruled without them! Rambling and farfetched laws are only a burden to the people, and they hinder cases more than they help them.[40]

There were two aspects to this argument. The first was a federalist argument that lower levels of government were more efficient at regulating local affairs and that centralization therefore did not serve the people. The second was that written imperial law was based on Roman law, which was of foreign origin and too closely intertwined with the Catholic Church and therefore was an alien force ill-suited to regulating German affairs.

Simon Grunau (c.1470–c.1530) told a story to illustrate the advantages of a localized justice system in his *Preussische Chronik* (*Prussian Chronicle*), written in the 1520s. A son shows his law books to his father and explains the difference between what is printed in big black letters and in small red letters. The former is "the text of law and the truth according to justice" and the latter "the words of law in which one can find deceit."[41] In his critique of the new written law, Grunau made a distinction between the law that was based in justice and legal verbiage that was designed to obfuscate and manipulate the law. In a comical twist, the father takes his scissors and cuts out all the small, red texts from the book, thus symbolically restoring justice based in local customs while cutting away the alien language associated with imperial law.

Johann Eberlin von Günzburg in his influential *Fünfzehn Bundesgenossen* (*Fifteen Confederates*) from 1521 took a similar position. In the eleventh pamphlet,

---

39 Simon, *Gute Policey*, 173–174. This is discussed in more detail in Chapter 2.
40 Luther, *To the Christian Nobility*, 451–452.
41 Grunau, *Preussische Chronik*, 2,318–319: "der text des rechtens unnd die warheit nach der gerechtigkeit;" "die wortter des rechtenns, auff wolche man kan ein bescheisserey finden." The *Prussian Chronicle* was printed for the first time in 1875–1889. It is considered the first chronicle of Prussia, but a number of segments, like the one discussed here, are works of fiction.

one of the two where Eberlin designed the utopian state of Wolfaria, he described its legal structure. Just like in Thomas More's *Utopia* (1516), there were no lawyers in Wolfaria.[42] Rather, Eberlin demanded the abolition of imperial law and of canon law: "We reject all imperial and priestly law."[43] Instead, Eberlin insisted that citizens should know common customs and traditional law: "Everybody should know common law, and everybody should know what is fair and what is unjust."[44]

Hutten tied his opposition to lawyers in general and to the practice of Roman law in particular to nationalistic and xenophobic reflexes common in his writings. In the dialogue *Praedones*, he concluded the discussion of the "robbing lawyers" with this invective:

> [Hutten.] And should we continue to tolerate such people in our midst? Let us instead emulate our forefathers, those brave warriors, having won their great victory over the Romans and restored liberty to their country, struck at all enemies without distinction but saved their most violent vengeance for Roman advocates. Whenever one of these ranters fell into their hands, they cut out his tongue, sewed up his lips, and said to him: "Now, viper, will you cease hissing?"[45]

Hutten's reminiscence of the heroism of his freedom-loving "forefathers" is typical of the nostalgia expressed by writers who scorned the rise of standardized legal codes at the territorial or imperial level, which were frequently framed as an unwanted foreign import. Hutten frequently reminded his readers to fight for their freedoms that were lost to the Romanists and to other foreign powers.

The term *freedom* in this context did not refer to individual conceptions of freedom discussed by Erasmus. Rather, it was reduced to the idea of outward freedom in the sense of German liberty (*libertas Germanorum*), that is the German independence from, and indeed supremacy over, other European nations, but also the liberation from foreign influences, like Roman law.[46] It was not just a political term, but also included the autarky of the German nation in culture and society.[47] Most frequently, the Roman Curia and the French kingdom were seen by German nationalists as the most serious adversaries of German freedom. Carolingian and Ottonian kings often served as models, but

---

[42] Strauss, *Law, Resistance and the State*, 21–23.
[43] Eberlin von Günzburg, *Ein newe ordnung*, fol. 4r: "Alle kayserliche vnd pfaffen recht thůnd wir ab."
[44] Eberlin von Günzburg, *Ein newe ordnung*, fol. 4r: "Jetlicher soll gemeine recht wissen/ vnd dz jetlicher wiß sin billichs vnd vnbillichs."
[45] Hutten, *Praedones*, fol. 29v. Translation Strauss, *Manifestations of Discontent*, 207.
[46] Hirschi, *The Origins of Nationalism*, 170.
[47] Hirschi, *Wettkampf der Nationen*, 320.

German Humanists also relied on other sources, including ancient Germanic tribes, to sustain their historical narrative of a willfully chosen and fiercely defended national independence.[48] Aventinus held Arminius, the chieftain of the Germanic Cherusci tribe, to be the leader who led his German people to independence from other nations.[49] As this freedom had to be fought for militarily, the notion of German freedom was often accompanied by the reference to Germans as a brave warrior nation. Writers like Hutten saw German freedom as perennially under threat. Hutten welcomed the new Emperor Charles V as "resurrector of German freedom" who would liberate Germany from Roman oppression and contain the influence of the French king.[50]

Many writers used nostalgic references to natural law to oppose the rising prominence of the written Roman law in Germany. The anonymous author of the rhymed pamphlet *Die welsch gattung* (*The Italian Kind*) from 1513 alleged that the Italians lacked natural law and argued that written Roman law was used to pervert natural law in Germany.[51] Some, like Hutten, blamed undue foreign influence for the demise of the native legal foundation and political structures, while others argued that self-interest, which in itself was on the rise due to inappropriate foreign influence, erased this idyllic state of things.[52]

The polemics against the Roman Church and its clergy predated Martin Luther but gained additional bitterness during the early years of the Reformation. Martin Luther himself developed a bleak view of the state of the Christian Occident, which he saw in the clutches of a manipulative and corrupt Roman Church: "All the estates of Christendom, particularly in Germany, are now oppressed by distress and affliction."[53] The Donation of Constantine (*Constitutum Constantini*), which was recognized as a forgery by Lorenzo Valla in 1440, played an important part in the anti-Roman propaganda. Ulrich von Hutten published Valla's text probably in 1518 as *De donatione Constantini*, complete with a sarcastic preface to Pope Leo X.[54] Luther used it as a weapon in his polemics against the papacy; he "saw the forgery as proof that the pope was Antichrist."[55] He referred to the text published by Hutten in his letter to Georg Spalatin in February 1520:

---

48 Hirschi, *The Origins of Nationalism*, 171.
49 Aventinus, *Bayerische Chronik*, 1,109.
50 Hutten, "Vadiscum," sig. k4v: "widerbringer der teütschen freyheit." See also Hirschi, "Konzepte von Fortschritt," 52.
51 Anon., *Die Welsch-Gattung*, 228, v. 2161–2167; see also Egenolff, *Chronic* (1533), fol. 86r.
52 Examples: Egenolff, *Chronic* (1533), fol. 86r–86v (discussed in Chapter 1); Münster, *Cosmographia* (1544), sig. a3v–a4r.
53 Luther, *To the German Nobility*, 378.
54 Setz, *Lorenzo Vallas Schrift*, 151–155.
55 Watts, "The Donation of Constantine," S94.

> I have at hand Lorenzo Valla's proof [. . .] that the Donation of Constantine is a forgery. Good heavens! What darkness and wickedness is at Rome! You wonder at the judgment of God that such unauthentic, crass, impudent lies not only lived but prevailed for so many centuries, that they were incorporated in the Canon Law, and [. . .] that they became as articles of faith.[56]

Later that year, Luther in *To the Christian Nobility of the German Nation* expressed his disbelief that so many learned people could believe such crude and clumsy lies and be manipulated by them.[57]

However, it is important not to frame anti-papal polemics as a strictly confessional issue. Pressure from Charles V to issue an edict against Martin Luther at the Diet of Worms in 1521 triggered a strong reaction by the Estates. In 102 articles, presented in four sets and resembling Luther's grievances, they chronicled the misdeeds of the Church at all levels.[58] An important argument was that the Church introduced its own corrupt values to a pristine German culture, just as the merchants did. Aventinus pointed out that the old Germans built neither churches nor altars, nor did they support priests as this was not part of their pristine culture.[59] To Johann Eberlin von Günzburg, the foreign origin of the Church was the key reason why it was beyond redemption:

> The courtiers and the mendicant friars bring all falsehood, stigmas, infidelity, and craftiness from foreign lands, particularly from Italy and Rome. In this way, loyalty and faith are broken, and henceforth one brother cannot trust the others anymore, in contrast to the traditional honesty of the German nation.[60]

Sellers of indulgences were condemned not just for their greed but also because they preached a false theology and taught reprehensible morals. Hutten bemoaned that members of the clergy were modeling an unworthy life for the common people and thus had a corrupting influence on them.[61]

---

[56] Translation Smith, *The Life and Letters*, 73. The original letter in Latin is in Luther, WA Br 2, Nr. 255, 42–45.
[57] Luther, *To the Christian Nobility*, 416.
[58] *Deutsche Reichstagsakten, Jüngere Reihe*, vol. 2, 670–704.
[59] Aventinus, *Chronica*, sig. H3r.
[60] Eberlin von Günzburg, *EJn klägliche klag*, sig. ++1r: "Die Curtisan vnd båttel münch bringen auß fremden landen/ besunder vß Jtalia vnd Rom allen falsch/ vssatz/ vntrew/ hinderlist/ do durch trew vnd gloub gebrochen wirt/ vnd schier ein brůder den anderen nit truwen darff/ wider alte redlichkeit teütscher nation."
[61] Hutten, *Von der wunderbarlichen artzney*, fol. H2v. Chapter 19 (sig. H1r–H4r) does not deal with syphilis and possible cures at all. Instead, it summarizes Hutten's general critique of contemporaneous German civilization.

More common were the complaints about the financial harm the Church inflicted on Germany and about its undue political influence. As Emperor Charles V pursued a quick condemnation of Martin Luther's teachings in early 1521, the imperial estates pushed back. They sent a document to the emperor entitled, "Articles How His Holiness the Pope Burdens the German Lands."[62] Here, the estates presented the full range of complaints raised at the time, from violations of the imperial constitution by the Church to the pope's plot to stoke the Turkish fear in order to suck funds out of the Germany with the empty promise of going to war against the Turks.

It was commonplace in Reformation-era literature to detail how the pope and the Roman Curia sucked money out of Germany in the form of indulgences, annates, pensions, and other rackets.[63] The Curia spent excessive amounts of money on a lavish lifestyle and on massive construction projects, like St. Peter's Basilica in Rome, at the expense of Germans: "they collect daily from Germans our sweat and blood."[64] Hutten's reference to German "sweat and blood" was part of a populist rhetoric designed to evoke an emotionally laden, nationalistic response. Martin Luther noted, "Now that Italy is sucked dry, the Romanists are coming into Germany."[65] Luther demanded that German princes resist, as the French king had done: "How is it that we Germans must put up with such robbery and extortion of our goods at the hands of the pope? If the kingdom of France has prevented it, why do we Germans let them make such fools and apes of us?"[66]

Hutten wrote a number of tracts where he chastised the undue influence of the Roman Church whose greed and moral depravity he scorned. Hutten viewed the Catholic Church as a foreign power which, in his nationalist rhetoric, victimized Germany and the Germans. In his 1519 pamphlet, *Drey ding findt man tzu Rhom wye das buchleyn Czeygeth an* (*Three Things that one Finds in Rome, as this Booklet Indicates*), he lampooned Trinitarian thinking by bundling Roman vices as well as absent virtues in groups of three:

> Three things keep Rome in dignity; holiness, pope, and indulgence.
> Three are treasured in Rome; women, horses, and documents.
> Three are easy to get in Rome; fever, pestilence, and poor people.

---

[62] *Deutsche Reichstagsakten, Jüngere Reihe*, vol. 2, 670–704: "Articul damit bäpstliche Heiligkait Teutsche land beschwärt."
[63] Hutten, "Vadiscum," sig. g4r.
[64] Hutten, *Clag vnd vormanung*, sig. c2v: "vnd nemen täglich ein von Teütschen/ vnser schweyß vnd blůt."
[65] Luther, *To the German Nobility*, 394.
[66] Luther, *To the German Nobility*, 395.

> Three one usually brings from Rome; bad conscience, spoiled stomach, empty wallet.
> Three are still soliciting in Rome; lots of money, many rules, many lies.[67]

Life at the Roman Curia was defined by palatial dwellings, extravagant food, carnal pleasures, gambling, deception, corruption, and graft. While *Drey ding* appeared in Leipzig in 1519, Hutten in the same year published the same text, with minor changes, as *Trias Romana*, this time in Mainz, the most important episcopal see north of the Alps. Hutten continuously recycled his material, and he fearlessly published his anti-Romanist and anti-clerical texts in the power centers of the Church.

Martin Luther followed suit with his own description of Rome as a depraved city under the corrupt leadership of the pope:

> The pope's arbitrary and deceptive reservation now creates such a state of affairs in Rome that it defies description. There is buying, selling, bartering, exchanging, trading, pretense, deceit, robbery, theft, luxury, whoring, knavery, and every sort of contempt of God. Even the rule of the Antichrist could not be more scandalous. Venice, Antwerp, and Cairo have nothing on this fair at Rome and all that goes on there.[68]

Luther likened Rome to the largest merchant and port cities that were generally seen as cesspools of sin.

The same anti-clerical rhetoric dominated Hutten's *Clag vnd vormanung gegen dem übermässigen vnchristlichen gewalt des Bapsts zů Rom/ vnd der vngeistlichen geistlichen* (*Lament and Warning Against the Excessive, Un-Christian Power of the Pope in Rome, and of the Irreligious Clerics*) from 1520. In his view, the pope was a heretic[69] who promoted false interpretations of Scripture that served his purposes.[70] In the subtitle, he declared his nationalist agenda, "for the use and benefit of the fatherland of the German nation."[71] In eloquent German verse, he bemoaned the outsize influence of the clerics in worldly affairs, much to the

---

67 Hutten, *Drey ding*, sig. a2r: "Drey Halten Rhom in wirden/ heyltumb/ Papst/ vnnd ablaß. | Drey Seyn kostlich gehalten tzy rhom frawen/ roß vnd bryeue. | Drey Seyndt wolfeyl zu Rhom/ fyber/ pestilentz/ vnnd arme leuthe. | Drey Bringt man gewonlich von Rhom/ böße gewysßen/ bößen magen/ leren seckel. | Drey Seyn noch tzu rhom solicitanti/ vyll geldes/ vyll vorschrifft/ vyl lügen."
68 Luther, *To the German Nobility*, 404.
69 Hutten, *Clag vnd vormanung*, sig. f4v.
70 Hutten, *Clag vnd vormanung*, sig. f1v. Luther (*To the Christian Nobility*, 392–393) made similar claims.
71 Hutten, *Clag vnd vormanung*, title page: "dem vatterland Teütscher Nation zů nutz vnd gůt."

detriment of the world. He added this commentary in the margins: "Such useless people and womanish individuals govern kings and princes today."[72]

Hutten addressed Elector Frederick of Saxony in a less polemical yet eminently political text, *Clag/ an Hertzog Friderich zů Sachsen* (*Grievance to Duke Frederick of Saxony*), written in 1520 but published in 1521. At the onset, he expressed great concern that the Roman Church was using sweet talk to lure Martin Luther to Rome "where he no doubt would be martyred."[73] He described the Roman Church as a "many-horned wild animal"[74] that was a burden to Christianity, led the war against truth, oppressed the pious and holy people, led the free to prison, deprived Germans of their goods and wealth, and "devoured the morals of the entire Christianity and spoiled it through its evil model and example."[75]

Hutten then turned to Frederick for help to fend off the influence of the Church and to protect German freedoms: "How dishonest, how disgraceful and crooked it is that the nation that is a queen of all nations should be subservient to anyone (let alone to idle clerics)."[76] Hutten reminded the Elector that the leadership of the German Empire over the Christian occident meant that Germans had to reject all attempts by the Church to interfere in German matters. Given the aggressive behavior by the Roman Curia, he urged Germans to "courageously abolish and cancel out the tyrannical papal regime."[77] Hutten followed up with an unusually detailed list of corrupt and wasteful practices with which German wealth was squandered.

The solution Hutten presented to Elector Frederick was unusually upbeat, given Hutten's generally bleak outlook. If the German estates ceased all payments to the Church, rejected its power grabs and ejected all corrupt clergy, a new era would arise in which Christian love ruled, the true Christian Church would be restored, and the German fatherland would rise. Like Sebastian Brant, Hutten did not promote a new political vision. Rather, he pushed for the restoration of an order he believed to have existed under the Carolingian and

---

72 Hutten, *Clag vnd vormanung*, sig. e4v: "Sölch vnnütz volck vnd weibisch leüt regieren Künig/ Fürsten heüt. His commentary in the margins specifies that he talks about "the tender and effeminate clerics" ("Die zarten vnd weibischen pfaffen.")
73 Hutten, *Clag/ an Hertzog Friderich*, sig. a2r: "da er vngezweyfelt gemartert würd."
74 Hutten, *Clag/ an Hertzog Friderich*, sig. a3v: "vilhörnig wild thier."
75 Hutten, *Clag/ an Hertzog Friderich*, sig. a3v: "hab verschlindt/ der gantzen Christenhait sitten durch sein böß exempel vnd vorbild verderbt."
76 Hutten, *Clag/ an Hertzog Friderich*, sig. a3v: "Wie vneerlich aber wie schentlich vnd vnredlich ist es/ das die Nation die da ist ain künigin aller Nation yemants (vil weniger den müssigen pfaffen) dienstbar sein sol."
77 Hutten, *Clag/ an Hertzog Friderich*, sig. b1r: "laßt vns kůnlich das bepstisch tyrannische regiment auffheben vnd abthůn."

Ottonian kings. Hutten's nationalistic project thus was anchored in a nostalgic vision of a better German past that needed to be recovered.

The illegitimate power the pope claimed over worldly affairs in the empire was a recurring theme in Hutten's writing. In his view, the pope sought to become "ruler of the world" and alleged that "nobody lives freely under his rule."[78] The pope accumulated his wealth at the expense of other Christians: "Many pious Christians have to die so that he can accumulate his wealth."[79] Members of the clergy bought political positions, both within the Church and in the secular realm, with the help of loans from the Fugger Company.[80] For the Fuggers, these were regular financial transactions, like trading merchandise or monopolizing the market.[81] The pope was overturning "the Christian order"[82] by usurping the emperor's power: "For isn't it a great humiliation, an insult, an improper affair, that the one who should be governing the world must fall to the pope's feet and has to kiss them with his mouth."[83] To Hutten, the emperor was the rightful leader of the Christian Occident who was supposed to guarantee German primacy over the other Christian nations, including Italy. Hutten pointed to the irony that Jesus kissed the feet of common people, but that the pope as his successor instead insisted on his own feet being kissed in his quest for global dominance. The list of the pope's infractions was long, and his behavior toward Germany prompted Hutten to call the pope a tyrant.[84] He repeatedly called on Germans to free themselves of the influence of the Roman Church, and he pleaded with Emperor Charles V, the "the restorer of German freedom,"[85] to lead this campaign.

A number of Lutheran pamphlets and broadsheets took up this viewpoint. An example is Martin Schrot's *Vrsprung vnd vrsach Gegenwertiger Vffrůr/ Teütscher Nation* (*Origin and Cause of the Present Unrest of the German Nation*), a song in 27 stanzas published as a pamphlet in Wittenberg in 1546 in the context of the Schmalkaldic War. Schrot implicated the pope, the Roman court, and Italians in general in a massive plot to suck financial resources out of

---

78 Hutten, *Clag vnd vormanung*, sig. a3r: "der welt regierer;" "vnder im leb niemant frey."
79 Hutten, *Clag vnd vormanung*, sig. a3v: "Vnd das er richtumb mög erwerben/ můß mancher frummer Christen sterben."
80 Hutten, *Clag vnd vormanung*, sig. d2r; also Hutten, "Vadiscum," sig. h1v.
81 Hutten, "Vadiscum," fol. 11r.
82 Hutten, *Clag vnd vormanung*, sig. b3v: "die Christlich ordenung."
83 Hutten, *Clag vnd vormanung*, sig. c4r: "Dann ist es nit ein grosse schmach/ | ein hochfart/ vnd vnförmlich sach/ | das der sol herschen in der welt | dem Bapst zů seinen fůßen felt/ | vnd můsß die küssen mit dem mund." Also Hutten, "Vadiscum," sig. k4v.
84 Hutten, *Clag vnd vormanung*, sig. f3r.
85 Hutten, "Vadiscum," sig. k4v: "widerbringer der teütschen freyheit."

Germany: "Indulgences you pursued, and you defrauded the entire world for sure. You cheated Germany out of huge amounts of money. Do you have no mercy now?"[86] At the core of the song, Schrot told the fable of 400 sheep in the stable of a butcher who gradually slaughtered all of them. But he only took a few sheep at the time while making empty promises of safety to the others who blindly trusted the butcher. He used his fable to call on the German estates not to trust the pope and the Italians and to unite against this foreign threat.

Schrot alluded to the most vexing problem, namely the pope's uncanny ability to suck financial resources out of Germany. Around 1510, the so-called Upper-Rhenish Revolutionary bemoaned the transfer of funds from Germany to Italy that was set up by the clergy: "Particularly the Italians extracted the money of the Germans through the priests."[87] Hutten concurred, addressing the Roman clergy in this passage:

> For so long, you have been carrying lots of money and goods out of the German land. In return, you brought here the shame of all vices, which to recount here does not befit me. Through you, the pope takes away from here that which we need and which is ours, through duplicity and evil guile.[88]

While this argument predated the Reformation, Luther and his disciples made it a staple of their anti-Romanist polemic.

In Hutten's view, annates, pensions, indulgences, and other rackets institutionalized by the Roman Church hurt the financial interests of the German nation.[89] Hutten accused the members of the Roman Curia of spending excessive amounts of money on a lavish lifestyle and on massive construction projects, like the St. Peter's Basilica in Rome, and to force Germans to pay for them. Local priests set a poor example by living in luxury as Hutten noted sarcastically: "Whoever wants to live comfortably should become a priest, as if it was appropriate for them to live that way."[90]

---

86 Schrot, *Vrsprung vnd vrsach*, sig. A2v: "Des Ablos hastu dich geflissen/ | Betrogen die gantz welt gar schier. | Deütschland vmb groß gelt beschissen/ | Jst jetz kein gnad bey dir."
87 Anon., *Der Oberrheinische Revolutionär*, 430: "Sunder die walen hand der tutschen gelt durch die priesterschafft ansich bracht." The anti-French and anti-Romanist polemic in this text is quite radical. See Knape, "Humanismus, Reformation," 115.
88 Hutten, *Clag vnd vormanung*, sig. e3v: "ir habt so lang getragen hin | vil gelt vnd gůt auß Teütschem land/ | her wider bracht all laster schand/ | die zůerzelen mir nit zimpt. | Durch eüch der bapst von hynnen nimpt | das wir bedörffen/ vnser ist/ | durch falscherey/ vnd bößen list."
89 Hutten, "Vadiscum," sig. g4r.
90 Hutten, *Von der wunderbarlichen artzney*, sig. H3r: "wer wol wil leben der sol ein pfaff werden/ als ob es inen gebürt der massen zů leben."

The looming conflict with the Turks played into this discussion as well. Italian Humanists in the fifteenth century held that the military deliverance of Christianity against the Turks was a task that fell to the Germans.[91] While Germans did not doubt the seriousness of the Turkish threat, many like Hutten also believed that the Roman Church used lies and deceptions to get at German money. One such ruse was to hype the Turkish threat to evoke fear among Germans:

> And this is a great skill of theirs that they have extracted money from us on many occasions in the name of the Turkish war. This war (you should truly believe) was begun with the general consent of all Christians, but these doubters and instigators are the only reason why it is not progressing. For it is useful to them that the Turks remain here for many serious reasons, but most importantly because it gives them a pretext to demand money from the Germans. For they do not solicit any money from the Italians, and rarely from other nations. Only the Germans seem opportune to them, whom they have been duping for so long and in so many ways.[92]

The pope and his clergy weren't just robbing the Germans of their money, they were also hindering the progress of the war against the Turks in order to perpetuate the pretext for asking Germans for more money. Elsewhere, Hutten alleged that the pope had no intention of actually going to war against the Turks at all.[93] Similarly, Luther counted the papal request for funding to fight the Turks among the "Romanist schemes" and noted that "the German Nation" was in a better situation to wage such a war.[94] Of importance in this context is that Hutten's and Luther's pushback against the financial drain at the hands of Italians followed a distinctly nationalistic rhetoric.

In later writings, Hutten's polemics against the pope and the Roman Church took on an increasingly confessional tone. In his short pamphlet *Eyn klag vber den Luterischen Brandt zu Mentz* (*A Complaint about the Lutheran Burning in Mainz*), published in Wittenberg probably in 1521, he bemoaned the public burning of

---

91 Hirschi, *Wettkampf der Nationen*, 301.
92 Hutten, "Vadiscum," sig. q1v: "Vnd ist dißes ein grosse geschicklicheit von jnen/ als sye auch im namen des Türckischen kryegs/ nun zům offtern mol gelt von vns gefürt/ welicher krieg doch (soltu fürwar glauben) wo yetzo auß gemeyner verwilligung aller Christen angefangen/ wurden allein diße vermaner vnd anrichter/ vff das er nit fürgangk behielt/ ein ursach sein. Dann jnn ist nutz/ das Türcken sein vnd bleiben auß vilen vnd dapferen vrsachen/ aber am fürnämlichsten auß der/ vff das sye von Teütschen gelt fordern mögen. Dann von Jtalianern heyschen sie keyns/ auch selten von andern nation. Allein Teütschen beduncken sye jn eben sein/ die sye so lang/ vnd in so manicherley gestalt äffen."
93 Hutten, "Die Anschawenden," sig. u2r.
94 Luther, *To the German Nobility*, 398.

Luther's books in Mainz on 29 November 1520[95]: "Here the writings of the pious Luther are burning. Because they concern your laws, and because they are the pure truth, as it gushed out of your mouth."[96] Hutten represented Luther as the person who spoke the divine truth. Yet, Hutten's argument was not theological in nature. Rather, he appropriated Luther for his nationalistic polemic and instrumentalized him for his project to emancipate Germany from the political influence of the Roman Church and to interrupt the flow of German financial resources to Rome. In the dialogue *Praedones* (*The Robbers*), Hutten had Franz von Sickingen proclaim that Hutten and Luther were awakening the German nation and helping it emancipate from Romanist influence.[97]

Both the relentless polemics by writers like Hutten and the success of Luther's early writings, which raised many of the same points, convinced many members of the imperial estates to bring their concerns about the financial burdens and abuses imposed on Germany by the Roman Church to the Imperial Diet held in Worms in 1521. They submitted a document to the emperor with a total of 102 articles.[98] No action was taken at Worms, and the Estates submitted a revised document at the Diet of Nuremberg in 1523.[99] However, the Latin version of the document was not prepared in time, and the papal nuncio left the Diet without it.[100]

---

95 There was a similar book burning in Cologne on 12 November 1520.
96 Hutten, *Eyn klag vber den Luterischen Brandt*, [1]: "Hie brendt des frummen Luthers gschrifft/ | Drumb das sie deyn gesetz betrifft. | Vnd das es ist die warheyt bloß/ | Wie die auß deynem mundt erschoß."
97 Hutten, *Praedones*, fol. 37r.
98 *Deutsche Reichstagsakten, Jüngere Reihe*, vol. 2, 670–704. A partial translation into English can be found in Strauss, *Manifestations of Discontent*, 52–63.
99 *Deutsche Reichstagsakten, Jüngere Reihe*, vol. 3, 645–688.
100 *Deutsche Reichstagsakten, Jüngere Reihe*, vol. 3, 645.

Chapter 21
The Global Spice Trade: Breaching Traditional Values and Violating the Divine Order

The newly developed German cultural nationalism, the growing readiness to challenge traditional, classical ideas and intellectual traditions, as well misgivings about growing global trade networks led to a critical examination of the booming Asian spice trade in Germany. Many physicians and herbalists questioned the book knowledge about food, spices, and medicinal herbs; rejected imported edibles for reasons to be examined here; and thus spawned something of a food-based nationalism. Herbalists and physicians researched locally grown German herbs and foods and collected the information in herbals and other books about food, diet, and medicine. The discussion surrounding food and its consumption also connected to traditional debates surrounding luxury and gluttony.

Traditionally, the deadly sin of gluttony most commonly referred to excessive drinking and eating. This notion of gluttony still dominated Sebastian Brant's *Narrenschiff* (1494); Brant dedicated Chapter 16 to this topic. Gluttony was a particularly serious sin because it also led to other deadly sins like sloth, lust, and wrath. Furthermore, it was associated with a number of health problems and with premature death. For Ulrich von Hutten, gluttony, and particularly excessive drinking, was part of the German national character: "Since ancient times, Germans have been drunkards and prone to gluttony. Furthermore, it has never been a disgrace with them to be drunk."[1] Martin Luther held excessive drinking to be the devil of the Germans, just as the Italians and French were haunted by their own demons.[2] Not only were Germans drunks, but they also did not see a problem with that and even bragged about their excesses. Hutten demanded "that we as masters of this world should not live so shamefully."[3] Excessive drinking posed a threat to the German leadership in the Christian Occident. Hutten conceded that others, like the Poles, drank heavily as well but that this was inconsequential. The Germans, on the other hand, had respect and ultimately an empire to lose: "We are not concerned that one day we may lose our empire with our drunken ways. I remain silent about the fact that we subjugated

---

1 Hutten, "Die Anschawenden," sig. y1v: "Es seind aber Teütschen von alter her trüncker/ vnd der fullery geflyssen. Jst auch bey jnn nye schand gewesen/ truncken sein."
2 Luther, "Auslegung des 101. Psalms" (1534), WA, 51, 257,5–10.
3 Hutten, *von der wunderbarlichen artzney*, sig. H1r: "dz wir als heren diser welt nit also schentlich solten leben."

foreign peoples, as the sober and reasonable people are ashamed to be governed by such a drunk people."[4]

However, in the writings of the early sixteenth century another aspect of gluttony came into focus, namely the undue enjoyment of food and the desire to consume fine, delicate, and unusual foods. Invariably, these finer foods were not grown in Germany but rather were imported. In the early sixteenth century, gluttony became increasingly linked to the import of spices and other foodstuffs from foreign lands, in particular from Asia. Lusting after imported delicacies thus was a component of the sin of gluttony. Ulrich von Hutten tied the growing preference for fine foods to the luxury debate and blamed imported foodstuffs for the decay of traditional moral values and a spreading disregard for the common good. Desiring delicate imported foods also fell into the category of *luxuria*, that is the sin of lustful craving for sexuality, for money and material goods, or for power. Sebastian Brant defined lust (*wollust*) not just in sexual terms but more broadly as vain earthly pleasure, as a "fleeting delight."[5]

Inversely, Hieronymus Bock praised the old Germans for their simple and wholesome culinary desires:

> The common man in the German land in former times did not value precious courses of food. They were satisfied with cabbage, vegetables, all kinds of beets, roots, and fruit, namely what the vegetable garden, the field, and the orchard yielded seasonally, and with that the common Germans throughout the ages were very content.[6]

Their diet of exclusively locally grown foods mirrored their simple and morally pure lifestyle.

Likewise, Hutten linked the desire for simple, domestically grown foods with moral purity, praising the bygone virtues of his own grandfather Lorenz von Hutten (1411–1498):

> I praise my grandfather because he never allowed fine spices [specery] to enter his house. And he wore more simple clothes than appropriate [for his status] even though many

---

[4] Hutten, *von der wunderbarlichen artzney*, sig. H1v: "Wir besorgen auch nit das wir mitt solchen trunckenen weisen ein mal vnser reich verlieren werden/ ich schweig das wir vns frembde völcker vnderthenig mechten/ den die niechtern vnd vernünfftigen leut schament sich von einem so trunckenen volck geregiert zů werden."

[5] Brant, *Narrenschiff*, ch. 50, v. 25: "zergenglich freüd."

[6] Bock, *Teütsche Speißkammer*, fol. 108r: "Der gemein man im Teütschen land/ achtet vor zeitten nichts sonders auff hohe köstliche trachten der speisen/ liessen sich mit kraut gemüß/ mit allerhand růben/ wurtzelen/ vnd dem obs settigen/ nemlich was der krautgarten/ der acher vnd baumgarten järlichs ertragen mochten/ mit dem selben waren die gemeinen Teütschen jeder zeit wol zůfriden." It is noteworthy that Bock mentioned Tacitus as a source in the margins.

precious garments were given to him because of his honorable deeds. Before our time, our young people were raised very harshly.[7]

In spite of his noble birth, Hutten's grandfather had the character to resist exotic spices and herbs as well as fancy finery. Instead, he stuck to native German foods and to simple, traditional garments. By contrast, contemporaneous Germans had abandoned the simple and moderate lives of their forefathers and had become soft and sickly, a result of a comfortable lifestyle marked by hard drinking and overeating. Hutten begged his fellow Germans to return to a simple, wholesome life: "Therefore let us remember our old virtues and leave behind such a tender life."[8]

Hutten despaired over the ongoing demise of the German culture as Germans had lost their tough, simple, virtuous, and manly ways. Hutten scorned the Germans who had lost their way because of a slothful and gluttonous lifestyle:

> These are the tenderly raised who sit on pillows and go in garments out of silk. And they excessively eat and drink everything that can be brought here by land or by ocean. They hold their meetings with wine, and they go clothed so tenderly that one had to bring the silk here from two thousand miles away. [...] It indeed was a despicable thing among the old Germans that a man should present himself in such a tender and womanish way.[9]

Hutten and others were very clear where to lay blame for the German malaise: merchants and the long-distance trade. Johannes Aventinus confirmed this in his *Chronica* from 1541: "The merchants spoiled everything; the burghers and courtiers learned it from them, and now everybody wants to be superior to the others with clothing and with the excess in food and drink."[10] The old German virtues were lost once the merchants arrived in more recent times. Aventinus

---

[7] Hutten, *von der wunderbarlichen artzney*, sig. H3r: "Des lob ich mein großuater der nie specery ließ in sein huß kumen/ vnd me andere den gewonliche kleider trůg so im doch offt vmb seiner erlichen dadten willen kostliche kleider geschenckt warden. Also seint vor zeiten vnsere jungen herttiglich vff erzogen."

[8] Hutten, *von der wunderbarlichen artzney*, sig. H3r: "Darumb laßt vns doch ein mal vnser alten tugenden gedencken vnd solch zertlich leben verlassen."

[9] Hutten, *von der wunderbarlichen artzney*, sig. H1v–H2v: "das seint die zart vff erzognen die vff den küssen vnd seiden kleideren gond vnd sitzen/ vnd alles dz fressen vnd sauffen das zů land vnd möre har mag bracht werden. Die meinen ratschlagen den bey dem wein/ vnd so zart gekleidet gon/ dz man in die seiden můß zwei tausent meilen har bringen. [...] Es war für war bei den alten teutschen ein verachtlichs ding dz sich ein man also solt zertlich vnd weibisch halten."

[10] Aventinus, *Chronica*, sig. H4v: "die Kaufleut haben all ding verderbt/ von den habens die Burger vnd Hoflewt gelernt/ will ye einer vber den andern sein/ mit den kleydern vnd mit dem vberflus in essen vnd trincken."

blamed the merchants for a life in excess and for the corresponding loss of virtue, modesty, and virility.

While the resentment toward merchants was widespread, merchants were most commonly censored for market manipulations, usurious practices and excessive, unearned wealth. Aventinus instead focused on their core business: trading merchandise, which in Aventinus's context meant bringing goods to a different place where they did not belong. To Aventinus, the very act of bringing goods into Germany contaminated Germans morally by instilling the desire for imported luxury goods, and in particular for food items like wine and delicacies. In the analysis of both Hutten and Aventinus, their contemporaries strayed from the simple traditional moral life and thus lost their moral compass. Imported spices and fine imported garments were untrue to the German heritage and led to a pampered and effeminate lifestyle.

Critics of global trade frequently sought to correct the popular perception that foreign and imported goods were better and more desirable than those grown or produced domestically. Sebastian Franck in his *Germaniae Chronicon* from 1538 described the basic pattern:

> The rare is well received. The unfamiliar bread tastes better. The alien is always better than the native. What is at the doorstep nobody cares about. This is how it is with the Germans as well; that is why they have nothing from themselves, so that there is barely a people that knows and owns less about itself.[11]

Germans were generally thought to favor imported foods over domestic varieties for reasons of prestige, a point that the herbalist Otto Brunfels condensed into this simple formula: "If it grows in our lands as well it is not valued."[12] In the section on valerian, he inverted the argument: "Valerian is also one of the nicely smelling roots which one would hold in much higher esteem if it were brought in from overseas."[13] The argument was two-fold. People would treasure this herb if they thought it was imported. More importantly, Brunfels inferred that valerian was equal to its imported counterparts. As a consequence, so

---

[11] Franck, *Germaniae Chronicon*, sig. bb2r: "Das selten kompt wol/ frembd brot schmeckt wol. Es ist immer zů das frembd besser dan das heymisch/ was vor der thür/ das hab mann niendert für. Also ist es den Teutschen auch/ daher haben sie so gar nicht von jn selbs/ das kaum ein volck ist/ das weniger von jm selbs weyßt vnd hat."

[12] Brunfels, *Contrafayt Kreüterbůch*, 313: "Aber dieweil es auch bey vns wechßt/ so gylts nichts."

[13] Brunfels, *Contrafayt Kreüterbůch*, 116: "Baldrian ist auch der wolryechenden wurtzelen eine/ welche/ wann sye über meer ynhär bracht were/ so möchte sie vileicht auch in höherem werdt sein."

Brunfels, Germans had lost faith in German herbal medicine and, much to their detriment, had gotten addicted to medicines from India and Arabia.[14]

A number of spice books pointed to viable native substitutes for imported spices, such as the native *Liebstöckel* (lovage) for pepper. Brunfels, for instance, chided the practice of importing pepper at great expense while *Liebstöckel* could be had at home for free.[15] Even spice books that did not polemically assail imported spices, like Leonhart Fuchs's (1501–1566) *New Kreüterbůch* from 1543, promoted *Liebstöckel* as a viable substitute for pepper.[16]

In Hutten's view, the desire to consume exotic foods was created and exploited by the Fuggers and by other merchant houses: "Our foods are not tasty to us anymore. We sell ours so that we can buy others for it, those that the Fuggers brought across the ocean."[17] By supplying exotic goods from overseas, the Fuggers ensured that Germans lost interest in domestic foods. Hutten also had harsh words for the Germans who succumbed to the seduction: "That is why all those are cursed who despise the precious and delightful foods that grow here and who instead bring foreign [foods] into our lands."[18] Hutten even expressed bad wishes for those who could not resist imported spices: "It is my highest wish that nobody will get rid of gout or the French disease who cannot live without pepper."[19]

The underlying argument was that everything Germans needed for sustenance was grown on German soil. Some spice books from the first half of the sixteenth century have the explicit goal of reacquainting Germans with their own native herbs and spices. Eucharius Rößlin (c. 1470–1526) justified his 1533 German edition of the *Kreutterbůch* (*Herb Book*) by Johannes von Cuba (1430–1503, a.k.a. Johann von Wonnecke Caub) with the remark that Cuba's work, originally written in the 1480s, was suited to combat the vanity of Germans by reacquainting them with old German herbs and spices in order to help them maintain their health.[20]

---

14 Brunfels, *Contrafayt Kreüterbůch*, 312–313.
15 Brunfels, *Contrafayt Kreüterbůch*, 291.
16 Fuchs, *New Kreüterbůch*, sig. Pp1r.
17 Hutten, *von der wunderbarlichen artzney*, sig. H3r: "aber vns schmacken vnsere früchten nit/ wir verkauffen die vnseren das wir andere darumb kouffen/ die/ die Fucker vber mör hat bringen."
18 Hutten, *von der wunderbarlichen artzney*, sig. H3v: "darumb seint verflůchet alle die vnsere so kostliche vnd liepliche bey vns erwachßenen speisen verachten/ vnd so frembde in vnsere lender füren."
19 Hutten, *De Guaiaci Medicina*, sig. g4v: "Meum igitur summum uotum est, ne unquam podagra, unquam morbo Gallico careant, qui pipere carere non possunt." This reference was omitted in the German version of the text.
20 Cuba, *Kreutterbůch*, fol. 1v. The original text by Johannes Cuba was written in the 1480s.

It is worth pointing out that the body of the text by Johannes von Cuba, which predates the advent of maritime trade with Asia, did not make critical references to the import of spices and herbs, unlike Rößlin's preface.

The 1529 Augsburg edition of the compilation *Apoteck für den gmeynen man* (*Pharmacy for the Common Man*) by Hieronymus Brunschwig (1450–1512) features a frontispiece showing a peasant cultivating the soil to grow native medicinal herbs (figure 11). A woman, perhaps his wife, stands next to him and harvests the herbs. God, in view in the top left corner, is guiding them with hand gestures. The illustration is framed by an inscription from Ecclesiasticus 38:4: "The Lord has created medicinal herbs from the ground, and a wise man will not shy away from them."[21] The title page thus instructs readers that they should look no further than the native soil to find appropriate medicines.

Paracelsus's *Herbarium*, which was written around 1525–1526 and was first published as a fragment in 1570, was explicitly motivated by the need to recover the knowledge of healing properties of domestic herbs that had been displaced by "Transmarina," that is substances imported from overseas.[22] Paracelsus insisted on the principle that native medicines to all nations were invariably the most effective to cure illnesses and that accordingly German herbs yielded the best-suited medicines for Germans: "In each country its own illnesses grow, as do its own medicines."[23] Otto Brunfels in his spice book added that early illiterate humans and even animals intuitively picked suitable native herbs for their own healing.[24] But this intuitive, innate knowledge was lost in part because of the pre-eminence of book knowledge, particularly as disseminated by the Arabs, and by merchants who recklessly imported useless and even harmful herbs and spices.[25]

In 1550, Hieronymus Bock published a handbook with the title *Teütsche Speißkammer* (*German Pantry*) in which he discussed all the edible plants and spices that grew on German soil. Bock sought to prove that Germany could provide all the nourishment Germans could ever need or want and that the importation of food items was a vain and damaging endeavor. In his dedication, he

---

21 Brunschwig, *Apoteck für den gmeynen man*, title page: "Der HERRE hatt die Ertzney vonn der erde geschaffenn/ Vnnd der weyse wirdt kayne schewhe darab haben." The short compilation was published in multiple editions and contains medical texts by Brunschwig and Michael Puff von Schrick (1400–1473).
22 Paracelsus, "Beschreibung Etlicher kreüter," 286; Moran, "The Herbarius," 104.
23 Paracelsus, "Beschreibung Etlicher kreüter," 288: "Einem jeglichen land wechst sein kranckheyt selbs/ sein artzney selbs." See also Moran, "The Herbarius," 104.
24 Brunfels, *Contrafayt Kreüterbůch*, sig. a5r–a6r.
25 Brunfels, *Contrafayt Kreüterbůch*, sig. b1v–b2v.

Figure 11: Hieronymus Brunschwig. *Apoteck für den gmeynen man. der die Ertzte zuersuchen. am gût nicht vermügens/ oder sonst in der not allwege nicht erraychen kan*. Augsburg: Heinrich Steiner, 1529. Title page. © Bayerische Staatsbibliothek München.

called the desire to import foodstuffs foolish, "since everything that we need can be found in abundance in the German land."[26] In his introduction, he asserted that he stocked his *German Pantry* with German foodstuffs, which provided everything to sustain the bodies of Germans: "For this reason I prepared

---

26 Bock, *Teütsche Speißkammer*, sig. A3r: "seintemal alles was vns von nötten/ im Teütschen landt vberflüssig funden würt."

the present pantry with everything that meets bodily needs with great effort, and I filled it with German foodstuffs."[27]

In his pioneering *New Kreütter Bůch* (*New Herb Book*), first published in 1539 and republished in multiple expanded editions, Bock stressed the importance of using simple herbs and spices grown in Germany. In the introduction of the second edition, Bock stated emphatically that he wanted Germans to avoid the spices and herbs of unknown origin because they were imported from distant countries at great expense. Instead, Germans should relearn to appreciate those of German origin "and be content with the common gifts from God which he gives to each country in abundance."[28]

Bock belonged to the first generation of herbalists who consciously established a new catalogue of nature that was based on empirical observation and detailed description rather than on the knowledge of the ancients.[29] Bock proudly declared that his book only contained descriptions of herbs "that I have seen and experienced myself."[30] The number of known and collected herbs rose rapidly: while Bock described 478 native herbs in his first edition of 1539,[31] he listed 806 plants in his last edition of 1551,[32] and Caspar Bauhin catalogued more than 6,000 plants in 1623.[33] Bock also set himself apart from authors who merely copied what others had written before. Those authors, in Bock's view, were driven by self-interest and a desire for fame.[34] Observing plants in their native habitat meant traveling throughout Germany to see them, as Bock explained in the introduction to the third edition:

> I do not want to discuss here my own danger, fear, worries, great labor, hunger, thirst, frost, heat, horror, long arduous journeys there and back, through many pathless areas in Germany, such as forests, mountains, valleys, and level fields, for what do other people have to do with that? Desire and the common good caused me to tolerate all this.[35]

---

27 Bock, *Teütsche Speißkammer*, sig. A4r; also sig. A4v–A5r: "Vmb gemelter vrsach willen/ hab ich gegenwertige Speißkammer mit allerhand/ was zůr leibs noturfft gehörig/ mit fleiß versehen/ zů bereit/ vnnd mit Teütscher wahr außgerüstet."
28 Bock, *Kreüter Bůch*, 1546, sig. a4v: "vnnd der gemeinen gaben Gottes/ welche er einen jeden Land vberflüssig gibt/ vns genügen lassen."
29 Ogilvie, *The Science of Describing*, 139.
30 Bock, *Kreüter Bůch*, 1551: sig. b1r: "was ich selbs gesehen vnd erfaren."
31 Bock, *New Kreütter Bůch*, 1539, fol. 4v.
32 Hoppe, *Das Kräuterbuch*, 44.
33 Ogilvie, *The Science of Describing*, 139.
34 Bock, *Kreüter Bůch*, 1551: sig. b1r.
35 Bock, *Kreüter Bůch*, 1551: sig. b3v: "Jch wil aber dißmals meine eigene gefahr/ als angst/ sorg/ grosse arbeit/ hunger/ durst/ frost/ hitz/ schrecken/ lange sorgliche reiß hin vnnd wider/ durch vil onwege des Teütschenlands/ als in Wälden/ Bergen/ Tälern/ vnnd Ebenen feldern lassen

Canvassing the countryside was the only way to expand the knowledge base of German herbs. Furthermore, stressing the difficult and strenuous nature of his travels served to authenticate his book and to guarantee its accuracy.[36]

Like Hieronymus Bock, Tarquinius Schnellenberg (d. 1561) praised the benefits of simple German medicinal herbs over questionable complex, composite medicines that were commonly imported from overseas. In the poetic preface of his *Experimenta. Von XX. Pestilentz Wurtzeln vnd Kreutern* (*Experience. On Twenty Roots and Herbs Against Pestilence*) from 1546, Schnellenberg praised the simple medicines grown in the endemic nature: "Nature speaks that it is gaining joy through basic medicines, which we call simplicia [simple herbs]. No doctor should be ashamed of them."[37] In his dedication, Schnellenberg stressed his strong preference for simple herbs grown in German soil: "As we have so many good and precious simple remedies in the German nation, they are more compatible with and closer to our nature than those called transoceanic or alien."[38] Citing Otto Brunfels, Hieronymus Bock, and Leonhart Fuchs,[39] Schnellenberg doubted the effectiveness of imported herbal medicines while promoting those indigenous to Germany. In the body of his text, Schnellenberg discussed twenty herbs or roots he considered suitable as remedies against the plague.

As the title of the book indicates, Schnellenberg confidently prioritized his own observations and experiences over the authority of the classical authors, as Bock had done before him. In the fourth chapter, he chided Pliny for claiming that the betony plant (Stachys officinalis) originated in Spain even though his own observation of at least two sub-species in Germany clearly made this a German native. Schnellenberg boldly asserted the primacy of empirical observation over the written tradition: "Therefore, the person seems to me to be much more consistent who observes simple herbs with his own eyes, engages and really deals with them, rather than just holding up a mere text. This person has to be seen as more credible and secure than the one who simply deals with texts."[40]

---

berůhen/ dann was haben andere leüt darmit zů thůn. Der Lust vnd Gemeiner nutz haben mich solches alles zů dulden/ dahin verursachet."
36 Ogilvie, *The Science of Describing*, 142–143.
37 Schnellenberg, *Experimenta*, sig. A3r: "Spricht die natur sich erfrewen thut/ | Durch einfeltige Artzney gut. | Die wir Simplicia thun nennen/ | Der darff sich kein Doctor schemen."
38 Schnellenberg, *Experimenta*, sig. A2v: "Sind dem mal wir nun so viel guter vnd thewrer Simplicia in Deutscher Nation haben/ vnser natur geheimer vnd neher denn die trans marina oder peregrina genant."
39 Heinrichs, *Plague, Print, and the Reformation*, 142.
40 Schnellenberg, *Experimenta*, sig. B4r: "Also deucht mich es viel bestendiger sein/ wer sichtbarlich die Simplica erfindet/ practiciert vnd darmit wirchklich vmbgehet/ vnd als denn

Schnellenberg not only preferred indigenous medicinal plants over alien, transoceanic ones, but he also prioritized native empirical knowledge over classical texts from across the Alps and from ancient times.

Like other writers, Hieronymus Bock conceded that contemporaneous Germans craved foreign, imported varieties even though native German varieties were at least as good and wholesome:

> Indeed, in the German lands many good and healthy herbs grow as well that are equal to foreign, alien spices. But we are not in the least content with that. We always have to send ships to India and Calicut for spices. This plays into the hands of merchants who know how to sell these spices to us. Yet in the German land, a noble, good, tender saffron grows that often surpasses the Oriental variety. Likewise, noble, fragrant juniper berries grow in the German lands, which one exports to foreign countries.[41]

Bock added a number of other spices that were exported from Germany, such as marjoram, rosemary, basil, thyme, and coriander. In other words, the German harvest could not only meet domestic needs but was abundant and diverse enough that many varieties could be exported. As in other contexts, it was the merchants with their global trade schemes that disrupted the self-sufficient German production of spices and herbs.

The counterpart to the argument that German lands could provide everything Germans needed was that imported foods were not able to yield what Germans needed nutritionally because they were not grown on German soil nor in a German climate. Otto Brunfels not only reiterated the value of domestic herbs but also pointed to potential negative health consequences of consuming imported varieties:

> For what reason should our herbs be not as good as those from Asia and Africa? How did we do before we imported such goods? And why is it these days that those who use such goods the least live the longest and have the fewest illnesses? We see the opposite in those who are at the pharmacy all the time who also are the sickest and

---

die Schrift dargegen hellt/ derselbige muß je glaublicher vnd sicherer geachtet werden/ denn der allein mit der blossen litera vmbgehet."

41 Bock, *Teütsche Speißkammer*, fol. 92v: "Zwar es wachsen im Teütschen land auch vil gůter vnnd gesunder wurtz/ die etwan denn außlendigen frembden specereien gleich sein möchten/ daran lassen wir vns aber keins wegs genügen/ wir müssen stets in Jndiam/ vnd gegen Calicuthen nach wurtz schiffen/ solches ist allein den kauffherren gespilt/ die wissen vns die specereien zů uerkauffen. Wolan im Teütschen land wachßt der Edel gůt zam saffran/ der offtermals den Orientischen vbertrifft. So wachsen auch im Teütschen land die edle wolriechende Weckolter beerlin/ so man von vns in frembde länder füret."

most infirm. While foreign herbs have a strong nature, they nevertheless are not attuned to our climate.[42]

Brunfels associated longevity with abstinence from imported herbs and spices and from pharmacy visits – which he both linked to illness and disease. He asserted that the composite medicines frequently dispensed by pharmacies were ineffective and even harmful because substances of opposite elemental and humoral properties were mixed together indiscriminately. Too many of the composites were based on herbs imported from Arabia and India, which were responsible for medical problems and premature death because these hot, imported herbs were ill-suited for the inhabitants of a cold climate.[43]

It is important to note in this context that none of these tracts in the early sixteenth century made a fundamental distinction between culinary and medicinal uses of herbs, between spices and medicines. The connection between food and medicine goes back to Hippocrates, and Galen stated that a good physician should also be a good cook. Paracelsus picked up this idea when he reminded his readers that "food, drink, and medicine should be treated as one and the same."[44] However, the healing properties of herbs and spices remained quite abstract as the texts under consideration here refrained from formulating recipes for healing purposes. Furthermore, the theory, as discussed in these texts, was quite divorced from medical practice,[45] which however cannot be the focus here. The same basic arguments Paracelsus used regarding the medical use of herbs also appeared in spice books. In the dedication to his *Kreuterbuch* from 1564, Adam Lonitzer (also Lonicer; 1528–1586) asserted that herbs served "not only for the maintenance of physical needs, or as nourishment for humans, but also for all kinds of diseases and fragilities, both for humans and for

---

42 Brunfels, *Contrafayt Kreüterbůch*, sig. b2v: "Dann vß was vrsach sollen vnsere kreüter nit als gůt sein als die vß Asien vnd Africa? Wie hat man gethan/ do man solich noch nit in diße land bracht? Vnd wie kompt es vff den heütigen tag/ das die am allerlengsten leben/ mynder kranckheyt haben/ so deren ding am allermynsten brauchen? Wie wir das gegentheyl sehen/ das die so on vnderlaß in der apothecken seind/ auch am aller syechsten vnd bresthafftigsten seind. Haben die frembden kreüter krefftiger naturen/ so seind sye aber dannocht nit vff vnser Clima attemperiert."

43 Brunfels, *Contrafayt Kreüterbůch*, sig. b2v. Similarly, Hieronymus Bock in the foreword to the second edition of his *Kreüter Bůch* from 1546 (sig. a4r–a4v) opposed composita because of their unknown foreign content and high expense.

44 Paracelsus, *Vom Holtz Guaiaco*, sig. B1v: "Dem nach so laß speyß/ tranck vnd die artzeney ein ding sein."

45 Lindemann, *Medicine and Society*, 281.

cattle."[46] In the heading of chapter five he repeated the claim that the herbs described here were "used in medicine and in the kitchen."[47]

The argument that imported herbs and medicines actually made Germans sicker, as Brunfels and others contended, was rooted in physiological theory, developed by Hippocrates (c. 460–370 BCE) and further developed by Galen (129–c. 200 CE). It held that all bodies were constituted by a balance of humors and that disease was caused by a state of bodily imbalance. Hippocratic theory indicated that it was best for humans to consume foods and medicines that were close in geographic origin and from the same climate zone.[48] The consumption of foreign foods, herbs, and spices, on the other hand, disrupted the humoral equilibrium and therefore led to disease.

Johann Vochs, an obscure physician from Cologne, was one of the pioneers of "medical localism" in Germany.[49] He was one of the first to promote the idea that locally grown herbal medicines were more effective than imported varieties.[50] Little is known about his life, other than him mentioning a medical career of almost forty years in his treatise *De pestilentia Anni praesentis et eius cura* (*On the Pestilence of the Present Year and Its Cure*) from 1507.[51] Like others after him, Vochs castigated the contemporary trade of spices and medicines, targeting especially the greedy foreign merchants who imported dangerous products, and simultaneously promoted native German medicines.[52] Vochs's impact appears to have been limited as there is no evidence that Paracelsus, Brunfels, Bock, and others knew of his work,[53] even though the 1537 reprint of his text by Johann Dryander had a limited reception.[54]

There was a broad theoretical consensus that consuming foods from different climate zones was unhealthy. When telling the journey to India by the eponymous protagonist in the prose narration *Fortunatus* (1509), its narrator

---

[46] Lonitzer, *Kreuterbuch*, sig. aa2r: "daß nit allein zu erhaltung des leibs notturfft/ oder dem Menschen zur speise/ sondern auch zu allerhand leibs gebrechen vnnd schwacheyten/ beyde dem Menschen vnnd Viehe."
[47] Lonitzer, *Kreuterbuch*, fol. 134v: "Von Beschreibung/ Natur/ vnd Eygenschafft/ allerhand Kreutergewächs/ so in der Artznei vnd Kuchen gebraucht." (On the description, nature and properties of all kinds of herbal plants, as they are used in medicine and kitchen.)
[48] Earle, *The Body of the Conquistador*, 26–30; Heinrichs, *Plague, Print, and the Reformation*, 59.
[49] Heinrichs, *Plague, Print, and the Reformation*, 54.
[50] For a discussion of Vochs's contribution see Heinrichs, *Plague, Print, and the Reformation*, 53–74.
[51] Heinrichs, *Plague, Print, and the Reformation*, 56.
[52] Heinrichs, *Plague, Print, and the Reformation*, 60–61.
[53] Heinrichs, *Plague, Print, and the Reformation*, 68–69.
[54] Heinrichs, *Plague, Print, and the Reformation*, 133.

speculated why people from India did not come to Germany: "The reason is, they hear say, how our country is meager because it is cold and does not have good foods, so they worry that they would die right away."[55] Likewise, forcibly moving human beings into different climate zones was problematic. The German conquistador Nikolaus Federmann noted that he left behind a native woman in Venezuela when he returned to Europe "because she, and all other Indios, do not live long outside their fatherland, and particularly in cold lands."[56] The woman was a gift to him from one of the native leaders during his military incursion into the interior of Venezuela in 1530–1531.

Furthermore, physical labor was understood to increase the body's vital heat. As a consequence, hard-working people, such as German peasants and artisans, required colder and moister foods.[57] Otto Brunfels argued that God created more tempered herbs that grew in Germany because they were better suited to the German temperament. While hot spices were not inherently unhealthy, they were only appropriate for people living in hot climates.[58] In his view, it was foolish to import "frembde materialia" (alien stuff), as each region grew the plants that were appropriate for the climate and for the complexion and temperament of the native population:

> It may well be, and it is the truth, that our herbs are not as pungent, tangy, and fragrant as those that come here over the ocean and from hot lands. But this also is not necessary. As we are of a different kind and temperament in our bodily constitution than the Arabs, so God also tempered the spices to our bodies and to our qualities, in the same way as all other foods and drinks.[59]

The elemental properties of German herbs thus correlated with the elemental properties of German bodies.

---

[55] Anon., *Fortunatus*, 107: "Ist die vrsach sy hören sagen wie vnsre land vnärtig seyen/ von keltin vnd auch nit gůte frücht haben/ hond sorg das sy gleich sturben." The point of reference is Germany here, in spite of the fact that the protagonists of the novel are based in Cyprus.

[56] Federmann, *Jndianische Historia*, sig. E4r: "darumb das sie vnd alle ander Jndios/ auß ihrem vaterland/ vnd sonderlich in kalten landen/ nit lang leben."

[57] Albala, *Eating Right*, 187.

[58] Earle (*The Body of the Conquistador*, 54–75) points out that Spaniards in the West Indies were keen on importing European foods and on growing them in their new colonies as European foods were seen as more wholesome for natives of Spain.

[59] Brunfels, *Contrafayt Kreüterbůch*, sig. b3v: "Nun mag sein/ vnd ist die warheit/ das vnser gewächsß nit so scharpff/ so kräfftig/ vnd so wolryechend wie die so über meer vnd vß hitzigen landen härbracht werden. Jst auch nit von nöten/ sonder wie wir des leibs halben/ auch einer anderen art/ vnd temperament seind/ weder die Arabier/ also hat vns Gott die kreüter auch getemperiet vff vnseren leyb/ vff vnsere qualiteten/ gleicher weiße wie alle andere speyß vnd dräncke."

This argument extended to the medicinal properties of herbs. In a clever chiastic argument, Brunfels contrasted the simple, yet effective German herbs with the ineffective ones imported from Calicut: "The ancients in former times healed one hundred illnesses with one herb. [...] Now we need one hundred herbs from all over Calicut to heal one illness, yet they do not help at all."[60] Ulrich von Hutten contributed a similarly pointed comment: "That is why we still see some Germans who live moderately according to old customs and live long lives. But those whose fingers are yellow because of the saffron and who swallow all spices are always sick and soon will die."[61]

Ulrich von Hutten railed against the import of spices and herbs in his famous syphilis tract, entitled *Von der wunderbarlichen artzney des holtz Guaiacum genant/ und wie man die Frantzosen oder blatteren heilen sol* (*On the Miraculous Medicine Called Guaiacum Wood, and How to Cure the French Disease or Pox*) from 1519. He warned of unscholarly doctors who "deliberately prescribe foreign medicine that was brought here from Egypt from the Nile river," thus endangering the patients' health and unduly enriching themselves.[62] Yet, he vigorously argued for the use of the guaiacum wood that was imported from the island of Hispaniola for the cure of syphilis, commonly referred to as *morbus Gallicus*.[63] His high praises for this imported wood seems ironic and was perhaps colored by the fact that he had contracted syphilis himself around 1509.[64] In fact, Hutten's text describes his symptoms and his suffering in vivid detail. While local varieties of food were generally considered most wholesome, medicines from far-off regions were sometimes considered highly effective.[65]

Seeking an elusive cure in the New World seemed plausible, however, as syphilis was widely believed to have originated there.[66] Hutten pointed out that the disease first appeared in Naples,[67] yet implied later in the text that the disease originated in Hispaniola, just like the guaiacum wood itself:

---

60 Brunfels, *Contrafayt Kreüterbůch*, sig. b3v: "Es haben vor zeyten die Alten mit einem eyntzigen kreütlin hundert kranckheyten geheylet. [...] Yetzundt brauchen wir wol zů einer kranckheyt hundert kreüter/ von etwann die gantz Calekutt/ vnd hylfft dannocht nit."
61 Hutten, *von der wunderbarlichen artzney*, sig. H3v: "Darumb wir noch etliche teutschen sehen die sich messig nach dem alten bruch halten lang leben/ aber den die finger von safferon gel seint/ vnd alle specery schlucken stetes kranck seint vnd bald dahin sterben."
62 Hutten, *von der wunderbarlichen artzney*, sig. E2r: "die vngelerten ertzt/ die also gewillig vßlendische artzney ingeben/ dz vß egypten von dem fluß Nilus har gefiert ist."
63 Hutten, *von der wunderbarlichen artzney*, sig. C1r; similarly Fries, *EJn clarer bericht*, sig. a3r.
64 Crone, *Paracelsus*, 113.
65 Earle, *The Body of the Conquistador*, 110.
66 Earle, *The Body of the Conquistador*, 112; Grafton, *New Worlds*, 177.
67 Hutten, *von der wunderbarlichen artzney*, sig. A2r.

> Its use came to us from the island called Hispaniola, located toward the sunset near America, the land that extends toward midnight in its length. And it was found in the past years along with the other newly found islands that were unknown to our ancestors. The inhabitants of the island commonly overcome the French disease as we do the chickenpox, and they used nothing other than this wood. When a noble Spaniard, who was a governor on the island, was seriously afflicted by the disease the natives recommended this medicine. He established its use in Spain. However, there were doubts initially whether it was as effective overseas as it was on the island.[68]

Hutten asserted that these initial doubts were unfounded as he supported its use in an unqualified fashion. His implication was that importing guaiacum from Hispaniola was legitimate as the disease originated on the same island.

Hutten reported an encounter with a physician in Frankfurt who had no opinion about guaiacum, as he did not know it. The anecdote ended with a critique of the physician, who lacked imagination:

> Then he started to talk about the books by Aristotle. I don't know what to say of what use they are. Finally I had to respond to him, dear old man, it may be that a new disease requires a new medicine that is still completely unknown to us. After he said many more foolish words that did not belong here, I said, you foolish old man, learn to give better answers in such serious matters affecting human lives.[69]

In spite of his general aversion to innovation, Hutten pushed hard for acceptance of the guaiacum wood to treat syphilis, no doubt motivated by his own advanced stage of the illness, which he described in great detail. The promise Hutten saw in the guaiacum wood was unfounded, however. There is no evidence that it affected the course of his illness, and Hutten died of it 1523.

---

[68] Hutten, *von der wunderbarlichen artzney*, sig. C1r: "Sein bruch ist zů vns kumen vß der Jnselen Spangnola genant/ die ligt zů dem nidergang der sonnen/ bey America dem landt da es sich zů Mitternacht hin erstrecket nach seiner lenge/ vnd ist auch in vergangenen iaren mitt den andern newlich erfundenen inselen erfunden worden die vnsern vorfaren vnerkant seint gewesen/ die ynwoner der Jnselen/ vberkumen gemeinlich all die frantzosen wie wir die parpelen/ vnd bruchten nüt darzů den diß holtz. Den ein edler hyspanier als in der Jnselen ein regent was/ von der kranckheit hefftig siechet/ haben im die inwoner dise artzney angezeigt/ vnd er hat seine bruch in hispanien bracht/ doch anfencklich gezweiffelt ob sein wirckung vber mere so gůt wer/ als in der Jnselen."

[69] Hutten, *von der wunderbarlichen artzney*, sig. E4r: "da fieng er an von Aristoteles biecher/ darzů nur dienent ich weiß selb nit wz zů sagen/ biß ich zů letzt můst sagen lieber alter es mag sein dz ein newer brest ein neuwe artzney erfordert/ vnd vnß dz noch gar vnbekant wer. Vnd noch vil sein anderen dorechten worten zů disen dingen nüt geherendt/ sprach leer du dorechter alter in solchen schweren dingen menschlich leben betreffen baß zů antwurten."

Lorenz Fries pointed to the divine provenance of the cure by guaiacum wood, "which God sent to us in fatherly love from foreign lands."[70] Paracelsus in his own syphilis tract entitled *Vom Holtz Guaiaco gründlicher heylung* (*On the Thorough Healing Through the Guaiacum Wood*) from 1529 disputed Hutten's claim, called his theory a sensationalist fuss and insisted that treatment with mercury ointment was a better cure for syphilis. Paracelsus claimed that the Fuggers promoted guaiacum for their own profit.[71] There is no evidence, however, for the claim that the Fuggers engaged in the trade with guaiacum at all. Rather, the Fuggers had a commercial interest in mercury, the competing cure for syphilis.[72] Such was the hype against the Fuggers at the time that Paracelsus's false allegation was widely seen as credible.

It was commonly assumed that it was part of the natural order and therefore part of God's plan to give mild foods to Germans who lived in a moderate climate zones, while those who lived in hot climates enjoyed spicy foods. Brunfels argued that different herbs with varying properties grew in different countries.[73] It was obvious to him that the Arabs in their herbals discussed their own native herbs, yet he bemoaned the fact that they also brought their books to Europe:

> As [the Arabs] wrote in foreign lands, they also cultivated the herbs and medicines of their land. This is not wrong by itself. For it is as easy for them to obtain spices and all kinds of exotic herbs as it is to get leaves and grass here. Furthermore, their own complexions and landscapes require this. It would be just as ridiculous for us to obtain our medicines in their land as it would be of equal disadvantage to them to fill their books with our herbs while despising their own.[74]

God gave spicy foods to the Arabs and moderate foods to the Germans, according to their climates and complexions. It made sense to Brunfels that the Arabs and Germans in their own respective books wrote about their own foods and spices.

---

70 Fries, *EJn clarer bericht*, sig. a2r: "welches vns gott vß vetterlicher liebe von frömden landen her gesendt hat."
71 Johnson, *The German Discovery*, 162.
72 Stein, *Negotiating the French Pox*, 103–104.
73 Brunfels, *Contrafayt Kreüterbůch*, sig. b4r.
74 Brunfels, *Contrafayt Kreüterbůch*, sig. b3r: "Darzů/ dieweil sye geschriben haben in frembden landen/ haben sye auch ires landts kreüter vnd artzeney gepflegt. Jst des selbigen halb nicht vnrecht gesein. dann gewürtz/ vnd allerley specerey/ ist ynen so leychtlich zů bekommen/ wie vns laub vnd graß. Hat auch solichs erforderet ire complexionen/ vnnd landtschafften. Dann gleicher weiß wie es vns spötlich/ was wir vnsere artzeney bey ynen holen/ also were es ynen nachteylig/ solten sye ire bůcher vß vnseren gewächßen zůsammen gesetzt haben/ vnd die ire veracht."

Ulrich von Hutten agreed with the herbalists discussed here that the German lands were more than capable to sustain Germans with food, spices and medicine:

> As our country has fed us well enough, why is it necessary to bring spices and medicine here from the far end of the world? That is why all those are cursed who despise the precious and delightful foods that grow here, and who thus bring foreign [foods] into our lands. For nature, as Jerome says, can easily feed itself and with its own goods.[75]

Like many others, Hutten believed that there was neither need nor justification to import food and spices from overseas and that the rising global system was harmful to Germans. Hutten's reference to Jerome clarifies that the arguments were not just social or economic in that long-distance trade also violated the natural and the divine order.

The widely accepted theological foundation of this insight was that God's creation provided ample sustenance for all creatures, including humans. Paracelsus held that God provided humans with bountiful nourishment through nature: "Thus God provided for the needs of humans marvelously through nature in many ways."[76] Hieronymus Bock expanded on this point:

> Thus, we in the German land are provided with heavenly gifts so well and perfectly, first with the holy divine word and then with the four elements, indeed as well as no other nation under the dear sun. So, the German soil in abundance gives and bears food and drink, feed and shelter, medicine, and more for us and for our cattle.[77]

The German soil offered ample sustenance as long as Germans lived in harmony with the four elements and in accordance to divine will.

In the view of Otto Brunfels, faithful Christians did not have to worry about food security because God met all their needs:

> Leviticus 25. Act according to my commands and value my laws so that you follow them. So that you may live securely on the land. For the land shall offer its foods to you so that you have enough to eat and to inhabit it securely. [...] Here is what Christ said, Matthew 6: You

---

[75] Hutten, *von der wunderbarlichen artzney*, sig. H3v: "So nun vnser landt vns notturfftig genůg speiset/ was ist es not specery vnd artzney von end diser welt har zůbringen/ darumb seint verflůchet alle die vnsere so kostliche vnd liepliche bey vns erwachßenen speisen verachten/ vnd so frembde in vnsere lender füren/ den die natur als Hyeronymus sagt mag sich leichtlich erneren vnd mit eleinen dingen." Similar argument in Hutten, *Praedones*, fol. 23r.

[76] Paracelsus, "Das Bůch von natürlichen dingen," 3: "Also hat Gott in vilerley weg/ dem menschen sein notturfft wunderbarlich durch die natur beschaffen."

[77] Bock, *Teütsche Speißkammer*, sig. A3v: "So seind wir je im teütschen landt mit himmlischen gaben/ erstlich des heiligen götlichen worts/ darnach mit den vier elementen gantz hoh vnnd treffenlich/ ja so wol als kein nation vnder der lieben sonnen versehen/ so gibt und tregt der teütsch erdbode speiß vnd dranck/ fütter vnd decke/ artznei vnd anders für vns vnd vnser vihe vberflüssig genůg." Bock made the same point in his *Kreüter Bůch*, 1546, sig. a4v.

should not worry and say, what shall we eat? What shall we drink? With what shall we clothe ourselves? For such things heathens strive. However, your Heavenly Father knows that you need all of that. First yearn for God's kingdom and for His justice, so all these things will come to you.[78]

God provided sustenance for true believers. For Brunfels, only the unfaithful had to worry about how to feed and clothe themselves as God punished those who disregarded his commands by causing harvest failure and spoiling stored food supplies.

The early Reformed Pastor Jakob Strauß shared this sentiment of a God who provided for his creation in a pamphlet from 1523: "God feeds the birds in the air and the fish in the water and dresses the flowers in the meadows."[79] Strauß left humans off this list as they experienced hunger because of their sinful nature, and in particular because they committed the sin of usury. If there was hunger it was either a result of divine punishment for an immoral and sinful life or a result of shameless and self-serving human market manipulations by godless merchants, such as usury and hoarding. The belief that food insecurity could be avoided by leading a god-pleasing life is a key reason why malnourishment and hunger per se was only a minor topic around 1500, as opposed to gluttony.[80] Pious Christians did not have to fear hunger because God provided for them, Strauß insisted: "Each pious Christian shall adhere to Christ's affirmative words without doubt, then he shall not lack nourishment."[81] Seen in that light, the yearning for foreign foodstuffs invalidated the divine gifts that offered sustenance to all Germans and thus disrupted the divine plan. Hieronymus Bock summed up these arguments and showed how God provided ample nourishment for Germans in their own country:

> That we Germans [...] are such thoughtless people that we fail to know ourselves and consider even less the noble gifts with which God provides for us daily, not just for our

---

78 Brunfels, *Almanach*, sig. A3r–A3v: "Leuit. xxv. Thût nach meiner satzung/ vnnd haltent meine recht/ das ir sye thût. vff dz ir im land sicher wonen mügt. Denn das land sol eüch seine frucht geben/ das ir zů essen genůg habt/ vnd sicher darinnen wonent. [...] Vff das auch Christus spricht Matt. vj. Jr sollt nit sorgen vnd sagen/ was werden wir essen? Was werden wir trincken? wo mit werden wir uns kleyden? Nach solchem allem trachten die Heyden. Dann eüwer hymmelischer vatter weißt/ das ir des alles bedürffent. Trachtent am ersten nach dem reich gottes/ vnd nach seiner gerechtigkeit/ so würt euch solichs alles zůfallen." Based on Leviticus 25:18–22 and Matthew 6:25–34.
79 Strauß, *Haubtstuck*, fol. 2v (Thesis 20): "Got speyset die vögel in lüfften/ die visch im wasser/ vnd beklaydet die plůmlein auff der haid."
80 Albala, *Eating Right*, 200. Chapter 16 in Brant's *Narrenschiff* is a good example for that.
81 Strauß, *Haubtstuck*, fol. 2v (Thesis 18): "Es soll ain yeder frommer Christ den zůsagenden worten Christi sonder zweyfel anhangen/ wirt jm nicht abgeen an seiner narung."

sustenance but frequently also in abundance. [...] And we ogle foreign countries from where we have foreign merchandise brought to us over water and land, with great effort and at huge expense, both for sustenance and medicine, as if we had nothing good growing in Germany. Thus, in our lands the endless graces and gifts of God are despised with which the Lord adorned His soil in the German lands, more so than in other countries in Europe. He equipped it in a fatherly way before we were created and still gracefully provides for it daily.[82]

In Bock's view, thoughtlessness and lack of self-knowledge caused Germans to covet foreign foods and spices and thus to reject God's gifts and to disregard the divine order.

The argument of God providing sustenance as long as humans complied with the divinely ordained natural order contained a health component. Different environments in different nations provided nutrition that was healthy for their respective populations. Hutten stated that humans in different climates had to eat differently and also needed different herbal medicines.[83] The common complaint raised in herbals and food books in the first half of the sixteenth century was that the onslaught of foreign spices displaced wholesome German products and obscured knowledge of domestic herbs and their healing properties. In that sense, German spice and food books tied into "a basic tenet of classical theory that individuals are best nourished by foods to which they are most accustomed, those that grow in their region and with long use have become most assimilated into people's bodies."[84] Thus an important part of the agenda of these books was to recover lost knowledge about domestic foods and herbs and to restore their prestige.

In sum, the fashionable spices and herbs imported from Egypt, Calicut, and India were generally seen as harmful as they led to the neglect of beneficial domestic herbs and had questionable health benefits in the cold German climate. To Brunfels, Bock, Paracelsus, Hutten and others, food culture was highly

---

[82] Bock, *Teütsche Speißkammer*, sig. A2r–A2v: "das wir Teütschen [...] so gar onbesunnen leüt seind/ in dem/ das wir vns schier selbs nit wol kennen/ noch vil weniger auff die hohen gaben/ damit vns Gott täglich nit allein zůr noturfft/ sonder auch zum dickern mal vberflüßig versihet/ acht nemen/ [...] vnd gaffen also bald inn frembde länder/ auß welchen wir mit schwerer arbeit vnd grossem kosten/ frembde wahr/ bede zur lebsucht/ vnd arznei/ als hetten wir nicht gůts im Teütschen land wachsen/ zu land vnd wasser zu vns fůren lassen/ dann werden die aller höchsten gnaden vnd gaben gottes bei vns verachtet/ mit welchen gott der herr seinen erdboden im Teütschen landt/ vor andere länder Europe/ wolgezieret/ auß gerüstet/ vnd gantz vätterlich vor vnser erschöpffung versehen hat/ vnd noch täglich gantz genediglichen versihet."
[83] Hutten, *von der wunderbarlichen artzney*, sig. F1v.
[84] Albala, *Eating Right*, 225.

localized by design. God created an ecological order by endowing different climate zones with different plants and thus different foods, each constituting a self-sufficient, sustainable ecological zone.[85] Divine creation by definition was sustainable. Its delicate balance was only threatened and disrupted by human intervention, such as the emerging global trade and the massive market manipulations by merchants. The mission of these books, like Hieronymus Bock's *Kreüter Bůch*, therefore was to reacquaint Germans with their own native herbs, which were a gift from God, and to wean them off the imported substances that were economically harmful and had dubious health benefits for Germans.[86]

I outlined three argumentative domains within which this discourse took place. (1) Global imports contributed greatly to gluttony, that is the lustful desire to indulge in fine and delicate foods. This gave rise to a pampered and effeminate lifestyle leading to the abandonment of traditional values and of a simple, virtuous and frugal lifestyle. (2) Imports caused an outflow of capital and aggravated market manipulations and fraudulent trade practices, which in turn intensified poverty and hunger in Germany. (3) God's plan provided for ample, wholesome, and above all, locally produced nutrition. The reliance on imported herbs and spices violated the divine design and led to an incompatibility with the humoral composition of the bodies of Germans, resulting in poor health and even premature death.

To be sure, all three argumentative contexts existed before and independent of the onset of early modern globalization. But the advent of global trade pushed these points into the forefront and made them a central part of an opposing German political and social discourse in the early sixteenth century. While the opposition to globalization was not formulated as a cohesive discourse, the German responses in the aggregate nevertheless point to deep-seated anxieties that were triggered by the cultural and social consequences of the emerging global system. We can discern a composite picture of a German culture in the early sixteenth century that overwhelmingly opposed globalization and its cultural impact. The potential for social, political and economic upheaval bolstered a conservative backlash against globalization specifically and against innovation in general.

---

[85] The seven classical climate zones were very much part of geographical thinking in Renaissance cosmographies, for instance in Lorenz Fries's *Uslegung der mercarten*, sig. A4r. The classical model was in flux, however, as evidenced by Fries's addition of an eighth climate zone in the North. Fries noted that these arctic territories had not been known to the ancients.
[86] Bock, *Kreüter Bůch*, 1546, sig. a4v.

Chapter 22
The Backlash Against Globalization: The Rhetoric of Moral Decline and the Nostalgia Project

The objective of Part III of this book was to trace the connection between the rise of global trade networks and the ascent of a globally networked elite culture on one hand and corresponding perceptions of moral decline and loss of social order on the other. Ulrich von Hutten was one of the most astute observers of the interrelationship and tension between the rise of global networks and the decline of local culture. In his view, the German culture had reached a low point because of the manifold pressures and influences from the outside. As a consequence, he wrote relentlessly against foreign influences and engaged in a nostalgia project to recreate a pure, ancient German culture he believed to have existed in an ideal past.

Nostalgia for valiant emperors of the past permeated Hutten's writings. The thought of Charlemagne and the Ottonian kings witnessing the German descent into effeminate and degenerate opulence filled him with shame:

> What would Charlemagne say now if he came back and saw his princes sitting around at court dressed in silk, while he wore armor all the time. And the Ottonians who conquered with great moderation and virtue [could see] how we grease up tenderly like women and how we take delight in flowers and fragrant, alien delicacies, much more than the women now do and previously did. Now this is done by the princes, priests, and the clergy.[1]

Hutten considered the Carolingian and Ottonian periods to be the heroic time when the old German morals and virtues and German masculinity and virility were still intact. Throughout his work, Hutten praised Charlemagne and the Ottonian kings as examples of German virtue and freedom,[2] and he called for a return of this older, purer culture as part of his nostalgia project and as a means of escaping the dystopian present. For many German writers, like Brant and Hutten, restoring the grand German past also served to complete the

---

1 Hutten, *von der wunderbarlichen artzney*, sig. H2r–H2v: "Was würt ietz Karolus sagen so er widerkem vnd sehe seine fürsten der massen in der seiden bey der fleschen sitzen/ so er alle zeit ein pantzer an im trůg. Und die otten die mit grosser messigkeit tugent eroberten so wir vnß so zertlich schmieren als die weiber/ vnd mit blůmen wol riechenden frömbden speceryen vns ergetzen vil mer den ietz vnd vormalß die weiber/ dz thůn ietz die fürsten vnd priester vnd die geistlichen."
2 Hutten, *Clag an Hertzog Friderich*, sig. a4v.

destiny of Germany as the last empire and to lead history to its logical endpoint under the strong and consensus-building leadership of Emperor Maximilian I.[3]

Brant, Hutten, and many other German writers around 1500 invented and projected an "authentic" German culture of the past that was placed in opposition to a contemporaneous world rife with harmful and deplorable foreign influences. Such nostalgia projects that construct memories of a simpler and purer life in the past appear to be quite universal. Justin Jennings describes how the introduction of snowmobiles, canned foods, and cable TV have led to a significant cultural change among the Yup'ik people of Alaska: "These changes have fueled nostalgia for the older way of life when people were more fit, generous, and disciplined, and when the world in general was quieter, more stable, and without boundary markers."[4] Uplifting stories of the past served as a "rhetorical attempt by the Yup'ik to publish themselves in opposition to the noisy, nasty, non-native world."[5] Contemporary right-wing populist rhetoric is laden with such attempts as well. Donald Trump's "Make America Great Again" campaign slogan conjured up an imaginary nostalgic space that is vaguely located in the 1950s. It was a world anchored in Christian values, secure masculinity, and ethnic purity, devoid of moral ambiguity and political correctness.

Much of Hutten's critique was dedicated to his analysis of how Germans lost touch with this idealized German culture of the past. While foreign influences were in part to blame, Hutten also held Germans themselves responsible for the demise of their own culture. He blamed Germans for throwing money after the Roman Church where it fed the sin of *luxuria*. To Hutten, Germans were not just victims of a sinful and corrupt Roman Curia, they also enabled it by providing the necessary financial resources. Germans were at fault "because we nourish and maintain this vice in Rome so profusely that some of it flows and spills over, as we hold on to this common pestilence of our morals and nourish and sustain this toxic, spreading addiction to a debased life."[6] Hutten's nostalgia project, that is the construction of a memory of a glorious German past, was designed to show what a pure, virtuous German culture could look like in the absence of oppressive foreign dictates.

---

3 See the discussion on Brant's vision of the end of history in Chapter 6.
4 Jennings, *Globalizations*, 137.
5 Fienup-Riordan, *Eskimo Essays*, 223.
6 Hutten, *Clag/ an Hertzog Friderich*, sig. b2r: "weil wir dise vntugent zů Rom daruon erneren vnd halten so überflüssigklich das da selbst her etwas überfleüßt vnd sich ergeüßt/ weil wir dise gemaine pestilentz der sitten halten/ vnd dise vergiffte vmb sich wachsende sucht des vntugentlichen lebens erneren vnnd vnderhalten."

Many contemporaries shared his bleak view of the state of German culture and morality and recognized him, along with Martin Luther, for his efforts to restore lost German values. Johann Eberlin von Günzburg praised Hutten and Luther as defenders of German virtue and faith in the first part of his *Fifteen Confederates* that were addressed to the new Emperor Charles V. As Germany undoubtedly was "the heart of Christendom,"[7] it was important for Eberlin to project a message of hope. To Eberlin, Luther and Hutten represented a rejuvenation of the old, native German values: "These two messengers from God are Martin Luther and Ulrich von Hutten. They are both German-born, highly erudite, and Christian men."[8] Hutten, in particular, was a fighter for the authentic old German ways: "Ulrich von Hutten employs the quill and the sword in order to re-awaken the old German honor, loyalty, faith, and truthfulness."[9]

In his dialogue *Praedones (The Robbers)* from 1521, Hutten identified four types of robbers: street robbers, long-distance merchants, legal scholars, and members of the Catholic clergy, as discussed in Chapter 20. Hutten was particularly concerned with the latter three categories as they were the result of undue foreign influences, were harmful for the common good, and compromised the morals of Germans. For these reasons, they triggered Hutten's xenophobic reflexes.[10] The Roman Curia was intent on unduly depriving Germany of its financial resources, while lawyers introduced foreign and alien legal concepts in the form of Roman law. Merchants were responsible for the spice trade, other forms of long-distance trade, monopolies, and other trade manipulations and profit-making schemes. What is more, they were un-German in their being and in their activities. As the previous chapters documented, the new global trade system didn't just have economic and political consequences. Rather, it created moral and ethical challenges that were rooted in the very nature of trade and of merchants as a class.

A number of authors argued that the entire urban merchant culture was a foreign invention and therefore un-German in nature. Ulrich von Hutten claimed that at the time when the morally pure old Germans lived, that is during the Carolingian and Ottonian periods, neither cities nor merchants were

---

[7] Eberlin von Günzburg, *EJn klägliche klag*, sig. +2r: "das härtz der christenheit."
[8] Eberlin von Günzburg, *EJn klägliche klag*, sig. +3r: "Djse zwen gottes botten sind Martinus Luther vnd Vlrich von Hutten/ sie sind baid teütsch geboren hoch gelert vnd christliche menner."
[9] Eberlin von Günzburg, *EJn klägliche klag*, sig. +3r: "Vlrich von hutten übt die fäder vnd das schwärt zů erwecken alte teütsche erberkeit/ in trew/ glouben vnd warheit."
[10] Hutten, *Praedones*, fol. 21v.

known in Germany.[11] He developed this idea most prominently in his dialogue *Die Anschawenden* (*The Observers*) where Sol and Phaeton debated the issue:

> S. In the beginning, there were no cities at all in the German lands. All buildings were separate from each other, and each had his dwelling alone and for himself. [...] During those times, no merchants came to them who would bring to them foreign goods. They did not desire them either, rather they used what grew in their area, and exclusively so. For their clothing was out of skins and furs of the wild [animals] in their area. Their food was grown out of the earth of their fatherland and raised in their air. They knew nothing of foreign goods, and nobody was cheated by small shopkeepers and merchants. The only principle was a strict integrity, to which everybody was adhering. Money was unknown to them. They had neither silver nor gold.
>
> P. This was the best time in the history of the Germans.
>
> S. Subsequently, foreigners from day to day came to them more and more. First, they traveled to those who lived along the seashore and started to trade with them. After that, they traveled further, until finally the new things were pleasing to the unfit, lazy, and curious ones and the habit of excess was accepted by the common population. This gave them the incentive to first build villages and then cities, which they later fortified with walls, bulwarks, towers, and moats, and within which they sealed themselves off. To this community all slothful, lazy and cowardly members consented.[12]

Hutten's vision of a peaceful, past German culture where walls, weapons, war, and political authority were unknown was shared by many contemporaries.

In the introduction to his *Cosmographia* from 1544, Sebastian Münster told a similar story of the simple and pure beginnings of German culture and of a German people who lived a simple, tough life:

---

11 Hutten, *von der wunderbarlichen artzney*, sig. H2r–H2v.
12 Hutten, "Die Anschawenden," sig. x2v: "S. Anfänglich seind keyne stätt gar im Teütschen land gewesen/ alle bew von ein ander abgesündert/ vnd hat ein yder seine wonung für sich vnd allein gehapt. [...] Zů den selbigen zeytten kamen keine kaufleüt zů jnn/ die jnn etzwas frembdes brächten. Sye begerten des auch nit/ sonder brauchten sich des ihenen so bey jnn wüchsße/ vnd des selbigen allein. Dann jre kleydung was von heüten vnd fellwerck der wilden bey jnn. Jre speyß auß vatterländischer erden gewachsen/ vnd in jren lufft erzogen. Sye wüsten nichtes von frembden gütteren/ vnd war zůr selbigen zeit nymant von den krämern/ vnd kaufleüten betrogen. Allein was ein strenge erberkeit/ noch der helt sich yderman. Gelt wz bey jnn vngesehen. Hatten kein silber noch golt. P. Dz ist die beste zeyt der teütschen gewest. S. Nachvolgens haben sich die außländer von tag zů tag mer und mer bay jnn zugethon/ vnd erstlich bey denen/ so am gestaden des möres gewonet/ angefaren/ mit jnn zů handelen angefangen. Darnoch seind sye auch weyter kommen/ so lang/ biß dz erstlich den vntüglichen trägen vnd fürwitzigen/ die newen ding gefallen/ vnd ist gewonheit des überflusses von gemeynen hauffen angenommen. Das hatt jnn anreytzung erstlich dörfie/ darnoch auch stätt zů bauwen gegeben/ die sye nachuolgens mit muren/ polwercken/ türnen/ vnd gräben beuestiget/ vnd sich also darein verschlossen. Jn welche versamlung alle trägen/ faulen/ vnd vnstreitbaren verwilliget."

They had no official coins in use; there were no crafts nor trade. Rather they gave goods for goods and compensated a good deed with another one. Nobody owned property nor anything else in particular. As air and the sky were commonly owned, so were earth and bodies of water free for everybody.[13]

They had no walls nor moats and moved about freely without concerns for thieves or murderers who were unknown at the time. People had to organize and defend themselves when "wild animals and foreign humans began to engage in robbery."[14] By likening foreigners to wild animals, Münster used a xenophobic topos that is still used in populist rhetoric today. While wild animals and foreigners provided the impetus to create an organized society, Münster described the evolution of a civilization in more positive terms than Hutten, yet with a similarly disturbing outcome. While Hutten blamed foreigners for the rise of a materialistic and effeminate culture and the simultaneous demise of a simple and wholesome ancient German culture, Münster saw dark, demonic forces at work that promoted the rise of vices and illicit desires in Germany. In an apocalyptic turn, Münster argued that dark forces had seduced Germans to desire a sinful life and forbidden occult knowledge.[15]

Johannes Aventinus in his *Chronica Von vrsprung/ herkomen/ vnd thaten/ der vhralten Teutschen* (*Chronicle of the Inception, Origin and Deeds of the Ancient Germans*) from 1541 presented an argument similar to that of Hutten. As the title indicates, the *Chronicle* traces the modest but honorable origin of Germans and their ancient virtues and customs; he too identified Tacitus as his main source.[16] In his *Bayerische Chronik*, Aventinus asserted that old Greek and Roman chronicles noted the simple and modest life of the Germans who preferred iron over gold, that is hard work over idle luxury.[17] The old Germans took shelter in simple huts because those who lived in comfort in well-built and comfortable houses would become "soft and womanish people."[18] Their lifestyle, food, drink, and clothing were simple as they just sought to meet their basic needs. According to

---

13 Münster, *Cosmographia* (1544), sig. a3r: "Sie hetten kein verzeichnete müntz im brauch/ do was kein gewerb noch kauffhandel/ sunder sie gaben war vmb war/ vnd vergolten ein gůtthat mit der andern. Es hett keiner etwas besunders oder eigenthům/ sunder wie der lufft vnd himmel gemein waren/ also was auch das ertrich vnnd die wässer frey bey jeder man."
14 Münster, *Cosmographia* (1544), sig. a3v: "die wilden thier vnd außlendigen menschen begunnen auff den raub zelauffen."
15 Münster, *Cosmographia* (1544), sig. a4r.
16 Aventinus, *Chronica*, sig. A3r–A3v.
17 Aventinus, *Bayerische Chronik*, 1,306.
18 Aventinus, *Chronica*, sig. J1r: "weych vnd weybisch lewt."

Aventinus, the old Germans managed to maintain their pure lives because they did not allow any merchants in their midst: "Merchants had no place among them. They did not allow wine nor other delicacies to be brought into their land. For they believed that the virtue or the strength of humans thus would be weakened, and that soft and timid people would result from that."[19]

Hutten clarified that the merchant class was not German in origin and that its arrival disrupted the peace in the land, which is why merchants were disliked and distrusted in Germany. Furthermore, the foreign luxury merchandise posed a threat to German morals:

> S. For they [the merchants] bring foreign goods to them, such as spices, silk, dyes, and other items, which are used for nothing other than useless splendor and luxury. They reverse the best and most manly morals of their nation with the introduction of foreign customs and of an effeminate life, which runs counter to the German manner and nature and which is hated not without reason.
>
> P. They have cause. For I can well imagine, as many of them conduct themselves in a tender and effeminate way, that many of them have little respect for strict virtue. Since they do not appreciate old customs and innate virtue, innovation and foreign customs will soon arise among them.[20]

To Hutten, the rapidly evolving urban culture of his time, governed by self-interest and Roman law, was a foreign innovation that was alien to German culture. Unlike most writers of the time, Hutten himself was not a product of this urban culture, which may explain his extraordinary disdain for it. As an impoverished imperial knight, he was a member of an old aristocratic class whose days of glory were in the distant past. His regressive nationalistic vision therefore was strongly structured around the empire and the landed nobility.

---

19 Aventinus, *Chronica*, sig. H4v: "Die Kauflewt hetten by jnen kein platz/ sie liessen auch weder Weyn noch ander ding/ so zum Geschleck dienet/ in ir land füren/ dann sie meynten die tugent oder krafft des menschen/ würden dardurch geschwecht/ vnd es würden weych zaghafft lewt dauon."

20 Hutten, "Die Anschawenden," sig. x2r: "S. Umb das sye außlendische war zů jnn bringen. als spetzerey/ seyden/ purpur/ vnd andere/ die zů nichtes/ dann einem vnnutzen pracht vnd überfluß gebrauchlich. verkeren die besten vnd manlichen sitten irer nation/ mit einbringung außlendischer gewonheit/ vnd eines weychen lebens/ dem die Teütsche art von natur wider/ vnd nit vnbillich gehaß ist. P. Sye haben vrsach. Dann ich kan selbs dencken/ die weyl ir vil sich also zart und weychlich halten/ das bey wenigen bleyb achtung strenger tugent. So dann ir alte gewonheit/ vnd angeborne tugend/ also abgeht/ mag bald newerung vnd außländischer brauch bey jnn aufkommen."

Many writers connected the moral decline to foreign influences and specifically foreign imports, as discussed in Chapter 20. To Sebastian Franck, the desire for foreign, imported goods and knowledge about things foreign in general created a moral issue, as he stated in his *Germaniae Chronicon* from 1538:

> Whoever pays attention to the Germans will find this curiosity, deficiency, and apish manner in them. They pay attention to all other things, search, examine, marvel, etc. before they do to their own affairs. They travel and wander through all lands up to the outermost islands in the New World. They espy everything with curiosity, yet do not know themselves. And they are not even lacking a club, as it is the manner of fools,[21] so that they rather marvel about, know, imitate, and query everything with curiosity before they even knew who they were themselves, whence they came, what their ancestors did, talked about, believed, or were. And so it happens with the Germans, as is customary in this world, that they always believe wrongly that the cow of the other has a bigger udder, and that better crops stand on the field of the neighbor. From this follows that the Germans know more to say about Indians than about Germans.[22]

People fell victim to their own curiosity and became enslaved by their illicit desires. More than with morality as a public policy issue, Franck was concerned with spiritual loss, like Sebastian Brant in his *Ship of Fools*, that led to an addictive desire for things foreign: "In sum, to a German is not pleasing what is his own. Instead, just merely out of curiosity, he likes foreign customs, manner of moving, clothes, language, and gestures."[23] Franck thus linked the desire for the foreign with the sin of curiosity. As a result, Germans foolishly spoke, behaved, and dressed like Frenchmen, Italians, and Spaniards.[24] In their desire to be like other nations, they disregarded their core essence and values in Franck's view:

---

[21] Sebastian Brant in the preface to the *Narrenschiff* identified the cap and the club as the insignia of the fool.

[22] Franck, *Germaniae Chronicon*, sig. bb2r: "Demnach wer der Teutschen acht hat/ der findt dissen fürwitz/ mangel/ äffische art an jn/ das sie aller ding echt haben/ sůchen/ nachfragen/ verwundern etc. dann jres eygen dings/ da faren vnnd durchwanderenn sie alle land/ biß zů den eussersten Jnseln/ inn new welt/ erspeen/ fürwitzig all ding vnd sich selbs wissen sie nit/ vnd gefelt jn so gar jr kolb nit/ wie doch der narren art/ das sie all ding ehe verwundern/ wissen/ fürwitzig nachthon vnd erfragen/ dann das sie wisten wer sie selbs weren/ woher/ was jr Vorälternn thon/ geredt/ glaubt oder gwesen weren/ vnd gehet hie nach der welt brauch mit den Teutschen zů/ daß sie jmmer zů wenen/ des ander kůe habe einn grösser euter/ vnd besser traid stand auff deß nachpaurn acker. Auß dissem ist geflossen/ das die Teutschen ehe von Jndianern wissen zů sagen/ dann von Teutschen."

[23] Franck, *Germaniae Chronicon*, sig. bb2r: "vnd gfelt einem Teutschen in summa nicht was sein eigen ist/ sonder nur auß fürwitz/ frembder sitten/ gang/ kleyder/ spraach/ geberde."

[24] Franck, *Germaniae Chronicon*, sig. bb2r.

Only the Germans disavow their language and dress and walk around in alien, strange disguise, as if they had done an evil deed so that one would only recognize them by their drinking and warfare. One knows a Hungarian, Bohemian, Frenchman, Italian, and Spaniard by his speech and language, but a German by his foolishness, laziness, careless drinking, and fighting. His habits, clothing, and speech are so varied and disparate that you cannot know who he is. You almost have to see it as a miracle how he is made and composed out of an Italian, Frenchman, Turk, and Pole. So much color and shape has their speech, clothing, gait, and language, like a people that apishly wants to mimic and speak like other peoples.[25]

Germans did not cultivate their own traditions because they did not know and care about them. To Franck, the Romans were justified to call Germans barbarians because they denied their ancestors and knew so little about their own history, culture, and traditions:

> Out of this carelessness it happened that we do not have nor know anything about ourselves, and that we know better how to talk about the Turks and Tatars than about ourselves and our ancestors. Not without reason, the Romans called us Barbarians, and they were not wrong in this case. Hardly a reasonable, polite word, saying, speech, and deed fell out of the mouth or hand of a Greek that was not recorded by the quill or preserved as a sacred object. But Germans would not know anything about Germans if it wasn't for the Latins taking careful records for us.[26]

With biting sarcasm, Franck painted a bleak picture of a German culture that blindly mimicked other cultures and imported their goods and customs because it lacked self-awareness and self-interest and was not one bit interested in its own history. This argument, of course, served to justify Franck's German chronicle, the *Germaniae Chronicon*, which was written to fill this gap. Franck conceded

---

[25] Franck, *Germaniae Chronicon*, sig. bb2v: "Allein die Teutschen verleugnen jre spraach vnd kleydung/ vnd geen in frembder seltzamer mummerey hereyn/ als haben sie einn böß stuck thon/ das man sie an nicht kan kennen/ dann an sauffen vnd kriegen. Ein Hunger/ Behem/ Frantoß/ Walhen/ Spanier/ kent man bei seiner spraach vnd kleydung/ aber ein Teutschen bei seiner torheit/ vnfleiß/ on sorg sauffen vnd kriegen/ sein sitt/ kleyd vnd spraach ist so vil vnd mancherley/ das du nit kanst wissen wer er ist/ vnd schier für ein wunder achten mußt das auß einem Walhen/ Frantzosen/ Türcken und Polecken gemacht vnnd zůsammen gesetzt sey/ so vil farb vnd gestalt hat jr rede/ kleyd/ gang/ spraach ein volck das äffisch alles allen lendern wil nachthon vnnd reden."

[26] Franck, *Germaniae Chronicon*, sig. bb2v: "Auß disser vnachtsamkeit ist kommen/ das wir nicht vonn vns selbs haben noch wissen/ vnd böß von türcken vnd Dattern wissen zů sagen/ dann von vns selbs vnd vnseren ältern/ das vns die Römer nitt gar vergebens Barbaros haben genent/ vnd in dem fall nit vnrecht thon. Es ist kaum ein vernünfftig höflich wort/ spruch/ red vnd that eim Griechen auß dem mund vnd hand gefallen/ es ist in die feder kommen/ vnd als heilthumb vffghebt worden. Aber vonn teutschenn wissen die teutschenn nicht/ so gar wan nit die Latini für vns sorgfeltig etwas hetten auffzeichnet."

that a generation of Humanists before him, like Willibald Pirckheimer, Conrad Celtis, Conrad Peutinger, and others, had started to compile documents for a German history. Franck, in his own words, was standing on the shoulders of these German Humanists in order to give to the Germans their own chronicle in their own language.[27]

The lack of self-knowledge was a major theme in the literature at the time. Sebastian Brant in chapter 66 of his *Ship of Fools* admonished Germans that a lack of self-knowledge among Germans turned travel to far-away places into a fool's errand. Sebastian Franck urged Germans to learn about their history in order to gain insight into themselves. The perceived lack of self-knowledge led Hieronymus Bock to the conclusion that Germans were thoughtless people who failed to see how God provided for them. Their lack of self-knowledge deprived Germans of insight into the divine order.[28]

In sum, the backlash against globalization is most discernible in three areas. First, Ulrich von Hutten and others recognized that the new global players, like the Fuggers, operated in a transnational space that defied national boundaries and jurisdictions of urban and territorial states. Transnational agency and the de-territorialization of power structures in fact were key contributors to the process of globalization.[29] Merchant-bankers threatened the urban order in which the guilds had played a central role, and they were largely seen as promoting their self-interest at the expense of the common good. The comprehensive literature promoting the common good in the first half of the sixteenth century has to be seen in this context, notably *Von dem Gemeinen nutze* (*On the Common Good*) published by the legal scholar Johannes Ferrarius in 1533.[30] This is a significant factor in the anxieties about social and political instability discussed in Part I.

Second, the emerging global system created anxieties about dislodging the moorings of traditional knowledge that was rooted in the knowledge of the ancients: "Experience gained in explorations and in contact with other cultures increasingly displaced classical sources in the authority for knowledge."[31] The new products from Asia that infiltrated European markets were not part of the knowledge base, myths, and traditions of the ancient world and thus could not be related to.[32] In short, the natural products imported from the non-European

---

[27] Franck, *Germaniae Chronicon*, sig. bb2v.
[28] Bock, *Teütsche Speißkammer*, sig. A2r.
[29] Osterhammel and Petersson, *Geschichte der Globalisierung*, 12.
[30] Ferrarius (*Von dem Gemeinen nutze*, fol. 19r–20v) associated usury and deceptive trade practices with the pursuit of self-interest.
[31] Barrera, "Local Herbs," 164.
[32] Smith, "Profits Sprout," 418.

world "lacked referents in the classical sources."[33] By creating new global connections and building a global trade network, explorers and merchants provided mounting empirical evidence to prove just how inadequate the world view of the ancients was, although they were not particularly interested in debating this question. Not surprisingly, the Humanist intellectuals discussed here, on the other hand, were not able and willing to question the very foundation of their intellectual framework and thus rejected the push for innovation presented by the emerging global system and its protagonists. European Humanists only gingerly started to explore the possibility that their knowledge base and cultural achievements may have been greater than those of the ancients.

Justin Jennings defined vulnerability and the re-embedding of local culture as two of the key hallmarks of globalization. The "interconnectedness of globalization, combined with the related erosion of the local," leads to doubts about the value of one's own cultural norms.[34] "The social changes that occur because of global flows can be traumatic, and some groups react to these changes by returning to local traditions," he writes.[35] As Thomas Hylland Eriksen explains, re-connecting with the local culture is part of globalization processes: "Globalization is *centripetal* in that it connects people worldwide; and it is *centrifugal* in that it inspires a heightened awareness of, and indeed (re)constructions of local uniqueness."[36] The focus on the local thus creates a counterweight to the uncontrollable global. The rise of German nationalism therefore has to be interpreted as part of an effort to reject the foreign, the imported, and the unknown in favor of local cultural and social norms rooted in traditional values.

Third, the emerging global system "fueled nostalgia for the older way of life when people were more fit, generous, and disciplined" and when the world was a simpler and more stable place.[37] What Jennings states for the Eskimo culture of the twentieth century is also true for the German culture of the early sixteenth century, as formulated most succinctly by Ulrich von Hutten. The solution presented by Brant, Hutten, Luther, Paracelsus, Brunfels, Bock, and others was to re-engage with their local culture and to present and (re)invent an authentic German culture in opposition to life in the modern world, which was rife with foreign influences. These pressures from the outside created nostalgia for the good old German ways – a romanticized vision of a time when life was simple but wholesome and of a pure and authentic German culture that never existed.

---

33 Barrera, "Local Herbs," 164.
34 Jennings, *Globalizations*, 139.
35 Jennings, *Globalizations*, 31.
36 Eriksen, *Globalization*, 142.
37 Jennings, *Globalizations*, 137.

The imported foreign spices as the feature of globalization most visible to German intellectuals became symbolic for undue foreign influence and for the threat that it posed to traditional German culture. Their texts both attest to a surge in long-distance connections and critically document how these new global connections affected German culture, thus providing both analysis and critique of early modern globalization and its repercussions for Germany.

Conclusion

Early sixteenth-century responses to the rise of a global system of trade and to the evolution of corresponding cultural and political changes constitute a politics of grievance that are eerily reminiscent of our current historical moment of resurging populism in the early twenty-first century. There is no doubt that the nationalist rhetoric, the defense of traditionalist and chiliastic monarchism, the rejection of the epistemological crisis of spatial exploration, and the broad polemic against long-distance trade constituted a backlash against early modern globalization. While populism is a useful term to describe the current dynamic, it is not a useful and indeed anachronistic term to describe the political backlash of the sixteenth century. The writers of the anti-globalist backlash may have considered the interests of the common man, but the writers themselves were part of an established, declining elite culture that challenged a rising new elite. While some authors tried to rile up public sentiment, particularly by using broadsheets in the vernacular, their impact on a broader public is difficult to assess. Nevertheless, it is conceivable that the anti-globalization rhetoric influenced the broad civic unrest in Germany in 1524–1525 that is commonly referred to as the Peasants' Revolt.

Then and now, populist rhetoric has defied conventional models of political cleavages, that is political or ideological dividing lines that bisect the populace into voting blocs. In the postwar West, cleavages in the political landscape were defined in terms of class politics and in traditional dichotomies like left and right or liberal and conservative. The gradual rise of populism after the demise of the Soviet Union rendered these categories obsolete as populist movements often pursue a seemingly eclectic mix of ideas from across the political spectrum. Inglehart and Norris argue that "the classic economic Left-Right cleavage in party competition is overlaid by a new cultural cleavage dividing Populists from Cosmopolitan Liberalism."[1] They read populism as a grievance and backlash against "an intergenerational shift toward post-materialist values, such as cosmopolitanism and multiculturalism."[2]

Two types of religious cleavages were operative then and still are in today's world. The most obvious one is the sectarian cleavage that played out in the Reformation. While a number of figures covered here played an important role in the Reformation, confessional affiliation per se was not a decisive factor for the issues discussed in this book. Rather, most issues cut across confessional

---

1 Inglehart and Norris, "Trump, Brexit, and the Rise of Populism," 4.
2 Inglehart and Norris, "Trump, Brexit, and the Rise of Populism," 3.

affiliations. More significant was the religious-secular cleavage that focused on the role religion, and by extension the clergy, played in public life. Its most obvious expressions were secularization and pluralization, as discussed in Chapter 16. Secularization and conflicts surrounding the role of religion and the church in society predated the Protestant Reform and in many ways were a prerequisite for it, but at the same time continued after the Reformation. Sebastian Brant in his *Ship of Fools* created a fully secular didactic text, yet infused it with biblical language and imagery to admonish immoral and socially reprehensible behavior and to create a framework of conduct for the urban middle classes in light of a profound transformation of their urban society, to which the church was unable to respond. It is the perceived permissiveness that spawned a conservative backlash against alleged transgressions, just as the political right today polemicizes against the separation of church and state and violations of what they frame as religious freedoms, but also against what they see as social excesses, such as reproductive rights, same-sex marriage, minority rights, women's rights, and gender fluidity.

As early as 1997, Maier redefined the most important political cleavage in spatial terms that is productive for our discussion here: "Despite traditional party labels, today's most important political division is between two de-facto coalitions: call them the party of globalization and the party of territoriality. One seeks to overcome geographical boundaries, the other to restore them."[3] In other words, globalists live in a post-national world, while territorialists are rooted locally and define themselves through their geographic ties and traditional cultural values.

A 2016 editorial in *The Economist* pinpointed "a new political faultline: not between left and right, but between open and closed."[4] Goodhart developed the shorthand Anywheres and Somewheres for the two groups, also making an allowance for a third group, the Inbetweeners.[5] He describes Anywheres as follows: "This is a worldview for more or less successful individuals who also care about society. It places a high value on autonomy, mobility and novelty and a much lower value on group identity, tradition and national social contracts."[6] In a U.S. context, Anywheres also value diversity and a multi-ethnic society. Anywheres "embrace transnational politics and economics."[7] Somewheres, by contrast, tend to be focused on their communities, often church and school,

---

[3] Maier, "The New Political Divide." See also Maier, "Territorialisten und Globalisten."
[4] *The Economist*, 30 July 2016, 7.
[5] Goodhart, *The Road to Somewhere*, 3–4.
[6] Goodhart, *The Road to Somewhere*, 5.
[7] Zielonka, *Counter-Revolution*, 32.

and are more socially conservative.[8] Social issues such as immigration, racial integration, abortion, LGBTQ rights, and school prayer are flashpoints to them. They often oppose institutions that are run by Anywheres, such as academia, the media, Hollywood, and more broadly the knowledge society. They distrust the post-national society and the post-industrial economy.

Western postwar governance, multilateral institutions, like the EU, and institutions of civil society until quite recently were largely controlled by Anywheres. The rise of the populist right in Europe and in North America has gradually questioned that model. First signs were authoritarian populist governments in Hungary and Poland, but the Brexit vote and the election of Donald Trump made clear that mature democracies were not immune and that the movement constitutes a paradigm shift and threatens the postwar order, both rhetorically and politically. The right-wing Heritage Foundation lambastes the twin evils of cosmopolitanism and multiculturalism: "The immigration crisis in America is the physical manifestation of our nation's intellectual confusion. The growing influence of dogmatic cosmopolitanism and multiculturalism has caused chaos in the public mind, which is reflected in the chaos we see on the ground."[9] Even mainstream leaders, like former British Prime Minister Theresa May, succumb to populist rhetoric. In 2016, she castigated cosmopolitans by stating that "citizens of the world are citizens of nowhere."[10] Among white nationalists, the label "cosmopolitan" has become an anti-Semitic dog whistle.[11]

In the introduction, I stated that Humanism pivoted toward pluralization and secularization and that Humanism introduced a high degree of tolerance for ambiguity, that is a tolerance for uncertainty of meaning, vagueness, or multiple possible meanings and interpretations.[12] For globalist Anywheres, a tolerance for ambiguity is a prerequisite to be able to operate in a transnational and transcultural context, both in the early sixteenth century and today. The grievance against the Anywheres documented in this book not only targeted their global activities but also reimposed a rigid intolerance for ambiguity. The Somewheres viewed the Anywheres as agents of decline and tried to close off Germany against foreign influences of any kind and developed a nationalist nostalgia mourning the passing of a simple and pure past. The same applies to today's right-wing populists as well.

---

8 Goodhart, *The Road to Somewhere*, 5.
9 Milikh, "Immigration, Citizenship."
10 Pezzini, "Rootless Cosmopolitans?" 199.
11 Greenfield, "The Ugly History."
12 Bauer, *Die Vereindeutigung*, 13.

If we compare today's anti-globalization backlash with that in Germany in the early sixteenth century, there are similarities but clearly also significant differences. As mentioned above, the protestations against globalization never amounted to a broad popular movement in the early sixteenth century, certainly in part because there were no mass media in place that could have promoted its rise. Furthermore, the political culture at the time did not provide mechanisms for popular movements to influence political processes, such as a public sphere or a fully developed civil society. As a result, the protestations against globalization remained an elite project and were largely without consequences, while the new commercial elites never had to make concessions. A good example is the ability of the global merchant houses to thwart attempts by the Imperial Diet to curb global trade and monopolistic practices in the 1520s.

Similarities include some of the anti-globalization rhetoric, which I will discuss below. Most importantly, the categories of Anywhere and Somewhere are useful to describe the political cleavages in Germany in the early sixteenth century. The "Party of Anywhere" was the driving force behind the global opening of the early sixteenth century. It included long-distance merchants, like the Fuggers and Welsers, and the members of their vast trade networks, investors, adventurers, explorers, mariners, mapmakers, and cosmographers. Intellectuals and publicists like Jobst Ruchamer, Conrad Peutinger, and Willibald Pirckheimer, travel writers like Balthasar Springer and conquerors like Nikolaus Federmann belonged to this group as well. The Iberian crowns provided critical support for the endeavors of the "Party of Anywhere" and profited handsomely, the Spaniards from taxing income generated in the conquest and colonization of the Americas and the Portuguese from controlling the spice trade with Asia in a system commonly referred to as crown capitalism.

The "Party of Somewhere," on the other hand, included most literary writers at the time, like Sebastian Brant, Hermann Bote, Ulrich von Hutten, Hans Sachs, the author of *Dyl Ulenspiegel*, and many others. They represented the old urban elites, that is members of old patrician families and of the guild system who supported the emperor unconditionally as the guarantor of political freedom and independence of the free cities. Brant, Bote, and Sachs were very much rooted in their communities, were tied to their native lands, and knew little about the world outside of their limited horizons. None had traveled beyond the German-speaking lands and showed no interest in them. They were influential people in their urban communities and were vigorous defenders of communal traditions, existing political structures, and social stability in their writings. Herbalists like Otto Brunfels and Hieronymus Bock promoted local herbs and foodstuffs over imports from lands far away. Many writers, Hutten in particular, engaged in an exuberant and irrational nationalism and rejected foreign influences as well as foreign goods. None of them welcomed innovation and change. Perceived change invoked false memories of a heroic past and a nostalgia for imagined former times. In their opposition to the evolving globalization, they bemoaned the passing of a more structured and tradition-bound world, just as their modern populist counterparts do.

No two figures captured the essence of this dichotomy more clearly than Jakob Fugger "the Rich" (1459–1525) and his contemporary Sebastian Brant (1457–1521). Albrecht Dürer (1471–1528) created a portrait of both of them, which captures their respective standings in early sixteenth-century society in a stunning fashion. The Dürer portrait of Fugger in oil from around 1520, a three-quarters bust, shows Fugger as a clean-cut and self-confident modern and fashionable man. He wears a simple but richly embroidered Italianate hat. His simple coat has a very broad fur collar, representing understated wealth. Dürer's portrait is lean, using simple clear lines and little ornamentation. Dürer's three-quarters portrait of Brant from 1520 is a silverpoint drawing. There are no clean, straight lines in this portrait. Brant's hat and coat are wrinkled, and the shirt that is visible underneath the collar is frilly. His slightly downward gaze lacks Fugger's self-confidence. The two portraits, executed at the same time, show two men who played very different roles in society. While Dürer represents Brant as a wrinkly, old-fashioned, and complicated figure, he shows Fugger as a virile modern man with a global outlook.

The analysis of a number of texts revealed distinct lines of conflict in German society from 1490 to 1540, peaking in the 1520s, between a rising secular elite of global players and their allies and associates on one hand and a traditional, localized elite that attempted to enforce the traditional order and power structure on the other. My investigation revealed that the discussion of globalization in the early sixteenth century in Germany resembles the debate in our current historical moment in important ways. While in the contemporary world, the populist "Party of Somewhere" appears to have gained the upper hand after decades of neo-liberal dominance, the rising globalist "Party of Anywhere" came to dominate German politics in the first half of the sixteenth century. In spite of a tireless effort, those protesting it in the absence of democratic structures never gained traction in the political process.

The three parts of this book deal with three interrelated realms in German society between 1490 and 1540 where pressures for change became apparent. Part I considers perceived threats to the political order and the protestations against them, above all a vigorous defense of the common good. Part II traces the intellectual and epistemological upheaval triggered by the spatial discoveries and the new methods of graphic and verbal representation of space. Part III, finally, examines the nationalistic backlash triggered by the rising global trade, abusive trading practices associated with it, and perceived undue foreign influences. Each of the three realms had its own players and stakeholders, although there was significant overlap as well.

The central theme of Part I is the overwhelming sense of political crisis that ran through the literature of this period like a red thread. The twin processes of secularization and pluralization were seen as the roots of the demise of traditional values. Manifestations were both immoral and antisocial individual behavior and the threat to social cohesion posed by the rise of self-interest pursued by the Anywheres. Anywheres and their activities therefore were perceived by the Somewheres as threatening the political and social stability. Somewheres invariably sought to stabilize the social and political systems, and in particular the central role of the emperor and the freedom of urban citizens, with little tolerance for ambiguity. They were invested in a rigid status quo while Anywheres responded more flexibly and positively to unstructured and often ambiguous and adverse circumstances that were difficult to control. Furthermore, secularization and pluralization created the intellectual foundation for the spatial explorations and expansions discussed in Part II and for the evolution of global trade networks discussed in Part III. The two political transformations therefore were thought to have been triggered by the rise of the long-distance merchant class and to shifts in the value system that governed political thinking.

The defense of the traditional social and political system primarily rested on the idea that it was part of natural law and thus God-given, as the first chapter argues. Pragmatists recognized that a more complex society offered more opportunities for transgressive behavior and therefore required more regulations and a growing body of written law, referred to as *Gute Policey* at the time. Critics, including Luther, pointed out that a more comprehensive written legal code was unable to incorporate local legal practices. The codification of customary law and its centralized administration therefore constituted a power grab by the territorial or imperial authorities, as the second chapter outlines.

The third chapter examines anxieties about perceived ruptures in the social and political order in literary texts, using *Dyl Ulenspiegel* and its reception among contemporaries as an example. Far from a benign jokester who pointed to shortcomings in contemporary society, Ulenspiegel's literalism subverted norms of communication and thus disrupted the formation of consensus through verbal communication. The chapter interprets *Dyl Ulenspiegel* as a warning against subversion and upheaval and as a call to rein in the activities of mischievous and lawless figures in the margins who threatened the established order through the protagonist's transgressive actions. Yet, even contemporaries reinterpreted Ulenspiegel as a harmless jokester who held up a mirror to his society.

The fourth chapter shows more broadly how many literary texts represented their reality as a dystopian topsy-turvy world. The carnivalesque, still a valid form of playful and temporary suspension of hierarchical structures in the fifteenth century, became an allegory for a world gone awry permanently in Brant's *Ship of Fools*. Other allegories of inversion, such as tales of the Land of Cockaigne or conduct books praising boorish behavior, became dystopian visions for a world that had become irreversibly corrupted. Rapid social and in particular economic expansion and progress, discussed in the fifth chapter, had a disorienting and anxiety-inducing effect on social and moral norms that could not be adequately reformulated to provide guidance to an urban audience. The idea of innovation and progress therefore was maligned as an agent for the destabilization of basic God-given political and social structures that already had been optimized, by design, functionality, and inner harmony. Literary texts at the time expressed an almost universal yearning for a stable social order that was embedded in a static vision of history and an unchangeable, permanent world view. The very concept of change therefore was alien to the nature of the political order.

Building on the general aversion against innovation, chapter six argues that literary texts so adamantly defended the existing order and, more importantly, fought transgressions against it because in their view a final political and social organization and order had been achieved, at least in theory. Many writers saw the empire of Maximilian I, by virtue of the *translatio imperii* doctrine, as an extension of the Roman Empire, which in turn was the fourth and final empire according to the vision in the Book of Daniel. To Brant, disrupting the political order therefore constituted an arbitrary violation of the course of history prescribed by the Biblical vision. As his model of history worked toward a stable and static end point, leading to the second coming of Christ, Brant viewed political, economic, and social change and innovation with a great deal of distrust and anxiety. In his vernacular texts, in particular in his *Ship of Fools*, he fiercely fought transgressions that might destabilize the political order and social organization and threaten his vision of the end of history. Similarly, the American political scientist Francis Fukuyama in 1989 published a provocative and much-discussed essay entitled "The End of History?" In it, he argued that the victory of western liberal democracy over communism may signal the endpoint of humanity's sociocultural evolution and the final form of human government.

Maintaining the common good as the backbone of communal organization over self-interest as the driver of the new economy perhaps was the most important objective of the political rhetoric, not in the least to salvage the static model of history. The final two chapters of Part I look at how the pursuit of self-interest was seen as a threat to the order and trace the heroic efforts to support the common good and how this can be seen as a struggle "between the people who see the world from Anywhere and the people who see it from Somewhere."[13] The outsize polemics in support of the common good is a strong indicator that it was seen as an endangered value. The loss of a shared good is also mourned in the latest manifesto on behalf of the common good, Robert Reich's *The Common Good* from 2018. Here, Reich argues that the idea of the common good has been vanishing from American political discourse since the 1970s and has been replaced by a more libertarian creed that places the individual ahead of the community: "What we have lost, I think, is a sense of our connectedness to each other and to our ideals – the America that John F. Kennedy asked that we contribute to."[14]

Just like Robert Reich's book, Johannes Ferrarius's *Von dem Gemeinen nutze* (1533) reads like a desperate declaration to fend off the excessive trade practices promoted by Conrad Peutinger, the chief apologist for the pursuit of individual interests, and generally practiced by the large merchant-banker corporations. To its contemporaries, the Fugger Company displayed a callous disregard for the late medieval social contract. Likewise, the excesses of the financial industry were lampooned in Oliver Stone's film *Wall Street* from 1987 from a similar point of view. Here, Gordon Gekko, the investor played by Michael Douglas, declares:

> The point is, ladies and gentleman, that greed – for lack of a better word – is good. Greed is right. Greed works. Greed clarifies, cuts through, and captures the essence of the evolutionary spirit. Greed, in all of its forms – greed for life, for money, for love, knowledge – has marked the upward surge of mankind.[15]

While the film's satire of the Reagan era works differently than the blunt didacticism of Brant and Ferrarius taking on the Fugger era, the sense of loss of a shared common purpose is real in both cases.

Part II outlines both the spatial explorations around 1500 as well as the changes in thinking about space and human interactions with it. Tolerating ambiguity was the prerequisite for scientific inquiry and spatial exploration that were based on empirical observation. The reliance on empirical observation in spatial exploration, cosmography, and map-making presupposed an openness to question preconceived notions and to tolerate uncertainty and ambiguity. This was the realm of the Anywheres. Many writers were not prepared to give up the certainties of their sheltered, localized environments, the world of Somewheres.

---

13 Goodhart, *The Road to Somewhere*, 3.
14 Reich, *The Common Good*, 4.
15 Clifton-Soderstrom, *The Cardinal*, 48.

They not only rejected the outcome, namely newly found territories and an emerging global grid of geographic knowledge, but they also challenged the endeavor of innovation, search, travel, and exploration itself. Examining this basic conflict between Anywheres and Somewheres and exploring their basic epistemological assumptions is the overarching theme of Part II.

Chapter 9 surveys German travel narratives, which range from pilgrimage accounts to reports by travelers who participated in trade missions or colonial conquests. The earlier texts dealt exclusively with narratives focusing on travel to Asia as Germans participated in some trade missions in the first decade of Portuguese navigation to India. Travel narratives beyond those by Columbus and Vespucci were hard to come by in Germany because no Germans traveled to the New World. Furthermore, the Portuguese and the Spaniards after 1500 increasingly saw it as proprietary information and therefore released it sparingly. While a number of Germans traveled to America starting in the 1520s, the first written account about their activities did not appear until after 1550. These were mostly first-person accounts that were based on empirical observation and personal experience. What these reports have in common is the uncritical and even positive attitude toward travel and spatial explorations and generally a lack of critical examination of their activities.

The tenth chapter deals with theoretical writings about space, mostly in the form of cosmographies and chorographies, which arose out of a renewed interest in chronicles in the fifteenth century. Diachronic narratives focusing on both Biblical and classical history were increasingly supplemented with descriptions of cities, states, and landscapes, starting with Schedel's *Nuremberg Chronicle* from 1493. If the German Empire, as the fulfillment of the vision of the four empires, was the end point of history, as argued in Chapter 6, the role of historical narratives indeed was diminished. Such hybrid texts fostered the rise of cosmographical and chorographical texts that privileged spatial, cultural and anthropological over chronological information. This process can be traced in the three subsequent editions of Christian Egenolff's chronicle, for instance. Sebastian Franck's *Weltbůch* from 1534 made critical steps toward fully establishing the new cosmographic paradigm. Franck also wrote a chronicle, evidence that Franck fully appreciated the two separate generic traditions.

The complex legacy of Ptolemy's *Geography* is the starting point for the eleventh chapter. On one hand, Ptolemy's grid system was very useful because it understood the globe as calculable spherical space that made the world knowable and describable. On the other hand, the Ptolemaic model was no longer able to support the rapid pragmatic expansion of spatial knowledge. A comparison between the 1507 and the 1516 world maps by Martin Waldseemüller vividly illustrates this. While the earlier map was designed according to the

Ptolemaic tradition, the 1516 *Carta marina* was based on contemporaneous information provided on navigational maps and in reports by travelers, merchants, and mariners, which ironically led him to drop the name America from the second map. Waldseemüller, Fries, and others, but also globe makers like Schöner adapted Ptolemy's grid in order to conceptualize a new world view where each spot on earth had precise coordinates and where new discoveries could simply be added to the grid without challenging it in principle. The gradual acceptance of this new way of thinking set up a backlash by those who remained loyal to a strict Eurocentric geography confined by Ptolemy's knowledge base.

The new pragmatic and empirical geographic method practiced by mariners and merchants and increasingly propagated by travel reports and cosmographies only gradually led to a new world view, but it became evident that Ptolemy no longer could serve as a heuristic model, as Chapter 12 argues. The discussion of newly discovered islands and territories ultimately forced a departure from Ptolemaic world view as it did not provide a niche to integrate this new knowledge. Cosmographers started to point out that the geographic horizon of the Ancients was quite limited and developed an awareness that their knowledge base was broader than that of the ancients. The key point is that this subset of Humanists, which we might call the "Party of Anywhere," pragmatically pursued geographic knowledge with great interest and curiosity and gradually shaped a new global outlook in a German intellectual context.

Many writers supporting the old local elites rejected this dynamic view of space and history as it ran counter to their ideal of a frozen history, stable order, and static notion of space. This group could be described as the "Party of Somewhere." Chapters 13 and 14 analyze this backlash against the spatial turn of the period around 1500. Among the most prominent passengers of Sebastian Brant's *Ship of Fools* were those who traveled far and wide. Brant created the image of the flawed traveler who sought to know the word without knowing himself – a theme picked up by Sebastian Franck and others. He even adjusted the myths of Hercules and Odysseus to connect their failures with their needless and indeed harmful travels. Brant also warned of the perils of measuring the earth, the work of cosmographers, as it only served lust and curiosity.

Chapter 14 investigates the function of travel and space in narrative texts. The anonymous *Fortunatus*, written in the 1480s, and Jörg Wickram's novel *Von Gůten vnd Bösen Nachbaurn* (*Of Good and Evil Neighbors*, 1556) form the bookends. *Fortunatus* still lives in the world of late medieval pilgrimages and fantastic voyages to the Orient, while Wickram's novel shows how travel and mercantile activities had become normalized by the middle of the sixteenth century. Literary texts written in-between viewed travel and the exploration of space very much like Brant did, namely as sinful activities that never served a moral purpose. In various texts, Hans Sachs presented the road as a physically and morally perilous place where strange people and spirits lurked. The basic moral flaw of the titular hero in *Dyl Ulenspiegel* was his mobility: he was a vagrant without geographic roots and therefore lacked a firm social identity. Its author rejected mobility as the source of Ulenspiegel's evil deeds.

Part II closes with a chapter on the struggle in German culture of dealing with the concept of the New World and in particular of integrating America into the knowledge base. We find huge discrepancies in both knowledge and perception of America, both across Europe and within Germany. The Portuguese and the Spaniards had first-hand knowledge as they sponsored many expeditions along the African coast, to India, and to the New World. The Portuguese immediately seized the economic opportunities their discoveries offered, while the Spaniards from the very beginning explored America with the intent of creating a colonial empire. The treaties of Tordesillas (1494) and Saragossa (1529) show how Portugal and Spain, but also the Catholic Church, developed a global understanding of the world along with global hegemonial aspirations. The large German merchant houses understood this world and were networked in it. However, printed German publications about America indicate that this knowledge was not shared and that America as a new continent did not become part of canonical knowledge until about 1540. As a consequence, the secretive actions of the German merchant houses were poorly understood in Germany, yet seen with a great deal of distrust as their economic impact was clearly felt in Germany. The anti-globalist rhetoric, discussed in Part III, therefore in part focused on the notion of territoriality. This is why the spatial expansion around 1500 as well as the political and epistemological struggles surrounding it are such an important part of the narrative developed in this book.

Part III is entirely focused on globalization around 1500, on its impact on Germany, and in particular on the populist backlash against it. Globalization was enabled by the groundbreaking explorations of the late fifteenth and early sixteenth centuries and by a reconceptualization of the world as a spherical space that could be explored and traveled endlessly, as discussed in Part II. This permitted European commercial interests, licensed by the Iberian crowns, to make direct connections with South and East Asia as well as with the Americas and to set up global trade networks. While the territorial state with a growing centralized administration was on the rise around 1500, the large transnational corporations, like the Fugger Company of Augsburg, clearly worked against that trend in favor of an unfettered access to global markets. This is the basic conflict between state regulators and transnational corporations that plays out in today's globalized world as well. Likewise, a capitalist economy was not fully formed yet, but the large merchant-bankers of the time contributed notably to its evolution.

There has been a growing consensus in scholarship that the period around 1500 can be seen as the first phase of globalization. Chapter 16 summarizes this discussion and establishes a methodological framework within which premodern globalization can be discussed. Globalization cannot be defined on the basis of empirical, quantitative evidence alone. According to Justin Jennings, two qualitative, cultural factors are more critical. First, there had to be a leap in interregional, long-distance interaction beyond established networks. Second, these global networks affected local cultures and prompted "social changes that are associated with the creation of a global culture."[16] Globalization therefore presupposes tolerance for ambiguity and promotes pluralization, that is in this context an openness toward foreign influences and imported, alien products. One effect of globalizing pressures also could be a grievance against global connections in favor of local particularities and practices. Part III traces this backlash that created a cleavage between the mostly pragmatic participants in the global trade and those who defended an insular German culture that was connected only locally, that upheld a traditional social structure, and that sought to create connections with a lost, morally pure past. Again, this cleavage can be described as conflict between the "Party of Anywhere" and the "Party of Somewhere." There was also a geographic dimension to this cleavage. Merchant cities like Augsburg, Nuremberg, Ulm, Memmingen, and others mostly supported the global trade while its antagonists mostly could be found along the Upper Rhine river in cities like Strasbourg and Basel.

In order to contextualize this backlash, Chapter 17 takes a look at the German involvement in the explorations of the period and at the German involvement with the expanding global connections. German corporations, such as the Fugger, Welser, Hirschvogel, and Vöhlin companies, created European trade networks before 1500 and maintained branch offices in many of the leading trading hubs. German companies also participated in the early Portuguese expeditions to Calicut, and several travel accounts describing them were published in Germany. This connection ended when the Portuguese Crown claimed a monopoly over the trade with Asia in 1506. While German merchants were not directly involved in the trade with Asia after that point, they supplied the Portuguese with most of the silver and copper used to purchase spices and other merchandise in Asia and were given the monopoly to distribute the imported spices in the Empire. While the volume of this trade did not exceed

---

16 Jennings, *Globalizations*, 21.

two percent of the gross domestic product,[17] the impact of this trade was keenly felt and debated in Germany, particularly the resulting shortage in silver coins and the monopolies the large merchant-bankers enjoyed.

The remaining five chapters describe various aspects of the grievance and backlash against global trade and other perceived foreign influences. Chapter 18 discusses negative responses to a range of trading practices, such as usury, hoarding, unfair competitive practices, and monopolies, which all led to inflation and hunger suffered by poor people, but also dishonest practices like using deceptive and dishonest measurements or selling merchandise that was spoiled, diluted, or otherwise of a poor quality. Chapter 19 looks at the objection to macro-economic conditions, such as outflow of financial resources, particularly gold and silver, to pay for imported goods. In an argumentation reminiscent of Donald Trump's economic nationalism, the perceived trade imbalance was seen as harmful to Germany while foreign merchants profited unfairly. Furthermore, monopolies helped German merchants generate excessive, unearned wealth. During the first three decades of the sixteenth century, a vociferous opposition to monopolies, particularly in the spice trade and in mining, prompted the Imperial Diet to take action. However, Jakob Fugger successfully pressured Emperor Charles V to rescind these measures, illustrating just how legitimate the polemics against Fugger were. This may have been the first intervention ever by a corporation to rewrite public policy, a pattern with which we are all too familiar today.

Chapter 20 explores the larger context of German nationalism that evolved in the fifteenth century, grouped around the ideas of national languages, national stereotypes, and civic patriotism, and culminated in openly nationalistic texts in the first three decades of the sixteenth century. These texts developed a xenophobic rhetoric around three key issues. Beyond the financial drain imported goods inflicted, the critique of merchants framed the merchant class as a whole as Italianate foreign import that disrupted the simple but honest local trading system the Germans had prior. Likewise, the Roman Church was increasingly seen as a foreign institution that sought to exert political control over Germany and fraudulently drained Germany of its financial resources. This complaint against the Church was shared widely beyond Lutheran circles in the 1510s and 1520s. The third issue was the rise of a written legal code based on Roman law that replaced the traditional, localized legal system rooted in natural law. Both law and lawyers were rejected as Roman imports. Ulrich von Hutten's xenophobic rhetoric resembles Trump's narrative where powerful alien forces, from immigrants to foreign traders, have undermined the well-being of

---

17 Parker, *Global Interactions*, 69.

America. The consensus held that traditional German freedoms were curtailed, that is the German independence from and preeminence over other European nations, but also the liberation from foreign influences, like Roman law and the Roman Church. The insistence on the *libertas Germanorum* resembled the sovereignty claims raised by Brexit supporters and in Trump's "Make America Great Again" campaign.

Chapter 21 picked up the theme of the nationalistic rejection of long-distance trade and importation of goods, specifically the repudiation of the global spice trade. The availability of exotic goods created a desire and addiction to the point where Germans dismissed domestically grown foodstuffs that were more wholesome and less expensive, leading to a decline of traditional German values. The consumption of fine, luxurious foods has always been seen as an elite project, extending to organic foods today. Inversely, Donald Trump's demonstrative consumption of hamburgers, the quintessential local American food, in the White House serves to connect with his populist base in the "Party of Somewhere."[18] As part of the backlash of the early sixteenth century, spice books stressed that everything Germans needed for sustenance was grown on German soil. Foods not grown on German soil nor in a German climate were seen as nutritionally inferior and even harmful because their elemental and humoral composition was not appropriate for cold German bodies. From a theological viewpoint, God's creation provided ample sustenance for all creatures as long as humans did not interfere with their unethical trade practices. The importation of foodstuffs therefore was in violation of the natural order and of God's plan that provided mild foods to Germans who lived in moderate climate zones while supplying spicy foods to those who lived in hot climates.

The anxiety about contemporaneous cultures invariably invokes false memories of a more wholesome and morally pure past. In this nostalgia project, fragments relating to former times are fused into a fake historical narrative that serves to justify a political backlash. Our current historical moment abounds with examples. Brexiteers allude to the glorious past of the British Empire, while "Make Amerika Great Again" evokes a purer America that controlled its borders and where white men were not emasculated by the emancipation of women, by civil rights for minorities, and by LBGTQ rights. As Chapter 22 argued, the backlash against pluralization and globalization devised a comparable nostalgia project that invented and projected an "authentic" German culture of the

---

[18] Trump served Hamburgers when the Clemson University football team visited the White House on 14 January 2019. He called it "great American food," and added, "If it's American, I like it. It's all American stuff."

past. Many considered the Carolingian and Ottonian periods to be the heroic time when the old German morals and virtues as well as German masculinity and virility were still intact and when neither cities nor merchants were known in Germany yet. This served as a counterpoint to a bleak view of the state of German culture and morality and to a contemporaneous world rife with harmful and deplorable foreign influences. This world was exploited by the new global players, like the Fuggers, who operated in a transnational space that defied national boundaries and jurisdictions of urban and territorial states. Furthermore, the emerging global system created anxieties about dislodging the moorings of traditional knowledge that was rooted in the knowledge of the ancients. It is this emerging global system that fueled nostalgia for an older way of life in Germany that was marked by a disciplined and moral life as well as by simplicity, generosity, and stability.

Obviously, this study could not answer all questions. The question of regional differences and of regional networks could not be fully addressed in this study. This study mostly excluded the northern half of Germany as the book culture of the late fifteenth and early sixteenth centuries was largely concentrated in the southern half of Germany. The Hanseatic League, the dominant trade network in the Baltic Sea and the North Sea in the late Middle Ages, was well past its peak influence during the period discussed here, and it largely failed to make a connection with the new networks that did their northern European business through Antwerp. To be sure, merchant cities like Hamburg or Lübeck still were active, but they did not play a role in the new networks.

The story largely played out in southern German cities. The large merchant-banker companies were concentrated in Swabian cities like Augsburg, Ulm, and Memmingen, in addition to the Franconian city of Nuremberg. These cities started to specialize in long-distance trade and established commerce-based networks in the fifteenth century. They formed natural constituencies in support of the rising global trade networks, the "Party of Anywhere." These networks were implemented gradually and pragmatically, but not discussed or theorized, with the exception of the rigorous written defense of the activities of merchant-bankers by Conrad Peutinger. The opposition, the "Party of Somewhere," mostly came from southwestern Germany, the region between Basel and Strasbourg, the Nuremberg writer Hans Sachs being an outlier even though his views were quite moderate and his writings not polemical. These cities were sites of traditional learning and were part of active regional trade networks but did not partake in the new global networks. There appears to have been little contact between the two groups, and the vocal criticism of the global trade ultimately had little impact.

Furthermore, this study focused on Germany only and did not look outside the boundaries of the Empire at the time. It would be of interest if similar anti-globalization polemics took root in other nations that did not directly participate in the global trade, like France. While the French Crown showed little interest in colonial ventures in the sixteenth century,[19] merchant cities in northern France became quite active in Portuguese possessions in Brazil, and French boats and fishermen traveled to the Grand Banks off Newfoundland. While France did not formally seize its first colonies until the early seventeenth century, the interest in colonial expansion in France reached back into the sixteenth century. The British colonial conquest had already begun in the last quarter of the sixteenth century. Italians, Spaniards, and Portuguese were involved in discoveries and colonial projects from the very beginning. Germany therefore appears to be the outlier as a largely landlocked nation with little interest in voyages of discovery and in colonial projects. We also have to consider that Germany had a decentralized political structure with multiple political and cultural centers and with highly autonomous cities, all the while other nations, like France, Britain, and Spain, were consolidating power in the hands of national royal houses in the fifteenth century. Germany was highly focused on internal issues and therefore was a much less likely actor in the creation of global networks.

We have to remember that German merchants participated only in one colonial project, the Welser project in Venezuela, which went virtually unnoticed in Germany and did not leave a lasting legacy. Nevertheless, it is unclear if this book presented a specifically German narrative or if some of the themes raised in Germany were discussed in other nations as well. Further research in how globalization pressures were perceived in other nations therefore would be desirable. Furthermore, it would be interesting to examine how this discussion played out in Spain and Portugal – nations that promoted exploration and expansion and profited from global trade.

This book leaves two important questions unanswered. Firstly, it would be important to ask the question of how early sixteenth-century globalization ended. This question is relevant for our time as the common belief after the fall of the Soviet Union was that globalization was going to be a lasting paradigm and that the "Party of Anywhere" would prevail eternally. Yet, we see a clear backlash against globalization in the resurgence of right-wing populism, symbolized by Brexit and Trump. While global trade has not ended, the enthusiasm for global expansion seems to have vanished as the "Party of Somewhere" has

---

19 Schwitter, "Das Desinteresse am Neuen," 68.

become influential in many developed nations. I would argue that the globalization of the early sixteenth century did not end either but that it was channeled into nationalist projects of colonization in which neither Germany as a nation nor German merchants participated.

While the early voyages to Asia were sponsored by commercial interests, including the Welsers and Fuggers of Augsburg, the Portuguese Crown soon sought to limit the participation of foreign merchants in the Asian spice trade by implementing the crown monopoly in 1506. The German merchants were reduced to the role of distributing the spices in the Empire, although the Fuggers remained important suppliers of German copper and silver at least into the 1530s. Later in the century, the key players in the Asia trade changed. The Portuguese gradually lost control over the spice trade with Asia in the second half of the sixteenth century as other players challenged their dominance, in particular the British and the Dutch. National trading companies, like the British East India Company or the Dutch Vereenigde Oostindische Compagnie, pushed into the trade. While these corporation had a global reach, they behaved like state actors and thus served a nationalist agenda.

The Spanish conquest and colonization of the New World was initially financed by large merchant-banker corporations as well. An example is the 1528 contract signed by the Welser Company with the Spanish Crown to colonize Venezuela and to build settlements and mining operations, a project that was never profitable. However, the Spanish Crown changed its policies in the 1530s. It gradually curtailed the interests of conquistadors and of commercial entities in order to develop an administrative apparatus in the colonies that served a nationalist agenda and that was entirely controlled by the Crown. The globally networked companies, like the Welsers, were squeezed out, to be replaced by bureaucrats loyal to the Crown. The innovative energy, the enthusiasm, and the venture capital driving the explorations around 1500 dried up and dissipated as colonization became an increasingly nationalist project administered by bureaucrats in the employ of the crowns of Spain or Portugal.

The southern German merchant houses also had a geographic disadvantage. The southern German merchants were well-positioned geographically to bring Asian merchandise from Venice to areas north of the Alps. The new trade route to Asia around Africa and the European discovery of America shifted commercial activities to the Atlantic; ports of entry now were Lisbon, Seville, and Antwerp. Southern German merchants were less well-equipped to participate in the Atlantic trade. Initially, they were able to engage in the Portuguese trade system because they provided much of the silver and copper for the Asian trade. However, the importance of German merchants declined as metals from the New World became available. At the same time, German merchants were forced to abandon their operations in the New World. As a result, German merchants had become marginalized players in the new globalized economy by the 1540s. The result was a restructuring of the business model of many southern German merchant houses, but by no means their demise.[20]

The second question is more interesting from the point of view of this book: What happened to anti-globalization discourses after 1540? When did the anti-globalization rhetoric subside, and under what circumstances? The backlash against globalization and grievances against its impact on Germany gradually waned in the 1530s. The why and how has not been researched; this would be worthy of further investigation. There is no indication that globalization critics managed to effect policy changes in spite of some efforts. The question of whether this movement had a lasting cultural effect can only be answered after further study. Protest movements sometimes just run out of steam, and perhaps the generation that followed Hutten, Brunfels, and others lost interest in the issue. The waning influence of the southern German merchant houses may have helped in this process. As imported spices made inroads into urban middle-class homes, perhaps the Asian spice trade became accepted and normalized. Jörg Wickram's novel *Von Gůten vnd Bösen Nachbaurn* (*Of Good and Evil Neighbors*), published in 1556, illustrates this process. It tells the adventures of a wealthy merchant from Antwerp who set up his business in Lisbon. Of significance is that both travel and long-distance trade were represented as perfectly normal and even honorable activities. Wickram's novel also shows how the focus of trade had shifted to the Atlantic world.

By the middle of the sixteenth century, the virulent phase of globalization had given way to economic nationalism, which had certainly gotten a boost from the rapid evolution of global trade. The conquest, colonization, and maintenance of trade networks increasingly became nationalist projects. The economic nationalism evolving around the middle of the sixteenth century was connected to the emerging idea that individual economic success benefitted the overall national welfare. This is an insight offered by Wickram's novel as well. The novel's protagonists act as individuals driven by their own inner moral compass rather than by social constraints. Their mercantile careers and accumulation of wealth are never challenged, and the question is never raised whether they served the common good. As Leonhard Fronsperger argued, merchants did not risk their lives traveling across the oceans to provide for others. Rather merchants were motivated by self-interest, and by providing

---

20 Häberlein, *The Fuggers of Augsburg*, 98.

for themselves and for their families they also provided for others.[21] The pursuit of the self-interest after 1540 therefore is connected with the pragmatic turn away from social concerns and with a renewed interest in the personal and private realm. Within this framework, there was little space to discuss the merits of globalization.

---

21 Fronsperger, *Von dem Lob*, fol. 18v.

Bibliography

Primary Literature

Agricola, Johannes. *Drey hundert Gemeyner Sprichworter/ der wir Deutschen vns gebrauchen/ vnd doch nicht wissen woher sie kommen*. Haguenau: Johann Setzer, 1529.

Alciato, Andrea. *Emblematum libellus*. Paris: Chrestien Wechel, 1542. [Reprint Darmstadt: Wissenschaftliche Buchgesellschaft, 1980.]

Anon. *Canon oder außlegung diser gegenwertigen Mappen/ Europa genant*. Nuremberg: Christoph Zell, 1533.

Anon. *Copia der Newen Zeytung auß Presillg Landt*. Nuremberg: s.n., 1514.

Anon. *Den rechten weg auß zu faren von Lißbona gen Kallakuth*. Nuremberg: Wolfgang Huber, 1506.

Anon. *Der Oberrheinische Revolutionär. Das buchli der hundert capiteln mit xxxx statuten*. Ed. Klaus H. Lauterbach. Hanover: Hahnsche Buchhandlung, 2009.

Anon. *Der Wûcherer Meßkram oder Jarmarkt*. Frankfurt am Main: Hermann Gülfferich, 1544.

Anon. *Die reyse van Lissebone om te varenna dat eylandt Naguaria in groot Indien gheleghen*. Antwerp: Jan van Doesborch, 1508.

Anon. *Die Welsch-Gattung*. Ed. Friedrich Waga. Breslau: M. & H. Marcus, 1910.

Anon. *Dyl Vlenspiegel. In Abbildung des Drucks von 1515 (S 1515)*. Ed. Werner Wunderlich. Göppingen: Kümmerle, 1982.

Anon. *Ein kurtzweilig lesen von Dyl Vlenspiegel geboren vß dem land zů Brunßwick. Wie er sein leben volbracht hatt. xcvi. seiner geschichten*. Strasbourg: Johann Grüninger, 1515.

Anon. *Ein kurtzweilig lesen von Dil Ulenspiegel geboren vß dem land zů Brunßwick. Wie er sein leben volbracht hat. xcvi. seiner geschichten*. Strasbourg: Johann Grüninger, 1519.

Anon. *Fortunatus. Studienausgabe nach der Editio Princeps von 1509*. Ed. Hans-Gert Roloff. Stuttgart: Reclam, 1981.

Anon. *Hie kompt ein Beüerlein zu einem reychen Burger von der gult/ den wucher betreffen*. Speyer: Johann Eckhart, 1522.

Anon. *Liber vagatorum Der Betler orden*. Pforzheim: Thomas Anshelm, 1510.

Anon. *Newe zeittung. Von dem lande. Das die Sponier funden haben ym 1521. iare genant Jucatan*. Erfurt: Matthes Maler, 1522.

Anon. *Von Vlenspiegel eins bauren sun des lands Braunschweick/ wie er sein leben volbracht hat/ gar mit seltzamen sachen*. Erfurt: Melcher Sachse, 1532.

Anon. *Vom wucher. Furkauff vnd Tryegerey*. Augsburg: s.n., c.1535.

Anon. *Wunderbarliche geschicht anzeygung/ so newlich in Portugal vnnd sonnderlich zu Lisebona geschehen sind*. Augsburg: s.n., 1531.

Apian, Peter. *Cosmographicus Liber Petri Apiani Mathematici studiose collectus*. Landshut: Johannes Weissenburger, 1524.

Augustine of Hippo Saint. *The City of God*. New York: Random House, 1993.

Aventinus, Johannes. *Bayerische Chronik*. In: *Johannes Turmair's genannt Aventinus Sämmtliche Werke*. Vierter Band, erste Hälfte. Bayerische Chronik, Buch I. Munich: Christian Kaiser, 1882.

Aventinus, Johannes. *Chronica Von vrsprung/ herkomen/ vnd thaten/ der vhralten Teutschen. 1541*. Nuremberg: Johann Petreius, 1541.

Beck, Balthasar. *Herbarius. Kreüter bůch von neüwem mit hochstem fleisß durch sůcht und gebessert. sampt drey neüwen Registern.* Strasbourg: Balthasar Beck, 1527

Bock, Hieronymus. *Kreüter Bůch. Darin Underscheidt/ Würckung und Namen der Kreüter so in Deutschen Landen wachsen.* Strasbourg: Wendel Rihel, 1546.

Bock, Hieronymus. *Kreüter Bůch. Darinn Vnderscheidt/ Namen vnnd Würckung der Kreuter/ Stauden/ Hecken vnnd Beumen/ sampt jhren früchten/ so inn Deütschen Landen wachsen.* Strasbourg: Wendel Rihel, 1551.

Bock, Hieronymus. *New Kreütter Bůch von vnderscheydt/ würckung und namen der kreütter so in Teütschen landen wachsen.* Strasbourg: Wendel Rihel, 1539.

Bock, Hieronymus. *Teütsche Speißkammer. Jnn welcher du findest/ Was gesunden vnnd krancken menschen zur Leibs narung vnd desselben gepresten von nöten.* Strasbourg: Wendel Rihel, 1550.

Bote, Hermann. *Das Schichtbuch. 1514.* In: Ludwig Hänselmann (ed.). *Die Chroniken der niedersächischen Städte.* Braunschweig, 2. Band. Leipzig: Hirzel, 1880. 269–493.

Bote, Hermann. *Hermen Botes Radbuch. In Abbildung des Druckes L ca. 1492/93. Mit dem Text nach Herman Brandes und mit einer Übersetzung von Heinz-Lothar Worm.* Ed. Werner Wunderlich. Göppingen: Kümmerle, 1985.

Brant, Sebastian. *An den allerdurchleüchtigsten Großmechtigsten Fürsten und Herren/ Herrn Carolum den fünfften Römischen Keiser vnnd Hyspanischen.* Strasbourg: Martin Flach, 1520,

Brant, Sebastian. *Daß Narren Schyff.* Basel: Johann Bergmann, 1494.

Brant, Sebastian. *Das Narrenschiff. Studienausgabe.* Ed. Joachim Knape. Stuttgart: Reclam, 2005.

Brant, Sebastian. *De moribus et facetijs mense. Thesmophagia.* Basel: Michael Furter, 1490. In: Silke Umbach (ed.). *Sebastian Brants Tischzucht (Thesmophagia 1490). Edition und Wortindex.* Wiesbaden: Harrassowitz, 1995. 37–71.

Brant, Sebastian. *Der richterlich Clagspiegel. Ein nutzbarlicher begriff: Wie man setzen vnd formieren sol nach ordenung der rechten ein yede clag/ antwort/ vnd vßsprechene vrteylen/ gezogen auß geistlichen vnd weltlichen rechten.* Strasbourg: Matthias Hupfuff, 1516.

Brant, Sebastian. "Eyn Chronick über Teutsch land/ zuuor des landes Elsas/ vnd der loblichen statt Straßburg/ durch Sebastian Brant versamlet." In: Caspar Hedio. *E/n Außerleßne Chronick von anfang der welt bis auff das iar nach Christi vnsers eynigen Heylands gepurt M. D. xxxix.* Strasbourg: Kraft Müller, 1539. 731–771.

Brant, Sebastian. "Doctor Sebastian Brannd vor reden in disen Layenspiegel." In: Ulrich Tengler. *Laÿen Spiegel von rechtmässigen ordnungen in Burgerlichen vnd peinlichen regimenten.* Augsburg: Johann Rynman and Johann Otmar, 1509. Sig. ¢2r–¢2v.

Brant, Sebastian. *Kleine Texte.* Ed. Thomas Wilhelmi. Stuttgart: Frommann-Holzboog, 1998.

Breydenbach, Bernhard von. *Peregrinatio in terram sanctam. Eine Pilgerreise ins Heilige Land. Frühneuhochdeutscher Text und Übersetzung.* Ed. Isolde Mozer. Berlin: de Gruyter, 2010.

Bronner, Teus. *Ein new lied/ von dem fürkauff/ vnd vnbillichem wucher der gesellschafften vnd kaufflewten.* Nuremberg: Gutknecht, 1542.

Brunfels, Otto. *Almanach ewig werend/ Teütsch vnd Christlich Practick/ von dem. xxvj. Jar an/ biß zů endt der welt aller welt.* Strasbourg: Johann Prüß der Jüngere, 1526.

Brunfels, Otto. *Contrafayt Kreüterbůch.* Strasbourg: Hans Schott, 1532.

Brunschwig, Hieronymus. *Apoteck für den gmeynen man. der die Ertzte zuersuchen. am gůt nicht vermügens/ oder sonst in der not allwege nicht erraychen kan*. Augsburg: Heinrich Steiner, 1529.
Bucer, Martin. *Das ym selbs niemant/ sonder anderen leben soll. vnd wie der mensch dahyn kummen mög*. Strasbourg: Johann Schott, 1523.
Bünting, Heinrich. *Itinerarivm Sacrae Scriptvrae. Das ist/ Ein Reisebuch, Uber die gantze heilige Schrifft/ in zwey Bücher getheilet*. Helmstedt: Jakob Lucius, 1581.
Carion, Johannes. *Chronica durch Magistrum Johan Carion/ vleissig zusamen gezogen/ meniglich nützlich zu lesen*. Wittenberg: Georg Rhau, 1532.
Celtis, Conrad. "Oratio in Gymnasio in Ingelstadio Publiae Recitata. (Public Oration Delivered in the University of Ingolstadt)." In: Leonard Forster (ed.). *Selections from Conrad Celtis 1459–1508*. Cambridge: Cambridge University Press, 1948. 36–65.
Columbus, Christopher. *The Four Voyages*. Ed. and transl. J. M. Cohen. London: Penguin Books, 1969.
Copernicus, Nicholas. *On the Revolutions*. Ed. Jerzy Dobrzycki. Transl. Edward Rosen. London: Macmillan Press, 1978.
Cortés, Hernán. *Praeclara Ferdinandi Cortesii de noua maris oceani Hyspania narratio sacratissimo*. Nuremberg: Friedrich Peypus, 1524.
Cuba, Johannes von. *Kreutterbůch von allem Erdtgewächs*. Ed. Eucharius Rößlin. Frankfurt: Christian Egenolff, 1533.
Cuppener, Christoph. *Ein schons buchlein czu deutsch. doraus ein itzlicher mensche. was standes er sey. lernen mag. was wucher und wucherische hendel sein*. Leipzig: Melchor Lotter, 1508.
Dürer, Albrecht. *Etliche vnderricht zu befestigung der Stett/ Schloß vnd Flecken*. Nuremberg: Hieronymus Andreae, 1527.
Eberlin von Günzburg, Johann. *EJn klägliche klag an den christlichen Römischen kayser Carolum/ von wegen Doctor Luthers vnd Vlrich von Hutten. Auch von wegen der Curtisanen vnd bättel münch. Das Kayserlich Maiestat sich nit laß sollich leüt verfüren. Der erst bundtsgnoß*. Basel: Gengenbach, 1521.
Eberlin von Günzburg, Johann. *Ein newe ordnung weltlichs standts das Psitacus anzeigt hat in Wolfaria beschriben. Der. XI. bundtsgnoß*. Basel: Gengenbach, 1521.
Eck, Johannes. *Tractat von baiden Sarmatien vnd andern anstossenden landen/ in Asia und Europa*. Augsburg: s.n., 1518.
Egenolff, Christian. *Chronic von an vnd abgang aller Welt wesenn*. Frankfurt am Main: Christian Egenolff, 1533.
Egenolff, Christian. *Chronica/ Von an vnd abgang aller Welt wesen*. Frankfurt am Main: Christian Egenolff, 1534.
Egenolff, Christian. *Chronica/ Beschreibung vnd gemeyne anzeyge/ Vonn aller Wellt herkommen*. Frankfurt am Main: Christian Egenolff, 1535.
Ersch, Johann Samuel, and Johann Gottfried Gruber. *Allgemeine Encyclopädie der Wissenschaften und Künste*. Leipzig: Gleditsch / Brockhaus, 1819–1889.
Fabri, Felix. *Tractatus de civitate Ulmensi. Traktat über die Stadt Ulm*. Ed., transl. and comm. by Folker Reichert. Konstanz: Edition Isele, 2012.
Federmann, Nikolaus. *Jndianische Historia. EJn schöne kurtzweilge Historia Niclaus Federmanns des Jüngern von Ulm erster raise so er von Hispania und Andolosia ausz in Jndias des Occeanischen Mörs gethan hat*. Haguenau: Sigmund Bund, 1557.

Ferrarius, Johannes. *Von dem Gemeinen nutze/ in massen sich ein ieder/ er sey Regent/ ader vnterdan/ darin schicken sol/ den eygen nutz hindan setzen/ vnd der Gemeyn wolfart suchen.* Marburg: Franz Rhode, 1533.

Fischart, Johann. *Das Glückhafft Schiff von Zürich.* Strasbourg: Bernhard Jobin, 1577.

Fischart, Johann. *Geschichtklitterung (Gargantua). Text der Ausgabe letzter Hand von 1590.* Ed. Ute Nyssen. 2 vols. Düsseldorf: Karl Rauch Verlag, 1963.

Fronsperger, Leonhard. *Von dem Lob deß Eigen Nutzen.* Frankfurt am Main: Martin Lechler, 1564.

Franck, Sebastian. *Chronica, Zeÿtbůch und geschÿcht bibel von anbegyn biß inn diß gegenwertig M.D. XXXI. jar.* Strasbourg: Balthasar Beck, 1531.

Franck, Sebastian. *Chronica Zeitbuch vnnd Geschichtbibell von anbegyn bis in dis gegenwertig M.D. XXXVI. iar verlengt.* Ulm: Hans Varnier, 1536.

Franck, Sebastian. *Germaniae Chronicon.* Augsburg: Westermair, 1538.

Franck, Sebastian. *Von dem grewlichen laster der trunckenheit/ so in disen letsten zeiten erst schier mit den Frantzosen auffkommen.* Augsburg: Heinrich Steiner, 1531.

Franck, Sebastian. *Weltbůch: spiegel vnd bildtniß des gantzen erdbodens.* Tübingen: Ulrich Morhart, 1534.

Fries, Lorenz. *Carta Marina Navigatoria Portugalien Navigationes.* Strasbourg: Johann Grüninger, 1530.

Fries, Lorenz. *EJn clarer bericht yetzt nüw von dem Holtz Guaiaco.* Strasbourg: Johann Grüninger, 1529.

Fries, Lorenz. *Uslegung der mercarten oder Cartha Marina.* Strasbourg: Johann Grüninger, 1527.

Frisius, Gemma. *De principiis astronomiae et cosmographiae.* Antwerp: Bontius, 1530.

Fronsperger, Leonhard. *Von dem Lob deß Eigen Nutzen.* Frankfurt am Main: Martin Lechler, 1564.

Fuchs, Leonhart. *New Kreüterbůch.* Basel: Michael Isingrin, 1543.

Geiler von Kaysersberg, Johann. *Christenlich bilgerschafft zům ewigen vatterland.* Basel: Adam Petri, 1512.

Geiler von Kaysersberg, Johann. *Des hochwirdigen doctor Keiserspergs narenschiff so er gepredigt hat zů Straßburg in der hohen stifft daselbst Predictant der zeit.* Strasbourg: Johann Grüninger, 1520.

Geiler von Kaysersberg, Johann. *Die brösamlin doct. Keiserspergs vffgelesen vom Frater Johann Paulin barfůser ordens.* Strasbourg: Johann Grüninger, 1517.

Geiler von Kaysersberg, Johann. *Doctor keiserszbergs Postill: Vber die fyer Euangelia durchs jor.* Strasbourg: Johann Schott, 1522.

Grunau, Simon. *Simon Grunau's Preussische Chronik.* Ed. M. Perlbach, R. Philippi, and P. Wagner. 2 vols. Leipzig: Duncker & Humblot, 1875–1889.

Grünpeck, Joseph. *Ein spiegel der naturlichen himlischen vnd prophetischen sehungen aller trübsalen/ angst/ vnd not.* Nuremberg: Georg Stuchs, 1508.

Hedio, Caspar. *EJn Außerleßne Chronick von anfang der welt bis auff das iar nach Christi vnsers eynigen Heylands gepurt M. D. xxxix.* Strasbourg: Kraft Müller, 1539.

Herr, Michael. *Die New welt, der landschaften vnnd Insulen, so bis hie her allen Altweltbeschrybern vnbekant/ Jungst aber von den Portugalesern vnnd Hispaniern jm Nidergenglichen Meer herfunden.* Strasbourg: Georg Ulricher, 1534.

Hopfer, Daniel. *Die Sprich Salomo das XI. Capitel.* Augsburg: s.n., 1534.

Hutten, Ulrich von. *Clag vnd vormanung gegen dem übermässigen vnchristlichen gewalt des Bapsts zů Rom/ vnd der vngeistlichen geistlichen.* Strasbourg: Johann Schott, 1520.

Hutten, Ulrich von. *De Guaiaci Medicina et morbo Gallico liber unus*. Mainz: Johann Scheffer, 1519.
Hutten, Ulrich von. *Dialogi Huttenici noui, perquam festini*. Strasbourg: Johann Schott, 1521.
Hutten, Ulrich von. "Die Anschawenden." In: *Gespräch büchlin herr Ulrichs von Hutten*. Strasbourg: Johann Schott, 1521. Sig. t1v–y4v.
Hutten, Ulrich, von. *Drey ding findt man tzu Rhom wye das buchleyn Czeygeth an*. Leipzig: Martin Landsberg, 1519.
Hutten, Ulrich, von. *Eyn klag vber den Luterischen Brandt zu Mentz durch herr Vlrich von Hutten*. Wittenberg: Johann Rhau-Grunenberg, c. 1521.
Hutten, Ulrich von. "Feber das Erst." In: *Gespräch büchlin herr Ulrichs von Hutten*. Strasbourg: Johann Schott, 1521. Sig. b1r–c1r.
Hutten, Ulrich von. *Gespräch büchlin herr Ulrichs von Hutten*. Strasbourg: Johann Schott, 1521.
Hutten, Ulrich von. *Praedones*. In: *Dialogi Huttenici noui, perquam festini*. Strasbourg: Johann Schott, 1521. fol. 20r–37v.
Hutten, Ulrich von. *Ulrichen von hutten eins teutschen Ritters von der wunderbarlichen artzney des holtz Guaiacum genant*. Strasbourg: Johann Grüninger, 1519.
Hutten, Ulrich von. *Ulrichs von Hutten verteütscht clag/an Hertzog Friderich zů Sachsen*. Augsburg: Erhard Öglin, 1521.
Hutten, Ulrich von. "Vadiscum oder die Römischen Dreyfaltikeit." In: *Gespräch büchlin herr Ulrichs von Hutten*. Strasbourg: Johann Schott, 1521. Sig. g1v–t1r.
Iustinianus, Flavius Petrus Sabbatius. *The Institutes of Justinian*. Ed. and transl. Thomas Collett Sandars. Clark, NJ: The Lawbook Exchange, 2007.
Köbel, Jacob. *Glaubliche Offenbarung/ wie viell fürtreffenlicher Reych/ vnd Kayserthumb auff erdtrich gewesen*. Augsburg: Heinrich Steiner, 1532.
Lauterbeck, Georg. *Regentenbuch Aus vielen trefflichen alten vnd newen Historien/ mit sonderm fleis zusammen gezogen*. Leipzig: Jakob Berwald, 1556.
Lonitzer, Adam. *Kreuterbuch. Künstliche Conterfeytunge der Bäume/ Stauden/ Hecken/ Kreuter/ Getreyde/ Gewürtze*. Frankfurt: Christian Egenolffs Erben, 1564.
Luther, Martin. "Ein Sermon vom Neuen Testament (1520)." In: *D. Martin Luthers Werke. Kritische Gesammtausgabe*. 6. Band. Weimar: Hermann Böhlau, 1888. 353–380.
Luther, Martin. *Martin Luthers Werke. Kritische Gesammtausgabe*. [Weimarer Ausgabe.] 127 vols. Weimar: Böhlau, 1883–2009. [Abbreviated as WA.]
Luther, Martin. *On Commerce and Usury (1524)*. Ed. and transl. Philipp Robinson Rössner. London: Anthem Press, 2015.
Luther, Martin. *To the Christian Nobility of the German Nation Concerning the Improvement of the Christian Estate*. In: Timothy J. Wengert (ed.). *The Annotated Luther*. Volume 1: The Roots of Reform. Minneapolis: Fortress Press, 2015. 376–465.
Luther, Martin. *Von Kauffshandlung vnd wucher*. Wittenberg: Hans Lufft, 1524.
Magnus, Olaus. *Ain kvrze Avslegvng vnd Verklerung der neuuen Mappen von den alten Gœttenreich vnd andern Nordlenden*. Venice: Magnus, 1539.
Mandeville, John. *Von der erfarüng des strengen Ritters johannes von Montauille*. Strasbourg: Johann Knobloch the Elder, 1507.
Meder, Lorenz. *Handel-Buch Darin angezeigt wird/ welcher Gestalt inn den fürnembsten Hendelstetten Europe/ allerley Wahren anfencklich kaufft/ dieselwig wider mit Nutz verkaufft*. Nuremberg: Johann vom Berg and Ulrich Newber, 1558.

Münster, Sebastian. *Cosmographia. Beschreibung aller Lender důrch Sebastianum Munsterum in welcher begriffen/ Aller völcker/ Herrschafften/ Stetten/ vnd namhafftiger flecken/ herkommen*. Basel: Heinrich Petri, 1544.
Münster, Sebastian. *Cosmographia. Beschreibung aller Lender důrch Sebastianum Munsterum in wölcher begriffen/ Aller völcker/ Herrschafften/ Stetten/ vnd namhafftiger flecken/ härkommen*. Basel: Heinrich Petri, 1548.
Münster, Sebastian. *Cosmographei oder beschreibung aller länder/ herrschafften/ fürnemsten stetten/ geschichten/ gebreüchen/ hantirungen etc*. Basel: Heinrich Petri, 1556.
Murner, Thomas. *Narrenbeschwörung*. Ed. Meier Spanier. Berlin and Leipzig: Walter de Gruyter, 1926.
Negelein, Paul. *Vom Burgerlichen Standt: Welcher massen derselbe in beharlichem Wesen erhalten/ vnd was darzu gehörig/ auch wie der widerumb zu schaden vnd untergang geraten möge*. Amberg: Michael Forster, 1600.
Oldendorp, Johannes. *Von Rathschlägen/ wie man gute Polizey vnd Ordnung in Stedten und Landen erhalten möge*. Rostock: Konrad Forstenow, 1597.
Osse, Michael von. "Politisches Testament." In: *Schriften Dr. Melchiors von Osse. Mit einem Lebensabriss und einem Anhange von Briefen und Akten*. Ed. Oswald Artur Hecker. Leipzig und Berlin: B. G. Teubner, 1922.
Osse, Melchior von. *Prudentia regnativa, Das ist: Ein Nützliches Bedencken/ ein Regiment/ so wol in Kriegs als Friedens Zeiten/ recht zu bestellen/ zu verbessern und zu erhalten: Allen Regenten/ dero Räthen vnd Dienern zu Anordnung ihrer Regierung vnd guter Policey zuwissen*. Frankfurt: Peter Kopf, 1607.
Paracelsus (Theophrastus von Hohenheim). "Beschreibung Etlicher kreůter/ auß dem Herbario Theophrasti Paracelsi, Bombast/ beyder Artzney Doctoris." In: *Ettliche Tractatus Des Hocherfarnen vnnd berümbtesten Philippi Theophrasti Paracelsi*, ed. Michael Toxites. Strasbourg: Christian Müllers Erben, 1570. 286–391.
Paracelsus (Theophrastus von Hohenheim). "Das Bůch von natürlichen dingen/ des Hocherfarnen vnd weitberümpten Theophrasti von Hohenheym beider artzeney Doctoris." In: *Ettliche Tractatus Des Hocherfarnen vnnd berümbtesten Philippi Theophrasti Paracelsi*, ed. Michael Toxites. Strasbourg: Christian Müllers Erben, 1570. 1–285.
Paracelsus (Theophrastus von Hohenheim). *Vom Holtz Guaiaco gründlicher heylung/ Darinn essen vnnd trincken/ Saltz vnd anders erlaubt vnd zu gehört*. Nuremberg: Friedrich Peypus, 1529.
Pauli, Johannes. *Schimpf und Ernst*. Ed. Hermann Österley. Stuttgart: Litterarischer Verein, 1866.
Peutinger, Conrad. *Sermones conuiuales*. Strasbourg: Johann Prüss, 1506.
Ptolemy, Claudius. *Claudii Ptolemei viri Alexandrini Mathematicae disciplinae Philosophi doctissimi Geographiae opus*. Strasbourg: Johann Schott, 1513.
Reisch, Gregor. *Margarita philosophica*. Freiburg: Johann Schott, 1503.
Richental, Ulrich von. *Das Konzil zu Konstanz, MCDXIV-MCDXVIII. Kommentar und Text*. Ed. Otto Feger. 2 vols. Starnberg: Josef Keller, 1964.
Rieger, Urban (Urbanus Rhegius). *Enchiridion odder handtbüchlin eines Christlichen Fürstens/ darinnen leer und trost aller Oberkeit seer nützlich/ allein aus Gottes wort auffs kürtzest zusamen gezogen*. Wittenberg: Hans Weiss, 1535.
Rollenhagen, Georg. *Froschmeuseler. Mit den Holzschnitten der Erstausgabe*. Ed. Dietmar Pfeil. Frankfurt am Main: Deutscher Klassiker Verlag, 1989.

Ruchamer, Jobst. *Newe vnbekanthe landte Und ein newe weldte in kurtz verganger zeythe erfunden.* Nuremberg: Georg Stuchs, 1508.
Sachs, Hans. *Das schedlich Thier der Eygen nutz/ mit sein verderblichen zwölff Eygen schafften.* Nürnberg: Pankraz Kempf, c. 1535.
Sachs, Hans. *Ein Dialogus/ des inhalt/ ein argument der Römischen/ wider das christlich heüflein/ den Geytz/ auch ander offenlich Laster etc. betreffend.* Nuremberg: Gutknecht, 1524.
Sachs, Hans. *Sämtliche Fabeln und Schwänke.* Ed. Edmund Goetze and Carl Drescher. 6 volumes. Halle: Niemeyer, 1893–1913.
Sachs, Hans. *Werke.* Ed. Adelbert von Keller and Edmund Goetze. 26 volumes. Tübingen: Laupp, 1870–1908. [Abbreviated as KG.]
Schedel, Hartmann. *Register des Buchs der Croniken und geschichten mit figuren und pildnussen von anbeginn der welt bis auf dise unnsere Zeit.* [*Nuremberg Chronicle.*] Nuremberg: Anton Koberger, 1493.
Scheidt, Kaspar. *Grobianus/ Von groben sitten/ und vnhöflichen geberden.* Worms: Gregor Hoffman, 1551.
Schmidel, Ulrich. *Neuwe Welt: Das ist/ Wahrhafftige Beschreibunge aller schönen Historien von erfindung viler vnbekanten Landschafften/ Jnsulen vnnd Stedten.* Frankfurt am Main: Siegmund Feyerabend, 1567.
Schnellenberg, Tarquinius. *Experimenta. Von XX. Pestilentz Wurtzeln vnd Kreutern/ Wie sie alle vnd ein jegliches besonder/ Für Gifft vnnd Pestilentz gebraucht mögen werden.* Frankfurt am Main: Weygand Han, 1546.
Schöner, Johannes. *Opusculum geographicum ex diversorum libris ac cartis.* Nuremberg: Johannes Petri, 1533.
Schrot, Martin. *Vrsprung vnd vrsach Gegenwertiger Vffrůr/ Teütscher Nation.* Wittenberg: Johann Krafft, 1546.
Schwarz, Matthäus. "Dreierlay Buchhaltung." In: Alfred Weitnauer (ed.). *Venezianischer Handel der Fugger. Nach der Musterbuchhaltung des Matthäus Schwarz.* Munich: Duncker & Humblot, 1931. 174–306.
Springer, Balthasar. *Die Merfart vnd erfarung nüwer Schiffung vnd Wege zů viln onerkanten Jnseln und Künigreichen.* Oppenheim: Köbel, 1509.
Staden, Hans. *Warhaftige Historia vnd beschreibung eyner Landtschafft der Wilden/ Nacketen/ Grimmigen Menschenfresser Leuthen/ in der Newenwelt America gelegen.* Marburg: Andres Kolb, 1557.
Stiblin, Kaspar. *Commentariolus de Eudaemonensium Republica (Basel 1555).* Ed. Isabel-Dorothea Jahn. Regensburg: Roderer Verlag, 1994.
Strauß, Jakob. *Das wucher zu nemen vnd geben.* Erfurt: Loersfeld, 1524.
Strauß, Jakob. *Haubtstuck vnd artickel Christenlicher leer wider den unchristlichen wůcher.* Augsburg: Steiner, 1523.
Tengler, Ulrich. *Laÿen Spiegel von rechtmässigen ordnungen in Burgerlichen vnd peinlichen regimenten.* Augsburg: Johann Rynman and Johann Otmar, 1509.
Tucher, Hans. *Nach Cristi vnnsers lieben herren gepůrt M.cccc.lxxix. jare. [...] Pin ich Hanns Tucher Burger zů Nüremberg [...] daselbest außgezogen [...] Die heyligen Stete [...] czů besůchen.* Augsburg: Schönsperger, 1482.
Turnauer, Kaspar. *Von dem Jüdischen vnnd Jsraelischen volck vnnd jren vorgeern. Durch Casparn Turnawer auß der Bibel gezogen.* Augsburg: Silvan Otmar, 1528.

[Verardi, Carlo; Columbus, Christopher.] *In laudem Serenissimi Ferdinandi Hispaniarum Regis, Bethicae & regni Granatae obsidio victoria & triumphus. Et de insulis in mari Indico nuper inuentis*. Basel: Johann Bergmann, 1494.

[Vespucci, Amerigo]. *Das sind die new gefunden menschen oder volcker Jn form vnd gestalt Als sie hie stend durch den Cristenlichen Künig von Portugall/ gar wunnderbarlich erfunden*. Nuremberg: Georg Stuchs, 1505.

[Vespucci, Amerigo]. *Dise figur anzaigt vns das volck vnd insel die gefunden ist durch den cristenlichen künig zů Portugal oder von seinen vnderthonen*. Augsburg: Johannes Froschauer, c. 1503.

[Vespucci, Amerigo.] *Diß büchlin saget wie die zwen durchlüchtigsten herren her Fernandus. K. zů Castilien vnd herr Emanuel. K. zů Portugal haben das weyte mör ersůchet vnnd funden vil Insulen/ vnnd ein Nüwe welt von wilden nackenden Leüten/ vormals unbekant*. Strasbourg: Johann Grüninger, 1509.

Vochs, Johann. *De pestilentia Anni praesentis et eius cura*. Magdeburg: Winter, 1507.

Waldseemüller, Martin. *Carta marina*. Strasbourg [?]: s.n., 1516.

Waldseemüller, Martin. *Der welt kugel. Beschrybung der welt vnd deß gantzen Ertreichs hie angezögt vnd vergleicht einer rotunden kuglen*. Strasbourg: Johann Grüninger, 1509.

Waldseemüller, Martin. *Universalis cosmographia secundum Ptholomaei traditionem et Americi Vespucii aliorumque lustrationes*. St. Dié: s.n., 1507.

Waldseemüller, Martin, and Matthias Ringmann. *Cosmographiae introductio cum quibusdam geometriae ac astronomiae principiis ad eam rem necessariis*. Saint-Dié: Walther Lud, 1507.

Wickram, Jörg. *Von Gůten vnd Bösen Nachbaurn*. Strasbourg: Knobloch, 1556.

Wimpfeling, Jakob. *Agatharchia. Id est bonus Principatus*. Strasbourg: Martin Schott, 1498.

Wimpfeling, Jakob. *Soliloquium pro pace Christianorum et pro Helvetiis ut resipiscant*. Strasbourg: Johann Knobloch, 1505.

Witzel, Georg. *Wider den Vnchristlichen Wucher/ vnd grosse Schinderey dieser itzigen bösen zeit*. Leipzig: Wolrab, 1539.

Zedler, Johann Heinrich. *Grosses vollständiges Universal-Lexicon aller Wissenschafften und Künste*. 64 vols. Halle and Leipzig: Zedler, 1731–1754.

Secondary Works Cited

Abu-Lughod, Janet L. *Before European Hegemony. The World System A.D. 1250–1350*. New York: Oxford University Press, 1989.

Albala, Ken. *Eating Right in the Renaissance*. Berkeley: University of California Press, 2002.

Ankenbauer, Norbert. *Paesi novamente retrovati – Newe unbekanthe landte. Eine digitale Edition früher Entdeckerberichte*. Wolfenbüttel: Herzog August Bibliothek, 2013. http://diglib.hab.de/edoc/ed000145/start.htm (last accessed on 11 May 2020).

Arrizabalaga, Jon, John Henderson, Roger Kenneth French. *The Great Pox. The French Disease in Renaissance Europe*. New Haven: Yale University Press, 1997.

Ashcroft, Jeffrey. "Black Arts. Renaissance and Printing Press in Nuremberg, 1493–1528." *Forum for Modern Language Studies*, 45:1 (2009), 3–18.

Asúa, Miguel de, and Roger Kenneth French. *A New World of Animals. Early Modern Europeans on the Creatures of Iberian America*. Aldershot, England; Burlington, VT: Ashgate, 2005.

Aurnhammer, Achim. "Sünder–Narr–Held. Korrekturen des Odysseus-Mythos bei Heinrich von Veldeke, Sebastian Brant und Martin Opitz." *Antike und Abendland*, 55 (2009), 130–151.

Aymoré, Fernando Amado. *Die Jesuiten im kolonialen Brasilien. Katechese als Kulturpolitik und Gesellschaftsphänomen (1549–1760)*. Frankfurt am Main: Lang, 2009.

Bachorski, Hans-Jürgen. "Wie der Narr ins Irrenhaus kommt. Diskursdifferenzierung im 16. und 17. Jahrhundert." In: Jörg Jungmayr and Christiane Caemmerer (eds.). *Das Berliner Modell der Mittleren Deutschen Literatur. Beiträge zur Tagung Kloster Zinna 29.9.-01.10.1997*. Amsterdam, Atlanta: Rodopi, 2000. 273–298.

Bächtold-Stäubli, Hanns (ed.). *Handwörterbuch des deutschen Aberglaubens*. 3rd edition. Berlin: de Gruyter, 2000.

Baeumer, Max L. "'Aufruhr' in der Volksliteratur des späten Mittelalters und im Selbstverständnis Luthers und seiner Zeitgenossen." *Monatshefte*, 74:4 (1982), 463–472.

Bakhtin, Mikhail. *Rabelais and His World*. Cambridge: MIT Press, 1968.

Barrera, Antonio. "Local Herbs, Global Medicines. Commerce, Knowledge, and Commodities in Spanish America." In: Pamela H. Smith and Paula Findlen (eds.). *Merchants and Marvels. Commerce, Science, and Art in Early Modern Europe*. New York, London: Routledge, 2002. 163–181.

Barrera-Osorio, Antonio. *Experiencing Nature. The Spanish American Empire and the Early Scientific Revolution*. Austin: University of Texas Press, 2006.

Bauer, Clemens. "Conrad Peutingers Gutachten zur Monopolfrage. Eine Untersuchung zur Wandlung der Wirtschaftsanschauungen im Zeitalter der Reformation." *Archiv für Reformationsgeschichte*, 45 (1954), 1–43 and 145–196.

Bauer, Thomas. *Die Vereindeutigung der Welt. Über den Verlust an Mehrdeutigkeit und Vielfalt*. Ditzingen: Reclam, 2018.

Beise, Arnd. "'machen die docter die bücher/ oder machn die bücher doctores.' Eulenspiegel unter den Gelehren." In: Bernhard Jahn, Dirk Rose, Thorsten Unger (eds.). *Ordentliche Unordnung. Metamorphosen des Schwanks vom Mittelalter bis zur Moderne. Festschrift für Michael Schilling*. Heidelberg: Winter, 2014. 33–48.

Bennett, Herman L. *African Kings and Black Slaves. Sovereignty and Dispossession in the Early Modern Atlantic*. Philadelphia: University of Pennsylvania Press, 2019.

Bentley, Jerry H., Sanjay Subrahmanyam, and Merry Wiesner-Hanks (eds.). *The Cambridge World History, Volume 6: The Construction of a Global World, 1400–1800 CE*. Cambridge: Cambridge University Press, 2015.

Bernstein, Eckhard. "Hans Sachs (5 November 1494 – 19 January 1576)." In: Max Reinhart and James Hardin (eds.). *Dictionary of Literary Biography. Vol. 179: German Writers of the Renaissance and Reformation, 1280–1580*. Detroit: Gale Research, 1997. 241–252.

Biehler, Birgit. *Der Eigennutz. Feind oder 'wahrer Begründer' des Gemeinwohls?* Epfendorf/Neckar: Bibliotheca Academica Verlag, 2011.

Bleuler, Anna Kathrin, Susanne Friedrich, et al. "Pluralisierungen. Konzepte zur Erfassung der Frühen Neuzeit." *Mitteilungen des Sonderforschungsbereichs 573 'Pluralisierung und Autorität in der Frühen Neuzeit,'* 1 (2007), 48–53.

Blickle, Peter. "Beschwerden und Polizeien. Die Legitimation des modernen Staates durch Verfahren und Normen." In: Peter Blickle, Peter Kissling, and Heinrich Richard Schmidt (eds.). *Gute Policey als Politik im 16. Jahrhundert. Die Entstehung des öffentlichen Raumes in Oberdeutschland*. Frankfurt am Main: Vittorio Klostermann, 2003. 549–568.

Blickle, Peter. "Der Gemeine Nutzen. Ein kommunaler Wert und seine politische Karriere." In: Herfried Münkler and Harald Bluhm (eds.). *Gemeinwohl und Gemeinsinn. Historische*

Semantiken politischer Leitbegriffe. Forschungsberichte der interdisziplinären Arbeitsgruppe 'Gemeinwohl und Gemeinsinn.' Berlin: Akademie Verlag, 2001. I, 85–107.

Blickle, Peter. *Die Reformation im Reich*. 3rd Edition. Stuttgart: Ulmer, 2000.

Blume, Herbert. *Hermann Bote. Braunschweiger Stadtschreiber und Literat. Studien zu seinem Leben und Werk*. Bielefeld: Verlag für Regionalgeschichte, 2009.

Borowka-Clausberg, Beate. *Balthasar Sprenger und der frühneuzeitliche Reisebericht*. München: Iudicium, 1999.

Brendecke, Arndt. "Der 'oberste Kosmograph und Chronist Amerikas.' Über einen Versuch der Monopolisierung von historischer Information." In: Frank Bezner and Kirsten Mahlke (eds.). *Zwischen Wissen und Politik. Archäologie und Genealogie frühneuzeitlicher Vergangenheitskonstruktionen*. Heidelberg: Winter, 2011, 353–373.

Breward, Christopher. *The Culture of Fashion. A New History of Fashionable Dress*. Manchester: Manchester University Press, 1994.

Broadberry, Stephen, and Bishnupriya Gupta. "The Early Modern Great Divergence. Wages, Prices and Economic Development in Europe and Asia, 1500–1800. *Economic History Review*, 59:1 (2006), 2–31.

Broecke, Steven Vanden. "The Use of Visual Media in Renaissance Cosmography. The *Cosmography* of Peter Apian and Gemma Frisius." *Paedagogica Historica*, 36:1 (2000), 131–150.

Brotton, Jerry. *A History of the World in Twelve Maps*. London: Allen Lane, 2012.

Brüggemann, Romy. *Die Angst vor dem Bösen. Codierungen des malum in der spätmittelalterlichen und frühneuzeitlichen Narren-, Teufel- und Teufelsbündnerliteratur*. Würzburg: Königshausen & Neumann, 2010.

Cañizares-Esguerra, Jorge. *Puritan Conquistadors. Iberianizing the Atlantic, 1550–1700*. Stanford: Stanford University Press, 2006.

Castells, Manuel. "Nothing New Under the Sun?" In: Øystein Sakala LaBianca and Sandra Arnold (eds.). *Connectivity in Antiquity. Globalization as Long-Term Historical Process*. London: Equinox Publishing, 2006. 158–167.

Cattaneo, Angelo. "European Medieval and Renaissance Cosmography. A Story of Multiple Voices." *Asian Review of World Histories*, 4:1 (2016), 35–81.

Classen, Albrecht. "Laughter as the Ultimate Epistemological Vehicle in the Hands of Till Eulenspiegel." *Neophilologus*, 92 (2008), 471–489.

Clifton-Soderstrom, Karl. *The Cardinal and the Deadly. Reimagining the Seven Virtues and Seven Vices*. Eugene: Wipf and Stock Publishers, 2015.

Cormack, Lesley B. "'Good Fences Make Good Neighbors.' Geography as Self-Definition in Early Modern England." *Isis*, 82 (1991), 639–661.

Correll, Barbara. *The End of Conduct. Grobianus and the Renaissance Text of the Subject*. Ithaca: Cornell Univeristy Press, 1996.

Cosgrove, Denis. "Globalism and Tolerance in Early Modern Geography." *Annals of the Association of American Geographers*, 93:4 (2003), 852–870.

Crone, Hugh D. *Paracelsus. The Man who Defied Medicine. His Real Contribution to Medicine*. Melbourne: Albarello Press, 2004.

Crowther, Kathleen. "Raising Cain. Vice, Virtue and Social Order in the German Reformation." In: Richard Newhauser and Susan J. Ridyard (eds.). *Sin in Medieval and Early Modern Culture. The Tradition of the Seven Deadly Sins*. Woodbridge: York Medieval Press, 2012. 304–320.

Curtius, Ernst Robert. *European Literature and the Latin Middle Ages*. Transl. Willard R. Trask. Princeton: Princeton University Press, 2013.
Dauser, Regina, and Magnus Ulrich Ferber. *Die Fugger und Welser. Vom Mittelalter bis zur Gegenwart*. Augsburg: Verlagsgemeinschaft Augsbuch, 2010.
Davies, Surekha. "America and Amerindians in Sebastian Münster's Cosmographiae universalis libri VI (1550)." *Renaissance Studies*, 25:3 (2011), 351–373.
Davies, Surekha. *Renaissance Ethnography and the Invention of the Human. New Worlds, Maps and Monsters*. New York: Cambridge University Press, 2016.
Denecke, Dietrich. "Strassen, Reiserouten und Routenbücher (Itinerare) im späten Mittelalter und in der frühen Neuzeit." In: Xenia von Ertzdorff and Dieter Neukirch (eds.). *Reisen und Reiseliteratur im Mittelalter und in der Frühen Neuzeit*. Amsterdam, Atlanta: Rodopi, 1992. 229–253.
Denzer, Jörg. *Die Konquista der Augsburger Welser-Gesellschaft in Südamerika (1528–1556). Historische Rekonstruktion, Historiografie und lokale Erinnerungskultur in Kolumbien und Venezuela*. München: C. H. Beck, 2005.
Deutsch, Andreas. "*Klagspiegel* und *Laienspiegel* – Sebastian Brants Beitrag zum Ruhm zweier Rechtsbücher." In: Klaus Bergdolt, Joachim Knape, et al. (eds.). *Sebastian Brant und die Kommunikationskultur um 1500*. Wiesbaden: Harrassowitz, 2010. 75–98.
Deutsche Reichstagsakten, Jüngere Reihe. Vol. 1–3. Gotha: Perthes, 1893, 1896, 1901.
Droege, Michael. *Gemeinnützigkeit im offenen Steuerstaat*. Tübingen: Mohr Siebeck, 2010.
Duby, Georges. *The Three Orders. Feudal Society Imagined*. Chicago: University of Chicago Press, 1982.
Dutschke, Manfred. "Bauernkrieg und bürgerliche Opposition. Die Reformationsdialoge des Hans Sachs und der Bauernkrieg." In: Walter Raitz (ed.). *Deutscher Bauernkrieg. Historische Analysen und Studien zur Rezeption*. Wiesbaden: Springer, 1976. 54–72.
Earle, Rebecca. *The Body of the Conquistador. Food, Race and the Colonial Experience in Spanish America, 1492–1700*. Cambridge: Cambridge University Press, 2012.
Eckert, Désirée. *Von Wilden und wahrhaft Wilden. Wahrnehmungen der "Neuen Welt" in ausgewählten europäischen Reiseberichten und Chroniken des 16. Jahrhunderts*. Hamburg: Diplomica Verlag, 2012.
Ehrlicher, Hanno. "Die 'Neue Welt.' Reisen und Alterität." In: Jörg Dünne und Andreas Mahler (eds.). *Handbuch Literatur & Raum*. Berlin: De Gruyter, 2015. 355–363.
Elias, Norbert. *The Civilizing Process. The History of Manners and State Formation and Civilization*. Transl. Edmund Jephcott. Oxford: Blackwell, 1994.
Entwistle, Joanne. *The Fashioned Body. Fashion, Dress, and Modern Social Theory*. Cambridge, UK: Polity Press, 2000.
Eriksen, Thomas Hylland. *Globalization. The Key Concepts*. New York: Berg, 2007.
Eser, Thomas. "Gewürze auf dem Behaim-Globus. Venture-Capital-Akquise um 1500." In: Frank Holl (ed.). *Gewürze – sinnlicher Genuss, lebendige Geschichte. Begleitbuch zur Sonderausstellung*. Rosenheim: Veranstaltungs- und Kongress-GmbH, 2010. 134–145.
Fäßler, Peter E. *Globalisierung. Ein historisches Kompendium*. Köln: Böhlau Verlag, 2007.
Fernández-Armesto, Felipe. *Amerigo. The Man Who Gave His Name to America*. London: Weidenfeld & Nicolson, 2006.
Fienup-Riordan, Ann. *Eskimo Essays. Yup'ik Lives and How We See Them*. New Brunswick: Rutgers University Press, 1990.
Findlay, Ronald, and Kevin H. O'Rourke. *Power and Plenty. Trade, War, and the World Economy in the Second Millennium*. Princeton: Princeton University Press, 2008.

Findlen, Paula. "Early Modern Things. Objects in Motion, 1500–1800." In: Paula Findlen (ed.). *Early Modern Things. Objects and their Histories, 1500–1800*. London and New York: Routledge, 2013. 3–27.

Fiori, Stefano. "Individual and Self-Interest in Adam Smith's Wealth of Nations." *Cahiers d'économie Politique / Papers in Political Economy*, 49:2 (2005), 19–31.

Flynn, Dennis O., and Arturo Giráldez. "Path Dependence, Time Lags and the Birth of Globalisation. A Critique of O'Rourke and Williamson." *European Review of Economic History*, 8 (2004), 81–108.

Forbes, Jack D. "The Use of Racial and Ethnic Terms in America. Management by Manipulation." *Wicazo Sa Review*, 11:2 (1995), 53–65.

Freyhan, Robert. "The Evolution of the Caritas Figure in the Thirteenth and Fourteenth Centuries." *Journal of the Warburg and Courtauld Institutes*, 11 (1948), 68–86.

Frübis, Hildegard. *Die Wirklichkeit des Fremden. Die Darstellung der Neuen Welt im 16. Jahrhundert*. Berlin: Reimer, 1995.

Funkenstein, Amos. *Theology and the Scientific Imagination From the Middle Ages to the Seventeenth Century*. Princeton: Princeton University Press, 1986.

Füssel, Stephan (ed.). *Hartmann Schedel. Chronicle of the World. The Complete and Annotated Nuremberg Chronicle of 1493*. Köln: Taschen, 2001.

Gärtner, Kurt. "Die Tradition der volkssprachlichen Weltchronistik in der deutschen Literatur des Mittelalters." *Pirckheimer-Jahrbuch*, 9 (1994), 57–71.

Gautier Dalché, Patrick. "The Reception of Ptolemy's Geography (End of the Fourteenth to Beginning fo the Sixteenth Century)." In: David Woodward (ed.). *The History of Cartography, vol. 3. Cartography in the European Renaissance*. Chicago: University of Chicago Press, 2007. Part 1, 285–364.

Geus, Klaus. "Ptolemaios – Reaktionär, Theoretiker, Plagiator?" In: Thomas Beck, Marília dos Santos Lopes, and Christian Rödel (eds.). *Barrieren und Zugänge. Die Geschichte der europäischen Expansion. Festschrift für Eberhard Schmitt zum 65. Geburtstag*. Wiesbaden: Harrassowitz, 2004. 36–50.

Gilomen, Hans-Jörg. "Christlicher Glaube und Ökonomie des Kredits im Spätmittelalter." In: Gerhard Fouquet and Sven Rabeler (eds.). *Ökonomische Glaubensfragen. Strukturen und Praktiken jüdischen und christlichen Kleinkredits im Spätmittelalter*. Stuttgart: Franz Steiner Verlag, 2018. 121–160.

Goldstein, Leonard. *The Social and Cultural Roots of Linear Perspective*. Minneapolis: MEP Publications, 1988.

Goodhart, David. *The Road to Somewhere. The Populist Revolt and the Future of Politics*. London: Hurst, 2017.

Grafton, Anthony. *New Worlds, Ancient Texts. The Power of Tradition and the Shock of Discovery*. Cambridge: Harvard University Press, 1992.

Green, Jonathan. "Text, Culture, and Print Media in Early Modern Translation. Notes on the Nuremberg Chronicle." *Fifteenth-Century Studies*, 33 (2008), 114–132.

Green, Jonathan. "Translating Time. Chronicle, Prognostication, Prophecy." *Renaissance Studies*, 29:1 (2015), 162–177.

Greenfield, Jeff. "The Ugly History of Stephen Miller's 'Cosmopolitan' Epithet. Surprise, surprise – the insult has its roots in Soviet anti-Semitism." *Politico*, 3 August 2017. https://www.politico.com/magazine/story/2017/08/03/the-ugly-history-of-stephen-millers-cosmopolitan-epithet-215454 (last accessed on 11 May 2020).

Greiff, Benedikt (ed.). *Tagebuch des Lucas Rem aus den Jahren 1494–1541. Ein Beitrag zur Handelsgeschichte der Stadt Augsburg.* Augsburg: Hartmann, 1861.

Grimm, Jacob, and Wilhelm Grimm. *Deutsches Wörterbuch.* 32 vols. Leipzig: Hirzel, 1854–1961.

Großhaupt, Walter. "Der Venezuela-Vertrag der Welser." *Scripta mercaturae*, 24 (1990), 1–35.

Grünberger, Hans. "Wege zum Nächsten. Luthers Vorstellungen vom Gemeinen Nutzen." In: Herfried Münkler and Harald Bluhm (eds.). *Gemeinwohl und Gemeinsinn. Historische Semantiken politischer Leitbegriffe. Forschungsberichte der interdisziplinären Arbeitsgruppe 'Gemeinwohl und Gemeinsinn.'* Berlin: Akademie Verlag, 2001. I, 147–168.

Häberlein, Mark. *Aufbruch ins globale Zeitalter. Die Handelswelt der Fugger und Welser.* Stuttgart: Konrad Theiss Verlag, 2016.

Häberlein, Mark. *The Fuggers of Augsburg. Pursuing Wealth and Honor in Renaissance Germany.* Charlottesville and London: University of Virginia Press, 2012.

Harbsmeier, Michael. *Wilde Völkerkunde. Andere Welten in deutschen Reiseberichten der Frühen Neuzeit.* Frankfurt am Main: Campus, 1994.

Harris, Steven J. "Long-Distance Corporations, Big Sciences, and the Geography of Knowledge." *Configurations*, 6:2 (1998), 269–304.

Harrison, E. L. "Virgil, Sebastian Brant, and Maximilian I." *Modern Language Review*, 76 (1981), 99–115.

Hartweg, Frédéric. "Sebastian Brants Anlehnung an die Antike in humanistischer Perspektive in *Narrenschiff* und *Tugent-Spyl.*" In: Peter Hvilshøj Andersen Vinilandicus and Barbara Lafond-Kettlitz (eds.). *Die Bedeutung der Rezeptionsliteratur für Bildung und Kultur der Frühen Neuzeit (1400–1750) III. Beiträge zur dritten Arbeitstagung in Wissembourg/Weißenburg (März 2014).* Bern: Lang, 2015. 137–149.

Hassauer, Friederike. "Volkssprachliche Reiseliteratur. Faszination des Reisens und räumlicher ordo." In: Hans Ulrich Gumbrecht et al. *Grundriß der romanischen Literatur des Mittelalters XI. 1. La Littérature historiographique des origines à 1500.* Heidelberg: Winter, 1986. 259–283.

Hauptmann, Andreas, Gabi Schneider, and Christoph Bartels. "The Shipwreck of Bom Jesus, AD 1533. Fugger Copper in Namibia." *Journal of African Archaeology*, 14:2 (2016), 181–207.

Hayden-Roy, Priscilla. "The Masquerade of History: Herman Bote's *Schichtboik.*" *Daphnis*, 22:4 (1993), 561–580.

Heimann, Sabine. "Curiositas und experientia. Reiseideologie und Reiserezeption bei Sebastian Brant." In: Dietrich Huschenbett and John Margetts (eds.). *Reisen und Welterfahrung in der deutschen Literatur des Mittelalters. Vorträge des XI. Anglo-deutschen Colloquiums, 11.-15. September 1989, Universität Liverpool.* Würzburg: Königshausen & Neumann, 1991. 264–276.

Heinen, Hubert. "Das Schlaraffenland und die verkehrte Welt als Gegenutopien." *Amsterdamer Beiträge zur älteren Germanistik*, 43:1 (1995), 241–253.

Heinrichs, Erik A. *Plague, Print, and the Reformation. The German Reform of Healing, 1473–1573.* London and New York: Routledge, 2018.

Heitzmann, Christian. "Wem gehören die Molukken? Eine unbekannte Weltkarte aus der Frühzeit der Entdeckungen." *Zeitschrift für Ideengeschichte*, 1:2 (2007), 101–110.

Henkel, Arthur, and Albrecht Schöne. *Emblemata. Handbuch zur Sinnbildkunst des XVI. und XVII. Jahrhunderts.* Stuttgart: Metzler, 1967.

Herz, Randall. *Studien zur Drucküberlieferung der "Reise ins gelobte Land" Hans Tuchers des Älteren. Bestandsaufnahme und historische Auswertung der Inkunabeln unter Berücksichtigung der späteren Drucküberlieferung*. Nürnberg: Stadtarchiv, 2005.

Hess, Peter. "Early Modern Globalization and Its Discontents. German Responses to the Emerging Global Networks in the Early Sixteenth Century." In: Simon Ferdinand, Irene Villaescusa, and Esther Peeren (eds.). *Other Globes. Past and Peripheral Imaginations of Globalization*. Basingstoke: Palgrave, 2019. 41–62.

Hess, Peter. "German Poetry, 1450–1700." In: Max Reinhart (ed.). *Early Modern German Literature*. Camden House History of German Literature, v. 4. Rochester, NY: Camden House, 2007. 395–465.

Hess, Peter. "Marvelous Encounters. Albrecht Dürer and Early Sixteenth-Century German Perceptions of Aztec Culture." *Daphnis*, 33 (2004), 161–186.

Hess, Peter. "The Poetics of Masquerade. Clothing and the Construction of Social, Religious, and Gender Identity in Grimmelshausen's Simplicissimus." In: Karl F. Otto, Jr. (ed.). *A Companion to the Works of Grimmelshausen*. Rochester, NY: Camden House, 2003. 299–331.

Hess, Peter. "Travel as Projection of Civic Virtue, Political Power, and National Identity. Johann Fischart's 'The Fortunate Ship from Zurich' (1577)." *Studies in Travel Writing*, 12:1 (2008), 29–48.

Hess, Peter. "Zum Toposbegriff in der Barockzeit." *Rhetorik. Ein internationales Jahrbuch*, 10 (1991), 71–88.

Hessler, John W. *The Naming of America. Martin Waldseemüller's 1507 World Map and the Cosmographiae introductio*. Washington, DC, and London: Library of Congress and D. Giles, 2008.

Hessler, John W., and Chet Van Duzer. *Seeing the World Anew. The Radical Vision of Martin Waldseemüller's 1507 & 1516 World Maps*. Delray Beach, FL: Levenger Press in association with the Library of Congress, 2012.

Hibst, Peter. *Utilitas Publica–Gemeiner Nutz–Gemeinwohl. Untersuchungen zur Idee eines politischen Leitbegriffes von der Antike bis zum späten Mittelalter*. Frankfurt am Main: Lang, 1991.

Hieber, Andreas. "Policey zwischen Augsburg und Zürich – ein Forschungsüberblick." In: Peter Blickle, Peter Kissling, and Heinrich Richard Schmidt (eds.). *Gute Policey als Politik im 16. Jahrhundert. Die Entstehung des öffentlichen Raumes in Oberdeutschland*. Frankfurt am Main: Vittorio Klostermann, 2003. 1–24.

Hirschi, Caspar. "Eine Kommunikationssituation zum Schweigen. Sebastian Brant und die Eidgenossen." In: Klaus Bergdolt, Joachim Knape, et al. (ed.). *Sebastian Brant und die Kommunikationskultur um 1500*. Wiesbaden: Harrassowitz, 2010. 219–250.

Hirschi, Caspar. "Konzepte von Fortschritt und Niedergang im Humanismus am Beispiel der translatio imperii und der translatio studii." *Germanisch-romanische Monatsschrift*, 58:1 (2008), 37–55.

Hirschi, Caspar. *The Origins of Nationalism. An Alternative History from Ancient Rome to Early Modern Germany*. Cambridge, New York: Cambridge University Press, 2012.

Hirschi, Caspar. *Wettkampf der Nationen. Konstruktionen einer deutschen Ehrgemeinschaft an der Wende vom Mittelalter zur Neuzeit*. Göttingen: Wallstein-Verlag, 2005.

Honegger, Peter. *Ulenspiegel. Ein Beitrag zur Druckgeschichte und zur Verfasserfrage*. Neumünster: Wachholtz, 1973.

Hoppe, Brigitte. *Das Kräuterbuch des Hieronymus Bock. Wissenschaftshistorische Untersuchung. Mit einem Verzeichnis sämtlicher Pflanzen des Werkes, der literarischen Quellen der Heilanzeigen und der Anwendungen der Pflanzen*. Stuttgart: Anton Hiersemann, 1969.

Hunt, Edwin S., and James M. Murray. *A History of Business in Medieval Europe, 1200–1550*. Cambridge: Cambridge University Press, 1999.

Imhoff, Christoph von. "Nürnbergs Indienpioniere. Reiseberichte von der ersten oberdeutschen Handelsfahrt nach Indien (1505/6)." *Pirckheimer-Jahrbuch*, 2 (1986), 11–44.

Inglehart, Ronald F., and Pippa Norris. "Trump, Brexit, and the Rise of Populism. Economic Have-Nots and Cultural Backlash." *Harvard Kennedy School Faculty Research Working Paper Series*, 29 July 2016. https://research.hks.harvard.edu/publications/getFile.aspx?Id=1401 (last accessed on 11 May 2020).

Iseli, Andrea. *Gute Policey. Öffentliche Ordnung in der Frühen Neuzeit*. Stuttgart: Verlag Eugen Ulmer, 2009.

Isenmann, Eberhard. *Die deutsche Stadt im Mittelalter 1150–1550. Stadtgestalt, Recht, Verfassung, Stadtregiment, Kirche, Gesellschaft, Wirtschaft*. Wien: Böhlau, 2012.

Israel, Uwe. "Sebastian Brant und Johannes Geiler von Kaysersberg." In: Klaus Bergdolt, Joachim Knape, et al. (ed.). *Sebastian Brant und die Kommunikationskultur um 1500*. Wiesbaden: Harrassowitz, 2010. 49–74.

Ivanov-Dogaru, Cristina. "Ambivalenz und Vielseitigkeit der Eulenspiegel-Figur." In: Carmen Elisabeth Puchianu (ed.). *Authentizität, Varietät oder Verballhornung. Germanistische Streifzüge durch Literatur, Kultur und Sprache im globalisierten Raum*. Passau: Verlag Karl Stutz, 2014. 95–106.

Jäger, Jens. "Texte aus Sebastian Brants "Narrenschiff" auf Flugblättern des 16. Jahrhunderts." *Daphnis*, 22:2 (1993), 493–502.

Jahn, Bernhard. "Raum für Schwänke. Zum Verhältnis von Raumstruktur und schwankhaftem Erzählen im *Dyl Vlenspiegel*." In: Bernhard Jahn, Dirk Rose, and Thorsten Unger (eds.). *Ordentliche Unordnung. Metamorphosen des Schwanks vom Mittelalter bis zur Moderne. Festschrift für Michael Schilling*. Heidelberg: Winter, 2014. 65–78.

Jahn, Bernhard. *Raumkonzepte in der frühen Neuzeit. Zur Konstruktion von Wirklichkeit in Pilgerberichten, Amerikareisebeschreibungen und Prosaerzählungen*. Frankfurt am Main: Peter Lang, 1993.

Janssen, Johannes. *Frankfurts Reichscorrespondenz nebst andern verwandten Aktenstücken von 1376–1519. Zweiten Bandes zweite Abtheilung. Aus der Zeit Kaiser Maximilians I. 1486–1519*. Freiburg im Breisgau: Herder'sche Verlagshandlung, 1872.

Jantz, Harold. "Amerika im deutschen Dichten und Denken." In: Wolfgang Stammler (ed.). *Deutsche Philologie im Aufriß*. 2nd ed. Berlin: Schmidt, 1962. Vol. 3, 309–372.

Jardine, Lisa. *Worldly Goods. A New History of the Renaissance*. London: Macmillan, 1996.

Jennings, Justin. *Globalizations and the Ancient World*. Cambridge: Cambridge University Press, 2011.

Johnson, Carina Lee. *Cultural Hierarchy in Sixteenth-Century Europe. The Ottomans and Mexicans*. New York: Cambridge University Press, 2011.

Johnson, Christine R. "Renaissance German Cosmographers and the Naming of America." *Past & Present*, 191:1 (2006), 3–43.

Johnson, Christine R. *The German Discovery of the World. Renaissance Encounters with the Strange and Marvelous*. Charlottesville and London: University of Virginia Press, 2008.

Johnson, Hildegard Binder. *Carta marina. World Geography in Strassburg*, 1525. Minneapolis: University of Minnesota Press, 1963.

Keller, Katrin, and Paola Molino. *Die Fuggerzeitungen im Kontext. Zeitungssammlungen im Alten Reich und in Italien*. Wien: Böhlau Verlag, 2015.

Kellenbenz, Hermann (ed.). *Die Fugger in Spanien und Portugal bis 1560. Ein Großunternehmen des 16. Jahrhunderts*. 3 vols. München: Ernst Vögel, 1990.

Kemper, Hans-Georg. *Deutsche Lyrik der frühen Neuzeit. Band 1: Epochen- und Gattungsprobleme. Reformationszeit*. Tübingen: Max Niemeyer, 1987.

Kemper, Hans-Georg. *Deutsche Lyrik der frühen Neuzeit. Band 2: Konfessionalismus*. Tübingen: Max Niemeyer, 1987.

Kießling, Rolf. "Problematik und zeitgenössische Kritik des Verlagssystems." In: Johannes Burkhardt et al. *Augsburger Handelshäuser im Wandel des historischen Urteils*. Berlin: Akademie-Verlag, 1996. 175–190.

Kirschner, Carola. *Hermen Bote. Städtische Literatur um 1500 zwischen Tradition und Innovation*. Essen: Item-Verlag, 1996.

Klaffke, Andreas. *"Es sey die alte Welt gefunden in der Neuen." Amerika in der deutschen Lyrik der frühen Neuzeit*. Marburg: Tectum, 2000.

Knabe, Wolfgang, and Dieter Noli. *Die versunkenen Schätze der Bom Jesus. Sensationsfund eines Indienseglers aus der Frühzeit des Welthandels*. Berlin: Nicolaische Verlagsbuchhandlung, 2012.

Knape, Joachim. "Der humanistische Geleittext als Paratext – am Beispiel von Brants Beigaben zu Tenglers *Layen Spiegel*." In: Andreas Deutsch (ed.). *Ulrich Tenglers Laienspiegel. Ein Rechtsbuch zwischen Humanismus und Hexenwahn*. Heidelberg: Winter, 2011. 117–137.

Knape, Joachim. "Der Medien-Narr. Zum ersten Kapitel von Sebastian Brants Narrenschiff." In: Klaus Bergdolt, Joachim Knape, et al. (eds.). *Sebastian Brant und die Kommunikationskultur um 1500*. Wiesbaden: Harrassowitz, 2010. 253–271.

Knape, Joachim. "Humanismus, Reformation, deutsche Sprache und Nation." In: Andreas Gardt (ed.). *Nation und Sprache. Die Diskussion ihres Verhältnisses in Geschichte und Gegenwart*. Berlin, New York: Walter de Gruyter, 2000. 103–138.

Kobuch, Manfred, and Ernst Müller (eds). *Der Deutsche Bauernkrieg in Dokumenten. Aus staatlichen Archiven der Deutschen Demokratischen Republik*. Weimar: Böhlau, 1975.

Kocka, Jürgen. *Capitalism. A Short History*. Princeton: Princeton University Press, 2016.

Kühlmann, Wilhelm. "Neo-Latin Literature in Early Modern Germany." In: Max Reinhart (ed.). *Early Modern German Literature*. Camden House History of German Literature, v. 4. Rochester, NY: Camden House, 2007. 281–329.

Kuper, Michael. *Zur Semiotik der Inversion. Verkehrte Welt und Lachkultur im 16. Jahrhundert*. Berlin: VWB Verlag für Wissenschaft und Bildung, 1993.

Kuttner, Robert. *Can Democracy Survive Global Capitalism?* New York: W. W. Norton, 2018.

Lach, Donald Frederick. *Asia in the Making of Europe*. 3 vols. Chicago and London: University of Chicago Press, 1965–1993.

Legassie, Shayne Aaron. *The Medieval Invention of Travel*. Chicago: The University of Chicago Press, 2017.

Lehmann, Hartmut. "Zur Erforschung der Religiosität im 17. Jahrhundert." In: Monika Hagenmaier and Sabine Holtz (eds.). *Krisenbewußtsein und Krisenbewältigung in der frühen Neuzeit. Festschrift für Hans-Christoph Rublack*. Frankfurt am Main: Lang, 1992. 3–11.

Lehmann, Martin. *Die* Cosmographiae Introductio *Matthias Ringmanns und die Weltkarte Martin Waldseemüllers aus dem Jahr 1507. Ein Meilenstein frühneuzeitlicher Kartographie*. München: Martin Meidenbauer, 2010.

Lehmann, Martin. "Amerigo Vespucci and His Alleged Awareness of America as a Separate Land Mass." *Imago Mundi: The International Journal for the History of Cartography*, 65:1 (2013), 15–24.

Lehmann, Martin. "The Depiction of America on Martin Waldseemüller's World Map from 1507 – Humanistic Geography in the Service of Political Propaganda." *Cogent Arts & Humanities*, 3:1 (2016), 1152785 (1–15). https://www.tandfonline.com/doi/full/10.1080/23311983.2016.1152785 (last accessed on 11 May 2020).

Leitch, Stephanie. *Mapping Ethnography in Early Modern Germany. New Worlds in Print Culture*. Basingstoke: Palgrave Macmillan, 2010.

Lester, Toby. *The Fourth Part of the World. The Race to the Ends of the Earth, and the Epic Story of the Map That Gave America its Name*. New York: Free Press, 2009.

Lindemann, Mary. *Medicine and Society in Early Modern Europe*. 2nd ed. Cambridge: Cambridge University Press, 2010.

Lobsien, Eckhard. "Die Pluralität der Welten im 16. und 17. Jahrhundert." In: Renate Dürr, Gisela Engel, and Johannes Süßmann (eds.). *Expansionen in der frühen Neuzeit*. Berlin: Duncker & Humblot, 2005. 131–151.

Lorentzen, Tim. *Johannes Bugenhagen als Reformator der öffentlichen Fürsorge*. Tübingen: Mohr Siebeck, 2008.

Lopes, Marília dos Santos. "Außerordentliche und kuriose Denkwürdigkeit. Die Endeckung der 'Newen Welt/ so jetzt America genannt wirdt' in deutschen Schrifen des 16. und 17. Jahrhunderts." In: Karl Kohut (ed.). *Von der Weltkarte zum Kuriositätenkabinett. Amerika im deutschen Humanismus und Barock*. Frankfurt am Main: Vervuert Verlag, 1995. 78–89.

MacGillivray, Alex. *A Brief History of Globalization. The Untold Story of Our Incredible Shrinking Planet*. New York: Carroll & Graf, 2006.

Maier, Charles S. "Territorialisten und Globalisten. Die beiden neuen 'Parteien' in der in der heutigen Demokratie." *Transit*, 14 (1997), 5–14.

Maier, Charles S. "The New Political Divide." *Project Syndicate. The World's Opinion Page*. July 3, 1997. https://www.project-syndicate.org/commentary/the-new-political-divide (last accessed on 11 May 2020).

McCants, Anne E. C. "Exotic Goods, Popular Consumption, and the Standard of Living. Thinking about Globalization in the Early Modern World." *Journal of World History*, 18:4 (2007), 433–462.

McGovern, John F. "The Rise of New Economic Attitudes – Economic Humanism, Economic Nationalism – During the Later Middle Ages and the Renaissance, A. D. 1200–1550." *Traditio*, 26 (1970), 217–253.

McGrane, Bernard. *Beyond Anthropology. Society and the Other*. New York: Columbia University Press, 1989.

McGuirk, Donald L., Jr. "The Presumed North America on the Waldseemüller World Map (1507). A Theory of Its Discovery by Christopher Columbus." *Terrae Incognitae*, 46:2 (2014), 86–102.

McLean, Matthew. *The 'Cosmographia' of Sebastian Münster. Describing the World in the Reformation*. Aldershot, England; Burlington, VT: Ashgate, 2007.

McNeill, William H. *A World History*. 4th ed. Oxford: Oxford University Press, 1999.

Mellor, Philip A., and Chris Shilling. *Re-forming the Body. Religion, Community and Modernity.* London: SAGE Publications, 1997.

Melters, Johannes. *"ein frölich gemüt zu machen in schweren zeiten ... " Der Schwankroman in Mittelalter und Früher Neuzeit.* Berlin: Erich Schmidt, 2004.

Menninger, Annerose. *Die Macht der Augenzeugen. Neue Welt und Kannibalen-Mythos, 1492–1600.* Stuttgart: F. Steiner, 1995.

Mertens, Bernd. *Im Kampf gegen die Monopole. Reichstagsverhandlungen und Monopolprozesse im frühen 16. Jahrhundert.* Tübingen: J. C. B. Mohr, 1996.

Mertens, Dieter. "Sebastian Brant, Kaiser Maximilian, das Reich und der Türkenkrieg." In: Klaus Bergdolt, Joachim Knape, et al. (ed.). *Sebastian Brant und die Kommunikationskultur um 1500.* Wiesbaden: Harrassowitz, 2010. 173–218.

Mignolo, Walter D. *The Darker Side of the Renaissance. Literacy, Territoriality, and Colonization.* Ann Arbor: The University of Michigan Press, 1995.

Milikh, Arthur. "Immigration, Citizenship, and Cosmopolitanism." *The Heritage Foundation*, 21 January 2016. https://www.heritage.org/immigration/commentary/immigration-citizenship-and-cosmopolitanism (last accessed on 11 May 2020).

Mirabella, Bella. *Ornamentalism. The Art of Renaissance Accessories.* Ann Arbor: University of Michigan Press, 2011.

Mittenzwei, Ingrid. *Der Joachimsthaler Aufstand 1525. Seine Ursachen und Folgen.* Berlin: Akademie-Verlag, 1968.

Moran, Bruce T. "The Herbarius of Paracelsus." *Pharmacy in History*, 39 (1993), 99–128.

Morison, Samuel Eliot. *The European Discovery of America. The Southern Voyages A.D. 1492–1616.* New York, Oxford University Press, 1974

Mozer, Isolde. "Vorwort." In: Bernhard von Breydenbach. *Peregrinatio in terram sanctam. Eine Pilgerreise ins Heilige Land. Frühneuhochdeutscher Text und Übersetzung.* Berlin: de Gruyter, 2010.

Müller, Gernot Michael. *Die 'Germania generalis' des Conrad Celtis. Studien mit Edition, Übersetzung und Kommentar.* Berlin: de Gruyter, 2012.

Müller, Jan-Dirk. "Alte Wissensformen und neue Erfahrungen. Amerika in Sebastian Francks 'Weltbuch.'" In: Horst Wenzel (ed.). *Gutenberg und die Neue Welt.* München: Wilhelm Fink, 1994. 171–193.

Müller, Jan-Dirk. "*Erfarung* zwischen Heilssorge, Selbsterkenntnis und Entdeckung des Kosmos." *Daphnis*, 15:2 (1986), 307–342.

Müller, Jan-Dirk. "Evidentia und Medialität. Zur Ausdifferenzierung von Evidenz in der Frühen Neuzeit." In: Gabriele Wimböck, Karin Leonhard, and Markus Friedrich (eds.). *Evidentia. Reichweiten visueller Wahrnehmung in der Frühen Neuzeit.* Berlin: Lit Verlag, 2007. 57–82.

Müller, Jan-Dirk. "Literarischer Text und kultureller Text in der Frühen Neuzeit am Beispiel des Narrenschiffs von Sebastian Brant." In: Helmut Puff und Christopher Wild (eds.). *Zwischen den Disziplinen? Perspektiven der Frühneuzeitforschung.* Göttingen: Wallstein, 2003. 81–101.

Müller, Maria E. *Der Poet der Moralität. Untersuchungen zu Hans Sachs.* Bern. Frankfurt am Main: Lang, 1985.

Neuber, Wolfgang. *Fremde Welt im europäischen Horizont. Zur Topik der deutschen Amerika-Reiseberichte der Frühen Neuzeit.* Berlin: Schmidt, 1991.

Neuber, Wolfgang. "The 'Red Indian's Body.' The Physiognomy of the Indigenous American Between Exoticism and Learned Culture in the Early Modern Period." In: Karl Enekel et al.

(eds.). *Modelling the Individual. Biography and Portrait in the Renaissance*. Amsterdam: Rodopi, 1998. 93–107.
Neuber, Wolfgang. "Verdeckte Theologie. Sebastian Brant und die Südamerikaberichte der Frühzeit." In: Titus Heydenreich (ed.) *Der Umgang mit dem Fremden. Beiträge zur Literatur aus und über Lateinamerika*. München: Fink, 1986. 9–29.
Obhof, Ute. "Der Erdglobus, der Amerika benannte. Die Überlieferung der Globensegmente von Martin Waldseemüller aus dem Jahre 1507." *Zeitschrift für deutsches Altertum und deutsche Literatur*, 135:4 (2006), 474–480.
Ogilvie, Brian. *The Science of Describing. Natural History in Renaissance Europe*. Chicago: Chicago University Press, 2006.
Olwig, Kenneth. *Landscape, Nature and the Body Politic. From Britain's Renaissance to America's New World*. Madison: University of Wisconsin Press, 2002.
O'Rourke, Kevin H., and Jeffrey G. Williamson. "When Did Globalisation Begin?" *European Review of Economic History*, 6:1 (2002), 23–50.
O'Rourke, Kevin H., and Jeffrey G. Williamson. "Did Vasco da Gama Matter to European Markets? Testing Frederick Lanes's Hypothesis Fifty Years Later." *Economic History Review, New Series*, 62:3 (2009), 655–684.
Ortiz Crespo, Alfonso. "The Spanish American Colonial City. Its Origins, Development, and Functions." In: Joseph J. Rishel, with Suzanne Stratton-Pruitt. *The Arts in Latin America, 1492–1820*. New Haven: Yale University Press, 2006. 23–37.
Osterhammel, Jürgen, and Niels P. Petersson. *Geschichte der Globalisierung. Dimensionen, Prozesse, Epochen*. Munich: C. H. Beck, 2003.
Osenbrüggen, Eduard. *Der Hausfrieden. Ein Beitrag zur deutschen Rechtsgeschichte*. Erlangen: Ferdinand Enke, 1857.
Ozment, Steven. *The Age of Reform (1250–1550). An Intellectual and Religious History of Late Medieval and Reformation Europe*. New Haven: Yale University Press, 1980.
Parker, Charles H. *Global Interactions in the Early Modern Age, 1400–1800*. Cambridge: Cambridge University Press, 2010.
Parthasarathi, Prasannan. *Why Europe Grew Rich and Asia Did Not. Global Economic Divergence, 1600–1850*. Cambridge: Cambridge University Press, 2011.
Peters, Ursula. "zins und gülte. Zur Ökonomie der Landleihe in der höfischen Dichtung." *Internationales Archiv für Sozialgeschichte der deutschen Literatur*, 42:1 (2017), 1–50.
Pettegree, Andrew. *The Book in the Renaissance*. New Haven, London: Yale University Press, 2010.
Pezzini, Barbara. "Editorial 'Rootless Cosmopolitans?' Visual Resources, an International Journal in Nationalist Times." *Visual Resources*, 33:3–4 (2017), 199–203.
Philipp, Michael. *Das 'Regentenbuch' des Mansfelder Kanzlers Georg Lauterbeck. Ein Beitrag zur politischen Ideengeschichte im konfessionellen Zeitalter*. Augsburg: Wißner, 1996.
Phillips, Seymour. "The Outer World of the European Middle Ages." In: Stuart B. Schwartz (ed.). *Implicit Understandings. Observing, Reporting, and Reflecting on the Encounters Between Europeans and Other Peoples in the Early Modern Era*. Cambridge: Cambridge University Press, 1994. 23–63.
Pieper, Renate. *Die Vermittlung einer neuen Welt. Amerika im Nachrichtennetz des Habsburgischen Imperiums 1493–1598*. Mainz: Philipp von Zabern, 2000.
Pieper, Renate. "Between India and the Indies. German Mercantile Networks, the Struggle for the Imperial Crown and the Naming of the New World." *Culture & History Digital Journal* [Online], 3:1 (2014), e003. doi: http://dx.doi.org/10.3989/chdj.2014.003

Pietsch, Christian. "Grundstrukturen historischer Abläufe bei Herodot, Platon und Polybios." *Germanisch-romanische Monatsschrift*, 58:1 (2008), 7–21.

Pietschmann, Horst. "Bemerkungen zur 'Jubiläumshistoriographie' am Beispiel '500 Jahre Martin Waldseemüller und der Name Amerika.'" *Jahrbuch für Geschichte Lateinamerikas*, 44 (2007), 367–389.

Pohle, Jürgen. *Deutschland und die überseeische Expansion Portugals im 15. und 16. Jahrhundert*. Münster: Lit Verlag, 2000.

Pomeranz, Kenneth, and Steven Topik. *The World That Trade Created. Society, Culture, and the World Economy, 1400–the Present*. Armonk, NY: M. E. Sharpe, 1999.

Pomeranz, Kenneth. *The Great Divergence. Europe, China, and the Making of the Modern World Economy*. Princeton: Princeton University Press, 2000.

Postel, Rainer. "Geschwinde Zeiten. Zum Krisenproblem im 16. Jahrhundert." In: Monika Hagenmaier and Sabine Holtz (eds.). *Krisenbewußtsein und Krisenbewältigung in der frühen Neuzeit. Festschrift für Hans-Christoph Rublack*. Frankfurt am Main: Lang, 1992. 13–21.

Prager, Debra N. *Orienting the Self. The German Literary Encounter with the Eastern Other*. Rochester, NY: Camden House, 2014.

Prietz, Frank Ulrich. *Das Mittelalter im Dienst der Reformation. Die Chronica Carions und Melanchthons von 1532. Zur Vermittlung mittelalterlicher Geschichtskonzeptionen in die protestantische Historiographie*. Stuttgart: Kohlhammer, 2014.

Otterspeer, Willem. *In Praise of Ambiguity. Erasmus, Huizinga and the Seriousness of Play*. Leiden: Leiden University Press, 2018.

Reinhard, Wolfgang. *A Short History of Colonialism*. Manchester: Manchester University Press, 2011.

Reinhard, Wolfgang. *Die Unterwerfung der Welt. Globalgeschichte der europäischen Expansion 1415–2015*. München: C.H. Beck Verlag, 2016.

Reinhardt, Volker. *Die Tyrannei der Tugend. Calvin und die Reformation in Genf*. München: C. H. Beck, 2009.

Reske, Christoph. *Die Produktion der Schedelschen Weltchronik in Nürnberg. The Production of Schedel's Nuremberg Chronicle*. Wiesbaden: Harrassowitz, 2000.

Ramachandran, Ayesh. *The Worldmakers. Global Imagining in Early Modern Europe*. Chicago and London: University of Chicago Press, 2015.

Reich, Robert B. *The Common Good*. New York: Knopf, 2018.

Richter, Sandra, and Guillaume Garner (eds.). *Eigennutz und gute Ordnung. Ökonomisierungen der Welt im 17. Jahrhundert*. Wiesbaden: Harrassowitz, 2016.

Rockenberger, Annika. *Produktion und Drucküberlieferung der editio princeps von Sebastian Brants Narrenschiff (Basel 1494). Eine medienhistorisch-druckanalytische Untersuchung*. Frankfurt am Main: Peter Lang, 2011.

Röcke, Werner. *Die Freude am Bösen. Studien zu einer Poetik des deutschen Schwankromans im Spätmittelalter*. München: W. Fink, 1987.

Roper, Lyndal. *Martin Luther. Renegade and Prophet*. New York: Random House, 2016.

Rosenfeld, Hellmut. "Brants Narrenschiff und seine Stellung in der Publizistik und zur Gesellschaft." In: Alfred Swierk and Susanne Besslich-Widmann (eds.). *Beiträge zur Geschichte des Buches und seiner Funktion in der Gesellschaft. Festschrift für Hans Widmann zum 65. Geburtstag am 28. März 1973*. Stuttgart: Hiersemann, 1974. 230–245.

Rosenthal, Margaret F. "Cultures of Clothing in Later Medieval and Early Modern Europe." *Journal of Medieval and Early Modern Studies*, 39:3 (2009), 459–481.

Rössner, Philipp Robinson. *Deflation–Devaluation–Rebellion. Geld im Zeitalter der Reformation*. Stuttgart: Franz Steiner, 2012.
Rössner, Philipp Robinson (ed.). *Economic Growth and the Origins of Modern Political Economy. Economic Reasons of State, 1500–2000*. New York: Routledge, 2016.
Rössner, Philipp Robinson. "Introduction." In: Martin Luther. *On Commerce and Usury (1524)*. Ed. Philipp Robinson Rössner. New York, NY: Anthem Press, 2015.
Rössner, Philipp Robinson. "Luther–Ein tüchtiger Ökonom? Über die monetären Ursprünge der Deutschen Reformation." *Zeitschrift für Historische Forschung*, 42:1 (2015), 37–74.
Rowan, Steven. "Chronicle as Cosmos. Hartmann Schedel's Nuremberg Chronicle, 1493." *Daphnis*, 15:2 (1986), 375–407.
Rublack, Ulinka. *Dressing Up. Cultural Identity in Renaissance Europe*. Oxford: Oxford University Press, 2010.
Rubiés, Joan-Pau. "Travel Writing and Humanistic Culture. A Blunted Impact?" *Journal of Early Modern History*, 10:1–2 (2006), 131–168.
Rupp, Michael. *'Narrenschiff' und 'Stultifera navis.' Deutsche und lateinische Moralsatire von Sebastian Brant und Jakob Locher in Basel 1494–1498*. Münster; New York: Waxmann, 2002.
Rüther, Stefanie. "Von der Macht, vergeben zu können. Symbolische Formen der Konfliktbeilegung im späten Mittelalter am Beispiel Braunschweigs und der Hanse." In: Christoph Dartmann, Marian Füssel, and Stefanie Rüther (eds.) *Raum und Konflikt. Zur symbolischen Konstituierung gesellschaftlicher Ordnung in Mittelalter und Früher Neuzeit*. Münster: Rhema, 2004. 107–128.
Rusterholz, Peter. "Till Eulenspiegel als Sprachkritiker." *Wirkendes Wort*, 27 (1977), 18–26.
Sahm, Heike. *Dürers kleinere Texte. Konventionen als Spielraum für Individualität*. Tübingen: Niemeyer, 2002.
Schulz-Grobert, Jürgen. *Das Straßburger Eulenspiegelbuch. Studien zu entstehungsgeschichtlichen Voraussetzungen der ältesten Drucküberlieferung*. Tübingen: Max Niemeyer, 1999.
Schulze, Winfried. "Das Wagnis der Individualisierung." In: Thomas Cramer (ed.). *Wege in die Neuzeit*. München: Fink, 1988. 270–286.
Schulze, Winfried. "Vom Gemeinnutz zum Eigennutz. Über den Normenwandel in der ständischen Gesellschaft der Frühen Neuzeit." *Historische Zeitschrift*, 243:3 (1986), 591–626.
Schumann, Eva. "Beiträge studierter Juristen und anderer Rechtsexperten zur Rezeption des gelehrten Rechts." *Jahrbuch der Akademie der Wissenschaften in Göttingen*, 2007, 443–461.
Schwarz, Alexander. "Leere statt Lehre im Eulenspiegel." *Daphnis*, 40:1–2 (2011), 89–113.
Schwitter, Thomas. "Das Desinteresse am Neuen. Frankreich und die Neue Welt 1492–1600." In: Kerstin Hitzbleck and Thomas Schwitter (eds.). *Die Erweiterung des 'globalen' Raumes und die Wahrnehmung des Fremden vom Mittelalter bis zur Frühen Neuzeit*. Basel: Schwabe Verlag, 2015. 61–84.
Scott, Tom. *Society and Economy in Germany, 1300–1600*. Houndmills, England; New York: Palgrave, 2002.
Scott, Tom. *Town, Country, and Regions in Reformation Germany*. Leiden, Boston: Brill, 2005.
Schmitt, Eberhard. "Atlantische Epansion und maritime Indienfahrt." *Pirckheimer-Jahrbuch*, 7 (1992), 127–144.
Seavoy, Ronald E. *Origins and Growth of the Global Economy. From the Fifteenth Century Onward*. Westport, CT; London: Praeger, 2003.

Senckenberg, Heinrich Christian von, and Johann Jacob Schmauß (eds.). *Zweyter Theil derer Reichs-Abschiede von dem Jahr 1495. bis auf das Jahr 1551. inclusive*. Frankfurt: Koch, 1747.

Setz, Wolfram. *Lorenzo Vallas Schrift gegen die konstantinische Schenkung. De falso credita et emmentita Constantini donatione. Zur Interpretation und Wirkungsgeschichte*. Tübingen: Max Niemeyer, 1975.

Shapin, Steven. *A Social History of Truth. Civility and Science in Seventeenth-Century England*. Chicago: University of Chicago Press, 1994.

Sieber, Siegfried. "Der Joachimsthaler Aufstand 1525 in seinen Beziehungen zu Sachsen." *Bohemia*, 4:1 (1963), 40–53.

Sievernich, Michael. "Entdeckung und Verdeckung des anderen. Zum 500-Jahr-Gedenken der europäischen Ankunft in Amerika." *Communicatio Socialis*, 24:1 (1991), 43–62.

Simmer, Götz. *Gold und Sklaven. Die Provinz Venezuela während der Welser-Verwaltung (1528–1556)*. Berlin: Wissenschaft und Technik, 2000.

Simon, Thomas. "Krise oder Wachstum? Erklärungsversuche zum Aufkommen territorialer Gesetzgebung am Ausgang des Mittelalters." In: Gerhard Köbler and Hermann Nehlsen (eds.). *Wirkungen europäischer Rechtskultur. Festschrift für Karl Kroeschell zum 70. Geburtstag*. München: C. H. Beck, 1997. 1201–1217.

Simon, Thomas. "Gemeinwohltopik in der mittelalterlichen und frühneuzeitlichen Politiktheorie." In: Herfried Münkler and Harald Bluhm (eds.). *Gemeinwohl und Gemeinsinn. Historische Semantiken politischer Leitbegriffe. Forschungsberichte der interdisziplinären Arbeitsgruppe 'Gemeinwohl und Gemeinsinn.'* Berlin: Akademie Verlag, 2001. I, 129–146.

Simon, Thomas. *'Gute Policey': Ordnungsleitbilder und Zielvorstellungen politischen Handelns in der Frühen Neuzeit*. Frankfurt am Main: Vittorio Klostermann, 2004.

Singer, Bruno. *Die Fürstenspiegel in Deutschland im Zeitalter des Humanismus und der Reformation. Bibliographische Grundlagen und ausgewählte Interpretationen. Jakob Wimpfeling, Wolfgang Seidel, Johann Sturm, Urban Rieger*. München: Fink, 1981.

Sixel, Friedrich Wilhelm. "Die deutsche Vorstellung vom Indianer in der ersten Hälfte des 16. Jahrhunderts." *Annali del Pontificio Museo Missionario Etnologico già lateranensi*, 30 (1966), 9–230.

Skrine, Peter. "Images of the Merchant in German Renaissance Literature." *Bulletin of the John Rylands Library*, 72:3 (1990), 185–197.

Smith, Duncan. "' ... beschreibung eyner Landtschafft der Wilden/ Nacketen/ Grimmigen Menschfresser Leuthen.' The German Image of America in the Sixteenth Century." In: Gerhard K. Friesen and Walter Schatzberg (eds.). *The German Contribution to the Building of the Americas. Studies in Honor of Karl J. R. Arndt*. Hanover, NH: Clark University Press, 1977. 1–19.

Smith, Jeffrey Chipps. "The 2010 Josephine Waters Bennet Lecture. Albrecht Dürer as Collector." *Renaissance Quarterly*, 64:1 (2011), 1–49.

Smith, Preserved. *The Life and Letters of Martin Luther*. Boston: Houghton Mifflin Company, 1911.

Smith, Stefan Halikowski. "'Profits sprout like tropical plants.' A fresh look at what went wrong with the Eurasian spice trade c. 1550–1800." *Journal of Global History*, 3:3 (2008), 389–418.

Smith, Stefan Halikowski. "The Mystification of Spices in the Western Tradition." *European Review of History*, 8:2 (2001), 119–136.

Sobel, Dava. *The True Story of a Lone Genius Who Solved the Greatest Scientific Problem of His Time.* New York: Walker, 1995.
Speth, Sebastian. *Dimensionen narrativer Sinnstiftung im frühneuhochdeutschen Prosaroman. Textgeschichtliche Interpretation von 'Fortunatus' und 'Herzog Ernst.'* Berlin, Boston: de Gruyter, 2017.
Spitz, Lewis William. *Conrad Celtis, the German Arch-Humanist.* Cambridge: Harvard University Press, 1957.
Spivak, Gayatri Chakravorty. *A Critique of Postcolonial Reason. Toward a History of the Vanishing Present.* Cambridge: Harvard University Press, 1999.
Stallybrass, Peter, and Allon White. *The Politics and Poetics of Transgression.* Ithaca: Cornell University Press, 1986.
Stein, Claudia. *Negotiating the French Pox in Early Modern Germany.* Farnham, Burlington: Ashgate, 2009.
Steinbrink, Matthias. *Ulrich Meltinger. Ein Basler Kaufmann am Endes des 15. Jahrhunderts.* Stuttgart: Franz Steiner Verlag, 2007.
Steiner, Benjamin. *Colberts Afrika. Eine Wissens- und Begegnungsgeschichte in Afrika im Zeitalter Ludwigs XIV.* Munich: De Gruyter Oldenbourg, 2014.
Steinmetz, Ralf-Henning. "Welterfahrung und Fiktionalität im Fortunatus." *Zeitschrift für deutsches Altertum und deutsche Literatur*, 133:2 (2004), 210–225.
Stieglecker, Roland. *Die Renaissance eines Heiligen. Sebastian Brant und Onuphrius eremita.* Wiesbaden: Harrassowitz, 2001.
Strauss, Gerald. *Law, Resistance and the State. The Opposition to Roman Law in Reformation Germany.* Princeton: Princeton Univ. Press, 1986.
Strauss, Gerald. *Luther's House of Learning. Indoctrination of the Young in the German Reformation.* Baltimore: Johns Hopkins University Press, 1978.
Strauss, Gerald. *Manifestations of Discontent in Germany on the Eve of the Reformation. A Collection of Documents selected, translated, and introduced by Gerald Strauss.* Bloomington: Indiana University Press, 1971.
Stock, Brian. "Antiqui and Moderni as 'Giants' and 'Dwarfs.' A Reflection of Popular Culture?" *Modern Philology*, 76:4 (1979), 370–374.
Strosetzki, Christoph. "Die Idee von Fortschritt und Zerfall im Europa der frühen Neuzeit." *Germanisch-romanische Monatsschrift*, 58:1 (2008), 1–5.
Subrahmanyam, Sanjay. "Introduction." In: Jerry H. Bentley, Sanjay Subrahmanyam, and Merry Wiesner-Hanks (eds.). *The Cambridge World History, Volume 6: The Construction of a Global World, 1400–1800 CE.* Cambridge: Cambridge University Press, 2015. 1–25.
Subrahmanyam, Sanjay. "The Birth-Pangs of Portuguese Asia. Revisiting the Fateful 'Long Decade' 1498–1509." *Journal of Global History*, 2:3 (2007), 261–280.
Sudhoff, Karl. "Vorwort." In: Karl Sudhoff (ed.). *Theophrast von Hohenheim gen. Paracelsus Sämtliche Werke.* I. Abteilung, 2. Band. Munich: R. Oldenbourg, 1930. V–XXXI.
Tally, Robert T., Jr. (ed.). *Geocritical Explorations. Space, Place, and Mapping in Literary and Cultural Studies.* Foreword by Bertrand Westphal. New York: Palgrave Macmillan, 2011.
Tally, Robert T., Jr. (ed.). *Literary Cartographies. Spatiality, Representation, and Narrative.* New York: Palgrave Macmillan, 2015.
Tally, Robert T., Jr. *Spatiality.* Abingdon, New York: Routledge, 2013.
Tang, Chenxi. *Imagining World Order. Literature and International Law in Early Modern Europe, 1500–1800.* Ithaca: Cornell University Press, 2018.

Tenberg, Reinhard. *Die deutsche Till-Eulenspiegel-Rezeption bis zum Ende des 16. Jahrhunderts*. Würzburg: Königshausen & Neumann, 1996.

Treue, Wolfgang. *Abenteuer und Anerkennung. Reisende und Gereiste in Spätmittelalter und Frühneuzeit (1400–1700)*. Paderborn: Schöningh, 2014.

Umbach, Silke. *Sebastian Brants Tischzucht (Thesmophagia 1490). Edition und Wortindex*. Wiesbaden: Harrassowitz, 1995.

Van Duzer, Chet. "A Northern Refuge of the Monstrous Races. Asia on Waldseemüller's 1516 Carta Marina." *Imago Mundi*, 62:2 (2010), 221–231.

Van Duzer, Chet. *Johann Schöner's Globe of 1515. Transcription and Study*. Philadelphia: American Philosophical Society, 2010.

Van Duzer, Chet. *Martin Waldseemüller's 'Carta marina' of 1516. Study and Transcription of the Long Legends*. Cham: Springer Open, 2020.

Van Duzer, Chet. "Waldseemüller's World Maps of 1507 and 1516. Sources and Development of his Cartographical Thought." *The Portolan Journal*, 85 (2012), 8–20.

Van Engen, John. "The Church in the Fifteenth Century." In: Thomas A. Brady, Jr., Heiko A. Oberman, and James D. Tracy (eds.). *Handbook of European History 1400–1600. Late Middle Ages, Renaissance and Reformation*. Grand Rapids: Eerdmans, 1996. Vol. 1, 305–330.

Vogel, Klaus A. "'America.' Begriff, geographische Konzeption und frühe Entdeckugsgeschichte in der Perspektive der deutschen Humanisten." In: Karl Kohut (ed.). *Von der Weltkarte zum Kuriositätenkabinett. Amerika im deutschen Humanismus und Barock*. Frankfurt am Main: Vervuert Verlag, 1995. 11–43.

Vogel, Klaus A. "Amerigo Vespucci und die Humanisten in Wien. Die Rezeption der geographischen Entdeckungen und der Streit zwischen Joachim Vadian und Johannes Camers über die Irrtümer der Klassiker." *Pirckheimer-Jahrbuch*, 7 (1992), 53–104.

Vogel, Klaus A. "Schedel als Kompilator. Notizen zu einem kaum bestellen Forschungsfeld." *Pirckheimer-Jahrbuch*, 9 (1994), 73–97.

Voltmer, Rita. "Krämer, Kaufleute, Kartelle. Standeskritischer Diskurs, mittelalterliche Handelspraxis und Johannes Geiler von Kaysersberg (1445–1510)." In: Dietrich Ebeling, Volker Henn, et al. (eds.). *Landesgeschichte als multidisziplinäre Wissenschaft. Festgabe für Franz Irsigler zum 60. Geburtstag*. Trier: Porta-Alba-Verlag, 2001. 401–445.

Vries, Jan de. "The Limits of Globalization in the Early Modern World." *Economic History Review*, 63:3 (2010), 710–733.

Wailes, Stephen L. "The Childishness of Till. Hermen Bote's Ulenspiegel." *The German Quarterly*, 64:2 (1991), 127–137.

Wallerstein, Immanuel. *The Modern World-System I. Capitalist Agriculture and the Origins of the European World-Economy in the Sixteenth Century*. New York and London: Academic Press, 1974.

Watts, Pauline Moffitt. "The Donation of Constantine, Cartography, and Papal 'Plenitudo Potestatis' in the Sixteenth Century. A Paper for Salvatore Camporeale." *MLN*, 119:1 (2004), S88–S107.

Weber, Matthias. *Die Reichspolizeiordnungen von 1530, 1548 und 1577. Historische Einführung und Edition*. Frankfurt am Main: Vittorio Klostermann, 2002.

Weitnauer, Alfred. *Venezianischer Handel der Fugger. Nach der Musterbuchhaltung des Matthäus Schwarz*. Munich: Duncker & Humblot, 1931.

Werhane, Patricia H. "The Role of Self-Interest in Adam Smith's Wealth of Nations." *The Journal of Philosophy*, 86:11 (1989), 669–680.

Werz, Bruno. "Saved from the Sea. The Shipwreck of the Bom Jesus (1533) and its Material Culture." In: Annemarie Jordan Gschwend and K. J. P. Lowe (eds.). *The Global City. On the Streets of Renaissance Lisbon*. London: Paul Holberton Publishing, 2015. 89–93.

Wesche, Jörg. "Der Narr ist ein Reisender. Frühneuzeitliche Vagantenregister im Gegenlicht der Literaturgeschichte." In: Franz Fromholzer, Jörg Wesche, and Julia Amslinger (eds.). *Lose Leute. Figuren, Schauplätze und Künste des Vaganten in der Frühen Neuzeit*. München: Wilhelm Fink, 2019. 17–30.

Westermann, Ekkehard, and Markus A. Denzel. *Das Kaufmannsnotizbuch des Matthäus Schwarz aus Augsburg von 1548*. Stuttgart: Steiner, 2011.

Wintroub, Michael. *The Voyage of Thought. Navigating Knowledge Across the Sixteenth-Century World*. Cambridge, New York: Cambridge University Press, 2017.

Wojciehowski, Hannah Chapelle. *Group Identity in the Renaissance World*. Cambridge: Cambridge University Press, 2011.

Wright, Clifford A. "The Medieval Spice Trade and the Diffusion of the Chile." *Gastronomica*, 7:2 (2007), 35–43.

Wunderli, Richard. *Peasant Fires. The Drummer of Niklashausen*. Bloomington: Indiana University Press, 1992.

Wunderlich, Werner. "Nachwort. Hermen Botes Radbuch. In Abbildung des Druckes L ca. 1492/93. Mit dem Text nach Herman Brandes und mit einer Übersetzung von Heinz-Lothar Worm. Ed. Werner Wunderlich. Göppingen: Kümmerle, 1985. 141–160.

Wunderlich, Werner. *Till Eulenspiegel*. München: Wilhelm Fink, 1984.

Wüst, Wolfgang. "Das Bild der Fugger in der Reichsstadt Augsburg und in der Reiseliteratur." In: Johannes Burkhardt, Thomas Nieding, and Christine Werkstetter (eds.). *Augsburger Handelshäuser im Wandel des historischen Urteils*. Berlin: Akademie-Verlag, 1996. 69–86.

Wuttke, Dieter. "Humanismus in den deutschsprachigen Ländern und Entdeckungsgeschichte 1493–1534." In: Dieter Wuttke (ed.). *Dazwischen. Kulturwissenschaft auf Warburgs Spuren*. Baden-Baden: Koerner, 1996. Vol. 2, 483–537.

Zäh, Helmut. "Konrad Peutinger und Margarete Welser. Ehe und Familie im Zeichen des Humanismus." In: Mark Häberlein and Johannes Burkhardt (eds.). *Die Welser. Neue Forschungen zur Geschichte und Kultur der oberdeutschen Handelshauses*. Berlin: Akademie Verlag, 2002. 449–509.

Zeydel, Edwin Hermann. *Sebastian Brant*. New York: Twayne, 1967.

Zielonka, Jan. *Counter-Revolution. Liberal Europe in Retreat*. Oxford: Oxford University Press, 2018.

Zwart, Pim de. *Globalization and the Colonial Origins of the Great Divergence. Intercontinental Trade and Living Standards in the Dutch East India Company's Commercial Empire, c. 1600–1800*. Leiden, Boston: Brill, 2016.

Index

Aelfric Grammaticus 12
Agricola, Johannes 280–282, 284, 285
Alciato, Andrea 183
Alexander VI 227, 239
Almeida, Francisco de 246, 247
Ambiguity 1–5, 155, 157, 341, 344, 346, 350
Apian, Peter 164, 165
Apollonius 190
Aquinas, Thomas 95
Aristotle 18–19, 39
Arminius 299
Augustine 25, 38, 77, 134
Aventinus, Johannes 136, 293, 294, 299, 300, 310, 311, 332, 333

Bacchus 186, 190
Bacon, Francis 126
Balboa, Vasco Núñez de 152
Bauhin, Caspar 315
Beck, Balthasar 249
Behaim, Martin 127, 243, 244
Bergmann von Olpe, Johann 182, 213, 214
Berthold von Regensburg 256
Bock, Hieronymus 269, 271, 309, 313, 315–317, 319, 324–327, 336, 342
Boemus, Johann 169
Böhm, Hans 79
Bom Jesus 248
Bote, Hermann 20–24, 28, 29, 43–45, 51, 57, 102, 103, 105, 106, 342
Brant, Sebastian 3, 9, 22, 24–26, 30, 37, 40, 42, 43, 49, 57, 66, 67, 70, 72, 74, 76, 78–80, 84, 88–93, 96, 98–107, 117, 119, 120, 134, 140, 141, 143, 180–187, 189–198, 200, 206, 211–215, 217, 225, 240, 260, 268, 277, 284, 286, 296, 303, 308, 309, 328, 329, 334, 336, 340, 342, 343, 345, 346, 348, 349
Breydenbach, Bernhard von 129
Bronner, Teus 266–267
Brunfels, Otto 27, 262, 269, 271, 311–313, 316–321, 324–326, 342

Brunschwig, Hieronymus 313–314
Bucer, Martin 32, 113, 119
Bünting, Heinrich 157
Burgkmair, Hans 130

Cabral, Pedro Álvares 155, 168
Cadamosto, Alvise 168
Capitulatio caesarea 89, 274
Carion, Johannes 16, 17, 85, 142–145
Carnival plays 58, 62, 66–67
Casa da Moeda 284
Casa de la Contratación 179
Caverio, Nicolo de 254
Celtis, Conrad 89, 140, 141, 172, 291–292, 336
Charlemagne 86, 87, 89, 291, 328
Charles V 93–94, 100, 222–223, 250, 274, 276, 277, 299–301, 304, 330, 351
Climate 164, 166–168, 218, 317–320, 323, 326, 327, 352
Clothing 46, 47, 50, 70, 71, 80, 205, 207, 223, 276–277, 310
Collaurius, Johannes 172
Columbus, Christopher 126, 130, 153–155, 158, 161, 162, 169, 182, 213–216, 219–221, 226, 236, 237, 244, 252, 347
Common good 26, 28, 95–106, 110–124, 268, 275–276, 280, 295, 309, 330, 336, 345–346, 356
Copernicus, Nicolaus 157
Copper 240, 246–248, 276, 284, 350, 355
Cortés, Hernán 169, 222–224
Cosmography 142–148, 149–180, 346
Council of Constance 258, 259, 289–290
Cuba, Johannes von 312–313
Cuppener, Christoph 261, 268

Der Wůcherer Meßkram oder Jarmarkt 259
Donation of Constantine 299–300
Drummer of Niklashausen 79
Dryander, Johann 135, 319
Dürer, Albrecht 223, 224, 343
Dyl Ulenspiegel 43–65, 106, 205–211, 342, 344, 349

Eberlin von Günzburg, Johann 287, 288, 297, 298, 300, 330
Eck, Johannes 173, 275
Egenolff, Christian 15–16, 86, 87, 143–146, 168–170, 237, 347
End of history 16, 92, 345
Erasmus 298
Ethics 7, 95, 256

Fabri, Felix 19, 20
Fashion 70–71, 79, 80, 184
Faustbuch 113
Federmann, Nikolaus 130, 134, 225, 227, 228, 250, 251, 320, 342
Feitoria de Flandres 247
Fernandes, Valentim 154, 238
Ferrarius, Johannes 9, 26, 28, 30–32, 35–38, 80–82, 99, 102–106, 119, 120, 124, 258, 268, 336, 346
Fischart, Johann 77, 106, 148
Fondaco dei Tedeschi 243
Foreign influence 7, 77, 289, 292–297, 311–312, 317–327, 328–334, 337–338, 341–344, 350–353
Fortunatus 201–203, 319, 348
Franck, Sebastian 17–18, 144–148, 169–171, 174–177, 180, 183, 198–200, 227, 311, 334–336, 347, 348
Free city 12, 88, 107, 110
Fries, Lorenz 149, 156, 165–167, 170, 254, 323, 348
Frisius, Gemma 164, 165
Fronsperger, Leonhard 33, 120–123, 275, 356
Froschauer, Johann 130, 217
Fuchs, Leonhart 249, 312, 316
Fuetrer, Ulrich 136
Fugger Company 99, 116, 174, 221, 228–229, 233, 238, 240, 243, 246–248, 250–251, 257, 261, 276, 278–282, 288, 304, 312, 323, 336, 342, 346, 349, 353, 355
Fugger, Jakob 76, 174, 240, 257, 276, 287, 323, 343, 351

Galen 318, 319
Gama, Vasco da 126, 129, 158, 168, 236, 237, 244, 246, 247, 254, 278

Geiler von Kaysersberg, Johann 192, 214, 258, 277–280, 286
Genre 8, 183, 267
German nation 6–7, 91, 289–292, 298
Globalization 2, 6, 8, 64, 233–242, 249, 327, 336–339, 342, 343, 349, 350, 352, 354–357
Gluttony 308, 327
Góis, Damião de 267
Grotius, Hugo 123
Grunau, Simon 297
Grüninger, Johann 156, 216
Grünpeck, Joseph 67
Grynaeus, Simon 173
Guaiacum 77, 221, 321–323

Hedio, Caspar 196
Hercules 185, 186, 190, 195–196, 348
Herr, Michael 173, 220, 225, 271, 272
Hie kompt ein Beüerlein 259
Hippocrates 318, 319
Hirschvogel Company 243, 246
History 78, 84, 85, 90, 91, 94
Hobbes, Thomas 103
Höchstetter, Ambrosius 161
Höchstetter Company 261
Homer 185
Hopfer, Daniel 262
Hörl, Veit 250
Hutten, Philipp von 250
Hutten, Ulrich von 77, 93, 95–96, 106, 119, 221–222, 240, 273, 278–279, 282–283, 286, 290–295, 298–307, 308–312, 321–324, 326, 328–333, 336, 337, 342, 351

Imperial diet 9, 40, 233, 273–277, 285, 287, 291, 300, 307, 342, 351
Importation, imported goods 6, 9, 70, 77, 203, 240–241, 243–244, 248–249, 251, 254, 268–271, 274, 276–283, 285, 288, 295–296, 298, 308–309, 311–322, 324, 326–327, 334–338, 342, 350–352, 356
Innovation 3, 6, 9, 30, 32, 76–84, 115, 126, 137, 211, 240, 273, 286–287, 322, 327, 333, 337, 343, 345, 347
Inter Caetera 239

Jerome 85
Justinian 196

Karlstadt, Andreas 224
Knobloch, Johannes 133
Köbel, Jacob 94
Koberger, Anton 137

Land of Cockaigne 67, 345
Lauterbeck, Georg 18, 19, 31, 32, 37, 84, 258
Libertas Germanorum 298, 352
Liber vagatorum 206, 207
Lonitzer, Adam 248, 249, 318
Luther, Martin 4, 26, 29, 38, 60, 83, 93, 96, 118, 119, 257, 258, 261, 262, 266, 279, 282, 283, 296, 297, 299, 300–303, 305–308, 330, 344
Luxury 41, 71, 183, 243, 249, 253, 257, 273, 276, 278, 279, 283, 293, 305, 308, 309, 311, 332, 333

Magnus, Olaus 174
Mandeville, Bernard 120
Mandeville, John 132, 133, 202, 247
Manuel I 245
Martellus, Henricus 162
Martyr, Peter 222
Maximilian I 50, 88–93, 100, 140–142, 145, 276, 286, 329, 345
Meder, Lorenz 272, 283
Medicine 269, 270, 308, 312, 313, 316, 318–319, 321, 324, 326
Melanchthon, Philipp 142
Meltinger, Ulrich 259
Mendoza, Pedro de 227, 251
Michelangelo 163
Miechowita, Maciej 173
Moctezuma 224
Montalboddo, Fracanzano da 131, 173, 219
Monopoly 9, 260, 273–275, 277, 279, 281, 285, 287, 330, 350, 351
More, Thomas 298
Münster, Sebastian 75, 86, 87, 177, 178, 267, 270, 271, 331, 332
Münzer, Hieronymus 141, 215

Murner, Thomas 206, 220

Nationalism 93–94, 234, 289–308, 337, 342, 351, 355–356
Natural law 15, 30, 296, 299, 344, 351
Negelein, Paul 124
Nostalgia 7, 83, 94, 298–299, 304, 328–338, 343, 352, 353

Odysseus 185, 190, 348
Oldendorp, Johannes 38, 40, 41
Osse, Melchior von 34, 35
Ovando, Nicolás de 223

Paracelsus 269, 270, 313, 318, 319, 323, 324, 326
Paul III 199, 227, 240
Pauli, Johannes 64, 65
Peace of Augsburg 3–5
Peasants' Revolt 9, 17, 21, 144, 285, 339
Pepper 202, 244, 246, 247, 249, 252, 268, 275, 283, 312
Petrarch 126
Peutinger, Conrad 8, 120, 161, 238, 257, 274–276, 286, 336, 342, 346, 353
Piccolomini, Enea 141
Pirckheimer, Willibald 286, 336, 342
Pizarro, Francisco 250
Plato 138, 190
Pliny 134, 139, 189, 316
Pluralization 2, 3, 5, 8, 97, 102, 119, 123, 241, 340, 341, 344, 350, 352
Policey 28–33, 40–43, 95
Polo, Marco 253
Progress 77–83, 91, 345
Ptolemy 6, 149–162, 166, 168, 172–180, 189, 252–253, 347, 348
Pythagoras 190

Reformation 4, 66, 94, 96, 111, 113, 119, 265, 299, 339, 340
Reformatio Sigismundi 256
Regiomontanus, Johannes 141
Reichsabschied 40
Reichspolizeiordnung 40, 274
Reisch, Gregor 172

Rem, Lucas 246
Ribeiro, Diogo 161
Ricci, Mateo 170
Richental, Ulrich von 290
Rieger, Urban 34, 38–40, 74
Ringmann, Matthias 150, 152–154, 157, 168, 216, 219
Rollenhagen, Georg 57, 58
Roman Church 95, 96, 295, 298–299, 301–307, 329, 330, 351, 352
Roman law 29, 194, 196, 295–299, 330, 333, 351, 352
Rößlin, Eucharius 312, 313
Ruchamer, Jobst 131–133, 135, 173, 183, 219, 220, 246, 342

Sabellicus, Antonius 140
Sachs, Hans 10, 37, 40–43, 58–66, 68–69, 96–98, 106–120, 203–205, 262–266, 280, 285, 286, 342, 349, 353
Schedel, Hartmann 134, 136–144, 148, 197, 347
Scheidt, Kaspar 65, 66
Schilling, Diebold 136
Schmidel, Ulrich 134, 227, 228, 251
Schnellenberg, Tarquinius 316–317
Schöner, Johann 127, 157, 348
Schriber, Hans 136
Schrot, Martin 291, 304, 305
Schwarz, Matthäus 257
Scientific Revolution 2–3
Secularization 2, 3, 5, 26, 96, 241, 340–341, 344
Self-interest 8, 22, 69, 88, 94, 95–124, 265–266, 275, 280, 285, 315, 333, 335–336, 344–346, 356, 357
Silenus 186, 190
Silk Road 247
Silver 240, 246, 247, 283–286, 350–351, 355
Smith, Adam 120, 121
Spalatin, Georg 299
Spatial turn 6, 127, 201, 208, 211, 348
Spice 6, 9, 71, 220–221, 240, 243, 248–249, 252–254, 261, 268–274, 278–279, 295–296, 338, 352

Spice trade 6, 237, 244, 247–248, 253, 271, 273, 276, 281–284, 308–327, 330, 342, 350–352, 355–356
Springer, Balthasar 129, 132, 246, 286, 342
Staden, Hans 134, 135, 227, 228
Strauß, Jakob 259, 325
Stuchs, Georg 218
Sublimis Deus 199, 227, 240
Sumptuary laws 47, 71

Tacitus 290
Telegony 185
Tengler, Ulrich 30, 42, 193–196
Topoi 26, 186
Traditional values 6, 72, 77, 119–120, 241, 309, 327, 337, 340, 344, 352
Translatio imperii 16, 85, 87, 88, 90, 143, 192, 345
Translatio studii 89, 192
Treaty of Saragossa 160, 227, 239, 349
Treaty of Tordesillas 161, 227, 239, 349
Tschudi, Aegidius 136
Tucher, Hans the Elder 129, 201–202
Turnauer, Kaspar 144

Valla, Lorenzo 299
Varthema, Ludovico di 253
Verardi, Carlo 182, 213
Vernacular 8–9, 30, 38, 89, 148, 194, 211, 216, 241, 290, 292, 339, 345
Vespucci, Amerigo 130, 145, 152, 154, 155, 157, 165, 167–169, 176, 211, 214–222, 226, 252, 347
Vespucci, Giovanni 161
Virgil 186
Vochs, Johann 319
Völhin, Conrad 161
Vom wucher. Furkauff vnd Tryegerey 260

Waldseemüller, Martin 127, 149, 150, 152–154, 156, 157, 161–163, 165–170, 173, 216, 219, 220, 252–254, 347, 348
Welsch gattung 294, 299
Welser, Anton 161, 274

Welser, Bartholomäus V 274
Welser, Bartholomäus VI 250
Welser Company 99, 116, 130, 161, 226, 228, 229, 238, 245–246, 249–251, 284, 342, 354, 355
Welser, Margarete 274
Welser-Vöhlin Company 244

Wheel of fortune 20, 72, 74, 91
Wickram, Jörg 201, 348, 356
Wimpfeling, Jakob 33, 34, 93
Witzel, Georg 257

Xenophobia 241, 249, 271, 289, 295, 298, 330, 332, 351

www.ingramcontent.com/pod-product-compliance
Lightning Source LLC
Chambersburg PA
CBHW031750220426
43662CB00007B/349